KU-790-790

Letterkenny I.T.

FRANCE
1814–1914

ROBERT TOMBS

LONGMAN
London and New York

Addison Wesley Longman,
Edinburgh Gate,
Harlow, Essex CM20 2JE, England
and Associated Companies throughout the world.

*Published in the United States of America
by Addison Wesley Longman Inc., New York*

© Addison Wesley Longman Limited 1996

All rights reserved; no part of this publication may be
reproduced, stored in a retrieval system, or transmitted
in any form or by any means, electronic, mechanical,
photocopying, recording, or otherwise without either the
prior written permission of the Publishers or a licence
permitting restricted copying in the United Kingdom issued
by the Copyright Licensing Agency Ltd.,
90 Tottenham Court Road, London W1P 9HE.

First published 1996

ISBN 0 582 49315 3 CSD
ISBN 0 582 49314 5 PPR

British Library Cataloguing in Publication Data

A catalogue record for this book is
available from the British Library

Library of Congress Cataloging-in-Publication

Tombs, Robert.
France 1814–1914 / Robert Tombs.
p.   cm. -- (Longman history of France)
Includes bibliographical references and index.
ISBN 0-582-49315-3. -- ISBN 0-582-49314-5 (pbk.)
1. France--History--19th century. 2. France--History--Third
Republic, 1870–1940. 3. Revolutions--France--History--19th century.
4. Republicanism--France--History--19th century. 5. National
characteristics, French. I. Title. II. Series.
DC251.T65   1996
944.06--dc20   95-43706
                                                    CIP

Set by 7 in 10/12pt Garamond
Produced by Longman Singapore Publishers (Pte) Ltd.
Printed in Singapore

CONTENTS

PART II: POWER

PART III: IDENTITIES

ACKNOWLEDGEMENTS

In writing this book I have been most fortunate in the generosity of friends, colleagues and students. Some, such as Albert Vaiciulenas and Sheila Lawlor, have probably forgotten the ideas they casually contributed at an early stage. Others have been generous in reading parts of the manuscript, contributing suggestions or information, or permitting me to draw on their published or unpublished works, especially Betty Bury, John Keiger, Steven Englund, Robert Alexander, Daniele Archibugi, Christopher Andrew, Tim Blanning, Alan Pitt, Alistair Reid, Lizzie Runham, Chloë Campbell, Claire Scobie, Ruth Pavey and Catherine May. Fellows of St John's, especially John Iliffe, Peter Clarke and Simon Szreter, have instantly supplied expertise and information over the lunch table. Joe Shennan has been a most supportive editor, and Andrew MacLennan a paragon among publishers. I am most grateful to all of them. They have, among other things, saved me from many embarrassing errors; those that remain, as well as the opinions expressed, are entirely my responsibility. I am of course immensely indebted to the work of many other historians, as will be evident to all specialists; and where this is not explicit in the text it is I hope sufficiently clear from the notes and bibliography. Without the boundless forbearance of my wife Isabelle, in addition to her intellectual contribution, this book could hardly have been written. I am deeply and additionally grateful to Betty Bury for allowing me to dedicate it to the memory of Patrick Bury, teacher and friend.

The publishers are grateful to Presses de la Foundation Nationale des Sciences Politiques for permission to reproduce Figure 5.1, from p. 26 of *Les Ministres de la République* by Jean Estèbe.

In memory of Patrick Bury

INTRODUCTION

> The French people seems to have advanced 2,000 years beyond the rest of humankind; one would be tempted to regard it . . . as a different species.
>
> *Robespierre*[1]

This book has two fundamental, connected and inescapable themes: the aftershocks of the French Revolution and the functioning of the French State. Fundamental, because they underlie the argument in every chapter. Connected, because the Revolution had profoundly changed the forms and functions of the State. Inescapable, because the Revolution and the State are what modern French history is about.

Can one sum up the history of a country so simply? Surely it must also be 'about' the ordinary lives, struggles, work, loves and leisure of millions of individuals – peasants, poets, women, children, families, orphans, communities – many of them little concerned for most of the time with revolutions, governments and wars? Yes indeed, and they will all appear in this book. But in what sense, if any, can they all be thought to have a shared history, and also a history distinct from the inhabitants of other areas of Europe? What kinds of events and changes could constitute such a history? The overall framework must, I believe, be political. A State and a nation are not natural phenomena but laboriously constructed and defended political edifices containing a wide diversity of ways of life, beliefs, customs, languages, and occupations. A 'national society', a 'national culture' and a 'national economy' are all to a greater or lesser extent manufactured, and were mostly manufactured during the nineteenth century, as all over Europe States were making sustained and fairly successful efforts to control their subjects' lives and even to change their beliefs and culture.

What the people composing each 'nation' significantly had in common was their relation to their State. Except in this sense, I doubt whether there is such a thing as a history of France, or of any other large nation-state, that does not under scrutiny break down into a collection of histories of regions or social groups, or else fade into a wider European or western history. France in the nineteenth century, more than most countries, contained a very diverse

1. Hunt (1984), p. 100.

conglomeration of peoples. The immense changes that took place during the nineteenth century, such as industrialization and urbanization, did little, at least in their early stages, to make France more homogenous or integrated. Undeveloped rural areas in Britanny or the Massif Central came to have even less in common with dynamic mining, manufacturing and commercial-farming regions such as Flanders or Alsace, while a textile town such as Lille grew more like its non-French counterparts such as Manchester, and resemblance was often cemented by economic links, immigration and conscious emulation. In short, what a woman dairy-farmer from Quimper had in common with a woman cotton-spinner from Mulhouse was that both were subjects of the French State, governed by its laws on work, suffrage and the family, and affected more generally by its revolutions and wars; in other ways, each had more in common with women in Cardigan or Zurich.

It is, therefore, as political history that the history of France ceases to be a collection of local studies or a regional sub-division of the common history of the European world from San Francisco to St Petersburg. One could say the same of other countries. But politics is more crucial in the French experience for two reasons, both bequeathed to the nineteenth century by the Revolution. First, the Revolution gave to the French State greater powers than in other western societies, and certainly greater ambitions to intervene in and even to remodel the 'society' over which it ruled. Second, the Revolution had left a nagging problem of legitimacy: who should rule and by what right? Finding a workable answer to this question was made far more difficult by the hatreds that emerged during the Revolution, and which were constantly being renewed by the tumultuous events of the century. This 'Franco-French War', as it is often called, meant that the inhabitants of France were involved in politics, whether as voluntary participants or as passive recipients, to an extent unique in Europe.

Politics are not simply the events that take place in palaces and parliaments. They concern vast and diverse efforts to organize the public, and many of the private, activities of the subjects of the State, from raising armies to regulating adultery, and from building barricades to subsidizing opera-houses. Politics also concern the responses of people, individually and collectively, to the State and to the other subjects of that State. They include the effort to understand and apply lessons from the past so as to shape the present and future through thought, argument, myth-making, ceremony and symbol.

In writing this book I soon realized, therefore, that there was not a single political narrative, but many, at different levels, obeying different logics and which, though connected, proceeded at different speeds. Rather than attempting to amalgamate them, I have separated them out. I hope that this has the advantage of showing how, beneath the political upheavals, there was often continuity, whether of institutions (such as the bureaucracy), of social activities (such as work), or of ideas, language and ritual. I have chosen to begin the story, in Part I, with major themes of political culture, and continue in Part II with the exercise of power. This is mainly an attempt to get away from the implication that a 'nation' and a State are organic growths, shaped and governed by geography, sociology or economics. Far from it: the shared experience of being French in this period came from inescapable political concerns (I have called them obsessions); from relations to a structure of power, the State; and from the conditions it caused to prevail throughout the diverse territories it ruled. Part III, on identities, looks at how the French thought about themselves and each other. Parts IV and V present political narrative at another level, that of national government: they divide at the point (1871) at which the 'era of revolutions' is replaced by a period of relative political stability, that of the Third Republic (1870–1940). This way of organizing the book is also intended to make it easier to consult selectively, with chapters and sections able to be read in isolation.

The unique political experience of France in our period was the long-drawn-out aftermath of the Revolution of 1789. France had undergone the trauma of a new kind of revolution. During it, and for generations after it, the French found themselves pioneers in trying to build a new political order without any agreed model. The combination of novelty, uncertainty, experiment and conflict in the political, ideological, international and socio-economic spheres makes nineteenth-century French history dramatic and frankly exciting. It was marked by an extreme degree of political instability. Since 1789 there have been three monarchies, two empires, five republics and fifteen constitutions. Every head of state from 1814 to 1873 spent part of his life in exile. Every regime was the target of assassination attempts of a frequency that put Spanish and Russian politics in the shade. Even in peaceful times governments changed every few months. In less peaceful times, political deaths, imprisonments and deportations are literally incalculable. This turmoil cannot be explained by social and economic deprivation: France was one of the richest countries in the world, and the strains of modernization were less severe than among most of its less agitated neighbours.

So what is the explanation? From the 1820s until roughly a generation ago, the answer seemed clear: the Revolution of 1789 had been the victory of the bourgeoisie over the nobility, the victory of a new world of capitalism over the old world of feudalism. That was a view of things that the historian-politicians Guizot and Thiers accepted in the 1820s and 1830s as the events were taking place; and it was a view equally accepted more than a century later by historians of Left and Right. What came next – and hence what fundamentally explained nineteenth- and twentieth-century French history – was the conflict between the victorious bourgeoisie, determined to defend and consolidate its power, interests and values, and the unprivileged lower-middle class and the exploited proletariat, embodied in republican and socialist movements which, however feeble and faltering their steps, were historically significant as the standard-bearers of the future. Hence the production of numerous and often indistinguishable monographs on republican and especially socialist history; hence too the relative neglect by French historians of fields such as 'high politics' and biography, dismissed as trivial, and right-wing and centrist politics, considered irrelevant.

Over the last 40 years this historical vision has faded. The political, intellectual and moral disintegration of the Marxist teleology of history has removed what was the triumphant conclusion and justification of the story: the proletarian socialist victory has proved illusory. This disintegration is reflected in a fundamental change in historical method: the axiomatic belief that ideas, individuals and politics were merely the spume on the great ocean swell of socio-economic change has gone; now, historians see language and culture (including those of politics) as reality itself. More specifically, revisionist historians of the Revolution have shattered the century-old view of it as a 'bourgeois revolution', a conflict of old and new classes. Alfred Cobban led off with the provocative assertion that the Revolution had not been the progressive victory of a modernizing bourgeoisie, but an anti-modern rearguard action by a traditional gentry of landowners and officials which set back economic and social change by a generation. There ensued one of the epic battles of modern historiography.[2] Cobban's whole interpretation did not survive, but neither did that of his orthodox opponents, repeatedly under-mined by the work of American and British historians such as George V. Taylor and Richard Cobb, and latterly of French historians, often converts from Marxism, led by François Furet. Instead of a socio-economic struggle, 'the Revolution is now', as William Doyle has put it, 'about perception and culture; society and economics were only real in the ways people understood them'.[3] Lynn Hunt has argued that the essence of the Revolution was the creation of a 'new political culture', 'the politicization of everyday life'. The rest, most historians now agree, was of secondary importance: the social and economic change brought by the Revolution, says Hunt, was 'not revolutionary'.[4] Furet sums it up concisely as a 'tremendous over-investment in politics'.[5]

These fundamental changes in understanding what the Revolution was must affect the way we analyse its long aftermath. What, in short, can the history of post-revolutionary France be about? This book attempts to explore some possible answers. The profound cultural, ideological and political turmoil of the Revolution – war, civil violence and religious conflict – had been suspended but not resolved: a new post-revolutionary order had still to be constructed. The State had been transformed, both in its powers and its ambitions: it was to be the creator of a new society, and the definer and protector of the common interest. Here the over-investment in politics had become institutionalized and therefore perpetuated, and so the expansion of politics into everyday life could never wholly be reversed.[6] The great problem facing successive generations was how to end the Revolution. And in a revolution, as in a novel, the end is the most difficult part to invent.

2. For a summary of the debate, see Doyle (1980), and for an incisive discussion of the main issues, see Blanning (1987).
3. Doyle (1992), p. 24.
4. Hunt (1984), pp. 213, 221.
5. In Feher (1990), p. 276.
6. An expensive business. De l'Ecotais (1992, p. 43) says that taxes and contributions cost the French $70 billion a year more than the Germans. We might consider this as literally the cost of the revolutionary/Napoleonic State today.

PART I

OBSESSIONS

R.T.C. LIBRARY, LETTERKENNY

CHAPTER 1

REVOLUTION

> Other peoples have had revolutions more or less frequently; but we have revolution permanently.
>
> *Parliamentary Enquiry, 1871*[1]

In their own eyes, and those of others, the French since 1789 have been the revolutionary nation. This, in complete contrast with their image in the eighteenth century as a law-abiding and tranquil people, was the principal distinguishing characteristic of being French in the nineteenth century: for good or ill the turmoil begun in 1789 had made French society and the French nation what they were. The Revolution was 'the only historical event that served as a chronological milestone for all French people . . . the great dividing point that separated the present from the past'.[2] But every new political crisis made it seem clearer that 'the Revolution' – not a succession of separate events, but one single process – had not ended in 1795 or 1815.

'The Revolution', the sudden violent remaking of society, was a new concept of politics. It upset old certainties, reversed relationships of power and intruded into every aspect of life. It opened up unlimited possibilities and unlimited dangers. A religious, even occultist, view of the universe often formed part of the outlook. 'Why discuss what it is like on the other side of the river?' asked the lifelong revolutionary Auguste Blanqui. 'Let us cross over and see.'

Paradoxically, there formed a 'revolutionary tradition'. It was traditional in two ways. First, 'the Revolution' was seen both as a continuing teleological process, developing from its beginning in the past to a culmination (whether desirable or undesirable) in the future, and also as a cyclical process, passing through certain logical phases observable in the past and likely to reproduce themselves again. Hence the idea of revolution 'advanced further', as Littré noted in 1850, in 'each generation'. Opposition to the Bourbons in the 1820s culminated in the unexpected revolution of 1830, followed by several years of attempted insurrections. This proved that revolution was not past history, but

1. Roberts (1973), p. 7.
2. Weber (1977), p. 109.

present politics. The revolutionary upheavals of 1848–51 and 1870–71 seemed to open further phases in the revolutionary cycle. The 1890s, marked by strikes and anarchist bombs, were believed by many to be the beginning of yet another period of revolution.

Second, ideas, symbols, myths and ritual actions were not fixed but were continually being elaborated over the century. By 1815, memories of the 1790s were fragmented and confused, varying greatly according to the divergent experiences of individuals, families and regions. Some of the most famous mythical symbols of the Revolution had yet to be propagated. Building barricades – the ritual signal of nineteenth-century Paris revolt – was practically unknown during the Revolution. The *tricoteuses* – those notorious women knitting at the foot of the guillotine – only appeared generations later, a cross-Channel reimport via the lurid imaginations of Carlyle and Dickens. Heroes, heroines and stirring events also had to be discovered, promoted and commemorated through speeches, newspapers, histories, novels, plays, textbooks, paintings, statues, street names and ceremonies. In short, the 'revolutionary tradition' had to be created, combining imaginative visions of revolution, rituals of political behaviour and ideological analyses.

The tradition could have a ludicrous side. In rural France in 1868, for example, flowers decorating churches caused riots because they included lilies, the Bourbon symbol, and these were taken to be a signal in a royalist plot to restore the monarchy and re-establish the Church tithe. In one village a crowd of 600 threatened to string up the priest if he refused to hand over all the offending bouquets.[3] In the 1870s, republicans still campaigned with the stories that royalists were planning to restore feudalism and the tithe: not an acre, not a centime, not a virgin was safe from the rapacity of the nobles and priests. As late as 1910, a panic was caused in sleepy Provence when a newsboy's shouts of 'la révolution au Portugal' were misheard as 'la révolution au Pont-du-Gard'![4]

But the revolutionary tradition was far more than mere hot air: it was a living political culture of deeds as well as words. The most telling measure of its power is the appalling total of killed or seriously wounded in political violence during the nineteenth century, which even a fairly modest estimate must place above 60,000.[5] The long and often bloody struggle to resolve the issues of the Revolution – by defeating it, controlling it or fulfilling it – has been called the Franco-French War. Why this 'war' continued so long and with such intensity is the principal theme of this book.

3. Corbin (1992:a), p. 16.
4. Weber (1986), p. 129.
5. Chesnais (1976, pp. 167–8), who is able to give only very tentative estimates, suggests approximately 17,000 casualties in 1830, 1848 and 1851. For 1871, the bloodiest conflict, there is no way of reaching a precise figure, but 40,000 is on the low side of the range of guesses. In addition are the casualties of 1815, 1832 and 1834 in Paris and the provinces, and the untotalled casualties in the century's minor riots and strikes.

VISIONS OF REVOLUTION

It created the politics of the impossible, turned madness into a theory, and blind audacity into a cult.

Tocqueville, 1850[6]

If the Revolution was principally a political and cultural phenomenon, as was suggested in the introduction, we need to explore how and in what form it was transmitted over successive generations. There were hopeful and fearful visions of revolution. The hope of a popular uprising, a *'lutte finale'* to create a society of harmony and justice, was endlessly inspiring. But in the aftermath of civil violence, endless war, invasion, occupation and catastrophic economic distress, the revolutionary experience was also transmitted to later generations as fear: revolution was uneasily nicknamed 'the tiger'. Fear could transform trivial political disagreement into something more serious. More than once 'France was caught in the trap of its own fantasies of social dissolution'.[7] Let us examine four principal fantasies, concerning blood, the crowd, religious conflict and apocalypses.

Blood

Marchons! Marchons! Qu'un sang impur abreuve nos sillons.

'Marseillaise'

Human blood has a terrible power against those who have spilt it . . . The Terrorists have done us immense and lasting harm. Were you to go into the last cottage in the farthest country of Europe, you would meet that memory and that curse.

Michelet [8]

What the Holocaust and the Gulag are for us, the violence of the French Revolution was for the nineteenth century: events that alter our understanding of politics and indeed of human nature. The lynching of aristocrats on street lamps, celebrated in the popular song 'Ca Ira', sung by the Left throughout the century; the parading of heads on pikes; the ritual of the guillotine; executions by drowning at Nantes in 1793; the trail of fire and slaughter in the Vendée in 1793 where 200,000 perished; the mass executions by grapeshot at Lyons; and – deepest trauma of all – the September Massacres of 1792, that butchery of prisoners in Paris with blade and bludgeon, which seemed to be the distillation of human savagery. On the other hand, republicans recalled the torture of prisoners by the Vendée rebels and the lynchings and summary executions of the 'White Terror' carried out in the south in 1815.

6. Paulson (1983), p. 2.
7. Furet (1988), p. 399.
8. Furet (1992), p. 374.

The nineteenth century inherited an inextricable mixture of fact, propaganda and fantasy, first spread by anti-Jacobin pamphlets in the later 1790s, and later by a flood of memoirs, histories, pamphlets, novels and plays. These conjured up a very intimate kind of horror: pikes and cleavers dripping with blood, hearts torn out and squeezed like sponges, livers eaten, intimacy violated by 'lecherous butchers'.[9] Some of the most nightmarish details were fictitious (trousers made of human skin; a young girl made to drink a cup of blood to save her father's life) but probably no less effective a reflection of collective fears.

Emotionally and ideologically, revolutionary bloodshed was hard to handle. One reaction was to sweep it under the carpet. While the private medium of the novel reflected fears of violence in the 1820s, in public performances the memory was repressed as too disturbing: censors usually cut out violent material. The 'Marseillaise' was banned for most of the century, for 'le sang impur of the Marseillaise bawled out' was an unambiguous revolutionary signal, a 'glorification of crime, frightful reminder of '93'.[10] Delacroix's painting Liberty leading the People (1830), with its rampaging mob trampling over corpses, was bought by the government and removed from public display. Bloody and violent spectacles were stopped or at least made less visible in the aftermath of the 1830 and 1848 revolutions. Animal baiting was forbidden in 1833 and so in 1850 was public cruelty to animals. Medical dissection of corpses was removed from public gaze. It became progressively more difficult to get into the morgue – a popular family outing – to gawp at the corpses. The consistent aim was to reduce popular brutality. Though executions remained public, they were moved to quieter places and to daybreak, and the guillotine was taken down from its platform and placed less visibly on the ground.

Moderate partisans of the Revolution felt obliged to explain away the bloodshed, especially when, after 1830, revolution recommenced. Some ascribed it to a minority – 'a handful of murderers' said the great republican historian Jules Michelet – or blamed the brutal traditions of the Old Regime that had carried over into the new era. Some blamed it on counter-revolutionary provocation. Many minimized its extent and alleged that the other side had been even worse, beginning a ghoulish and enduring polemic in which Right and Left accused each other of killing the most.

If moderates wished to muffle reminders of violence, extremists of Right and Left kept fantasies of bloodshed alive. In the 1830s, collecting weapons for the next revolution conferred radical chic. Secret societies in the 1840s named their sections 'Robespierre' or 'Marat'. Lyons republicans struck a medal in 1848 inscribed 'The people have arisen and 1793 may yet return', and threatening death to 'aristocrats, moderates, egoists'.[11] In 1871, a revolutionary club in Paris demanded the execution of a hostage every 24

9. Taine (1878), vol. 2, p. 303.
10. A Lyons moderate, quoted in Agulhon et al. (1992), p. 184.
11. Ibid., pp. 185–6.

hours. Such bar-room bravado was portentously reported by worried bureaucrats and eagerly spread by alarmist conservatives.

Horrifying stories were readily believed. The same hallmarks recurred: blood, torture, mutilation, sadism (including violence by and towards women), even cannibalism. After February 1848, it was reported that brand new guillotines had been delivered to Lyons. In June 1848, soldiers taken prisoner by the insurgents in Paris were said to have been sawn in two or burnt alive. The December 1851 insurrection inspired hair-raising stories of torture, murder and mutilation reminiscent of the September Massacres of 1792. Bands of syphilitic revolutionaries at Clamecy were reported to have raped the daughters of the bourgeoisie in the presence of priests about to be burnt at the stake. In 1871, the Paris Communards were accused of using poison and dum-dum bullets, and torturing prisoners. Their killing of hostages (arguably rather few in the circumstances of the wholesale slaughter of their own men) was seen as another proof of the enduring horrors of revolution, especially as the killing of priests and the gruesome mass lynching of 50 prisoners by an angry crowd in the Rue Haxo in eastern Paris recalled the September Massacres.

Such lurid accounts, mythical or real, partly explain the harsh reprisals taken by government forces against defeated insurgents in 1848, 1851 and especially in 1871, the crushing of the Paris Commune. This was the bloodiest 'White Terror' in French history. Thereafter, the level of political violence fell to a fairly normal west-European level – far more killing than in Britain (including Ireland), but far less than in Russia or America. Yet the old fears persisted. As before, fact and fantasy made a potent combination. Zola's 1885 novel *Germinal* reflected a gut fear of revolutionary violence, and portrayed the revolting butchery of a shopkeeper by the angry wives of striking miners – far worse than anything that ever really happened in these years. Yet strikers in the 1880s still sang 'Ca Ira' and the 'Carmagnole', the blood-curdling songs of the 1790s, and verbal violence was the norm. In 1886 at Anzin a mine manager really was lynched. Zola also portrayed troops firing on strikers; and on May Day 1891 troops really did so at Fourmies, killing nine.

Expectation of violence could lower the threshold at which clashes and reprisals really occurred. Yet it also inspired efforts to head them off. The 'silent majority' was horrified by memories of the 1790s – a horror reflected in popular songs and plays, which were consistently hostile to the Terror. Liberals, moderate republicans and many socialists stressed their determination to avoid a return to 1793, and declared hopefully that Terror belonged to the past. After the 1830 revolution the new regime resisted popular left-wing demands to execute the ministers of Charles X, and in 1848 reluctance to engage in a battle with 'the mob' may have helped persuade Louis-Philippe to abdicate. He knew the risks of tangling with revolution: his father, and the fathers of three of his prime ministers, had died on the guillotine. The new Republic in 1848 immediately abolished the death penalty for political offences to prove its rejection of the Terror. Lamartine, its leader, pleaded (with bullets whistling round his head, he related) against the adoption of the red flag, 'that flag of blood!'. The 1871 Paris Commune had the guillotine publicly burnt, and its socialist members opposed the establishment of a Committee of Public Safety because of the frightening memories it evoked. Even 'extremist' leaders in 1848 and 1871 risked their own lives trying to shield prisoners.

Every nineteenth-century revolution shunned deliberate and organized terror. They frightened the property-owning classes none the less. Whatever the intentions of politicians, violence, counter-violence, threats of violence and fear of violence remained characteristics of French political and social life.

The crowd: 'people' or 'mob'?

> The people come! Their flowing tide
> Is rising endlessly with the waxing moon.[12]

The power of the crowd, an essential image of revolution from Delacroix to Eisenstein, impressed contemporaries as a force of nature: a torrent, a flood, an ocean, overwhelming all barriers. 'The tide is rising, the tide is rising!', one panicky minister kept repeating in February 1848. For revolutionaries 'the bare-armed fighters' were invincible if they could be set in motion: 'with rifles in their hands and paving stones under their feet they have no fear of all the strategists of the monarchical school', proclaimed the Commune leader Delescluze in 1871. Was this elemental force 'the people', the source of legitimacy and virtue, collective hero of revolution and national defence, which stormed the Bastille in 1789 and fought off the foreign invader at Valmy in 1792? Or was it 'the mob' (for which there seem to be as many words in French as Eskimo words for snow: *la foule, la populace, la multitude, la canaille, la racaille, la tourbe*), savages responsible for terror and crime, as conservatives asserted? Was revolution the liberation of the people or the unleashing of the mob? Or were 'people' and 'mob' somehow the same?

For democrats, the people were the source of natural wisdom and uncorrupted virtue. For the great republican historian Jules Michelet, they were the true essence of the nation. The popular novelist Eugène Sue portrayed the whole of history as the saga of the people's struggle for justice. For Victor Hugo, revolution was a 'transfiguration' of the people: 'these bare feet, these bare arms, these rags, this ignorance, this abjection, this darkness can be used in the conquest of the ideal'. A revolution carried out by them could not go wrong: 'Revolutions have a mighty arm and sensitive fingers: they strike hard and choose well'.[13] Yet even democrats were wary of the mass, especially when, after the political revolutions of 1830 and 1848, riots continued and were linked with what was called 'the social question', the problem of urban poverty.

12. Hugo, in Fritz (1988), p. 98.
13. Hugo (1967), vol. 2, pp. 122, 358.

Hugo, Michelet and Sue were ambivalent: there was 'the people', who made history, but there was also 'the mob', who committed crimes and threatened society. If 1789, 1830 and even 1848 were accepted by moderates and even some conservatives as revolutions for justice and liberty, subsequent revolts were illegitimate 'revolts of the belly' rather than for an ideal, threatening to overthrow liberty, order and property – in short 'civilization'. Thiers, conservative liberal and historian of the Revolution, made the classic distinction in a notorious speech in 1850: 'the people' were not the same as *la vile multitude*. The 'mob' was believed to come primarily from the 'dangerous classes', the vicious criminal poor who obeyed the impulse of their 'passions'. They were 'as far outside civilization as the savage tribes portrayed so well by Fenimore Cooper. But these barbarians are among us.'[14]

Most barbarous of all was thought to be the involvement of women and children, beings incapable of reason, wholly subject to emotion, and hence capable of uninhibited savagery. This is how Georges Clemenceau, in Zolaesque vein, thought he remembered the violence on 18 March 1871 at Montmartre: 'Children perched on top of a wall were waving indescribable trophies, dishevelled women were waving their naked arms in the air, and uttering harsh, inarticulate shouts.'[15] The role of women in revolution was always sensitive. As pleasing paint and plaster embodiment of abstractions such as Liberty or the Republic, they were omnipresent. As real individuals they were an embarrassment to men of all political tendencies, who tried to keep them out of the limelight, bandaging the wounded and serving refreshments. In historical and literary accounts, they are pushed into a conventional feminine role: 'the weakness of their sex is stressed insistently, as if the political impact of a woman could only be ephemeral and fatal to herself'.[16] The alternative description is of them as *mégères*, defeminized and dehumanized, savage, sexually corrupted and dangerous. The invention of the revolutionary myth of the *tricoteuses* is precisely paralleled by that of the *pétroleuses* of 1871: the women revolutionaries believed to be setting fire to buildings with bottles of *pétrole*. The authorities never managed to find a real *pétroleuse* – which did not weaken the belief in their existence – but they shot a number of suspects and prosecuted others, and the accusations against them show perfectly the male perception of female revolt: they were assumed to be prostitutes, because this ultimate form of female corruption was assumed to be an essential element of a woman's rejection of male authority and the established social order. The *mégère*, the *pétroleuse*, was thus the nadir of perverted female nature: weak intellect, strong emotion, and physical fragility leads to mindless violence, helpless debauchery, hysterical savagery. They thus ceased to be civilized women and became 'femelles', wrote one contemporary, becoming women again only when they had been killed. In reality, women's most potent revolutionary act was probably in the early

14. Sue (1989), p. 31.
15. Watson (1974), p. 48.
16. Aubry (1988), p. 200.

stages of revolt, by coming into the streets en masse, when their presence, along with their children, demoralized troops and made military action to clear the streets practically impossible: this was a very effective use of femininity, using weakness as a weapon.

To blame political revolt on the savagery of the 'dangerous classes' was, of course, a convenient explanation as far as property owners were concerned, for it denied it any legitimate cause. It was far from being a reassuring belief, however. Fear of the 'dangerous classes' persisted at least until the end of the century. The 'mob' was accused of wanting revolution as an opportunity for crime on a grand scale: not all republicans were thieves, went a common jibe, but all thieves were republicans. It was a widespread myth that revolutionary ringleaders offered their followers 'three hours of pillage' as their post-revolutionary reward, as to a conquering army. Proof of these fears was the naive relief of property owners when no such orgy took place, as in February 1848: 'People in the street could not be more polite: never ever have I seen the lower classes more thoughtful'.[17] However, memories of the most radical themes of the 1790s – the *Loi Agraire*, the Maximum, the 'conspiracy of Equals' – combined with the egalitarian utopias of romantic socialism of the 1830s and 1840s, and notorious if misunderstood phrases such as Proudhon's 'Property is theft' (1840), created the stereotype of the *partageux*, the revolutionaries who aimed to share out property. While this was a caricature, popular socialism did promise immediate and tangible benefits: the poor would have white bread to eat, and wine instead of water. The fundamental basis of such promises was the belief that there would be abundance for all once wealth was redistributed fairly, and the 'idlers' became 'producers'.

The *partageux* were a potent theme of alarmist propaganda among property owners large and small. In June 1848, peasants with shotguns and pitchforks mounted guard on their barns and haystacks when they heard rumours (in at least one case started as a joke) that the 'reds' from Paris were on the rampage through the countryside.

The nineteenth century was fascinated by crime, in the press (*La Gazette des Tribuneaux*, founded in 1825, specialized in it), fiction, songs, policemen's memoirs, and the popular theatre situated on what was nicknamed the 'Boulevard du Crime'. Eugène Sue's hugely popular serialized novel *Les Mystères de Paris* (1842) dealt with the adventures of the virtuous poor and the criminal underground in the lower depths of Paris. Hugo's *Les Misérables* (1862) also visited the secret worlds of crime and revolution. The same metaphors and fantasies recur in such fiction: conspiracies, underground lairs, secret tunnels, sewers, secrecy, darkness and filth – menacing counter-societies hidden within or beneath the visible world. Such writing reflected, perhaps inspired, real fears. When Tocqueville saw the revolutionary Blanqui in 1848 he described him as looking as if he had 'passed his life in a sewer and to have just left it'.[18] In June 1848 and again in

17. Apponyi (1948), p. 29.
18. Tocqueville (1948), p. 138.

1871 it was believed that revolutionaries planned to blow up Paris from underground. Soldiers were sent down the sewers to prevent catastrophe, and cut numerous copper cables thought to be connected to explosives until the post office complained that its telegraph network was being wrecked. Similar themes still recurred a generation later, though in modern, 'scientific' terms in the works of Hippolyte Taine, Gustave Le Bon and others who in the last decades of the nineteenth century developed the idea of 'crowd psychology', according to which individuals en masse were overcome by 'mental contagion'.[19] Taine used the old metaphors of the underworld, but now referring explicitly to the depths of the psyche: 'the monsters who crawled in chains in the lower depths of the heart emerge together from the human cavern, not only hateful instincts with their fangs, but also filthy instincts with their slime'.[20] Although the political and social crises that gave rise to fantasies of the criminal mob had by this time disappeared, the fantasies themselves persisted in the counter-revolutionary writing of the late nineteenth and twentieth centuries, often with a new racist twist. As will be seen in Chapter 8, treatment of criminals remained unusually harsh, aiming to eliminate dangerous elements permanently.

Religious war: the cosmic dimension

The French Revolution is a political revolution that operated in the manner . . . of a religious revolution.

Tocqueville[21]

We have torn human consciences away from belief . . . We have put out the lights in the sky and they will never be lit again.

René Viviani, 1906[22]

The Revolution, whether by a tragic combination of unforeseen circumstances or because of the essentially anti-Catholic nature of its Enlightenment ideology, turned into a war of religion. Determination to force through in 1790 a fundamental reform of Catholicism, the Civil Constitution of the Clergy, led to opposition, schism, resistance by popular counter-revolutionary Catholicism and finally a 'dechristianization' campaign involving the desecration of churches, a new secular calendar, substitute 'civic religions', the killing of 2–3,000 clergy and the exile of over 30,000,[23] the savage persecution of their supporters and the latter's no less savage (if less extensive) retaliation against republicans. This religious conflict left an enduring division. It gave a cosmic dimension to the obsession with revolution, which, for many on both Right and Left, concerned not merely political or social change, but the ultimate

19. Barrows (1981), p. 77.
20. Taine (1878), vol. 2, p. 303.
21. Tocqueville (1967), p. 69.
22. Lefranc (1973), p. 164.
23. Gibson (1989), p. 52.

purpose of human life. This was perhaps the unique characteristic of modern French political culture.

Until the 1850s, when positivism and atheism became common among radical republicans and socialists, the conflict lay not between belief and unbelief but rather between dogmatic and conservative Catholicism on one hand and a variety of progressive religious cults ranging from liberal Protestantism to occultism on the other. Most leading left-wing thinkers from Robespierre onwards, and especially socialists, including Saint-Simon, Leroux, Buchez, Blanc, Fourier, and democrats such as Michelet, Quinet and Hugo, saw the Revolution in religious terms, as an attempt to create a truly moral society – the kingdom of God on earth. Conservative Catholics saw it as a diabolical attempt to destroy the Church. The struggle concerned 'the soul of France', and whether it would be a desert of atheism/arcadia of free thought or stronghold of piety/prey of the Inquisition.

The conflict had been suspended, not solved, by Napoleon I, whose 1801 Concordat with the pope restored freedom of worship and financial support to the Church, but at the price of making the clergy practically civil servants: his post-revolutionary order demanded a strong but obedient Church. This equilibrium was threatened by the Bourbon Restoration, when a revival of Catholic militancy seemed to endanger political liberty. Stendhal in *Le Rouge et le Noir* portrayed the clergy as the real holders of power, and popular rumour cast Charles X as a secret Jesuit.

The revolution of 1830 brought crowd attacks on Catholic churches and religious houses across the country. However, shared opposition by republicans and the Church to the July Monarchy in the 1840s led to brief reconciliation between Catholicism and the Revolution in 1848, when priests blessed trees of liberty and several were elected to the Constituent Assembly. The honeymoon was short. Its end is symbolized by the killing of the Archbishop of Paris, Denis Affre, as he tried to mediate between rebels and the authorities in June 1848, shot perhaps by a stray bullet, perhaps by a soldier, perhaps by a rebel. The Church rallied to counter-revolution, supporting Louis-Napoleon Bonaparte's 1851 coup. This won it the execration of defeated republicans. Hugo denounced the new archbishop for celebrating a *Te Deum*:

> Murder at your side follows the prayer divine
>   Crying: shoot the rabble dead!
> Satan holds the cruet, and that is not wine
>   That stains your chalice red.

The conflict was even further aggravated during the 1850s and 1860s. Catholic leaders supported papal rule in central Italy and die-hards welcomed Pius IX's assertion in 1864 of an embarrassingly reactionary theology in the Syllabus of Errors, condemning 80 'modern errors', including religious toleration, the secular State, and 'progress, liberalism and the modern world'. At the other end of the intellectual spectrum, Darwinian biology, advances in geology and scientific materialist theories seemed to be providing a non-supernatural account of the existence of life. Historical criticism of the Bible was introduced to the wider public by Ernest Renan's *Vie de Jésus* (1863), which presented Jesus not as God but as 'an admirable human being'. Positivism, a scientistic philosophy which rejected metaphysics, won many followers during the 1860s, while French Catholicism embraced sentimental and mystical popular religion marked by a series of apparitions of the Virgin Mary. This to the Left was contemptible demagogic exploitation of ignorant credulity, an intellectual offence to add to the Church's political iniquities.

Nemesis came after the fall of the Empire in 1870. New republican authorities introduced anticlerical measures, especially to secularize schools. In Paris in 1871, during the Commune insurrection, anticlerical violence recalled that of the 1790s: schools were closed, 120 priests and religious arrested and accused of treason, and churches were vandalized, Notre Dame itself narrowly escaping the torch. Another archbishop of Paris, Georges Darboy, was killed, and 23 other clergy were shot as hostages or lynched. The mocking interrogation of Darboy by a Blanquist police chief was widely reported: 'What is your occupation?' 'Servant of God.' 'Where does your master live?' 'Everywhere.' 'Clerk, write that the prisoner claims to be the domestic of someone named God, of no fixed abode.'

Persecution was of course condemned by moderate republicans, but for them too the Church was an incorrigible enemy of progress. Their views were confirmed during the struggle against royalism during the 1870s. The unexpected – to some, providential – victory of royalists in the 1871 elections seemed to make the restoration of a Catholic Bourbon possible, and led to an upsurge of vocal and imprudent Catholic royalism. Public prayers in parliament, the dedication of France to the Sacred Heart and the building of the Sacré Coeur basilica in left-wing Montmartre, the encouragement of mass pilgrimages to Lourdes and Paray-le-Monial with the singing of royalist hymns ('Dieu de clémence, O Dieu vainqueur, Sauvez Rome et la France, Au nom du Sacré-Coeur') seemed to align Catholicism at its most demagogic with the most reckless forces of reaction. When in 1877 French bishops petitioned the government to support the pope (whose sovereignty had ended with the invasion of Rome by Italian troops in September 1870), this clerical alliance seemed to be threatening France with another war: 'le cléricalisme, voila l'ennemi', cried the republican leader Gambetta.

When the republicans finally consolidated their power in the 1880s, anticlericalism inevitably became State policy in a restrained but unrelenting secularization campaign (*la laïcité*) in which the principal battleground was the school system (see p. 141). Popular anticlericalism remained strong among organized and politicized workers: in the 1880s striking anarcho-syndicalist miners dynamited churches, and strikers in Limoges smashed religious statues. At least until 1905, when the Church was finally disestablished, religious conflict was at the heart of the perennial struggle between revolution and reaction.

Apocalypses: 'the final struggle'

C'est la lutte finale,
Groupons-nous et demain
L'Internationale sera le genre humain.

Eugène Pottier, 'L'Internationale', 1871

A final struggle that would abolish injustice and liberate and ennoble mankind was an essential part of the revolutionary vision. Its heady if rather desperate euphoria was perfectly expressed by a member of the Paris Commune, Jules Vallès, in March 1871:

> What a day! That clear warm sun which gilds the cannon's mouth, the smell of flowers, the rustle of flags, the murmur of the revolution . . . Whatever happens, if we must again be beaten and die tomorrow, our generation is consoled! We are paid back for twenty years of defeat and anguish.[24]

The Commune embodied the seduction of the revolutionary gesture: outsiders could see it as doomed, but those involved seem to have been unable to face this stark fact. In retrospect, the ten-week revolutionary victory was sentimentalized as a lost golden age, 'the cherry time', in the words of a famous song by the Communard Jean-Baptiste Clément. Although the bloody repression of the Commune ended one kind of revolutionary fantasy, it was replaced in the 1890s by the anarchist vision of '*le grand soir*', when a revolutionary general strike would bring bourgeois society crashing down: 'Soon perhaps darkness lit by the flickering flames of the Great Evening will cover the earth. Then will come the dawn of joy and fraternity.'[25]

The counter-fantasy of the Right – a mirror image of '*la lutte finale*' – was a White Terror, a 'great sweeping-out'[26] that would restore 'order' by eliminating disruptive elements from society. The notorious (if much exaggerated) 'White Terror' of 1815 was carried out by special summary courts martial (*prévôtés*), but thereafter until 1848 political offences were left to judicial process. But the June 1848 revolt led to summary executions, mass arrests and wholesale transportation of suspects to Algeria by special act of parliament – eloquent proof that these events seemed on a different plane from those of the early 1830s. The December 1851 insurrection – again seen as a criminal *jacquerie* (peasant revolt) – led to further special measures: summary trials by 'mixed commissions' and more mass transportation to Algeria. From the 1850s until the Second World War, transportation to penal colonies became the standard punishment for serious criminals as well as for political prisoners.

The appalling climax came in May 1871. The Paris Commune, condemned by conservatives and liberals as beyond the political pale, a saturnalia of

24. *Le Cri du Peuple*, 28 March 1871.
25. *Le Libertaire*, 1899, in Steenhuysen (April/June1971), pp. 63–76, at p. 65.
26. Phrase used in army report, 1871. Tombs (1981), p. 122.

violence and crime by international revolutionaries and the 'dangerous classes', led to the most savage purge of the century, as far in excess of its cause, in Richard Cobb's phrase, as an appalling level-crossing accident at the end of a school outing to the seaside.[27] At least 10,000 people were killed in Paris between 21 and 28 May, a massacre unparalleled in nineteenth-century Europe, and some 40,000 were arrested. A high proportion of those killed were shot after the fighting had ended, often after drumhead court martial. Foreigners, volunteers, ringleaders or suspected members of the 'dangerous classes' – 'ex-convicts, drunkards, pimps, déclassés, in short, all the vermin of the faubourgs'[28] – were specially targetted. Much of the massacre was known to the public and reported in the press, to the applause of conservatives, who saw it as a solution to the revolutionary threat. 'The ground is strewn with their corpses', Thiers told parliament. 'May this terrible sight serve as a lesson.' The novelist Edmond de Goncourt thought it was 'good that there was neither conciliation nor bargain . . . such a purge, by killing off the combative part of the population, defers the next revolution by a whole generation'.[29] The slaughter was followed by the transportation to New Caledonia of some 5,000 of those considered most dangerous. The conflict of 1871 'which created the most fear and shed the most blood', suggests Furet, was 'the ultimate exorcism' of revolutionary violence in France.[30]

Liberals usually warned against the apocalyptic visions of both Left and Right, which they saw in Aristotelian terms as 'anarchy' and 'despotism'. These were the characteristic nightmares of liberals throughout the century. Revolution might be necessary and justified, as in 1649 in England or 1789 in France, but unless it was quickly controlled, limited and ended, as in 1688 in England and 1775 in America, irrational expectations and 'passions' would lead to uncontrollable disorder and 'anarchy'. France risked becoming 'a vast Tipperary'. The economy would collapse, the hungry would loot shops and *châteaux*. What had happened in 1789–93, they feared, had barely been averted in 1848–51. But anarchy, they believed, was by nature temporary: into the vacuum would burst its antithesis, despotism. 'The worst thing about anarchy is not so much the absence of the government destroyed as the birth of new governments of an inferior type . . . Conquering and sovereign bands form . . . the innate enemies of work, subordination and law.'[31] These conquering bands included in Taine's view the Terrorists of the 1790s, and also the Napoleons, I and III, following in a long line of post-revolutionary despots that went from Caesar to Cromwell. If many liberals admired the genius and dazzling achievements of Napoleon I, and praised his services to France, the orthodox view was to lament the despotic excesses that led finally to Waterloo: in the words of a popular song, 'Gloire au soldat qui nous

27. Cobb (1976), p. 129.
28. Montaudon (1898–1900), vol. 2, p. 276.
29. Goncourt (1969), p. 312.
30. Furet (1992), p. 506.
31. Taine (1878), vol. 2, p. 263.

donna la gloire, Haine au tyran qui nous donna des fers'.[32] Not a few liberals
supported Louis-Napoleon Bonaparte's dictatorship as an emergency solution
to 'anarchy' in 1851, but his disastrous defeat at Sedan in 1870 proved again
that the despotic remedy was as dangerous as the anarchic disease. They
were confirmed in their view that only reason and moderation could ward off
revolutionary apocalypse.

THE REVOLUTIONARY PASSION PLAY

> But yonder, whiff! there comes a sudden heat,
> The gravest citizen seems to lose his head,
> The king is scared, the soldier will not fight,
> The little boys begin to shoot and stab,
> A kingdom topples over with a shriek
> Like an old woman, and down rolls the world
> In mock heroics stranger than our own.
>
> *Tennyson*

The 'revolutionary tradition' involved actions as well as words: what Richard
Cobb has aptly called the 'revolutionary passion play' – a rubric of actions,
words and symbols which revolutionary events followed and through which
they were understood to be revolutionary. Perhaps loosely based on
memories and accounts of the great *journées* from 1789 to 1795, it developed
new features from the 1820s onwards. Contemporaries as different as
Tennyson and Marx noted its self-conscious, even histrionic, features: 'mock
heroics' in which history was repeated 'as farce'.[33] Yet the 'passion play'
threatened all regimes at least until 1871; it brought out genuine heroism in
thousands of obscure and largely forgotten people, and cost thousands their
lives. The 'passion play' was not exclusively Parisian: Lyons especially, and
Marseilles, Limoges and other cities staged their own versions. But while
there could be revolt anywhere, there could be revolution only in Paris. The
drama was played out in familiar settings, whose geography was an essential
part of the tradition: spaces, high ground, rivers, bridges, government
buildings, popular neighbourhoods.

The first act of the passion play was fomenting revolution. Conspiracies,
revived by the secret society the Charbonnerie in the 1820s, were durably
attractive to a handful of activist intellectuals and radical workers, though
almost invariably unsuccessful. Setting up elaborate and fanciful secret
societies – 'winds', 'families', 'seasons' – taking oaths, holding secret meetings,
collecting weapons and ammunition, and even holding clandestine
rehearsals, gave a mystique to political opposition, especially when restricted
suffrage or legal restrictions made open politics hopeless. The most tireless

32. Aubry (1988), p. 231.
33. Similarly, the playwright Jean Gênet recalled rather scornfully that the student
'revolutionaries' of May 1968 seized and occupied the Odéon theatre.

fomenter of revolution was Auguste Blanqui, one of the leading revolutionaries of the 1830s–1840s with Raspail and Barbès, but unique in his obsessive
singlemindedness and the length of his career. His importance was largely as
a model of perseverance, for he had little direct impact on events. The son of
a minor noble who served as a sub-prefect under Napoleon, at nine Blanqui
experienced the Allied invasion when Prussian troops were billetted on his
family, and at seventeen (in 1822) watched the guillotining of four sergeants
for plotting against the Bourbons. In 1827 he was injured in his first riot, and
in 1832 received his first prison sentence. He spent the rest of his life (he died
in 1881) planning revolution, often from prison where he spent in all 34
years. For him, revolution (always linked with the cause of French
nationalism) was an aim in itself: he despised reform, and refused to plan for
a post-revolutionary society, for he assumed that 'every revolution is
progress'.[34] He tried to create an elite underground army to launch a surprise
attack on the State, detonate a mass uprising, and lead a revolutionary
dictatorship which would 'cross the river' to the undiscovered utopia. 'When
one demolishes the old world', he wrote, 'the new is awaiting discovery in its
ruins; one final hammer-blow and it is triumphantly displayed.'[35] None of his
attempts succeeded; most were fiascos. He was an inept planner who
fantasized about the forces at his command. That he retained among generations of would-be revolutionaries and many historians a heroic image
(despite weighty accusations of treachery) says much about the mystique of
violent revolution in France, and its real limitations.

Risings were staged in Paris in 1832 (at the funeral of a nationalist leader,
General Lamarque), 1834 (in response to strikes and a workers' rising in
Lyons), 1839, 1849, August and October 1870 and January 1871. Shots would
be fired during demonstrations or at public buildings; running battles started
in the streets; barricades built; barracks attacked to seize arms. These tactics
resulted in bloodshed, but none succeeded in setting off a revolution. Nor did
the many assassination attempts (usually by loners) that occurred under every
regime – eight against Louis-Philippe alone. However, secret-society activists
may have contributed to pushing largely peaceful mass demonstrations over
the edge into violence in February 1848 and March–April 1871. Sometimes
governments themselves were suspected of provoking violence, especially in
June 1848 and March 1871. On neither of these occasions was that so, though
in 1849 the authorities certainly expected trouble and perhaps welcomed it.

The second act of the passion play was mass disorder in the capital, as in
July 1830, February 1848, June 1848, September 1870 and March 1871. These
were largely spontaneous outbreaks, and usually took both governments and
revolutionaries by surprise. Most people wanted to avert violence, but the
appearance of crowds in the streets could have uncontrollable consequences.
In February 1848, an outbreak of shooting, possibly caused by a nervous
soldier, possibly begun by a left-wing activist, led to troops firing on the

34. Paz (1984), p. 33.
35. Pilbeam (1993), pp. 253–64, at p. 253.

crowd, and the start of a true ritual of revolution, with corpses being paraded round the streets in torchlight processions to arouse popular anger. The tocsin was rung, drums beaten, streetlamps smashed to give cover of darkness, weapons seized from gunsmiths' shops or the prop-rooms of theatres, paving stones ripped up to slow the movement of cannon, and barricades hastily thrown up. Barricades were seen for the first time in 1795, then again during election riots in 1827. Thereafter they became the unmistakable symbol of Parisian revolt. In the first stages, they were built as a signal, to bring people into the streets, or as a gesture of defiance, and even to provoke a reaction from the government. Sometimes they were intended as an obstacle to hamper troops. Some were solidly built and garrisoned to turn neighbourhoods into miniature fortresses. Their construction was a collective ritual, in which passers-by were expected to participate: 'Your paving-stone, citizen!'. Even their very materials – 'a people's cast-offs' said Hugo – could romantically be seen as symbolizing popular resistance: 'that door! that fence! that awning! that doorframe! that broken stove! that cracked saucepan!'[36] In June 1848 and 1871 hundreds were built all over central and eastern Paris.

Who the hundreds or thousands were who turned out to make a revolution is fairly clear from records of casualties, medal-winners (in case of success) or prosecutions (in case of failure). Although such figures are incomplete and imprecise, they give an adequate general indication. Most were skilled working men in their mid-twenties and thirties, relatively settled, married and reasonably law-abiding, employed in the craft industries in which Paris and Lyons specialized: metalworking, joinery, building, printing, textiles, clothing and footwear. What is striking is how stable the picture is, especially between the two different generations of 1848 and 1871.

They were literate, politicized and often members of political or workers' organizations; in 1830 many were former soldiers of Napoleon. What made them turn out for some *journées* and not others was a combination of political demands and economic grievances, principally related to unemployment, especially when these could be blamed on the State. Above all, they turned out in response to what were seen as duplicitous, threatening or provocative acts by the government: in July 1830 the Ordinances of Charles X, in February 1848 the banning of a political meeting, in June 1848 the abolition of the National Workshops, in March 1871 the attempt to disarm the Paris National Guard. In short, their actions always had political aims (they were not bread riots) and were defensive, to preserve what were regarded as rights and to stave off what were feared to be threats.

The third act of the passion play saw the response of the government and its armed forces, always decisive. Governments were reluctant to use excessive force, which could inflame the situation. But to remain inactive, or to offer concessions, might be taken as proof of weakness. To use inadequate force – committing too few troops, for example – could lead to military

36. Hugo (1967), vol. 3, pp. 198–9.

Table 1.1: Participants in Parisian insurrections

	July 1830[1]	June 1848[2]	May 1871[3]
Skilled workers (total)	73.3	60.0	54.4
of whom:			
wood	8.6	10.9	8.0
building	14.8	12.4	15.7
metals	19.2	14.8	11.9
leather	18.0	6.3	5.4
textiles/clothing	8.4	6.5	3.9
luxury goods	1.0	8.5	6.9
printing	3.3	0.6	2.7
Unskilled workers	4.2	13.4	14.9
White collar	3.1	6.7	8.0
Middle classes	2.0	7.3	7.6
of whom:			
small business	2.0	4.1	4.3
professional	0.0	3.2	3.3
Others (total)	17.2	12.6	6.0
of whom:			
servants	12.3	?	4.9
others	4.9	12.6	1.1

[1]1830: % of casualties whose occupations are recorded
[2]1848: % of those accused of insurrection
[3]1871: % of those arrested during and after insurrection

Sources: Merriman (1975), pp. 33–4; Charle (1991), p. 134; Rougerie (1964), p. 127.

débâcle, with soldiers running away or even joining the insurgents. The reaction of the citizen militia, the National Guard, could be decisive: if the National Guard sided with the crowd, the regular troops might well do the same. For governments, therefore, there was no obviously safe role in the passion play. Consequently, decisions and self-confidence tended to oscillate wildly. The reactions of Louis-Philippe and his advisers in February 1848 are a textbook example of what not to do. A public meeting was banned by a government too confident of its strength. Soldiers sent to hold back crowds fired shots, which caused the inevitable angry reaction. The troops were then withdrawn, leaving the streets to the insurgents. The king reviewed 'loyal' National Guards and was booed, which left him shaken and pessimistic; he was in any case reluctant to fight a real battle. He then changed his government three times in rapid succession, appointed a new army commander, abdicated in favour of his infant grandson, and then made a dash for the English Channel, leaving his supporters in complete confusion. The imperial government on 4 September 1870 attempted no resistance at all, and the Thiers government on 18 March 1871 was no more decisive. Personal weaknesses aside, there seems clearly to have been a conviction that beyond a certain point a popular revolution was irresistible, and that to try to withstand it was folly. Fear of the angry crowd was doubtless important, especially given conservative nightmares of the violence of 'the mob'. Especially between 1830 and 1871, conservatives sometimes felt that history was running against them, and they were 'dancing on a volcano'.

The fourth act was the popular offensive. Crowds invaded the real and symbolic centres of government and dispersed (there was, in fact, never any serious attempt to capture or kill) the personnel of what had just become the Old Regime. The Tuileries Palace was stormed in July 1830 and February 1848, and the lower house of parliament at the Palais Bourbon in February and May 1848 and September 1870. At the Tuileries, people swarmed into the state apartments; jubilant citizens took it in turns to sit on the throne, then burnt it. Volunteer guards prevented looting, though in 1830 the wine cellar suffered. At the Palais Bourbon, crowds of armed citizens and National Guards crammed sweating and shouting into the chamber, scrambled into the tribune, occupied the president's chair, rang his bell and attempted to make speeches, pass resolutions, or force the deputies to do so. The same was done at the Hôtel de Ville in October 1870, when perorating revolutionary leaders walked up and down on the cabinet table at which the government were seated. However, if instead of giving in or fleeing for safety, as the scenario required, deputies and ministers sat tight – self-consciously and nervously imitating Roman senators facing the Goths – there could be a lengthy stalemate, as in May 1848 and October 1870. And if loyal forces mustered, the invaders might be ejected. In May 1848, the sound of the drums of approaching National Guards caused the invading revolutionaries to retreat; in October 1870, troops were smuggled into the Hôtel de Ville through a secret tunnel, and after negotiations, the revolutionaries backed down.

The fifth act was choosing a revolutionary government by acclamation: candidates showed themselves on balconies and lists of names were scattered among the crowd to be cheered or booed. This, for revolutionaries, was real democracy. It was best done at the Hôtel de Ville, the ancient city hall, centre of Parisian government. In 1830, it was the appearance there of the Duc d'Orléans that marked his popular acceptance as king. On 24 February 1848, and again on 4 September 1870, left-wing deputies led the crowd from the Palais Bourbon to the Hôtel de Ville to proclaim a republic led by themselves. The Marxist Jules Guesde sat in parliament in the 1890s in the hope that when proletarian revolution broke out, he would be ready and waiting to follow this tradition: but the call never came. In both 1848 and 1870 revolutionary governments made the Hôtel de Ville their headquarters. Naturally the Paris Commune of 1871 sat there, like its predecessor of 1793; and, in a symbolic act of defiance, the defeated Communards burnt it down rather than surrender it, so ending a tradition.[37]

But if the Hôtel de Ville was the symbolic centre of popular power, the

37. General de Gaulle cautiously avoided reviving it in Aug. 1944.

various ministries were the nerve centres of government, and they had to be occupied for power to be exercised: this was the final act. In September 1870, the young radical Gambetta raced in a cab to arrive first at the Ministry of the Interior, and sent telegrams to all the prefects in the provinces naming himself as minister: so minister he remained. The main race in 1830, 1848 and 1870 was to install a moderate government and so forestall more extreme elements. When Paris fell into the hands of a revolutionary government, it proved difficult for opposition to rally in the provinces. In 1830 and February 1848, prefects, generals and local councils either slipped quietly away or protested their loyalty to their new rulers. Local politicians were often quick to secure their own positions, occupying power in their own districts and expecting Paris to recognize them in return. No one tried to organize resistance. Even the royal princes with the army in Algeria in 1848 simply resigned and left. Merely to exist was to have established a certain legitimacy that rallied officials and electors eager to avert 'anarchy'. Existence, indeed, was the major form of legitimacy that nineteenth-century governments could claim, and it was far from negligible: 'the Republic exists', proclaimed Thiers in 1873; 'to think of overthrowing it would be another revolution, and the most dangerous of all'.

Even when revolution occurred, government had to be carried on. Bureaucracy survived. The State never did disintegrate. Irrespective of ideology, there was always a shared desire to restore 'order'. In 1830, ministers and leading liberals searched for compromise even as fighting went on in the streets; it was a similar story in 1848 and 1870. This instinctive determination to control and limit revolution was as important a part of the 'revolutionary tradition' as the readiness to make it.

News of revolution in Paris caused repercussions in the provinces. Popular grievances were settled robustly – that was what liberty and revolution meant: tax offices, enclosed forests, churches, *châteaux*, foreign-built railways, immigrant workers, and money lenders were all at different times targets of popular violence. A period of broadening political mobilization followed as more groups seized the opportunity to press their demands by every means from founding newspapers or clubs and campaigning for election, to demonstrations, strikes or riots. Fears of instability aggravated the economic situation in 1830 and 1848, leading to a vicious circle of increasing discontent. After months or even years, this was invariably ended by a crackdown by the post-revolutionary regime: 1834, June 1848, 1851, 1871. These were 'founding massacres', in Alain Corbin's phrase, the use of force to prove that a new regime was viable.

The provinces would not follow the lead of Paris unconditionally. Paris revolutionaries had to find leaders who could be accepted as a credible national government. Even so, among conservatives of all classes fear and resentment of 'red' Paris accumulated: 'ten times in eighty years Paris has sent France governments ready made by telegraph, and she has had enough of it!' shouted a royalist deputy in 1871. Twice a Parisian revolt was resisted: in June 1848 and in March–May 1871. In June 1848, over 100,000 provincial

National Guards turned out to suppress the 'Reds', pictured as brigands and terrorists who would spread fire and slaughter across France. In 1871, the National Assembly, shorn of many of its Parisian members and meeting in Versailles, pressed the government to resist and crush the insurrection.

After the bloody defeat of the Parisians in May 1871, the founding massacre of the Third Republic, the revolutionary passion play ceased performance: 'in this Paris in flames', judges Furet, 'the French Revolution bade farewell to history'.[38] The force of the crowd was no longer to be the ultimate decider in the political process which it had been since 1789. Later revolutionary situations failed to produce revolutions. The Boulangists made no attempt to march on the Elysée in 1889. When the Dreyfus affair set Paris in turmoil, it was confined to demonstrations and petty riots. The nationalist Paul Déroulède's attempted coup in 1899 was a fiasco. Circumstances had changed: universal suffrage backed up by modern armed forces had made revolt on the barricades an anachronism and a death trap. Significantly, Déroulède appealed to the army, not to the crowd.

EXPLAINING REVOLUTION

> Our century is singular in that it apprehends by memories, as it makes politics with memories.
>
> *Joseph Fiévée, 1818*[39]

Trying to understand the Revolution and its recurring aftershocks was the inescapable problem of nineteenth-century political thinkers. Every French political tendency of the century had to define its position with regard to the Revolution, and this meant explaining it. These explanations will be broadly summarized here under the headings counter-revolutionary (covering all those who rejected the Revolution in principle), centrist (those who considered at least part of the Revolution and its heritage as beneficial) and republican (who regarded it unambiguously as a new dawn of democracy and justice).

Counter-revolutionary explanations

> Revolution . . . is the cry of Satan, 'I shall not obey,' erected into a principle, a right.
>
> *Catechisme de la Révolution, 1878*[40]

The most influential counter-revolutionary thinkers explained the Revolution as essentially anti-Catholic. Louis de Bonald, Joseph de Maistre and (less intelligently) Abbé Barruel saw it as a Satanic enterprise to destroy the Church

38. Furet (1992), p. 506.
39. Mellon (1958), p. 2.
40. Roberts (1973), p. 8.

by undermining the French monarchy, its secular protector. Protestants, freemasons and the *philosophes* were partners in the conspiracy. God had allowed them to succeed as a punishment for France's eighteenth-century impiety: king, court, nobility, clergy and people had all suffered. Out of this suffering could come repentance and salvation.

This explanation overshadowed other counter-revolutionary analyses. Burke's eloquent defence of tradition, and his prophetic warnings of the dangers of trying to make society anew, had great impact when published in French in 1790. Other conservatives within France in the later 1790s and 1800s attacked the excesses of revolution in the language of Enlightenment rationalism. But the most powerful voices among royalist émigrés denounced the Revolution in the name of God.

The hallmark of the extreme Right – 'ultraroyalist' under the Restoration, 'legitimist' after 1830, 'monarchist' or 'conservative' after 1870, 'liberal' or 'nationalist' in the 1890s, for it changed labels as its political situation deteriorated – was never to accept that the Revolution had been beneficial, or that the 'principles of 1789' were valid, even if, for pragmatic reasons, they were prepared by the 1890s to abide by the republican constitution. Those on the Left realized this: 'You accept the Republic . . . But do you accept the Revolution?' They did not: the Revolution, for them, had brought into France godlessness, revolt, individualism and egalitarianism, all disruptive of morality and social order, and the causes of France's decadence.

Like the Left, the counter-revolutionaries saw the Revolution as constantly breaking out in new forms. The design of Italian nationalists on the Papal States in the 1850s–1860s, the 'Roman Question', was seen as a new revolutionary threat to the existence of the Church. But France, instead of doing her duty as 'eldest daughter of the Church', actually helped the nationalists. Defeat by Germany in 1870 and the horrors of the Paris Commune were interpreted as renewed punishment by an angry deity as in the 1790s: 'The daughter betrayed the mother; the daughter is chastised.'[41] Catholic leaders, in fulfilment of a 'national vow' of expiation made in 1870, built the Sacré Coeur basilica on Montmartre, dominating revolutionary Paris.

A new counter-revolutionary explanation of the Revolution was formulated at the end of the century by Charles Maurras, leader of the neo-monarchist Action Française. He too saw revolution as the individualist rejection of authority. But for him it had its roots in Judeo-Christian monotheism which, believing in direct contact between each soul and God, made individual conscience supreme: 'Your idea of justice is a Jewish idea; and your idea of pity and compassion is another Jewish idea, since it flows from an evangelical source . . . Moreover, all individualistic theory is of Jewish making.'[42] This subversive idea had destroyed the Graeco-Roman world, except that the Catholic Church (not really Christian) and the French monarchy had preserved and transmitted classical culture and constituted a source of

41. 1871 pamphlet, in ibid., p. 11.
42. Sutton (1982), p. 37.

authority that every society needed. The Protestant Reformation had renewed the individualist threat, and the Revolution had done so again. Jews, Protestants and democrats (especially freemasons) were carriers of the plague. Maurras exercised a huge influence on Catholic nationalists from the 1890s until the 1940s, when the supporters of the Vichy regime explained France's defeat as a consequence of the individualism and democracy introduced by the Revolution.

Centrist explanations

I regarded the French Revolution overall as a necessary and salutary crisis.

Duc de Broglie, 1867[43]

In this category are all those – royalist, republican or Bonapartist – who by choice or necessity accepted part of the heritage of the Revolution, rejecting both counter-revolution and continued revolution. Intellectual leadership came from liberals, who included many of France's most distinguished writers and orators. Experience of the Revolution and the Empire was at the root of nineteenth-century French liberalism. Its seminal thinkers – Germaine de Staël, Benjamin Constant, Pierre Royer-Collard, the *Idéologues* – had all welcomed 1789, fled the Terror, supported the moderate Republic after 1795, and accepted Napoleon's dictatorship with reservations and sometimes open criticism. They were preoccupied in political and historical writing both with justifying 1789 and condemning and diagnosing the disasters of 1793 and 1799.

For liberals, 1789 had been the justified and inevitable abolition of absolutism, 'feudalism' and privilege. However, they did not agree as to why it had happened. De Staël and Constant in the 1800s saw its cause as the advance of enlightened ideas. For Augustin Thierry, the conflict was racial in origin: the nobility were the descendants of the conquering Franks, the Third Estate were descendants of the defeated Gauls. Other liberal writers were the first to explain the Revolution as a class conflict: François Mignet and Adolphe Thiers, writing in the 1820s, explained the confrontation between the Third Estate and the privileged orders in 1789 as a struggle between bourgeoisie and aristocracy.

All agreed that the introduction of legal and religious equality and representative government by an enlightened elite had fulfilled the Revolution as early as August 1789. But it had not ended: there had ensued years of religious and political conflict, civil and foreign war, terror and oppression. Why? Liberals offered four explanations. First, the refusal of some of the aristocracy to accept the Revolution had precipitated conflict: die-hard reaction was dangerous folly. Second, the Revolution had encouraged utopian political and social projects, exciting irrational 'passions', and causing the irruption of the masses into politics: 'Human beings are sacrificed to

43. Girard (1985), p. 72.

abstractions', lamented Constant in 1813, 'a holocaust of individuals is offered up to "the People" '.[44] Third, the stresses of war had led to increasingly authoritarian government, under the Jacobins and finally under Bonaparte. Fourth – an argument made by Alexis de Tocqueville in *L'Ancien régime et la Révolution* (1856) – the Revolution had swept away restraints on State power by abolishing local and corporate privilege, and hence fulfilled an ambition pursued during 'twenty generations' by the Old Regime.

Revolutions, they believed, might be necessary, but their aims must not be visionary and they must be speedily ended. Monarchs and courtiers must not resist justified and necessary change like the Stuarts. The individual must be protected and despotism restrained. Popular 'passions' must not be aroused; hence their anger with socialists in 1848. Politics should be safe, in Thiers's words, from both the court and the street. And war must be prevented, or 'the tiger' of revolution would slip its leash. After 1830, when liberals held power, this seemed a negative creed – anti-democratic, selfish, unpatriotic – and it cut them off from majority aspirations in the country. When in 1848 a new revolution came, this time directed against them, liberals were dumbfounded, and universal male suffrage showed them to be leaders without followers.

A very different kind of centrist analysis of the Revolution was that of Bonapartism. Though centrist in the sense of accepting part of the revolutionary heritage and deploring both counter-revolution and revolutionary extremism, their analysis was far less subtle than that of the liberals, far less cautious, and far more politically successful. They shifted the focus of the Revolution away from 1789 and 1792–93, seen as preliminary chaotic phases, to the Consulate and Empire, when the charismatic genius of Napoleon, 'Robespierre on horseback', tamed, organized and defended the achievements of the Revolution against internal and external enemies:

> I saved the Revolution, which was on the point of death. I washed off its crimes, I held it up to the eyes of Europe resplendent with glory. I planted new ideas in the soil of France and Europe: their march cannot be reversed.[45]

The Bonapartist history of the Revolution thus became a populist, patriotic and military saga with vast popular appeal to later generations.

Republican explanations

> The Revolution was in the people; there was its heart, its core.
>   *Esquiros, Histoire des Montagnards, 1847*[46]

Republican histories of the Revolution, pioneered in the 1830s and 1840s by Blanc, Cabet, Buchez, Esquiros, Lamartine, and above all Michelet, differed

44. Johnson (1991), p. 70.
45. Last testament, 1821.
46. Fritz (1988), p. 101.

from those of liberals in seeing revolution as the act of the people. The storming of the Bastille, not the deliberations of the Estates General, was the inaugural revolutionary act. Mass action was not a perversion of the Revolution, but its very essence; for its true aims were popular sovereignty and equality. The popular struggle was seen as ancient (some accepted Thierry's theory of a Gauls-versus-Franks struggle) marked by generations of sufferings and reverses, which had culminated in the popular victories of 1789–94 and opened a new era in world history. The French people, sanctified by long struggles for freedom, transformed itself through the Revolution from a subject race into a nation of free citizens – the only true nation, whose sacrifices would in time redeem mankind, said Michelet: France 'says to the world, Take, this is my blood'. The Revolutionary Wars of the 1790s were seen as a struggle to defend the Revolution against international reaction, and to liberate the less enlightened peoples beyond French borders: the battle of Valmy in 1792 was as great a revolutionary symbol as the storming of the Bastille. This view explains the incandescent nationalism of republicans during the first half of the century and beyond. It also provided a patriotic view of the Revolution which, by stressing the struggle against foreign enemies, could eventually form the basis for a national consensus: right-wing nationalists rallied to this patriotic version of the Revolution from the 1890s onwards.

Yet analysis of the Revolution reflected serious political divergences among republicans. Many moderate republicans and early socialists condemned 1793 and the Terror, and accepted the liberal view of a Revolution gone wrong; but others regarded Robespierre and the Jacobins as heroes, and their dictatorship as the climax of the Revolution. This was a recurring debate from the 1820s onwards, with ominous implications for any future republican government. It was particularly important in the 1860s, when the elderly Edgar Quinet and the youthful Jules Ferry helped to turn mainstream republicanism in a liberal direction by interpreting the Revolution as a struggle for freedom, betrayed by the Jacobin Terror. Republicans must reject the Terror if they were ever to be an acceptable government for France. 'Whoever will demonstrate that the Terror was not necessary, whoever will rid democracy of that dream of dictatorship which sometimes stirs it like a temptation and sometimes obsesses it like a nightmare, will deserve much from the future.'[47] But other republicans continued to justify the Jacobin dictatorship as necessary to defend the Revolution against treason and foreign aggression: this was the point of the radical Clemenceau's famous declaration in 1891 that 'the French Revolution is a bloc from which nothing can be removed'. For them, the 'dream of dictatorship' had not wholly dissipated, as Clemenceau demonstrated in 1917.

A second source of profound disagreement was the social meaning of the Revolution. From the 1840s onwards some socialists – notably Blanc, Buchez and Esquiros – adapted and extended the liberal idea of class struggle

47. Ferry, in Furet (1992), p. 480; see also Furet (1986).

between bourgeoisie and nobility by explaining the most radical phase of the Revolution as a new class struggle between the victorious bourgeoisie and the still oppressed masses. Robespierre was cast in the unlikely role of popular hero. This interpretation became the basis of socialist and later communist historiography. It explained the recurring outbreaks of revolution in the nineteenth century as episodes in a continuing class war against the capitalist bourgeoisie, whose 'Bastilles have yet to be taken', wrote a socialist paper in 1880.[48] The Revolution could only be ended by a proletarian victory creating social as well as political justice: *'la République démocratique et sociale'*.

THE DECLINE OF THE REVOLUTIONARY TRADITION

I shall always love cherry time:
From that time I have an open wound in my heart!
Jean-Baptiste Clément, Le Temps des cerises

We must all beware of the Utopias of those who, dupes of their imagination or ignorantly behind the times, believe in a panacea . . .
Gambetta, 1872[49]

There are at least two widely accepted views of when the French Revolution finally ended, in the sense that the political culture engendered by the Revolution – fears, hopes, resentments, ideas and political practices – ceased to dominate political life. The first is the 1870s, when, after the defeat of the Paris Commune, the Third Republic legally enshrined the 'principles of 1789'. To date the end of the Revolution in the 1870s, however, begs many questions. What about the persistence (however unsuccessful) of would-be revolutionary movements in the 1880s and 1890s, Marxist, anarchist, Blanquist and nationalist? What about the Dreyfus case (1894–99) which again brought the conflict between Republic and Church to a head? What about the radicalization of politics caused by the First World War and the Bolshevik Revolution, which brought the 'revolutionary tradition' up to date and thus helped to revive counter-revolution? What about the struggle between the Vichy regime, which renounced the very name Republic, and the Resistance?

These are the reasons that lead other historians to suggest the post-Second World War period as the real end (if end there can be) of the era of the Revolution,[50] with counter-revolutionary forces defeated, and with 'thirty glorious years' of economic and social modernization sweeping away the traditional 'stalemate society' in which ancient grievances and quarrels had so long survived. To complete the process came de Gaulle's creation of the Fifth

48. Gildea (1994), p. 46.
49. Bury (1973), pp. 98–9.
50. For example, Hayward (1991), pp. 269, 291–5. He does suggest, however, that 'the Revolution is not entirely over'.

Republic in 1958, bringing unprecedented political stability. The withering away of the Communist Party after 1970 and even François Mitterrand's election in 1981, showing that, unlike most of its predecessors, the regime could survive major political change, have been suggested as the years in which the last ripples of 1789 died out.

Whichever of these alternatives is preferred, there are several points to bear in mind concerning the evolution of the 'revolutionary tradition'. It was at its peak between 1830 and 1848, a period which combined narrowly-based governments with limited suffrage, the high-point of Romantic 'political messianism' (as Talmon called it), the first phase of economic transformation, and weak and unreliable armed forces – themes to be examined later in this book. Other countries coped with similar problems with fewer, or no, revolutionary outbursts: France really did have a uniquely revolution-prone political culture. Yet even so, all the major outbreaks were largely unexpected and unplanned reactions to government actions: few people ever positively wanted a revolution, and those who did had little success in bringing one about.

Much has been said above about the aggravation of conflict by fear. But over the long term, fear acted as a moderating factor. Most people wanted to avoid another Terror and also to avoid a counter-revolution, with a return to power of nobles and priests. As soon as it was consulted, the electorate (whether narrow or broad) voted for safety, against those who seemed the disturbers of the fragile equilibrium: against the ultraroyalists in 1816; against the liberals in 1820; against the ultras again in 1827; against the reds in 1848, 1851 and 1870; against the royalists in 1877; against General Boulanger in 1889 and so on. All parties, if they wanted to win significant support, had to reassure public opinion: this can be seen from Louis XVIII's promise of 'pardon and forgetfulness' to Louis-Napoleon's 'the Empire means peace', and from Thiers's 'conservative republic' to Mitterrand's *force tranquille*. As Thiers liked to say, *'la France est centre-gauche'*.

Yet from the 1880s onwards, many on Left and Right believed that revolution was still possible. Blanquism continued to retain the support of nostalgic revolutionaries, especially in Paris, though its principal activities became commemorative and symbolic, such as the annual commemoration of the Commune at the 'mur des Fédérés' at the Père Lachaise cemetery, when *'Le Temps des cerises'*, a music-hall song that had become a lament for the lost revolution, was wistfully sung. This was a 'revolutionary tradition' in the most literal sense, but significantly although Blanquists continued to look out for revolutionary situations they never attempted to practise their old insurrectionary tactics: they were now 'liturgists', says Hutton, not revolutionaries.[51] The mystique remained most attractive to relatively marginal groups such as non-organized workers, intellectuals and students. Anarchists carried out sporadic and sometimes spectacular acts of violence (a bomb was thrown into the Chamber of Deputies in 1893, and the president of the

51. Hutton (1981), p. 36.

Republic, Sadi Carnot, was murdered in 1894). But these were uncoordinated and politically futile acts. The anarchist dream of a revolutionary general strike was no more practical: indeed, many of its proponents regarded it as a 'myth' (in the term used by the theorist Georges Sorel) to inspire the masses. This was, suggests Steenhuysen, the 'behaviour of defeat', a consolation for powerlessness.[52] French socialism was periodically divided and marginalized by its rhetorical attachment to an impossible revolution, which contrasted with its acceptance in practice of the 'bourgeois Republic'. Moreover, the revolutionary tradition tended to lose its bearings politically, with some of its most determined supporters allying with former royalists and Bonapartists to form a nationalist 'revolutionary Right'. On the Left, the newest and most attractive revolutionary ideology was Marxism, embodied by the Parti Ouvrier Français (POF), commonly known as 'Guesdists', from the name of the leader and principal theorist, the journalist Jules Guesde. It fitted well into the emotive but since 1871 directionless revolutionary tradition, for it promised revolution in the future and prescribed patience in the present. Its 'scientific' approach to revolution as possible only when the 'proletariat' had attained overwhelming social and political dominance (something that was clearly a distant prospect in France) provided an incontrovertible justification for abandoning the tradition of the spontaneous rising of the 'people' on the barricades while maintaining a rhetorical commitment to a guaranteed revolutionary victory in a never defined future.

Once universal male suffrage had been established in 1848, the revolutionary tradition lost its chief justification: it was no longer the only way of asserting popular sovereignty. After 1848–51 there were no more major revolutionary conflicts in peacetime: 1870–71 and 1940–44 were intimately linked with defeat in war, which destroyed the existing regime and left a vacuum. Without the war of 1870, the 'revolutionary tradition' would probably have ended in 1851, with the triumphant Bonapartist claim to have both ended and preserved the Revolution. The crucial impact of war on France explains why that was the second great obsession.

52. Steenhuysen (1971), p. 74.

CHAPTER 2

WAR

France . . . eminently bellicose and warlike, how ardently she will accept the duel of war!

Etienne Cabet, 1840[1]

The most explosive consequence of the French Revolution was war. 'Militarized nationalism', notes Schama, was its 'heart and soul'.[2] The level of economic and manpower mobilization was unprecedented, and had lasting political and ideological consequences: in Mann's terms, the 'four greatest modern state crystallizations – capitalism, militarism, representation and the national issue – were institutionalized together'.[3] For a generation before 1815 France was almost continuously at war. During the century after 1815 she was marked by war more than any major European country, undertaking eight wars or expeditions in Europe,[4] engaging in conflict with all the other continental Great Powers, and fighting innumerable colonial campaigns at a cost in French soldiers' lives of about 350,000[5] – a toll exceeded only in Russia, whose population was of course far greater. To this must be added civilian losses, very high in 1870–71. Fundamental political changes stemmed from war: the fall of the old monarchy; the rise and fall of Napoleon; the Bourbon restorations of 1814 and 1815; the fall of the Second Empire in 1870 and its replacement by the Third Republic; the fall of the Third Republic in 1940 and of the Vichy regime in 1944; and the installation of the Fifth Republic in 1958.

Constant expectation and fear of war and preparation for it deeply affected political, cultural and economic life. Politically, for example, the fatal conservatism of the July Monarchy in the 1840s was largely due to fear that a

1. Cabet (1840), 6th letter, p. 15.
2. Schama (1989), p. 858.
3. Mann (1993), p. 214.
4. The European engagements were: Spain (1823), Greece (1827–28), Antwerp (1831), Ancona (1832), Rome (1849), Crimean War (1854–55), Italian War (1859) and Franco-German War (1870–71).
5. Chesnais (1976), p. 178, who estimates 250,000 in European and 100,000 in colonial wars.

nationalistic left-wing government would precipitate a disastrous war with Europe. Opposition to the Second Empire in the 1860s was strengthened by fear of Napoleon III's bellicosity. Electoral setbacks of republicans in 1871 and 1885, of royalists in 1875–79, and of nationalists in 1889 owed much to fear that their victory would lead to war. During the 1860s the republicans and during the 1910s the socialists gained support by opposing military expansion. The expectation of war provided the context for nationalism, left-wing anti-patriotism and the Dreyfus affair.

Beyond party politics, the themes of victory and defeat, patriotism and martial virtue and the contrary vices of selfishness and materialism, fears of national military decline and projects for regeneration were emphasized in the arts and philosophy, and pressed on a wider audience by the press, the popular arts and the schools, whose textbooks told the history of France as principally a history of war. The army, especially after the introduction of universal conscription in 1889, became, with the primary schools, an instrument for inculcating national culture and identity. It was also a huge burden, imposing the most stringent conscription in Europe, and by far the highest per capita defence expenditure of any of the continental powers. The concept of citizenship as masculine was reinforced by the stress on military service. Sport was regarded as an aspect of military training. Even sex was mobilized to serve military interests, with inducements to breed more future soldiers. The first French social law, to regulate child labour in 1841, was justified as protecting future 'defenders of the fatherland'. The economy too was affected by war. The costs and losses of the Napoleonic Wars and the war of 1870 both had fundamental consequences. Tariffs, demanded as protection for strategic industries and food supplies, and military influences on railway building and foreign investment significantly affected development.

FRANCE AFTER WATERLOO, 1815–70

France had reached the apogee of power during the Revolutionary and Napoleonic Wars, dominating Europe, reaching and even exceeding her 'natural frontiers', the Rhine and the Alps. Then had come stunning collapse, final defeat at Waterloo, and loss of territory, power and wealth. Occupation by huge foreign armies left memories of humiliation and material exactions, and the knowledge that the European powers, regarding France as a potential threat, might repeat the invasions of 1814 and 1815.

Every government after 1815 came under pressure to reverse this decline. Left-wing French nationalists believed that France was hemmed in by a European Old Order that was the enemy of the Revolution and hence of the French nation, and that France must somehow break down the 'coalition' against her. From 1830 until 1848, the main likelihood seemed to be that the wars of the 1790s would be renewed, with France again fighting to spread revolution, to avenge Waterloo and destroy the hated 'treaties of 1815'. These treaties had redrawn the French border so that invasion routes – Rhine crossings, Alpine passes, frontier fortresses – were in unfriendly hands. Hence the determination to assert influence in buffer zones, especially Belgium and northern Italy, and also in Spain, Switzerland and the Rhineland. Hence too the dream of statesmen under several regimes to regain the 'natural frontiers', the Rhine and the Alps, both to ward off invasion and to win the popularity that such a coup would bring.

To a remarkable extent, Napoleon III took over this programme during the 1850s, defeating Russia and Austria, creating an independent Italy, winning the 'natural frontier' of the Alps and making France the 'arbiter of Europe'. But these very successes brought France to a confrontation with Germany in the 1860s, which changed the prospect entirely: from then on, relations with Germany have dominated many aspects of French life.

Facing the 'Holy Alliance', 1815–48

War or the desire for war dates from 1789 . . . when foreign governments, the governments of despotism, of aristocracy, realized that it meant liberty and equality in France.

Lafayette, 1831

The Bourbons had returned to France after Waterloo in 'the baggage train of the allies' – a stigma they never lived down. Their opponents considered them to be 'lackeys of the Holy Alliance' (the anti-revolutionary alliance proposed by Tsar Alexander I), brought back in order to eradicate the Revolution and repress democracy in France. Every grievance – from press censorship to unemployment, from foreign economic competition to immigration – could thus be blamed on the anti-French machinations of the 'Holy Alliance', abetted by the treacherous Bourbons and their clique.

For the Bourbons and their supporters, the defeat of Napoleon had indeed been the defeat of revolution, but a salutary defeat that set the country back on the road to peace and stability; the Allies of Waterloo were their allies too, and the aim of French diplomacy was to bring France back within the European state system as a trusted partner. A war against the European Powers would be a mortal catastrophe which would again unleash revolution inside and outside France. The desire of the foreign minister Chateaubriand to 'wither the laurels of Waterloo' and 'busy the French with glory' in the Bourbon cause led to his dismissal after the successful but risky intervention in Spain in 1823. Yet the invasion of Spain, even though to restore the Spanish Bourbons, proved popular as a sign that France had recovered her prestige, not least by annoying Britain, and opposition to the Bourbons flagged. It was becoming an accepted view – one that would lead France into a series of disasters over the next half-century – that domestic popularity required success abroad. Charles X was much more ready for adventure, and dreamed of regaining Belgium and the Rhine frontier. He intervened in Greece in 1829 and in 1830 attacked Algiers; not the least advantage was that this again was an act of defiance to Britain. However, none of this was enough to repair the disastrous handling of domestic politics, which resulted in the overthrow of the Bourbons in July 1830.

The 1830 revolution had European significance. For French nationalists, the fall of the 'lackeys of the Holy Alliance' had annulled the defeat of 1815. 'The cannon of Paris', they proclaimed, 'has silenced the cannon of Waterloo.' Sympathetic uprisings broke out in Belgium and Poland. A general revolutionary upheaval in Europe, backed up by French bayonets, seemed inevitable, even desirable: 'perhaps this looks very much like a general war ... but the opposition does not mind a general war', wrote the left-wing *National* (13 August 1831). National Societies formed to make preparations; National Guards drilled. Victory was seen as certain with the help of revolutionary and nationalist movements in other countries, which were only waiting for France to give the signal. Hence the persistent popular support for Belgian, Italian and especially Polish independence – Poland being 'the France of the north', a bulwark against the Cossack hordes. Louis-Philippe and his ministers tried to steer a middle course between the revolutionary and conservative positions. France after 1830 must be seen as having recovered her standing in Europe, and though careful not to precipitate war, they sent troops into Belgium (to enforce evacuation by the Dutch) and Italy (to counterbalance Austrian influence). But for nationalists, these were cowardly half-measures, merely postponing the inevitable conflict.

During the 1830s and 1840s, nationalists believed that the struggle was widening to prevent the future domination of the world by Britain, Russia or America. Napoleon's prediction that possession of Constantinople would give 'dominion of the world' was often quoted. The need to prevent France falling behind explains much of the interest in Algeria, Egypt, and the Pacific: less for any immediate need than in anticipation of a great future struggle. But Louis-Philippe, supported by most of the small electorate, refused any initiative that risked economic upheaval, military complications or, most of all, confrontation with the Great Powers. In 1836 he backed out of military involvement in Spain and in 1840 refused to allow his government, led by Thiers, posing as the leader of the national cause, to pursue a policy of support for Mohammed Ali, the pro-French pasha of Egypt. The 1840 crisis brought France to the brink of a war in Europe against all the Great Powers: the army was increased and Paris massively fortified. Demonstrations of patriotism broke out in theatres and the streets: the government even had to permit public singing of the 'Marseillaise'. There were strikes, demands for suffrage reform, and another attempt to assassinate the king. These events – followed a few months later by the ceremonious return of Napoleon's remains from St Helena, which brought out huge crowds – give a glimpse of the power of nationalist feeling among the urban population, and how even the prospect of war brought with it the threat of revolutionary upheaval.

Prudence was encouraged by the army high command, whose 'appetite for European conflict remained small'.[6] They were painfully aware of France's

6. Cox (1994), p. 45.

military weakness, and planned no great liberating invasions: their only hope was a fighting retreat from the frontiers towards Paris. Their view of war was a realistic one, which had an effect on all governments but, being secret, no effect on public opinion. Nationalists thought France was everywhere falling behind. Many thought that a racial competition was in progress between Teutons, Slavs and Latins to be the future masters of civilization. There were three great interconnected revolutionary struggles, wrote the socialist Considérant: of races and nations, for political liberty, and for socialism.[7]

While the king's and Guizot's attempt to put French foreign policy on what they considered a rational basis was successful inside the small electorate, and helped Guizot to win a safe parliamentary majority in 1846, it aroused the utmost bitterness and contempt among nationalists, who accused the regime of cravenly putting the material interests of a corrupt 'bourgeoisie' above the greatness, honour and liberty of France and her protégés. These recriminations damaged the regime's prestige, especially among the urban middle class, the National Guard and the army whose support was vital. 'It is above all the mistrust caused by the government's handling of the *foreign question* that makes us desire the reign of Democracy so strongly; that is the main cause of our internal agitations', wrote the socialist Cabet in 1840.[8] The government proved practically powerless in the crisis of 1848: as one critic had predicted, it suffered 'a revolution of contempt'.

The republican opposition, which took power in February 1848, found itself under even greater pressure: the wave of revolutions in Europe led to expectations, as in 1830, of a great revolutionary war, and rebels in Italy were encouraged by the hope of French aid. Volunteers flocked to the National Guard, to the new Garde Mobile, and to volunteer forces on the frontier. Amateurish attempts were made to invade Belgium, Germany and Italy. The provisional government, many of them nationalists, suddenly became aware of the dangers of a European war with France in a state of political, social and economic chaos. The State was almost bankrupt. The army consisted of only 85,000 men fit for duty. The foreign minister Lamartine reassured foreign governments in private while using cautiously patriotic rhetoric in public. Words failed to satisfy the mainly Parisian revolutionary Left, and on 15 May 1848 the new Constituent Assembly was invaded by a crowd demanding aid for Poland and the immediate dispatch of an army to the Rhine to threaten Prussia. This would have begun both a new domestic revolution and the great international conflict so long feared or hoped for. As in the 1830s, the threat was defeated by repression of the Left. Soon the question of foreign war was overshadowed by social conflict, but it was nevertheless on another 'national' question, the expedition to Rome in June 1849, that the Parisian Left made their last (for two decades) unsuccessful attempt at insurrection.

7. Considérant (1849:b), passim.
8. Cabet (1840), 6th letter, pp. 20–1.

The cult of glory

> Glory is such a powerful cement, it surrounds a throne with such a brilliant aura, it
> sinks such deep roots for a new dynasty, that it would perhaps be politic to seek it
> for its own sake.
>
> *General Lamarque, 1831*[9]

The glories of war were epitomized by the wars of Napoleon. As Michelet put
it, 'above the Revolution rose the Empire, and buried it beneath its banners,
victories and laurel-wreaths'.[10] Why so many Frenchmen were willing to
regard those wars with nostalgic pride, and even to contemplate their
renewal, is worth consideration. On one hand, the costs in blood and
treasure had substantially been borne by France's allies and subject peoples.
For certain regions and industries, war had meant prosperity, ended by the
defeat of 1814. Some of these regions – the east, Paris and the Rhône basin –
had rallied to Napoleon in 1815, and remained thereafter nationalist and
left-inclined. Liberals saw Napoleon's defeat (however much they criticized
aspects of his reign) as the defeat of the Revolution by reactionaries. Former
soldiers and officials, several hundred thousand of them, transmitted heroic
legends of the war, and in turn became heroes of popular literature. Finally,
the sufferings and costs of the wars, and of any future war, were discounted
by blaming the other side. France had been defending the Revolution against
a reactionary attack led by perfidious Albion; Napoleon, in his own account
and that of his admirers, had been a reluctant warrior. He was, notes
Schroeder, 'one of the most remarkable, persuasive and impudent liars in
history'.[11] If war recommenced, the reasons would be the same: passionate
advocates of war such as Carrel and Lamarque invariably argued that it was
inevitable, because the reactionary powers were planning to attack. If or
when war came, it would be a glorious crusade of liberation, both at home
and abroad, and victory was guaranteed. For Napoleon, as he himself
asserted, had only been defeated by treachery when on the brink of final
victory. The next time there would be no hitch: a French army had only to
march to the Rhine and raise the tricolour, and the peoples of Europe would
welcome them as liberators.

Glory would unite all classes in a fraternal national spirit, the antithesis of
the materialistic egotism of the bourgeoisie – what Tocqueville called the
'little democratic and bourgeois stew-pot' and Michelet called 'the reign of
gold, of the Jew'.[12] It would sweep away the timid and unpatriotic and place
in power a popular 'national' government. This might be republican,
Bonapartist, or even royal: Louis-Philippe's dashing soldier-heir, the Duc

9. Chamber of Deputies, 15 Jan. 1831.
10. Crubellier (1991), p. 331.
11. Schroeder (1994), p. 469.
12. Tocqueville (1985), p. 143; Michelet (1876 [1869]), p. xxvii.

d'Orléans, was much fancied for this role. Perhaps fortunately, he was killed in a road accident in 1843. If glory was a powerful cement, its lack was corrosive. In Tocqueville's words: 'if the idea is allowed to grow that we, once a strong and great nation . . . allow everything to go on without us . . . [it] would . . . lead to the burial of the monarchy itself beneath the ruins of our national honour'.[13] However, there were safer and cheaper ways of creating an aura of glory than a European war: completing Napoleon's Arc de Triomphe, placing his statue in the Place Vendôme, making his ageing marshals ministers and bringing his remains back to the Invalides. Still relatively safe, though vastly more expensive, was the conquest of Algeria, in which the king's sons took a well publicized part. Economic gain and colonial settlement were far less important than glory and the hope of putting patriotic fire into the bellies of the nation.

The glories of war and the prestige of the warrior were reiterated in every medium. Royalty now always appeared in military uniform, and surrounded themselves with soldiers: even at Charles X's coronation, a consciously archaic gesture, four of Napoleon's marshals played leading ceremonial roles. Several of Louis-Philippe's governments were nominally headed by marshals, and all his sons served actively in the armed forces. Leading contemporary artists – Horace Vernet, Gérard, later Meissonnier, Neuville and Détaille – specialized in battle scenes. Louis-Philippe hung them in a special Salle des Batailles at the restored Versailles. At a more popular level, soldiers were a major theme of the coloured cartoon *images d'Epinal*, and of many prints by Charlet and Raffet. There was a spate of patriotic plays about Napoleon in the 1840s. The fictional character Chauvin, 'the soldier-ploughman', had very wide currency, combining the characteristically French virtues of soldier and peasant – a literary and sentimental theme that lasted well into the twentieth century.[14] Songwriters took up bellicosity as a favourite theme, at a time when singing clubs were a highly popular pastime and a means of spreading ideas. Historians recounted the triumphs and heart-rending defeats of the French, in the hope of rekindling patriotic fervour and causing readers 'to feel enthusiasm and emotion for something other than . . . the price of railway shares'.[15]

Artistic portrayals of war reflected the Romantic taste for pathos, tragedy, sacrifice and inspiring heroism. Combat was a glorious moral contest, won by courage and dash. French victory had been, and would again be, the reward of French intellectual and moral superiority: 'The French soldier is everywhere acknowledged to be the first for élan, for movement, for improvization in hand-to-hand combat . . . The French soldier is the first soldier in the universe on a battlefield, provided that he is marching forward.'[16] The French army was superior because it encapsulated the unique unity and brotherhood of the nation:

13. Rémusat (1958), vol. 3, p. 449.
14. Puymège (1993).
15. Saint-Aulaire, in Bury and Tombs (1986), p. 149.
16. Griffith (1989), p. 121.

His father showed him the people, the army that was passing, the bayonets glistening, the tricolour flag . . . 'Look, my son, look well, there is France, there is the Fatherland! All are like one man. One soul and one heart. All would die for one.[17]

This was not only literary cliché, for it also affected military thinking, giving rise to a French tradition of making war some of which survived at least until 1914. This emphasized spontaneity, not planning; guts, not brains; morale, not numbers; a taste for the grisly joys of cold steel, not advanced technology. Combat was a fantasy of pleasure: in the words of one general: 'One goes into battle as if to one's mistress: the same palpitations, same embraces, same hopes and same uncertainties.' Wounds were always 'glorious', but not obscene. Death was an enviable apotheosis: 'Happy the man who died amid these pomps! / For God, my lads, gives you a fine decease!' sang Béranger encouragingly.[18]

The resonance of all this in the country was enormous. Béranger's songs, for example, had a vast circulation, and he became one of the most genuinely popular writers of the early nineteenth century, from cottage to Academy. The appeal of war was not solely vicarious and literary. In 1815, thousands spontaneously flocked to Napoleon's banner. The 1830 street fighting was equally spontaneous. Hundreds of thousands joined the National Guard when war seemed likely in 1830 and 1848. Wearing a uniform part-time, as in the National Guard, had attractions for the middle class and even the Left, who had an exuberant taste for thigh-boots and gold braid up until the Paris Commune of 1871 when some revolutionary fighters ran up extravagant military tailors' bills.

But in less exciting years, the tedious life of a peacetime army had little prestige. Conscription was always detested. Its long duration, up to seven years, ruined peasant family economies, delayed marriage and disrupted middle-class careers. About a quarter of those called up – sons of the upper classes, and prosperous peasants and artisans – avoided it by paying for a substitute. Self-mutilation, desertion, magic spells or registering new-born boys as girls were cheaper but less reliable remedies. Violence between soldiers and civilians was common, with civilians, especially in rural areas, frequently the aggressors. As in Britain, the rank and file came disproportionately from the poorer highland areas: men who could not afford to buy themselves out or who volunteered as a career. Officers came disproportionately from Paris and the traditionally military east, both patriotic and liberal regions. They were not highly paid and as a profession had modest social status: 'the uniform does not open salon doors'.[19] Garrison life meant threadbare boredom, drink, debt, duels, pox and suicide.

17. Michelet, in Citron (1989), p. 20.
18. Béranger (1857), vol. 2, p. 89.
19. Serman (1982), p. 136.

Revenge for Waterloo, 1849–70

> I detest the treaties of 1815 that some today would like to make the basis of our
> foreign policy.
>
> *Napoleon III, 1866*[20]

It was not the Republic, but Louis-Napoleon Bonaparte, later Napoleon III,
who went furthest in pursuing the objectives invoked by the nationalist Left
since 1830. He intended to 'end the era of revolutions' by (among other
things) satisfying nationalist ambitions inside and outside France. This would
finally expunge Waterloo. Aided by the turmoil caused by the 1848
revolutions and by friction among the other Great Powers, he intervened in
Rome in 1849 to save the papacy from revolution, but also as a first step
towards reasserting French hegemony in Italy. In 1853–54, in alliance with
Britain, he defeated Russia in the Crimean War. The war was ineptly
managed by all but the French were certainly the least incompetent. The war
removed Russian influence from European affairs, destroyed what remained
of 'the Coalition' of powers that had opposed French ambitions since 1814,
and thus set the scene for extensive and revolutionary changes in the
geography and power structure of Europe.

Deciding to resolve the long-running Italian problem, the emperor carefully
provoked a war with Austria in May 1859. The campaign was no better
organized than that against Russia, but the army, experienced in the Crimea
and north Africa, proved able to muddle through. In June the armies
floundered bloodily into each other at Magenta and Solferino, both won by
the aggressiveness of the battle-hardened French troops. The Austrian army
retreated, defeated but not destroyed, to its fortresses, leaving the French the
prospect of a long and bloody campaign. Meanwhile, Prussia began to
mobilize its forces to impose a ceasefire, and throughout Germany there were
alarming signs of nationalist support for Austria. Though the French people
may have been reassured of the invincibility of their army, Napoleon and his
generals dreaded a second front on the Rhine, and a quick peace was signed
at Villafranca in July. Italy's archaic political structure collapsed following
Austria's defeat and a Kingdom of Italy was established in 1860. It paid for
Napoleon's help by handing over Nice and Savoy to France: the 'natural
frontier' on the Alps.

The Italian adventure won the emperor acclaim among the nationalist
urban masses. The middle classes sulked, but in the Faubourg Saint-Antoine,
cradle of Parisian revolution, so great was the enthusiasm that Napoleon's
carriage could hardly pass as he left for the front; the crowd tried to
unharness the horses and haul it by hand to the Gare de Lyon. Not since 1848
had he met such warmth in the capital, to which he replied by amnestying all
political offenders. Like his uncle, he had won the support of Paris workers
by a nationalist war. The military superiority of the French army and nation
seemed amply demonstrated, with new military heroes such as the colonial

zouaves, the 'Red Devils', whose exotic uniform was soon copied by armies all over the world.

Austria's defeat encouraged Prussia, in alliance with the new Italy and with the connivance of Napoleon, to force the Austrians again into war in 1866 to decide the mastery of Germany. Napoleon hoped for an opportunity to gain more of the 'natural frontier' on the Rhine, but was deterred from military intervention by the unpopularity of another war, and by realization of the French army's numerical weakness, especially as a large part of it was chasing guerrillas in Mexico. His hopes were finally wrecked by the rapid and crushing Prussian victory at Königgrätz (Sadowa) in July 1866. This won Prussia control of northern Germany and raised the possibility of her incorporating the whole of non-Austrian Germany in the foreseeable future. Napoleon secretly sounded out Bismarck on the possibility of acquiring compensation on the Rhine, if not by acquiring German territory (which Bismarck ruled out) then by buying Luxembourg or possibly annexing Belgium: he needed to show that his policy had gained something for France. It came to nothing, but reports of Napoleon's intrigues caused alarm in Germany, Belgium and Britain.

The French government had been forced to recognize the inadequacy of the army. The most optimistic estimate was that France could eventually field 450,000 men, whereas the Prussians could raise at least 800,000.[21] Napoleon decided to increase it: from this time until the First World War the army would be a central political issue and a major social, cultural and economic influence. Unlike the new Prussian system, which conscripted annually a large number of men for a relatively short period, who then constituted a large trained reserve, the French system since 1832 had conscripted, by ballot, a limited proportion of the available men and kept them with the colours for a long period – up to seven years. The reserve of trained ex-conscripts available in time of war was therefore relatively small. The defenders of the system, who invariably quoted Napoleon I, believed that long service made better soldiers, obedient, cool under fire, skilled in fieldcraft, and adept in *'le système D'* – *'se débrouiller'*. Recent events in the Crimea, Italy, China and Africa gave force to the argument. Moreover, old soldiers were thought to be more reliable in case of civil disorder, having lost their ties with civilian society. Last but not least, selective conscription was popular with all those who escaped it.

Napoleon and his minister of war, Marshal Niel, designed reforms to ensure a wartime strength of one million men. Service was reduced from seven years to five for those selected, with a further four years in the reserve. Those who drew a 'good number' or bought exemption were no longer to get off scot free, but would serve for four years in the reserve and then another five in a territorial army, the Garde Nationale Mobile. This was perhaps the most widely unpopular act of the whole reign and, reported one official, 'the most serious blow to the Emperor's popularity'.[22] Taxpayers bemoaned the cost: in

21. Holmes, R. (1984), p. 92.
22. Case (1954), p. 235.

the 1869 elections, 678 out of 700 candidates demanded a reduction in military spending, which amounted to over a third of the budget. Economists, employers and small farmers declared that there would be a crippling loss of labour. Families lamented the loss of their sons. Reports of public discontent streamed in from local authorities. Pro-government deputies insisted on watering down the bill: 'we have got to vote this law as the Emperor wants it, but we'll fix it so that it can't work'.[23] Garde Mobile training was reduced to fifteen days per year, and no more than 24 hours at a time. Even this caused riots in Paris and the south. Republican leaders had lost their enthusiasm for wars of liberation that increased the popularity of the detested emperor. They feared that Napoleon might use a stronger army for further adventures, as well as for repression at home; whereas if France were ever attacked, they believed that a *levée en masse* of patriotic citizens could see off any invader. 'Do you want to turn France into a barracks?' shouted the republican Jules Favre to Niel in the course of the angry debates. 'Take care', retorted Niel, 'that you don't turn it into a cemetery!'[24] With weapons, it was a similar story of watered-down reform. The Prussian victory in 1866 was widely ascribed to their breach-loading rifle. At the emperor's insistence, a superior French model, the Chassepot, was rapidly introduced. Deputies breathed a sigh of relief and refused funds for new artillery – a fateful decision. The emperor himself put up the money for an experimental machine-gun.

Most professional and armchair strategists still took France's military superiority for granted. We have seen the general belief that Frenchmen were born soldiers. Moreover, the core of the army were hardened by colonial warfare and by their victories over Europe's greatest military powers, Russia and Austria. The Prussians, by comparison, were seen as dim-witted, beer-drinking, pipe-smoking peasants, led by inexperienced officers good only at military theory and usually portrayed in French cartoons as wearing spectacles. Moreover, it was taken for granted that if war did come France would not fight alone: the nationalist Left had preached for decades that France was regarded as a liberator by Poles, Italians and even Germans; and diplomats convinced themselves that Austria, Italy and Bavaria would join France in cutting Prussia down to size. The French army, therefore, would march straight across the Rhine, put the dumbfounded Prussians to flight, stroll into Berlin and redraw the map of Europe as France had wanted since 1815, securing its 'natural frontiers' by taking in the Rhineland, Luxembourg and – why not? – Belgium too.

The fatal belief had grown in both France and Germany that war, or at least some major trial of diplomatic strength, was inevitable. Ministers such as Rouher and Ollivier had put a brave face on developments since 1866, arguing that German national unity accorded with the 'principle of nationalities', was probably inevitable and held no threat for France. But Niel's military reforms belied these prudent words. A Bonapartist government

23. Howard (1967), p. 33.
24. Ibid., p. 33.

could not allow Prussia to overtake her in power: recent history showed the
danger of foreign policy humiliation, and Napoleon III was determined not to
end like Louis-Philippe. In this context, the 1870 dispute with Prussia over
influence in Spain (see p. 422) seemed to many French nationalists to give a
perfect opportunity for putting Prussia in her place by diplomatic humiliation
or, if necessary, war. A vocal group in parliament and the press demanded
that the government should take a tough line. The government, politically
weak, was over-sensitive to parliamentary and newspaper pressure. When the
crisis was under way there were bellicose demonstrations in the Paris streets:

> A large crowd . . . with the flag carried in front . . . singing the Chant des Girondins
> and the Marseillaise. Cries of Long live the Emperor! Long live the Army! Long live
> France! . . . Applause from the cafés and private homes answered them. Some
> individuals who tried to object were manhandled.[25]

This popular bellicosity recalls the 1830s, 1840, 1848 and 1859. Now,
however, the left-wing opposition opposed it, convinced that another
successful war would be 'the final blow to the republican cause'.[26] The 'Chant
des Girondins' runs: 'Mourir pour la Patrie, C'est le sort le plus beau, le plus
digne d'envie'. It was soon to be the fate of several hundred thousand men,
women and children.

The army was ready, the war minister assured the government, 'to the last
gaiter-button'. This may have been true of gaiter-buttons. It was true of little
else. It cannot be said that nothing went according to plan, because there was
no plan; but nothing went right. Mobilization was slower and more chaotic
than admirers of the army's professionalism had expected: one hapless
general telegraphed 'Have arrived at Belfort. Can't find my brigade. Can't find
the divisional commander. What shall I do?'[27] Rather than marching into
Germany (for which they had been provided with maps), they were soon
pushed back from their own frontier, overwhelmed by vastly superior
numbers of German troops at the battles of Spicheren and Woerth in August;
only half the French reservists had yet managed to get to their units. The
regular army fell back to the fortress of Metz, where it was surrounded. A
second army, composed mainly of reservists and the untrained Garde Mobile,
was sent, under the nominal command of the emperor (never much of a
general, and now incapacitated by agonizing bladder disease) to relieve Metz:
it was the Charge of the Light Brigade on a vast scale. They marched forlornly
north to try to outmanoeuvre the Germans, but were caught and surrounded
at Sedan. Remarked one general presciently, 'Nous sommes dans un pot de
chambre, et nous y serons emmerdés'.[28] Heroic attempts to break out failed
bloodily, and the French were subjected to merciless shelling from the
superior German artillery, which outranged their own guns. The emperor

25. Case (1954), p. 263.
26. Audoin-Rouzeau (1989), p. 45.
27. Horne (1965), p. 42.
28. Howard (1967), p. 208.

rode painfully round the battlefield looking for an honourable death that might save his dynasty, then, having failed even in that, ordered surrender: he and 130,000 men became prisoners of war. There had been no defeat so humiliatingly complete since Pavia in 1525. It was, in very many ways, the end of an era.

FRANCE AFTER SEDAN, 1870–1914

Sedan was as important as Waterloo, and more profound in its effects on France's status and pride. For, unlike Waterloo, it had been both crushing and humiliating. After Waterloo, France could still be seen as potentially the mistress of Europe; after Sedan, she seemed truly in decline. It began a long process of self-examination and conscious self-regeneration that would profoundly affect the lives of all French people.

The people's war, September 1870 – January 1871

The whole French nation must be made sick of fighting.

German officer[29]

Defeat of the Empire and proclamation of the Third Republic on 4 July revived a left-wing bellicosity largely silent since 1848: once again, the war was one of republic against monarchy, and the tone was set by veteran nationalists of the 1830s and 1840s such as Hugo, Blanqui, Quinet and Blanc. Again, they demanded a revolutionary war, as in the 1790s, to be fought through a *levée en masse*. The nation in arms would be invincible, as in 1792, not only by weight of numbers, but also because of the superior courage and determination inspired by patriotism: war was above all a moral contest. To some extent, this view was shared by the new Government of National Defence, led militarily by the young Léon Gambetta, the left-wing war minister, but not by the professional soldiers, for whom moral superiority came from long military training and *esprit de corps*.

The autumn of 1870 witnessed a burst of patriotic activity from all parties. Throughout the country the Garde Mobile took shape, and in Paris citizens of all ages and conditions clamoured to be admitted to a revived National Guard, whose uniform (at least the *képi*) became a standard item of male attire. Women served as nurses and some demanded weapons. The Orleans princes enlisted under assumed names. The legitimist Papal Zouaves persuaded Gambetta to let them enlist while their Garibaldian enemies also joined up.

During October and November it was still possible to be optimistic. The struggle centred on two great fortresses: Metz, where the bulk of the imperial regular army was besieged, and Paris, the seat of the government and the core of national resistance. The army in Metz, commanded by the popular

29. Howard (1967), p. 228.

Marshal Bazaine, made two vain attempts to break out. Their military position rapidly became hopeless; perhaps it always had been. Their horses died or were eaten, making it impossible to move artillery and equipment. Bazaine feared that France was in the throes of revolution, and hoped to be able to make terms with the Germans, perhaps to restore the Empire, certainly to keep his army intact. Like most professional soldiers, he did not believe that France could win the war once the regular army had been defeated. Consequently, he surrendered on 29 October. This released 200,000 German troops to take part at a crucial moment in the campaign in central France. It also had a serious effect on French morale.

The other fortress, the real focus of the war, was Paris, garrisoned by a vast, largely untrained horde of over 400,000 National Guards, soldiers, sailors and Gardes Mobiles. Its fate would be decisive, such had been its importance in French life since the Revolution, and especially under a Republic, when the Parisians in effect became the sovereign authority. There the government remained, except for Gambetta (who escaped by balloon) and a delegation at Tours, whose efforts were directed to raising armies to relieve the capital. As long as Parisians pressed the government to hold out, the war would continue. There was, however, no obvious way of winning it. Logically, the situation called for negotiations with the Germans. But the harsh terms they offered, especially annexation of territory, were unacceptable to the hundreds of thousands of amateur Parisian soldiers, who, brought up on misleading legends of victories won by the people in arms in 1792, regarded themselves as invincible and talk of defeat as treason.

The spirit of resistance was most vehemently expressed by the extreme Left. Their nationalism, based on the idea that the French nation (they meant Paris and the cities) was the champion of world revolution and the foe of reaction throughout Europe, was now in its last great flowering. Conservatives accused them of using the predicament of France to promote their political aims; it would be truer to say that they made no distinction between the triumph of the nation and that of the Revolution. Their aim was a victory that would vindicate the Republic and leave power in the hands of the armed people and their leaders. They set up a network of committees and clubs, ran newspapers, and got themselves elected to ranks in the National Guard. They demanded a more vigorous pursuit of the war, a mass sortie and a Commune – a revolutionary Parisian government. The moderate republicans of the Government of National Defence feared and detested these men, but felt obliged to appease them.

French hopes depended on Gambetta's new armies in the provinces, a motley collection of regulars, reservists, conscripts and volunteers. The principal force, the army of the Loire, was assembled south-west of Orléans with the intention of marching to the relief of Paris. The surrender of Metz, which released two more German armies, made their task impossible in the long run. But on 9 November the French captured Orléans. This news, sent to Paris by carrier pigeon, caused the commanders there to launch a sortie to try to join up with the army of the Loire. The politicians, for understandable reasons, were demanding the impossible of their troops. The Paris sortie on 29 November was halted only a little way beyond the French lines; on 2 December the army of the Loire was defeated. The men had suffered terribly from the weather and were demoralized to the point of disintegration. A German officer wrote:

> It is lamentable and irresponsible to send an army like that into action. They have no idea what soldiering is . . . the artillery fires into the air and hits practically nothing. They have no cavalry. Their weapons are appalling. Despite [their] undeniable bravery, [they] can hardly put up any resistance.[30]

The last real hope of victory had gone. Yet still resistance continued in a melancholy epic of cold and hunger. All Gambetta's armies were beaten one after another: on the Loire, in the north and in the east. The Parisians were determined to fight on, under shell-fire, freezing, existing on adulterated bread, horsemeat and the occasional dog, rat or zoo elephant: it was mainly cold and malnutrition that killed about 40,000 people, mainly, as always, babies and the old. They attempted one more sortie, by 90,000 men, on 19 January 1871. It was planned more to prove to the National Guard that the situation was hopeless than to fulfil any strategic purpose: 'Those National Guard clowns want to get their heads blown off', a general was reported as saying, 'We'll give them the opportunity.' The sortie of course failed. There was one more riot on 21 January, when some left-wing National Guards again tried to storm the Hôtel de Ville and were driven off. The government signed an armistice a week later. The city had only a few days' food left. Gambetta wished to fight on in the provinces, but was overruled by the government in Paris.

Defeat caused immediate recriminations which echoed the familiar reproaches of the 1830s and 1840s. For revolutionaries, the blame lay on a weak government, and the cowardice of unpatriotic bourgeois and peasants. For conservatives, the Left had disrupted the war effort by their indiscipline and agitation, and showed again that war brought revolution in its train. For the generals, the insistence on throwing untrained and ill-armed men into battle had been disastrous. These bitter divisions contributed to the outbreak of civil war in Paris in March 1871, when the National Guard took control of the city (see p. 427). The revolutionaries tried putting into practice their belief in the spontaneous power of the *levée en masse*. It proved to be an illusion, not only because they lost, but also because their brief defence of Paris was made possible only by rapidly abandoning spontaneity in favour of conventional military organization and professionalism.

L'année terrible of 1870–71 had repercussions even wider than those other great traumas, the defeat of Napoleon and the 1848 revolution. All the French armies had been defeated, and hundreds of thousands of soldiers, with arms, equipment and colours, taken into captivity. The Germans had overrun the

---

30. Roth (1990), p. 296.

country from the Rhine to the Channel, and had even marched under the Arc de Triomphe. On the French side it had not been a war of professional generals and diplomats, but of amateur soldiers, democratic politicians and journalists. The Germans, alarmed that it had turned into an uncontrolled 'people's war', had taken reprisals against civilians, culminating in the deliberate bombardment of Paris, in order to force them to abandon resistance – they should leave the people nothing but their eyes to weep with over the war, advised the American general Sheridan. Material destruction, confiscations of goods and money, arrests of hostages and reprisals had been added to patriotic humiliation. The Empire, the chosen regime of the great majority, had been destroyed, and its successor existed on German sufferance. The Paris Commune and ensuing civil war had shown that the country had been divided rather than united by the defeat, and seemed to threaten a total political and social breakdown. German peace terms, enshrined in the Treaty of Frankfurt, were seen as a crime, an insult, and a source of weakness: they included the cession of Alsace and part of Lorraine, with a population of 1.6 million and some of France's major mining and industrial areas, an unprecedented indemnity of 5 billion francs, and military occupation until it was paid.

This bitter clash of nations, so different from the limited wars of the previous 20 years, left a long and fatal inheritance of resentment. French and German nationalism were characterized by mutual antagonism, and both fed on the memories of 1870–71. France adopted the role of injured party seeking revenge. The new Republic was marked with a nationalist stamp, with the regeneration of the nation as a theme running through its actions, and the legend of resistance as its heritage – these were the images, says Agulhon, 'on which the regime would live'.

Regenerating the nation

> You have no idea of the sombre atmosphere in which we grew up, in a humiliated and wounded France . . . bred for a bloody, inevitable and perhaps futile revenge.
>
> *Romain Rolland*[31]

The unexpectedness and completeness of France's defeat – 'the ancient world in its darkest hours affords us no spectacle of such a collapse'[32] – caused agonized self-interrogation not only among politicians and intellectuals, but also among those who rarely gave a thought to the state of the nation. Unlike 1814–15, when France had finally been worn down by a coalition of most of Europe but was still arguably the strongest continental power and the moral and intellectual leader of Europe, 1870 had been, as Zola was later to call it, a débâcle, a collapse, inflicted by a single nation, Germany, and principally by Prussia, previously regarded as in every sense inferior: Prussian immigrants swept the streets of Paris.

31. Digeon (1952), pp. 519–20.
32. *Le Soir*, 19 March 1871.

How could this be explained? Fairly easily, we might think: bad preparation, incompetent leadership, inferior numbers and obsolete artillery accounted for most of it. But this was not enough to satisfy those who believed that wars were won by moral qualities. Germany, many influential voices reluctantly admitted, had proved a superior society. The Prussian schoolmaster, or the German university, or Protestantism, or feudal traditionalism had been its secret weapons, not Krupp steel cannon. Conversely, French society, institutions and traditions had been found wanting. 'The débâcle of 1870 was the scientific demonstration of our incurable rottenness . . . [we] ignoble people of slaves, faces marked by the German hobnails, backs furrowed by blows of the stick . . . minds worn out by literary masturbation.'[33] Not only the French army, but the whole of society, needed reform and regeneration. This was agreed over the whole political spectrum. How it should be done, however, was a source of deep division.

Republicans blamed the defeat in the first place on the Second Empire, not only for its military and diplomatic errors, but because it had corrupted the nation. It had stifled freedom and civic courage, encouraged crass materialism and self-interest, and hence weakened patriotism. But behind the Empire stood older enemies, and above all Catholicism, with whom Napoleon III had made an unholy alliance. Catholicism was the antithesis of modernity, Enlightenment and science. It promoted cowardice, meekness and hypocrisy. It turned its victims' attention from their patriotic duty.

Catholics and conservatives, of course, took a quite different view. It was irreligion and revolution that had sapped the nation's strength, destroyed unity and discipline. 'A democratic country', pronounced the leading philosopher Ernest Renan, 'cannot be well governed, well administered, well ordered'. It encouraged selfish materialism, which Renan called 'the sickness of France', the antithesis of patriotic sacrifice. How, asked General du Barail, could one expect a man to die for his country if he did not believe in life after death?

Each side drew evidence from the war. For republicans, national honour had been saved by Gambetta's indomitable efforts in the provinces and the heroic resistance of the ordinary people of Paris, holding out on a diet of rats and sawdust, desperate to fight but betrayed by stupid or treacherous generals. For conservatives, the heroes had been the provincial Garde Mobile of peasant soldiers and aristocratic officers, especially the Catholic Bretons marching into battle with the Sacred Heart sewn to their tunics, and the former Papal Zouaves charging heroically to their deaths at Patay, the battlefield of Joan of Arc. These rival patriotic traditions would help to fuel the quarrel between Left and Right during the next generation. Yet above this quarrel, bitter though it was, lay a shared acceptance of the virtue of patriotism, a cult of the army and a hatred of Germany.

33. Digeon (1952), p. 355.

Attitudes to Germany had been transformed. Popularly regarded as the peaceful home of cuckoo clocks and dreamy philosophers, French intellectuals from Germaine de Staël in the 1800s and Victor Cousin in the 1820s to Renan and Taine in the 1860s had looked to it as the home of modern thought and art. The war gave rise to a contrary set of images: arrogant officers, brutal soldiers, efficiency, discipline, technology, looting, destruction, violence. Bismarck replaced Kant as the archetype. To call someone a 'Prussian' became legally defamatory.[34] Germanophile intellectuals such as Renan painfully reconsidered their sympathies. At a popular level too the press and literature had also to come to terms with this new perception.

A widely held view was that there were 'two Germanies': the peaceful, traditional Germany, especially in the south, and a 'young, chauvinistic, reactionary and utilitarian'[35] Germany, especially Prussia. The new Germany (so went the theory) had conquered the old, and it had then conquered France. This success was usually explained in a way that flattered French pride. The Germans had won because of their cultural and moral inferiority: brute force, machine-like obedience, ruthlessness, trickery. They were merely 'Mohicans who had been to Polytechnique'.[36]

How far should France imitate these 'new Germans', and in what way? Conservatives admired their monarchical institutions and the military role of the nobility, and this remained a persistent theme in the ideas of Taine and Maurras well after the practical possibility of monarchy in France had faded. Republicans wished to emulate what they understood of their education system. Nearly all agreed that they should copy their army. Here again, in spite of ideological differences, there was considerable agreement on a practical programme: universal military service. The small professional army had been defeated, but so had the spontaneous *levée en masse*. The post-war period would see the adoption of a third way: a trained mass conscript army. But the traditional ideas of war, combat and French superiority would be salvaged and reapplied.

'Revenge' as fantasy and mobilizing myth

Let us think of it always; let us speak of it never.

Gambetta (attrib.), 1871[37]

The ostensible aim of regeneration was *la revanche*, of which recovery of Alsace-Lorraine became the symbol. There was a public 'cult of memory'. War memorials and the black-veiled statue of Strasbourg in the Place de la Concorde became the sites of annual ceremonies. Museums were built, and shrines to heroic actions preserved. Over 1,000 books were published.

---

34. Weber (1986), p. 106.
35. Prévost (1906), p. 359.
36. Digeon (1952), p. 97; see also Pick (1993), p. 93.
37. Bury (1973), p. 68.

Feelings were strongest in the regions most affected by the war and most resentful of the occupation, especially Paris, the centre and the north-east; south of the Loire, feeling was less. Revenge, which the statesman Delcassé revealingly called France's 'principle raison d'être', was never a policy, however. For how could it in practice be obtained? France's military inferiority was evident, and imposed what was delicately called *recueillement* (silent meditation) in foreign affairs: in cruder terms, doing nothing that might annoy Germany. Royalists dreamed that a restored monarchy might be able to arrange a peaceful return of the provinces by hobnobbing with the kaiser. Colonialists later thought of swapping them for Madagascar or Indochina. No government ever considered starting a war to reconquer them. Yet 'revenge' did preclude any true reconciliation with Germany, not least because Germany would demand an explicit renunciation of Alsace-Lorraine, which had become an untouchable nationalist symbol.

Revenge was first of all a fantasy. 'France lived revenge, mimed it without ever putting it into practice.'[38] To think of revenge – and also, *pace* Gambetta, to speak and write of it – was a way of circumventing the reality of humiliation and vulnerability by imagining a reversal of roles: France would be the victor, her greatness and virtue at last vindicated, her superiority reasserted. But it was always to be in the future, never at once.

Popular war literature provided fantasy revenge. Its focus neglected the depressing overall story of the war and the major battles to concentrate on dramatic personal stories of brave individual resistance, in which the defeat of France was glossed over by a host of imaginary small victories. The realities of modern warfare – numbers, technology, supply, firepower, casualties – were ignored in favour, as in the past, of a moral and non-material view of war as exciting and ennobling adventure, in which ordinary French men, women, and often children (for there were many children's books) worsted brutal and stupid Germans by their courage and intelligence. The didactic and escapist intentions are clear: defeat was an aberration, and next time there would be victory. This was a reflection of 'a terrible inferiority complex, on a national scale'.[39] It took several years for more consciously realistic, and pessimistic, war literature to appear, sometimes written by men who had served in the war. Zola, Maupassant, Daudet and others wrote works that were complex and ambiguous: sometimes anti-army, anti-war, anti-bourgeois but also anti-German. For Maupassant, this was 'a problem without a solution'. Such works did not replace those preaching revenge, whose most famous exponent was Paul Déroulède, a soldier turned nationalist agitator whose whole poetic *oeuvre*, distributed at innumerable school prize-givings, was dedicated to inspiring patriotic fervour.

Revenge was also a mobilizing 'myth', an instrument to justify and rally support for a range of actions to regenerate and strengthen the nation. These included not only far-reaching military reforms, discussed below, but an effort

38. Roth (1990), p. 629.
39. Digeon (1952), p. 64.

at mobilization which extended into society as a whole. A fundamental step was the extension of primary education to train a nation of republican soldier-citizens to serve France from childhood to middle age: without schooling, an inspector told recalcitrant factory children, they would be 'bad Frenchmen and bad soldiers, who would run away on our day of revenge'.[40] The republicans made it free, secular and compulsory in 1881–82. The republican philosopher Littré wrote: 'we must bring up [our children] in suspicion and hostility; we must teach them that military drill is their primary task; we must drum into them that they must be ready to kill and be killed'. Textbooks, pictures, maps and exercises were designed to hammer the message home. The compulsory civic instruction textbook, introduced in 1882 as the lynchpin of republican education, was headed 'By the school for the Fatherland', and had as its first chapter 'Military service. The Fatherland', and its second chapter, on taxation, began 'Taxes are necessary to maintain the army'. Composition subjects such as 'A Good Frenchman' were set: 'A young sergeant undergoes an amputation for a wound received in Tonkin. He wakes up and looks at the wound: "Better that than to be Prussian", he says.' Girls had to learn 'to admire courage and despise cowardice' and practise writing edifying letters to their brothers in the army.[41]

Gambetta's minister of education, the scientist Paul Bert, set up a Military Education Commission, including Déroulède and the military painter Detaille. Gymnastics was made compulsory in 1880. *Bataillons scolaires* were founded in 1882, in which children would learn drill with miniature rifles; Jean Macé, the leading republican educationist and organizer of the influential Ligue de l'Enseignement (motto: 'For the Fatherland, by book and sword') wrote the introduction to their training manual. The Ligue des Patriotes, later to play a major political role under Déroulède, was set up with Gambetta's blessing in 1882 to encourage pre-military training through rifle-shooting and gymnastic clubs. In a few years it had over 100,000 members, 25–30,000 in Paris alone. The introduction of organized sport in France in the 1880s and 1890s had explicit militarist overtones. Fencing, and duelling too, enjoyed an extraordinary vogue. By 1911, sporting clubs had about 900,000 members, more than half of them from specifically military training clubs, which placed them among the largest organizations in the country.[42]

The problem with keeping pace with German power was that her economy and above all her population were growing much faster: a source of great worry and debate from the 1880s onwards. A range of measures attempted to increase French manpower. The very concept of nationality was affected in 1889, with automatic naturalization of French-born children of foreign parents so as to make them liable for military service. Vaccination of children was made compulsory in 1893. Attempts were made to involve women as breeders of soldiers, and also to reinforce certain ideas of what constituted

40. Heywood (1988), p. 279.
41. Hamon (1986), p. 204; Girardet (1983), pp. 78–9.
42. Arnaud, in Tombs (1991), p. 183.

legitimately male and female roles, often defined and 'protected' by law (for example, on work, concerning which extensive legislation was passed in 1892). Although some suggested regarding parenthood as an aspect of military service, with women who had fewer than four children 'no better than deserters', politicians did not make serious attempts to interfere with reproduction until after the carnage of the First World War, when prosecutions for abortion were made easier and birth-control information energetically suppressed. Before 1914, reliance was placed on patriotic alarmism ('for every future soldier born in France, four are born in Germany') and exhortations to renounce contraception ('with a few kilos of rubber the kaiser can suppress thousands of future soldiers').[43] Inducements were also given, such as cash prizes and in 1913 paid maternity leave, for 'by protecting maternity and early infancy we assure the primordial element of our national defence'.[44] Some feminists were prepared to embrace this nationalist vision of women's social role, and point out how much more Germany was doing, in the hope of winning benefits and (a vain hope, as it turned out) asserting their right to citizenship.

National defence and the 'cult of the army'

> The daily passage of the regiment empties every shop and leaves the whole street tingling with pride and love.
>
> *American visitor, 1899*[45]

The destruction of both the imperial regular army and Gambetta's raw forces seemed proof to most politicians and soldiers that they had to copy the German model of mass conscription. Republicans now favoured universal military service as just, democratic, and a desirable form of civic training, and once they were fully in power, they reduced the normal term of service to three years by the law of July 1889 and to two years in 1905. The total military obligation, however, was extended to 25 years, including time in the reserves and territorial army. Because of its low birth rate, France imposed a much heavier burden on her male population than any other country: by the eve of the First World War, 84 per cent of Frenchmen of military age actually performed military service, compared with only 53 per cent in Germany, 29 per cent in Austria and 20 per cent in Russia.[46]

During the 1870s and 1880s a large programme of rearmament with modern artillery and rifles was carried out, and a huge system of fortifications built to guard the eastern frontier. A proper general staff was created, training improved, and systematic mobilization planning begun. These were years of obvious vulnerability, and the 'war scare' of 1875 (manufactured by Bismarck

43. Ronsin (1980), p. 130.
44. Offen, in Tombs (1991), p. 204.
45. Feldman (1981), p. 44.
46. Doise and Vaïsse (1987), pp. 34, 81; Ferguson (1992), pp. 725–52, at p. 734.

for domestic political reasons) caused panic. By 1882, men, arms and fortifications were in place, and the danger of German aggression seemed to recede. Military spending settled at about 40 per cent of the total State budget in the 1880s.

The army was treated by republicans and conservatives alike as the guardian and symbol of the nation, lauded as the repository of its finest virtues and the finishing-school of patriotism. It was indeed the country's largest remedial class, and did, as Eugen Weber has shown, help to turn peasants into Frenchmen (see p. 309). Compared with other conscript armies (there was no comparison with professional armies such as the British and American), living conditions were about average, and were often thought good by young peasants: 'the best time of my life . . . we had meat twice a day'.[47] The suicide rate was much lower than in the Saxon or Austrian armies.[48] Some prominent officers, most notably Boulanger and Lyautey, tried to make military service more humane and more genuinely educative. But many middle-class boys, no longer able to buy exemption, found the army brutal and sterile. Georges Courteline wrote witty satires on the claustrophobic surrealistic idiocy of conscript life (where the reply to every problem was a bawled 'Je m'en fous!'), but a much bleaker denunciation of brutality and corruption came in novels by Georges Darien, Abel Hernant and Lucien Descaves. A different kind of anti-militarism came from socialists and anarchists, for whom the army was a tool of repression at home and in the colonies: occasional shootings of rioting strikers gave point to their anger. Extreme left-wing newspapers and activists were regularly prosecuted for incitement to mutiny.

What was the result of all this propaganda, counter-propaganda and military experience? Rather mixed. Conscription was never popular. Its extension to three years in 1913 was one of the most controversial measures of the period, yet it was accepted. The army was publicly worshipped; General Boulanger and colonial soldiers Négrier, Marchand and Sergeant Bobillot were popular heroes much exploited by advertisers. Yet officers as a group were poorly paid and not highly regarded, and ordinary soldiers were often shunned (as for the Foreign Legion, only in the late 1930s had its image so much improved, with the help of the cinema, that it could dispense with its regimental brothels). When in 1897–99 the Dreyfus affair put the army's status to the test, after much huffing and puffing it came off worst. The 'affair', the great political quarrel of the end of the century, stemmed from spy mania caused by obsessive military competition with Germany, and would scarcely have caused so much anguish had it not called into question the honour and credibility of the army – unscrupulously played upon by the High Command, who implied that war with Germany might result from too probing an enquiry into the facts. The consequences of the affair for the army are debated. Apart from a few resignations, the institution itself was protected

47. Weber (1977), p. 301.
48. Gillis (1989), p. 169 n. 5.

by successive governments. Most historians have suggested that it soon recovered from the ordeal, though Porch argues that it did durable damage to morale and competence, even during the years of 'national revival' when the perceived danger of war with Germany renewed the army's national role.[49]

An examination of popular culture – picture postcards, early cinema – shows that though soldiers were shown, they were never in warlike occupations: it was the army of Courteline, not that of Déroulède. Popular songs usually reflected the same frivolity: 'En rev'nant d'la revue', the most famous, was a catchy celebration of a boozy family outing to the 14 July parade. Even Aristide Bruant, the bohemian singer from Montmartre, had jaunty military songs in his repertoire. But there was rarely any evocation of war against an identifiable enemy: a specific war, especially against Germany, seems to have attracted a kind of taboo.[50]

Whatever the popular taste for brass-band militarism, most people profoundly feared a real war. This was the major political factor. In 1871, the republicans almost lost power to royalists due to their commitment to continuing the war; but led by Thiers and Gambetta they convinced the country during the 1870s that the Republic now stood for peace and recovery, and the royalists for danger. This certainly helped the conversion by 1876 of the silent majority of the electorate to acceptance of the Republic as the safest regime. The fall of the republican leader Jules Ferry in 1885 was precipitated by the fear of war that his colonial policy inspired. General Boulanger, though propelled to celebrity as 'le général Revanche', was forced from office by parliament and subsequently rejected by the electorate in 1889 because a jingoism that was thrilling on the parade ground was a frightening prospect if translated to the Elysée Palace. 'Boulanger, c'est la guerre', warned Le Figaro; 'No Sedan!' one poster insisted unanswerably.[51]

From 'National Revival' to war, 1905–14

> I thought of war, of war that will purify, of war that will be holy, that will be balm for our sick hearts.
>
> Ernest Psichari[52]

The 'National Revival' was a nationalist reaction to the Moroccan crises of 1905 and 1911 which brought France into serious conflict with Germany for the first time since the 1880s. It affected a small, mainly male, Parisian and middle-class minority. Intellectuals and educationists persisted in wanting to regenerate the country. Some younger republican politicians and businessmen wanted to improve the efficiency of the economy and system of government. Some writers and students were attracted by romantic militarism,

49. Porch (1981).
50. Sorlin, in Tombs (1991), pp. 81–2.
51. Carroll (1931), p. 122; Sirinelli (1992), vol. 2, p. 483.
52. Psichari (n.d.), vol. 2, p. 67.

among them the fifteen-year-old Charles de Gaulle who wrote a story, set in 1930, in which 'General de Gaulle' defeats a German invasion and liberates Lorraine. Two young journalists, writing under the pseudonym Agathon, published in 1913 a survey entitled *Les jeunes gens d'aujourd'hui*, which concluded, probably accurately for the sort of *jeunes gens* covered (law and politics students in Paris), that nationalism and sport were fashionable. Young officials within the Foreign Ministry, a generation that had been brought up on the themes of 'revenge' and muscular patriotism, seemed not unwilling to put their lessons into practice, trying to sabotage efforts by ambassadors to calm German feelings. But the National Revival had limited echoes in the population at large. Candidates thought to favour war did not do well in elections. Alsace-Lorraine had become an embarrassing subject. The 1905 crisis caused panic (see p. 476).

A quite different sort of *jeunes gens* from those of Agathon were those belonging to the parties of the extreme Left. Not only anarchists, but syndicalists and the leftist fringe of the socialist party attacked the army, war, colonialism and nationalism. The parliamentary socialists were less strident, but they too criticized colonial expeditions, tried to establish a joint anti-war strategy through the Second International, and opposed increases in the army. Their opposition to the three-year military service bill helped win them 20 or 30 seats in the 1914 general elections. Their leader Jaurès advocated the replacement of the standing army with a citizen militia trained for home defence, and predicted that a future war would see 'human masses rotting in disease, distress, pain, under a hail of shells'.[53] Mainstream republicans were alarmed, nationalists such as Péguy were apoplectic, and the Interior Ministry updated its blacklist of agitators (*le carnet B*) to be arrested in case of war.

Among intellectuals some remarkable realignments took place that suggest that the National Revival was more than merely a student fashion. Two archetypical examples are Gustave Hervé and Charles Péguy. Hervé, the most notorious exponent of quasi-anarchist anti-militarist 'anti-patriotism', courted prosecution in his paper *La Guerre Sociale*. But in 1912 he began to espouse 'revolutionary militarism', in which the army and the nation were seen as potentially revolutionary forces, just as for Armand Carrel in the 1830s. With Péguy, Michelet is the model. Péguy was a fervent apostle of hitherto incompatible traditions: Catholicism and republicanism, revolution and tradition, Dreyfusism and nationalism, poetry and football. The Morocco crisis was his road to Damascus: 'everyone realized' that Germany was again the enemy, and that France must prepare to defend civilization against barbarism. He looked forward to a purifying crusade of justice against corruption, a reincarnation of 1792. This led him to attack the socialists in the name of the Revolution: 'the policy of the National Convention means Jaurès in a tumbril and a roll of drums to drown that big voice'.[54] Happiness, he said, would be to 'enter Weimar at the head of a good platoon of infantry': Weimar, symbol

53. Field (1986), pp. 45–57, at p. 49.
54. Péguy (1957), pp. 1251, 1238.

of German culture, vanquished by the sacred bayonets of France. Interesting in a different way was Ernest Psichari, a young colonial army officer, who won literary acclaim in 1913 with terse evocations of invigorating masculinity in the desert, tinged with discreet homoeroticism and disgust towards 'Americanized' civilization: 'A sick man does not suffer from the fetid smell of his room. But if a healthy man comes in from outside he . . . will vomit.' Like Déroulède, who had 'taken the képi as one takes the veil', Psichari discovered in the army a quasi-religious order: 'a great force from the past, the only one – with the Church – that remained virginal, immaculate'.[55]

When war came, victory would be rapid, and it would be a revolutionary and a moral victory. Péguy consciously echoed the voice of Michelet and his contempt for 'peace at any price'. His dreams of the apocalyptic struggle for a new world could have come from nationalists 80 years before. But in his obsessive litanies there is a desperate nihilism that is related to the intellectual and political concerns of his own time. Only in death can there be peace:

> Happy those who have died, for they have returned
> To the first clay and the first earth.
> Happy those who have died in a just war.
> Happy the ripe ears and the gathered corn.[56]

Most prophets of war die in their beds, but Péguy and Psichari were killed in the opening battles of 1914. Hervé used his journalistic talents to support the war effort in 1914–18, when he was dubbed France's leading brainwasher; and he later turned to fascism.

Senior officers nursed fantasies even more dangerous than those of poets. Colonel de Grandmaison, head of the operations section of the War Ministry, was the eloquent spokesman of an updated philosophy of the offensive at all costs, the rhapsodies of the 1830s and 1840s in modern jargon: 'psychological factors are paramount in combat . . . for all others – weaponry, manoeuvrability – influence only indirectly by provoking moral reactions'.[57] The French soldier, combining inbred national superiority with resolute leadership, could smash the German army, irrespective of its numbers, fortresses and firepower. 'The character of our soldiers adapts itself marvellously to present requirements. Numbers no longer decide victory.'[58] Only the unimaginative, such as Colonel Pétain and the socialist leader Jaurès, pointed out that 'fire kills'. Joffre, from 1911 the dim chief of the general staff, went along with Grandmaison's rhetoric, which had the advantages of maintaining morale and glossing over problems concerning inadequate artillery, neglected fortresses, insufficient reserves and confused tactics. The stress on the moral advantage of the offensive was whistling in the dark.

55. Psichari (n.d.), vol. 2, pp. 25, 178.
56. Péguy, 'Eve', 1913.
57. Porch (1981), p. 215.
58. Ibid., p. 228.

However, the generals also pressed in 1913 for an increase in the standing army by increasing military service to three years. This came in response to German increases in their own standing army in 1913, themselves responses to earlier French improvements. The government's public case was that a larger standing army was needed to prevent a surprise German invasion. Their real reason, which was kept secret, was that the French army wished to be able to launch a knock-out blow immediately war was declared. One reason was to convince Russia of French determination and so persuade them to agree to speed up their own attack.[59] For the logic of the Franco-Russian alliance was to divide the German armies by rapid and simultaneous mobilization.

The German solution to the Franco-Russian alliance, formulated in 1905, was the Schlieffen plan: to defeat France rapidly, before Russia could mobilize, by a surprise attack through Belgium, outflanking the French fortresses, taking Paris, and attacking the French army in the rear. They could then turn on Russia. The military modernization of Russia, aided by 400–500 million francs per year in French loans, as well as the French three-year law, diminished the prospect of success month by month; the German government did not have the money to keep ahead in this race, and the high command became dangerously pessimistic and reckless. Though the Schlieffen plan was secret, there were many clues: German military publications and training exercises, the acquisition of motor lorries and the construction of mile-long platforms at country railway stations near the Belgian border. The French had even been given an early draft of the plan, possibly a fake, by an officer code-named 'Vengeur', his face swathed in bandages except for his waxed moustache. Reluctantly, the high command accepted that there would be a diversionary German attack through eastern Belgium, but refused to believe that their main attack would swing round to the west. This contradicted their own views, and was therefore impossible.

They persisted in their plan, lovingly reworked over sixteen years and now the 'recklessly offensive'[60] Plan XVII, for a mass attack into Lorraine, heavily fortified by the Germans. One reason was that this was part of the deal with the Russians, but there were more important reasons. Most French generals had convinced themselves that modern warfare favoured the offensive. The French national character, they believed, responded best to the attack, which would paralyse the cumbersome Germans. They had the excellent 75 millimetre cannon, made for mobile warfare. They had increased the standing army which was ready for instant attack. And, as nearly everyone agreed, modern war would be quick, decided by the first great clash of arms. In short, they were admirably prepared to win the war of 1870; so they nearly lost that of 1914. In 1905 and in 1911 – as in 1830, 1840, 1848, 1866 and 1887 – the generals had told the government that if war came they would lose: an unanswerable argument for peace. In 1914, as in 1870, the generals were confident: the politicians could permit themselves risks.

59. Krumeich (1984), p. 26.
60. Stevenson (1988), p. 33.

When war did come in August 1914 it was neither expected nor welcomed by French men and women. Nor was it opposed. Defending the nation was a duty that they had been brought up to fulfil, against an enemy whose identity had been known for 40 years. During the third week in August, French soldiers streamed towards the lost provinces to fulfil the dreams of generations of nationalists. Behind their brass bands and tricolour flags, led by officers with plumes and white gloves, marched the infantry splendid in red trousers, light cavalry in sky-blue tunics, cuirassiers in breastplates and helmets like those of Waterloo, and with tactics like those of Magenta. The result was the worst carnage of the whole war, four times the death rate of 1917; nearly a million men were killed or wounded. Victory was not to be quick or easy; and it would not solve France's national or international problems.

War was essential in beginning the Revolution and in ending it. But the end was not in 1815 or 1914, although the unity brought by war – the 'sacred union' proclaimed by President Poincaré in August 1914 – seemed for a time to have bridged the old divisions (see p. 480). But it was not until after another war, that of 1939–45, which altered Europe and the world almost beyond recognition, reduced the German threat, began a painful and bloody process of decolonization and placed France willy-nilly under American protection, that the long obsession with her role, status and security began to be a secondary issue.

CHAPTER 3

A NEW ORDER

R.T.C. LIBRARY, LETTERKENNY

The epoch of '89 has thus marked in the history of humanity the great separation between the Old Order and the New Order.

Considérant [1]

We pass the day asking whether we shall be governed in the evening by Babeuf, or by Gregory VII, or by both men jointly.

Quinet [2]

The Revolution had specifically rejected the past as a source of legitimacy and had destroyed the traditional order of 'feudal' society. But the Revolution too had been swept away by defeat. Consequently, it became a commonplace during the first half of the nineteenth century that France was passing through 'an epoch of transition, of decadence'[3] full of dangers and possibilities: 'Aristocracy was already dead when I was born and democracy had not yet come into existence . . . I was living in a country which for forty years had tried out everything and settled permanently on nothing.'[4]

Many thought in retrospect that 1815 had begun to repeat the cycle begun in 1789: from Bourbon absolutism (1814–30) via Orleanist liberalism (1830–48) to republican anarchy (1848–51) and finally Bonapartist despotism, ending again in war and defeat in 1870. The cycle had to be stopped, the Revolution ended, and a stable new order created. Each political tendency had its own new order to propose: ' "The Revolution is finished." That is the cry of triumph, the slogan, the promise of all.'[5]

Most people assumed that any new order must be based on common values. Not only did the nineteenth century have, as Girardet notes, 'an incorrigible will to believe', it also thought that society should believe the

1. Lovell (June 1992), pp. 185–205, at p. 201.
2. Babeuf was the proto-socialist leader of the 1796 'Conspiracy of Equals'; Gregory VII (d. 1085) the imperious pope.
3. Flaubert (1979), p. 513.
4. Tocqueville, 1837, in Hayward (1991), p. 141.
5. Prévost-Paradol, 1862, in Pitt (1995), p. 134.

same things. 'Is it not in the spiritual order, and only there, that the principle of union is found?' asked the Catholic Félicité de Lamennais. The liberal Benjamin Constant ringingly proclaimed the opposite view: 'diversity is life; uniformity is death'. This disagreement, argues Girardet, is a fundamental ideological divide of the last two centuries, which does not coincide with the conventional distinction between Right and Left.[6]

Constant, however, was in a minority: most influential voices called for uniformity. The urge to unity was in part inherited from the Old Regime, which had so long struggled to consolidate territories and religion. But the Revolution, with its ideologies of the general will and the sovereignty of the nation, and its own struggles against internal and external enemies, had stressed 'the One and Indivisible Republic'. Awareness of the fragility of that unity in reality, and the universal fear of renewed conflict, meant that all regimes and parties after the Revolution embraced in varying degrees the unitary aspiration. Individual freedom was only legitimate within a framework of common purpose: 'the continuous subordination of egoism to altruism', in the words of the philosopher Auguste Comte. The social and economic transformations and political instability of the nineteenth century made the creation of a firm ideological base for social and national unity seem all the more urgent.

Here the similarity of opposites is plain: the theocratic counter-revolutionary philosopher Joseph de Maistre influenced the socialist visionary Henri de Saint-Simon, the positivist Auguste Comte and the socialist atheist Pierre-Joseph Proudhon, the most innovative political thinkers of the first half of the century. Comte attributed 'great revolutionary catastrophes' to the 'spiritual disorganization of society', and, taking Maistre as his guide, aimed to create a modern equivalent of the 'moral communism' of medieval Christendom, based on science.[7]

While thinkers and politicians aspired to create uniform values, they disagreed about what those values should be; and consequently the very attempt to create uniformity was itself a constant source of conflict. Throughout the century, religious, political and social prophets jostled each other to preach their creeds. There were fundamental disagreements: first, concerning the very nature of human beings; second, over the relation of individuals with society; third, over the interpretation of history.

First, and most fundamental, concerned human nature itelf. Was that nature fallen, corrupted by original sin, as Catholics believed, or originally innocent and perfectable, as Enlightenment thinkers, and especially Rousseau, had asserted? This was the fundamental philosophical divergence between Catholicism and the Revolution, and it shaped basic attitudes to society and politics. For Catholics, sinful man needed the guidance of the Church and the authority of a paternal Christian State. Revolution was a revolt against God and against the reality of human nature. The very desire for individual liberty

6. Girardet (1986), pp. 172–3, 150.
7. Hayward (1991), p. 82.

– the 'spirit of revolt' – was a source of evil: the duty of man was to submit to divine providence and obey lawful superiors. From Maistre (d. 1821) to Maurras (d. 1952), philosophers called for authoritarian government, ideally a Catholic monarchy. At the other end of the spectrum, utopian socialists such as Fourier (d. 1837) believed that if people were simply released from oppression, and allowed the freedom to follow their natural desires, a perfect community would be created. The Saint-Simonian socialist mystic Enfantin (later a successful railway entrepreneur) believed that the end of evil was at hand and that Satan was about to mend his ways. In more sober terms, the republican Jules Ferry was no less convinced: science showed humanity 'not as a fallen race dragging itself painfully in a vale of tears', but 'an unending procession marching towards the light'.[8]

Liberals sought to harmonize faith and reason, and to develop rational systems of government that could balance liberty and order. Republicans, many of them, at least during the first half of the century, *spiritualistes* or non-Catholic Christians, sought to reconcile Christianity and Revolution, and to develop a new civic morality with its own festivals. Everyone agreed that it was necessary to moralize the masses. Protestants seemed to many to have succeeded in combining individual liberty with faith, and, in spite of being a tiny minority within France, they were prominent in all progressive political and philosophical movements. But Catholic liberals, a small and rather beleagured elite, were repeatedly forced to choose between their Catholicism and their liberalism. The influential liberal priest Lamennais was condemned by Rome and abandoned the priesthood in the 1830s; Montalembert, leading young Catholic politician of the 1840s, compromised his liberalism and died disillusioned but obedient to the Church in 1870; at the beginning of the twentieth century, the Christian democratic group *Le Sillon*, led by Marc Sangnier, was condemned by Rome in 1910.

The cleavage over human nature meant disagreement over democracy. Conservatives rejected it as outrageous. Liberals stressed necessary constraints, checks and balances on a dangerous and unpredictable force. Republicans, from the 1840s onwards, insisted on universal (male) suffrage as a right, whatever the status or level of education of the elector. (The lack of a vote for the female half of humanity should perhaps have posed an important philosophical problem, but it did not.) The Second Republic (1848–51) seemed to demonstrate the dangers of unbridled democracy leading to social and political polarization and violence. There emerged two solutions: first, Bonapartism, whose populist authoritarianism tamed the mass electorate and proved that democracy need not be revolutionary; second, the Third Republic, which accepted the sovereignty of male suffrage, but whose constitution also featured checks and balances, and whose governments undertook compulsory mass education after 1880 to inculcate moderation into the electorate.

A second line of divergence concerned the individual and society.

8. Pitt (1995), p. 119.

Individualism – significantly, a derogatory word in French – was regarded with suspicion. Constant made a celebrated distinction between 'the liberty of the ancients' (the right to participate fully in the political life of the community, as in the marketplace of ancient Athens) and the 'liberty of the moderns' (the right to be left alone to pursue one's private affairs). The liberty asserted by the French Revolution had been the 'liberty of the ancients': the right, and duty, to be a patriotic citizen. The stress on the private liberty of 'the moderns', and the liberal ideal of the 'hidden hand' that transformed the totality of private efforts for self-betterment into the general good never commanded anything near a consensus in France. *Laissez-faire* was regularly denounced as a cover for anti-social egotism. As Nicolet notes, a fundamental fact about France was that it was the only country in Europe that never accepted the Scottish Enlightenment, the 'birth certificate of modernity', with its principles of economic liberty, utilitarianism and liberalism.[9] Constant (who had studied in Edinburgh) was a fairly lonely exception. Furthermore, even many liberals rejected major tenets of Anglo-Saxon liberalism, such as free trade.

Consequently, debate about how to reconcile individual rights with the pre-eminent needs of people, nation and State took place between more or less 'organicist' tendencies. Throughout the century denunciations of 'individualism', 'materialism' and the 'bourgeoisie' – almost synonymous concepts – came from traditionalists, socialists and nationalists alike, all steeped in a mixture of Golden Age nostalgia and organicist utopianism. 'Every evil has come from the bourgeoisie. Every aberration, every crime. It is the capitalist bourgeoisie that has infected the people' wrote Péguy in 1913.[10] Traditionalists, speaking in the name of Catholic paternalism, sought to restore (in the words of Richelieu, minister of Louis XVIII) those 'chivalrous centuries [when] religion, honour and virtue . . . served as your guides'.[11] Socialists fantasized about conflict-free communities: what Pierre Leroux in the 1840s called 'communionism'. Nationalists lauded sacrificial devotion over self-indulgence, and denied the significance of individual consciousness compared with the historic majesty of the group: 'the individual is destroyed and rediscovers himself in the family, the race, the nation' wrote Barrès.[12]

The third point of divergence, which summed up and expressed the others, was the interpretation of history, and especially the history of the Revolution. As was seen in Chapter 1, each tendency had its own interpretation: for counter-revolutionaries, a revolt against divine providence; for centrists, a necessary progress that had got out of hand; for republicans, a popular struggle as yet unfulfilled. As well as dramatizing and emotionalizing political debate, these differing interpretations, as will be seen, determined what sort of post-revolutionary new order was aspired to.

  9. Nicolet (1982), p. 479.
 10. Girardet (1986), p. 118.
 11. Ibid., p. 112.
 12. Girardet (1983), p. 187.

It was not simply a question of 'Left' versus 'Right'. Although Left and Right form the most common of all political analyses, they conceal as much as they reveal. As will be seen in Chapter 5, these were constantly shifting terms, as new alliances were made and labels adopted and discarded. In trying to identify fundamental 'obsessions' which display similarities between, as well as cleavages within, 'Right' and 'Left', I suggest a different approach, identifying six visions of a new order: Catholic, liberal, republican, socialist, Bonapartist and national.

A CATHOLIC ORDER

France must be converted or she is finished.

Albert de Mun

The extreme Right in France was not merely traditionalist or conservative (though it later appropriated that word): after the Revolution there seemed no traditions to conserve. Its aim rather was to cut out the revolutionary rot and create anew. Although the restored Bourbon king proclaimed himself Louis XVIII in 1814 (as though the dead child dauphin had reigned from his prison cell as Louis XVII), and wrote of 'divine Providence . . . recalling us to our States after a long absence' (as if the Revolution had been merely a wearisome interlude), few were fooled: the Right never made the mistake of underestimating the Revolution. Though after 1830 it took the name 'legitimist' (which remained its usual label until the death of the last direct Bourbon heir in 1883), simply to restore the 'legitimate' Bourbon monarchy – especially the irreligious and incompetent monarchy of the late eighteenth century – would not be enough. This was proved by the failure of the Bourbons in 1830: monarchy, noted Chateaubriand, had ceased to be a religion. Only Catholicism could sustain a counter-revolutionary order; a throne could only be secure in alliance with the altar. Indeed, Catholicism became increasingly the senior partner, as major thinkers from Maistre via Lamennais to Maurras proclaimed.

The clergy tended to be intellectually dim (Lamennais, with his stunning *Paroles d'un croyant* (1834) was an exception, but it marked his break with Rome). But a succession of mainly lay writers, artists, and composers – Chateaubriand, with his *Génie du Christianisme* (1802); the political ardour of Montalembert in the 1840s; the pugnacious journalistic talent of Louis Veuillot in the 1850s and 1860s; the oratory of de Mun in the 1890s; the vitriolic writings of Maurras in the 1900s; the late-nineteenth-century literary revival of Claudel, Péguy and Mauriac; and the liturgical music of Franck, Saint-Saëns, Fauré (and later Duruflé, Poulenc and Messiaen) – all sustained a Catholic intellectual, political and artistic tradition more than able to hold its own against the intellectual offensive of the Left.

During the 1850s and 1860s, the 'Roman question' revived fervour, for it concerned both the Catholic patriotic ideal of France as 'eldest daughter of the Church' and defender of the papacy, and the conservative view of the papacy as the keystone of counter-revolution. World history – the cosmic struggle of good (the Church) and evil (the Revolution) – seemed to have reached a crisis: Rome was seized by Italian troops in 1870, and so France was punished by defeat and revolution. A millenarian ultramontanism, with mystical visions and mass pilgrimages, reached a climax in the 1870s. At last, the restoration of 'Henri V' seemed likely. The most fervent royalists, including the pretender himself, behaved as if this was not a matter of politics, but of Providence: 'it is for France to speak, and God to act', he declared. He refused to make any concessions to public opinion, insisting on replacing the tricolour with the Bourbon white flag, as a symbol that France had renounced the Revolution and was placing itself in the hands of a paternal monarch: 'I cannot consent to begin a strong and healing reign by an act of weakness'. Plans for restoration had to be shelved.

A Christian 'moral order' was conceived as part of the divinely appointed natural order: the paternal authority of God, the king, and the head of each family. Society was an organic hierarchy, not, as Enlightenment thought supposed, a contract between equals. Legitimists stressed the importance of 'natural' elites, intermediary bodies and local government, where the influence of clergy and landowners could be exerted. After their national defeat in the 1870s, royalists held on to seats on departmental *conseils généraux*, and were vocal supporters of 'decentralization', which really meant the devolution of power from the State bureaucracy to local *notables*.

A paternalist social order was the aim of a vast range of charitable societies, which were meant to moralize and Christianize the poor and maintain a healthy respect for the caring upper classes. Bishops and laymen were early and outspoken critics of capitalist exploitation, especially when it interfered with religious activity or seemed a cause of immorality. Frédéric Ozanam's St Vincent de Paul Society (founded in 1833) organized a network of visitors and aid for working-class families. Two aristocratic army officers, the Comte de Mun and the Marquis de La Tour du Pin, in the aftermath of the civil war of 1871, set up Cercles Ouvriers to promote Catholic corporatism in opposition to secular individualism. They had about 60,000 members by 1900, more than all the socialist parties combined. Some major Catholic employers were leading exponents of paternalist management. The Church heartily encouraged this inter-class solidarity as a truly Christian response to social and political problems, and conversely it condemned class war. Pope Leo XIII's encyclical *Rerum Novarum* (1891) urged the creation of corporate organizations of both employers and workers to combat the class-war teaching of socialism. The success of these mobilizing efforts should not be underestimated: in 1891, for example, 20,000 Catholic workers visited Rome, and over 300,000 pilgrims went annually to Lourdes.[13] Relatively successful too were Catholic agricultural *syndicats*.

Counter-revolutionaries were incorrigibly convinced that the masses would

13. Weber (1986), p. 189.

respond favourably to firm paternalist authority. This was rarely true. Except in the west and parts of the Midi, where a distinctive Catholic populism survived at least until the 1880s, workers and peasants were suspicious of clergy, nobility and 'counter-revolution', associated with 'feudalism' and the tithe. They showed this by supporting Bonapartism after 1848, and republicanism and socialism during the Third Republic. When the conservative 'moral order' government tried to rule with a strong hand in 1877, it was defeated.

Counter-revolutionaries continued to rely on the Church, and, from the late 1880s onwards, attempted to jump on to the nationalist and anti-Semitic bandwagon. This was really an admission of their failure to win over the country. With the restoration of a Catholic monarchy becoming increasingly unlikely, they hoped desperately for an authoritarian, nationalist and preferably military state, whether monarchical or formally republican. By the time of the Dreyfus affair (1894–99), the alliance of 'throne and altar' had largely been replaced by an alliance of 'the sabre and the holy-water sprinkler'. Attempts to reconcile Catholicism with liberal democracy were scarcely yet even embryonic: the '*ralliement*' (the attempt, encouraged by the pope, to reach a *modus vivendi* with the Republic in the 1890s) had met grass-roots resistance from both sides; while the Catholic populism of priest-politicians and priest-journalists was strongly tinged with anti-liberal and antisemitic nationalism.

Counter-revolutionary authoritarianism was revived by Charles Maurras and his Action Française movement at the end of the century. This was a cerebral and paradoxical creed: Maurras did not believe in God, but he did believe in Catholicism, 'the only idea of God that is tolerable in a well organized society'; he admired the pope, not Jesus, whom he considered 'essentially a charlatan'.[14] He wanted monarchical and ecclesiastical power to purge France of the corruption of 1789. Maurassian nationalism exerted strong influence between the two world wars, and was to have a final poisonous flowering after France's defeat in 1940, when the last attempt at counter-revolution was made under the protection not of the troops of Wellington and Blucher, but those of Hitler and Mussolini. This 'divine surprise', in Maurras's words, elevated Marshall Pétain as ersatz monarch, preaching the virtues of authority, the family, religion and the soil. His 'National Revolution' made a final attempt to expunge the traces of 1789, the 'individualism' and disorder on which (as in 1870) France's defeat was blamed: 'May the peaceful Revolution of 10 July 1940 finally close the era of bloody revolutions begun on 14 July 1789'.[15]

14. Sutton (1982), pp. 18, 34.
15. Amalvi (Spring 1987), pp. 17–39, at p. 29.

A LIBERAL ORDER

> France wanted a revolution that would not be revolutionary, and that would give it both order and liberty.
>
> *François Guizot*[16]

Liberals did not want to expunge the Revolution, but to safeguard what they considered its positive achievements – liberty, reason, equality before the law, constitutional government – and prevent it from again degenerating into fanaticism, tyranny and war. Divine-right monarchy was obsolete, but popular sovereignty had proved terribly dangerous: 'the consent of the people cannot legitimate what is illegitimate', declared Benjamin Constant.[17] A *juste milieu* between revolution and counter-revolution was required. If this could be achieved, constitutional labels did not greatly matter: empire, monarchy or republic could be accepted as long as they espoused liberal principles. This pragmatism helped liberals to exert influence on successive regimes and provide one of the principal elements in France's post-revolutionary development.

The perpetual danger in politics was to lurch from one extreme to another: 'the clear path, known to everyone, is this: ANARCHY, DESPOTISM, RESTORATION'.[18] A struggle to break free of oppression could easily overflow into anarchy, which would eventually be ended by an authoritarian restoration of order and a new despotism. Liberal writers found many historical examples: the Rome of the Caesars; Cromwell's England (a favourite theme for paintings and plays as well as works of history); Renaissance Florence; the Dutch Republic. But the best example was closer: the French Revolution showing the excesses of democratic 'anarchy' leading to Napoleon's 'despotism' and finally the Bourbon Restoration. Government must therefore be scientific and moderate; its task was not to change 'society', but to let it regulate itself and protect it from 'utopias, lunacies and despair'.[19] Hence the consistent liberal stress on the study of society and its workings. They wished to limit the power both of the State and of the masses and to safeguard individual liberty, including that of property, 'the security', said Constant, 'for a thousand kinds of happiness'.[20] But how could this be done?

To provide a practical answer was the self-imposed task of the Doctrinaire group, led by Royer-Collard and Guizot, the dominant voice in liberalism in the 1820s and, after 1830, the major influence in government, which Guizot led from 1840 to 1848. The intellectual descendants of the *Idéologues* (the last generation of the Enlightenment *philosophes*) who had supported the

16. Agulhon *et al.* (1992), p. 96.
17. Hayward (1991), p. 123.
18. Thiers (1831), p. 155.
19. Royer-Collard, in Auspitz (1982), p. 23.
20. Hayward (1991), p. 128.

Revolution in its more moderate forms, they rallied with misgivings to Napoleon, acquiesced in the Bourbon Restoration, and provided the intellectual and political pillar of 'Orleanism', the liberal regime of the duc d'Orléans, who became King Louis-Philippe in 1830. Their ambition was to formulate a liberal political 'doctrine' of legitimacy for a post-revolutionary government.

For Guizot, a devout Protestant, sovereignty belonged only to God, not to king or people; just government must be based not on dangerous claims to absolute sovereignty, but on reason. For reason to prevail, those who exercised the vote – which he saw not as an individual right but as a public function – must be those capable of reasoning: an educated and public-spirited 'middle class', free of the prejudices of the old nobility and the turbulent passions of the uneducated masses. The only practical way of identifying these rational citizens was by a property test: a degree of wealth indicated education, prudence and independence. Moreover, as a good Calvinist, Guizot knew that wealth honestly acquired was a proof of virtue. His notorious call to 'Enrich yourselves' was not an invitation to a materialist debauch: 'by work and thrift' was the never-quoted ending of the phrase. That, for Guizot, was the proper way to earn the capacity to vote without threatening the rational stability of the State.

The self-confidence of the 'Orleanist' order, bitterly attacked by Right and Left in the 1830s and 1840s, was above all based on an interpretation of history. History was progress towards liberty, finally embodied in France in the ideas of Enlightenment and the claims of the Third Estate, which had defeated monarchical, clerical and noble oppression in 1789. After a regrettable but perhaps inevitable period of conflict, the 1830 revolution had ended the process by establishing constitutional representative government, the epitome of progress and modernity already complete in America and Britain. There was a historical pattern: Charles I prefigured Louis XVI; the Puritans, the Jacobins; Cromwell, Napoleon; James II, Charles X; and the Glorious Revolution of 1688 anticipated 1830. France was clearly on the right track: they had seen the future and it worked. History had ended: progress was assured.

All liberals agreed on this, and the July Monarchy never lost their support in principle. But there was much on which they did not agree, especially when after 1830 they were actually in power – a terrible fate for intellectuals. At once they fragmented into factions. Behind the personal rivalries and competition for office there were significant intellectual divergences and a fear that the regime was failing in its historic role. All critics agreed that it was falling increasingly, especially during the 1840s, into the corrupting hands of an egotistical 'bourgeoisie' that cared about nothing in liberalism except its defence of property – a far cry from Guizot's dream of a public-spirited 'middle class'. The liberal but theocratic Catholic Lamennais protested that 'a society is not a bazaar'.[21] Men as different as Thiers and Tocqueville agreed

21. Girardet (1986), p. 150.

that the regime had to find a way of inspiring the nation. A central theme of Tocqueville's writing was the danger of atomization in modern societies, and one remedy he and others saw for France, as was seen in the previous chapter, was 'glory'. Guizot himself felt some of that disillusion in the late 1840s: 'no one judges the moral state of our time more severely than I; no one is more convinced than I that the evil is profound and extensive'.[22] Yet he and his supporters, including the king, would make no concessions, in particular by widening the franchise. He insisted that it adequately represented society, and to extend it would let in the irrational 'passions', nationalist and democratic, that had led to the catastrophes of 1792–93. He was convinced that history was on his side: there is no better proof of the utopian and dogmatic nature of his liberal 'new order'.

Its collapse in February 1848 was a permanent defeat not only for the liberals, but for liberalism, which was never again able to construct its post-revolutionary order, but could at best influence other parties. Most liberals were unable to comprehend the 1848 revolution and what followed. Guizot never came to terms with it, and the historian Augustin Thierry wrote in his last work in 1853, 'Where now can be placed the future of France, which seemed obviously to me to be the alliance of monarchical tradition with the principles of liberty? . . . These uncertainties overcome me, and have replaced in my mind the most complete faith.'[23] Incomprehension was accompanied by fear of social upheaval and popular violence: 'I hate and fear the mob', noted Tocqueville, who believed that a class war had begun. Liberals fragmented, abandoning or compromising their principles to attach themselves to legitimism, Bonapartism or even moderate republicanism as ramparts against socialism. They were, admitted Tocqueville, 'like river oarsmen . . . called upon to navigate their boat in mid-ocean'.[24] Guizot permanently abandoned politics for theology, and many other liberals retreated to a cultural ivory tower and wrote books, many of them very good.

Liberalism survived and revived. Rosenvallon has argued that Thiers, only briefly sharing the general disarray, created a new focus for liberalism in the defence of property against socialism, both by debating in parliament with the socialist Proudhon and through a widely read pamphlet, Du Droit de propriété (1848), which immediately went through four editions and is said to have sold 100,000 in an English edition too.[25] No less important, by breaking with Bonaparte in 1851 and being imprisoned (however briefly) at his coup d'état, Thiers and other liberals such as the Duc de Broglie were able to emerge during the 1860s as the spokesmen of a revived liberal opposition, warning against the dangers of the second round of Bonapartist populism and demanding 'necessary liberties' to make political life possible. This proved the rallying point of opposition in the 1860s, and had a permanent

22. Tudesq (1964), vol. 2, p. 924.
23. Girard (1985), p. 173.
24. Tocqueville (1948), p. 89.
25. Bernstein (1971), p. 173.

effect on republicanism, which itself evolved in a liberal direction. Indeed, the liberal and republican opponents of Napoleon III seemed to be moving towards a degree of consensus, and the Empire itself had to offer liberal reforms in the 1860s. Taking the view of their forbears that labels were of little importance, most were willing to support a 'liberal empire' while assuming that when the emperor died, France would become a republic. Writers close to Thiers, including Rémusat, Broglie, Laboulaye and the youthful Prévost-Paradol whose book *La France nouvelle* (1868) was one of the most influential of the period, elaborated the agenda for liberalization, now including universal male suffrage with a restraining upper house of parliament. America, as much as England, was now seen as the prototype. Tocqueville's view that democracy was inevitable was now widely accepted: it was, wrote Prévost-Paradol, as natural as old age and death.

Many of their expectations were realized, though in a far stormier way than anticipated: through war with Germany, the collapse of the Empire, French surrender and the bloody civil war of the Paris Commune. Thiers, participant in the 1830 revolution, critic of Guizot, enemy of socialism, opponent of the Empire, was at last in command. His 'new order' was at first sight a contradiction in terms: a 'conservative republic'. To this, he believed, all sensible men could rally; this 'government that divides us least' would keep at bay the extremists of both Right and Left. However, Republicans and Royalists, affected by the crises of 1870–71, were convinced that France needed to be regenerated, and so had far more ambitious ideas for new 'moral orders'.

Hence, although the constitution of the Third Republic, finally adopted in 1875, embodied the principal features outlined by Thiers and other liberals in the 1860s, and led to a durable system of liberal republican government, it did not mark that final 'ending of the Revolution' aimed at by generations of liberals since 1790. Rather, it provided the arena for successive conflicts between two broad and changing coalitions of Left and Right, in which liberals played a marginal role. Some, as after 1848, retired again to a Parnassian ivory tower, from which Flaubert poured scorn on the idiocy of 'bourgeois society', and Renan and Taine mused elegantly on the decadence of France. A new generation, beginning with Renan and Taine, and continuing into the 1920s with Le Bon, Tarde, Boutmy and Leroy-Beaulieu, despaired of parliamentary politics and concentrated on creating a new bureaucratic and business elite to govern and protect society behind the scenes of the political Punch-and-Judy show. Private schools (on the English public-school model) and the independent Ecole Libre des Sciences Politiques, set up by Boutmy in 1872, aimed to train a new ruling class: 'refaire une tête du peuple', said Boutmy. To a remarkable extent they did so, with important and lasting consequences. France in the 1990s is perhaps the only democratic country to have literally a ruling elite.

There also remained a liberal current – never a party, but always a presence – that, consciously following Thiers's example, attached itself to republicanism: it took the label 'progressist' in the 1890s, and was personified by Raymond Poincaré, from the 1900s to the 1920s the bulwark of *juste milieu* republicanism, opposing the nationalist Right and the socialist Left. Thus, though not in its own name, liberalism profoundly influenced the republican new order as it emerged in practice.

A REPUBLICAN ORDER

My aim is to make humanity without God or king.

Jules Ferry

For republicans – who included a wide variety of opinions, from liberal to nationalist and socialist – the Revolution was the central event of history, 'the absolute point zero',[26] a revelation of truth and progress beginning a new epoch in the development of humanity, even if it had been temporarily defeated by reaction. However much they might disagree over its precise implications, origins, heroes and villains, they agreed that it had ceaselessly to be made and remade, and its fundamental significance fulfilled. This fulfilment, whether violent or peaceful, was the only way of creating a stable new order in France: 'the only way to prevent revolutions is to make them', wrote a republican in 1879.[27]

Republicans inherited the awkward proto-totalitarian legacy of Rousseau and the Jacobins, the rhetoric of the 'liberty of the ancients', with its stress on political participation, civic virtue and patriotic sacrifice, and also the logically contradictory eighteenth-century ideas of social contract and natural rights, which stressed the sanctity of individual property. They also, from the 1830s onwards, had to face the problem of the 'social question' and the appearance of socialism. While in opposition, the precise social programme of republicanism could remain vague. But in power, especially in 1848, it caused division and conflict within republican ranks. Once permanently in power after 1879, the response of the circumspect governing republicans, led by Gambetta and Ferry, was to stress the patriotic duty of the individual to the nation and to defend the rights of private property, especially small property – 'the world of the small that is democracy', in Gambetta's words – against both socialism and big capitalism, while also proclaiming a duty of 'solidarity' towards those in need. This was later elaborated as 'solidarism', the radical republican response to the socialist challenge of the 1890s, sponsored by the first radical prime minister Léon Bourgeois. Based theoretically on the idea that there existed an implicit contract between society and its members by which they owed each other 'solidarity' (an idea taken from the sociological school of Durkheim and Bouglé), it advocated a range of measures to protect the individual against adverse economic circumstances without weakening private property and enterprise.

26. Nicolet (1982), p. 57.
27. Ibid., p. 89.

A quasi-religious conception of the Revolution and the Republic – not directly inherited from the revolutionaries of the 1790s, many of whom had rallied to Napoleon or the restored Bourbons – was reinvented in the middle decades of the nineteenth century. This saw the Revolution as the seizure by the nation of its sovereign right. The nation was the only legitimate source of power; the vote was a right of all (male) citizens. The Republic – by definition, the reign of popular sovereignty – was the only legitimate form of government, which could be installed by force if necessary, but never validly opposed or overthrown, even by majority vote, for the people could not abandon its inalienable rights. The sovereign people or nation consisted not merely of a collection of individuals, but a community of equal citizens. This had two immensely important implications. First, that the Republic was 'One and Indivisible': unity of belief and aspiration was the proper and desirable goal. Second, that the Republic's main focus was not the individual (for which liberalism was criticized from the 1830s onwards), but 'society', which depended on fraternity and solidarity: two key terms.

Education had been a key theme of republicanism since the 1790s. It took on extra significance for the post-1848 generation, who had experienced the failure of the Second Republic and its abandonment by the majority of voters, who had flocked to Bonapartism. For loyal republicans, this proved that universal suffrage was not automatically the solution to political problems. Few (mainly on the extreme Left) questioned universal suffrage in principle, but the need to guide and enlighten it seemed clear. Education would dispel Catholic obscurantism and become the motor of modern republican progress. Here was felt the influence of positivism, the fashionable scientific philosophy of August Comte reinterpreted in the 1860s by Emile Littré, for whom education was the means of 'regeneration'. It would enable the full fruits of popular sovereignty to ripen, as the whole electorate became capable of informed and rational choice. It would make what positivists termed 'reaction' impossible. It would ensure that the potential for social perfection inherent in the Revolution was fulfilled through peaceful progress.

Young republicans growing up under the Empire, including the future leaders Gambetta and Ferry, were influenced by the liberal opposition of the 1860s. Legality, constitutional guarantees, 'necessary liberties', parliamentary control – the staples of liberal, but not previously of republican, thought – became new weapons in the republican political armoury in the struggle against Bonapartism. Positivism encouraged this development too: it rejected 'metaphysics' and 'anarchy' in favour of hard-headed 'scientific' analysis.

By the 1870s, when republicans got their chance to govern, the new order they offered was an effective if logically inconsistent amalgam of revolutionary traditions moderated by the political experience and intellectual developments of the previous quarter of a century. The two key figures here were Gambetta and Ferry, both, and especially the latter, strongly influenced by positivism. Their primary concern was to make a viable republic: to prove for the first time that a republic could govern effectively and survive. Moderate republicans extolled 'the spirit of the Revolution', now confined to history, but condemned 'the revolutionary spirit', which refused to accept that the age of the barricades was finished. In the short term, the republicans in government – soon nicknamed 'opportunists' – wanted to win the trust of the electorate and defeat both 'reaction' and 'anarchy'. In the long term, they had an ambitious strategy – the utopian aspect of their new order – to create a republican society, led by a republican political class drawn from what Gambetta called 'new social strata', a democracy based on shared secular values taught by republican schools, on scientific faith in reason and progress, on political equality and on the steady extension of property. Ideological and class conflict would have no place in the republic of harmony. 'Class', said Gambetta, was 'a bad word that I never use'. History would come to an end with the fulfilment and end of the Revolution, for when 'universal suffrage functions in full sovereignty', said Gambetta, 'no further revolution is possible'.[28]

Their Third Republic, however moderate its methods and liberal its constitution (the 1875 constitution, accepted at first with reluctance by republicans, was largely drawn up by liberals), was not to be the 'neutral' non-ideological regime that 1860s liberals such as Thiers, Broglie and Prévost-Paradol had envisaged. Rather, it was 'a party, a faith, an ideal' which Catholics and monarchists, however law-abiding, could never share, and from which they were to find themselves excluded. For the new order envisaged by the 'absolute Republic' (as Rudelle calls it) was not to accept France as it existed, but, however gradually, cautiously and democratically, to remake France in its own image, without God or king.

This remained the essential vision of the republican new order. Conflicts within republican ranks, and they were bitter, concerned (apart from the inevitable rivalries of individuals, parties and interests) the speed and vigour with which a republican society should be created. This, broadly speaking, was what separated opportunists from radicals. Radicalism first emerged in the 1860s to protest against coexistence between moderate republicans and the liberalizing Empire and found its classic expression in Gambetta's 1869 Belleville Programme, based on an ultra-democratic rejection of State and Church oppression. Radicalism re-emerged in the 1870s to express a similar impatient demand for purer and truer republicanism, and its new programme, rather similar to the Belleville Programme, was Clemenceau's Montmartre Programme of 1881. The debate came to focus above all on the vigour of *la laïcisation* (secularization) which all republicans saw as the indispensible, even the principal, step towards creating a truly progressive democracy. They also disagreed on the extent to which the State should intervene in economic and social life in the name of the republican values of justice and equality, and to defend small property owners against 'financial feudalism' – a debate taking in pensions, nationalization and endless attempts to introduce income tax. Radicalism became a huge and amorphous movement from the 1890s onwards, frequently attacked (and not without reason) for becoming

28. Rosenvallon (1985), pp. 367, 364.

increasingly 'centrist', opportunist and self-serving; yet as the embodiment of republican tradition it was always able, however uncomfortably, to straddle the gap between liberalism and socialism and prevent the complete fragmentation of republicanism.

A SOCIALIST ORDER

Socialism . . . is the opposite of egoism and individualism.

Petit Manuel Republicain, 1849[29]

Socialists displayed the obsession with a utopian new order in a particularly pure form. Socialist ideas emerged (the word itself dates from about 1831), along with liberalism, Bonapartism and republicanism, from the fertile debris deposited by the Revolution. Far from being a response to the economic and social problems of industrialization (still in the future), it was a moral response, typical of the Romantic idealism of the 1830s and 1840s, to what was seen as the egoism, materialism and atomization of post-revolutionary society.

Socialists, like liberals and republicans, traced their modern history from the Revolution. They accepted the common interpretation of the Revolution as a class struggle between the aristocracy and the bourgeoisie. But they believed that the Revolution was still only in its first stage: 'the revolutionary task is accomplished', wrote Victor Considérant in 1847, 'the democratic task has hardly begun'.[30] For the Revolution had emancipated the bourgeoisie, but not the 'proletariat', whom Blanqui defined as the 30 million who worked for a living. It would only be complete when this next stage had taken place, with the creation of a 'democratic *and social* Republic', a perfect society of fraternity, justice and harmony. 'Fraternity alone is the generative social principle', wrote Pecqueur in 1842. 'Equality and liberty define and clarify fraternity.'[31]

As we have seen, the utopian ambition to end history was not confined to socialists. What distinguished them was not only their willingness to give their imagination freer reign, but also to recast the social and economic system, which liberals and republicans believed could and should be left to develop according to its own immutable laws. As Lefranc neatly puts it, socialists were pessimistic about things, and optimistic about man.[32] They were above all optimistic about the 'people', who, unlike the 'bourgeoisie', they saw as having preserved unspoilt the natural human virtues of fraternity and equality. They agreed, however, in being extremely pessimistic about the present (whether in 1820 or 1890), which, following the destruction of the old order, was wallowing in chaos, materialism and anarchic individualism – the marks

29. Levêque (1992), p. 312.
30. Lovell (June 1992), p. 190.
31. Ibid., p. 198.
32. Lefranc (1973), p. 186.

of bourgeois society. This they saw as the antithesis of morality and justice. Work, which was a moral activity, was debased as a mere saleable commodity, subject to the destructive effects of competition. Saint-Simon's division of society into producers and idlers (*oisifs*) was long accepted as the fundamental class division, responsible for poverty and oppression. Producers were not only workers and peasants, but also what Proudhonists later called the 'working bourgeoisie', including managers, shopkeepers and (of course) writers. Idlers were all those who lived off rents and investments, and also the hangers-on of a parasitic and oppressive State: kings, priests, bureaucrats, policemen and professional soldiers. The optimistic belief – never wholly abandoned by French socialists in spite of violent rebuffs – that socialism could be brought about by the consent of the productive majority, helped to integrate socialism, which never lost its moralistic tone, into the democratic republican tradition, and perhaps explains why class hatred was more violent on the Right than on the Left, who liked to dream of a great fraternal conciliation.

While all agreed about the inevitability of the glorious future, and most expected it soon, routes to utopia varied. There was one fundamental and persistent division: between those who saw the State as the instrument of change, and those who mistrusted the State and wanted to act independently of it. This division corresponded to a different judgement of the Revolution. Advocates of State action, from Blanqui and Blanc in the 1830s and 1840s to the Marxists of the 1880s and after, admired Robespierre and the Jacobins, and envisaged a revolutionary dictatorship (temporary, of course) to remodel society. Those who wished to act outside the State, from Fourier and Proudhon to the anarcho-syndicalists of the end of the century, either deplored and feared revolutionary violence or at least (as in the case of the anarchists) regarded a Jacobin-style revolution as merely the substitution of one set of oppressors for another.

The great period of socialist imagination was the 20 years after 1830, which inspired hopes that the Revolution might be fulfilled, and then disappointed them by inaugurating a 'bourgeois monarchy'. However, the first stirrings went back to the Restoration and the influential writings of Saint-Simon (*Le Système industriel*, 1820–22), and when Fourier appealed to the king, the tsar and the Rothschilds to support his model socialist community. For this was peaceful, philosophical socialism, convinced that if it could only set up a working model of Utopia, based on science, sociology and religion, then princes, paupers and merchant bankers would flock to join. Charles Fourier (d. 1837), the most extravagant visionary of all, planned his socialist phalansteries around the satisfaction of pleasure, which would be ensured by a minute scientific planning of the community so as to provide a mix of 810 human types, ages and tastes. Modern science and industry would produce 'Harmony', an earthly paradise of peace and plenty, sex, gastronomy, flowers and cats, in which the oceans might be turned into lemonade, there would be 37,000,000 poets equal to Homer, women would be equal to men, brothels would be respected institutions, and the planets could be shifted as required.

Etienne Cabet (in *Le Voyage en Icarie*, 1840) portrayed a more regimented society: uniform clothing and uniform opinions, people's courts, vast factories, identical housing blocks, and, instead of gastronomy, rations delivered from central kitchens – as history has shown, a more plausible utopia.

Such perfect communities were based on religious foundations, seen (perhaps rightly, given the results in practice) as indispensable to their working; indeed, socialism was usually one facet of an extreme nationalist and religious millenarianism. It was commonplace to claim during this period that socialism or communism were Christianity in practice. 'JESUS-CHRIST est COMMUNISTE!!!' proclaimed Cabet.[33] If paradise was to be built on earth, they did not believe that it was confined to this planet. Their very unorthodox Christianity was supplemented by a wonderful range of occult beliefs: spiritualism, the transmigration of souls after death to other planets, reincarnation (Fourier calculated that people would have 400 earthly lives) and, in the case of the grimly austere and ferociously atheistical Blanqui, the hallucinatory belief that our lives were eternally repeated in an infinity of identical planets.

Fourier's phalansteries and Cabet's *Icaria* attracted considerable following (Cabet's newspaper *Le Populaire* was one of the largest left-wing papers in the 1840s). Enfantin, a follower of Saint-Simon, set himself up in 1832 as 'Supreme Father' of a mystical socialist community at Ménilmontant, on the outskirts of Paris, whose life was marked by a 'characteristic mixture of humanitarian ardour and fatally humourless solemnity',[34] and which was swiftly closed down by the government. Cabet set up short-lived Icarian communities in the United States in the late 1840s, as did Fourier's disciple Victor Considérant in 1854. A 'Familistery' (more straight-laced than Fourier's original inspiration) was set up near Bourges by an idealistic stove-manufacturer, Godin, in 1859. After many vicissitudes, it was still manufacturing heating equipment in the 1980s.

These strange totalitarian idylls had a durable influence. Other socialists, especially Marxists, dismissed 'utopianism', but their refusal to specify their own vision of a socialist society let echoes of Fourier and Cabet linger in the imagination of socialists and anti-socialists alike. Waving corn, combine harvesters, free love and ballet in the evening remained the dream of many a militant. While 'ask any good narrow-minded bourgeois about a socialist', wrote Considérant in 1848, 'and the uniform answer will be that he is dangerous and immoral, motivated by the desire to burn and pillage, to partition property and collectivize women'.[35] Clemenceau dismissed socialism more succinctly as 'barracks or convents'. Perhaps the most influential of all French socialist thinkers, Proudhon, was as opposed to barracks and convents as Clemenceau, however. Inspired by republican moralism and rejecting

33. Charlton (1963), p. 80.
34. Ibid., p. 73.
35. Bernstein (1971), p. 165.

Catholicism, he was also, unlike most republicans, fearful of the oppressive nature of the State and of the stultifying effects of the kind of socialism envisaged by Cabet and Blanc. Influenced by the corporate traditions of Lyons artisans, he saw socialism as a federation of 'associations' (workers' cooperatives and democratic local communities) which would make the bureaucratic central State wither. Like Fourier and Cabet, he believed that his system would be quick and easy to establish, but unlike them he tried to work out the economic means of bringing it about: namely, a popular credit bank that would provide cheap capital to set up the associations.

There were other French socialists – called at the time communists, and referred to by subsequent historians as 'republican socialists' or 'Jacobin socialists' – who condemned all this as escapism, and directed their attentions to taking power. Their intention was to repeat and continue the Revolution, and this time to use it to create socialism through the power of a revolutionary State. Blanqui, who epitomized them, refused to speculate about a post-revolutionary society, but another major socialist theorist, Louis Blanc, advocated in *L'Organisation du travail* (1840) the establishment by the State – which should become the controller of the economy – of 'social workshops' that would replace private industry.

The 1848 revolution seemed to give socialists, especially Blanc, Blanqui and Proudhon, an opportunity, if in very different ways, to carry out their plans. Socialism became a political force, first through the activism of Paris workers, then through the organization of the démocrate-socialiste party. However, repeated defeats and repression from May 1848 to the coup d'état of December 1851 altered the context and tone of French socialism. The naive apoliticism of the earlier generation finally made its exit to the bluer skies of Texas or Illinois. Yet basic features remained. Political defeat and repression convinced many 'republican socialists', including Blanqui and his little band, that the seizure of the State and the destruction of reaction and Catholicism were the essential first steps. But Proudhon and his many followers were equally convinced that political action had proved useless and that they must act directly, setting up associations in the workplace; this also attracted moderate trade unionists, permitted by the Second Empire to engage in non-political activity. Many socialists and workers, however, were willing to combine the two pragmatically, working both for a republic and for cooperative organization of industry. The Paris Commune of 1871 showed all these elements: strong republicanism, anticlericalism, and measured encouragement of cooperatives. The Commune, though looking back to an earlier generation of socialists for most of its ideas, was far more political and less 'utopian' than the Parisian Left had been in 1848.

After the defeat of the Commune, it was not until the 1880s that socialism became again a significant presence. Some old elements remained, particularly Proudhonism and Blanquism (Blanqui himself died only in 1881). There was, however, a significant newcomer: Marxism. In an atmosphere of defeat, its utopianism, conventionally expressed but guaranteed by 'science', was central to its appeal: 'men and women ... will drink good wine and leave water to the livestock', *Le Socialiste* promised in 1886.[36] It took over the mantle of Statist socialism as the Parti Ouvrier Français (1879), commonly known as Guesdists after their leader, and it eventually attracted those Blanquists who had not moved towards nationalism. With its dogmatic stress on political action and central leadership, it fitted easily into the old Jacobin socialist tradition, notwithstanding its repeated (and vain) declarations that the old issues of anticlericalism and republican defence were irrelevant to the only question that mattered: class war.

The anti-Statist tradition of Proudhonism also persisted, receiving a new lease of life from the vogue for anarchist rejection of 'bourgeois' society and the 'bourgeois Republic' from the 1880s. This took moderate forms: in the 'possibilism' expounded by Paul Brousse, which refused authoritarian ideologies and practised, with some success, democratic municipal socialism; and in the very popular '*mutuellist*' movement (roughly equivalent to British friendly societies) which had 3.7 million members in 1913.[37] The revolutionary form was anarcho-syndicalism, led by Griffuelhes and Pelloutier and embodied in the Confédération Générale du Travail (CGT), set up in 1895, which aimed at revolution through a general strike: 'spontaneous and creative action', as Griffuelhes put it in 1907.[38]

During the 1880s and 1890s, the socialists were perennially split into rival parties, divided over tactics, organization and the question – increasingly theoretical but still emotive – of whether revolution or gradual reform was the route to socialism. Attempting to reconcile and unite all socialists were several influential 'independents' – intellectuals such as Jean Jaurès and later Léon Blum, former revolutionaries such as the Communard Benoît Malon, and converts from radicalism such as Alexandre Millerand – who appealed to the moral and idealistic tradition of the Revolution as the liberator of all mankind, and presented socialism as the 'human religion of the new age'. Combining idealism with political acumen, they wished to infuse the Republic with social concerns that would appeal to all men of good will, appeal to a wider spectrum of voters, and establish a distinctive socialist message that marked them off from their rivals and partners in opposition, the radicals and nationalists.

In 1896 the various groups brushed aside years of doctrinal quarrels by agreeing on Millerand's Saint-Mandé programme, which managed to reconcile distant and non-violent revolutionary aspirations with present-day reformist parliamentary practice. But it was not until 1905 that a single party, the Section Française de l'Internationale Ouvrière (SFIO), could be established on the basis of a similar uneasy compromise. Its rhetoric continued to paint a vision of the future as mystically utopian, and no less beguiling, than Fourier's lemonade-washed world, but far less precise. As Jaurès wrote in 1890:

36. Stuart (1992), p. 483.
37. Gueslin (1992), p. 200.
38. Lefranc (1973), p. 89.

when socialism has triumphed, when the state of concord has succeeded the state of struggle . . . all men will have the fullness of pride and joy . . . They will understand life . . . history . . . the universe [which] cannot be brutal and blind, but which has spirit everywhere, soul everywhere . . . [in] an immense confused aspiration towards order, beauty, liberty and goodness.[39]

Order, always order!

THE BONAPARTIST SYNTHESIS

Outside the ideas and principles . . . which I made triumph I see nothing but slavery or confusion for France and Europe alike.

Napoleon Bonaparte, 1821[40]

Bonapartists claimed that Napoleon I had been a surpassing genius who had understood and mastered the new post-revolutionary age: modern France had been 'regenerated by the Revolution of 1789 and organized by the Emperor'. He had successfully ended the Revolution by preserving its central values, protecting it against its enemies, purging it of its excesses and establishing the new post-revolutionary order: strong government embodying popular sovereignty, a meritocracy devoid of 'privilege', ruled by 'the greatest genius of modern times' who is arguably the most influential political thinker and actor in modern French history. Waterloo and the intervening regimes had mutilated his great work; the first step towards creating stable government was therefore to return to the emperor's system. Then, France could pursue the other aims that Bonapartists said the emperor had always intended: peace, prosperity and the liberty of nations.

More than the other restorations that marked the nineteenth century, the Second Empire claimed to be a pure restoration: the faithful re-application of the political system that had been interrupted only by the overwhelming strength of the reactionary foreign 'Coalition' aided by faint-hearts and traitors within. In fact, like the new orders proposed by other political movements, that of Bonapartism was progressively formulated during the first decades of the nineteenth century, and, suggests Furet, with greater imaginative freedom than any of the others. The Bonapartist utopia, a synthesis of pragmatism and fantasy, of propaganda and popular aspiration, of public subsidies, police regulation, paternalist populism and national glory, was the simplest, the least subtle, and the most effective on offer.

Napoleon himself on St Helena deliberately inspired idealized accounts of his reign and his intentions, through memoirs and published conversations which obtained a huge circulation among the political class, most famous of them Las Cases's *Mémorial de Sainte-Hélène* (1823). As Napoleon's jailor, Sir Hudson Lowe, wryly observed, he created an imaginary Napoleon, an

39. Jaurès (1947), pp. 204–5.
40. Deathbed testament, in Herold (1961), p. 255.

imaginary Europe and even an imaginary St Helena.[41] Napoleon's apologia was that of a man devoted to France and the Revolution, who had, by grasping the essence of the Revolution's ideas, been able to end internal conflict and lay the foundations of the modern society that the Revolution had made possible. He had been forced against his will into perpetual wars against the enemies of the Revolution. But even defeat had brought apotheosis: for the triumph of 'reaction' had proved Napoleon right, and his sufferings on the 'rock' of St Helena gave him the romantic appeal of a new Prometheus, as Victor Hugo put it, who had stolen the fire of Heaven. 'Every day strips me of my tyrant's skin.'[42]

A 'cult of Napoleon' grew up, partly spontaneous, partly inspired by Bonapartist propaganda and independent admirers, partly encouraged for their own purposes by opponents of the Bourbons. Propagated through pictures, songs, memoirs, plays, and popular almanacs peddled throughout France, it combined a view of the Empire as a golden age of prosperity and glory with a contrastingly bleak view of France since 1815, ruled by 'the fat pig' and his nobles and priests, and then after 1830 by the timid, pear-shaped Louis-Philippe. It appealed widely to small peasant proprietors (always fearful of feudalism and threats to their *biens nationaux*), artisans, the lower-middle classes, and not least the very poor, among them former soldiers, many maimed and reduced to beggary. The centre of the cult was a sentimental image of the 'Little Corporal' as the friend of the people: the man who was notorious among his entourage for lack of human feeling was presented as a Santa Claus in jack-boots. This providential saviour would one day return, as he had from Elba in 1814. Sightings of Napoleon, rumours that he was returning to liberate France with armies of Americans or Turks, and stubborn refusal to believe in his death were common even as late as 1848.

Shorn of its millenarian and democratic elements, the Napoleonic cult held considerable attraction for the elite. Its association with glory and victory seemed an indispensable element of national reconciliation and unity, even among those who criticized the Empire. Though it was conventional to deplore Napoleon's excesses, in the same breath his genius and achievements were praised to the skies, and his acts placed beyond ordinary morality or rationality in the realm of romantic genius. Hugo, the self-appointed national conscience, who went through a period of royalist and anti-Bonapartist fervour, finally gave in to romantic admiration in his ode *To the Column* (1827), and later fictionalized his conversion in the character of Marius in *Les Misérables*.

However, the cult of Napoleon did not seem to have a political future after Napoleon's death in 1821 and that of his only son in 1832. But his nephew, Prince Louis-Napoleon Bonaparte, remedied this by proposing himself as a future ruler. His *Des Idées Napoléoniennes* (1839) turned the outpourings from St Helena, seasoned with some Montesquieu and buttressed by recent

41. Herold (1961), p. xxxiv.
42. Ibid., pp. 274, 281.

historical writing, into a coherent political manifesto, perhaps the most fateful of the century, not least because he himself believed it. Napoleon, he argued, was one of those Great Men who marked human progress like 'milestones' because they had been able to understand and embody the ideas of their time. Napoleon, 'the messiah of the new ideas', had been the 'executor' of the Revolution, which 'dying but not defeated left to Napoleon the accomplishment of its last wishes': to put its principles on solid bases; to reunite the French people; and to repulse the attacks of 'feudal Europe'. All this he had done, argued Louis-Napoleon, in spite of the wars that had been forced on him, founding a new State and new social order based on equal opportunity and merit: 'a man was asked what he had done, not from whom he was born'. He had rebuilt the economy, and succoured the poor. He had healed the wounds left by the Revolution by uniting Frenchmen in patriotism, and by himself being 'national', above party rivalry. He had governed with authority, but in order to lay the foundations for liberty in due course. He had created a hereditary monarchy because of its pragmatic advantages, but it was a 'democratic' monarchy: 'the nature of democracy is to personify itself in one man'. Finally, he had sought to extend these benefits to all of Europe, and create a confederation of free nations, but had been sadly 'misunderstood'.

To this vision – a gloss on the self-justification emitted from St Helena, and which patriotic Frenchmen eagerly swallowed – Louis-Napoleon Bonaparte added an entirely new element: a 'socialist' one. If his uncle had been 'Robespierre on horseback', he was 'Saint-Simon on horseback'. Like so many of his generation, he had been influenced by the Saint-Simonians, and had contacts with socialists such as Blanc and Proudhon. In *Des Idées*, asserting that Napoleon I had succeeded in fostering industry and 'extraordinary prosperity', he drew the conclusion that a strong State, emphatically different from the liberal conception, could be 'the beneficent motor' of progress through great public works. In his celebrated *L'Extinction du Paupérisme* (1844), advocating among other things quasi-military agricultural colonies for the unemployed, could be seen 'the influence of Saint-Simonianism and of Louis Blanc, though the book is more reformist, statist and military than socialist'.[43]

Underlying all this was the implication that the ideas of Napoleon could best be carried out by another Bonaparte. This only became feasible in 1848 after the failure of the other contenders. But then it won an unprecedented tide of popular support. This was partly the mystique of the name. But it was also because, as Louis-Napoleon said, 'my name is in itself a programme': Bonapartism had political content, as well as mythical prestige. 'The Bonapartes must remember', his mother had told him, 'that all power comes to them from the people's will.' Louis-Napoleon did remember: 'He has a bee in his bonnet about the people', noted one Orleanist lady scornfully.[44]

The token of that mutual tie was the plebiscite, one of the essential

43. Bluche (1980), p. 228.
44. Girard (1986), p. 16.

elements of Bonapartism. Napoleon I had used the 'appeal to the people' (however bogus) in 1800, 1802, 1804 and 1815; Louis-Napoleon used it to legitimate his coup d'état in 1851, his restoration of the Empire in 1852, his liberalization of the regime in 1870, and above all to demonstrate his own position as charismatic embodiment of the people's will. Plebiscites were condemned by all other parties, none of whom had enough confidence in the electorate or themselves to risk them. This recipe for strong government, manipulating popular opinion and legitimized by it, lived on after the fall of the Empire in 1870 to become, from the 1880s onwards, common to all conservative and monarchist tendencies, and indeed it influenced all who advocated a powerful government at the head of a dynamic State. It was finally revived by another man who regarded himself as the embodiment of the nation, who despised parties, and who defended public order against extremes of Left and Right: Charles de Gaulle.

A NATIONAL ORDER

Irreversible tendencies are pushing Europe towards a new organization... everywhere the cause of the peoples is triumphing.

Anon., La Coalition, 1860

That the Revolution was an event of universal, not only French, significance, and that its victory or defeat would change the face of the world, seemed as clear to counter-revolutionaries who fought against it as to those who followed the tricolour flag. Nationalism – which gives *primacy* to national values over all other values, in Girardet's useful definition[45] – has been a potent theme of post-revolutionary French political culture because of this identification of the French nation with universal values, because of the proclamation in 1789 of the nation as the source of political legitimacy, and (as was seen in Chapter 2) because of the lasting tension between France and the rest of Europe that followed defeat in 1814–15. These three elements produced three corresponding characteristics in later French nationalism: the conviction that France had a uniquely important role in world history; the insistence on unity within the nation; and the perception of an intimate connection between France's domestic well-being and her relations with the outside world. All ideas of a post-revolutionary order had to take account of these issues.

The central place of nationalism in political culture means that every party has been tinted by some shade of it, and in a later chapter we shall examine aspects of national identity and nationalist politics. As every party has used nationalist language, there has rarely been a titular 'nationalist party'. At times, however, particular groups have trumpeted their claims to be the exclusive defenders of the national cause and made this the centre of their rhetoric. In

45. Girardet (1983), p. 9 n. 1.

particular, the 'national question' was a major concern of liberals, republicans and socialists during the first half of the nineteenth century, and they often appropriated the title *parti national.* At the end of the century, nationalism was a label attached increasingly to anti-liberal and anti-democratic parties.

For the Left the Revolution had made the French nation unique in two ways. First, she was the Messiah of the new age. They saw her influence, her ability to survive attack, and her power to impose her will, as crucial to the progress of humanity. For the socialist workers' paper *L'Atelier* (March 1841), 'the distinctive character of French patriotism is, by making France more and more formidable, to make her the hope of the oppressed, the terror of oppressors, the model of nations'. Second, the Revolution had made her the most fully developed of nations, perhaps the only true nation. Whereas most other peoples were merely 'races' (that is, biological phenomena) or arbitrary agglomerations of subject peoples, 'France had made France', as Michelet explained, by her long struggle for freedom culminating in the Revolution, which turned the nation into a true community based on liberty, equality and patriotic fraternity.

As revolutionary standard-bearer and 'universal fatherland' (Michelet), it was France's destiny to create and lead the new world order, both by peaceful persuasion and, if necessary, by the force of her 'sacred bayonets', without falling into 'humanitarian claptrap'. 'We shall never make the Chinese and the Arab regard us as brothers . . . so long as we have not made them accept, willingly or by force, our civilising ideas', wrote the socialist *Atelier* (May 1841). When the new order was complete, in the form of a 'universal republic', its centre would naturally be France. Then, the French nation would, some thought, have 'embraced the universality of peoples'.[46]

This nationalism was an essential characteristic of those who wanted to pursue the Revolution in the generation after Waterloo. Conversely, internationalism was a necessary part of conservatism, whether the visionary Christian order dreamt of by Bonald or Tsar Alexander I, or the pragmatic attempt to reintegrate France into the international States system worked on by Talleyrand and later Guizot. At least until the 1860s, this marked one of the principal divisions between Right and Left, and was a central element in the opposition to both the Bourbon Restoration and the July Monarchy. Left-wing liberals, republicans, most socialists and Bonapartists (anyway overlapping categories) saw their hopes for political change within France as depending on France's ability to create a new world order, almost certainly by force: 'it is no use demanding reforms . . . in our social order', declared *L'Atelier* (March 1844) 'if we cannot impose [them] on the outside world'.

It was Napoleon III who actually tried to bring about, or at least to begin, this new national order. This, he believed, had been his uncle's 'great idea': to create a Europe of national 'agglomerations' under the leadership of France. He announced officially his support for the 'principle of nationalities', the idea, based on a dictum of Napoleon I, that with the destruction of the

46. *L'Atelier*, March 1841; see also Todorov (1993), ch. 3.

old order of monarchical states, a new order must be based on free national states and 'natural frontiers'. As was seen in Chapter 2, this led to the 1859 war with Austria, and indirectly into the 1870 war with Germany, in which the European order was indeed changed, with immense consequences, though not those hoped for and expected by the nationalists. Napoleon and his entourage went even further at least in their imaginations: in 1863 the Empress Eugenie proposed to the Austrian ambassador a radical redrawing of the map of Europe, which included forcing Russia back into Asia, 'suppressing' Turkey, setting up a Poland ruled by the King of Saxony, giving Saxony to Prussia and the Balkans to Austria, who would in return hand over Italy, and so on.[47] This was fantasy on a heroic scale, though scarcely more so than the notion of creating a puppet empire in Mexico – which Fourier had pronounced 'the natural capital of the world' and Saint-Simonians saw as the bridge to China and Japan – for a Habsburg archduke, which actually happened in 1864, with disastrous results; or Napoleon's manoeuvring in the late 1860s to annex Luxembourg, Belgium and/or the Rhineland, that familiar nationalist dream.

This adoption by Napoleon III of the visionary agenda long advocated by the Left caused much heart-searching. Republicans realized that they did not want a new order created by Napoleon which would not bring about the 'universal republic' of their dreams, and they began to use a new pacific language. Where Armand Carrel had proclaimed in 1831 that the Left 'had no fear of a European war', and Michelet had identified the army with the nation, Hugo in 1869 declared that wars were caused only by despots and armies: 'Get rid of the army and you get rid of war'.[48]

Although the war of 1870 brought a strong left-wing nationalist revival, the devastating defeat by Germany brought about a much modified world-view. The fantasy of a mighty France, supported by the peoples of Europe, creating a new order faded before the reality of a weakened and vulnerable France facing the menace of Germany: on this, and on the recovery of Alsace-Lorraine, patriotic attention focused. A new radical nationalist movement emerged in the 1880s which had in common with the old 'parti national' of the 1840s the stress on unity and the rejection of pluralism, cosmopolitanism, materialism and individualism. But it no longer thought of liberating other nations as a way of putting France at the head of a new European order. Its nationalism was more than ever inward-looking, aiming to purge the nation of its enemies within, increasingly identified as Jews, international socialists and democrats. This amalgamation of the traditions of both the counter-revolutionary Right and the anti-liberal Left created a 'national socialism' (as Barrès termed it) that would fuel the extreme Right throughout the twentieth century. On the other hand, as will be seen in Chapter 11, the pursuit of a colonial empire received a new impetus from the defeat of 1870. 'We had to dispel the widely credited myth that France, after

47. Barker (1967), appendix.
48. Speech to Lausanne Peace Congress, 4 Sept. 1869. Hugo (1938), p. 290.

her disasters, had resigned herself to introspective and impotent withdrawal', explained Jules Ferry in 1882.[49] The vision of the French Republic as fulfilling a great world mission never lost its allure.

CONCLUSION: THE SEARCH FOR A 'MORAL ORDER'

Citizens, can you imagine the future? City streets flooded with light, green branches on the thresholds, nations brothers, men just . . . One might almost say: there will be no more events. All will be happy.[50]

My critics, protested President Thiers, the ancient mariner of French politics, in 1873, complain that France has not regained 'moral order'; but 'moral order' means 'division', so they should be glad that France was enjoying 'material order' – peaceful streets and economic prosperity – 'which was certainly something'.[51] It was not enough for his critics, however, who voted him out of office and established a royalist government that proclaimed its determination to restore true 'moral order' in France – a label that stuck. As we have seen, this insistence on the need for a moral order, that is, a social and political consensus based on shared values, was by no means confined to conservatives. Indeed, it is one of the most characteristic features of nineteenth-century French social and political thought.

Every ideology in nineteenth-century France was in this sense utopian: not only 'utopian socialism', but utopian conservatism, utopian liberalism, utopian republicanism, utopian nationalism. For all aimed at creating a future and final form of society. None was content with administering the present, or even improving it – cultivating that contemptible 'material order' that Thiers commended. This struggle was not between a 'party of movement' and a 'party of order', to use the terminology of the 1830s, taken up by some later historians. Ideological diversity was far more complex, which is why it never proved possible – as generations of nineteenth-century politicians from Louis XVIII, via Guizot, Thiers, Gambetta and Ferry to Clemenceau and Poincaré hoped – to create a two-party system, with French whigs and tories standing for progress and conservatism within a compromise political framework. Instead, what each party aimed at, at least in the 'fervour of heart and the power of dream', was the creation of a 'moral theology of politics'.[52] Ironically, attempts to create moral unity kept the flames of dissent burning. The rival utopianisms had fundamental common features. All held an 'image of harmony, balance and fusion: that of a society One, indivisible, homogenous, for ever protected from troubles and divisions . . . the

49. Andrew and Kanya-Forstner (1988), p. 16.
50. Hugo (1967), vol. 3, pp. 215, 218.
51. Message to Assembly, 24 May 1873.
52. Girardet (1986), p. 153.

reassuring certainty of total reconciliation'. Based on rival interpretations of history, they all aimed to bring politics, and even history itself, to an end: 'the world of the Golden Age is that of stopped clocks'.[53]

53. Ibid., pp. 153, 129.

CHAPTER 4

PARANOIA

We have now come down very low, very far into death . . . There is great darkness.

Michelet[1]

We cannot understand the obsessions of French political culture without taking account of the fantastic. Analysis in terms of interest and calculation, capital and labour, or profit and loss leaves much of the iceberg hidden. Major political battles were fought against partly imaginary antagonists, and were based on beliefs about the workings of society and politics that were at best travesties of reality. Nowhere can this be better seen than in the paranoid obsession with conspiracies, a lurid world of myth inhabited not only by cranks and simpletons, but by serious and influential thinkers and statesmen.

Conspiracy theories perpetuated 'the language of civil war' in politics. They portrayed not a society pluralistically divided by legitimate beliefs and interests, but a 'binary divide' between a united, patriotic and wholly legitimate 'us', and a diverse unholy alliance of traitors and criminals – 'them'.[2] The struggle was dramatized into a historic battle for the soul of France and the future of the world. For each side, the struggle finally was between 'one true France' and an 'anti-France'. The idea, dear to all, of the unique messianic mission of France (whether revolutionary or Catholic) meant that she had both friends and enemies everywhere, even within her own borders. Throughout the century there was an extraordinary similarity in the way various parties imagined 'the enemy': the fantasy of an ancient conspiracy for world dominance was a common feature; so was fascination with the hidden and the secret; so was the language and the imagery – cellars, tunnels, darkness, spiders' webs, tentacles, sadism, sexual perversity.

1. Girardet (1986), p. 41.
2. Parry (1993), pp. 223–4, 231.

THE GREAT REVOLUTIONARY CONSPIRACY:
FREEMASONS, PROTESTANTS, JEWS

In that French revolution, everything, even its most frightful crimes, everything was foreseen, thought out, planned, resolved, decided . . . by men who alone pulled the strings of deep-laid conspiracies.

Abbé Barruel[3]

The theory that the Revolution was the outcome of conspiracy was contemporary with the event itself. The most influential version was formulated by the Abbé Barruel in his *Mémoires pour servir à l'histoire du jacobinisme* (1797), which accused the freemasons of causing the Revolution in order to destroy monarchy throughout Europe and undermine the Catholic Church. Alexandre Dumas's novel *Joseph Balsamo* (1846) set the decisive meeting in an underground chamber in a ruined castle in Germany in May 1770. Versions of the original fantasy circulated throughout the nineteenth century, and no doubt still have some believers.

French freemasonry was, and to some extent remains, a federation of clubs for aspiring left-wing politicians, a place for networking rather than conspiracy, and a discreet refuge for political discussion when the atmosphere outside is unfavourable. As such it performed a useful and even influential function: by the beginning of the twentieth century, nearly all radical and most socialist leaders were members. For its enemies, however, it was a vast, ancient, occult and terrifying subversive organization, whose rank and file blindly obeyed the mysterious orders of the higher ranks, and whose inner circles were held together by blood-curdling initiation rites and oaths.

The defeat of France in the war of 1870, and the civil war of 1871 – when some Parisian freemasons had tried to mediate between the insurgents and the government – revived the old myth of the revolutionary conspiracy: the widely read *Les sociétés secrètes et la société*, published in 1874 by Nicholas Deschamps (interestingly, a Jesuit) saw freemasonry behind German unification, with Bismarck as 'leader and instrument'.[4] The association of freemasonry with republicanism, and especially with anticlerical radicalism during the Third Republic confirmed for conservatives its pernicious and conspiratorial nature. In the aftermath of the Dreyfus case, which brought so many conspiracy theories together, the 'affaire des fiches', in which freemasons were found to have supplied the Ministry of War with details of the religious beliefs of army officers so as to block the promotion of Catholics, seemed to confirm all the suspicions concerning masonic plots, now seen as linked with Jewish conspiracies. If anything, paranoia about masonic influence increased in the early twentieth century and during the First World War, when freemasons were believed to have infiltrated the

3. Girardet (1986), p. 33.
4. Roberts (1973), pp. 15–16.

government and the police, and favoured pacifism and subversion: hence the repression of freemasonry as well as the persecution of Jews after 1940 by the reactionary Vichy regime, which gave political paranoia free rein.

Protestantism was also identified with the Left, since the Revolution granted full civil and political equality in 1790, and because (especially in parts of the south of France) the political conflicts of the 1790s followed the lines of a much older Protestant-Catholic antagonism. From 1815 onwards, Protestants tended to support whichever political party opposed clericalism and legitimism. This was, needless to say, open and legal. But in the minds of Catholic conservatives, it was a further ramification of the great conspiracy: the continuing Revolution was a manifestation of Protestant hatred of Catholicism, a continuation of the Reformation. Protestant powers, they asserted, were behind the catastrophic events that threatened the independence of the papacy and the status of France. Palmerston, 'his disciple Gladstone' and their Teutonic counterpart Bismarck controlled the 'secret societies' and had brought about Italian unification and the victory of Prussia, followed by the anti-Catholic *kulturkampf* in Germany. 'The French Revolution is a branch of Protestantism, and from that branch there hangs today, ripe, that arch-Protestant fruit called Prussia', wrote the leading Catholic journalist, Louis Veuillot, in September 1870.[5]

Jews were relative latecomers to the Great Revolutionary Conspiracy. Most vocal antisemitic paranoia came from the Left during the first half of the century, with Jews being seen as the incarnation of cosmopolitan capitalism. During the 1860s, there were accusations that Jews, led by Disraeli in association with freemasons and Protestants, were helping to plot the rise of Bismarck's Prussia. But it was not until the sensational publication of Edouard Drumont's weird bestseller *La France Juive* in 1886 that antisemitism became a major theme of conservative paranoia. The 1880s and 1890s saw the creation and energetic propagation of anti-Jewish mythology in many parts of Europe, and its exploitation as a pillar of a new conservative populism. Organized Jewry was accused of plotting to take over the world, a vision most notoriously embodied in the Protocols of the Elders of Zion, forged by the tsarist police in association with French anti-Dreyfusards during the mid-1890s from an original idea in a trashy German novel, and given huge circulation. Alongside this fantasy went the infamous 'blood libel', the accusation that the blood of Christian children was used in secret Jewish rites, similar to the Satanism said to lie at the heart of freemasonry. This too circulated very widely in France, for example, in the Abbé Desportes's *Le Mystère du sang chez les Juifs de tous les temps*, published in 1889.

The Dreyfus affair (1894–99) gave a particularly French twist to antisemitic paranoia. That Captain Alfred Dreyfus had sold secrets to Germany was proved, for many who believed the accusation, by the fact of his 'race': if Jews were eternal aliens, and enemies of Christian civilization, then patriotism and loyalty were naturally beyond them. Moreover, powerful Jews were

5. Ibid., p. 9.

accused of forming a 'syndicate' to protect themselves from the discredit of Dreyfus's crime by bribing politicians, witnesses, officers, journalists and judges to proclaim him innocent. Even when the guilty man, Esterhazy, confessed, it only proved that he too had been got at. By this logic, every demonstration of Dreyfus's innocence was really further proof of his guilt and of the sinister machinations of the syndicate. And even if Dreyfus did turn out to be innocent of spying, he and his supporters were in a deeper sense guilty of 'the worst of crimes', said the nationalist writer Maurice Barrès: 'having served for five years to undermine the Army and the Nation'. For those who thought like Barrès, the Dreyfus case was only one episode in a long secret war: when the nationalist thinker Charles Maurras was found guilty in 1945 of collaborating with the Nazis, he cried: 'It is Dreyfus's revenge!'.

International socialism was a modern addition to the Great Conspiracy. The International Workingmen's Society (l'Internationale), a weak and relatively moderate confederation of labour and socialist parties set up in London in 1864, was quickly fitted into existing conspiracy theory. In several widely read books, notably Oscar Testut's *L'Internationale* (1871) it was declared to be behind the 1871 Paris Commune. Its secretary Karl Marx, cast as the Commune's chief manipulator, was said to be Bismarck's henchman; some suspected Gladstone of being involved somewhere too. In any case, it was another attempt by the foreign revolutionary conspiracy to destroy France. It had burned Paris; it had destroyed churches and killed priests – proof enough that it was pursuing the old Satanic design. Though many expressed scepticism (including government ministers), the official parliamentary enquiry into the Commune stressed the role of the Internationale, and a law was passed in 1872 outlawing it. The fear of an international revolutionary working-class conspiracy – reflected, for example, in Zola's *Germinal* (1885), when the Russian Souvarine destroys both coalmine and miners and then goes 'quietly on his way to exterminate, wherever there was dynamite to blow up cities and men' – fed the panic concerning anarchism and anarcho-syndicalism in the 1890s, a 'collective psychosis' leading to exceptional repressive measures.[6]

It all made sense. Everything was connected. 'The Revolution is universal' and so incorporated a wide variety of conspirators from Voltaire to Lenin: Palmerston, Gladstone, Disraeli, Marx and Bismarck controlled a vast anti-French and anti-Catholic Protestant-Masonic-Jewish conspiracy. 'Free-masonry, solidarism, the International, biblical, trade union and protestant societies, rationalists and radicals of every hue . . . sons of the same father, Satan, they are brothers by their doctrine.'[7] More sophisticated in its expression and less exuberant in the degree of its paranoia was Charles Maurras's concept of 'anti-France'; but the identity and aim of the enemy was the same: Jews, Protestants, freemasons were all bearers of the bacilli of individualism, revolution and democracy, which threatened to destroy France and Catholicism, the pillars of western civilization.

6. Machelon (1976), p. 401.
7. Roberts (1973), p. 41.

THE GREAT REACTIONARY CONSPIRACY: THE JESUITS

Men in black, whence come you?
We come from underground
Half fox, half wolf,
Our rule is a mystery profound
                              Béranger, 1819[8]

The idea of a counter-revolutionary plot inspired by secret Catholic organizations was elaborated in the 1820s: 'the Congregation', a mythical all-powerful clerical secret society, was a fantasy inspired very loosely by a real existing Congregation and by a genuine semi-secret society set up to oppose Napoleon, the Chevaliers de la Foi. Many opponents of the Bourbons believed, like Stendhal's anti-hero Julien Sorel, that 'the Congregation' secretly pulled the strings of power and patronage. And behind the Congregation – indeed, in real control of the papacy and the Church itself – were the Jesuits. Demands during the 1820s to expel the Jesuits from France provided one of the most excited debates of the Restoration, being supported by prominent liberals, leading opposition newspapers and by some traditionalist Gallicans, most famously the extravagantly reactionary Comte de Montlosier, opposed to Roman control over the French Church. The fears inspired by the Society of Jesus (of whom there were well under 500 in France) went far beyond the reality of Jesuit activity or even ecclesiastical influence as a whole: the Jesuits were accused of having conspired since the sixteenth century to seize absolute power for their order, not only in France but throughout the world.

Over the centuries, it was asserted, they had built up a vast, ruthless and wealthy organization with thousands of secret members ('short-robed Jesuits') who included, it was said, Charles X and his unpopular minister Polignac. In response to these attacks the Jesuits were expelled in 1828, which did not prevent anticlerical attacks during the 1830 revolution.

A second wave of paranoia emerged in the 1840s, sparked off by a political quarrel over Church schools. The minister of education Villemain saw Jesuit agents everywhere and went mad under the strain. Excitement was orchestrated by two leading left-wing historians, Jules Michelet and Edgar Quinet, and one of the most popular novelists, Eugène Sue: the Jesuits were seizing power everywhere through their manipulation of the confessional, money, patronage, education and women. The Jesuits wielded 'the greatest concentration of power' in the world; their superior-general was 'the man best informed on everything important that happens in the world', and their Rome headquarters contained 'the most gigantic biographical compilation . . . since the world began'.[9] For Michelet, the Jesuits represented spiritual and

8. Béranger (1857), vol. 1, p. 516.
9. Cubitt (1993), pp. 211–12.

political death, the antithesis of the free Christianity of which he dreamed, and they interfered with the just rights of republican patriarchs over their women and property: 'The confessor's thoughts reach into the bedroom . . . slide into the bed between husband and wife and there watch and supervise the most secret privileges of wedlock'.[10] These fears were disclosed by the two historians – braving the poison and daggers of Jesuit agents – in immensely popular and melodramatic lectures at the Collège de France in 1843. Even more popular was Sue's novel *Le Juif Errant*, serialized in *Le Constitutionnel* in 1844, whose circulation rose from 3,600 to 20,000. Sue told of the attempts by the Jesuit agent Rodin to seize the fortune of the Rennepont family. This extravagant fantasy was taken as investigative journalism, and Sue's early death in 1857 was ascribed by many to a Jesuit 'electric galvano-chemical current': the penalty for exposing their dreadful secrets to the world.

The Jesuits were again expelled in 1845. But when in the late 1850s the threat to papal independence stirred up Church–State quarrels once again, anti-Jesuitism returned to prominence. In 1861, the Monita Secreta (the Jesuit equivalent of the Protocols of the Elders of Zion) was published in French. Napoleon III's liberal education minister, the relatively anticlerical Victor Duruy, warned him that the Jesuits were 'the worst enemies of your son; they are preparing a battle'.[11] In 1871, the Paris Communards, living out the myth, searched monasteries and convents for arms caches and secret tunnels, accused priests of sexual crimes, vandalized churches, and eventually shot a score of Jesuits and other clergy. Moderate republicans, in power in the 1880s, carried on the campaign by legal means. Gambetta's close associates, Paul Bert and Eugène Spuller, wrote anti-Jesuit tracts. Jules Ferry again expelled the Jesuits (they kept coming back) from France in 1880. But this was not the end of the story. Radicals demanded more stringent measures to root out Jesuitism, even if few went quite as far as the veteran revolutionary François-Vincent Raspail and his son Benjamin, who, boldly scorning plausibility, ascribed the Paris Commune, the International, the September Massacres and the battle of Waterloo to Jesuit plotting. The Dreyfus affair provided grounds for a more plausible accusation: the Jesuits, through their influence over Catholic army officers, were running the anti-Dreyfus plot in order to destroy the Republic.

Anti-Jesuitism, in short, was the quintessence and core of anticlericalism. It was possible in theory to be dispassionately anticlerical on purely political grounds: that the clergy had too much independent influence and money, for example (though this was far from self-evidently true). In general, however, anticlericalism fed on the paranoia of anti-Jesuitism: leading anticlericals believed the lurid myths of priestly wickedness, or at least found it expedient to go along with them. It was the Jesuits, they maintained, who were really in control of the papacy, the other clergy, and so of the whole Catholic Church, with which, in consequence, there could be no compromise.

10. Rémond (1985), p. 69.
11. Cubitt (1993), p. 145.

CONCLUSION: THE USEFULNESS OF CREDULITY

I believe so that I can understand.

St Anselm

Conspiracy theories, so strikingly symmetrical on Left and Right, were not merely the foible of a Romantic age attracted by the occult, a creation of Stendhal, Dumas or Sue. They were a symptom of a period of change and uncertainty, in which the real causes of events remained opaque and the future mysterious and threatening. It is hard to decide which side outdid the other in credulity. The similar fantasies that the rival myths contained – concerning power, secrecy, organization, the control of knowledge, money, sex, patronage, manipulation of opinion – had common sources in shared worries about characteristic features of contemporary society, reaching a peak at times of political, social and ideological crisis: the 1820s, 1840s, 1880s–1900s, 1930s.

As Girardet suggests,[12] these myths were the 'negative projection of tacit aspirations'. The utopian ambitions of one party were seen by the others as sinister conspiracies; the order and unity that all wanted were a nightmare if imposed by its enemies; and each party fearfully ascribed to the enemy the power it dreamed of possessing itself. These fears affected behaviour, not only by maintaining excitement, encouraging extremism and justifying illiberal measures to repress imaginary conspiracies, but also by actually helping to create conspiratorial behaviour intended to counteract the supposed conspiracies of the other side. During the Third Republic freemasons spied on army officers whom they suspected of conspiring under Jesuit direction to subvert the Republic: reality imitating fantasy.

Conspiracy theories had several functions. They explained the incomprehensible through a 'logic of manipulation':[13] mysterious things happened because someone made them happen. A scapegoat was thereby found for the unexpected and the undesirable, an excuse, in Cubitt's words, for the non-arrival of utopia. This was both frightening – and so could mobilize support to combat the threat – and reassuring, for it showed that peace and harmony were normal and attainable once the conspirators were defeated. Thus, conspiracy theories both expressed anxieties and reduced them to order. Finally, they created and perpetuated a dualist vision of politics, making it possible to identify political friends and enemies amid a 'blizzard of historical change'[14] that otherwise tended to obscure and weaken that simplistic division into Left and Right, pro-revolution and counter-revolution, that gave spurious meaning and coherence to modern French history.

12. Girardet (1986), p. 61.
13. Ibid., p. 31.
14. Cubitt (1993), p. 308.

PART II

POWER

CHAPTER 5

POWER AND THE PEOPLE, 1814–1914

While you owe justice to everyone . . . you keep your favours those who have unmistakably proved their fidelity.

Emile Combes[1]

The unique characteristic of the organization of power in nineteenth-century France was the coexistence of an active centralized administration with powerful elected assemblies. The latter, reduced to impotence under Napoleon, were re-established by Louis XVIII in the 1814 constitutional Charter as a condition of his restoration. Based on the English model, the Chamber of Deputies and Chamber of Peers (Senate after 1851) were intended to protect civil society against central authority. Many contemporaries believed, however, that a genuine parliamentary system could not function in the shadow of the over-mighty bureaucracy, which had the means to influence voters and deputies. At certain times – during the 1840s, when parliament was colonized by state officials who made up 45 per cent of deputies, and in the 1850s, when it was made subordinate to executive authority – this seemed to be proved. But from the 1880s until the 1960s, the republican parliament successfully asserted its power over ministers, and even over much of the bureaucracy.

Looking at the whole period, there was an inextricable entanglement of bureaucracy and politics, as the powers of the administration became weapons in factional conflicts, and jobs in the administration the prizes of political victory. So ubiquitous and ambitious was the post-revolutionary State that it tended to politicize the whole of society, as shown by the outstandingly high electoral turnout of peasant voters once manhood suffrage was established in 1848: more of the total French population voted (over 30 per cent) than in any other country up to 1890.[2] Stanley Hoffmann has suggested that 'the story of the successive balances and imbalances between [State and society] is far more interesting than the story of the often accidental succession of regimes and revolutions'.[3]

1. Larkin (1974), p. 139.
2. Flora *et al.* (1983), vol. 1, p. 92.
3. Hoffmann (1974), p. 443.

THE BUREAUCRACY

France . . . is a bureaucracy tempered by revolutions.

Report to parliament, 1900[4]

The most popular constitution that could be devised for France would have as its first and only article that all Frenchmen are civil servants and are paid by the State.

Germaine de Staël[5]

The creation of a centralized system under Napoleon between 1800 and 1811 was a logical response to the decentralization, disorder and conflict of revolution and to the need to mobilize resources for war. It was also a conscious reaction against the limitations of the Old Regime system: haphazardly overlapping authorities, local privileges, tenured officials and interference by an independent judiciary. The new system was marked by centralization of authority in the ministries in Paris, which transmitted their instructions 'swift as an electric current' (as Napoleon's interior minister Chaptal optimistically put it) to the prefects, who governed 83 uniform departments with neutral geographical names ('High Pyrenees', 'Lower Seine' etc.) which in 1789 had replaced the historic provinces such as Burgundy and Normandy. All officials were under the absolute control of their superiors, who could appoint, move, promote and dismiss at will. Their actions were free from the constraints of the civil law and the interference of the civil courts, being subject only to a supreme administrative court, the Conseil d'Etat, composed of government appointees.

The pivot of the system was the prefect, who accumulated administrative and political functions like a colonial governor, or, as Napoleon himself put it, like 'a low-level emperor'. He alone was responsible for law and order, political loyalty, and civil administration in his department. Below him came the sub-prefect (in each *arrondissement*) and the mayor (in each of the 36,000 *communes*), appointed by the prefect until 1882. The range of activities controlled by these officials was enormous, including things which in many other countries, if they were done at all, were done by local squires, parsons and their wives in their official or private capacities. For example, they appointed to many public jobs, including schoolteachers (after 1850), village constables (*gardes champêtres*), roadmenders and postmen. They assessed taxes, and controlled the budgets for church repairs, schools, roads and bridges. They made by-laws, awarded contracts and licences, decided the use and disposal of the vast common lands, immensely important to the rural population both rich and poor, and the distribution of water, vital in the arid south. They set food prices at times of shortage, provided poor relief, obtained compensation for fire, drought or flood, provided scholarships and

4. Larkin (1995), p. 80.
5. Johnson (1963), p. 266.

got boys out of the army. They could choose to turn a blind eye to popular disturbances and petty delinquency such as forest offences or poaching. The importance of these questions is shown by the many bitter disputes in rural areas to decide the composition and boundaries of *communes*, including demands by villages to secede and form their own.

Prefects and mayors had potentially enormous authority and influence in their little empires: a world where 'everyone knows the mayor and the vice-mayor, while the leader of the "fanfare" is a celebrity and the captain of the "pompiers" a hero',[6] and which, little changed by the 1930s, was immortalized in Gabriel Chevallier's comic masterpiece *Clochemerle*. About one-quarter of all *communes* had fewer than 80 electors.[7] Inevitably, in the unstable and cut-throat post-revolutionary world, marked by political antagonism, social instability and economic change, local political factions and clans needed to control the use of that authority, and ideally appropriate it by manning the *prefectures* and *mairies* themselves. Those who were important in this society were those 'closest to the power of the State'; to be or become a *notable* meant the 'seizure of the State and private use of its sovereign power'.[8] This became the very substance of local politics, as much under the limited suffrage of the constitutional monarchies as under the manhood suffrage of the Republics and the Second Empire: everyone, from aristocratic landowner to landless labourer, had much to gain or lose. What the distant 'national' politics in Paris meant at the grass-roots level was a benevolent or malevolent presence in the *prefecture* or *mairie*, and the consequent prospect of jobs, favours, profits, honours, protection – or their loss.

In practice, the Napoleonic ideal of 'the electric current' passing from centre to periphery was often perverted: the administration, rather than controlling, was controlled; rather than asserting the sovereign will in the provinces, it was made to protect local interests against the centre. There were several reasons for this. There was always and inevitably a gap between what Rosenvallon calls 'theoretical rationalization' (the belief that sending out an instruction was the solution of a problem) and actual results. The central bureaucracy in Paris was always quite small: 2–3,000 people in about ten ministries, each divided into something like ten sections of only 20–30 people to cover the whole country. When late in the period a few new ministries were added (such as the Ministry of Labour in 1906) the effect was often to duplicate the functions of existing departments. Agricultural matters, for example, were covered by the Ministries of Agriculture, Commerce, Interior and Public Works. The different departments were fiercely jealous of their empires, and happily pursued conflicting policies. That characteristic French institution, the *cabinet ministeriel* (minister's private office) also began to grow at the end of the century, adding what has been called 'an irregular amateur bureaucracy'.[9]

6. Bodley, *France* (1898), vol. 2, p. 40.
7. Ibid., vol. 2, p. 90.
8. Charle (1991), p. 43.
9. Burdeau (1994), p. 153.

Inevitably, they were forced to rely greatly on their officials on the spot: 'we know nothing of what is going on', lamented one minister.[10] Local officials were frequently, and increasingly as the century progressed, overwhelmed with instructions, circulars, decrees and questionnaires: in 1907, new social legislation inspired 266 ministerial instructions to prefects. The staff of the *prefectures* was also small: in the 1890s, a department of 500,000 inhabitants might be supposedly administered by 100 people. Moreover, from the beginning, the prefects' powers were deliberately curtailed: law courts, tax collection and the army were kept outside their control. Finally, nineteenth-century governments, wary of their independence, usually moved prefects frequently to limit their personal influence, hence neatly negating the whole purpose of the office. As for mayors, in theory the grass-roots arm of the State, they became increasingly close to their *administrés*. In 1882, all *communes* (except Paris) were finally allowed, after repeated demands, to elect their mayors, and they elected people like themselves who would look after their interests: already in 1866, 37 per cent were farmers, and in 1913 46 per cent, and 78 per cent in the smallest *communes*. In short, rather than being agents of the State, mayors had become agents of their communities.

Civil servants early became (and remain[11]) a byword for apathy and incompetence. The satirist Henri Monnier described a civil servant's day in the 1820s: '9 a.m., arrival of staff, changing of clothes, gathering round the stove; 10 a.m., reading of newspapers, breakfast, sharpening of pens; 10.30, opening of drawers, private conversation', and so on.[12] This was partly because throughout our period appointment and promotion was essentially by favouritism, not performance, and partly because low pay was offset by an amiable tolerance of the kind of eccentricity and indolence satirized in Courteline's *Messieurs les Ronds-de-cuir* in 1893. No government, and no regime, was willing to rationalize and professionalize the bureaucracy, which despite its Napoleonic reputation and the thorough training of its technical branches (bridges and highways, and mines) was far less well organized by the mid-nineteenth century than that of Germany or Britain, because the only way to keep it under ministerial control seemed to be to continue with arbitrary appointment, favouritism and occasional wholesale purges of the politically unreliable: 'liberty of opposition does not exist for the servants of the State', as Freycinet stated in 1886.[13] The growing size of the civil service and the growing technical needs of the expanding departments (education, communications, social services, colonies) caused a piecemeal introduction of competitive examinations and educational qualifications in some departments. The education needed for entry became expensive and specialized. Interestingly, governments repeatedly backed away from establishing a State-

10. Ibid., p. 102.
11. Late-twentieth-century *fonctionnaires* in major Paris ministries are not unknown to spend a good deal of their time at the office doing their laundry and cooking.
12. Thuillier and Tulard (1984), p. 40.
13. Machelon (1976), p. 332.

run training school, fearing to create a professional *mandarinat*; this meant that a private establishment, the Ecole Libre des Sciences Politiques (founded 1872) was able to establish a dominating position. It efficiently prepared a small wealthy, mainly Parisian elite for an increasing proportion of posts. For example, by 1914 some 45 per cent of the staff of the key departments in the Foreign Ministry were graduates of the school. Prior self-selection reduced the number of candidates for nationwide entrance examinations – only about 30 entered annually for the prestigious Inspection des Finances at the turn of the century – and contacts and social suitability continued to count.

The second half of the nineteenth century saw major changes: expansion, mainly in teaching and the post office, which led to an increase in civil service numbers from 135,000 in 1845 to 500,000 in 1900; and the late-nineteenth-century recruitment of women, described as 'a bit slow, but punctual, docile and meticulous'[14] and of course cheap. Expansion and the refusal of governments to pass a *statut des fonctionnaires*, a legal framework to guarantee uniform rights and conditions demanded since 1848, led to serious conflict between government and civil service employees in the 1900s. Anarcho-syndicalist bureaucrats (an intriguing hybrid) dreamed of replacing parliamentary government with delegates of civil service trade unions. A *statut* was only achieved in 1946.

Because of these practical limitations, the central administration generally had to compromise with local *notables*, rather than trying to bypass them. Before 1851, this meant appointing local men of wealth and influence as prefects, sub-prefects and mayors. If they supported the government, the local powers of the State were handed to them in return. During the Second Empire, in contrast, prefects often fought to weaken the influence of legitimist or Orleanist *notables*, and win over local electors to Bonapartism. In several regions Bonapartists won a political clientele for themselves that outlasted the regime they served: Janvier de la Motte spent the fortunes of two wives and ran his Normandy *prefecture* into deficit doing favours for voters. Another Bonapartist dynasty were the Cassagnacs in the Gers department, Gascon-speaking populists who obtained grants, buildings and railways, and even invited Napoleon III and Eugénie to stay. They long outlasted their imperial patrons. As a despairing prefect reported in 1878, 'Over twenty years they have been filling [Lower Armagnac] with their creatures, tax inspectors, justices of the peace, engineers, teachers, postmen, road menders, constables. All are Bonapartist.' More than half a century after the fall of the Bonapartes, Paul Julien de Cassagnac was still being elected deputy and *conseiller-général*.[15] After 1870, as parliament and elected local councils increased their powers, prefects became in practice the subordinates of local politicians, whose re-election they were expected to assist and on whose favours their careers now depended. This series of compromises was how the bureaucracy and parliament managed to coexist.

14. Thuillier and Tulard (1984), p. 73.
15. Soubadère, in Feral (1990), p. 629; see also Zeldin (1973), vol. 1, p. 544.

This symbiotic relationship between local *notables*, politicians, governments and bureaucrats is a characteristic of French political society: it has become a general practice for national politicians to build up an independent power base by accumulating local offices (for example as a member of a departmental *conseil général* and/or a mayor). A recurring political theme has been 'decentralization', which means in fact giving administrative power to local elites. Demanded by opposition politicians (especially paternalistic legitimists) to help them resist central government – it was an important uniting element of the opposition to the Empire in the 1860s, when central authority was particularly heavy-handed – it was resisted repeatedly by governments until the 1980s when the socialists, in the euphoria of victory, introduced a major decentralization law. This has had, to put it mildly, predictably mixed results.

ASSEMBLIES

The rules of party warfare . . . I take to be that I may call my opponent a villain though I know him to be honest, that I may abuse his measures though I know them to be useful, that I may deny his facts though I know them to be true, that I may attack his arguments with sophistry and even with falsehood. All this he will do to me, and therefore it is fair that I should do it to him.

Adolphe Thiers, 1854[16]

From 1789, when the archaic Estates General transformed themselves into the National Assembly, elected bodies remained a permanent part of political life, though their role, composition and significance varied greatly. For royalists of 1789, and for their nineteenth-century legitimist successors, assemblies were called into existence by the monarch to give the nation's consent to laws and taxes, but were subordinate to the sovereign, who truly embodied the State. With their organic conception of society, and their nostalgia for the Old Regime, they favoured assemblies that would represent tradition, hierarchy and regional diversity: a Chamber of Peers to represent the great historic families, the great prelates, and the great officers of the Crown; a Chamber of Deputies dominated by lesser *notables*; and they hankered throughout the century for local assemblies representing the provinces. All this, they hoped, would maintain the power of the old elites. It did not work out in practice. The Revolution and the Empire had created a new elite that feared a return to the Old Regime, and so, however restricted the franchise, opposition to the Bourbon monarchy emerged. (The 1817 law gave the vote to men who paid 300 francs per year in direct taxes, 110,000 in all, mainly landowners, who were reduced to 89,000 by giving tax rebates – a rare example of a government deliberately cutting its opponents' taxes.) Even the Chamber of Peers, which contained liberals ennobled by Napoleon and Louis XVIII shortly after his restoration, was troublesome by the 1820s. A law of 1825

16. Senior (1878), vol. 1, p. 213.

gave large taxpayers, mostly landowners, a second vote, intended to counter-balance smaller landowners and urban *notables*, who were feared, in many cases correctly, to have liberal sympathies. This too failed to prevent an ultimately fatal conflict between king and parliament in 1830, when the liberal majority claimed the right to reject a government appointed by the king.

Liberals viewed an elected assembly as the principal emanation of national sovereignty, but believed that it should be checked and balanced by a second chamber, whether hereditary as in Britain or appointed from among the great and the good, and also by a separate executive, ideally a constitutional monarch. The franchise should be exercised on behalf of the whole nation by those who had the 'capacity' to vote wisely, which they believed in practice meant those rich enough to be educated and conservative. After the 1830 revolution, the revised constitutional Charter only cut the property qualification for voting to 200 francs (with a reduced rate for military officers and the intellectual establishment), which raised the electorate to 166,000: about 33 voters per 10,000 inhabitants. By the late 1840s, as the number of wealthy men increased with economic growth, this had reached 248,000, compared with over 600,000 in England with a much smaller population. Louis-Philippe and his chief minister Guizot refused electoral reform during the 1840s, whether by reducing the tax qualification or by recognizing other sorts of 'capacity', such as university degrees or rank in the National Guard. This refusal left unenfranchised a considerable middle and lower-middle class, literate, politicized and dangerously disaffected; and this helped bring about revolution in 1848.

For republicans the elected 'Representatives of the People' expressed the sovereign will of the nation. This was a much more idealistic and absolute view than the pragmatic liberal approach. Republican purists believed in government by a single-chamber parliament which would combine legislative, executive and where necessary judicial powers. By the 1840s, they advocated 'universal' (male) suffrage, and the February 1848 revolution introduced it, increasing the electorate at a stroke to 9,900,000; no party supported votes for women until the early twentieth century. The results of 'universal' suffrage were bitterly disappointing to the Left, for the new electorate were mostly peasants whose ideas and interests were not necessarily those of urban republicans, and who were open to the influence of conservative *notables* and the clergy. The first truly self-assertive act of the mass electorate was to elect Louis-Napoleon Bonaparte president of the Republic in December 1848. Though republicans were disappointed, they did not abandon their faith in democracy; rather it was conservatives who, following a rise in socialist support in several parts of the country in 1849, passed the law of 31 May 1850 which reduced the electorate by eliminating all those with judicial records and requiring a long residence qualification. This disfranchised nearly 3,000,000 people, including more than half the voters of Paris, and showed the instinctive fear and impotence of liberal and conservative *notables* in the face of a mass electorate.

Quite different was the attitude of Bonapartists, especially of Louis-Napoleon Bonaparte, later Napoleon III. He was intuitively confident of the support of the masses, but suspicious of party intrigues. He considered himself, not parliament, the embodiment of the will of the people. Assemblies were there to endorse the decisions of the charismatic leader; otherwise they were hotbeds of self-interested factionalism. After his 1851 coup d'état Bonaparte reduced the elected chamber (demoted in title from Assemblée Nationale to Corps Législatif) to a subordinate and silent role. It was balanced by a tame appointed Senate, its debates could not be published, it had no power over governments, and ministers could not sit as deputies. The executive power, with the administrative bureaucracy as its instrument, was once more to rule freely as in the days of the First Empire.

However, in the 1860s, when Napoleon's regime was weakened by political and diplomatic setbacks, parliament progressively regained its function as the arena for public criticism, as the government restored its pre-1851 prerogatives, including the publication of debates and the right to question ministers. As opponents began to win more seats, parliamentary politics proved the most effective weapon against 'caesarism': the populist manipulation of the mass electorate. Legitimist nobles, Catholic clergy, Orleanist notables and republican politicians joined the opposition, and they were more than the State could take on. Many republicans were now converted, for the first time, from the rhetoric of revolution to electoral and parliamentary politics. Many liberals, realizing that they too could win elections, were reconciled to universal suffrage. By thus unwittingly converting his opponents, Napoleon III became something he had never intended: the godfather of a parliamentary democracy. In 1869, he agreed to appoint a government 'faithfully representing the majority of the Corps Législatif' and led by a former republican deputy, Emile Ollivier.

After the fall of the Empire, the Third Republic built on this foundation, but developed – again in a way that was unintended by the makers of its 1875 constitution – into a new phenomenon: government by parliament, with deputies taking over many of the attributes of the executive. Parliamentary committees (commissions), made permanent rather than ad hoc in 1902, exercised quasi-ministerial powers of formulating policy, introducing legislation and drawing up budgets. The Chamber, free of the threat of dissolution after the defeat of President MacMahon in 1877 (see p. 441), brought down governments frequently. Even the Senate unilaterally asserted its power at the end of the nineteenth century, the first time since the 1820s that a second chamber had played a significant role. This was a double irony: first, because republicans theoretically disapproved of upper chambers; second, because the Senate had been designed in 1875 to be a stronghold of conservative notables, being indirectly elected principally by local politicians from rural areas and small towns. But it quickly became the voice and stronghold of socially conservative provincial republican orthodoxy, 'a retreat for elderly men of education . . . whose favourite pastime is . . . to recite to one another essays on abstract, legal or historical questions, with an occasional reference to topics of the hour'.[17] As such it proved a solid barrier against any attempt to alter the republican status quo, such as by income tax or the horrors of women's suffrage.

Assemblies provided an arena for great ideological battles, when deputies could bring down a government by a timely question (*interpellation*). They were also a marketplace for the broking of power and patronage: this was the gilded age both of parliamentary oratory and of parliamentary corruption. But what no assembly under any regime did was to provide a means for *alternance*, the peaceful alternation of parties in power, for which generations of French parliamentarians regarded Westminster as a model. This inability to integrate opposition, it has been argued, was the key problem of post-revolutionary politics.[18] The goal of French governments was to exclude their opponents permanently from power, because those opponents ultimately sought to overthrow the existing regime. So the power of the bureaucracy was routinely used to try to stifle the rise of opposition, or the Crown could try to ignore the parliamentary majority, or, as under the Third Republic, all the republican parties could periodically suspend their own quarrels to keep out 'the Right'. So, although governments changed frequently, they changed only within certain pre-defined limits. Under every regime, there existed a 'disloyal opposition' which was excluded, and expected to be excluded, from any share in power and patronage, such as legitimists after 1830 or republicans before 1870. Their function was to express root and branch rejection of the regime (including on behalf of those whose repugnance was so great as to refuse to take any part in its political life at all) and also to constitute a government-in-waiting ready to take power in case of revolution, as happened in 1830, 1848 and 1870.

Yet it was one of the saving graces of nineteenth-century France that amid the most serious crises an elected assembly was seen as the natural solution, and rapid elections the only way to re-establish legitimate authority. This, no doubt, was partly due to the prestige of liberal ideas, and partly to the realization by every party that they could not command general obedience or consent. The electorate proved time and time again a moderating force in its determination to avoid a descent into civil war.

ELECTIONS

Homme élu, homme foutu.
              Popular saying

Parliament, therefore, was both arena and marketplace at national level; elections had a similar function at local level. It was at the local level that politics first came to rural France: first dramatically, during the Revolution,

17. Bodley (1898), vol. 2, pp. 57–8.
18. Lagoueyte (1989), p. 13.

with disputes over land and the Church; and then again more calmly and permanently after 1831, when local councils were made elective, with a comparatively large electorate of over 10 per cent of ratepayers. The tensions between landowner and labourer, priest and layman, nobleman and bourgeois; the rivalry of one district with another, or of a clan with its neighbours; the hatreds inherited from the Revolution or earlier all found an arena in the municipal elections of each of the 36,000 *communes*. On a larger scale, similar rivalries were acted out in the *conseil général* of each department, and of course in elections to parliament.

Attempts to control elections were made by governments throughout the period. Although the intensity with which they were used fluctuated, the methods did not greatly alter, in spite of the expansion of the electorate. Because the administrative system placed such wide powers in the hands of the State and its local agents, many kinds of gerrymandering, intimidation and bribery were undertaken. Constituency boundaries were carefully drawn and redrawn. Polling stations were shifted. Electoral registers were tampered with – a speciality of the Restoration. If necessary the counting of votes could be falsified or (especially under the Third Republic) elections could be annulled. The mayor and his minions kept a close eye on how their neighbours voted, and not until 1914 was the ballot truly secret. As was seen above, there were many carrots and sticks at their disposal. Jobs could be offered, ranging from procurator-general to village policemen, from peer of the realm to postman. Decorations likewise. Concessions ranged from railway contracts to tobacconists' licences. Railway lines could be re-routed. Subsidies could be offered to impecunious local authorities for schools, churches, roads and bridges. The local fire brigade might receive new helmets. Scholarships were available to the children of useful allies, as was rapid compensation for natural disasters. Everything was possible if people voted the right way. The mayor of a village in Lozère sent a list of 'well known republicans' to the prefect in 1889, so that

> this list will be used in distributing compensation to flood victims . . . this will be the best way I know of opening the eyes of the others, especially as before the elections I told them often enough that there would be no compensation if the commune did not produce a republican majority.[19]

Opponents could suffer more than simply absence of favour. Throughout our period, State employees risked demotion or dismissal if their loyalty was insufficiently demonstrated in times of crisis. Publicans could lose their licences if they allowed their premises to be used for opposition meetings. Police powers could be used to seize or ban newspapers, forbid meetings and demonstrations, harass and arrest activists, and tear down opposition posters. Especially under the Republic, bishops and priests faced legal action, reprimands or suspension of stipends if they supported anti-government

19. Jones (1985), p. 301.

candidates. One Second Empire prefect is said to have permitted brothels to be opened in an aristocratic quarter of Marseilles in order to punish the Catholic legitimist residents. Files were kept on voters' political sympathies. Secret police funds paid spies to infiltrate opposition organizations and even *agents provocateurs* to start violence at meetings; they also subsidized pro-government newspapers and bought off or even bought up those of the opposition.

In the period of the Restoration and July Monarchy, when 75 per cent of constituencies had under 600 electors and many deputies were elected by fewer than 200 voters, electioneering was on a personal scale. Invitations to dinner at the *prefecture*, cosy chats, promises of decorations and jobs could win sufficient support to secure a seat for a government supporter or persuade a sitting deputy to vote with the government. Prefects and deputies were partners in the broking of power between the localities and central government, and the prefect was often the senior partner, in practice choosing the candidate and then keeping him his seat. Universal suffrage meant operating on a wider scale: although some prefects did manage to maintain wide personal contacts within their departments, political rather than personal methods became more important: running newspapers, setting up public works projects, financing electoral campaigns. But elections remained principally about personal relations and group solidarities: opinion in traditional communities was consensual, not a privately developed view of things.

Louis-Napoleon Bonaparte discovered that a mass electorate could be made to support strong government, and he immediately restored manhood suffrage after his 1851 coup. He used all the resources of the State machinery – intimidation, propaganda, jobs, subsidies, favours, protection – to maintain overwhelming support among the peasant electorate. A mere majority was not enough: Bonapartism required overwhelming acclamation. He called plebiscites in 1851, 1852 and 1870 to demonstrate his legitimacy, and the prefects chose 'official candidates' whom they openly supported in elections. One liberal termed this 'directed universal suffrage'. Unlike in 1848 and 1849, voting was not about bringing in the millenium, it was about making a bargain, something that peasants understood: getting a good price for votes, as for cattle. Until mid-century, the State was principally something that *took*, especially taxes and conscripts; increasingly thereafter it also *gave* roads, schools, jobs. Peasant voters in many parts of the country were looking to the emperor's government and his mayors and prefects as the main source of local power and protection: they, not local landowners, were now the people who counted most. In short, Napoleon, in trying to free himself from the grip of the *notables*, was freeing the electorate from that same grip.

For the first ten years or so of the Second Empire, the prefects had an easy task, and the huge electoral majorities of those years left many politicians with an exaggerated idea of what prefectoral pressures could achieve. In fact, such methods only succeeded when the voters were well disposed; they were also facilitated by the early practice of voting unanimously: relatives, neighbours or workmates went ceremoniously to the polls in a body to publicly

express corporate solidarity. In tranquil times, under all regimes, a considerable part of the electorate saw sense in good relations with the government,
and could be persuaded to support pro-government candidates, especially if
tangible favours resulted. It was equally in the interest of prefects to ensure
victory by backing a candidate who already had influence and popularity in
the district. As a prefect wrote to one of 'his' deputies in 1834, 'we cannot get
any Tom, Dick or Harry elected. Our skill consists solely in working out precisely
who among the men on our side enjoys most favour among the mass of
electors.'[20] The deputy was seen as his constituents' envoy to Paris, all the
more effective if he was *persona grata* in the corridors of power. Moreover,
much of the electorate feared upheaval and preferred those in power to possibly
dangerous alternatives. The successes of Villèle in the early 1820s and Guizot in
the 1840s were results of this, as much as of their use of patronage. The
defeat of General Boulanger and his supporters in 1889 and of the anti-
Dreyfusards in 1902 owed more to the electors' prudence than to the
determined and even ruthless efforts of the State machinery to silence and
intimidate the opposition.

But when governments frightened or offended numerous or powerful
sections of the electorate, all the prefects' bribery and bullying proved vain:
the ultraroyalists in the late 1820s, and their royalist grandsons in the 1870s
discovered this to their cost. Even Napoleon III's prefects discovered in the
1860s that they could not stifle the growing opposition. Pressures from the
prefects could be counterbalanced by pressures from local *notables*, which
were sometimes too strong to be overcome, both under the limited pre-1848
suffrage and under universal suffrage. Certain families had veritable electoral
fiefs, supported by legions of kinsmen, friends and dependants. Landowners
expected support from their tenants, whether won by threat or inducement,
and universal suffrage sometimes strengthened their position. One explained
that he gave tenancies on easy leases, allowed free pasture in his fields and
left his woods open for friends to help themselves. Many were willing
enough to repay such generosity at the ballot box. Big industrialists expected
similar deference and in factory or mining towns dependent on one
employer, who provided not only jobs but houses and welfare benefits, they
had the means to enforce it. Schneider, owner of the Le Creusot ironworks,
had been a supporter of Napoleon III in the 1860s, and was still a deputy in
the 1880s, by then the only conservative in Burgundy. Such people could
stand up to pressure from the prefects. But they too required at least an
acquiescent electorate, willing to regard them as protectors against an
unfriendly authority, as in the Catholic south and west. If bureaucrats or
notables tried to force their choices on a resentful electorate, elections
became bitter and sometimes violent affairs.

Elections cost money, and there were no controls on electoral expenses. A
few visits, dinners and an election address was all that was required before
1848, and sometimes this was organized by friends with the candidate

20. Vidalenc (1953), p. 69.

remaining modestly absent. Under universal suffrage, and especially during the Empire and the Third Republic, voters had to be wooed, and elections became festive occasions: 'If there's enough drink, we'll be all right', as one election agent put it. Posters and leaflets were reckoned at about 7,000 francs in the 1880s, but food and endless rounds of drinks for weeks beforehand put the average cost up to 30–40,000 francs – four times a deputy's annual salary. Sometimes barrels of wine were placed at the polling stations; and in one 1902 election voters were said to have averaged 500 free glasses of wine each in the months preceding the vote. Some candidates went even further, especially wealthy royalists fighting an uphill battle against the Empire or the Republic, when costs might reach 100,000 francs. However, bribery was usually less crude than in English elections in the mid-nineteenth century, one reason doubtless being that French candidates could promise State patronage rather than paying cash on the nail.[21]

The electoral system encouraged the primacy of local issues and influences. For most of the century, it was *scrutin d'arrondissement* based on small single-member constituencies: 'little, stinking, stagnant pools', Aristide Briand called them. Most in the 1830s had under 600 electors, and even in the 1880s some had only 3,000. After 1848, the mass electorate increasingly preferred local men – landowners, businessmen, lawyers, doctors – who knew their constituents and served their interests. If they did so successfully, they could expect a long tenure, and not infrequently could pass their seats on to their sons. Briefly in 1848, 1871 and 1885–89, this cosy system was replaced by *scrutin de liste*, in which electors cast votes for several candidates on a party list in large multi-member constituencies. This diluted local influences and was supposed to highlight national issues and national personalities, especially as leading politicians could stand in any number of constituencies simultaneously, and thus shed their lustre on less famous political allies who would be elected on their coat-tails. Such elections could turn into quasi-plebiscites, and could thus strengthen a government emerging from them: for example, Thiers in 1871 was elected on 26 departmental lists, the only time a parliamentary election has ever clearly designated a head of government. General Boulanger seemed to be heading in the same direction in 1889 (see p. 452), and this put an end to the system: the republican majority decided that it was a danger to democracy and that parish-pump politics were safer.

The three- or two-ballot system was the other important organizational feature of French elections. Introduced in 1815 and interrupted only in 1848–51, 1871 and 1885–89, it produced a result in the first round only if a candidate obtained an absolute majority of votes cast; otherwise a second (and until 1848 a third) round was held to elect the candidate with the highest number of votes.[22] From the 1880s onwards – a period of multiplying

21. For details see Weber (1991), pp. 183–4; Guiral and Thuillier (1980), pp. 70–83; Zeldin (1973), vol. 1, pp. 580–1.
22. There were subtle variations over the years, especially when or whether losing candidates had to withdraw.

parties – two-round contests became increasingly common. This had important consequences. Diversity of parties and independence of candidates were further encouraged because in the first ballot any number of candidates could stand without risking a split vote and the victory of a common enemy. So diverse tendencies of republicans, radicals, socialists or royalists could continue to exist and attract a handful of votes, and indeed were encouraged to persist in order to stake a claim to consideration. The essential thing was to agree on a single compromise candidate for the second round: in the first round one voted for, in the second round *against*. The ability to do this was what decided elections, locally and nationally, far more than changes in voters' preferences, which remained remarkably stable in numbers and geography: between 1877 and 1928, it has been argued that the relative strength of 'Left' and 'Right' altered by only 0.5 per cent. Local parties had to be free to negotiate deals with their rivals (including payment of election expenses), thus limiting national centralization of organization or programme. The need for a unifying slogan put emphasis on the basic ideological shibboleths around which diverse groups could unify: defence of the Charter, defence of order, loyalty to the monarchy, defence of the Republic, defence of or hostility to the Church. 'Our programme is known', radicals proclaimed in 1901, 'it was laid down by our forefathers . . . it unites all the sons of the Revolution, whatever their differences, against all the men of counter-revolution.'[23] Precise commitments were divisive and hence best avoided.

The republican party from the 1870s to the 1900s was the most successful at last-minute unity. 'Republican discipline' meant not opposing a republican candidate where there was a risk of letting in a monarchist or Catholic. Hence, in emergencies Marxists voted for capitalists and millionaire mill-owners campaigned for socialists, all in the sacred name of the Republic; but candidates elected in such circumstances were not committed to supporting a particular government (elections never chose governments) or legislative programme. The royalists proved less disciplined, and hence always won fewer seats in the second ballot than their overall electoral strength would have justified, through splitting their vote. In short, the two-ballot system meant a proliferation of political groups, local independence from central party control, and a premium for unity round the great ideological issues.

PARTIES AND PRESSURE GROUPS

There are so many parties in France, and so many divisions within the parties, that there is no longer a single word of the political vocabulary that is perfectly clear.

Jules Simon, 1868[24]

23. Nordmann (1977), pp. 42, 44.
24. Dubois (1962), p. 367.

When you choose a deputy, choose a very Red one; because afterwards, they fade.
Popular saying

There were many types and levels of political organization. First, at the national level, a 'party' was a loose affinity of like-minded people: *'le parti libéral'*, *'le parti de mouvement'*, *'le parti républicain'*, *'le parti de l'ordre'* and many others. Agulhon's definition of the republican party – 'the totality of people who identify themselves as republicans by their convictions and their votes' – could be adapted to each.[25] Second, at the organizational level, a party was embodied in a huge variety of local associations of activists, often with social as well as political functions, from drinking clubs to religious confraternities. Third, in parliament, there were multifarious groups of deputies. And fourth, especially later in the century, there was a wide range of often very sizeable economic and political pressure groups which were not necessarily aligned with the political parties. Let us look at each of these categories in turn.

National parties

At the national level, there was a kaleidoscope of names over the century, with no equivalent of the ever-changing but ever the same Whigs and Tories. At the most basic level, there was Right and Left: 'the obsessive hammering of those twin terms articulates 150 years of political struggle', in Rémond's phrase, and without them he considers it impossible to make sense of political history.[26] A wide variety of ideas and organizations – and even tastes in art and food[27] – have invariably tended to be classified somewhere along an imagined Left/Right spectrum. However, what was a useful simplification for labelling friends and enemies at election times is of limited use for historical analysis. As was seen in Part I, attitudes to the Revolution (the original sense of Right and Left) were too complex to be easily summarized. Certain major political traditions, such as liberalism, were sometimes on the Left and sometimes on the Right. Certain crucial political themes, such as the aspiration to moral order, we have seen to be shared by both Left and Right. So, despite many aspirations to create one, there has never been a two-party system durably polarized in terms of Right and Left.

There have been various attempts to elucidate these mysteries. André Siegfried suggested that French politics underwent *'sinistrisme'*, a slow shifting of the whole body politic to the Left. Thus, in the 1820s, all but a tiny minority were royalist; in the 1890s, all but a minority were republican; by 1914, the radicals, formerly the extreme Left, were now the centre, and the socialists had become a new force on the Left. However, this ostensible

25. Hamon (1986), p. 2.
26. Rémond (1968), vol.1, p. 13.
27. The *Nouvel Observateur* ran a survey some years ago that suggested that camembert was a left-wing, and brie a right-wing cheese.

movement to the Left was largely nominal. It was, wrote Siegfried, like an opera chorus singing 'March! March!' without actually moving.[28] François Goguel[29] noted that the phenomenon could equally be regarded as 'dextrisme', the movement of parties towards the Right. Thus socialists, revolutionary extremists in 1840, had become parliamentary moderates by 1914, and radicals, representatives of the urban working class in the 1870s, had become the pillars of agriculture and business. Goguel, wishing to stress the dualism of French politics (the 'centre' is regularly broken up by polarization), suggested that the fundamental division was between two 'temperaments': a 'party of movement' and a 'party of established order'.

Other historians have analysed the subdivisions *within* Right and Left. René Rémond[30] has argued that 'the Right' consists of three durable traditions. First, legitimist and Catholic, supporters of the Bourbons from 1814 to the 1880s, thereafter primarily devoted to the defence of the Church and the promotion of Christian social values. Second, liberal and Orleanist, champions of the principles of 1789 and the 1830 revolution, and above all supporters of individual liberty and parliamentary government whatever the regime. Third, Bonapartist and nationalist, supporters of strong populist government, whether under Empire or Republic. With pleasing Gallic symmetry, Georges Lefranc[31] has suggested a similar tripartite division for the Left. First, a liberal parliamentary Left, that of the democrats of the 1830s and 1840s, who by the 1870s formed the bedrock of the moderate republican 'opportunists', similar to the Orleanist Right in their support for parliamentary government and economic liberalism. Second, the democratic and anticlerical Left, once revolutionary, devoted to the welfare of '*les petits*' against 'financial feudalism', but hostile to socialism and united by fervent anticlericalism. Third, the socialist and communist Left, tiny clandestine groups before 1848, periodically underground again during the 1850s and 1870s, and emerging as a significant electoral force in the 1890s. Party labels changed, alliances formed and broke, but these essential tendencies remained.

What sense can be made of this undeniably complex history? It may be useful to recall that we are dealing with political phenomena at different levels: as ideologies, collective identities and political organizations. Rémond and Lefranc attempt to synthesize these three elements into a single model; this is a helpful simplification, but inevitably has the disadvantage of simplification, which is that on closer examination many things do not quite fit. For example, Orleanism and Bonapartism form elements of Rémond's 'Right', but until 1830 they were undoubtedly on the 'Left'; while Bonapartism and republicanism, radicalism and socialism, carefully delineated in the models, in reality often intertwined. Hence, at the risk of complexity, this book deals separately with ideology, identity and organization. At the level of

28. Siegfried (1930), p. 76.
29. Goguel (1946).
30. Rémond (1968).
31. Lefranc (1973).

ideology, there are persistent themes – even obsessions, as discussed in Part I – that dominate thinking about politics: for example, attitudes to the Revolution. At the behavioural level, political identities, as discussed in Part III, often had a strong regional and religious link, causing a visceral attraction to or, no less important, revulsion from certain political traditions: loyalties were 'biological rather than ideological'.[32] Thus, for example, Protestants in the Midi would consistently identify with the least Catholic candidate, which over the century meant successively being Bonapartist, liberal, republican, radical and socialist. Conversely, Catholics in the Midi voted consistently for legitimists, though in the 1900s some voted for socialists, seeing them as less anti-Catholic than the radicals. Peasant dislike of urban politicians led them in several regions to support socialists, then Bonapartists and then radicals. Algerian settlers' dislike of Napoleon III's Arab policy led them to vote consistently for the republican Left, even for the thoroughly racist reason that Jews voted for moderates. Such rather wayward continuities of obsessions and identities did not translate simply into support for a single political party, or even consistent support for 'Right' or 'Left'.

Parties as we are considering them in this section are organizations for winning votes: so while both ideas and identities of course remain important, there is also an indispensable practical need for adaptation, compromise and tactical manoeuvre in order to win, or at least survive, by adopting credible slogans and even changing party labels to seem up-to-date and so maximize electoral support. Sometimes these adaptations were caused by seismic shifts in the political landscape. For example, monarchists increasingly realized after 1870 that a republic was inevitable for the foreseeable future; in the 1893 elections the old monarchist Right collapsed, as its electors either abstained in despair or voted for 'moderate' republicans. Hence, without altering their deepest ideas and loyalties, monarchists who wanted to stay in politics stood as 'republicans'. Many republican politicians, wishing to distance themselves from unpopular opportunist governments in the 1880s, adopted the label 'radical'; so many genuine socially concerned radicals thereupon called themselves 'radical-socialist' or even 'socialist', though without necessarily joining a party, subscribing to a programme or accepting party discipline. The label 'republican', without qualifying adjectives, was thus left, oddly, to conservatives, who, especially in marginal constituencies, successively dropped not only the label 'monarchist', but also 'conservative' ('un mot qui commence bien mal'), 'right' and even 'liberal'.

In short, continuity in ideas and in identities was very imperfectly disguised by fluidity in labels. The continuity explains why, for example, converts from monarchism to republicanism in the 1890s were still treated with suspicion by 'real' republicans, for the basic ideological chasm still remained: 'You say you accept the Republic, that is nothing! Do you accept the Revolution?' demanded the radical Léon Bourgeois.[33] The answer, of course, was no: ex-

32. Jones (1985), p. 211.
33. Siegfried (1930), p. 57.

monarchist 'republicans' maintained their preferences for 'order', authority, the Church, property, low taxes, the landed interest and the army. Voters were well able to decode the political symbols and identify what lay beneath the surface, judging a candidate by his origins, family, friends and coded language. So the 'republican' Right continued to be elected in the same regions as the old monarchist Right, just as new socialists were elected in old strongholds of Jacobinism.

However, during the 1880s and 1890s the old ideological division between Right and Left grew temporarily less sharp. A new brand of populist nationalism, which first coalesced around General Boulanger in 1886–89, seemed to combine the popular urban radicalism of the Left with the authoritarian militarism of the Right: Barrès called it 'national socialism'. After the defeat of Boulanger, the most 'moderate' elements of the 'Left', led by Méline, were drawn closer to the least intransigent elements of the 'Right' by their shared fear of radicalism and detestation of socialism. For a few years, it seemed that a new centre coalition was in the making, loyal to the republican constitution and willing to compromise over the religious question. But the Dreyfus affair and its aftermath (1894–1906) forced the whole political class, however reluctantly, to choose sides again (see p. 464). This largely revived the traditional Right/Left division, though with some redrawing of the boundary: some long-time republicans found themselves on the 'Right' because they opposed a retrial of Dreyfus. The Left was now synonymous with the Dreyfusards: those who chose democracy, the values of the Enlightenment, individual rights, anticlericalism and the Republic. The Right were the anti-Dreyfusards: those who chose authority, support for the army, tradition, Catholicism and race, and condemned, if not invariably the Republic in principle, certainly the parliamentary Republic as it existed.

These observations permit us to clarify one final problem: the frequently remarked phenomenon of the missing centre. Goguel stresses the point that there was a Right ('party of established order') and a Left ('party of movement'), but no centre. There were plenty of centrists (often calling themselves 'moderates') but no centre party, though there was often a 'centre-right', a 'centre-left' and sometimes a 'third party'. This is partly because the centre tended to split ideologically at times of stress, usually over religion or fundamental concepts of political legitimacy. But it is also because the centre was the most politically pragmatic of all tendencies: it tended almost by definition to accept the status quo and try to work within the system, and hence was successively reincarnated as the 'moderate' wing of royalism, Orleanism, Bonapartism and republicanism.

Party organization

At a local level, party organization usually meant a committee. Local worthies, especially at election times, set them up *ad hoc* to choose candidates and canvas support. They might loosely coordinate their action nationally: the prototype was the liberal federation Aide-toi le ciel t'aidera in the 1820s.

Committees raised the money to publish election propaganda, provide drinks for voters and perhaps run a newspaper. According to party, the local *château*, church, prefecture, newspaper office, gentlemen's *cercle*, freemasons' lodge, popular drinking club, charitable society, literary society, business organization, freethinkers' group, trade union or at the end of our period sports club (bicycle club for the Left, automobile club for the Right) might provide a focus for meeting and recruitment. Once electoral success came, local councillors, deputies and senators would naturally provide leadership. Rank and file activists would be the local middle class. Civil servants were prominent in the government party; landowners and clergy in the Right; teachers, white-collar workers, small landowners, businessmen and trade union leaders in the republican, radical and socialist parties. Patronage provided a cement for this structure, and made activists jealous of their independence from the centre as well as of interlopers. Even socialists and their relatives, for example, colonized the public services of the towns they controlled.

Parties did not develop permanent national organizations until the turn of the century. The law, which until 1901 placed restrictions on associations of more than 20 people, and also widespread suspicion of organized parties as improper, hampered organization. The political stimulus of the Dreyfus crisis, helped by the 1901 Law of Associations, caused parties to be set up almost simultaneously by the radicals, socialists, Catholics (Action Libérale Populaire) and conservative republicans (Fédération Républicaine). Conservatives tended to dislike the word 'party', which smacked of faction and even worse of the Left, and preferred words like 'federation', 'union' or 'alliance'. The radical party (officially, the Parti Républicain Radical et Radical- Socialiste) was the archetype of the federation of local committees: at its founding conference in June 1901 there were delegates of 476 committees, 155 freemasons' lodges and 215 newspapers.[34]

The alternative model to 'parties of *notables*', which were strongly focused on winning elections and defending local interests and were run by local worthies, was the 'party of militants', inspired more exclusively by ideological enthusiasm. During the first three-quarters of the century, there were clandestine groups of Right and Left, whose goals were a coup d'état or insurrection. The temporary lifting of repression, especially in the aftermath of revolution, produced a mushrooming of clubs, consciously inspired by the practices of the 1790s, always more effective at oratory than action. Such activities were marginalized after 1870, as free electoral politics, safer and more effective, exerted an irresistible attraction; but the militants were determined not to succumb to the fleshpots of 'bourgeois' politics. Several small socialist groups emerged in the 1870s and 1880s, such as the Fédération des Travailleurs Socialistes (1879), the Marxist Parti Ouvrier Français (1883), and the Blanquist Parti Ouvrier Socialiste Révolutionnaire (1890), whose common history was marked by labyrinthine amalgamations and secessions

34. Nordmann (1977), p. 43.

(see p. 292), and who eventually joined with independent socialists in 1905 to form the Section Française de l'Internationale Ouvrière (SFIO). Party activists attempted, without complete success, to control policy-making and discipline their parliamentary members, who they insisted were merely delegates of the party who must obey its instructions. This led to friction with some prominent socialist deputies and the resignation or expulsion of several party leaders, including Millerand, Briand and Viviani. In practice, the '*notable*' and 'militant' patterns tended to converge, becoming after 1900 large national organizations led by professional politicians, the new *notables*.

A different type of political organization emerged from the 1880s onwards: the *ligue*. The prototype Ligue des Patriotes (1882) was followed by the Ligue des Droits de l'Homme (1898), the Ligue de la Patrie Française (1899), Action Française (1899), and several others after the First World War. Some were relatively mass organizations with larger memberships than conventional political parties. They did not aim primarily at parliament and only rarely at insurrection, but rather at mobilizing opinion and organizing extra-parliamentary activity from sports events and lectures to riots.

France was not a society of truly mass organizations, especially in politics. Relatively low urbanization, legal barriers, suspicion of factionalism, instability of organizations and localism doubtless provide much of the explanation. By 1914, the SFIO had between 35,000 and 75,000 members; the centre-right Action Libérale Populaire claimed 250,000. The contrast with Germany or Britain is striking. The German SDP had 1.7 million, and the British Conservative Primrose League over 2 million members.

Parliamentary parties and pressure groups

At the parliamentary level, these were in effect clubs of deputies, whether named after the individual organizer or the meeting place ('Groupe Target', 'Rue de Poitiers'), or indicating their position on the political spectrum ('*extrême Droite*', '*Centre-Gauche*'). It was usual to belong to several: many deputies liked to keep a foot in more than one camp. Parliamentary groups did not directly tally with national parties. The republican party in the 1870s, for example, was in the Chamber of Deputies split into *Centre-Gauche*, *Gauche républicaine*, *union républicaine*, *Gauche radicale* and *extrême Gauche*; and in the Senate into a different set of groups. A generation later, the republican line-up had changed, and included five rival (and tiny) socialist groups. Not until the beginning of the twentieth century did parliamentary parties begin roughly to match party organization in the country. Only in 1910 were ten political *groupes*[35] officially recognized in the Chamber, and all deputies required to join one, though this compulsion led

35. They were: Action Libérale, les droites, gauche démocratique, gauche radicale, députés indépendents, républicains progressistes, républicains radicaux-socialistes, républicains socialistes, parti socialiste, and the ineffable 'députés n'appartenant à aucun groupe'.

to the creation of a group of 'deputies not belonging to any group' for the determinedly independent, nicknamed *les sauvages*.

Parliament contained far more than these principal political groups, however. There were small clubs, including dining clubs, devoted to tactical planning and not a little self-advancement. Most prominent radicals and socialists belonged to masonic lodges. There were over 50 groups large and small relating to general, constituency or sectional interests, named after the cause they supported.[36] The largest included the Groupe Viticole, Groupe Antialcoolique, 'Défense du personnel des chemins de fer', 'Défense des intérêts agricoles' etc. These interest groups cut across the political groups: the Groupe Ouvrier in the 1890s included socialists, nationalists and radicals; the Groupe Agricole, with over 200 members, also drew on several parties. These groups sometimes negotiated directly with each other over legislation, bypassing both the political parties and the government. They also tried to pack the parliamentary commissions drafting legislation.

Parliamentary groups had links with organizations in the country. These included industrial and agricultural associations, which became important during the 1880s and 1890s, stimulated by economic depression, labour militancy, and issues such as protectionism. Naturally, they represented contrary interests and policies. In the 1880s the Association de l'Industrie Française (the successor of the 1860s Association pour la Défense du Travail National, set up to oppose Napoleon III's free-trade policy) campaigned for tariffs, while the Association pour la Défense de la Liberté Commerciale campaigned for free trade. The largest and most important pressure groups were those which could command electoral as well as financial power, such as industrial, wine-making and agricultural lobbies, these last probably the largest such organizations in the country, totalling over 900,000 members by 1911, which dwarfed the trade unions and political parties. These pressure groups, as well as printing propaganda, organizing petitions and holding dinners for deputies, could also bring out crowds of workers and peasants to demonstrate and vote. But here too, opposing interests tended to balance each other: for example, during the great wine crises of the 1900s, wine growers from the south (represented in parliament by the Groupe Viticole) wanted to limit the sugaring of wines which increased output, but the sugar-beet growers of the north (represented by the Groupe Sucrier) wanted it to continue. Though in the 1890s centrist politicians tried to persuade businessmen to take a more direct role in politics, most appeared to prefer the traditional means of using professional politicians, often lawyers, as their spokesmen, or the newer method of acting through professional organizations, such as the Comité des Forges or the Union des Industries Métallurgiques et Minières, run by full-time officials who were also active in official consultative bodies. While the precise influence of these bodies is little known, it seems likely that, in spite of their own conflicts of interest, they were able to influence legislation

36. Le Chartier (1911), ch. 9.

on taxation, regulation and tariffs. The wine lobby in particular has been called the 'spoilt child of the republic'.

There were also ideological pressure groups aiming at mass mobilization and/or behind-the-scenes influence. Among the most prominent of these were the Ligue de l'Enseignement and the Parti Colonial (a federation of pro-colonial societies). They often had significant membership inside parliament: about one-third of the Chamber were members of the Ligue de l'Enseignement in the 1880s; and the Groupe Coloniale, linked with the Parti Colonial, numbered over 200 deputies by 1901. It was a particularly effective lobby, often taking over the direction of government policy.

Political parties were rarely so effective. They could not impose a legislative programme or voting discipline, and there was always a considerable number of maverick deputies. There was no defined party leadership in the British sense. It was difficult to work out the loyalty of some deputies and so calculating party gains and losses at elections was always approximate. The rapid increase in the numbers of deputies calling themselves 'radical' or 'socialist' in the early 1900s was one reason for consolidating the formal organization of those parties, which were losing all cohesion. This was due to the importance of local and sectional issues, patronage and the electoral system. Once deputies paid lip-service to the great ideological shibboleths, they were largely free to follow their own and their constituents' interests and ideas, if any. Even those parties, particularly the radicals and socialists, that purported to have relatively well-defined programmes could never control their deputies or ministers, much to the annoyance of party militants.

An indispensable part of holding on to a constituency was to serve the interests, personal and collective, of the voters: this was the curse of the deputy's life throughout the century, but also the source of his relative independence. Villèle in 1815 was already pestered by his electors for personal services (including getting rid of an unwanted mistress); a century later mass politics had turned this into an industry, and deputies tried to cope with the torrent of requests with pre-printed letters of recommendation. As well as helping individual voters and their families, deputies had to help the community as a whole: much money could be spent on gifts, charitable donations and subscriptions to local societies. In 1909 one candidate's electoral circular listed all his friends and contacts in high places, and concluded: 'We ask our readers whether all these contacts, all this support . . . are not useful for all the schools, roads, railways and all the personal services electors can hope to expect'.[37] Deputies were the mediators between citizens and the omnipresent State machinery. If they were effective, they often had a free hand in their other political activities. For example, the leading socialist Alexandre Millerand, who worked hard to defend the interests of the wine traders of his constituency (Bercy), was able to break with the socialist party in 1904 and move towards the other end of the political spectrum without a murmur from his electoral committee.

37. Zeldin (1973), vol. 1, p. 579.

This independence had its price, literally. Without permanent national party organization until the early twentieth century, politicians and their immediate backers were largely on their own financially. Prominent politicians ran or controlled their own newspapers, in the absence of a party publicity machine. Those in opposition might have to face opponents secretly subsidized by the government. Providers of money were sometimes politically motivated (in a spectacular and notorious case in the 1880s, the nationalist General Boulanger literally sold out to wealthy royalist backers); more often they were economic interest groups. Many deputies were paid consultancy or legal fees by economic organizations, and were expected to represent their interests in parliament. Many held directorships. There was probably little basic change here throughout the period. Thiers, for example, received money from opposition sources to found the newspaper *Le National* in 1830; he was later lent money in order to meet the property qualification for election to parliament; and eventually became a director of the Anzin Mining Company, whose interests he energetically represented in a pro-tariff campaign in the 1860s. Clemenceau received money from the crooked financier Cornelius Hertz to subsidize his newspaper *La Justice* in the 1880s and 1890s: this implicated him in the 1893 Panama scandal, which nearly ended his career. Such financial arrangements were not necessarily corrupt, though they were often embarrassing. There was indeed corruption under all regimes, as some politicians sought to get rich, and economic interests sought political favours; opposition parties naturally argued that such corruption was the norm, and was an essential characteristic of the regime they disliked. The July Monarchy, the Second Empire, and the Third Republic were all the targets of similar criticism. The most notorious of all the scandals of the period, the Panama scandal, showed that many politicians accepted money from business interests, but that those paying did not receive much in return. Socialist deputies, determined to stay clean, spent as little as possible on their election campaigns and even borrowed to meet them, hoping to pay off the debt from their parliamentary salaries, from which they also had to pay a levy to the party.

Parties could not control ministers; neither could ministers control parties. Governments throughout the century were at the mercy of unstable majorities, and found it impossible to force through legislation. A few exceptional men in exceptional circumstances managed to command a majority for a relatively long period, though significantly many of these periods ended in crisis: Villèle (1822–27), Perier (1831–32), Guizot (1840–48), Thiers (1871–73), Ferry (most of the time from 1880 to 1885), Meline (1896–98), Waldeck-Rousseau (1899–1902), Combes (1902–5) and Clemenceau (1906–9). But the average life of a government was only about eight months. Under the Restoration, the July Monarchy and the Empire, the Crown used its patronage to discipline parliamentarians, with varying degrees of success, and could also occasionally use the threat of a dissolution to protect its ministers. But during the Third Republic no president dared after 1877 to dissolve the Chamber. As has been seen, much local patronage slipped into the hands of deputies themselves, which increased their independence.

Every prime minister could have echoed Perier's words, 'Anyone can support the government when it is right; what I need is people who will support the government when it is wrong'. Generations of leaders – Villèle, Perier, Thiers, Gambetta, Ferry, Méline, Clemenceau, Poincaré – longed for a two-party system. Certain parties – the démocrates-socialistes in 1849, and the various socialist parties during the Third Republic – attempted to formulate a clear class-oriented programme. Conservatives and moderates dreamed of a French Tory party, which would be united, electable and able to defend respectable conservative interests without, as French conservateurs were constantly tempted to do after 1830, trying to overthrow the regime. Yet it is striking how secondary class politics remained, and how rarely class set the political agenda. This was because of the strength of purely ideological issues – monarchy, republic, religion, nation – to which socio-economic issues had no clear link. There was no such thing as a republican, Catholic, royalist or nationalist policy on taxation, tariffs, factory legislation or farm policy, for example. Moreover, major socio-economic issues affected sectional rather than class interests, and for this reason too did not contribute to the re-definition of politics on class lines. The sempiternal struggles over excise duties on alcohol and over tariffs cut across classes, uniting landowners with labourers, capitalists with workers. The Association de l'Industrie Française represented both the usually republican mill-owners and the usually conservative ironmasters, and it had links with both right-wing and left-wing deputies. Similarly, the parliamentary Groupe Viticole included royalists, moderate republicans and socialists. Governments could win parliamentary support by pleasing these pressure groups. During the July Monarchy and the Third Republic – the two parliamentary regimes par excellence – heterogenous majorities based on shared interests tended to replace ideologically based majorities during the gap between general elections. During the Third Republic, the incoherence and hence immobility of the system (governments introduced an income-tax bill sixteen times without being able to pass it) caused criticism of the parliamentary system as such. In the late twentieth century, the decline of ideological conflict has not meant the creation of parties of interest, but the disintegration of party politics altogether.

REIGNING AND RULING

Louis XVIII has not been restored to the throne of his ancestors: he has simply ascended the throne of Napoleon.

Joseph de Maistre

It was commonly said that the French were a monarchical people at heart who needed and liked authority. That the Revolution, after going through chaos, terror and oligarchy, had culminated in Napoleon's Empire, and that after him the Bourbons had been popularly acclaimed, seemed proof. The monarch's main task was to preserve 'order', one of the most highly charged words in the nineteenth-century political vocabulary. He had also to provide unity and consistency in a body politic riven by factionalism, and ensure dignified representation for the State in a Europe where monarchy was practically universal. So whether monarchist or republican, every constitution – 1814, 1830, 1848, 1852, 1875 – provided for a strong executive power. Most politicians would have agreed with Guizot's dictum, 'The throne is not an empty chair'. Yet, because his role was so important, and his powers so extensive, the occupant of Napoleon's throne must not appear to abuse them and threaten the delicate balance of rights and interests – the abolition of 'privilege', sanctity of property, religious tolerance – that had emerged from the Revolution. In Thiers's 1830 phrase, 'The king reigns, he does not rule'.

To reconcile Thiers's axiom with that of Guizot proved difficult. A neutral monarch meant a neutral State, yet as has been seen, for all parties the State was both a weapon and a prize. Under every regime up to and including the present Fifth Republic the relations between head of state, government and parliament have been problematic, sometimes fatal, and usually deliberately vague. Constitutions might specify that ministers were 'responsible' for policy, but without saying how or to whom, whether the whole cabinet was collectively responsible, or whether policies could be privately approved by individual ministers and the head of state. Monarchs who used their prerogative powers, even on the advice of their governments, came under personal attack. Louis XVIII set the precedent by dissolving a disobedient ultraroyalist parliament in 1816. Charles X, using, in his view, his emergency powers to save the State from creeping revolution, precipitated the revolution of 1830. Louis-Philippe, doing his duty as he saw it to safeguard a fragile political equilibrium against the dangers of war and revolution in the 1840s, was accused of 'personal government' and subverting the spirit of the constitution. Louis-Napoleon Bonaparte, elected president in 1848 under a constitution based on the separation of executive and legislative powers, was in deadlock with parliament by 1851 which he solved by a coup d'état. This left him in full charge of government: ministers were individually responsible to him, not to each other or to a muzzled parliament. His attempt in the 1860s, as Napoleon III, partially to liberalize his regime caused a confusion of responsibility that contributed to the outbreak of a catastrophic war with Germany, and his own fall.

The Bonapartist trauma left most politicians with a heightened mistrust of executive power, and this had enormous consequences for the development of political ideas and political practice: as the republican Jules Ferry argued in the 1860s, 'If you want to be an industrious, peaceful and free people, you have no business with a strong power ... France needs a weak government'.[38] Thereafter, any attempt to assert executive power met

38. Furet (1992), p. 477.

determined resistance. Ironically, Thiers himself as president of the Republic was accused of reigning and ruling by ignoring the will of the parliamentary majority. His political wings were clipped by the so-called '*loi chinoise*' which prevented him from speaking in parliament, a precaution that has become a permanent part of French constitutional practice, and he was overthrown in 1873. In 1875, the liberal royalists who framed the constitution of the Third Republic set up a strong president – a republican monarch – as a barrier against democracy: he had a seven-year term of office (which despite its evident disadvantages has become a permanent constitutional feature), commanded the armed forces, appointed ministers and if necessary dissolved the Chamber of Deputies. But, unlike Bonaparte in 1848, he would be elected by parliament, not by the people, a precaution that survived until de Gaulle reintroduced direct popular election in 1962. When President MacMahon tried to use his constitutional powers in 1877, dismissing a government too left-wing for his taste, appointing a royalist successor, and dissolving the Chamber – all perfectly legal – he was accused by republicans of attempting a coup d'état. This time, violence was avoided; but such was the outcry that he resigned in 1879 and none of his successors dared to use their full constitutional powers. The main qualification of his replacement Jules Grévy was that in 1848 he had opposed having a president at all.

Though presidents of the Republic were able to use influence behind the scenes, especially in areas traditionally the responsibility of the head of state such as foreign policy (they had the constitutional power to make treaties), and to arbitrate between parliamentary factions, they did not govern. The role of head of government devolved to a *président du conseil des ministres*, often translated as prime minister, but without the power or means of action of modern prime ministers: his office was unrecognized by the constitution, he had little control over parliament and no staff, he simultaneously held another portfolio, and in short he was often no more than the convenor of an ephemeral cabinet of independent and insubordinate ministers, each of whom looked after his own business and did not share cabinet responsibility. In spite of his title, he did not even chair cabinet meetings: the president of the Republic did that. Grévy, in refusing to appoint the recognized leader of the republican party, Léon Gambetta, as *président du conseil* in 1880, deliberately reduced the prestige of the office and prevented any direct link being established between party leadership, popularity in the country and leadership of the government. Gambetta himself was opposed by the Chamber when in 1882 he appeared to be trying to strengthen the powers of the executive; he was the first of many who failed in that attempt. From the fall of Thiers in 1873 until de Gaulle after 1958, no individual reigned and ruled, and the electorate was never given the opportunity to choose its government: indeed, the name of the prime minister was rarely mentioned in election campaigns 'either to praise or to blame him'.[39] Choice of prime ministers was a matter not for the electors but for backstairs bargaining

39. Bodley (1898), vol. 2, p. 135.

between politicians. Executive authority was fragmented between ministers, leading deputies, the head of state (monarch or president), the prime minister, pressure groups and civil servants, frequently pursuing contradictory policies. They were not only protected, as Thiers had wished long before, from the pressures of 'the court and the street', but shielded from the profane gaze of the electorate. Finally, when in 1940 and again in 1958 this system appeared to have failed the country in time of crisis, the reaction was to give full powers to an individual 'saviour'. Finally, this was institutionalized in the Fifth Republic's constitution and its constitutional conventions, which have created what is often called a republican monarchy.

THOSE WHO RULED

We offer the spectacle of a tranquil people and agitated legislators.

Edouard Laboulaye[40]

The eighteenth century had seen the emergence of a new elite, including nobles and commoners, landowners and bourgeois, based on wealth and education. The Revolution gave the coup de grâce to the traditional society of orders, gave male citizens equality before the law and redistributed land, wealth and power. The Empire consolidated the changes. A jealous, quarrelsome, insecure and pushy conglomeration of ancient and not-so-ancient noble families, *nouveaux riches*, circumspect ex-revolutionaries (who could say, like Siéyès, 'I survived'), soldiers and officials, often decked out with Napoleon's brand-new orders and exotic titles, formed the top of the socio-economic pile. The term *notables* had been used under Napoleon to denote those the government needed to take notice of. The Bourbon Restoration added to them the die-hard émigrés, an awkward addition. These *notables* were the people with power in France after 1815; and their sons and grandsons held on to it at least until the end of the century.

To be a true *notable* required sharing in State power, hence the bitterness with which it was disputed, and the mutual detestation, especially, of the returned émigrés and those who had survived and prospered during the Revolution and the Empire. The period between 1814 and 1848, the period of *notable* rule *par excellence*, saw an overlapping of bureaucratic and political office: officials became deputies, and politicians became officials. This was intended to consolidate government power and it also, of course, consolidated that of the *grands notables*, whose grip on influence and patronage increased. Most *notables* were landowners. After the so-called 'bourgeois revolution' of 1830, over 90 per cent of deputies were landowners, and by 1846 titled nobles once again formed nearly a third of the Chamber, more than in the late 1820s.[41] A high proportion of deputies came from

40. Halévy (1937), vol. 2, p. 95.
41. Lagoueyte (1989), p. 90; Higonnet and Higonnet (1967), pp. 204–24, at p. 222.

families of officials, including those of the pre-revolutionary *noblesse de robe*. Businessmen were greatly under-represented in parliament, and showed no collective wish to be otherwise.

When citizens were equal before the law and where nobility had only honorific significance, worth and importance were signified by wealth. In official documents, 'rich' becomes the indispensable adjective denoting suitable candidates for office. Wealth was more respected when it was unearned; so inherited ownership, especially of land, was the principal mark of notability and also, theorists hoped, a proof of education, independence, experience, and an interest in the public weal. Yet many wealthy office-holders, scornfully nicknamed '*les satisfaits*' or '*les ventrus*' (the pot-bellies), simply provided routine pen-pushers and docile lobby fodder for govern-ments. The low regard with which most politicians were held, and the assumption that they were motivated by self-interest, was thus established from the first years of the Restoration. One of Béranger's famous songs, '*Le Ventru*' (1818), summed up the deputy's achievements, not least with a knife and fork:

> All in all I've managed things well;
> A district attorney am I;
> I've got jobs for two of my brothers,
> And fixed up my three sons too.
> I've a hundred invitations
> For when the chamber meets again:
>   What dinners,
>   What dinners
> The ministers have given me!

The 1830 revolution made a significant change in those occupying the highest offices of State. These were no longer reserved for nobles, whose leading role steadily dwindled and practically ended in 1877. Instead, semi-professional politicians, whose qualifications were mainly intellectual or technical, came to prominence. One of the Third Republic's many nicknames was 'the Professors' Republic' (10 per cent of its ministers were teachers) but the July Monarchy had already been in part an intellectuals' monarchy, with leading positions for the historians Guizot (son of a provincial lawyer) and Thiers (a nobody from Marseilles) and the philosopher Victor Cousin (son of a worker). A fairly dazzling list of thinkers took supporting roles, including Tocqueville, Hugo, Lamartine, Royer-Collard, Rémusat and Broglie. However, the largest group of political office-holders under all regimes were lawyers, who, although they often practised at the bar, were as much career politicians as jurists. In 1881, 45 per cent of deputies had trained as lawyers; in 1914, 38 per cent of ministers were lawyers.[42]

There were clear social differences between parties: those of the Right had

42. Estèbe (1982), p. 107.

more nobles and landed proprietors, those of the Left more commoners and professional men. Manhood suffrage was introduced in 1848, but the first elections in April returned a high proportion of *notables*, including 190 former deputies and 68 of their families.[43] However, the growth of republican and *démocrate-socialiste* parties brought into parliament in 1849–50, along with one or two token workers, a significant number of middle-class men: journalists, doctors, lawyers. The Second Empire, by eliminating the Left, reversed this process. Although the Empire helped to liberate peasant voters from the sway of local *notables* by providing an alternative source of power and protection, it provided for the voters' choice another set of *notables*, many of whom had been in politics during the July Monarchy. However, Napoleon, eager to modernize the country, encouraged for the first time the participation of businessmen, whose numbers in the Chamber increased from 17 to 24 per cent.[44] He also, as Louis-Philippe had done, appointed some to ministerial office (usually commerce or finance), most notably the banker Achille Fould. Otherwise, he used State officials both as ministers and deputies (more than one-third of the 1852 Chamber), often from Parisian mandarin families, and a few new men willing to go along with the emperor's ideas. The prominence of officials was a sign of the deliberate downgrading of politics; the same was to occur during the Vichy regime and the neo-Bonapartist Fifth Republic, both of which also frowned on party politics. But the Empire shows clearly one of the drawbacks of having to rely on a narrow governing elite of *notables*: its own officials and politicians obstructed many of Napoleon III's schemes on grounds of prudence, cost and orthodoxy. There was little he could do: as Guizot had said, one could carry out a coup d'état with soldiers, and win a plebiscite with peasants, but one could not govern with soldiers and peasants.

The elections of 1871, in the aftermath of defeat by Germany, returned for the last time a very high proportion of nobles and country gentlemen, largely because the royalists campaigned for peace, but also because in a time of political confusion, as in 1848, voters turned back, with more or less enthusiasm and deference, to the *châtelains* and squires. The republican victories of the 1870s showed that this was a temporary phenomenon for most of the country, and marked the 'end of the *notables*'[45] as the dominant political group: nobles, 34 per cent of the 1871 Chamber, were only 10 per cent of the (also conservative) 1919 Chamber. Locke has analysed the political affiliations of deputies with titles or the *particule* 'de' (showing at least aspiration to noble status) in the 1872 National Assembly, and his findings show how marked the differences between parties were.[46] Slightly simplified, his figures are:

43. Tudesq (1964), vol. 2, p. 1065.
44. Figures in Charle (1991), p. 76.
45. Halévy (1937).
46. Locke (1974), p. 70.

Legitimists:	60 per cent with titles or *particule*
Bonapartists:	39 per cent
Orleanists:	32 per cent
Centre-Left:	15 per cent
Left:	6 per cent
Extreme Left:	0

Gambetta proclaimed that 'new social strata' (*nouvelles couches sociales*) were forming a new republican governing class. Yet although Gambetta (lawyer, son of an immigrant grocer) and several of his disciples were pretty plebeian, many republican leaders were not far removed from the squirearchy. They included Ferry, Freycinet (who was said to have visiting cards variously engraved 'Freycinet', 'de Freycinet' and 'Comte de Freycinet' for use in different milieux), Grévy, Waldeck-Rousseau (son of an 1848 deputy), Poincaré (grandson of a July Monarchy deputy) and Clemenceau, the radical leader, who came from an old landowning family in the Vendée and grew up in a *château* decorated with busts of Robespierre. Some 80 per cent of ministers came from the richest 2 per cent of the population,[47] and a remarkable number of leading republicans were intermarried, like their aristocratic conservative rivals. The consolidation of the Third Republic nevertheless brought major change in the political class. Republican politicians, especially at the lower levels, came increasingly from the small-town middle classes, especially from the traditionally republican east and south: doctors, teachers, shopkeepers, civil servants, and of course lawyers; 70 per cent of all deputies between 1871 and 1898 had university degrees, mostly in law.[48] There were relatively few industrialists, landowners, peasants or workers. Socialist leaders came mostly from the same background: Jaurès (professor), Millerand (lawyer), Brousse and Vaillant (doctors), and Guesde (journalist). Not until major socialist and radical gains in the early years of the twentieth century did lower-middle-class deputies enter the Chamber in considerable numbers. Workers, however, were always very few (5 per cent in 1893), and peasants, the largest electoral and social group, almost entirely absent. But although administered by the bourgeoisie and often attacked as a 'bourgeois Republic', the regime needed to win the support of peasants and workers, and the rival socio-economic interests it had to placate caused it to follow rather eclectic economic policies.

Christophe Charle, in his magisterial study of the elites of the Third Republic, concludes that famous phrases such as 'the end of the *notables*' and 'new social strata' exaggerate the degree of the change. The new elite, he concludes, if not entirely open, at least managed to seem open.[49] It was certainly more open in its recruitment than in Britain, Germany or perhaps even America. An increasing proportion of upwardly mobile sons of middle-

47. Charle (1991), p. 260.
48. Mayeur (1984), p. 78.
49. Charle (1987), pp. 70–2; see also Charle (1991), p. 137.

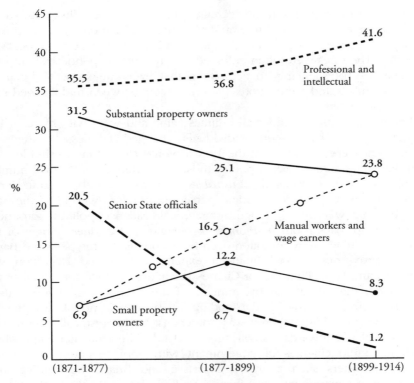

Figure 5.1 Changes in social origins of ministers, 1871–1914 (The occupation shown is that of the father at the time of the future minister's birth)

Source: Estèbe (1982), p. 26

and working-class families entered government in the generation before 1914. In Third Republic France, parliament and government became ways of joining the upper class, rather than signs that one already belonged.

More significant than their social origins was how deputies gained and kept their seats: they were decreasingly *notables* sitting by virtue of their local social and economic status, and increasingly *élus* dependent on the favour of their electors. Universal suffrage tended to spread professionalization to rank-and-file deputies, because the demands made on them by their electors required full-time attention. Under the Third Republic, the average age for entering parliament was only 34, and once there deputies made it their career, and often a long career: 40 or 50 years in politics was not uncommon. The substantial increase in the parliamentary salary in 1906 (from 9,000 francs, set in 1848, to 15,000 francs) was a landmark in the process of professionalization. Politicians shared a camaraderie based both on common origins (the socialist Millerand and the conservative republican Poincaré, for example, had attended the same Paris *lycée*) and on a common way of life, emphasized by the spread in the early twentieth century of the highly significant practice of calling each other *tu*. This camaraderie had its rules of etiquette, for example not to use certain expressions especially in the wrong place: 'At the tribune we can tolerate anything from each other, but in private life such language is unacceptable', said an indignant Thiers on one occasion in 1849.[50] The rules were often enforced throughout our period by duels (an effective way of silencing an accusation that everyone knew to be true): usually harmless and rather grotesque encounters between middle-aged men of sedentary habits.

Though governments under all regimes came and went with more or less rapidity, as we have seen, individuals changed far less: changes of government were usually what the British would call cabinet reshuffles, but with the prime minister being one of those reshuffled. A fairly small number of politicians were considered *ministrables*: they were the ablest professionals among the tongue-tied *notables* and parish-pump hacks who filled the back benches. They were distinguished by oratorical brilliance, political adroitness, technical grip, back-room *bonhomie*, or oleaginous blandness. Some of the most successful are now forgotten even by historians. Prototypes were Baron Louis, an ex-priest turned financial expert, who served Napoleon, the Bourbons and Louis-Philippe; or Charles Duchâtel, in office for a total of ten years under the July Monarchy, minister of the interior from 1840 to 1848, who had 'an admirable understanding of business', noted Tocqueville, 'always ready to oblige when it was not against his interest; full of contempt and benevolence towards his colleagues'.[51] Under the Third Republic, which combined rapid changes of government with unprecedented institutional stability, ministers such as Ferry, Delcassé and Briand held office in a succession of governments, and those who had ideas were thus able to have an effect on long-term policy. The champion was Freycinet, Gambetta's assistant in 1870, head of five governments and a member of four others between 1877 and 1892, and a minister for the last time in 1916. When not holding office, this inner circle of *ministrables* often exerted as much or more influence as members or chairmen of key parliamentary committees.

The State administration also began to professionalize, but without greatly widening its social composition. High officials became more detached from the rest of society, and far more rarely went into politics after 1870. While politicians became more middle-class and provincial, their senior officials remained rather mandarin: especially in the prestigious *grands corps* (*inspection des finances, conseil d'état, cour des comptes*, etc.) they remained heavily Parisian in origin, with a high proportion (30–40 per cent in many departments) recruited from civil service families.[52] Except at times of major political rupture senior officials held their posts far longer than ministers, often for a generation: Franqueville, for example, director of the bridges, highways and railways department from 1855 to 1876 was said to have been the 'real minister of public works' for nearly a quarter of a century. This is

50. Malo (1932), p. 408.
51. Yvert (1990), p. 129.
52. For statistics see Charle (1987), passim.

doubtless a feature of parliamentary systems; but in France the difference was extreme under all regimes except the Empire. There certainly emerged a civil-service view of policy which officials could press on inexpert politicians. In the Foreign Ministry in the 1900s, for example, nationalist views instilled at *Sciences Po* caused young officials to make repeated, and often successful, attempts to influence policy, and even to sabotage actions of which they disapproved. The inner circle of ministers, leading deputies, senior officials and pressure groups – a few thousand men – made policy behind the scenes with little involvement of the electorate or even parliament.

Major changes in the governing group came rarely, but catastrophically. In 1815, the civil service was purged; in 1830, the victims had their revenge, and purged the purgers: 79 prefects, 246 magistrates, 81 generals and 19 ambassadors were sacked. The period 1848 (when all the prefects were sacked) to 1852 saw repeated arrivals and ejections. In 1870, the Bonapartist administrative and political personnel was liquidated: again, every prefect was sacked. In 1877–82, the republicans finally forced out monarchist politicians and officials: no minister who had held office before 1877 ever held it again; *conseillers d'état* were retired, all but two prefects were removed, and over 600 judges and 1,700 public prosecutors were sacked or resigned.[53] Thereafter, changes were less great. There was a partial purge in 1889 (during the Boulanger crisis), and a considerable change in ministerial personnel at the time of the Panama scandal in 1893. The upheaval of the Dreyfus affair (1894–99), bringing resignations, dismissals and the rapid growth of the radical party (in government from 1898), also meant a considerable change of personnel.

The history of the governing elite in this period can be summarized as a change from a monopoly of politics and administration by landowning *notables* (leavened by a few intellectuals in key positions), characterized by amateurism, partisanship and favouritism, to joint rule by professional officials and politicians. *Notable* rule proved vulnerable because it tended to become isolated from the country and caused dangerous resentments, not least among excluded *notables*. So in 1830 and 1848, few risked defending the falling regimes. Already, the governing elite was showing a detachment from political symbols, and claimed to be serving the State and France, not any particular regime: as one prefect wrote to the new government in February 1848, 'Released from my oath of allegiance, I come, as a good citizen, to pledge myself to the government of the Republic. The loyalty with which I constantly served the fallen dynasty proves my devotion to duty.'[54]

To have *'le sens de l'état'* was the highest professional virtue, and it also gave them a chance to hold on to their jobs, and help defend 'order', 'society' and property. This was the context of Thiers's appeal to accept the Republic in 1850 as 'the government that divides us least'. Thus, the fall of a regime did not cause a collapse of the State machine, which, purged of its most compromised elements, rallied to the new government and looked forward to

---

53. Machelon (1976), pp. 283–300; Charle (1980), pp. 236–9.
54. Charle (1980), p. 242.

accelerated promotion. The history of the Second Empire showed that an increasingly professional administrative class would rally to a regime promising order and efficiency, but not unconditionally: it restrained policies judged dangerous, and once again abandoned the regime as it fell. The Third Republic, an attempt to assert the superiority of society over the State through parliamentary rule, saw back-benchers representing the country far more closely than under previous regimes: a source of strength for a regime which, said Siegfried, represented the 'needs, inclinations and even the failings' of the French people.[55] But the political and policy-making processes, dominated by *ministrable* politicians and officials, remained opaque to outsiders and frequently ground to a halt. There were potential dangers in too great a social and cultural divergence between the mandarins (the State) and the politicians (the regime), as became clear from the 1880s onwards. Officials disliked cuts in their budgets, despised politicians' concessions to pressure groups and electoral special pleading, and often regarded their ministers as incompetent: after the First World War officials were tempted to dispense with the confusions and frustrations of parliamentary democracy, and after 1940 many of them seized the chance. De Gaulle, as in so many other areas, was able to create a lasting synthesis in the 1960s, this time between 'technocrats' and a presidential democracy that exercised power through an extraordinarily small professional politico-administrative elite and systematically downgraded parliamentary politics.

55. Anderson (1977), p. 80.

CHAPTER 6

THE GOVERNMENT OF MINDS

The great mystery of modern societies is the government of minds.

Guizot[1]

As was seen in Chapter 3, an obsession of French political culture was the need for unity: 'Without unity we perish. How can we not feel this?' insisted Michelet.[2] True and durable unity required a unity of belief and values, *l'ordre moral*: what Auguste Comte called the 'unity of a common doctrine'.[3] This seemed an essential part of ending the Revolution. Only the State could create such unity; indeed, it could not permit any other agency to do so. There was tension here with the liberal principles to which all regimes during this period, if in varying degrees, were committed. This tension distinguished France from its liberal neighbours, where the advance of liberalism during the century brought the dismantling of State regulation of belief and opinion, regarded as oppressive and archaic, as in religious qualification for public office and religious conformity in education. In France, on the contrary, the State tended to strengthen its role, a tendency associated not with archaism, but with progress. This has left durable traces, for example in State patronage and regulation of cultural life, which developed what has been called *'l'état culturel'*,[4] and the educational treatment of ethnic minorities, whether Breton in the nineteenth century or Muslim Arab in the late twentieth. Cultural convergence has always been the ideal.[5]

The instruments of State action here, as in other fields, had mostly been established by Napoleon. They covered the Churches, education, artistic and intellectual activity, and the press. Napoleon had set up standardized

1. Rosenvallon (1985), p. 223.
2. Girardet (1986), p. 142.
3. Ibid., pp. 142–3.
4. Fumaroli (1992).
5. The bitter 1990s dispute over whether Muslim girls should be permitted to wear veils at school is highly significant. Rosenvallon has suggested that control over education is the acid test of whether power has truly been decentralized in late-twentieth-century France.

organizations for recognized religions – dioceses and parishes; directories and consistories – under the supervision of the Worship Department (*direction des cultes*). The most important feature was the regulation of the Catholic Church under the Concordat of 1801 and the unilaterally imposed Organic Articles of 1802. These allowed freedom of worship, re-established the episcopal hierarchy, and paid for buildings and clerical stipends, but at the price of making the Church subordinate to the State, which chose the bishops. Napoleon and many of his successors considered the clergy to be quasi-functionaries owing obedience to their paymaster: the bishops 'purple prefects', the priests 'gendarmes in cassocks'.

The education system – the *Université*, created in 1806 by Napoleon – was also a branch of the central State, under ministerial control and with its senior teachers having civil service status. The role of its higher institutions – *lycées, facultés* and *grandes écoles* – was primarily to train for State service; curricula, examinations and diplomas (culminating in the *Doctorat d'Etat*) were controlled by the State. The development of primary education after 1830 always had the purpose of socializing and moralizing the masses. The national theatres, the fine arts school, the Salon (the annual art exhibition), and prizes and scholarships came under State control. The Institut de France (the combined academies) organized a wide range of scientific and philosophical activity, as well as attempting to regulate the language. The press was, of course, censored. These activities were far from being all negatively repressive: there were many juicy carrots – jobs, commissions, prizes – as well as sticks.

Fundamentally, this system continued until the 1880s, and much of it thereafter. But there were two great changes in the 1880s. First, the almost complete abolition of press controls in 1881, which, along with technical innovations and transport improvements, permitted after a vast increase in the circulation of cheap Parisian and regional newspapers, destroyed any monopoly on news and opinion. Second, the attempt to create a new source of ethics. A principal feature of the Napoleonic system was the use of religion as the moral underpinning of society, and the Church as the main instrument of moral control; but under the Third Republic the State began to substitute itself for the Church, and its own ideology – secular, nationalistic, liberal and democratic – for religion.

VARIATIONS ON THE NAPOLEONIC SYSTEM

State, Church and people, 1802–80

> Whoever believes in nothing is a danger to society.
>
> *Restoration deputy*

The Concordatory system remained until 1905:[6] all regimes until then

6. It still applies in Alsace-Lorraine.

considered the Church too valuable an ally, and too dangerous a rival, to loosen the ties. Even during the Bourbon Restoration, the closest to a love match between Church and State, there was never any intention of restoring the status and autonomy enjoyed by the Gallican Church under the Old Regime: liberal royalists restricted Church secondary schools and expelled the Jesuits. For all regimes until the Third Republic, the Church was the principal means of reaching and influencing the great mass of the rural population. The clergy, from the point of view of the State, were a moral police force, whose duty included preaching good order, morality and obedience to the laws. Even non-believers, like their hero Voltaire, saw the benefits: belief in the afterlife kept the poor honest and helped soldiers to die for their country. The Church was also, again for the mass of the population, a guarantee of the legitimacy of the State, and so each regime in turn – First Empire, Restoration, July Monarchy, Second Republic and Second Empire – insisted that the clergy should offer public prayers for the regime after Sunday mass, in formal recognition of its legitimacy, and State officials usually attended church on important occasions.

The Church had its own pastoral, moral and educational priorities that were never identical with those of even the friendliest regime. This meant that the Church as a whole – excepting some individual clergy and laity especially in certain parts of the country – were willing to rally sooner or later to every successive regime if they were allowed to proceed with their major tasks. The Church in many ways gained from such accommodation. It had been devastated by the Revolution, and still in 1814 its institutional framework – clergy, seminaries, schools, church buildings – was in ruins. With the money and opportunities provided by successive regimes, it regained and exceeded its previous numerical strength.

Missions (Protestant as well as Catholic) to reconvert the nation were held throughout the first half of the century, with impressive ceremonies, hellfire sermons and mass participation. Churches, whose insipid architecture still disfigures the urban and rural landscape, were thrown up, as were schools and seminaries. Some old monastic orders returned, and new religious congregations sprang up to do social work. Charities and pious confraternities organized the laity. With the support of the Bourbons, the less enthusiastic support of the July Monarchy, and with important State aid after 1850, the Church recruited clergy and built up a major school network.

In this uneasy but profitable partnership each party considered itself the senior. The Catholic revival, though facilitated by State support, built on a purely religious revival that had begun during the late eighteenth century, and was intensified by the turbulence and sufferings of the revolutionary period. A missionary campaign, which began under the Restoration but continued throughout the first half of the century, was intended to revive religious practice and ecclesiastical discipline. Zealous priests, many of them newly recruited in the early years of the Restoration, waged a stern campaign to stamp out 'immorality', which came increasingly to be seen as sexual: dancing was a clerical bugbear, for it was believed to lead to dangerous familiarity between girls and boys. They tried to purge traditional collective festivities, such as pilgrimages and patron saints' days, of their enjoyable aspects, such as drinking and (again) dancing. At the end of the century, bicycling for girls was similarly condemned. So was Sunday work, and lending money for interest. Unmarried working women inspired suspicion. Birth control became a major problem from the middle of the century. All this tended to strain relations between the clergy and their parishioners, especially the men. Priests would often publicly refuse the sacraments to offenders, which could have severe social consequences. Offended parishioners sometimes complained to the civil authorities, and judgement was given, significantly, by the Conseil d'Etat, the principal civil service tribunal. The Conseil always, until the 1880s, upheld the priests' authority in such disputes, however high-handed their actions. Although the State found wrangles over dancing and suchlike a nuisance and even a threat to public tranquillity, the moral authority of the priest was seen as too important to be undermined. When this changed from 1881 onwards, it was an unmistakable sign of the changed attitude of the State towards the Church and public morality.

However, the change had its roots a generation earlier, during the 1850s and 1860s when, as we saw in Chapter 3, there had developed a bitter political and intellectual conflict between Catholicism and the Left. Unpardonable for republicans was the Church's support for Louis-Napoleon Bonaparte. Bonaparte based his regime on managed popular support, which implied an alliance with the Church. This the Church was willing to give, for fear of a godless revolution, to ensure French support for the papal government in Rome, and simply, as usual, to go along with the prevailing tide. Bonaparte followed the principles of his uncle, whose Concordat was generally regarded as a political masterstroke in consolidating support from the mass of the peasantry. The *budget des cultes* rose from 39 to 48 million; clerical stipends were raised, new churches built, including vast soulless piles in Paris, and Catholic schools multiplied. But Napoleon's support for Italian independence in 1859 led to bitter attacks on the imperial government by the pope, echoed by some of the French clergy and the more militant members of the laity, often supporters of the Bourbons. The most popular and outspoken Catholic newspaper, Veuillot's *L'Univers*, once fulsome in its praise of the emperor, was banned in 1860. The alliance of Church and Empire was thus shaken, though not broken. The Church was unable to mobilize opinion: the mass of Catholic voters was indifferent to the fate of the pontifical regime, while the Left, of course, was utterly hostile to the papacy. The Church had nowhere else to go. To the Left in the generation after 1851, Catholicism was politically discredited as the apologist of reaction at home and abroad, and intellectually discredited as the pedlar of obscurantism and popular superstition. The younger generation of republicans regarded the Catholic Church as the most dangerous enemy of democracy and enlightenment. From the point of view of Catholics, republicanism again, as in the 1790s, meant godlessness and hostility to the Church.

Looking at the period between 1814 and 1880, a number of general comments can be made. As an institution the Church was growing ever stronger during the first three-quarters of the nineteenth century. In 1821 there was a priest for every 814 people; in 1848 one for 752, and in 1877 one for 657.[7] The numbers of baptisms and Easter communicants (a basic test of conformity) rose until about 1880, which marks probably the highest ever point of institutional religious participation. Moreover, the Church became a major provider of social services through dynamic new religious congregations, especially of women, engaged in teaching, nursing, foreign missions and other social work.

Yet as a political instrument the Church was less effective than its friends or enemies believed. Few of the clergy wanted to get deeply involved in politics; Catholics in all but a few regions did not regard the clergy as political guides anyway. Many resented clerical interference in politics, as in other aspects of everyday life. Most seem to have been indifferent to political issues concerning the Church. Even the imprisonment of Pope Pius VII by Napoleon in 1809 had caused little stir among ordinary Catholics, and the progressive abandonment of the cause of papal government in central Italy by his nephew Napoleon III caused similarly little reaction in the 1850s and 1860s. Even as a moral mentor the Church's influence was limited. Anathemas against dancing, festivals, Sunday work and birth control had little effect, except to deter many from attending church.

This paradoxical combination of strength as an institution and relative weakness as a political and moral guide is explained by the non-ethical and apolitical nature of popular religion: it was a ritual transaction with the supernatural to bring good fortune in this world and the next (see p. 245). The priest was the organizer of necessary rites and public ceremonies. Private conduct and politics were regarded by many Catholics as none of his business.

State, Church and school, 1806–c.1880

> The Fatherland alone has the right to educate its children.
>
> *Robespierre, 1794*

The respective roles of the State and the Church in education was one of the major recurrent controversies of the nineteenth century. Its importance is a consequence of the almost universal belief in the effectiveness of schooling in moulding children 'like wax', and permanently affecting their values and beliefs. Hence, whoever controlled the schools was thought to hold the key to the future, for good or ill. As noted above, the Napoleonic *Université* originally provided secondary and higher education aimed principally at training a small number of sons of the upper classes for State service. Primary education was neglected as of little significance. The ethos of the *Université* was 'Voltairian', that is secular, often anti-religious. During the Restoration,

7. Gibson (1989), pp. 67, 122–4.

controversy was caused by ultraroyalist attempts to bring the *Université* under the influence of the Church, and prevent State schools from being 'hotbeds of irreligion': Bishop Frayssinous was Grand Master of the *Université* from 1824 to 1828. This alarmed and angered much of the post-revolutionary elite, who did not wish their sons to be exposed to the reactionary Catholic influence that they themselves detested. Alternatively, the Church attempted, under both the Restoration and July Monarchy, to break the monopoly of the *Université* by taking boys not destined for the priesthood into its seminaries: in effect, establishing its own secondary schools. This too angered non-Catholics, because it seemed to be creating divisions within the future ruling class or even creating a Catholic ruling class that would be available to a counter-revolutionary regime. The danger was doubled if the teaching was provided by religious orders, worst of all the Jesuits, which were 'unauthorized' by the State and did not submit to State supervision.

Similar fears persisted throughout the century. Governments under the Restoration, the July Monarchy, the Empire and the Republic all limited or forbade teaching by unauthorized orders, and prevented major infringement of the *Université*'s monopoly. As Thiers put it in 1849, the State must 'strike youth in its own effigy' and 'prevent young Frenchmen [from being taught] to hate the government of their country'. However, the *Université* lost its monopoly of secondary education after the 1848 revolution, when Catholic liberals successfully demanded 'freedom of education'. Under the Third Republic, the suggestion that all future officials or military officers should be required to attend State schools was never adopted. However, except for a few years under the royalist and Catholic governments of the mid-1870s, the Church was never permitted to open universities, and Catholic 'institutes' could not confer degrees, which remained the monopoly of the State. Similarly, the *Université* controlled school diplomas, principally the *baccalauréat* (giving access to higher education), and so determined the curriculum even in private schools.

Primary education was a quite different matter. Only in 1833, with the Loi Guizot, did the State begin to establish a publicly regulated system, requiring every *commune* to set up a school. Guizot, the minister of public instruction, believed that 'universal instruction is henceforth the guarantee of social order and stability'.[8] Unlike the secondary system, this did not require conformity with the post-revolutionary 'Voltairian' values of the State, because the pupils of the primary schools were not destined for positions of authority. Indeed, the primary system of mass education (including *écoles primaires supérieures* giving practical training to older children) remained completely separated from the secondary and higher systems for the elite until the 1930s, and this may partly explain the hierarchical character of the French system today. The primary school was intended to moralize the masses, not provide them with an intellectual or practical education that was considered inappropriate: 'faith must be their only philosophy'. This was best left to the Church, as part of the

8. Giolitto (1983), vol. 1, p. 10.

moral police duties of the clergy, who often regarded schoolteaching as a part-time activity of their sexton. At least until the 1850s, resources and standards, especially in the rural areas, were abysmal. But in an economically static society, this seemed of little importance, and was even thought prudent: 'the child who has been to school too often does not want afterwards to follow the plough'.[9]

The sudden creation of a mass electorate in 1848 altered the terms of the debate. The primary schools now became the means by which the future electorate would learn its political values, and the 43,000 primary school teachers – *instituteurs* – became the State's own channel for communicating with the electors in every *commune*. The new Republic's minister of public instruction, Hippolyte Carnot, prepared for the 1848 elections a 'manual of civic instruction' – a republican catechism, said critics – which primary school teachers were to read and explain to the local electors. He also proposed to introduce free and compulsory primary education which would 'make the whole of France as republican in heart and mind as it is today in its institutions'. This was the first step towards the creation of the image, exaggerated in most cases, of schoolteachers as enthusiastic missionaries of republicanism and socialism among the gullible peasantry: the 'black hussars' of the Republic, as they were later to be called. The teachers rivalled the clergy – 'veritable anti-curés', one conservative called them – as the only body of comparable size in touch with the mass of the population.

Conservatives, who won control of parliament in 1849 but were alarmed by the growing popularity of the Left, passed on 15 March 1850 one of the most revealing and important measures of the century, the Loi Falloux, named after the Catholic minister who introduced it. Primary education was limited to the three Rs, and placed under the control of the clergy: 'the masses need imposed truths . . . that good philosophy that teaches man that he is here to suffer'. The *instituteurs* – 'thirty-seven thousand socialists and communists . . . each reading aloud in a café . . . the nasty little newspaper to which he subscribes' – were purged and brought under prefectoral control. Moreover, local authorities were permitted to hand their primary schools over entirely to the Church to be run by religious congregations, but with the costs paid by the State. Mass education and religion were to be a bulwark of the established order. The other element of the law was a compromise between Catholics and 'Voltairians' over secondary education. The Church was given freedom to establish secondary schools that could present candidates for the *baccalauréat*, and so could keep the sons of the Catholic elite in a Catholic atmosphere. However, State secondary and higher education, the domain of the *Université*, remained free of Church control: 'the middle classes of society, which desire as a right free philosophical discussion, would revolt against imposed doctrines'.[10]

9. Thiers, in Bury and Tombs (1986), pp. 121–2.
10. Quotations from debates of education commission, Chenesseau (1937), pp. 30, 33, 153–4.

The Falloux Law was a peace treaty between Catholic and non-Catholic conservatives willing to sink their differences in the face of the threat of democracy and socialism. It made it starkly plain that Church schools had become a political tool of conservatism. This finally ended the brief honeymoon that Catholicism had enjoyed with the new Republic immediately after the February Revolution. The law permitted the expansion of Church-run schools, both independent and publicly funded, which increased resentment on the part of lay *instituteurs*, who were brought under clerical control or, in thousands of cases, lost their jobs. The anticlerical and left-wing sympathies of the teaching profession which conservatives feared were actually aggravated or created by the law. The friction between the Church and Napoleon III over the Roman question led to steps being taken to limit the extension of Church schools. The emperor appointed the historian Victor Duruy, son of a worker, a militant secularist, as minister of public instruction in 1863, and he proved to be one of the great holders of that office. He revived the pre-Falloux secular tradition of the *Université*, modernized the curriculum, widened free primary education and required *communes* to open separate schools for girls. Catholic alarm turned to outrage when he introduced public secondary courses for girls in 1867. Girls' education had hitherto been largely a Catholic monopoly; Duruy's call to remove it from the hands of 'people who are from a different age and a different country'[11] seemed the thin end of a wedge that could shatter one of the Church's most solid pillars. In an age of male secularism and anticlericalism the religious sensibility of women was seen as a last bastion of Christianity and the best way of passing Christian values to future generations. Duruy's measures were a sign of things to come. But first came a short reprieve, when in 1875 the Catholic royalist majority in the National Assembly went beyond the Falloux Law by allowing the Church to set up universities. By the mid-1870s, the peak of Catholic educational extension, some 24 per cent of all primary-school boys and 30 of secondary, and 57 per cent of primary-school girls and over 70 of secondary, attended schools staffed by religious orders. It was a short-lived victory.

THE STATE AGAINST THE CHURCH, 1880–1905

> When you need to appeal to the energy of men educated by [religious] teachers . . . when you speak to them of their civic duties . . . of devotion to the Fatherland, you encounter a softened, debilitated human type, resigned to every misfortune as if to decrees of Providence.
>
> *Gambetta, 1871*[12]

For the first time since the 1790s, instead of paying at least lip-service to Catholic ethical and spiritual values as the foundation of morality in society,

11. Yvert (1990), p. 253.
12. Rémond (1985), p. 188.

representatives of the republican State condemned them for undermining the
ethical standards of a modern democratic nation. The schools question turned
into a French *kulturkampf.* Republican activists held beliefs – deist, liberal
Protestant or positivist – that were hostile to Catholicism, and sometimes to
Christianity. Gambetta's minister of public instruction, Paul Bert, a doctor,
contrasted 'superstition' with 'science': the latter led men to work and
progress, while the former made them 'lie prostrate and pray'.[13] All their
educational aims – the promotion of scientific rationalism, of national unity,
of progressive political attitudes, of a new rational morality, of individual
self-reliance – they saw as blocked or undermined by Catholic education,
which, they believed, made children superstitious, submissive, hypocritical
and unpatriotic. National unity was destroyed by the existence of separate
Catholic schools and universities. Moreover, the clergy were less concerned
with enforcing the use of French in non-French-speaking regions, always a
major issue for republicans. Girls, overwhelmingly educated by nuns, were
not being trained as fit helpmeets for the new breed of free-thinking
republican citizens, and progressive-minded mothers for their children.

A republican religion

The Republic set out to replace the Church's authority with its own. In the
words of Ferdinand Buisson, a liberal Protestant, future Nobel Peace Prize
winner and chairman of the Ligue de l'Enseignement, the biggest republican
pressure group, this should take the form of 'a secular religion of moral
idealism, without dogmas, without miracles, without priests'.[14] The State
machinery turned against the Church. From the 1880s onwards, complaints
against the clergy were invariably upheld by the Conseil d'Etat. In strongly
anticlerical regions, some republican local authorities, rather than attending
religious services and insisting on the priests' praying for the Republic (as had
happened in 1848), began to harass and disrupt traditional public ceremonies.
Priests were prosecuted for vagrancy when they took collections, for
obstruction if they conducted processions through the streets or for causing a
public nuisance when they rang church bells. 'Civil funerals' became a rallying
symbol, a ceremonial affirmation of the rejection of religion: as high officers
of the Legion of Honour had the right to a military escort at their funerals, the
government, unwillingly before 1880, very willingly afterwards, had to
associate the State with this gesture. At a humbler level, freethinkers' societies
(*sociétés de libre pensée*) were set up to organize ceremonial civil funerals for
their members; they also expanded their activities to holding sausage-eating
feasts on Good Friday, when Catholics fasted, and jeering at religious
processions. To unmask schoolteachers who were secret Catholics, in 1905 some
teachers' conferences were held on a Friday with a compulsory meat dinner.[15]

13. Ibid., p. 191.
14. Chevallier (1982), p. 108.
15. Prost (1968), p. 210.

Collective festivities had centred round saints' days, and though the merrymaking involved had annoyed many priests, at least a nominal religious connection had remained, often with attendance at mass as the opening act of the festival. The Church thereby remained an important part of community life. Previous regimes had used this tradition – for example in celebrating the sovereign's feast day, even the unlikely 'St Napoleon' – to assert their legitimacy. But the Republic set out not to use but to replace the Church. This occasionally meant taking over a popular religious festival: in Cordes in the 1880s, the anticlerical mayor organized a traditional pilgrimage banned by the bishop as 'superstitious', and it took place behind the tricolour flag amid shouts of 'Vive la République!'[16] More radical, however, was to replace religious festivals with a republican one – again, somewhat reminiscent of the 1790s. In 1880, after much discussion, 14 July, the day of the fall of the Bastille and the 1790 Fête de la Fédération, became the fête nationale. It was not accepted immediately, especially in Catholic regions, but the government and local authorities made efforts to attract popular participation with dancing (the curés' bête noire), fireworks and above all a military parade. In Paris, this was always a grand affair. The soldiers, the flag and the music were the big attraction: jingoistic patriotism was at the heart of the new republican religion, as one music-hall song expressed it in 1886: 'Sans hésiter nous voulions tous fêter / Voir et complimenter l'armée française!' One of the rare prosecutions of a novelist during these years, Lucien Descaves for Sous-Offs (1889), was for 'insulting the army'. Prosecutions for 'insulting religion', on the other hand, ceased.

The Republic created other quasi-religious symbols. The Pantheon, the temple of Great Men, was taken from the Church to enshrine the Republic's secular saints. In 1885, Victor Hugo was 'Pantheonized' after an immense public funeral: 'They are throwing out God to make room for M. Hugo'.[17] He was followed in 1889, centenary of the Revolution, by three heroes of the revolutionary wars and a victim of the 1851 coup d'état. Statues to great ancestors of the Republic, or its more recent servants, were mass produced for an orgy of what Maurice Agulhon has called 'statuemania', providing objects of veneration in thousands of towns and villages. Official artists decorated the public rooms of hundreds of new mairies, where secular marriages were solemnized, with edifying allegories of liberty and justice and scenes from the Republic's history.

After 1880, the State looked with disapproval on religious practice, at least for men. The careers of civil servants, especially in sensitive departments, and soldiers were not unlikely to suffer if they, or even their families, were practising Catholics or if their sons attended Catholic schools.[18] In this climate, conventional conformity fell.

16. Faury (1980), p. 439.
17. L'Univers, in Nora (1984–93), vol. 1. p. 495.
18. This issue has now been studied thoroughly by Larkin (1995).

The battle of the schools and disestablishment

> Never shall we accept that the education of the people should be a private industry.
>
> *Jules Ferry*[19]

Significant though all this was, by far the most controversial instrument in the battle for minds was the school. While it had been, as we have seen, a major issue under every regime since the Revolution, it now attained unprecedented political importance. The republicans had just secured power, yet were aware of the continuing strength of their enemies: education was part of a struggle for the soul of France, and its votes. Jules Ferry, one of the leading republicans of the 1870s and 1880s, a positivist and a freemason, with a perceptiveness similar to those of his great predecessors Guizot and Duruy, took the usually minor portfolio of public instruction in four governments between 1879 and 1883. 'We shall have on our side', he wrote in 1882, 'all these new generations, these countless young reserves of republican democracy, trained in the school of science and reason, and who will oppose to the retrograde spirit an impassable obstacle of free minds and emancipated consciences.'[20] Moreover, France had experienced a devastating defeat, which it was commonplace to describe as 'the victory of the German schoolmaster', supposed to have instilled not only technical competence, but patriotism and self-reliance. Finally, republicans also saw improved education as the way to bring about economic advance and social improvement, and forestall the dangers of socialism.

There were two specific characteristics of French republican thinking on education that distinguished them from other parties and countries. First, Statism: education was not a private enterprise, but a State service aiming to 'penetrate every heart and every spirit . . . to the very marrow of their bones', as Bert put it. Second, its anticlericalism, a far more important issue than any purely educational consideration, such as modernizing the curriculum or teaching methods, or social goals, such as the widening of opportunities. Although schooling was such a major ideological issue, France spent no more of her GNP on schools than Britain, and markedly less than Germany; the proportion of children attending school and the literacy rate was slightly lower than in Britain and considerably lower than in Germany.[21]

Beginning in 1879 with the establishment of training colleges for lay women teachers, republican policy continued over the next four years with the exclusion of the clergy from central and local educational bodies, the abolition of Catholic universities, the institution of a system of girls' secondary education, the institution of a free, obligatory and secular primary system in which religious teaching was forbidden, and finally the progressive secularization of the teaching body itself, eliminating nuns and brothers from

19. Chevallier (1982), p. 277.
20. Meyeur (1973), p. 113.
21. Hamerow (1983), p. 166.

State schools. Church schools, however, were remarkably successful in holding their ground. They managed to survive the abolition of fees, the expulsion of the teaching orders from State schools, and the closure of private schools run by religious orders. Although over 1,800 schools had been closed down by 1911, only a minority of their pupils went to State schools. Most went to lay-directed Catholic private schools, which in some strongly Catholic regions had by 1920 more pupils than the State system.[22]

However single-minded, Ferry was also prudent. If not a pluralist, he was certainly a liberal who rejected persecution, and he was also a practical politician who knew that many of his constituents went on pilgrimages. Even within the State system, teachers were instructed not to offend the consciences of parents. In many theoretically secularized schools in strongly Catholic regions, teachers continued to give illegal religious instruction and even take their pupils to mass. Nevertheless, there were some serious conflicts in Catholic regions, especially over the introduction of 'godless' textbooks. Parents boycotted State schools, and turbulent priests had their stipends docked.

Even though it was waged with restraint, this was genuinely a struggle for the soul of France between two institutions with paradoxically similar goals, similar methods but quite different ideologies. State and Church schools followed parallel rather than opposite paths. Both stressed order, obedience, hard work and duty. Both were intensely patriotic – in State schools, 'patriotic ideology underpinned and held together all their teaching'[23] – but their patriotism had a different content and different heroes. State schools stressed the revolutionary heritage of political and material progress in which France led the world. Church schools taught an older saga of Clovis and St Louis, of a kingdom founded by divine providence to protect the Church. The Catholic view was expressed in textbooks such as *Petit-Jean*, repeatedly re-edited and updated from 1846 to 1930, and the republican in the immensely successful *Tour de France de Deux Enfants* (1884 and often re-edited). Both taught history and ethics through the adventures of two young orphans; and although there were overlaps (such as Joan of Arc, a heroine for both) the ideological message was very different. In *Petit-Jean*, patriotism was religious and conservative. In *Tour de France*, it was secular and moderately progressive, and was intended to replace Catholicism with what Bert called 'the religion of the Fatherland'.

The Church, aware from the 1890s onwards that it had no choice but to accept the *fait accompli* of the Republic, tended to retreat into what has been called a 'Catholic counter-society'. Although, encouraged by Pope Leo XIII, all but a die-hard minority recognized the Republic, the Church tried to organize the lives of its flock in such a way as to preserve them from anti-Catholic influences, while strengthening the Church as a social and even political force. Catholicism retreated to its regional heartlands – the west, southern

22. Statistics in Larkin (1974), p. 100; Cholvy and Hillaire (1985), vol. 2, p. 122.
23. Maingueneau (1979), p. 101.

Massif Central, rural north and east – and elsewhere to its residual social core: women and children. Church primary and secondary schools were the foundation of the counter-society. The rival school systems became the focus of two rival sociabilities. They organized different celebrations: 14 July versus the local saint's day. They formed rival sports clubs, boy-scout movements and choirs. They got into fights, as in Louis Pergaud's famous novel *La Guerre des Boutons* (1912), in which boys organize elaborate provocations (such as putting old clothes on a church statue) and reprisals. There were familiar and often old-established spiritual and charitable confraternities, which the clergy increasingly brought under its own control, rather than leaving leadership in the hands of lay members. Then there were new kinds of societies, including Catholic trade unions and very successful sports federations.

Political representation proved more problematic. Leo XIII urged acceptance of the Republic – the *ralliement* – in 1893 (see p. 456), and some Catholic politicians hoped vainly to set up a powerful Catholic party like the German Centre Party. But as in the past, being a Catholic did not necessarily imply political obedience, and church-goers included several shades of opinion from royalist to socialist. However, Catholics who cooperated with non-Catholics, especially if they stressed democracy or class conflict, were strongly discouraged by the hierarchy: the Christian democrat group Le Sillon was condemned by Pius X in 1910, and *'abbés démocrates'* who were elected to parliament, such as Abbé Lemire, met strong opposition from their superiors.

Moderate republicans resisted the demands of the extreme Left for a total break with the Church, however. The Concordat remained, with the Church financially supported by the State, which in return maintained a large degree of control over it: the consequences of setting the Church free seemed too dangerous. Diplomatic relations were kept with the Vatican, particularly useful when the pope favoured concessions. But this changed in the aftermath of the Dreyfus affair, which aroused extreme political passions in which the Church became deeply implicated (see p. 462). A fresh bout of conflict erupted between the Republic and the Church, regarded once again as a source of political and moral danger. This time the republicans, especially the radicals and the socialists, felt strong enough to scrap the Concordat. By this time, many republicans of all shades believed not only that the State had replaced the Church as the moral guardian of society, but also that, in consequence, if the Church was abandoned financially by the State it would quickly wither away.

The State and the intellectual

Throughout our period, what may loosely be called intellectuals were prominent in French public life. Probable reasons are not difficult to find. Already during the eighteenth century, the *philosophes* expressed criticism of the Church and the absolute monarchy, and many contemporaries believed that the Revolution was a consequence of this intellectual undermining of the Old Regime; indeed, revolutionary leaders claimed to be practising the principles of Rousseau. The power of ideas seemed clearly proved. The fall of the Republic and then of the Empire, far from ending the attempt to build a new society, made it seem essential, as we saw in Chapter 3, to create a new order, for which intellectuals eagerly proposed a vast range of blueprints. This was also the period of Romanticism, when 'genius' claimed moral and political authority: '*Lettrés*! [scholars] you are the living instruments, the visible leaders, of a redoubtable and free spiritual power'.[24] Finally revolutions, and in particular the 1830 revolution, brought forward professional politicians, many with intellectual qualifications, as we have seen. So, for example, while Britain produced a Disraeli, a unique and exotic literary species within that gentlemanly establishment, France was successively governed by the journalist Thiers, the historian Guizot and the poet Lamartine. Consequently, governments were much involved in intellectual and cultural life. Patronage and direct administrative control attempted to enrol artists in favourable image-making, or at least to prevent open attacks. As well as the press in all its forms, art exhibitions, theatres, opera houses, museums and lecture rooms were objects of official solicitude, or where necessary, sanctions. Many of the great political and intellectual names were at times in bruising conflict with the State, including Guizot, Cousin, Michelet, Quinet, Renan, Flaubert and Zola.

However, the term *les intellectuels*, popularized by Barrès (who used it in a derogatory sense), is particularly associated with the Dreyfus affair. Emile Zola's crucial intervention with his open letter *'J'accuse'* (13 January 1898) was an individual act; but what was new at this time, and provided a model and inspiration for later generations, was the collective and concerted action of many less prominent figures – writers, professors, scientists, doctors – through the press, petitions and organizations such as the (Dreyfusard) Ligue des Droits de l'Homme and the (anti-Dreyfusard) Ligue de la Patrie Française. Their actions did much to turn the Dreyfus 'case' into the Dreyfus 'affair', a great moral, ideological and political crusade. This emergence of *les intellectuels* as a distinct category has been explained as an attempt by an enlarged and more anonymous professional class to claim legitimacy, respect and political influence. The Third Republic, by freeing the press and expanding education, had enlarged the intellectual professions: their numbers had roughly doubled. But they were not particularly grateful. Journalism had become a desperately cut-throat business; academia, increasingly specialized and self-contained, and relatively meritocratic and democratic, was often disgusted with the compromises and corruptions of the 'bourgeois' Republic and its professional politicians. These intellectual professions were trying to widen their audience among the general public, and the Dreyfus affair was an opportunity to intervene in politics 'outside the official channels' and demonstrate their 'non-conformism' with the political establishment.[25]

24. Hugo to French Academy, 1841, in Bénichou (1988), p. 307.
25. Charle (1991), p. 271.

Even though divided by ideology and by conflict of interest (for example, between more junior and more established intellectuals, who tended to be Dreyfusard and anti-Dreyfusard respectively), they were all attempting to define a political agenda in terms of their own beliefs, interests and professional values, for example by stressing the centrality of ideas, culture, education and science, and, as Charle puts it, elaborating their own identities as right-wing or left-wing intellectuals. In that sense, the phenomenon of *les intellectuels* may be compared with the contemporary emergence of what has been identified in Britain as 'professional society', in which intellectuals and technical experts increasingly influenced the actions of the State.[26] The greater radicalism of French intellectuals which lasted through most of the twentieth century may be explained, Charle has suggested, by awareness of a gulf between their conviction of the importance of their 'vocation', inherited from the glorious ages of Voltaire or Hugo, and the prosaic reality of their 'real social status' as merely one section of the middle class.[27]

CONCLUSION: THE 'TWO FRANCES'?

> It is always the same men struggling with the same enemies. What our forefathers wanted we still want.
>
> *Clemenceau, 1891*[28]

> There are two Frances, and theirs is the bad one.
>
> *Bishop of Amiens, 1895*[29]

It became common to speak of 'two Frances', that of the Revolution, and that of its opponents, increasingly identified with Catholicism. Two ideologies, two political cultures, two traditions, two histories, two patriotisms. This polarization, however – in spite of Clemenceau's vision of the unchanging struggle – only became clear at the end of the century, when the disappearance of political alternatives (Orleanism, Bonapartism) left a secularist democratic republic face to face with the forces of Catholicism, and when the recurring conflict over schools seemed to encapsulate a political struggle for 'the soul of France'. It is only at this time that an unmistakable division between 'two Frances' takes shape on the map, as will be seen in later chapters, affecting both public and private life: religious loyalties coincide with political loyalties, and also (for example) with the level of the birth rate. The integrating effect of two school systems, of two rival networks of sociability, and of two powerful sources of propaganda (including mass-circulation newspapers) probably made more people than ever aware of which side of the great divide they were supposed to be standing on.

26. Perkin (1989).
27. Charle (1990), p. 64.
28. Amalvi (1987), pp. 17–39, at p. 27.
29. Ibid., p. 32.

However, we must not assume that everyday life conformed very strictly to the dictates of ideological purity, especially outside the more 'red' or 'white' areas. Schools, notes Heywood, were more successful at capturing the bodies than the minds of their pupils. Larkin has shown that even among career-conscious civil servants, political correctness was frequently fudged: some republican *fonctionnaires* sent their sons to Catholic schools in the hope of keeping them from 'bad habits'.[30] As we shall see in Part III, gender and class created other dividing lines and solidarities that complicated the picture of two Frances; while on the other hand, a growth of nationhood (however differently 'the nation' was interpreted) promoted a sense of common loyalty to the 'one and indivisible'.

30. Heywood (1988), p. 294; Larkin (1995), p. 76.

CHAPTER 7

THE STATE AND THE ECONOMY

Property: More sacred than religion.

Flaubert[1]

ECONOMIC AND SOCIAL CONSEQUENCES OF THE REVOLUTIONARY PERIOD

The Revolution's institutional changes had durable consequences for economic development. The intention of the legislators of the revolutionary and Napoleonic periods, influenced by Enlightenment ideas, had been to sweep away archaic relics of 'feudalism' and rationalize and liberate economic activity. This meant uniformity in law, markets, money, taxation and measurement; freedom to work and trade; and the recognition of property, on the Roman Law model, as an 'inviolable and sacred right', unencumbered by ancient regulations and communal customs. Corporations, collective action and restrictive trade practices were forbidden, and workers' combinations criminalized. These principles were formulated in the d'Allarde and Le Chapelier laws (1791), the Code Civil (or Code Napoléon) of 1804 and the Code de Commerce of 1807.

Because of these changes the Revolution has often been described as opening the way to free enterprise and capitalism. This is at best a half-truth. In the 1780s, France had been one of the two leading western economic powers; the turmoil of the revolutionary period caused a 'complete disorganization of economic activity' and a 'quasi-blockage' of growth for a generation.[2] Moreover, many limitations on economic activity remained, as they did in all countries, for example restricting the formation of companies, and preserving common rights to certain land uses. More importantly, the new laws favoured small property and landownership. They hardly considered capitalist enterprise, except to restrict company formation severely, which 'effectively limited most businesses to the scope of family

1. Flaubert (1991), p. 548.
2. Asselain (1984), vol. 1, p. 114.

firms'.[3] These restrictions were only removed by Napoleon III in 1867. The abolition of feudal land tenures and the sale of the *biens nationaux* (vast amounts of land confiscated from the Church and émigrés) added to the number of landowners, large and small. High inflation and economic disruption doubtless made real property seem the best and safest investment; it also made people wary of banks and paper money.

Those who had made large fortunes from trade, speculation and military contracts, such as the Foulds and the Periers, quickly put their cash into broad acres. So did prosperous bourgeois and peasants with savings. In the Nord department, for example, peasant ownership of land increased from 30 to 42 per cent of the total between 1789 and 1802.[4] Several million peasant families owned some land (though mostly too little to live on so that they had to rent other land or work part-time as labourers), and this proportion steadily grew. The persistent demand for land meant that its price tripled during these years. The provisions of the Code Civil on inheritance, which gave all children the right to a share, tended to hamper the growth of larger holdings. After 1815 the size of holdings fell as the number of owners increased by some 55 per cent: from something over 5 million to something over 8 million by the 1860s. In the 1880s there were 3.5 million mainly small *exploitations* (roughly, farms), three-quarters of them under ten hectares – a figure that remained fairly stable.[5] So France was more than any of its neighbours a society of medium and small farmers, many of whom owned the soil they tilled. The contrast even with Italy is striking, and far more with Britain:

Table 7.1: Employment in agriculture (*c.* 1900)
(% of agricultural labour force)

	employer or self-employed	wage earner
France	61.4	38.4
Italy	45.7	55.3
England & Wales	21.6	63.6

After Flora (1983), vol. 2, ch. 7

In short, the practical consequences of the Revolution had not been to create an expansive capitalist economy, but rather to have 'consolidated for a century and a half the system of small-scale peasant agriculture based on subsistence and the intensive use of family labour'.[6] The lower productivity of French compared with British agriculture was in itself sufficient to account for

3. Trebilcock (1981), p. 136.
4. Moulin (1988), p. 52.
5. Ibid., p. 77; Beltran and Griset (1988), pp. 64, 66. Price (1987), pp. 146–50, gives a more sceptical view of peasant landownership.
6. Moulin (1988), p. 65.

the entire difference in national income between the two countries, according to O'Brien and Keyder.[7]

The extent of landowning was a fundamental economic, social and political fact about France between the 1790s and the 1950s. Much has been written about the attitudes to which it is supposed to have given rise: avid attachment to land; determination to maintain independence; suspicion of modernization and industrial investment; preference for service-sector jobs, especially in the civil service, as a means to social mobility; and resentment of large-scale enterprises. Some of this is doubtless accurate, and provides often entertaining anecdotes. But whether we regard such attitudes as a determinant of economic behaviour, or as a consequence and rationalization of the objective economic opportunities that existed, the indisputable fact is that the unique pattern of ownership and the types of economic activity that emerged from the revolutionary period proved durable. In Claude Fohlen's opinion, it 'fixed society and the economy in such a way as to do the greatest damage to industrialization'.[8]

By 1815, the economy bore the marks of years of war. British blockade had severed the rich colonial and Mediterranean trade that had stimulated growth in the eighteenth century. The seaports and their manufacturing hinterland went into a lasting decline. Not until the 1840s did exports recover the levels of the 1780s.[9] France had been cut off from British technology, and by 1815 was outclassed in mechanized industry, particularly textiles. The impetus given to certain industries such as metals and clothing by the war had largely benefited territories that were no longer part of France: Belgium and the Rhineland. Besides, with the coming of peace, these industries faced a chilly climate of shrinking demand and severe international competition. Production of iron fell below the level of 1789. Agriculture too had suffered during the long period of disruption: production had increased by only 0.3 per cent per year, less than the growth in population, and productivity was probably lower than in the 1780s. Here too there was to be a 'long quasi-stagnation'.[10]

SURVIVAL AND ADAPTATION, 1815–1914: THE FRENCH MODEL

> Our habits are economical, prudent, perhaps timid . . . we like to grow moderately rich by small profits, small expenditures, and constant accumulation.
>
> *Victor Cousin*[11]

Economic evolution followed, perhaps inevitably, from these circumstances in a striking example of what Adam Smith might have seen as the operation of

7. O'Brien and Keyder (1978), p. 190.
8. Fohlen, in Cipolla (1973), vol. 4, p. 31.
9. Asselain (1984), vol. 1, p. 137.
10. Ibid., vol. 1, p. 124.
11. Sherman (1977), pp. 717–36 , at p. 733.

the hidden hand. In agriculture, industry and commerce in the generations after Waterloo, millions of French producers followed what I shall term the French model of economic growth that avoided the salient features of the British model, namely a revolution in agriculture, rapid fall in the rural population, corresponding urbanization, technological transformation of sectors of industry, large-scale production for export and growth of a mass domestic market. Comparison of the numbers employed in agriculture and manufacturing shows this strikingly. In Britain, the manufacturing labour force overtook the agricultural before 1840; in Germany and Belgium, around 1900; in France, in the 1950s.[12]

The French experience was until fairly recently disparaged by historians as 'retardation'; it is now more positively appraised as 'happy adaptation'.[13] This change is above all due to statistical research which shows that while *in total production* of basic commodities such as coal, iron and steel the French economy was outdistanced during the century not only by Britain, America and Germany but also in the 1900s by Russia, when measured *per capita* its performance in production, growth, and productivity is round the European average and compares favourably with the other early industrializer, Britain, in so far as such statistics are reliable. The slow *overall* growth of the economy was due therefore not to incapacity to produce wealth, but to unusually slow population growth. Moreover, revisionist analyses of British economic history question the extent of the 'industrial revolution', consider the British experience not as the standard pattern of economic development, but as 'idiosyncratic',[14] and stress its serious long-term flaws. Therefore, the traditional unfavourable comparison with Britain seems doubly questionable.

There were three unique characteristics of the French model. First, economic growth within a remarkably stable economic, social and technological framework: small-scale agriculture and manufacturing by relatively traditional and labour-intensive methods, carried out by a heterogenous and mobile workforce, in an overwhelmingly rural and small-town environment with very few large cities. Second, 'Malthusianism': birth control, a symptom of complex attitudes towards social and economic change (see p. 321). Long before those in any other country, French families began to limit the number of their children, and the population stagnated and in some years from the 1880s onwards even declined. As an economic factor the birth rate was probably neutral, neither helping nor hindering per capita growth, though of course it reduced the total quantity of production by limiting the number of producers and consumers even though an unusually large number of adult women and immigrants (France was Europe's great importer of people) provided labour. Third, the role of the State, without which French economic history is incomprehensible. Determination to maintain order and protect society against economic shocks was the

12. Mitchell (1978), pp. 51–61.
13. Asselain (1984), vol. 1, p. 146.
14. Crafts (1985), p. 165; for a critical history of the British record, see Lee (1986).

characteristic attitude of the post-revolutionary State, as far removed from the British evolution towards free trade as from the later Russian policy of promoting modernization at all costs.

In order to examine the operation of the French model, we shall look first at its patterns of growth in a chronological framework, and second at the role of the State; 'Malthusianism' in its social and cultural context will be discussed in Chapter 16.

The chronology and pattern of growth

The French economy went through five principal phases of growth during our period: 1815–40, irregular but sometimes fast; 1840–60, fast; 1860–82, slowing down; 1882–96, stagnation; 1896–1914, fast.[15] Within these periods, the highest overall growth rates occurred in the late 1830s, the late 1850s and the 1900s. The main turning points were 1860 and 1896, between which occurred a long period of slow growth, and so, for convenience, we shall consider the two long nineteenth-century periods before and after 1860.

Before 1860

As has been seen, the handicaps facing the economy in 1815 were largely due to the Revolution and war. Growth over the next 45 years was due first to the expansion of the traditional agricultural and industrial systems, and then after 1840 to huge investment in railways, a phenomenon common to the whole developing world. Annual industrial growth averaged 2.5 to 3.0 per cent, and growth in total national income 2.0 per cent.[16]

The agricultural sector, released from the constraints of war, underwent in these years its fastest period of growth until the transformation of the 1950s. The agricultural labour force increased; the amount of land under cultivation expanded to an all-time peak in 1860; the old system of fallow was replaced by more productive crop rotations. Production rose on average by 1.2 per cent per year.[17] This took place without any revolution in method and within the small-scale peasant farming system, although the most productive farms, in the north and the Paris region, were larger than average. The rural population continued to grow until it reached its highest ever total in the 1840s. Some 20 million people, nearly 60 per cent of the total labour force, remained dependent on agriculture. Whether it was held on the land by the attractions of land ownership or the lack of opportunity to earn a living elsewhere is a matter of debate. Either way, O'Brien and Keyder conclude that a major rural exodus would have been beyond the political or economic capacity of France.[18] Yet in staying put, much of the rural population needed supplementary sources of income to make ends meet. This income came

15. Crouzet (1974), pp. 167–79, at p. 171.
16. Beltran and Griset (1988), p. 12.
17. Asselain (1984), vol. 1, p. 139.
18. O'Brien and Keyder (1978), p. 195.

from rural industry (a wide range of activities from spinning flax to smelting iron); from traditional rights (common lands, forests, communal grazing); and from temporary migration, especially from poor, often highland, regions in the south-western half of the country (the famous stonemasons from the Creuse; the 'Bougnats', coal-merchants cum bar-keepers from Auvergne; chimney sweeps from Savoy; domestic servants from Brittany). All in all it was a remarkably durable if precarious system, marked by great regional disparities in living standards: for example, in large upland areas of central and southern France, chestnut porridge was the staple winter diet, due to the scarcity of bread.

Industry also rapidly increased output. Outpaced by Britain in the mass production of textiles, metals and machines, and lacking cheap domestic coal, French industry concentrated on areas where it had advantages. One was producing traditionally made consumer goods for local use: soap, candles, sugar, paper. The other – and this was a major characteristic of the French model – was hand-crafting luxury goods for export to the wealthy markets of Europe and America, above all Lyons silks (France's largest export item throughout our period) and the fashionable wares known as *articles de Paris* : furniture, clocks, jewellery, books, clothing. These goods accounted for roughly half French exports in mid-century. In producing them, entrepreneurs benefited from a skilled workforce paid less than in Britain, and a valuable reputation for fashion and quality. Plentiful rivers and forests meant that water-powered production remained widespread, as did charcoal smelting of iron in little water-driven forges producing a few tons a year. These obsolescent methods could be turned to good account: charcoal smelting gave expensive but purer steel until the 1860s, suitable, for example, for high-quality cutlery and surgical instruments. Hand-operated looms could make more ingenious patterns in silk. Thus, technological handicaps and high costs could be surmounted through high-value-added labour-intensive products. Units of production and firms remained small, with many self-employed workers in tiny workshops: economies of scale were irrelevant. The 1840s were 'decisive years',[19] a time of record industrial expansion, probably the highest of any period until the 1950s; and growth continued after the 1846–48 crisis, during the 1850s. Many signs of 'modernization' are detectable, with the growth of some large mechanized units (for example, in engineering, metallurgy and cotton) and improvements in banking, transport and education.

In France, unlike Britain, there was no move towards freer trade: on the contrary, tariffs and quota barriers were strengthened. According to liberal theory, protectionism must have slowed economic change: that, after all, was its purpose. In the case of railway building, France, unlike Germany, preferred to develop and use its own products rather than importing from Britain. This slowed down the process and delayed some of its benefits, but on the other hand built up domestic metallurgy and engineering industries.

19. Pinkney (1986).

Interruptions in the course of growth were caused partly by agricultural depressions, which reduced domestic demand, as in 1816–17, partly by international financial crises, such as 1825, or by a combination of both, as in 1847. They were aggravated and prolonged by political instability in 1830 and 1848–51: businesses postponed orders and investments. Nevertheless, measured in terms of output and production per head, the French model seemed to be working satisfactorily by 1860, when both industry and agriculture had enjoyed several years of unparalleled prosperity: though well behind Britain and Belgium in national income, France was comparable with Denmark and Germany, and well ahead of Italy.[20]

After 1860

Three decades of slow or stagnant growth, beginning in 1860 and worsening after 1880, pose the great problem of modern French economic history. Many contemporaries, and many historians subsequently, have blamed Napoleon III's experiment with trade liberalization begun by the 1860 Anglo-French commercial treaty, which eventually exposed France, and especially French agriculture, to low-cost imports with which no west European producer could compete: wheat prices fell by 45 per cent between 1860 and 1895.[21] On top of this came a series of disasters: cotton shortage due to the American civil war; the damaging war of 1870 and the loss of Alsace-Lorraine; post-war political upheaval; and finally the devastation of two major export products by silk-worm disease (*la pébrine*) and the vine-killing insect, phylloxera. Was it therefore Napoleon III's unwise abandonment of the French model, plus very bad luck, that caused the trouble? As Thiers had said, 'when you ruin the land, you ruin everyone'. Hence, was it the reintroduction of industrial tariffs in the 1870s and 1880s, then the Méline tariff on agricultural imports of 1892, raised in 1897 and 1910, that enabled a recovery of the whole economy, which a few years later was restored to vigorous health?

The chronology seems to fit. However, there is evidence that the problem was not only due to a mixture of free-trade dogma and bad luck, but to basic failures in the French model itself. Already in the 1860s, growth was causing strains in both agriculture and industry.[22] In the 1870s and 1880s, the agricultural sector was not only unable to compete with American and Russian grain, but it also proved slower than the British to adapt by specializing, for example in livestock, or to widening the range of its exports (which, as in manufacturing, concentrated on luxury goods, especially wines and spirits). As agriculture was relatively larger than in Britain, its problems had a correspondingly bigger impact on the economy as a whole. Industry too lost competitiveness. With a weak domestic market it had failed to invest in modern production techniques, and finally this took its toll: hundreds of outdated firms collapsed during the 1880s. The vital export of luxury goods

20. Statistics in Crafts (1985), p. 54.
21. Asselain (1984), vol. 1, p. 161.
22. Verley (1988), pp. 73–110.

was damaged by international recession, changes in fashion and foreign competition whose price advantages finally got the better of the relatively traditional French production methods. In newer products, such as machinery, France was almost absent from international markets and unable to provide for its domestic needs. With a few exceptions, its large-scale industry was weak. To sum up, in 1860 France accounted for 60 per cent of the Continent's exports; in 1913, 12.6 per cent.[23]

Fundamental to the whole performance of the economy were basic characteristics of the French model: low average productivity in both agriculture and industry, and hence low incomes and low consumption. Comparison with her competitors shows that in both areas she still lagged behind Britain, and was outpaced by Germany:

Table 7.2: Labour productivity in industry
(annual product per worker, in pounds sterling, 1905–13 value)

	1855–64	1885–94	1905–13
France	51.1	68.2	83.3
Britain	56.4	78.4	90.4
Germany	39.5	68.9	106.8

After Crafts (1985), p. 88

Table 7.3: Per capita national income
(in US dollars, 1970 value)

	1870	1890	1910
France	567	668	883
Britain	904	1,130	1,302
Germany	579	729	958

After Crafts (1985), p. 54

The luxury industries, however superb the craftsmanship of their workers, and however high the wages of an elite, were vulnerable to trade recessions, fashion changes and off-season slumps. The low level of technology in industry as a whole meant that when forced to cut costs or improve productivity employers could only cut wages or jobs. The contrast with highly mechanized industry is eloquent: Lancashire cotton workers were paid twice as much in the 1890s as those in the Vosges or Normandy, but unit labour costs were still 30 per cent lower. French wages were held down either by direct cuts, or through constant pressure on piecework rates, or by using semi-skilled labour and outworkers, usually women, at starvation wages: a

23. Caron (1979), p. 105.

skilled (male) craftsman making cars at Renault in 1910 earned as much in an hour as a woman seamstress could make in a day. Pressure on wages caused endless industrial conflict throughout the period. This frequently developed into grave political disturbance, and had a long-term effect in creating confrontational industrial relations and political radicalism. Moreover, low wages seriously hampered the development of a mass market. The purchasing power of a French worker in 1913 was not only much lower than a British or American worker, but was quite low on the western European scale.

Table 7.4: Industrial wages in 1913 based on purchasing power parity (Great Britain = 100)

USA	126–134
Britain	100
Sweden	82–92
Germany	68–75
Belgium	65–68
France	60–64
Italy	45–49

After Zamagni (1989), p. 119

Beginning in the late 1890s, there was a period of recovery and rapid growth marked by large investment in modern industries – 'a change of habit?', ask Lévy-Leboyer and Bourguignon – including aluminium, electrical goods, motor vehicles and even aircraft. However satisfactory the performance of the economy seems up to the 1920s, with the conquest of new and the reconquest of old markets, and the development of new industries, there were still persistent weaknesses: reliance on luxury exports, relative underinvestment, small-scale production, low wages and above all a large, uncompetitive and relatively low-income agricultural sector. This meant that many of the problems seen in the 1880s and even earlier would appear again in the 1930s.

The role of the State

The State played a crucial role in the development and survival of the French model. Yet it did not have an economic policy in the modern sense, by which governments accept as a prime responsibility the supervision and even management of economic activity, for this did not develop until after the Second World War. During the nineteenth century it was widely believed that the economy operated according to laws that could not be flouted; and that it was not the function of government to try to alter society or redistribute wealth. An important sign of these beliefs was that inflation, the greatest redistributor of wealth, was almost nil, with an unusually high proportion of the money supply in gold coin. On the other hand, only a minority of extreme liberals (usually academics) favoured dogmatic *laissez-faire* principles, with no role for the State. Consequently, the State's economic action was marked over the whole period by continuity, rather than innovation. It stemmed from a traditional conception of sovereign functions: grandeur, national defence, social order. In the words of the minister of the interior in 1830, 'The government's prime objective must be the constant, permanent maintenance of material order . . . in society. Material order may be disturbed by lack of jobs for the labouring population.' In this case, the solution was money for job creation; at other times it was the use of troops to suppress protests; or it was the provision of protective tariffs and subsidies. The objective, notes Rosenvallon, was the same.[24]

Overall, politicians and officials throughout the period (the most notable exceptions being Napoleon III and some of his advisors) had very mixed views concerning economic change. They envied and feared British and later German power and wealth, and felt obliged to emulate to some extent their industrial methods. But they had deep misgivings concerning the risks – social, economic, cultural, moral and political – involved in urbanization, industrialization and big business. The concept of 'industrial revolution' originated in France during the 1830s, and 'revolution' was an ominous concept. Their response was to maintain a high degree of supervision and control over economic activity, even though this resulted in hesitant, confused and even contradictory actions. They feared that uncontrolled enterprise would cause instability, leading to bankruptcy and unemployment: 'there is reason to fear that the suffering which the working class must go through will leave them open to evil influences'.[25] These fears were confirmed by the 1847 crisis, widely blamed on reckless growth, and also encouraged until the 1860s by a pessimistic analysis of British society and expectations of social revolution there. Yet State ambitions usually remained limited to encouraging self-help (such as savings banks), managing crises and protecting the French model against internal or external threats.

Social policies show no wish to change social structures, but to limit the damage caused by economic modernization. There was no fundamental change in thinking between the 1841 law on child labour, when the State asserted its right to protect children against both their employers and their parents, and the 1898 law on industrial accidents, when it asserted the right to intervene in contracts between consenting adults. Even the radicals' 1890s programme of solidarism was concerned with defending the individual not altering the system. When ministers did entertain occasional interventionist projects in the late nineteenth century, such as agricultural modernization, old age pensions, health or factory regulation, there was invariably a gap between ambitious ends and parsimonious financial means: in 1886 the public hygiene department did not possess a flush lavatory, and in 1892 there were only 92 factory inspectors for the whole country. Moreover, for practical

24. Rosenvallon (1990), p. 221.
25. Sherman (1977), p. 725.

and political reasons small farms and businesses had to be exempted from many charges and regulations, and they accounted for a large proportion of the whole economy.

Taxation was crucial to State action: significantly, it changed little from Napoleon I to the Second World War. Revenue came mainly from '*les quatre vieilles*' direct taxes (complicated levies based on land, rent, commerce, and doors and windows); from a range of no less complex duties (on alcohol, salt, legal transactions etc.); and from the tobacco monopoly. Income tax was delayed until 1917, and even then remained of secondary importance. The system, considers Gueslin, was designed for a nation of small landowners, businessmen and shopkeepers who were jealous of their rights and regarded the State as an enemy despite special tax concessions.[26] The secretive and the thrifty could avoid or evade much of the burden, which was partly assessed on 'external signs of wealth' such as carriages and servants; a recurring objection to income tax was that local bureaucrats and political rivals would learn the real financial position of families. In short, the political and economic weight of small farms and small businesses set narrow limits on State revenue. As much of the budget was spent on the army (23.4 per cent in 1913–14), the resources for economic and social policy were tiny: the ministry of industry and commerce received 1.7 per cent of the total.[27]

The principal form of State intervention, over which controversy continually raged, was protection against foreign imports through tariffs, quotas and prohibitions, which successive governments, with the single exception of Napoleon III in the 1860s, imposed in varying degrees throughout the period. In spite of criticisms by major exporting industries (particularly silk and wine) which favoured free trade, and by liberal theorists – the economist Bastiat suggested sarcastically that the State should require householders to keep their blinds closed to protect the rapeseed lamp-oil producers from unfair competition from sunshine – there was support for protection in principle from all political parties, much of agriculture and most of industry. The arguments remained practically unchanged throughout the period, and they had considerable force. Strategic considerations were prominent during a century when, as was seen in Chapter 2, France was, or seemed, perpetually in danger of war. It seemed folly to allow vital industries such as coal, iron or agriculture to dwindle because they could not compete with foreign imports. In wartime, that would place the country at the mercy of its enemies, the most dangerous of whom, Britain, could withhold coal and iron, and whose navy could cut off shipments of Russian wheat. Hence coal, of which France was chronically short, was made even scarcer and more expensive by import tariffs to protect home producers.

The domestic arguments for protection were equally weighty. The French economy was (this was the stock description) 'balanced': it included every form of agriculture and industry, unlike the British, which specialized in a

26. Gueslin (1992), p. 58.
27. Broder (1993), p. 187.

small range of mass-produced goods. Britain could sacrifice lesser interests for the sake of greater, even agriculture could be decimated as the price for free trade in textiles, whereas in France every sector was important. Free trade would 'smash [French prosperity] like a glass'. It was no good saying that France could sell more of her specialized exports, silk and wine, in return for exposing her cotton and woollen industries to British competition: 'Would you grow mulberry trees in Lille and Rouen? Would you make wine in Lille and Rouen?' And, again unlike Britain, the French economy was composed of millions of small producers who could not face international competition and yet whose interests could not be sacrificed. Whatever the theoretical advantages of free trade, it would create social tensions that France dared not contemplate. The precedent of the 1786 commercial treaty with Britain was ominous: 'there was a wretched population in the streets of Rouen, starving, rioting and cursing the authors of the 1786 treaty',[28] and three years later, revolution! These arguments from the 1850s appeared again in the 1860s, when Napoleon III aroused an outcry by his personal decision to conclude liberal trade treaties with Britain and other trading partners. They were equally familiar in the 1890s, when new agricultural tariffs were introduced, and still raise echoes in the 1990s.

Protection worked. Before the 1860 free-trade treaty, only 3 per cent of French imports were manufactured goods. The 1890s tariffs on agricultural products reduced imports by 31 per cent in ten years.[29] It cannot be doubted that protection maintained the prosperity, or at least the survival, of a large range of otherwise uncompetitive activities, as was its intention. It also led to retaliation against French exports, hence damaging the more competitive activities. But whatever the balance of costs and benefits, by the 1890s it was politically, socially and economically indispensable.

The State gave other forms of assistance to businesses under threat from market forces. Late in the century, one department was subsidizing canals to help them resist competition from rail, while another department was favouring rail; as late as the 1890s sailing ships were subsidized against steam; gas maintained its privileged position against electricity in lighting Paris; and the momentous groundwork was laid for subsidies to farmers through a separate Ministry of Agriculture set up in 1881 by Gambetta, a true administrative Frankenstein. After the First World War, one reason for limiting the introduction of tanks into the army was that the cavalry was an important consumer of hay; while the need to drain the wine lake was an important reason for continuing the often-criticized wine ration to soldiers.

Another traditional State activity was the development of roads (the pre-motorcar network was mainly completed by 1880), waterways (until the 1840s) and railways (between the 1830s and the 1880s). This was done by direct spending (the State paid about 3 billion francs, one-third of the total cost of railway construction), supervision of construction, subsidies and profit

---

28. Quotations from Thiers's famous protectionist speech of 27 June 1851.
29. Asselain (1984), vol. 1, p. 136; Broder (1993), p. 147.

guarantees to companies. Here, strategic, political and economic aims were mixed: to move troops between the northern frontiers and the Mediterranean ports, to strengthen the central power of Paris, to open up remote parts of the country through country roads and branch lines, to stimulate the internal market, to protect small business and agriculture by controlling fares, to protect existing economic interests, and not least to win votes. Consequently, the network had serious shortcomings, for example for carrying coal from the mines to industry.

Colonial expansion was always in part motivated by the desire to expand and protect overseas markets, and as in Britain it eventually became one of the principal ways by which the State influenced, for good and ill, the structure of the economy. Industries that were losing competitiveness in European markets were kept going for generations through protected trade with the colonies, while sinking gently into featherbedded stagnation and irredeemable obsolescence. By 1913, in open market conditions French exports outdistanced those of Britain and Germany only in Belgium and Haiti; but in her colonies she had 65 per cent of the market.[30] As in Britain, this made it possible to postpone necessary economic modernization, and made it all the more painful when it could be postponed no longer.

It was, however, through its activities in areas only indirectly connected with economic activity that the State had the most dramatic effect on the working lives of its subjects: war and the maintenance of order. If both were essential activities of all States, in France, emerging from a quarter of a century of revolution and war, they were issues of unparalleled sensitivity. Most States spent large sums of their subjects' money on military adventures that good liberals hoped had become obsolete. France was different in the frequency of major wars fought between 1792 and 1815, and then again between 1854 and 1871. These took place at crucial moments for economic development, and, no less important, ended with devastating defeats. The first period set the French economy back a generation. The second caused an outflow of capital during the 1860s which contributed to the slowdown after the remarkable economic growth of the 1850s; and then the defeat of 1870–71 resulted in vast expenditure, a huge indemnity to Germany, a tripling of the national debt, and the loss of one of the country's most modern industrial regions, Alsace-Lorraine. This did much to turn a slowdown into prolonged stagnation. The disproportionate military effort made by France from 1870 onwards, in the expectation of another war with Germany, must have had damaging effects on investment and the labour force. In addition there were the direct costs of colonial expansion.

The 1870 war and the indemnity (5 billion francs, equal to two and a half years' State budget) increased taxation and government borrowing, thus making money for industrial investment scarce and expensive. The problem was compounded by a well-meaning but ill-conceived public works programme, the Freycinet plan, begun in 1879, mainly to increase roads and

30. Caron (1979), p. 110; see also Marseille (1984).

railways. It was intended as an economic stimulus and a vote winner: it proved to be too expensive, was abandoned (causing more bankruptcies in the engineering sector), and left a heavy burden in public debt and uneconomic railway lines. Public spending reached the highest level of the century, and total public debt reached an equivalent of 125 per cent of annual gross domestic product[31] – two and a half times its level in the 1990s. In consequence, interest rates remained high, discouraging business investment, argue Lévy-Leboyer and Bourguignon. Moroever, State borrowing absorbed a high proportion of available savings. Investors had their existing taste for safe fixed-interest bonds with tax-breaks rather than company shares confirmed, and even preferred (with government encouragement, publicity and tax concessions) to shovel money into Russian State loans, where much of it was spent on German imports and all was lost in 1917. The inevitable result of this was a high level of taxation. The French central government spent 13.3 per cent of the national product in 1913, compared with the British 7.1 and the German 6.2 per cent.[32] All in all, it was a record of avoidable self-mutilation matched only by Russia.

In the policing of economic activity and the maintenance of social order the State left a deep imprint. The legislators of the Revolution, by the d'Allarde law (1791) and Le Chapelier law (1791), forbade as anti-social all corporations, monopolies, restrictive practices and combinations of citizens, including both employers and workers. In practice, employers were brought within the umbrella of the State through its official chambers of commerce and various consultative councils. Workers were a different matter. Those owning no property and working for wages, the 'proletariat' (as they were called from the 1830s onwards), were a worrying and undesired phenomenon, seen as hard to control but easy to excite, lacking that proper attribute of citizenship, a material stake in society. There were many signs of this mistrust of workers, which may have been another aspect of the mistrust of industrialization mentioned above. They were required to carry *livrets* (identity documents cum work records), a much resented requirement which, although often ignored, remained in theory until 1890. Only employers were allowed until 1849 to elect the *conseils des prudhommes*, instituted by Napoleon I to resolve industrial disputes. In legal disputes over wages with employers, courts were required until 1864 to accept the employers' testimony. All workers' organizations were punishable under the penal code until Napoleon III decided to 'tolerate' them in 1864; only in 1884 were trade unions fully legalized. Governments habitually feared that workers' protests were being fomented by political enemies: fear of revolution was never absent from their calculations. The July Monarchy's harsh repression of the silkworkers' protests in Lyons in 1831 and 1834 was motivated partly by the belief that legitimists or Bonapartists were instigating the unrest to undermine the regime. The Second Empire feared republicans or socialists. The Third

31. Lévy-Leboyer and Bourguigon (1990), pp. 88–9.
32. Trebilcock (1981), p. 159.

Republic feared socialists, anarchists and later communists. These fears were self-fulfilling, for the politicization of economic protest was usually a consequence of the State's response, which was a mixture of repression and attempted mediation. As will be seen in Chapter 15, this was a major cause of class consciousness.

From a rational economic viewpoint, a disorganized and alienated workforce was in no one's interest. The difficulties faced in the 1890s and 1900s by French firms trying to modernize methods in these confrontational circumstances were great. The political consequences, and their repercussions on the economic system, were far worse. As has been seen, the 'French model' was vulnerable to slump. A militant and alienated industrial workforce, faced with falling incomes and unemployment, was a constant political danger, as the 1830s, 1848 and 1871 most dramatically showed. This political instability worsened economic crises by destroying confidence, so that an economic slump that might last for months elsewhere lasted for years in France, as in 1846–52, and did long-term damage to economic growth, as well as to the lives of French people.

The key to State policy was its concern to maintain order at home and power abroad. Protectionism was adopted because the prospect of a huge economic, social and political backlash against free trade persuaded most politicians that (in Guizot's words in 1845) 'every sensible government must adopt it'. Above economic liberty and the free rights of property, the State consistently aimed at protecting the social order by cushioning it against economic shocks; it favoured established interests, large and small, against change, risk and disorder. Napoleon III was the notable exception, as in so much else, and he followed his own agenda, which made him the most popular and the most detested of rulers. It included free trade, visionary economics and war (below Chapter 20).

CONCLUSIONS: BENEFITS AND COSTS OF THE FRENCH MODEL

> Our industry fights the continent's industry by throwing in hardship after hardship, just as Napoleon under the empire fought Europe by throwing in regiment after regiment.
>
> *Balzac*[33]

The French produced roughly the same amount of wealth per capita for themselves as their neighbours did during our period. But they did so by different, and in some ways less traumatic, means. They defended and to a considerable extent preserved peasant farms, a large rural population, small firms and traditional production of high-quality labour-intensive goods. Allowing for changed circumstances, these features of the French model are

33. Chevalier (1958), p. 454.

as clear at the end of the century as at the beginning: for example, in the
1900s, nearly 40 per cent of the French industrial labour force was
self-employed, compared with 16 per cent in Germany and 9 per cent in
England.[34] Though by the early 1900s, cars and aeroplanes had partly
replaced Lyons silks and Paris fashion goods as leading export successes,
they were in a sense themselves a new line in *articles de Paris*, expensive
luxuries crafted for a small wealthy clientele: mass production methods made
little progress and were bitterly resisted by workers. Even after the vast
transformations of the 'thirty glorious years' after 1945, important traces of the
French model still remain, for example the importance of agriculture, food
processing and luxury goods. It is the impressive performance of the modern
economy that makes the pessimistic diagnoses of incorrigible 'retardation'
commonly made by historians in the 1950s seem misplaced. It is certainly
arguable from the perspective of the 1990s that the French economy 'aged
better' than that of the other industrial pioneer, Britain.[35] So is 'happy
adaptation' the verdict?

Most people in France preferred and indeed insisted on a defensive
response to change, marked by tariffs, regulation, subsidies, and birth control.
In other countries, people would certainly have done likewise, had they had
a choice: the fates of Irish or Italian emigrants, landless German labourers
forced into Silesian mines, and English handloom weavers made redundant
by the miracle of steam were not ones that they welcomed. The French more
often did have a choice. Owning a plot of land, however modest, was an
incentive and a means for small farmers, artisans, industrial workers and
traders to resist economic change. Their numbers meant that governments
worrying about elections (especially after the introduction of manhood
suffrage in 1848), public order and even revolution, dared not ignore
demands for protection of *les intérêts acquis* (vested interests).

But this 'happy adaptation' was not without its economic costs, social
penalties and political dangers. The persistence of a large peasant agricultural
sector meant that much of the population consumed comparatively little from
the market, both through poverty and the self-sufficiency of subsistence
family farming supplemented by barter. Until around 1870, notes Weber,
'many peasants bought only iron and salt, paid for all else in kind and were
paid the same way, husbanded their money for taxes or hoarded it to acquire
more land'.[36] Peasant farmers, though vulnerable to natural disasters and
economic cycles, were tenacious; they tightened their belts and tried to hold
on. Consequently, a mass market for manufactured goods was slow to
develop as a motor of economic growth. The industrial sector remained
characterized by many small firms, a concentration on luxury exports (hence
a 'precarious' trade balance[37]), little innovation in production methods even

34. Flora *et al.* (1983), vol. 2, ch. 7.
35. Asselain (1984), vol. 1, p. 201.
36. Weber (1977), p. 35.
37. Caron (1979), p. 115.

in new products such as cars, and inattention to changes in the market.[38] Average wages were low. In many important areas (such as machinery, shipbuilding, machine tools, locomotives) French industry was weak or even non-existent.

For all these reasons, the French model was prone to serious and prolonged depression. The rural economy, seriously overmanned in the 1840s, was ravaged by bad weather and crop disease in 1846. The industrial economy showed itself to be equally vulnerable to the side effects of this crisis, which caused a collapse in demand, financial chaos and mass unemployment. Another very long depression marked the third quarter of the century, as neither industry nor agriculture could adapt easily to innovation or face competition in foreign and domestic markets. Essentially similar problems re-emerged in the depression of the 1930s, which began the demise of the classic French model. In Crouzet's view, this was the inevitable 'dead end'.[39]

Even though they preferred it, we might wonder with hindsight whether the long grinding struggle for economic survival by generations of artisans and peasants – Balzac's 'hardship after hardship' – led to more disappointment than satisfaction, and simply delayed change until a later generation. But this is really another way of asking whether French peasants were happier than English factory workers: an unanswerable question. Perhaps the only objective test of overall economic well-being is life expectancy. In 1914 that of France was well below advanced agricultural societies such as Scandinavia or Ireland, and had also been overtaken by industrial England (whose babies died less frequently and whose adults could expect to live some two years longer on average by 1914) and was soon to be overtaken by Germany.[40]

There is a final cost that risks being overlooked in a purely economic and social discussion: industrial and demographic weakness meant a visible decline of international power. A wish to buttress her position was not irrelevant to decisions that led France into war in 1870 and, indirectly, in 1914, though one might think that on her earlier record a mightier France might have been no more likely to avoid war. In 1940 the result is unambiguous: France had become incapable of resisting Germany economically, and therefore militarily, and in consequence politically and perhaps psychologically. This catastrophe marked the end of the old France in many different ways, and not least the end of her traditional economic model.

38. Laux (1976), pp. 201–3.
39. Crouzet (1990), p. 378.
40. Flora et al. (1983), vol. 2, p. 92; Hamerow (1983), p. 81; Mitchell (1978), pp. 39–43.

CHAPTER 8

POWER AND THE DISEMPOWERED

That majority of the inhabitants of France composed of women, children, paupers, criminals and the insane had in common dependency on the decisions of others for the regulation of their lives. In looking together at the parallel histories of this diverse category in its relations with the holders of power, it will be possible to see how certain ideological, socio-economic and political developments taking place in all western societies were affected by specifically French preoccupations and conditions, and how, therefore, the experiences of French people differed from those of others.

WOMEN

What is man's vocation? It is to be a good citizen. And woman's? To be a good wife and a good mother.

Jules Simon, 1892[1]

Throughout the developing world during the nineteenth century, similar changes were taking place in ideas about women and their role, in the realities of their lives, and in their claim to certain rights and responsibilities. Socio-economic changes were international, and were realized to be so. Events in other countries, whether in legal reforms, in organization or in ideas, were studied. The vehement assertion of a 'domestic ideology', which exalted the female role as mother, educator and chaste domestic angel, while reiterating the undesirability and inappropriateness of her acting outside her own 'separate sphere', was dominant in all western societies and all classes.

The development of an urban and industrial economy led far more women to work outside the domestic-based round of farmyard, spinning-wheel and kitchen, often in the most modern industries such as textiles, or in the growing tertiary sector ranging from skivvying, via retailing, to teaching and medicine. There were demands for improved education for girls, whether in preparation for work or for domesticity. Yet economic growth also made it

1. McMillan (1981), p. 12.

possible, as male incomes rose, for more women to accept the idealized unpaid domestic role that denoted respectability. In politics, broadly defined, the fading during the first three-quarters of the century of traditional forms of spontaneous popular protest and the growth of formal organizations tended to exclude women. On the other hand, the acceptance that women's 'separate sphere' included moral causes and philanthropy led to the emergence of 'women's issues' and women's organizations. Though sharing in these general developments, the experience of French women had unique characteristics. We shall return to this in other chapters, especially those concerning identities. This chapter is concerned particularly with the State, the law, work and politics.

The post-revolutionary concern with creating moral order placed particular importance on the educative role of the mother. All parties saw women as crucial in moulding the beliefs of future generations. How women were educated and by whom, their relations with their husbands, and their ability to fulfil their domestic vocation were seen as matters of immense importance to society: hence the strongly expressed desire to see women remain within their 'natural' sphere. 'Woman worker: blasphemous phrase', exclaimed Michelet. This attitude influenced the actions of men in positions of power, who finally controlled the status and opportunities of women at work, in marriage, in education and in politics.

In contrast with the rhetoric, however, a uniquely high proportion of French women compared with other countries, especially older and married women, had paid jobs. Round the turn of the century 32 per cent of manufacturing workers (an all-time record) and 38 per cent of workers in the service sector were women.[2] This was because of the chronic shortage of labour in France generally, and of the economic importance of the textile and clothing industries, large employers of women. The French model of economic growth also meant the continuance of a multitude of small family farms on which millions of women continued a traditional type of agricultural activity, concentrating on conventionally defined women's work centred on the house, farmyard and vegetable garden. Views vary on whether this provided a degree of independence and dignity or whether it meant in practice low status and exploitation within the family.[3] Away from the farm, the large number of small businesses also involved many thousands of women: in 1900 over 160,000 kept shops.[4] Hundreds of thousands were involved in part-time craft manufacture. The slow decline of rural domestic industries such as spinning, knitting and weaving undermined the family economy, especially after 1880: daughters were among the first to take the strain by leaving for domestic service and other work in towns. Another aspect of this socio-economic system was one of the most unusual features of French women's lives, which has already been referred to and which we shall return to in Chapter 16: their uniquely low rate of childbirth.

2. Stearns (1975), p. 27; Dupâquier and Kessler (1992), p. 75.
3. Segalen (1983) takes an optimistic view; Weber (1977) far less so.
4. Crossick and Haupt (1984), p. 110.

As French women were so important in a range of economic activity, we might expect them to have been in advance of women in other countries in their political and trade union activity. But, on the contrary, in the most obvious symbol of equality, the vote, French women were a generation behind the rest of Europe, only being enfranchised in 1944. Indeed, so weak was the suffrage movement before 1914 that a prominent American suffragist compared it with Persia, Cuba, Turkey and the Philippines.[5] This disparity between economic and political status is the principle paradox that we have to explain.

Work, education and marriage: conditions and attitudes

Why did women's importance in the workforce not lead to greater social and political equality? The answer lies in the type of work they did, the attitudes of employers and male workers, and the education deemed appropriate for them.

A minority of women workers (reaching 24 per cent in 1906[6]) were employed in mills and factories: however grim the conditions, these were the most secure and best paid jobs, but they aroused particular alarm among the advocates of *la femme au foyer*, who considered work outside the home a grave moral and social danger. It was not only or mainly that the work was dangerous or debilitating, but that it was thought to favour promiscuity and moral disorder: 'a woman, once become a worker, is no longer a woman'. Especially in the south, convent-like workshops supervised by nuns were set up to safeguard the purity of young unmarried girls working to earn a dowry: in 1900 up to 100,000 worked in them under religious discipline.[7] Strict factory dormitories for girls were also common. From mid-century living conditions improved in these model establishments: flea-powder was supplied for bedding and sheets were changed as often as every two months.[8] In general, women factory workers were subject to far stricter discipline than men.

Far more typical of women's work in France, and regarded as more appropriate, was piecework at home (36 per cent of workers in 1906) or in the small workshops of the luxury trades. These formed one of the pillars of the economy, but as has been seen were marked by intensive use of cheap labour: female sweat was the lubricant for France's export successes. Conditions, hours and wages were often appalling and impossible to regulate even if the will had been there. But it was not. Male employers and workers considered that women were not family breadwinners and so they were systematically paid at rates that could not support them. This of course suited employers, but also meant that male workers wished to exclude cheap female

5. Hause and Kenney (1984), p. 20.
6. Rebérioux, in Aron (1980), p. 62.
7. Heywood (1988), p. 123.
8. Ibid., p. 305.

labour from 'male' occupations, and so throughout our period there was strong male resistance in many industries to accepting women as workmates. In 1872, the average female industrial salary was only 43 per cent of that of men, and in 1911 almost unchanged at 47 per cent.[9] Yet, for example, only half of Parisian seamstresses in 1900 were in fact married, the rest being spinsters, widows or abandoned wives, sometimes with dependent children. Lower pay than men with similar productive skills condemned them to exhausting overwork, ill health, poverty, or financial dependence on men in marriage, *concubinage* (cohabitation) or prostitution. This is the sense of the misogynistic socialist Proudhon's notorious pronouncement that women's real choice was to be a housewife or a harlot. Many were forced to be both, for some forms of *concubinage* were similar to prostitution. 'The socio-demographic characteristics of *concubines* and prostitutes are practically identical': most commonly they were recent migrants working in the clothing trades.[10] If abandoned by their men, they were often pushed fully into prostitution, the only high-earning female occupation. 'Women's occupations' inevitably had a glut of labour. An important feminist theme was therefore to broaden the scope of work considered 'appropriate', and to improve education and training, though still within the general bounds – accepted after all by most women – of women's 'sphere', which meant principally teaching, light industry and services.

It was, however, through the Church that a rapidly growing number of French women were able to pursue an expanding range of unequalled opportunities for challenging, creative and relatively autonomous careers. Female religious orders grew throughout the century: in 1815 there were about 15,000 nuns; by 1878, over 130,000. This expansion came entirely in social work, for which some 400 new women's religious orders were established.[11] They engaged in teaching, hospital and home nursing, foreign missions, and running prisons, orphanages, factory workshops and hospices. Relatively little is known about the details of this activity, but it clearly gave many dynamic women wider responsibilities than anywhere else in French society. The most celebrated was the formidable Sister Rosalie (d. 1856), who set up and ran a network of social services in the poorest district of Paris in mid-century 'with a charismatic power and a single-minded devotion that made her a legend'.[12] However, in marked contrast to the role of the Churches in Protestant countries, which led lay women to carry their moral and philanthropic concerns into political campaigning, Catholic religious orders placed a vast range of women's activity under ultimate male authority, and removed these professional women from the public political arena.

Girls' education was long regarded as of secondary importance. By 1847,

9. Rebérioux, in Aron (1980), pp. 65, 77.
10. Fine, in Dupâquier *et al.* (1988), p. 444.
11. Mills, in Tallet and Atkin (1991), p. 43. I am using the term 'nun' for all female religious, and 'order' for all regular congregations.
12. Gibson (1989), p. 126.

2 million boys but only 1.25 million girls attended primary schools, and girls' literacy always lagged; roughly speaking, they were a generation behind. Only from 1867 were *communes* required to set up separate girls' primary schools, though as the teaching was different (several hours' sewing per week for girls) the reform was two-edged. Duruy's experiment with public lectures for girls in the 1860s outraged Catholics, as has been seen. State secondary education was not systematically extended to girls until the Camille Sée law of 1880: a bold and shocking step, intended, wrote one conservative newspaper, to dispense a 'vain and superficial science in the place of divine precepts'.[13] But courses remained feminine – no Greek, Latin or philosophy, but morality, needlework and music – and they did not lead to the *baccalauréat*, the road to higher education. Money was always short, even though women teachers were of course paid less. As always, the availability of money is the real test of political wills and priorities.

If it did not crucially matter to men in authority how well or how much girls were taught, it mattered very much who taught them. 'By whom are our daughters and our wives educated?' asked Michelet. 'By our enemies.'[14] The Falloux Law of 1850 increased the role of the Church in education, and this was most strongly manifested in teaching girls. By the 1860s, 54 per cent of girls but only 22 per cent of boys attended schools run by religious orders.[15] There was a clear double standard: many middle-of-the-road parents did not wish their sons to receive a religious education, but were happy for their daughters to do so – it fitted with the Romantic idealization of femininity as pure, credulous and irrational. On the other hand, patriarchal anticlericals fretted about the subversive influence exercised by prurient confessors on their women: 'A humiliating thing, to obtain nothing of what was once yours except under authorization and by indulgence, to be observed, followed in the most intimate of intimacies by an invisible witness who regulates you and allots you your share'.[16] Education would liberate women from the priests and put them under the proper control of their husbands and fathers, as adequate wives and mothers for progressive, rational citizens. They would then be not an instrument of reaction, but of progress: 'He who holds the woman holds all', as Ferry put it neatly.[17]

Left and Right, therefore, shared this limited view of the aim of women's education: primarily to make good wives and mothers. 'We want above all to keep women faithful to their husbands', wrote one pundit in 1864, 'so we hope that the girls will bring to the world an angelic provision of ignorance that will be immune to all temptations'.[18] The near duopoly enjoyed by State and Church largely crowded out private initiatives to take girls' education further, as in the many private schools and colleges of the United States or

13. Szramkiewicz and Bouineau (1989), p. 511.
14. Rémond (1985), p. 69.
15. Rendall (1985), p. 148.
16. Michelet, in Cubitt (1993), p. 239.
17. Auspitz (1982), p. 43.
18. Zeldin (1973), vol. 1, p. 355.

even Britain. Though there were no insurmountable legal barriers, it required dauntless individual determination to transgress the conventional limits, such as that of Julie Daubié, a primary school teacher who put herself in for the *baccalauréat* in 1861 and took a degree in 1871: the first woman to do so. The first woman doctor qualified in 1875; the first women lawyers in 1892 (and male students rioted). But social constraints remained: by 1914 there were only 4,254 women at university, at least half from abroad, compared with 37,783 men; only about 70 women graduated annually.[19]

Most women's career was marriage, which a dominant consensus proclaimed to be their natural and sufficient destiny. Unmarried women, except nuns, especially if economically independent, were regarded with suspicion. Midwives and lay schoolmistresses, for example, met considerable petty persecution from priests in the early part of the century, and later, unmarried women teachers were required to lead a nun-like existence. Subordination to the husband was consecrated by the Code Napoléon: 'The husband owes protection to his wife, the wife owes obedience to her husband'. He alone exercised 'paternal power' over children and common property, though the law carefully protected the dowry, part of the contract with the wife's family. Dowries were usual until the later part of the century, and for army officers were required by military regulations.

Among the propertyless, especially in towns, formal marriage was often not entered into: 'free unions' were common, partly due to cost, but this could leave the woman very vulnerable. Love and desire were not ignored by the law, but it did not necessarily connect them with marriage: rather, the social institution of marriage had to be protected from the disruptive ravages of (illicit) sex. The law forbade action to identify the father of an illegitimate child: bastardy was the woman's fault, and must not be allowed to threaten the family or status of the father. The lesson was underlined by the ineligibility of unmarried mothers to receive public assistance until 1869. The Code Napoléon regarded male adultery as reprehensible only if the mistress was installed in the marital household, though a wife's adultery was punishable by prison (the husband could have her released at his discretion); indeed the Penal Code regarded as excusable the killing of a wife discovered *in flagrante delicto*. All this gave errant and vindictive husbands a good deal of scope. Still in the 1880s, even men who mistreated and abandoned their wives could have them imprisoned if they lived with another man. The radical politician Clemenceau, who had lived apart from his American wife for years, sent the police to arrest her when he learnt that she was having an affair, and had her deported. The lunatic asylum was a not uncommon fate of women regarded by their families as delinquent: committal was easy to obtain. Perhaps not surprisingly, when divorce, abolished by the Restoration in 1816, was reintroduced by the Third Republic in 1884, it was used more by women than men.

19. Hause and Kenney (1984), p. 24; see also Zeldin (1973), vol. 1, p. 344.

Politics

The political history of French women shows equally marked specificity. Traditionally, as in other countries, they had been prominent in direct action when family or community issues, particularly food supply or prices, accommodation, collective rights and the defence of the 'moral economy' were concerned. Such actions were common in the first half of the century, with serious disturbances over food supply in 1816–17, 1828, 1831, 1839–40 and 1847–48, and endemic troubles over communal forest and pasture rights. It was usually women who started direct action, which took certain characteristic forms: it aimed to provide food at a 'just price', the women rarely used weapons but rather their bare hands, and often to cause ridicule rather than injury, for example by tearing clothes.[20] It was women too who sometimes received harsh prison sentences. Women were often leaders in resistance to machinery in the 1830s and 1840s, especially when it threatened domestic industry. As long as workplace and home remained close together, and especially when a whole neighbourhood or community was affected by an economic crisis or industrial dispute, women remained prominently involved; arguably, this kind of involvement produced the most determined and sometimes violent resistance. Rent and debt to shopkeepers remained prominent issues for urban women: they were the most common cause of trouble with the law in Belleville at the end of the century. During the revolutions of 1848 and 1871 (when the problem of rent arrears was very serious) women demonstrated, for example with *charivaris* of saucepan-banging, or threatened violence against landlords who demanded rent or tried to evict tenants or take possession of their personal property. But overall women tended to be marginalized over the century. Food supply became more regular (there were food disturbances only in 1868 and 1897). Work and home grew more separate as many old craft industries declined in the 1880s and 1890s. Politics became more organized and formal, revolving round elections, parties, and trade unions – all predominantly masculine.

Nineteenth-century feminism began during the 1830s and 1840s as an aspect of socialist plans to create communities to supersede the family. Several sects had high ambitions for women; the Saint-Simonians fantasized about the coming of a female Messiah. Hundreds of women attended socialist meetings, and there was a newspaper, *La Tribune des Femmes*. The rather tragic figure of Flora Tristan, semi-aristocratic wandering intellectual, has come to seem typical of this period. She was convinced of her Messianic mission but, rarely taken seriously, she saw her experience as representative of women as outsiders. During the 1848 revolution, women's political clubs and workers' societies were set up, such as the Société Fraternelle des Ouvrières Unies, founded by the socialist Jeanne Derouin, a textile worker turned schoolteacher. A few women's delegates sat on the Luxembourg Commission to study social questions. But with the breakdown of the Second

---

20. Perrot, in Dufrancatel *et al.* (1979), pp. 134–5.

Republic this activity, and especially association with socialist groups, proved to be a dead end. After the June 1848 uprising, women's societies were dissolved on grounds of public order (they attracted constant male heckling) and women were forbidden to speak at meetings or petition parliament. Derouin and another socialist Pauline Rolland were arrested and imprisoned. The authoritarian Empire of the 1850s silenced feminist voices, associated with dangerous radicalism, at a time when in the United States and Britain women were playing a leading part in the immense moral and political issue of slavery.

The Paris Commune gave a number of radical women the freedom to pursue educational experiments and hold political meetings. Several fairly prominent left-wing feminists, notably André Léo, Paule Minck and Louise Michel, took an active part. At grass-roots level, the Commune was a traditional revolt of 'the people' (as opposed to a movement organized round male-run parties or labour organizations) and women were able to make their voices heard: literally, as speakers in clubs, and through a political society, the Union des Femmes pour la Défense de Paris et les Soins aux Blessés. But for male Communards there was no question of political equality, and women sympathizers were almost invariably cast in the conventional role of nurses and auxiliaries. Conservatives reacted to any hint of female revolutionary activity with extravagant contempt and horror, as was seen in Chapter 1. Several women were court-martialled and imprisoned for participation in the insurrection, including Louise Michel, who for a generation afterwards remained the heroine of the revolutionary Left.

The feminist mainstream had quite different roots and associations. From the 1860s, a new generation of republican feminists appeared, associated with Protestantism, freemasonry and the republican campaign against the Second Empire. Out of this arose a new wave of feminism, and in 1871 the Association pour le Droit des Femmes was founded by Maria Deraismes and Léon Richer. In 1882 Richer founded the Ligue Française pour le Droit des Femmes, with Victor Hugo as president, whose sympathy for women was genuine if, especially in old age, combined with an astonishing amount of what would now be termed sexual harassment. Yet these activists were not only feminists: they were militant republicans and anticlericals, often closely linked by friendship or family to the republican establishment. Consequently, the republican political struggle took priority. The republican electorate contained a mass of provincial middle-class and peasant men – not the most progressive element. Republicans idealized patriotic 'fraternity', which stressed the male character of citizenship linked with military service. Their arch-enemy was Catholicism, and this provided an unanswerable argument for refusing citizenship to women. Richer, the pioneer male feminist, thought that it would be dangerous for the time being to give French women the vote: 'They are in great majority reactionaries and clericals. If they voted today [1888] the Republic would not last six months.'[21] This objection – embodied in the blocking power of the Senate – denied women the vote for another 60 years.

21. McMillan (1981), p. 84.

Republican feminists believed that progress could best be made by cooperating with the republican State. Various reforms were secured to give married women a somewhat more adult status: in 1881 and 1885 they were given the right to open savings accounts and draw out money without their husbands' consent; in 1893, legally separated wives regained their legal independence and divorced women were able to use their own names; in 1907 married women were allowed the use of their own earnings. Less successful was the determined and courageous campaign waged against regulated prostitution in the 1870s and 1880s, modelled on similar efforts in Britain. Male radicals for a time supported it as a stick with which to beat the Paris Prefecture of Police. But most republicans were not interested in the issue.

Hubertine Auclert broke away from Richer and Déraismes in 1876 in order to campaign for the vote. She was willing to use Anglo-Saxon suffragette tactics, but had few followers. The outstanding figure among left-wing feminists round the turn of the century was Madeleine Pelletier. The daughter of small Paris shopkeepers, one of the first women doctors, a freemason and left-wing socialist, she admired the English suffragettes and stressed the importance of political as well as legal and social equality. She also flouted conventional views on sex and the family, advocating rights to contraception and abortion, and despised conventional feminity and wore male clothes. Her practical influence, however, was small; and most French feminists found the tactics of British suffragettes shockingly extreme.

The mainstream of the movement remained moderate. In 1897 a serious feminist newspaper, *La Fronde*, was set up by Marguerite Durand, wife of the prominent radical and later nationalist politician Laguerre. Before 1914, there were several large federations of womens' organizations of various political hues. The Conseil National des Femmes Françaises (1909), presided over by Sarah Monod, member of a prominent republican family, had about 100,000 affiliates belonging to 123 societies. The Union Française pour le Suffrage des Femmes (1909) attempted to create a unified movement, symbolized by having as its two vice-presidents the extreme-right-wing Duchesse d'Uzès and a female trade unionist. By 1914 it had 65 affiliated groups and 12,000 members. Both had strong establishment links. Many of their activities were connected with a wide range of often Protestant philanthropy, including suppression of regulated prostitution and temperance. They saw these causes as more important than the vote, not unlike English women's groups some 50 years earlier. The Catholic women's movement remained firmly hostile to women's suffrage, in spite of the Left's fear that it would benefit the Right. Some of the largest women's organizations were Catholic and conservative, such as the Fédération Jeanne d'Arc (about 350,000 members in the 1900s) and the Ligue Patriotique des Françaises (about 320,000). They were concerned with 'the rechristianization of France, not the emancipation of women'.[22] In short, McMillan suggests that the mainstream women's

22. Hause and Kenney (1984), p. 63.

movement in France was 'very largely a "purity crusade" '.[23] This was demonstrated by the campaign for the suffrage just before the First World War: whereas 250,000 marched to demand votes for women in London in 1908, the biggest French suffrage demonstration before the war, in July 1914, brought out only 5–6,000 people.[24]

Women who saw a more hopeful future in socialism were disappointed. As long as the largest socialist party of the late nineteenth century, the Marxist POF, was itself politically marginal, largely concerned with community politics in the textile regions of the north, it was sympathetic to women's claims. Once it began to concentrate on elections, it lost interest. In spite of their numbers in the industrial labour force, women were only 3 per cent of party membership, and two-thirds of these were wives of male members. The leading left-wing feminist Madeleine Pelletier complained that 'only the woman who comes along with her husband, her father or her brother is welcomed without objections, but against the admission of a woman coming on her own impediments are always found'. Sometimes a written demand by a male member of her family was required before a woman was allowed to speak.[25] Women socialists were reminded that the priority was the class struggle, and anything that distracted from this – namely feminism – was, as the Marxist leader Guesde put it, 'an encumbrance'. Only after the future revolution could women's problems be resolved. Most socialist women seem to have accepted this, refusing to cooperate with republican and conservative women, and even denying that there was a gender issue as well as a class issue. The Groupe des Femmes Socialistes de la Seine (1913), for example, did not feature sex discrimination in its programme.

The labour movement took a similar view to the Marxists, but added to it an ingrained reluctance to accept that women, especially married women, were or should be truly workers. The powerful Lyons printing union not only refused Emma Couriau's application to join, they also expelled her husband for not making her give up her job; officially until 1910 and in practice until 1919, the main printers' union refused women members. Such an attitude combined a long-standing fear of cheap female labour, a striving among skilled workers for domestic respectability, and the ambition to raise men's wages high enough to support a whole family. This had been reiterated generations earlier by the most influential and representative of French socialists, Proudhon, for whom socialism had come 'to restore the household' by returning women to 'the tranquillity of the domestic hearth'.[26]

Three principal characteristics emerge from this survey of the relations of women with holders of power inside and outside the State. First, an obsession – seen in so many other aspects of post-revolutionary France – with maintaining or creating 'order'. This required a patriarchal family

23. McMillan (1981), p. 89.
24. Hause and Kenney (1984), p. 20.
25. McMillan (1981), p. 87; Perrot, in Dufrancatel et al. (1979), p. 151.
26. Rendall (1985), p. 235.

structure and the subordination of women, who were regarded as instrumental in maintaining and civilizing the family and educating future generations. It involved both an idealization of the wife and mother, and a violent and panicky rejection of women who seemed to infringe the ideal. Most women and men of all parties and classes accepted the primarily domestic role of women within the social order.

Second, the extent and importance of women's work did not confer corresponding new powers or rights. Their most responsible work was almost entirely absorbed by the Church through female religious orders, or the State through the school system. In either case professional women were subordinated to male-dominated hierarchies, both of which agreed on denying women's suitability for social or political equality. In Daubié's words, 'the encroachment of the cloister and the usurpation of men' were obstacles to the development of a large feminist movement. For women manual workers, the hostility or indifference of organized male labour, and the fragmented and badly paid occupations prominent in the French model of economic growth, were handicaps not only to the development of feminism, but also to the attainment of a decent life.

Third and probably most important was the difficulty that women found in getting a hearing for their own interests and concerns amid the clamour of the 'Franco-French war'. The rhythms of male politics dominated: the brief victory of 1848, the authoritarian hiatus of the 1850s, the republican struggles of the 1880s, 'class war' in the 1890s and the Church question in the 1900s. Women had to, and most wanted to, take part in the struggles between Right and Left, Catholicism and anticlericalism, nation and class; consequently there could be no single united women's movement, but on the contrary, there was a huge range of antagonistic women's organizations. The kind of consensus campaigning on moral and social issues such as slavery or drink from which feminism emerged in America and Britain was impossible in France. Also, although every party from extreme Right to extreme Left by the 1900s contained both pro- and anti-feminists, the issue was crowded out by other political concerns. Consequently, the two major feminist campaigns of the late nineteenth century, against regulated prostitution and for the vote, both ended in failure. The prostitution campaign ran into the sands of legislative indifference. A bill to give women the vote in local elections was under consideration in 1914, but was interrupted by the war. After the war, the Senate was to veto suffrage bills in the name of republican defence. Not until after the Second World War, when the old battles and forces of the Third Republic had faded, did women manage to win the vote.

CHILDREN

Affect a lyrical tenderness towards them – when there are people present.

Flaubert[27]

Children, like women, formed part of an idealized vision of a patriarchal, preferably rural, family in a 'new domestic ideology'.[28] Although this ideal had tenuous contact with reality, what seemed to be a departure from it – the employment of children (like that of women) in urban industry – aroused fears for the future of society and the well-being of the nation. The State was therefore brought to intervene to protect children, which it did with limited success.

. Children in pre-industrial societies, like women, had always worked, except for a privileged minority. They continued to do so in agriculture, domestic rural industry and factories. Industrialization in fact reduced the amount of labour they performed, as more children attended school and more women became full-time housewives able to care for them; but it intensified and concentrated their work, and made it more visible. Traditional work was regarded by nearly all commentators through a nostalgic haze: 'Almost naked, without clogs . . . he keeps an eye on a cow or a few geese, he lives in the open air, he plays. The agricultural work . . . only serves to strengthen him . . . in the gentle surroundings of his family.'[29] Factory work was seen not only as unhealthy and stultifying, which of course it usually was, but as corrupting, exposing the innocent child (or woman) to the temptations of money, drink and sex. The conservative philanthropist Louis Villermé described mill children off duty: 'Loud conversations, bursts of laughter, raucous singing, shouting, the clink of glasses, the banging of fists on tables . . . Most of the talk revolves around pleasure and debauchery.'[30] The work of children in industry, said a powerful body of critics, was producing a decadent and debilitated generation. Such alarm was not confined to France. Indeed, these ideas consciously fed on foreign, especially British, examples and writings. But in France certain concerns were particularly acute. The growth of corrupted and indisciplined urban children seemed a threat to a fragile social and political order: 'Everyone knows that breed the Paris *gamin*, who in demonstrations always shouts the first seditious slogan, in riots always carries the first stone to the first barricade, and who has almost always fired the first shot'.[31] These fierce and fearless children – immortalized by Delacroix in *Liberty Leading the People* and by Hugo in the character Gavroche in *Les Misérables* – had to be tamed and moralized.

27. Flaubert (1979), p. 512.
28. Heywood (1988), p. 3.
29. Ibid., p. 7.
30. Ibid., p. 193.
31. Canler (1882), vol. 1, p. 177.

Moreover, cities and factories were blamed for poor physical conditions which made boys useless as soldiers – another major French preoccupation for more than a century after the 1830 revolution. This ignored the awkward fact that the most unhealthy and backward children were those in the idealized bucolic Edens of the centre, west and south. It was there above all that young men were too sickly to serve as soldiers: during the 1820s, about a quarter of boys liable for conscription were refused as being below the minimum height to handle a musket (only just over 5 feet).[32] The highest infantile death rates occurred in old cities such as Rouen, not factory boom-towns like Mulhouse and Saint-Etienne. Similarly, the bigger mechanized mills were less noxious than the little sweat-shops. This is perhaps one reason why there was no demand among working-class families for measures to regulate child labour. More importantly, they needed children's earnings to be able to eat; children at work sometimes allowed the mother to stay at home; often children worked alongside parents or relatives and could be kept under control. In some industries family working was a very old-established practice.

Yet in 1841, the first ever French social protection law was passed by the minister of commerce, the self-made cloth manufacturer and former worker Cunin-Gridaine, to regulate child labour in factories. It was an important departure for the State, which substituted itself for the authority of the father, one intention being to ensure 'robust workers' and 'defenders of the fatherland'. The law was pushed through by a small group of politicians, officials and experts, quite without the pressure of public opinion that brought about similar measures in England. Heywood suggests that no earlier action was taken because of the strains of the Napoleonic Wars followed by post-war economic stress. However, the law proved ineffective. Evasion by employers, parents and children was easy. Moreover, very small workshops, family businesses, agriculture and of course domestic piecework were exempt: in other words, where most French children worked. A long hiatus in legislation followed during the Second Empire. A new law, with provision for professional inspectors, was passed in 1874, and somewhat extended and tightened in the 1890s. One of the motives was stated by an inspector: 'the Prussians could all read and write'.[33] While this legislation, in Heywood's opinion, had some effect, real change was caused by the decline in demand for child labour after mid-century as mechanization proceeded, and by the increased provision of schooling, largely free by the late 1860s, and both free and compulsory from the 1880s. By the end of the century, the areas of poorest school attendance and lowest literacy were, as always, the rural areas, where children's work was still required at certain times of year by peasant agriculture.

Far worse off were those children whose families failed to look after them, or who had no families (orphans, foundlings, of whom there were 128,000 in

32. Aron *et al.* (1972), p. 218.
33. Heywood (1988), p. 279.

1833 alone[34]), and children sent to board with wet-nurses or paid foster parents – a sad fate heart-rendingly embodied in another Hugo character, Cosette. The death rate for all these children was fearfully high: up to 70 per cent for infants boarded out, while illegitimate children had more than double the death rate of legitimate children.[35] It is hard not to see this, as many contemporaries did, as legal infanticide; and of course there was illegal infanticide too. Surviving foundlings (as in other countries) were practically sold as apprentices or indentured workers when they were twelve. The State, again motivated by demographic, police and military concerns as well as by humanitarianism, eventually took a succession of cautious protective measures, but the need was very great, and resources very small. The plight of children – 'above all the orphan, the foundling, the child separated from its parents, or the child rejected by family and peers' – became an important literary theme; partly no doubt inspired by awareness of real and painful social problems, it also became a symbol of wider alienation in a world of worrying instability.[36]

It was difficult in a society that in principle idealized the patriarchal family officially to recognize its shortcomings by aiding single mothers or fatherless children (thus condoning immorality – only in 1869 did the law cease to forbid aid to be given to single mothers), or by interfering with paternal authority in order to protect children against their own parents' ill-treatment or neglect. Rather, the State supported paternal rights: fathers could have children under sixteen committed to prison or reformatory on request. In 1874 the law began to regulate wet-nursing, a cause of high infant mortality. Law proved far less effective than war: disruption of the wet-nursing business in 1870–71 forced mothers to breast-feed their own children and reduced mortality by half.[37] Only in 1889 did the law act against serious parental ill-treatment. Child victims remained as much objects of fear and shame as of compassion, subject to the rigorous discipline of 'cloister, prison, regiment'.[38]

THE POOR, THE SICK, THE DEVIANT

> The barbarians who threaten society are not . . . in the steppes of Tartary: they are in the *faubourgs* of our manufacturing towns.
>
> *Journal des Débats, 1831*[39]

Nowhere more starkly than in the treatment of deviants and the indigent can the obsession to create and maintain 'order', both material and moral, be seen. The Old Regime had combined charity, mainly ecclesiastical, with

---

34. Hamerow (1983), p. 79.
35. Zeldin (1973), vol. 1, p. 361; Weber (1977), pp. 182–3; Fuchs (1984).
36. Lloyd (1992), p. 241.
37. Kanter (1986), pp. 13–30, at p. 20.
38. Perrot, in Dufrancatel *et al.* (1979), p. 245.
39. Chauvaud (1991), p. 145.

elementary public order, trying to clear society's casualties off the streets and lock them away in vast forbidding institutions, most notorious among them the Parisian *hôpitaux-généraux*, Bicêtre and the Salpêtrière, still in use. The Revolution, in its hopeful dawn, rejected this harsh and hopeless response: social ills were to be cured, not merely contained. In the early 1790s, plans were discussed to create a universal provision of 'assistance' to the needy. It never materialized; the old ecclesiastical charities collapsed but were not replaced by a new State system. However, the utopianism of the 1790s remained the source for the rationalizing philanthropy of the first part of the nineteenth century: while those in temporary difficulty would be assisted by public welfare (*bienfaisance*), those with longer-term problems – which included the deaf, the blind, homeless children, the crippled, the aged, prostitutes, the mad and the criminal – would be isolated in social laboratories, 'enclosed worlds of correction'.[40]

In reality, the immensity of the problem (by one estimate there were in the 1830s 2 million poor, 300,000 beggars, 100,000 travellers and 300,000 found-lings[41]) left the State helpless. Its ambitious reforms, minute regulations and constant reorganization of Byzantine but inoperative bureaucratic structures contrasted absurdly with the facts: provision was left increasingly to the voluntary initiative of local authorities, *notables* and charities. In 1840, the responsible ministry had to set up the most basic enquiry to find out the extent of the problem and what was actually being done at the grass roots to relieve it.

Assistance to the poor, therefore, was so limited, disorganized and uneven that even the harshness of the English Poor Law was often praised by comparison. The first element, *bureaux de bienfaisance*, existed to give aid (medicine, clothing, work) to the poor in their own homes, intending, in contrast with the Malthusian rigours of the English system, to maintain the family structure. But bureaux were regularized only in Paris by 1849, and in the provinces aid depended on the initiative and slim resources of mayors and priests. Over most of the country there was no reliable public assistance at all, and emergency aid (such as bread distribution and 'charity workshops' for the unemployed) had to be improvized at times of crisis. The second element consisted of enclosed institutions, which, like English workhouses, were feared and hated, but which, unlike English workhouses, were very unevenly spread. *Hospices* (for the sick, the old, homeless children and the destitute), *dépôts de mendicité* (for beggars) and foundlings' homes (some with the famous *tours* – revolving wall niches permitting babies to be handed in anonymously) perpetuated many of the archaic practices of the Old Regime with unshakeable institutional inertia. They combined chaotic administration with anarchic mixture of function. Bicêtre and the Salpêtrière were typical in functioning simultaneously as hospitals, asylums and prisons, mixing up inmates of all ages and conditions. This was far from the utopian

40. Gueslin (1992), p. 93.
41. Castel (1988), p. 14.

dream of social laboratories. Moreover, they were regarded as very expensive (though total social spending totalled only 0.3 per cent of national income in mid-century), and successive governments struggled to cut costs. The *tours*, for example, were progressively closed in the 1840s because they were too successful in attracting foundlings; and asylums were told that they could not accept all the mentally ill. Self-help was more attractive to liberal theorists and taxpayers, and in 1835 a law established *caisses d'épargne* (savings banks), useful for those who had savings.

Ideological and political conflict over policy towards the poor came to a head following the 1848 revolution. Socialists demanded radical changes to abolish poverty and inequality; liberals and conservatives resisted what they saw as utopianism that would fan the flames of popular unrest. Both reactions were understandable in the face of overwhelming social and economic crisis, which in Paris culminated in the June insurrection of 1848 when the government decided to close down the new National Workshops (see p. 382). Socialists continued to demand that social rights, especially the right to work, should be enshrined in the new Republic's constitution; liberals asserted that such 'rights' were 'a fatal and dangerous mass of benefit promised but unfortunately impracticable'.[42] The two sides battled inside and outside parliament, led by the printer and socialist writer Proudhon, whose pamphlet *Sur la propriété* had become famous, and the conservative liberal Thiers, whose response *Du Droit de propriété* sold in huge numbers. Similar debates raged over universal credit and workers' cooperatives: conservatives would only agree to temporary assistance to the unemployed within the limits of what could be afforded and within the framework of the existing system of property. Public assistance was not to be the road to socialism or vast public spending.

A second debate concerned the role of charities: Catholics were eager to ensure that the Church should play a leading part in helping the poor, as a way of maintaining its influence in society and 'moralizing' the masses. The Society of St Vincent de Paul, founded in 1833 by the law student Frédéric Ozanam, organized groups to visit poor families to bring both Catholicism and charity. Similarly, conservative paternalists wanted private charity to continue as a means of social control, making the poor grateful for the solicitude of the rich: 'it is essential', wrote the director of a Rouen charity in 1854, 'to establish moral links between the rich and the poor which would prevent the latter from giving themselves up . . . to despair and especially to the evil temptations aroused by envy'.[43] The National Assembly set up a Commission on Public Assistance in 1849, at the request of the Catholic philanthropist Armand de Melun, though significantly Thiers was chosen to draft its report. It was a compromise, rejecting both liberal *laissez-faire* and radical State action, stressing self-help, and leaving a large place for religious and private charities. It suggested many piecemeal measures – child welfare,

42. Bury and Tombs (1986), p. 119.
43. Price (1987), p. 113.

poor relief, housing, encouragement to self-help societies and pension funds, job creation in State industries, colonial settlement – few of which actually reached the statute book. Those that did, such as the law on unhealthy dwellings, permitted, but did not require, local authorities to act. Self-help institutions, for example *sociétés de secours mutuels*, did grow, setting a pattern that prevailed throughout the period and continues to mark French social provision even today. However, they merely scratched the surface of poverty. By 1863 there were 4,721 mutual aid societies with 676,000 members, but the benefits paid amounted only to 0.02 per cent of GNP, hardly 10 per cent of hospital costs. Similarly, the law of 1850 setting up State-guaranteed mutual pension funds – quintessential liberal self-help – covered only 2 per cent of the workforce by 1903, and half the beneficiaries received less than 50 francs per year. What alleviated the lot of the poor after mid-century and ended mass social crises such as that of the late 1840s when nearly 400,000 people in Paris alone were receiving subsidized bread, was not social policy, but the development of the economy and the end of subsistence crises.[44]

During the Second Empire, although Napoleon III showed interest in experimental reforms, they remained largely symbolic. Only in the 1890s and 1900s, under the stimulus of political competition between moderate republicans, radicals and socialists, was there a significant push towards social reform. The radical party, through one of its leading intellectuals Léon Bourgeois, formulated the concept of 'solidarism' (see p. 460), which inspired a range of less than sweeping legislation. A not very effective law on industrial accidents was adopted in 1898, after 20 years of discussion. After another lengthy wrangle, a rather feeble old age pension law was introduced in 1910. The provision of cheap public housing (*habitations à bon marché*) began in the 1890s and 1900s. The 'Pasteur revolution' brought by the discovery of bacterial infection stimulated a greater State involvement in health, in the law of 1902. All in all, however, when compared with Germany or even Britain, the French State, in spite of its central role in society and its extensive powers, played a limited role in social security and health: public assistance rose from 1.4 per cent to 2.2 per cent of the State budget. 'In this domain as in others', concludes Rosenvallon, 'French society oscillated endlessly between the love of big ideas and the reality of petty compromises.'[45]

Another social novelty of the Revolution that reached maturity during the nineteenth century was the prison and its offshoots. Prisons were to be the 'hospitals of moral order', wrote a commentator in 1845,[46] to reform and correct the maladjusted and delinquent. As Foucault has argued in an influential book,[47] the late eighteenth century replaced the bloody liturgy of

44. Rosenvallon (1990), pp. 168–9; Price (1987), p. 51.
45. Rosenvallon (1990), p. 166.
46. Zysberg, in Perrot (1980), p. 196.
47. Foucault (1977).

public torture and death, which represented expiation for sin and a reassertion of the power of the monarch, with the prison, which had previously been merely a place of administrative internment or temporary passage but which was now reinvented as a place of work, social training and moral redemption, supposedly the quintessence of bourgeois capitalist society. Enlightenment philanthropists such as the Duc de La Rochefoucault-Liancourt, active in the early years of the Revolution, returned to prison reform after the 1815 Restoration.

Here too utopian ideals collided with parsimonious reality. In spite of voluminous decrees and regulations, prisons remained as in the past 'anarchic, disorderly and idle'.[48] Children, debtors, political prisoners, rioters, prostitutes, strikers, old lags, and sometimes merely the sick and the old mixed together in communal dormitories and courtyards instead of meditating lugubriously on their misdeeds in the silent, solitary cells of purpose-built 'Panopticons', where reformers wished them to languish under the unwinking eye of their jailors. Such expensive new buildings were rarely forthcoming, and the biggest prisons were in the ancient confiscated monastery buildings of Fontevrault and Clairvaux (still in use in the 1990s). Furthermore, for serious criminals the *bagnes*, chain-gangs of now landlocked galley slaves run by the navy, still existed untouched by new ideas: they killed their inmates by overwork and disease, but did not bother them with moralizing.

The fear of crime loomed larger during the 1830s and 1840s with the threat of the 'dangerous classes', conceived as a horde of barbarians spawned by vice and poverty in the bulging cities, and threatening 'civilization' with crime, disease, insanity and revolution. These years saw the first outbreaks of cholera, repeated political disturbances, and a perceived increase in crime. To older instruments for controlling and disciplining the lower classes – the *livret* and arbitrary police powers to intern 'vagabonds' – were added new weapons: public lunatic asylums were set up under prefectoral supervision largely for the disorderly poor; street traders and beggars had to carry large numbers; foundlings had to wear riveted identity collars. Hopes that prisons would reform criminals – 'the illusions of certain philanthropists', in Tocqueville's words – were replaced by a determination that they would control and punish, and cost less money. Education provision was cut, and the government ordered in 1839 that work should not be considered as therapy but 'as punishment . . . without interruption and as much as their strength permits'.[49] In the late 1840s the number of prisoners was higher than ever before or since: some 50,000 at any one time, including 25,000 long-term prisoners; about 160,000 people saw the inside of a cell some time every year. The numbers held in lunatic asylums also greatly increased: twenty-fold between 1800 and 1840; fifty-fold by the end of the century.[50] A combination of concern with public order and the desire to support the authority of fathers

48. Duprat, in Perrot (1980), p. 68.
49. Perrot (1980), p. 281.
50. Ibid., pp. 279–80; Rosenvallon (1990), p. 122.

and husbands over their families embodied in the 1838 law on insanity, meant that people (mostly women) could be committed to asylums on a wide variety of grounds with few safeguards.

Enlightenment revulsion from the punitive barbarities of public torture and mutilation was intensified by horror at the carnage of the Revolution. The masses had to be weaned away from bloodshed. In 1832 branding was abolished, as was the pillory in 1848. The notorious *chaîne* (the weeks-long procession of prisoners for the *bagne*) which attracted crowds of jeering or sympathetic onlookers was abolished, and the prisoners moved in enclosed *voitures cellulaires*, separated from each other and the public. In 1832 the guillotine was taken down from its scaffold to make it less visible; in 1833 executions were moved from the popular afternoon to inconveniently early morning, and in Paris relocated from the central Place de Grève to the remote and empty Barrière Saint-Jacques. In spite of these expedients, public guillotinings continued to attract large and disorderly crowds for more than a century, until the Second World War. This astonishing French peculiarity survived thanks to an alliance of conservatives, who believed in deterrence, and abolitionists, who wished to keep capital punishment as repugnant as possible.

The 1848 revolution caused only partial and temporary change in the treatment of criminals. The new Republic abolished the death sentence for political offences, partly to prove that it did not intend to follow in Robespierre's footsteps, and many expected that complete abolition would follow: cutlers in Grenoble delayed executions for a time by refusing to sharpen the guillotine blade. Corporal punishment was forbidden in prisons. The cellular system of solitary confinement remained the ideal, although there was evidence that far from being salutary it caused breakdown and death; prisoners preferred even the *bagne*. The republican government was more concerned with workers' protests that labour in prisons and charity workshops were harming their jobs than with the condition of criminals and ex-prostitutes: 'prisoners will be treated as prisoners', it promised. For some republicans, crime was less excusable in a democracy. The June 1848 and December 1851 insurrections greatly increased fears of the 'dangerous classes', and thousands of prisoners were transported to penal settlements in the colonies.

Though this was an exceptional measure, in fact transportation had been discussed for some years as a way of disposing of habitual criminals for good: 'Those who contravene honour, order, law, are enemies, veritable conspirators, who wish to place the country under the shameful and tyrannical yoke of their vices; unworthy to have a country, they must be expelled to a distant and uninhabited land'.[51] During the Second Empire, this was done: 22,000 people were transported. The *bagnes* were moved to Guiana, which Louis-Napoleon Bonaparte hoped would be 'more efficient, less costly and . . . more humane'. There was a fatuously optimistic belief in

51. Perrot (1980), p. 306.

the regenerative quality of agricultural work in virgin territory. Colonies were set up in France too for young offenders and homeless children 'whose precocious corruption frightens society; little socialists who already declare themselves hostile to law, property and family'.[52] The colonial *bagnes* proved effective only as a means of elimination, due to high mortality. Transportation was also a manifestation of the wish to carry out a great purge of 'certain vicious elements which have infiltrated the masses'.[53] This reached a climax after the fall of the Paris Commune of 1871, when thousands of 'dangerous people' were shot and nearly 5,000 more transported to a special penal colony in New Caledonia. The Third Republic managed to go a stage further, perfecting a system now clearly resting on the fully developed alternatives of moralization or permanent exclusion. From childhood, the primary schools, backed up later by the army as 'school of the nation', were to moralize the masses and teach them that education, work and thrift were the ways to self-improvement in a fair and democratic Republic. For juvenile delinquents reformatory schools would teach work and discipline. For adult delinquents cellular prisons or insane asylums would save those who could be saved. But since the 1860s, criminologists had taught that many were born criminals: 'degeneracy' was seen as a growing danger of the modern urban world. The police and prosecuting authorities had practically arbitrary powers for dealing with vagrants and prostitutes, and to hold suspects before trial. Prosecutions for vagrancy increased: in 1890, there were 32,822 convictions, but only 33 hostels for the homeless; thousands of vagrants were transported to the colonies.[54] Crime rates, certainly those of violent crime, were probably falling by the 1890s, but fear of anarchists and young delinquents (*apaches*) led to panicky calls for ever harsher treatment. Judicial records and scientific identification (through measurement and later fingerprints) made it possible to identify habitual criminals, who, by a law of 1885, which Nye considers 'one of the most Draconian' in French history,[55] were liable to *relégation* (transportation for life to the penal colonies). Transportation continued until 1938 (only Portugal and Russia had comparable institutions), perpetuating in the twentieth-century Republic a system 'as inhumane . . . as that of the galley slaves of the century of Louis XIV'.[56]

Control of prostitution was stern and arbitrary. The State considered it as a necessary and inevitable safety valve for men, but regarded the women as a virulent element of the 'dangerous classes' who had to be disciplined and controlled. Public order and (male) health (the late nineteenth century became obsessed with syphilis) were the priorities. Under what was sometimes known as the 'French system', most thoroughly developed in Paris from the 1820s to the 1880s, women registered by the police as prostitutes

52. Ibid., p. 238.
53. Zysberg, in Perrot (1980), pp. 198–9.
54. Castel (1988), p. 34; Chauvaud (1991), pp. 191–2.
55. Nye (1984), p. 95.
56. Zysberg, in Perrot (1980), p. 200.

R.T.C. LIBRARY LETTERKENNY

were outside the common law and under the arbitrary authority of the police. These *filles soumises* were required to submit to medical inspection; they could be interned without trial, in Paris in the notorious hospital-prison of Saint-Lazare. Women suspected of working outside the system (*insoumises*), who grew in number from the 1880s onwards, could be arrested, interned and arbitrarily registered as common prostitutes. The *police des moeurs* ensured a disciplined functioning of the sex industry. This gross caricature of patriarchal authority, one of the starkest examples of the disregard of individual rights by the State in the name of public interest, became the principal target of feminists and anti-authoritarian radicals in the later part of the century, but it continued throughout our period, and indeed in large part until 1960.

Why these seeming contradictions between consciously progressive humanist republican democracy and ruthless and archaic treatment of deviants? France was not wholly different from her neighbours, who shared many of the same fears stemming from exaggerated perceptions of the social dangers of urbanization, which ironically reduced crime, especially violent crime. Foucault points to detestation of 'anomaly', of 'departure from the norm'.[57] Liberal and republican society, sure of its rightness, tended to be intolerant of those who would not conform to its rules: the 1885 law, for example, was pressed for by freemasons, local councils and republican leaders such as Gambetta. Moreover, assumptions about 'degeneracy' encouraged a pessimistic harshness, which professionalization of those in charge – including doctors, policemen and psychiatrists – seems to have amplified. Yet in France some of these common features are clearly exaggerated. Fears of disorder, anarchy and national decline were greater and hence measures were harsher. A mixture of Old Regime survivals, the Revolution's refusal to allow the functions of the State to be trammelled by the law courts, and the consideration of deviant groups as non-citizens without civil rights, permitted a remarkably arbitrary use of State power. The prefects, the police and the examining magistrates could arrest, detain, intern and banish without redress in the courts. At bottom, the key to understanding the treatment of deviant groups seems to be that familiar obsession with order: 'that *order* that [prisoners] have lacked all their lives. It is to that *order*, principle of all good, that they must be brought back by every means.'[58]

57. Foucault (1977), p. 299.
58. La Rochefoucauld–Liancourt, in Duprat in Perrot (1980), p. 89.

CHAPTER 9

PARIS: SEAT OF POWER

Paris regards itself, rightly, as proxy for the whole population of the national territory.
Bulletin de la République, 1848[1]

Paris had an importance in French life during the century after the storming of the Bastille unparalleled in its previous history or in any other country. As General Lamarque reminded parliament in April 1831: 'In the days of our forbears, its occupation had little influence on the rest of France; Charles VII and Henri IV did not cease to be kings by ceasing to reign over Paris; [but] two recent examples have proved that this great capital . . . [now] takes with her the destiny of all our provinces'. With the permanent destruction of the 'religion' of monarchy after 1789, and the lack of any universally accepted symbol of legitimate authority thereafter, kings and governments could no longer reign if they ceased to hold Paris: the city and its people became, in effect, the sovereign body of France. Power from 1789 to 1795 had depended on the balance of forces in the capital. It was in Paris that thrones had been lost and won in 1814–15 and 1830: Lamarque's 'two recent examples'. King Louis-Philippe recognized this in 1830 when he remarked that being cheered by the Paris National Guard was 'better for me than coronation at Rheims'.[2] Events in 1848–51 and 1870 were again to prove the rule. The processes by which sovereignty was asserted – the 'revolutionary passion play' – have already been examined (see pp. 20–6). But to understand how this could happen, and why it ceased to happen, needs further consideration of how and precisely where power was concentrated in Paris.

A necessary, though not sufficient, element was socio-economic: Paris stood out for its size and economic importance in a society of small towns and villages. In 1850 it contained 1.2 million people, more than France's other fourteen large towns combined, and 20 per cent of the total urban population; the next biggest cities, Marseilles and Lyons, had under 200,000 each. It accounted for one-quarter of the wealth of France.[3] Clearly, under

1. Girard (1964), p. 299.
2. Ibid., p. 184.
3. Bourillon (1992), pp. 20–1; Marchand (1993), p. 207.

any political system such a city would carry weight. In turbulent times cities were difficult to control. Lyons, the second industrial city, was also a centre of serious unrest and even insurrection in the 1830s, and in 1870–71 several towns and cities wavered on the brink of revolt. During the 'year of revolutions' in 1848, Vienna, Berlin, Munich, Milan, Rome, Prague and Budapest were similar centres of conflict over power, as at other times were Brussels, Madrid and Warsaw. Yet the differences are greater than the similarities: only Paris repeatedly – 1830, 1848 and 1870 – successfully and alone decided the government of its country.

There were four essential elements in Parisian power. First, its large, literate and radical working- and lower-middle-class population. Most Parisians until the last years of the century were wage-earners or small self-employed artisans. Various attempts have been made to explain their political attitude by reference to their socio-economic condition. The artisan trades have often been described as declining, and Johnson has shown how certain trades (such as tailoring) underwent organizational changes in the 1830s that brought many of their members to support socialism in 1848.[4] However, the idea of a general artisan decline is a dubious concept, as both Judt and Berlanstein have demonstrated.[5] Attempts to show, on the other hand, that workers in more modern, larger-scale 'proletarian' industries were more militant are not convincing; moreover, genuinely large enterprises were always few.[6] In any case, no economic factor can explain Paris's unique history.

What was crucial, as in different ways Amman, Sewell, Gossez and Traugott point out, was the high level of membership of political, trade and even military organizations.[7] In other words, it was the high degree of politicization – already visible in working-class support for Napoleon in 1815 – attained by a closely knit and probably uniquely literate working-class population that counted. Political organizations (clandestine or legal), trade societies, economic and political hybrids such as the National Workshops of 1848, or official organizations such as the National Guard could thus mobilize considerable numbers rapidly, especially in the face of economic hardship, mass unemployment, a threat to subsistence and above all perceived government provocation. The rituals of the 'revolutionary passion play' taught people what to do, and success encouraged repetition. Finally, Parisians had a strong sense of their unique status as leaders and guardians of popular rights.

The second key element was physical control of the city. The Parisian citizen militia, the National Guard of the Seine, is an important element: indeed, its heyday is identical with that of Parisian suzerainty. Charles X, Louis-Philippe and Louis-Napoleon often wore its uniform for ceremonies in tribute to its symbolic importance. Founded in 1789, revived in 1814,

4. Johnson, in Price (1975).
5. Judt (1986), pp. 27–9; Berlanstein (1984), pp. 15–21.
6. Tilly and Lees, in Price (1975).
7. Traugott (1985); Gossez (1956), pp. 439–58; Amman (1975); Sewell (1980).

disbanded in 1827, restored in 1830, democratized in 1848, run down in the
1850s, vastly expanded in 1870–71, briefly in control in 1871, it was a
part-time police and defence force. Its companies acted as social clubs, for
many men enjoyed playing at soldiers and occasionally being invited to
hob-nob with the royal court; its military bands played a considerable part in
the city's musical life, and were the origin of the Paris Conservatoire. Most
guardsmen tried to avoid routine duty (which required about 5,000 men
daily) although absence could earn a spell in the National Guard prison, the
'Hôtel des Haricots'. Governments too were usually willing to run down
membership in quiet times.

   In times of trouble, however, the Guard played an important military, and
an even more important political role, and Paris could not be controlled
without its cooperation. Eastern Paris, largely working class, was almost
outside government authority even in normal times. The regular army
garrison before 1848 varied between 10,000 and 25,000 men,[8] plus about
2,000 gendarmes, to the Guard's normal 40,000. In the 1830s, left-wing
insurrections were suppressed with the help of the Guard, in which only
middle-class citizens were normally required in practice to serve. In May and
June 1848, and in October 1870, moderate republican governments were
defended from revolutionary opponents by loyal National Guards. As a
citizen militia, it exercised considerable moral authority. But the
independence that made it valuable also made it dangerous. It reflected
Parisian middle-class opinion, usually moderately left-wing. Before 1848
middle-class National Guards who did not have the vote in parliamentary
elections used it as a political forum. It elected its company and battalion
commanders, and was therefore only tenuously under government control: 'I
swear to support, to defend our institutions, and if necessary to attack them',
declared one (fictional) officer. Revolutionary leaders such as Barbès in the
1840s, and Blanqui and Flourens in 1870 were elected to senior ranks. In
1827, Charles X disbanded the Paris National Guard after its men shouted
slogans – 'A bas Villèle! A bas les Jésuites!' – during a royal review; his
government thus lost a possible ally and gained many certain enemies during
the July Revolution. In February 1848, shouts of 'A bas Guizot! Vive la
Réforme!' from a force which until then had been the regime's staunch
defender demoralized Louis-Philippe and his advisers, while in the streets
National Guards prevented gendarmes from dispersing crowds. In short, the
Guard was the most direct means by which governments lost that basic
attribute of sovereignty, the monopoly of legitimate violence.

   In the aftermath of revolutions, control of the Guard became crucial. The
Left campaigned successfully to democratize membership in 1848 and 1870,
which meant giving arms and organization to urban workers and their
leaders. This split the force between bourgeois conservative and working-
class radical legions, corresponding broadly to the west and east of the city.

8. According to Delmas (1992), pp. 538–42, 13,000 in July 1830, 16,000 in 1839,
23,000 in 1848.

In the spring and summer of 1848, culminating in the June insurrection in which 200 guardsmen were killed on the government side (one-third of all loyalist casualties), it became a focus of political conflict, with some of its units on either side of the political divide. This happened again in 1870 after the downfall of the Second Empire. The Prussian siege of Paris turned the Guard into a Parisian army of some 320,000 men, and the revolt of its left-wing batallions in March 1871 established the Paris Commune, its apogee and death-knell. It was bloodily smashed by the regular army in May 1871 and then permanently disbanded.

The third key element was the centralization of political and administrative power in Paris. Most politicians lived in Paris before 1871: the core of the political class was permanently there. The system of central appointment of prefects and other officials has been described above. Local *notables* in post-revolutionary France needed State office to maintain their influence, and this came from Paris; local prestige of the sort enjoyed by Old Regime governors, English lords lieutenant or indeed American state governors was no longer enough to ensure authority in a divided society. Consequently, not only was there no effective rallying point for any provincial resistance to a Parisian coup, but local officials frequently fell over themselves to express their loyalty to the new regime in Paris.

The fourth element was the prestige of the capital city. Many provincial conservatives might hate, resent and fear Paris, but they could not contest its uniqueness. Their demands for 'decentralization' in the 1860s, and attempts to move the seat of government (conservatives insisted on parliament's meeting at Versailles from 1871 to 1880) were back-handed tributes to its potency. They recognized the danger of a government residing in a city it never fully controlled, threatened by 'the paving stones of the mob'. Progressives, on the other hand, were eager to hail Paris as the centre of civilization, and to follow its political promptings: it was 'the sacred city', republican deputies told the National Assembly in 1871, where 'the sovereign [i.e. the people] resides . . . the intellectual, moral and political centre of France'. Though the rise and fall of the 1871 Commune destroyed Paris's political hegemony, events there (such as General Boulanger's by-election victory in 1889) continued to be regarded as of special importance. The vast rebuilding programme begun by Napoleon III had as one of its results the creation of an 'Americanized' epitome of modernity. This image, tirelessly explored by artists, continued to be systematically promoted by a prestige-conscious State in the stunning Universal Exhibitions of 1867, 1889 (marked by the building of the Eiffel tower), and 1900. Thus the status of Paris, both as the leading international cultural centre and as France's only cultural centre, was consolidated: for example, over three times as many international conferences were held in Paris as in London (the second most important venue) in the 1900s.[9] No less magnetic was its unique if more raffish allure as the 'New Babylon', the city of fashion and pleasure.

9. Tapia, in Kaspi and Marès (1989), pp. 38–9.

The heart of national sovereignty had to be defended. In a modern war, as Napoleon's fate in 1814 showed, possession of Paris was decisive. Napoleon said that he could have survived if Paris had been fortified, and so during the war scare of 1840 huge defences were begun. However, opponents of the July Monarchy raised an outcry: a ring of forts surrounding Paris would be new 'Bastilles' to shelter unpopular governments from the people, serve as prisons and act as bases for counter-revolution. The government had to agree to build a huge rampart round the city to protect Parisians against a possible domestic as well as a foreign enemy. In fact, neither in 1848 nor in 1870–71 did the fortifications help the government control the city in time of rebellion; but in 1871 the Paris Commune was able to resist attack by the Thiers government's forces for five weeks because of the shelter given by the forts and ramparts begun by an earlier Thiers government in 1840. However, the fortifications did fulfil their main purpose of keeping a foreign enemy at bay. The Prussians in 1870 defeated all the French armies in the field, but were unable to win the war as long as Paris held out. They were forced to besiege the city until starvation and bombardment forced Parisians – 'whose wickedness was the guilty cause of the war' said the Prussian crown prince – to capitulate. This was the most spectacular and heroic, and the last, example of the sovereignty of Paris over France: the war could not end until the Parisians surrendered, and could not continue after they had done so.

The real attempt to make the city physically controllable was made by Napoleon III and his prefect Georges Haussmann in the 1850s, following the turbulence of 1848–51. Their ambitious urban remodelling – which inspired a superb effort to record the old city by nostalgic early photographers – was undertaken for several reasons, including to modernize the city, shed prestige on the regime and create jobs. But it also aimed to lance the abcess of revolt. Conflict had its geography: a political geography, around the three main centres of power (the Louvre–Tuileries palaces; the Chamber of Deputies at the Palais Bourbon; and the city hall, the Hôtel de Ville); a social geography in and around the main working-class districts of east-central Paris and (with the extension of the city and its growth in the 1850s and 1860s) in the new industrial working-class suburbs; and a physical geography (strategic roads and crossings like the Porte Saint-Denis; squares where crowds could assemble and battles could be fought such as the Place de la Bastille; barriers such as the Saint-Martin canal; and high ground that could be fortified, such as Montmartre, the Montagne Sainte-Geneviève and the Père-Lachaise cemetery). These were familiar battlegrounds for several generations.

Napoleon and Haussmann intended to hamstring future insurrection. Wide, straight roads such as the Boulevard de Sébastopol, the Rue de Rivoli, the Rue Mazas, and the Avenue du Prince Eugène drove through the grubby and picturesque warrens of central Paris, and surrounded and cut off the revolutionary Faubourg Saint-Antoine, cradle of revolution from 1789 to 1848. This aimed to contain disturbance and allow police and troops freer access, and if necessary room to shoot. The ancient crowded central district round

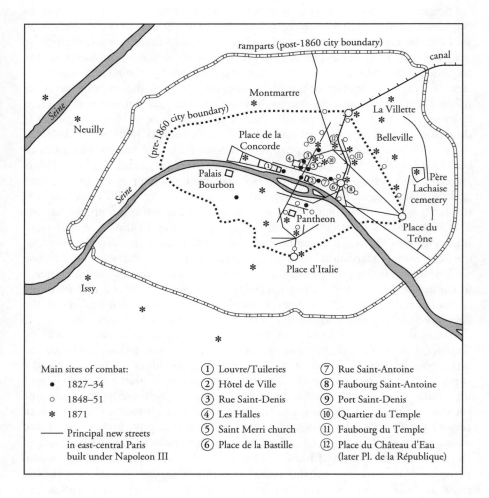

Figure 9.1 Paris

Main sites of combat:

- • 1827–34
- ○ 1848–51
- * 1871

—— Principal new streets
in east-central Paris
built under Napoleon III

① Louvre/Tuileries
② Hôtel de Ville
③ Rue Saint-Denis
④ Les Halles
⑤ Saint Merri church
⑥ Place de la Bastille

⑦ Rue Saint-Antoine
⑧ Faubourg Saint-Antoine
⑨ Port Saint-Denis
⑩ Quartier du Temple
⑪ Faubourg du Temple
⑫ Place du Château d'Eau
(later Pl. de la République)

the Hôtel de Ville and the Ile de la Cité, scene of riots in the 1830s, was razed
and turned into a protected official enclave. Massive barracks were sited in
trouble spots. A large part of the working-class population was deliberately
moved out from the centre into the suburbs: a lengthy process more or less
completed since the 1960s. The consequences of 'Haussmannization',
however, were disappointing to its architects. First, it contributed to the
Empire's abiding unpopularity in Paris by disrupting neighbourhoods and
raising rents, prices and transport costs. Second, the new largely
working-class suburbs to the north, east and south of the city (such as
Montmartre and Belleville) proved hot-houses of political militancy. Finally,
when successful revolt did occur in 1871, the new strategic pattern of
Haussmann's streets and squares actually helped the rebel National Guard to

defend the city against the regular army, which had difficulty in crossing the open spaces under fire.

However, Paris did eventually fall to the national government in May 1871, the first time that an insurrection in control of Paris had been subsequently defeated, and the last time that a Parisian revolution would be seriously attempted. This can be seen as the last of an escalating series of defeats of the revolutionary forces in the capital since 1848, most crushingly in June 1848 and December 1851. What had changed since February 1848, the last successful Parisian revolution? First, universal male suffrage, proclaimed in February 1848, replaced the sovereignty of Parisians with that of the whole country. Provincial and conservative forces, Catholic and rural, often viscerally hostile to revolution and suspicious of cities, gained a powerful voice. Moreover, the government that defeated the Paris Commune in 1871 (like that which defeated the June revolt of 1848) had recently been elected and its confidence, far from collapsing like that of Charles X in 1830 and Louis-Philippe in 1848, was bolstered by the electoral proof of widespread support. By the same process, Paris rebels were marginalized: electoral results showed them to be an isolated faction even within Paris, not the vanguard of the sovereign people. Hence their revolt seemed both illegitimate and doomed. Moderates stayed neutral or rallied to the government: neither the June rebels nor the Paris Commune attracted leaders with a national reputation. The army obeyed orders. Purely class motives were ascribed to the rebels – June 1848 was a 'servile revolt', in Tocqueville's words, against 'society' and 'civilization' – which further hardened opposition, especially when conservative propaganda got to work. Consequently, last-ditch support for the insurgents in June 1848 and May 1871 was fairly small, probably 10–20,000. Crowds would turn out to build barricades, fight or at least cheer the combatants when the enemy was a monarchy supported only by a small electorate; far fewer would do so, however great the provocation, when the enemy was a Republic elected by universal suffrage. 'Republics are lucky', Louis-Philippe is supposed to have said, 'they can shoot people.'

Technological, material and even tactical changes also contributed to the taming of Paris. Railways brought reinforcements rapidly in June 1848, and helped to maintain a besieging army of 130,000 government troops in April and May 1871. The Old Regime pattern of economic crisis, combining mass unemployment and food shortages, ceased to apply after 1848, except in the exceptional wartime circumstances of 1870–71. Army commanders developed deadly street-fighting tactics after 1830 and 1848: not to storm barricades frontally, but to work round them and fire down on the exposed defenders from adjacent buildings. Although caught napping in March 1871, they withdrew their troops from the quagmire of revolutionary Paris and bided their time before returning in overwhelming force: as Thiers put it, 'the strategy that worked for Windischgraetz', the Austrian general who retook Vienna in 1848. This was a bloody lesson that revolutionary leaders took to heart: barricades in the streets of Paris no longer worked.

The defeat of the Paris Commune confirmed that a major shift of political power had taken place, and perpetuated it institutionally. The Paris National Guard was permanently disbanded. The city was placed again under the authority of two prefects (Jacques Chirac was the first mayor since 1871). Parliament remained in Versailles pending proof of Parisian docility. A large military garrison and an expanded police force guaranteed order: for the May Day demonstrations in 1890 there were 38,000 troops – more than three times the garrison in July 1830. In a broader political context, the power of the provinces, and particularly rural France, was embodied in the Senate, in which Paris and the other cities were deliberately under-represented. The Third Republic's political class ceased to be predominantly Parisian. Paris itself was changing, irrespective of politics. The growth in the service sector and the administration, combined with movement of industry and population out to the periphery meant that by the end of the century workers had become a minority of its population. In 1902, the Paris city council was won for the first time by the nationalist Right. Henceforth, Paris was often a nuisance to governments, but not a threat.

CHAPTER 10

POWER AND THE SWORD

Regular or irregular, government will always function beneath the hand that holds the sword.

Taine[1]

For 80 years we have lived in turmoil . . . and the army, tossed around from one régime to another . . . no longer knows how or to whom it should be faithful.

General du Temple, 1874[2]

Since the Revolution France has often been governed by soldiers – Napoleon, Cavaignac in 1848, Trochu in 1870, MacMahon from 1873 to 1879, Pétain and de Gaulle – but never by the army. This is not the least important of French paradoxes. In no major European countries other than Spain and Russia was armed force so frequently used at home. In 1814–16, in the turbulent period between 1827 and 1852 and in 1871 it was the final decider of which regime France should have. It was also frequently used in these years, and in the 1880s, 1890s and 1900s, to suppress social conflict. Yet it never exercised autonomous power. Two of France's neighbours demonstrate how differently things could turn out: in Spain, the army frequently intervened to arbitrate or alter the political system; in Germany it possessed autonomous power within the State structure. In France, in spite of political instability, the army never attempted to impose its own political solution, and indeed at crucial moments it stood aside or even proved impotent in the face of political challenge to the established order. And in spite of its prestige and considerable influence, it always remained obedient to the civilian authorities in major matters. Why did the dog not bark? Why was the army *'la grande muette'*?

The fundamental reason was that in a country perpetually in a state of at least cold war with its neighbours the defence of the frontiers was the army's overriding task. This determined the kind of army it was, and what it could do. It had to be large and hence raised by conscription; and this meant that,

1. Taine (1878), vol. 2, p. 311.
2. Jauffret, in Tombs (1991), p. 245.

in spite of efforts to professionalize it, it remained a heterogeneous body. It had to be commanded by competent professional officers, qualified by their military experience, and again necessarily a large and heterogeneous corps. These realities the restored Bourbons soon realized, finding it impossible to raise a large enough volunteer army. The Gouvion-Saint-Cyr law of 1818 established a conscription system (though avoiding that detested word) whose three principal features were to last half a century: long service, a selective call-up based on a ballot, and the possibility for those who drew a 'bad number' to pay for a substitute. The law also guaranteed that one-third of officers' commissions would go to NCOs. After the fall of the Bourbons, the Soult laws of 1832 and 1834 confirmed the recruitment system and gave officers tenure of their ranks, which protected them from arbitrary punishment, and also set up a career structure covering pay, promotions and pensions – a system that lasted for 150 years. Officers were the only servants of the State to have these privileges. By protecting the officer corps from political interference, it also protected the civil State from the officer corps, which was able to pursue its professional aims without needing to become involved in politics.

Moreover, strategic necessity lessened the army's capacity or desire to intervene in internal conflicts. Much of it had to be deployed near the frontiers or in the colonies; and so Paris, as has been seen, usually had a relatively small garrison in spite of its political sensitivity. The experience of revolutions in 1830 and 1848 weakened and disorganized the army and made it visibly incapable of intervening outside its borders or even defending the country in case of attack, which seemed frighteningly likely on both occasions. The conclusion that the army should stay clear of political conflicts was widely drawn.

The army was a far more heterogeneous body than in Britain or Germany. Even before the Revolution, large-scale continental campaigning since the seventeenth century had made it a large force led by a relatively open professional officer corps, and the Revolution and the succeeding wars had offered promotion to competent soldiers of many backgrounds. Although throughout the nineteenth century many senior officers, their promotion assisted by connections, money and education, came from the upper classes, most officers (especially lieutenants and captains in the line infantry and cavalry, the backbone of the army) were career soldiers from middle-class or skilled-working-class families who had risen through the ranks: about 60 per cent overall. Political sympathies were no less diverse. Royalists, Bonapartists and republicans were scattered through the army. In the late 1820s, for example, long-serving officers looked back nostalgically to their old commander Napoleon, while new arrivals (especially in elite units such as the Royal Guard) were partisans of the restored Bourbons. This conflict of loyalties emerged during the 1830 revolution, when several infantry units abandoned the government, and many Carlist officers were expelled from their units by pro-revolutionary officers and NCOs, whose liberal fervour was buoyed up by hope of promotion.

Similarly, in the 1870s there were officers and ambitious NCOs who felt that their career prospects were linked either with the old or the new regime. Ideology, personal loyalty and ambition all counted, but their effect was to prevent any political consensus. So prudent, patriotic and ambitious officers gave their loyalty to the army itself, as the embodiment of the nation, and not to any regime. The civilian game of politics was unworthy of a soldier; it was also risky, and usually unprofitable. Very few officers gained glory and promotion by rash public political activity, especially of an oppositional nature, though careful cultivation of the powers that be did no harm. General Joffre, who became chief of the general staff in 1911, was the supreme example: he combined adequate military competence with loyal republicanism. The example of how not to do it was given by General Georges Boulanger, who successively and then simultaneously swore devotion to royalists and radicals and himself went into politics, earning the jealousy and contempt of many of his brother officers, several of whom pledged to support the republican government against him. In short, the interests of the army, and of its individual members, were better furthered by steering clear of political parties, and keeping their opinions to themselves.

The unremitting manpower needs of continental preparedness and colonial warfare meant that the army always had to be for the most part a conscript force. Until the 1880s, this was regarded by soldiers, politicians and civilians as at best a necessary evil: hardened professionals were considered militarily superior and politically more reliable. Attempts were made, by imposing long periods of service (up to seven years), encouraging volunteers and re-enlistment by large bounties (the payment for volunteering in someone else's place was the equivalent of two to four years' wages for a farm labourer), moving units round the country, and mixing together recruits from different regions, to make the army as far as possible a professional body separate from society. The aim was to create an obedient instrument – 'passive obedience' was the watchword – not a politicized one. Trying to create a political force could backfire. The Bourbons recruited a privileged Royal Guard which included former émigrés and Swiss mercenaries, but caused intense resentment in the rest of the army. This contributed to the half-heartedness with which the army defended, or failed to defend, the Bourbons in July 1830. In December 1851, President Louis-Napoleon Bonaparte staged the only military coup of the century. It is important to note that the army merely obeyed orders during the coup: although Bonapartism was certainly the political creed closest to military hearts (though a slightly higher proportion of soldiers voted 'No' in the 1851 plebiscite than civilians) the army took no political initiative. Bonaparte was very careful to preserve the political and legal proprieties: the army would only act on purportedly legal orders from its hierarchical superiors. This remained the rule. After the defeat of 1870 the army had to be expanded to keep pace with Germany, and this greatly changed its character. The introduction of universal short-term service in 1889 increased the proportion of young conscripts. The overriding requirement for rapid wartime mobilization meant that from the 1880s units had to be based and recruited in a particular area, and hence they maintained links with the civil community. Reservists and territorials rejoining for training brought lax discipline and civilian attitudes. From 1904, most soldiers served with local units. All this made the army even less apt for a political role, just at a time when right-wing politicians began to think it should play one.

So during the years of political division from 1870 to 1905 the army stolidly continued to be '*la grande muette*'. Even when one of its most distinguished officers, Marshal Patrice de MacMahon, was made president of the Republic, and in 1876–77 found himself in direct political conflict with the Left, neither he nor any senior general seriously considered a military coup. The republican leader Gambetta made confidential enquiries at this time about the political loyalties of all senior officers and every regiment in the army: information probably supplied in part by freemasons. The reports concluded that there was no serious danger of a coup, because a large number of officers, especially those of lower rank, were republicans, while royalists were divided among themselves. Moreover, Gambetta inspired personal loyalty because he had led the stubborn military resistance to Germany in the winter of 1870–71, a loyalty strengthened by the fact that many officers who had served under his orders looked to him (and hence to the Republic) for advancement and protection. In any case, MacMahon himself expressly ruled out military support for a Bourbon restoration, although his own sympathies were legitimist. Interestingly, a crucial question concerned the national flag: the Bourbon pretender insisted on restoring the white flag, but the army was attached to the tricolour, which was associated with military victory. If it was taken away, said MacMahon, 'the rifles would go off by themselves'. In other words, the army's own corporate loyalty, symbolized by its flag, was more important than any dynastic or religious consideration.

Republican governments from the 1870s onwards continued to collect secret reports on the political opinions of officers, assembled in a card index that caused a scandal when disclosed in 1904. This surveillance, if shabby, was effective: those with an eye to promotion and a pension realized that they should be circumspect. Only retired officers sometimes bandied about talk of a coup d'état. Besides, republican politicians gave national defence and military preparation as high a priority as any soldier could have wished, and they paid sufficient attention to professional military opinion not to discriminate too severely against able officers who were discreet about their political and religious beliefs. General de Miribel became chief of the general staff in 1881 and General de Castelnau deputy chief of the general staff in 1911, although both were conservative Catholics and nobles. Peaceful coexistence between army and Republic was thus possible. Although several monarchist generals were removed following the peaceful defeat of MacMahon in 1879, the army was never exposed to the kind of purges that civilian services suffered after political upheavals; even after the Dreyfus affair (see pp. 462–68), in which its commanders had been so deeply involved, the army was largely spared. Not a single general could be persuaded by right-wing politicians to attempt a coup during that troubled time. In February

1899 the popular army-worshipping nationalist leader Paul Déroulède actually tried to provoke a coup by grabbing the reins of General Roget's horse and shouting 'To the Elysée!', but the general led his men into the nearest barracks and closed the gates – a reaction that perfectly symbolizes the political attitude of the army throughout the period.

While the army kept aloof from party politics, it could not avoid involvement in the maintenance of public order, when prefects used their authority to requisition troops to assist the police. For obvious reasons, the danger of mass political disorder has been a preoccupation of every French government. The organization, training and deployment of its coercive forces, *la force publique*, showed that the priority was the defence of the State, rather than the protection of individuals. Many small towns and villages had no resident police at all. Except for village watchmen (*gardes champêtres*) and some municipal police forces, the police were nationally organized and controlled. The rural police, the *gendarmerie*, 22,000 strong in 1913, was, and remains, part of the army. City police forces, a mixture of military and civilian, were ultimately under the control of the prefects, and acted in a quasi-military fashion, rather than as 'bobbies on the beat'. Civilian police forces, however, were very small: under the authoritarian Second Empire, Lille had only 52 policemen and Marseilles only 103 – far fewer than Manchester and Liverpool.[3] The army and (until its abolition in the 1870s) the National Guard were indispensable auxiliaries in case of even minor unrest. Even fire brigades were armed auxiliary police forces, and in the cities were (indeed still are) military or naval units. The National Guard was fairly numerous, on the spot and cheap. Governments hoped that as respectable property-owning citizens, they had an interest in suppressing disorder. More important, because it was a body of citizens not a mercenary force it had moral authority: its appearance, unlike that of policemen and soldiers, often calmed disturbances. Moreover, regular soldiers were reluctant to become entangled in civil disturbances. They did not like shooting at their own people, and also did not want to end up on the losing side in a revolution: men of the 66th regiment, for example, were punished for having fired on the rebels in Paris in 1830, and reprimanded for not having done so in Lyons in 1831. When faced with crowds in the streets they preferred to leave the initiative to the National Guard, whom they regarded as better able to gauge the political situation. 'There is danger for the government in counting too much on the service the army can render. It will act with confidence and vigour if the National Guard is on its side, otherwise its effectiveness should be little counted on', wrote the army's public-order expert in 1839. However, the National Guard was not always on its side (in 1830, 1848, 1870–71), and although militarily this was not always important, politically and psychologically it could be crucial. When small groups of soldiers were surrounded by huge, usually friendly crowds, who appealed to them as brothers, often offering them food and drink, the prescribed military response – to open fire – was humanly

3. Emsley (1983), p. 95.

impossible. Soldiers sometimes handed over their weapons or joined the crowd. These experiences confirmed the reluctance of army commanders to become involved in political conflict if there was any doubt about where political legitimacy lay, and precisely what their military objective was: 'To disperse . . . the troops by platoons in the open spaces and streets', the army believed, 'is to gamble with the life and strength of the soldier, and to compromise military honour and the safety of the state itself'.

Even if troops did act, their technical means of doing so – which for the whole of our period meant more or less gentle cavalry or bayonet charges as the mildest step, and then musketry and finally cannon fire – could do more harm than good, as bloodshed provoked anger and condemnation. This was realized by governments, soldiers and revolutionaries. Unplanned exchanges of fire fatally escalated the crisis facing the July Monarchy on 23 February 1848; revolutionaries may sometimes have deliberately provoked shooting with this intention. If shooting started, troops could not even be sure of winning a pitched battle with the population in cities. Buildings and barricades inhibited manoeuvre, communication and firepower. Weapons seized from gunsmiths, barracks or friendly soldiers soon put the crowd – which always contained many former soldiers trained to shoot – on fairly equal terms with troops. In June 1848, however, the army did crush a Parisian uprising, and it did so again on an even larger scale in May 1871. But in these cases, the legitimacy of the newly appointed government – in 1848 led by a republican general, Cavaignac – was relatively clear. Furthermore, on those occasions governments no longer tried to minimize violence and the army was given military *carte blanche*. Instead of standing about in the streets trying to control crowds, they attacked rebel positions in overwhelming force, supported by artillery. In both cases, commanders were careful not to ask too much of their men, or expose them to high casualties. In a real urban battle, numbers, organization and discipline gave the army a decided advantage.

After 1871, there were no more pitched battles, but there were several shootings of strikers. In 1869–70, the 1880s, 1890s and 1900s troops were frequently requisitioned by prefects to maintain order, especially in coal-mining areas where a large part of the population was involved. They were mainly used to protect company property or prevent violence against strike-breakers. Prefects often used them to put pressure on one side or the other to compromise: on employers, by threatening to withdraw troops, for example. On several occasions outnumbered troops fired on strikers, usually in response to stone-throwing, most notoriously at Fourmies where nine people were killed in 1891 in the first serious bloodshed of the Third Republic. Syndicalists round the turn of the century regularly attempted to persuade soldiers to refuse to obey orders in such circumstances, and engaged in a sustained anti-military campaign, which doubtless contributed to the huge increase in deserters. There is every reason to believe that the army, taught to regard itself as the national army, was very reluctant to do such duty. Wrote one officer in 1904, he was 'always questioning his conscience . . . and fearing to be blamed if he acts too much or too little'.[4] General Boulanger, when minister of war, made himself popular with the Left by suggesting that troops were probably sharing their rations with striking miners. In 1880 and 1902–5, the army found itself on the other side of the political fence, closing down monasteries and occupying churches; several officers resigned their commissions. The only case of outright mutiny, however, came in quite different circumstances: when several local units demonstrated their sympathy for mass protest of southern wine growers in 1907 (see p. 471). The exceptional nature of this mutiny highlights the army's habitual obedience, but also showed that a locally recruited conscript army could not be counted on to quash civil disturbance.[5]

What above all influenced its capacities and conduct was that more than any other continental army it was a fighting force. Its preoccupations were preparing for war in Europe and fighting continuous colonial campaigns. Officers wanted to maintain the strength and cohesion of the army for battle, not dissipate it in internal factionalism. Moreover, ambitious officers realized that the quickest way to advancement was through combat, not politics: the brightest graduates of Saint-Cyr chose the colonial army. 'What drove us to expand in faraway places', wrote a former colonial governor in 1897, though with some exaggeration, 'was above all the need to find something to occupy the army and navy.'[6] What the army as a whole wanted was a government that would maintain order at home and promote the army's interests. The Restoration and the July Monarchy pared military spending, reduced the army and stressed their commitment to peace in Europe. Neither inspired widespread loyalty among the troops. The Second Empire and the Third Republic provided huge budgets and fought big wars: as long as they kept winning the loyalty of the army was assured. Since the time of the first Napoleon, war and the prospect of war was therefore a key to the obedience of the army and hence an important pillar of the equilibrium of the State. However, political loyalty did not mean complete obedience: in what it considered its own domain, the colonies, the army and sometimes the navy proved perpetually insubordinate, as will be seen. Nor did it mean that the army would defend a regime losing control at home. Politically the army remained *la grande muette* largely because, had it attempted to speak, it would have produced not a single voice but a cacophony.

4. Porch (1981), p. 108.
5. Ibid., p. 119.
6. Andrew and Kanya-Forstner (1981), p. 10.

CHAPTER 11

POWER BEYOND THE HEXAGON: THE EMPIRE

The conservation of the colonies is necessary to the strength and greatness of France.

Tocqueville, 1843[1]

The second French colonial empire, acquired in the century after Waterloo in replacement of that lost during the half-century before, was the conscious projection overseas of several remarkably consistent nationalist pre-occupations. Most fundamental was a perception of weakness. Empire was intended to counteract decline in Europe by the discovery of a chimerical 'French India'; to secure a place in a new world order; to cure decadence at home by creating pride and a sense of purpose; and to express the cherished self-image of France as prophet and teacher of mankind. This primarily ideological motivation of French imperialism recalls the late-nineteenth-century German *Weltpolitik* of acquiring a 'place in the sun', but in its desire for empire as a cloak for weakness it resembles the desperate expansionism of Italy and Russia. It is essentially different from the pragmatic British accumulation of territories, motivated by finance, trade, strategy, ideology and accident, which J.H. Seeley famously described as a 'fit of absence of mind': French colonialists always thought they knew what they were doing.

Enthusiastic individuals and groups (certain politicians, the armed forces, journalists, missionaries, business interests, geographical societies) played a disproportionate part in the process. There were no major economic interests at stake and negligible pressure for emigration, so the public and most politicians usually remained indifferent. But unpredictable bursts of jingoism occurred when colonies brought France into conflict with European rivals – periodically Britain, from 1830 to 1905, and then Germany, after 1905. In these circumstances policy frequently escaped the control of politicians, as enthusiasts, usually soldiers or sailors, precipitated unauthorized expansionary adventures, and ministers, far away and ill-informed, had to decide whether to support or disavow the men on the spot. In either case, they risked the mercurial wrath of parliament and the press, which habitually feared the costs and dangers of expansion, but also resented the humiliation of retreat.

1. Todorov (1993), p. 195.

IDEAS OF EMPIRE

England has set foot in no country without setting up her counting-houses. France has nowhere passed without leaving the perfume of her spirituality.

Louis Blanc[2]

France would not easily be content to count for no more in the world than a big Belgium.

Jules Ferry, 1882[3]

The belief that colonial expansion was part of a global struggle between European nations was the starting point of imperialist thought. Napoleon popularized the idea of a conflict of super-states for world domination. Tocqueville took it up by predicting the rise of America and Russia. The first focus was the Mediterranean and the Ottoman Empire: Napoleon (echoed by many others) declared that Constantinople was the key to world hegemony. France's casual conquest of Algiers – for years considered a liability – was seen by the late 1840s as a step towards making the Mediterranean a French lake: 'a position seized in advance for a time unknown', parliament was told in 1846, 'when, on the great battlefield of the sea, we shall sooner or later have to contest the influence of our rivals'.

In practice, however, the men and money expended on colonial conquests actually reduced French power in Europe: 'Algeria is between the Rhine and you, Algeria is between Poland and you', declared Lamartine. In 1840, the army in Algeria, vulnerable to the British navy, was regarded by Palmerston as a hostage for French good behaviour. The Mexican expedition of 1862–67 made it impossible for France to intervene in the Prusso-Austrian war of 1866. Colonial expeditions, as Déroulède and Clemenceau asserted in the 1880s, weakened France in Europe and made her dependent on German goodwill. Imperial dreams were haunted by the fear that France had missed the great prizes: Russia and Britain were conquering Asia while France was merely occupying the Sahara desert, lamented the republican Quinet. Over the decades, Algeria, Indochina, Mexico, west Africa and Morocco were successively imagined as a 'French India', the last unclaimed prize in the global contest which France had to seize in order to remain great in the 'Anglo-Saxon world of the future'.[4] The economic value of colonies was proclaimed in the crudest and most fanciful terms – mountains of gold, vast markets – but these were politicians' fantasies of power, not businessmen's assessments of profit.

A second theme was empire as a remedy for decadence. France, defeated at Waterloo and again at Sedan, was physically damaged and psychologically

2. Andrew, in Bull and Watson (1984), p. 337.
3. Andrew and Kanya-Forstner (1988), p. 16.
4. Prévost-Paradol (1869), pp. 408, 416.

enfeebled. It was necessary to rekindle patriotic fervour by proving to the world and also to the French themselves that they were still more than 'a big Belgium'. Imperialism was its own justification here: any adventure would serve to raise France from what Quinet called 'the sepulchre of Waterloo'. The 1840 crisis over Egypt was seen by many as a moment of truth: would France stand up to the threats of its rivals, or would it give in and abdicate its world role? Similarly, it was argued in 1848 that Algeria had to be held and developed, or it would be a sign that, as one deputy argued, 'France is incapable of founding anything, that she is in decline, that she has no choice but to descend from the first rank of nations'. The new Republic duly annexed it. After 1870, the same thinking appeared among younger republican patriots: in Gambetta's words, 'it is through expansion, through influencing the outside world, through the place that they occupy in the general life of humanity, that nations persist and last'.[5] In language reminiscent of Thiers or Tocqueville in the 1840s, Republicans warned against 'the policy of the fireside'. France's new mission would be to 'carry wherever she can her language, her way of life, her flag, her arms, her genius'; to fail in this would be 'the high road to decadence', descending 'from the first rank to the third or fourth'.[6] Colonies would enable France to recover a leading role in the world without risking another disastrous conflict with Germany. The empire was seen as a place of regeneration, especially for soldiers who, hardened and purged of the sicknesses of urban civilization, would provide France with leaders; indeed, nearly every soldier who played a significant national role – including Bugeaud, Cavaignac, Saint-Arnaud, MacMahon, Boulanger, Lyautey and Joffre – had proved themselves in the colonies. The popular image of the empire was as a military adventure: colonials, notes Girardet, were almost always portrayed in uniform. In the 1900s, colonial heroes figured in the literature of consciously modern, strenuously healthy patriotism, along with sportsmen and aviators.

The third theme of imperialist thought was France's civilizing mission. This provided the moral underpinning which, in the minds of nationalists, distinguished French conquests from the selfish aggression of other colonial powers, especially Britain, the 'social vampire' motivated by 'mercantile egoism'.[7] This justified the use of force in France's case, as Tocqueville regretfully admitted:

> The idea of . . . possessing Africa . . . with the aid and support of the native population, an idea that is the dream of noble and generous hearts, is chimerical, for now at least . . . Once we have countenanced the great violence of conquest, I believe we must not recoil before the specific acts of violence that are absolutely necessary to consolidate it.[8]

5. Girardet (1972), p. 78.
6. Girardet (1983), pp. 100, 106–7.
7. Considérant (1840), pp. 8, 66.
8. Todorov (1993), p. 203.

The socialist anthropologist Gustave Flourens, later killed fighting for the Paris Commune, taught in the 1860s that the lower races should and would inevitably 'disappear' in the face of higher Aryan civilization.[9]

The belief in a unique French mission was shared in different ways by Left and Right. Catholics pressed for backing in the name of France's traditional role as protector of Catholics. They repaid such support by becoming the willing instruments of French influence, more valuable, it has been said, than the Foreign Legion. The nationalist Barrès reported in 1914 that 'Beneath the banner of Christ [they] preach the love of France with an ardour no description can exaggerate'.[10] The Third Republic officially adopted the concept of liberation through conquest, 'tinging with messianism the glory of victorious combat'.[11] Ferry declared that 'the superior races have a right . . . a duty to civilize the inferior races'.[12] The Alliance Française was founded in 1883 as a secular missionary organization to 'make our language known and loved' and hence contribute to 'the extension beyond the seas of the French race which is increasing too slowly on the continent'.[13] Colonization became the extension and fulfilment overseas of the process of cultural assimilation and republicanization that was turning peasants into Frenchmen inside France. Significantly, among republican colonialists were leading exponents of the gospel of mass schooling at home, such as Paul Bert, Gambetta's minister of education and later governor-general of Annam and Tonkin, and Albert Sarraut, a prominent radical who went from being governor-general of Indochina to minister of education in 1914. Interestingly, his ideas on the kind of education appropriate for Vietnamese peasants was almost identical with that thought appropriate for French peasants half a century before.

The imperial mission was expounded through the republican schools: 'France is kind and generous to the peoples she has subdued'.[14] In theory, non-European peoples welcomed French rule: the famous textbook by the republican historian Lavisse related, for example, that the explorer de Brazza proclaimed to the joy of the natives that 'wherever the French flag flies, there must be no slaves'.[15] The most intelligent would adopt the universal values and culture of France, and would themselves be 'assimilated' into a greater French nation. The story that African children were taught in school about 'our ancestors the Gauls' was probably a myth,[16] but one uncomfortably close to home.

The French mission proved a seductive justification for colonialism, and one that few rejected in principal. Liberal economists attacked empire as a waste of effort and resources in the 1840s. Some nationalists for a time took a

9. Flourens (1863), p. 35.
10. Andrew and Kanya-Forstner (1981), p. 41.
11. Citron (1989), p. 62.
12. Porch (1981), p. 136.
13. Andrew and Kanya-Forstner (1981), p. 27.
14. Citron (1989), p. 63.
15. Ibid., p. 63.
16. Weber (1991), pp. 15–16.

similar view in the 1880s, as expressed in Déroulède's famous outburst comparing the lost provinces of Alsace and Lorraine with compensatory colonial gains: 'I have lost two sisters, and you offer me twenty servants'. But very few – anti-militarists and anarchists in the 1880s and 1890s – denied that French colonialism was progressive and beneficent in principle, even if it sometimes fell short in practice. As the socialist leader Jaurès put it in 1903, 'If we have always fought against warlike policies of colonial expansion . . . we have always supported the peaceful expansion of French interests and civilization'.[17]

ACQUIRING THE EMPIRE

On returning to France after many years overseas, one is struck by the public's profound indifference to all aspects of the colonial contribution to our national greatness.

Francis Garnier, 1869[18]

While thinking about empire showed remarkable continuity over the century, there were four broad phases of acquisition: from *c.* 1820 to 1848; the 1850s and 1860s; the 1880s; and from 1890 to the end of the First World War. The first phase, *c.*1820–48 – the Restoration, July Monarchy and Second Republic – saw prudent and parsimonious governments trying to reassert French prestige after Waterloo without conflict with major states, while trying to fend off left-wing accusations that they were indifferent to national greatness. The principal region of interest was the Mediterranean, where French influence was long established. The momentous step was the punitive expedition against the Dey of Algiers in 1830, aimed at winning prestige for the doomed government of Charles X. Boatloads of sightseers came from France to watch the bombardment. The troops were supposed to return within six weeks; they stayed for 130 years. In campaigns from 1832 to 1847 the whole of Algeria was occupied, and the Second Republic in May 1848 fatefully declared it to be 'a land forever French'. The dream of becoming the dominant Mediterranean power and taking part in what Tocqueville called the 'new world of Europe enveloping Asia' led to involvement in the Ottoman Empire. France suffered a humiliating diplomatic reverse in 1840 (see p. 364). However, successive French governments clung for more than a century to claims to special influence in the Middle East.

There was also cautious consolidation of footholds in Africa, the Pacific and South America. However, no government was willing to commit major resources to what remained tentative experiments. This contradiction between great ambitions and cautious acts inaugurated what was to be a characteristic of French colonialism: local initiatives to force the government's hand. The

17. Andrew and Kanya-Forstner (1988), p. 27.
18. Ibid., p. 15. Most unattributed quotations in this section are from this source.

great names of imperial history are ambitious, visionary and insubordinate soldiers: Bugeaud, Faidherbe, Brazza, Galliéni, Lyautey. From the Mediterranean to the Pacific (in 1844 Tahiti was the scene of a trivial but damaging conflict with Britain) soldiers and sailors acted without or against orders in the expectation that nationalist opinion would force governments to back them up. Most notorious was Marshal Bugeaud in Algeria, who advised that 'one should burn instructions so as to avoid the temptation of reading them'. In 1847 he invaded Kabylia in defiance of orders, reporting to the minister of war: 'My troops . . . have already left . . . If we succeed, France and the government will have the honour. If we fail, the responsibility will be mine alone.' This was an offer that few politicians over the century were strong enough to refuse. Guizot, although an opponent of jingoism and aimless expansionism, spoke for all his successors: France must not 'appear uncertain and timid'. This attitude gave the military their chance.

The second phase was that of the Second Empire, which in the colonial domain as in others added an unpredictable twist to inherited policies. Napoleon III intended to restore France to a leading position in the world, inspired by visionary maxims of Napoleon I and some of the apocalyptic predictions of romantic nationalism – a dangerous combination. Although he began with little interest in the footholds in Indochina, Madagascar and the Pacific inherited from the July Monarchy, his opportunism led him into a series of adventures. Victory in the Crimean War (1854–55), which combined European and imperial aims, had placed him in a tempting position of predominance. 'For the sake of national greatness', he declared in 1861, 'we must maintain our incontestable rights everywhere in the world, defend our honour wherever it is attacked, lend our assistance wherever it is sought in support of a just cause.' There were campaigns in Indochina, China, Syria, Senegal and Mexico. This last adventure, 'the great idea of the reign', was aimed at providing France on the cheap with a major protectorate, ruled by the Habsburg Archduke Maximilian as emperor, that was expected to be a vast sphere of political and economic influence, the key to central America, and a possible canal route to the Pacific. However, Mexican guerillas, United States pressure and intense unpopularity at home forced a humiliating withdrawal in 1867 leaving Maximilian to face a firing squad. The new colony in Indochina was nearly abandoned too. As the emperor had admitted in 1863, there had been no preconceived plan, but merely response to circumstances. When circumstances deteriorated, with opposition at home and the threat of war in Europe, colonial losses were cut.

The third phase followed the war of 1870. A serious revolt in Algeria, the Arab reaction to the French defeat, was ruthlessly crushed. Young republicans, led by Léon Gambetta and Jules Ferry in the 1880s, were determined to restore French greatness and their arguments were echoed by the small but persistent groups of colonial enthusiasts. They promised trade, wealth, fertile lands for colonization, a new race of hardy frontiersmen, and the always beckoning mirage of 'a French India' somewhere near the Sahara desert. But at the same time, the 1870 defeat created widespread fear of any act that might conceivably lead to another major war anywhere. Moreover, militant nationalists, led by Déroulède's Ligue des Patriotes, insisted that all France's men and money should be concentrated in Europe, against the German enemy beyond 'the blue line of the Vosges'. Hence, attempts promoted by Gambetta and Ferry to pursue colonial expansion in Tunisia and Indochina, and to defend French influence in Egypt, met angry opposition in parliament and the press, leading to Ferry's political downfall in 1885. Yet, such was the ambivalence of public attitudes to empire, the abandonment of Egypt to British influence in 1882 was also unpopular, bringing down the Freycinet government and poisoning Franco-British relations for a generation. Despite setbacks, ambitions in west and north Africa, Madagascar and Indochina were doggedly pursued behind the scenes in Paris by politicians, officials and lobbies, or by determined soldiers on the spot. 'Since the government was foolish enough to send me 500 men', declared one officer in 1883, 'I set out to accomplish on my own what it lacked the nerve to make me do. They will now be forced to carry on.'

The fourth phase, 1890–1920, saw 'a renewed expansionist wave [that] extended the . . . empire to its final territorial limits'.[19] Initiative shifted from men on the spot to Paris as politicians and journalists increasingly espoused the colonialist lobby's views. The 'scramble for Africa' convinced many that if colonies were valuable for France's European rivals, they must be valuable to her too. The conquest of Madagascar was undertaken in 1894 'to teach England a lesson'; the hare-brained Fashoda expedition to the Sudan of 1896–98, sent to try to forestall the British, was retroactively approved by the Chamber by 477 votes to 18, which even the socialist Jaurès described as 'not a political vote but a national one'. The greatest colonial cause, however, became Morocco, all the more desirable because it was Germany that stood in the way. 'How many people have been converted to the Moroccan cause only by the . . . irritating opposition of Germany!' Ultimately, therefore, for the French as for Bismarck, their map of Africa was really a map of Europe.

Those in charge of policy in Paris were from the 1890s onwards the leaders of the Parti Colonial: an association of colonialist politicians, intellectuals, officials, soldiers and businessmen. The leaders were Théophile Delcassé (minister of colonies, 1894–95 and foreign minister, 1898–1905) and Eugène Etienne (deputy for Oran, real leader of the colonial lobby and several times junior colonial minister between 1887 and 1892). They were determined to extend and unify territory held in north and west Africa, to gain full control of Indochina and to force the British out of Egypt. Soldiers on the spot cooperated by making things easier to justify. Lyautey changed place-names on the map: 'to spare diplomatic susceptibilities, Béchar will no longer be called Béchar, if you get my meaning'.[20] There was no collective cabinet control; most politicians remained uninterested in the details of imperial policy. Dangerous initiatives – the Fashoda expedition in 1896 and the

19. Ibid., p. 23.
20. Porch (1981), p. 148.

occupation of Fez in 1911 which caused potentially disastrous confrontation with Britain and Germany respectively – were undertaken by colonialist ministers and officials without the government as a whole knowing what was happening; Fez was approved by three colonialist ministers while the rest of ·the government was on holiday. 'We have behaved like madmen in Africa', complained President Faure after Fashoda, 'led astray by irresponsible people called colonialists.'[21] The colonialists themselves drew the conclusion that a compromise with Britain was necessary and in 1904, again without briefing his cabinet colleagues, Delcassé negotiated an agreement (later known optimistically as the *entente cordiale*) by which the two agreed to a compromise in north Africa, with Egypt being recognized as a British sphere and Morocco a French. This momentous reversal of policy was motivated by alarm and anger at German designs on Morocco, the focus of nationalist ambitions in the 1900s. As in the past, 'we were yearning to recover from both the moral and the material blows we had suffered, both in our own eyes and in the world's'.[22] The occupation of Fez precipitated the dangerous Agadir crisis in 1911, but also strengthened the new relationship with Britain in the face of what now seemed a common threat from Germany. British support enabled France to secure Morocco as a protectorate in 1912, the last major acquisition until the spoils won in the First World War brought the empire to its apogee.

RULING THE EMPIRE

All that interests the French public about the Empire is the belly dance.

Jules Ferry, 1889[23]

Rarely in the chequered history of European imperialism did idealistic rhetoric diverge so widely from the practice of ruling. This was partly due to the importance of the army in acquiring and governing the empire: in Porch's pithy phrase, the civilizing mission was hampered by the fact that most of its agents had acquired their notions of civilization in a barracks.[24] The habitual lack of interest in colonial affairs of the public and most politicians – when shown a map, the new minister of colonies in 1905 exclaimed 'I didn't know there were so many!'[25] – made it impossible to recruit a civilian colonial service of adequate quality. The colonies remained a dumping ground for failures: 'a barber, a peanut-vender, a navvy with the right connexions, can be named an administrator of native affairs'. This was not mere hyperbole: in 1887, 61 per cent of officials were officially rated incompetent, and of those

21. Kanya-Forstner (1969), p. 263.
22. Charles-Roux, 1906, in Baumgart (1982), p. 57.
23. Keiger (1983), p. 14.
24. Porch (1981), p. 137.
25. Marseille (1984), p. 367.

recruited in 1900–14, barely half had a secondary education.[26] Such officials were incapable of doing much for the conquered peoples in their charge or keeping soldiers and settlers in check, especially as political authority was divided between rival ministries in Paris (navy, war, interior, foreign affairs, commerce and after 1894 colonies) each ferociously guarding what one minister termed its 'prey'.

The soldiers' motives were a mixture of nationalism and ambition: they wanted France to have an empire and they wanted action and promotion for themselves. They used colonial territories as a live battle-training ground. Ruthless methods camouflaged by high-minded rhetoric proved a deadly combination for colonial peoples, especially when carried out by men who included a liberal sprinkling of careerists (the most ambitious officer cadets chose the colonial army), drunks and psychopaths. Atrocities were frequent. One that came to public notice in 1845 was the suffocation by smoke of several hundred Arabs sheltering in caves at Dahra, in Algeria: 'I have all the exits hermetically sealed and I make a huge cemetery',[27] reported Colonel Saint-Arnaud, later famous as a participant in the 1851 coup d'état. Such reports were denied, excused or ignored. Half a century later, horrors continued without serious censure from governments that wanted colonies, needed the army to obtain them, and were too weak to control it on the ground; only the extreme Left protested energetically. Despite the legend of Brazza and the liberating tricolour, the army tolerated and even used slavery in central Africa into the 1890s. Slave markets operated at army posts, military expeditions used quasi-slavery to obtain porters, and officers gave slaves as booty to their native troops – especially women, euphemistically known as *épouses libres*. Forced labour and military conscription remained until after the Second World War. Colonial subjects who were not French citizens – the great majority – were subject to arbitrary administrative punishment. Large numbers of refugees sought shelter in British west African colonies, which organized military defences against the depredations of French troops; and thousands fled from harsh repression in Indochina to neighbouring British colonies in the 1920s and 1930s.[28]

The ideal of 'assimilation' was an aggravating element, whether among the Muslims and Jews of north Africa or the peoples of equatorial Africa and Indochina. Those who rejected 'civilizing ideas' were dismissed as fanatical. Social and political practices were overturned; for example, communal property was handed over to individuals. The proclamation of Algeria as part of France in 1848 showed the hollowness of the idea and some of the contradictions of republican principles. Although 'universal suffrage' was proclaimed as an inherent right, not subject to any qualification of wealth or education, it was not extended to the non-white inhabitants of the Algerian departments. The Crémieux decree of 1870 made it possible for all Algerian

26. Porch (1981), p. 144.
27. Todorov (1993), p. 205.
28. Asiwaju (1976).

Jews, though not Muslims, to accede to French citizenship; non-citizens remained until the Second World War largely deprived of legal rights. Clearly, the 'universal' values of 1789 were subject to an ethnic (as well as gender) hierarchy. The Jews were slow to take up an offer that cut them off from their own communities; but nevertheless Jewish emancipation fanned ferocious antisemitism among settlers during the 1880s and 1890s, led, interestingly, by left-wing republicans. The Muslim majority received few political rights. Indeed, the advent of the Third Republic increased the political voice of settlers, who returned deputies to the French parliament. They also controlled local government, which reproduced in particularly gross form the clientelism and corruption of the metropolis. Arabs and Kabyles were more than ever vulnerable to land-grabbing.[29]

Economics were a secondary consideration of French imperialism, as its high-minded exponents often boasted. The 'French Indias' and El Dorados such as Timbuctoo quickly proved illusory. The 'Malthusian' French were not eager settlers: only in the hunger-stricken 1840s was there much interest in colonization, and even in Algeria a high proportion of whites came from Italy and Spain. Railways and roads were painfully and expensively built, but with disappointing results, especially when hampered by interministerial rivalry, such as that which left a gap of several hundred yards at the border between Algeria (ministry of the interior) and Tunisia (ministry of foreign affairs). The process of conquest itself wrought economic havoc, especially in west central Africa. Consequently, trade was slow to follow the flag: businessmen were chary of imperialist fantasies. Only a few industries – soap, sugar, silk, mining – were interested in colonial trade or investment before 1900. Lyautey found the contrast between Singapore and Saigon disturbing: the former full of banks and businesses, the latter with only soldiers, cafés and administrative buildings.[30] However, after 1900 investment and trade did become more important. Marseille, arguing that the economic significance of the empire has usually been underestimated, points out that by 1914 it was second only to Russia as a field for investment, and that colonial trade was important for certain industries: in exports, for example, 86 per cent of bleached cotton and 39 per cent of refined sugar went to the empire in 1906.[31] If put in perspective, this is less impressive than it sounds. Only 10 per cent of total foreign trade was with the empire, far less than before the Revolution.[32] Only 9 per cent of total foreign investment was in the empire, mainly in Algeria and Indochina (to the neglect of the vast tracts of west and central Africa), small compared with the 25 per cent in Russia (or the 45 per cent of British overseas investment in her empire). Moreover, a high proportion of colonial investment was State spending, not private. Economic development was very patchy: though sugarcane and wine were produced, there was hardly any

29. Prochaska (1990).
30. Porch (1981), p. 137.
31. Marseille (1984), pp. 50–7.
32. Andrew and Kanya-Forstner (1981), pp. 14–16.

cotton; the Ivory Coast colony produced 47 tons of cocoa to the British Gold Coast's 51,000 tons. When the empire became genuinely important economically between the World Wars, its main function, as in Britain, was to provide a protected market to keep uncompetitive industries profitable.

CONCLUSIONS

We remain because we are here, because we want to believe that it is possible to continue the conquest without great effort, because we do not want to lose the benefits of the sacrifices already made, because we consider the interests of the nation and the natives who immediately attach themselves to this kind of enterprise, and finally because the honour of the army and the prestige of the flag, sometimes the existence of governments, are at stake.

Colonial official, 1910[33]

Empire was directly linked to fundamental ideological and political concerns of the post-revolutionary period: consolidating support for shaky regimes by appealing to national pride; uniting a nation riven by political conflict; asserting a special world mission for France as a remedy for self-doubt and decadence; and strengthening France in the face of perceived military, economic, demographic and cultural threats. The acquisition of the empire displayed idealism and ruthlessness: it was a sacred cause that ultimately justified any methods. The desire for empire for its own sake, not primarily for trade or settlement, made it peculiarly dependent on military force and on the initiatives of small groups of enthusiasts occasionally backed up by jingoistic outbursts of a public that had little knowledge of or concrete interest in colonies.

Before 1870, nationalists dreamed of leading Europe as well as playing a part in the 'civilization' of the non-European world. After Sedan, their visions were increasingly projected outside a German-dominated continent towards an imperial role that would compensate for continental weakness. The Third Republic made imperialism a crowning aspect of its emancipating mission, and was eventually able to win the support in principle of nearly the whole political class. An empire second only to that of Britain became the principal channel by which French culture and political ideas ('the values of 1789') reached the wider world. French culture indeed proved attractive to much of the colonial elite, even if they rejected French rule. One of the most notable examples, the Senegalese writer and politician Léopold Senghor, expressed his ambivalence neatly: 'I know no people more tyrannical in its love for mankind. It wants bread for all, culture for all, liberty for all; but this liberty, this culture, this bread, are to be *French*.'[34] Imperialism was thus intimately linked with the great events of French history and with the hopes and fears of nationalists perhaps to a greater extent than anywhere else, including Britain.

33. Porch (1981), p. 134.
34. Andrew, in Bull and Watson (1984), p. 338.

After the two World Wars, in which the empire had helped France to survive, popular support for it increased substantially. And yet it still remained of major interest only to a minority. This perhaps explains some seeming contradictions: decolonization in the 1950s was uniquely traumatic and bloody, yet the ordeal has left few traces on public memory; and governments engage quietly in neo-colonialist activities without arousing public concern.

PART THREE

IDENTITIES

How people thought of themselves and each other forms the subject of this section. These identities changed in broadly similar ways throughout the European world, affected by common economic and social changes, and by ideas and fashions that crossed frontiers and were often consciously imitated. Can there in that case be a specifically French history of identities? As in other areas of life, the key is the aftershock of Revolution. It focused attention on the proper boundaries between public and private life. It strengthened the normative obsession of the State and its auxiliaries, including, in this area, doctors and scientists. Its interventions in the workings of society influenced the formation of regional, class and national identities. It fuelled the struggle between Catholicism and *laïcité*. The chronology of change was influenced by political events. All this sustained a specifically French variant of the history of identities.

CHAPTER 12

PRIVATE IDENTITIES: SELF, GENDER, FAMILY

SELF

Man can barely know himself, and he is never more than guessed about by others. The most simple person would have a thousand secrets to reveal to us.

Guizot[1]

There are many signs in the early nineteenth century of a sharper individual consciousness – what Corbin calls 'individuation' – which we might associate, among other things, with the upheavals of the Revolution and the Romantic fashion for introspection and singularity. Children were given a wider variety of names, and more adults learned to sign theirs; during the Restoration, that time of Romantic yearning, people began to carve their initials on the trees and rocks of the Fontainebleau forest.[2] Large numbers of people kept scrapbooks and diaries, and more and more wrote letters. Mirrors, once rare and even taboo, became commonplace: for the first time, most people knew what they looked like. In other ways, they became concerned for their appearance: grooming, fashion and even cleanliness became increasingly widespread concerns, though at the end of the century the aristocratic Pauline de Broglie recalled that 'no one in my family ever took a bath'.[3] Cheap photographs in the 1860s (the photographer Disdéri sold 2,400 per day) and travelling street photographers provided a record of the changing self, and also photographic postcards of models to emulate. Collecting, as an external expression of one's own taste and intellect, became more widely fashionable. Travel, not the familiar Grand Tour but exploration of the exotic and even the dangerous, became another means of self-expression and self-discovery: Hector Berlioz, for example, wandered among the brigands of the Roman Campagna in 1831 to find inspiration for his music. All these things were signs of a clearer and far more widespread self-consciousness, self-scrutiny and self-dramatization. An aspect of modernity: a shared desire to be different.

1. Zeldin (1973), vol. 2, p. 768.
2. Corbin, in Perrot (1990) – a fascinating piece to which this section owes much.
3. Weber (1986), p. 59.

Religious practices reflected and spread self-awareness. While examination of conscience and spiritual exercises were not new, at least for a pious elite, subjectivity in religious devotion seems to have become more widely practised. Again, the stresses of the Revolution, with its religious persecutions, the consequent need actively to choose religion rather than merely conforming, and the mission campaigns of the Restoration to win back the masses to Christianity provide much of the explanation. Conversion or apostasy became a great Romantic drama of the soul, as in Chateaubriand's return to Catholicism, impelled by personal emotion: 'I wept and I believed'. The nineteenth century became the golden age of confession, no longer simply a formal annual obligation, but a pilgrimage to self-knowledge and catharsis. The greatest of confessors, Jean-Marie Vianney, the *curé* of Ars, spent seventeen hours a day during the 1840s and 1850s confessing over 50,000 penitents a year who queued for a week for what was clearly often a traumatic assessment of their lives and worth: 'My boy, you are damned!'[4] It could also be an enjoyable opportunity to talk about oneself with a sympathetic listener, as the primly pious Parisian teenager Pauline Brame recorded in her diary in the 1860s.[5] A religious vocation became a spiritual choice, not merely a family convenience for unmarriageable children. Prayers too became increasingly personal intercessions, rather than dutiful conformity or mechanical ritual: the nineteenth century was the golden age of the *ex-voto* offering to thank God or the saints for personal favours, such as those which cover the walls of Notre Dame des Victoires in Paris or the basilica at Lourdes.

The Romantic movement – a subject too vast to discuss here – stressed the importance of individual experience and insight, and art itself (for the creator and the 'consumer') was seen as a way to self-knowledge. A greater availability of books to buy or borrow (40,000 Parisians used lending libraries) and the consequent decline of communal reading aloud made literature – whether works of piety, textbooks, almanacs, children's books, biographies, novels, poetry or history – a more solitary activity. The huge new success of poetry and novels, especially those serialized in the press, made it possible to reflect imaginatively on one's own life and the lives of others, and provided heroes, heroines and villains with whom readers could identify and compare. Eugène Sue's hugely popular *Mystères de Paris* (serialized in 1842–43) drew masses of letters from working-class readers as the story progressed. Drawing on their own experiences and feelings, they told him how he must and must not deal with his characters, 'as if the workmen and artisans of Paris had taken it in turns each day to guide Sue's pen'.[6]

Science and medicine were increasingly influential in elaborating ideas of the self. They defined norms of health and illness, sanity and insanity,

4. Boutry and Cinquin (1980), p. 66.
5. Perrot and Ribeill (1985).
6. Chevalier (1973), p. 405.

prudent and dangerous behaviour. 'Physiognomy' defined the role of body and soul in the creation of personality and character. A succession of pioneering French psychiatrists, from Pinel to Charcot, created the idea of the hidden personality, the unconscious mind. Self-awareness brought characteristic troubles: the Romantics spoke of *l'ennui* and *le mal du siècle*; Baudelaire wrote of 'spleen', one of many franglais imports. Hamlet was discovered as the archetypal introspective: 'être ou ne pas être'. Ambition, encouraged at all levels of society by the theoretical equality of opportunity proclaimed by the Revolution, but frustrated by the socio-economic realities of a relatively unchanging society, was considered dangerous by doctors because it created insecurity and a sense of failure. Self-consciousness brought an awareness of loneliness, whether a result of social and geographical mobility, or a feeling of isolation within a friendless or loveless environment, so different from the literary models. The nineteenth century discovered solitary drinking and alcoholism. It became obsessively concerned with the supposed ravages of solitary sex. The new asylums were filled by a horde of people diagnosed as insane. The suicide rate probably increased until the end of the century: it came in waves, affecting those at the top and the bottom of the social pile; loneliness was the commonest cause.

GENDER

Man must nourish woman. Both spiritually and materially, he must nourish her who in turn nourishes him with her love, with her milk, and with her blood.

Jules Michelet, 1845[7]

If men understand nothing of women's hearts, women understand nothing of men's honour.

Alexandre Dumas fils, 1885

The circumstances that were stimulating self-consciousness were also elaborating conceptions of the natures of women and men and their proper self-expression. The Revolution momentarily brought women on to the political scene as it dissolved conventional barriers and hierarchies, and removed the distinction between private and public life, opening everything to public scrutiny and political interference. There was an almost immediate reaction: the Jacobins barred women from politics. The Civil and Penal Codes set limits to public intrusion, protecting family and household both from the waywardness of their members and from outside interference. A 'domestic ideology' became almost universally accepted. The family was cast as the basic unit of society. On its healthy functioning all else depended. This microcosm was a monarchy, ruled by the father; but its soul was female – the mother alone could provide love, gentleness and care. So important was this task that she was urged to devote all her energies to it. Withdrawn from the

7. McMillan, in Tallet and Atkin (1991), p. 60.

distractions of the outside world, domesticity would be the 'separate sphere' in which she would find fulfilment. She would exercise profound influence as wife and mother: whether as society hostess presiding over the salons where great men met, as a softening and civilizing influence over her husband, or as moulder of the next generation by giving her children their first indelible lessons in morality. If men monopolized 'power', women were said to exercise 'powers'.[8] Hardly anyone disagreed in principle with this concept. The fact that many women, including mothers, had to take jobs outside the home was regarded at best as a regrettable necessity, at worst as a scandalous aberration. Industrialization would, in fact, make domesticity realizable for more people, first for the growing middle classes, and also for better paid workers.

The separation of a public male sphere from a private female sphere was justified as a consequence of the different natures of the sexes. The Romantic sensibility dramatized and idealized this conventional difference: the model woman was sensitive, fragile and pure; the ideal man strong, courageous and wise. The simpering smile and heavenward gaze of the former, the set jaw and pugnacious glare of the latter were embodied in innumerable drawings and photographs. Women's nature, as analysed by men, was marked by extreme fragility: their inferior intellect, greater emotional sensitivity, and physical vulnerability exposed them to psychological and moral dangers. Unless protected and controlled by men, they risked hysteria, insanity, depravity: 'a mere nothing troubles them . . . their nervous system is far more malleable than ours', declares one of Flaubert's characters.[9] This amounted to a dual nature. On one hand, woman as saint, accepting the martyrdom of her body, nourishing man with her blood and milk, and devoting her emotional resources to chaste love and charity. The model was the Virgin Mary, who began to appear miraculously to a succession of young French girls from the 1830s onwards. On the other hand, woman as sinner, as Eve, the source of temptation for men, and herself incapable of sternly resisting temptations of the flesh, 'always stronger among primitive natures and ineffectively held in check by the vacillating will power of their pliable, deadened minds', as Maupassant gallantly put it. Cultural representations of these two opposing stereotypes were everywhere. Anything that challenged them caused controversy. Two of the most famous paintings of the century fell into this category: Delacroix's *Liberty leading the people* (1830) and Manet's *Olympia* (1863). Both were attacked for a shocking de-idealization of female imagery, the second clearly deliberate. *Olympia* was immediately identified as a prostitute: she looks the spectator coolly in the eye. This Manichean attitude towards women was of course not specifically French; but the combination of Catholic tradition and the legacy of Revolution with its myths of female savagery may have made the contrast between pure and impure particularly lurid in French imaginations.

8. Perrot, in Reynolds (1986), p. 44.
9. Leclerc (1991), pp. 132–3.

Female figures provided ubiquitous political icons: numerous 'Mariannes', demure, maternal or warlike republics with flashing eyes and 'powerful bosoms', even figuratively leading men into battle, as in Delacroix's epic. But real women were not meant to be politically prominent: flesh-and-blood militancy was alarming to men of all parties, and was commonly associated with the counter-image of women, marked by debauchery, hysteria and savagery. The *mégère* (the harpy) was a figure of male nightmares (see p. 13). Several historians have recently argued that the Paris Commune saw a significant attempt by women to defy the conventional stereotypes and assert a new concept of female citizenship, especially the right to bear arms. The evidence is slight: at most a handful of the very bold or the very eccentric ever tried to fight. Perhaps more significant is that the few who notoriously did, such as the Russian Eliseveta Tomanovskaya, known as Elisabeth Dmitrieff, or 'Générale Eudes', wife of a leading Blanquist, could not imagine their role except as a comic-opera caricature of masculine militarism, ostentatiously festooned with bandoliers and pistols. In other words, there was less and less of a model for being a political woman. Outstanding individuals such as the socialist writer Flora Tristan and the radical novelist George Sand (Aurore Dupin), both active in the 1840s, had found it difficult to find a viable political role either among women or men, or, indeed, a viable lifestyle. The most enduring model of action, that of the working-class woman rebel, associated with spontaneous community action to provide food for the family in times of dearth or high prices, was superseded, as Perrot has observed, as revolution became more militarized, and political action generally became based less on community and 'people' and more on party, trade union and 'class'.[10] Male militants were often irritated or shocked by what they saw as frivolous and indisciplined female actions: when women in the north of France as late as 1899 and 1905 organized noisy nocturnal *charivaris* and on one occasion raised their skirts in unison to embarrass a sub-prefect, strait-laced male socialist organizers put a stop to it. With a few marginalized exceptions – such as the tie-wearing cigar-smoking Hubertine Auclert, founder of the suffrage movement, and regarded as mad – women in politics during the Third Republic found it prudent to emphasize their respectability, moderation and conventional femininity, and to express horror at the feminist extremism of America and Britain. This is a strategy still followed by Chanel-clad politicians a century later.

In everyday life, women and men were increasingly separated over the century, and hence what seemed appropriate and natural for each in modern 'civilized' society steadily diverged. In pre-industrial societies, all but a privileged minority of both sexes worked manually, and the work they did, if different, was complementary and closely associated: men tending the fields, women the animals; women spinning, men weaving. Industrial society enabled more people to gain or aspire to relative affluence, in which female leisure, or at least abstention from paid employment, was for women a sign

10. Perrot, in Dufrancatel *et al.* (1979).

of respectability and for men, including better off workers and farmers, a
mark of success, like buying a piano. In the northern textile industry, for
example, wives of mill-owners ceased to take part in the business, and new
houses were built well away from the mill: they became 'ladies of the
leisured class'.[11] The unusually large number of adult women who took paid
work in France were confined by convention and law to 'women's work',
glutted with labour and badly paid, while men monopolized (with the partial
exception of textile manufacture) the new, expanding and better paid sectors.
'For the man, wood and metals. For the woman, the family and textiles' a
workers' pamplet pronounced in 1867. In short, women at work were
hemmed in by stereotypes about their 'nature', and their segregation at work
in turn reinforced the conventions of what was appropriate.

Changing forms of sociability also tended to segregate the sexes. Certain
shared activities declined, notably the rural *veillée* (evening work gatherings
accompanied by story-telling) and participation in religious services and
festivals. New activities were for men: the village clubs (*chambrées*) from the
1830s onwards, and the urban bars (*cabarets*), centres of social life which
multiplied hugely after the Third Republic removed licensing restrictions.
Political organizations, which began to affect the mass of the population from
1830 onwards, and particularly after 'universal' (male) suffrage arrived in
1848, were also concerns of men. New kinds of religious, philanthropic and
charitable organizations also separated men and women. From the 1880s
onwards, the increasing appeal of organized team sport principally involved
boys. Primary schools also became increasingly segregated after 1867. Of
course, boys and girls continued to meet, and dancing and later bicycling (a
craze from the 1890s onwards) gave exciting opportunities, which moralists,
especially the clergy, went to extreme lengths to prevent on the grounds that
dancing led to sex and cycling caused nymphomania. But these activities
were for a specific and exceptional purpose, courtship, and did not counter
the everyday separation of women and men. Indeed, the degree of
supervision and control of the activities of girls, for example, may have
reached its peak very late – just before the First World War.[12]

It would, however, be misleading to think of women as merely the
malleable victims of male stereotyping. The 'separate spheres' could be a
form of protection and even a source of empowerment. Girls working under
the supervision of nuns were at least safeguarded from harassment by male
foremen, including sexual – a scourge that until very recently historians have
overlooked.[13] Perrot has shown how certain activities and places were taken
over by women. The urban working-class housewife (*ménagère*), a new
phenomenon, often controlled the family budget and made city streets,
markets, shops (small retailing was very much a female sector) and
communal laundries her domain. These were centres of news, gossip and

11. Smith (1981).
12. Corbin, in Perrot (1990), p. 576.
13. Louis (1994).

'practical feminism'.[14] Interestingly, the order-obsessed Second Empire tried to make laundries more impersonal, and remove them from city centres. Women transmitted village and regional stories, remedies and beliefs into urban culture, resisting the hegemony of nineteenth-century science and rationalism; and they kept their rural soups and stews, despised by professional male chefs who prized the 'richness' of fats and sugar.

Great effort, not only in France, went into reinforcing gender stereotypes. Secondary schools and universities, by the very fact of their exclusive (until the 1880s) or overwhelming maleness, maintained the appearance of masculine intellectual superiority. Girls' education had a clearly different content and purpose, and it engendered different expectations and ambitions. As one text set for dictation put it in 1886, 'Young girls must be taught from their earliest years that calm, self-possessed bearing which is at once a mark of modesty and of grace. They must early be taught those habits that will make them sedentary.'[15] Religion became increasingly a powerful creator of gendered identity (see p. 243). Irreligious men considered piety necessary and normal for women: it kept them chaste and satisfied their supposedly infantile appetite for sentimentality. Military service, especially after it became practically universal in 1889, powerfully contributed to masculine identity. It was closely linked with the republican tradition of 'fraternity', and the republican political victory in the 1870s, followed by determined efforts to universalize its rationalist, secular and patriotic values, served to reinforce and perpetuate the idea of an exclusively and characteristically male public sphere. A republican citizen was a soldier and a 'freethinker'; the republican tradition, its ceremonies, its heroes, its discourse, emphasized revolutionary struggle and war, both past and future, with stress on preparation for 'revenge' against Germany. One result was that duelling had an extraordinary vogue in late-nineteenth-century France just as it was dying out in most other countries. It was regarded as a quintessential activity of a French gentleman, courageous, hot-tempered and sensitive about honour. Young men rushed to take fencing lessons, and newspapers had duelling columns. Up until the First World War most prominent politicians had to fight at some time or another, even those on the Left, such as Jaurès and Millerand; Clemenceau was particularly adept and ruthless. Though deliberately not usually very dangerous, duels were sometimes bloody, even fatal. Unless the rules of honour were broken, there were no prosecutions. Women were of course excluded from all these masculine political activities. However, certain other types of violence, fitting the stereotype of emotional irrationality, were condoned for women too. The most famous case was that of Henriette Caillaux, wife of a prominent politician, who in 1914 murdered the editor of *Le Figaro*, and was acquitted: 'her poor [female] nervous system' had been under stress 'and finally the boiler blew up'. Hundreds of women were acquitted of murder on similar grounds.[16]

14. Perrot, in Dufrancatel *et al.* (1979), pp. 140-8.
15. Segalen (1983), p. 91.
16. Berenson (1992), p. 32; see also Harris (1989), p. 208.

Changes in conceptions of the self and of the nature and relations of the 'sexes profoundly affected love. The crucial developments, Corbin tells us, were the elaboration and then decline of Romanticism, which 'reinvented' love between about 1820 and 1860.[17] Romanticism, centred on the supreme importance of individual emotion, idealized love as a quasi-religious experience: 'Love is life, if it is not death'.[18] The double standard applied to male and female sexuality, by which men where permitted greater freedom than women, was a reflection of the duality of 'idealized' and 'degraded' love. This corresponded to the perceived fragility of women's psyche, noted above, more vulnerable to degradation. These ideas influenced and standardized what was considered normal and proper behaviour between young men and women, which had previously varied greatly between regions and social groups, sometimes being remarkably permissive.

Idealization of the 'angelic' woman was omnipresent in literature and art of the Romantic period: in religious imagery, poetry, songs, the theatre, novels, serial fiction and picture postcards. Men and women imitated these dominant cultural models. Diaries and the private letters of lovers to their 'angels' displayed 'a violence of passionate language' and a quasi-sacramental fervour, full of avowals, suffering, redemption and expectation of final bliss.[19] Idealized love required suffering and frustration. Berlioz, that archetypal romantic, was plunged into the depths of despair when he fell in love from a distance with Harriet Smithson playing Ophelia at the Odeon theatre. Even the sober Guizot contemplated suicide when lovelorn, as did Hugo's Marius when he thought he had lost Cosette.

Marius and Cosette in *Les Misérables* provide a quintessential example of Romantic love: 'love has no half-way point; either it ruins or it saves. All human destiny is in that dilemma.' They fall in love at a distance without ever speaking; they are separated and their love seems hopeless; they are innocent and chaste to the point of imbecility ('that celestial blindness of modesty'); and their eventual union ('that blessed and holy hour') is a cosmic and religious experience: 'God willed that the love Cosette found was one of those loves that saves . . . Two lovers hid in the dusk . . . with the birds, with the roses . . . and during that time immense motions of the stars filled the infinite.'[20] But such idealized adoration was not carnal:

> Marius, the pure and seraphic Marius, would have been rather capable of going to a whore than of lifting Cosette's dress even up to her ankle. When once, in the moonlight, Cosette bent to pick something up and the opening of her blouse showed the beginning of her breast, Marius turned away his eyes.

Desire for an angel – 'naivety, simplicity, whiteness, candour, brightness . . . a

17. Corbin, in Perrot (1990), p. 571.
18. Hugo (1967), vol. 3, p. 30.
19. Corbin, in Perrot (1990), pp. 570, 574.
20. Hugo (1967), vol. 3, pp. 29–34.

condensation of auroral light in female form'[21] – is taboo; sex, as Hugo implied, is for whores.

This was the bane of Romantic love, that castrating and chilling idealization. When Michelet lamented the frigidity of married women, Adèle Esquiros replied that men were either too respectfully undemonstrative, or else 'brutal, gross and savage'.[22] Because sex was seen as a degradation, it was something to which women 'submitted', carried away by male strength or their own uncontrollable impulses: 'an inexorable fall from the heights of angelic yearning to the pit of the brothel'.[23] After Louise Colet seduced Flaubert, she lay with 'her eyes lifted up to heaven, her hands joined, offering up her crazy words'. Sartre commented that 'in 1846 a woman of bourgeois society who had just behaved like an animal was required to play the angel'.[24] Yet the stain was indelible. Eugène Sue's fictional heroine, the wonderfully named Fleur-de-Marie, both angel and whore – 'one of those pure and angelic faces that keep their ideality even in the midst of depravity'[25] – accepted that redemption was impossible, became a nun and died of a broken heart.

These images projected male anxiety about their own sexuality, and a fearful fascination with that of women, seen as potentially devouring and insatiable. Mérimée's *Carmen* (1845) (where Cosette is 'whiteness', 'light', she is 'all in black'[26]), Manet's *Olympia*, and Zola's *Nana*, which sold 45,000 copies on its publication day in 1880 (and was also the subject of an earlier painting by Manet), are archetypes: women independent, intimidating, in control. They usually have to die: like poor Fleur-de-Marie, from remorse; or killed by a former lover, like Carmen; or from disease, like Nana from smallpox or like Dumas the Younger's 'dame aux camélias' (1852) from consumption brought on by excitement and pleasure. Men suffered from an alarming sense of sexual inferiority, says Corbin, and needed constant reassurance of their prowess, or at least 'mathematical proof of constant regularity': Vigny, Hugo, Flaubert and Michelet all engaged in careful sexual book-keeping.[27] Doctors warned that over-indulgence caused 'depletion' and frightful physical decline. Warned a doctor dolefully in 1879, 'each time that the individual consummates the act of procreation, he gives a portion of his life in order to create a new life'.[28]

The disintegration of the Romantic imagination becomes tangible from mid-century. The serialized publication of Flaubert's *Madame Bovary* in 1857, and its sensational prosecution for 'outraging public and religious morality', is an almost too perfect portent, both in what Flaubert wrote and in what his readers read into it. What was it that was too dangerous for their wives or

21. Ibid., vol. 3, p. 33.
22. Zeldin (1973), vol. 1, p. 293.
23. Jean Borie, in Corbin in Perrot (1990), p. 579.
24. Ibid., p. 580.
25. Sue (1989), p. 40.
26. Mérimée (1973), p. 120.
27. Corbin, in Perrot (1990), p. 581.
28. Corbin (1995), p. 137.

servants to read? In France, disillusionment with Romantic idealism was linked with the failure of the 1848 revolution, which seemed to demonstrate the hollowness of the extravagant moral, political and social optimism of the Romantic Left. At the same time, fear of social upheaval in the wake of the violence of 1848 and 1851 seemed to make intellectual and artistic dissent more dangerous. A friend warned Flaubert that he was 'attacking society by one of its pillars' – the family. The worried response of 'society' was not mere prudishness (as would have been the case across the Channel), but fear of its own vulnerability at a time when sin was equated with socialism. The novel was a story of Romantic yearnings leading to adultery and suicide – the sad fate of a farmer's daughter educated beyond her 'sphere', pleaded Flaubert's defence council, which made it admirably moral. In fact, Flaubert, with disdainful irony, had inverted all the clichés of Romantic love. The heroine Emma is beautiful but strong and 'masculine' – Baudelaire thought her a 'bizarre androgyne' – while her feeble lovers display 'that natural cowardice that characterises the stronger sex'. Morality too is inverted: Flaubert writes of 'the stains of marriage and the disillusion of adultery' – surely, protested the prosecuter, it had to be the other way round. None of the characters, complained critics, was good or even nice. As Flaubert himself realized, he could have avoided prosecution by putting in, at the end, 'a *venerable priest* or a *good doctor* to reel off a lecture on the dangers of love',[29] but he deliberately refused the moralistic role claimed by Romantic art, which he dismissed as 'official aesthetics'. Furthermore, the style shocked readers by its deliberately non-Romantic language, its refusal to idealize with euphemisms: it was an everyday story of countryfolk, mentioning pots of jam, corsets, snoring. 'Art without rules', said the prosecutor with absurd appropriateness, 'is like a woman who takes off all her clothes.'[30]

The significance of these quibbles is the fact that 'romantic love had ceased to exist as a coherent model', says Corbin. Emma yearned for love with 'some great solid heart [so that] virtue, tenderness, pleasure and duty' could be combined; but she never found it. For the next 50 years, only fragments of Romanticism survived: 'a vague, shifting complex of sensations, reveries, souvenirs and fears supplanted the irresistible impulse towards the ideal'.[31] In short, the contemporary history of sexuality began.

The world of Zola's *Nana* (serialized 1879) and Maupassant's *Bel-Ami* (1885) was entirely different from that of Marius and Cosette: gone were the burning eyes and elevated gaze. Whereas the seraphic Marius averted his gaze from his beloved's cleavage, Bel-Ami, succeeding solely through beefy good looks and calculated indifference, carries out brisk seductions, neatly stripping his 'prey' with 'the light fingers of a chambermaid'.[32] Adultery became an obsessive literary theme, and even a joke, with Feydeau's frenetic

29. Leclerc (1991), p. 204.
30. Ibid., p. 195.
31. Corbin, in Perrot (1990), pp. 571–3.
32. Maupassant (1975), p. 325.

clownish philanderers. Though still a criminal offence and a legal excuse for murder, the courts now regarded it with less seriousness. Even prostitutes had to pretend to be adulterous amateurs. Corbin believes that married women, at least of the Parisian upper classes, in reality as well as in fantasy, were less worried by transgression, less ignorant and more accessible – especially in Haussmann's new Paris, with its streets, parks and department stores where respectable and non-respectable women could wander anonymously, the intriguing ambiguity of their status reflected in many paintings by Renoir, Manet, Degas and Seurat. France (in reality Paris) acquired that most enduring of French stereotypes: that of *l'amour.*

Marriage too became more affectionate and erotic, believes Corbin, with 'shared pleasures replacing selfish assault', although with medical opinion approving 'virile energy and speed' in lovemaking, the change was probably less than revolutionary.[33] Gustave Droz's 1866 bestseller *Monsieur, Madame et bébé* – interestingly, the word *bébé* was a franglais import – urged the combination of cosy domesticity and the joy of sex: 'It is nice being an angel, but, believe me, it is either too much or not enough . . . You have fine spiritual qualities, it is true, but your little body is not bad either, and when one loves, one loves completely.'[34] The very success of the book (121 editions between 1866 and 1884) shows how startling the message remained. Fears and neuroses had not been banished by the decline of Romantic love; perhaps even the contrary. If the image of the 'angel' had weakened, Eve was still present, and with her the male fear of women. 'Exhaustion' was a constant danger: the poor shrinking male was obsessed by his inadequacy faced with the voluptuous, insatiable – though of course less intelligent – female. Men felt safer fighting duels, suggests Nye. The sword was mightier than the penis.

Jean-Martin Charcot, the renowned psychiatrist, staged for 30 years after 1863 what amounted to public performances by mentally disturbed women, which influenced the portrayal of women in the acting of Sarah Bernhardt, and in the novels of Edmond de Goncourt, Zola and Huysmans. The big star was Ernestine, an adolescent rape victim, who was brought on to re-enact her experience: 'the complex game of exhibitionism and voyeurism . . . dramatized a sick relation to desire on the part of both participants and onlookers'.[35] The obsession with syphilis, which reached a peak towards the end of the century in medical discourse, literature and politics, seems also to have represented more than just a concern with a genuine problem of public health: it dramatized the danger of sexuality, provided a pretext for repression, and marked the culmination of a series of campaigns to ascribe a range of social and national ills to sexual indulgence. The prominence of prostitution, both as a common social phenomenon and an obsessive theme in literature and art, dramatizes the difficulty of relations between the sexes.

33. Corbin, in Perrot (1990), pp. 598, 591.
34. Zeldin (1973), vol. 1, p. 295.
35. Corbin, in Perrot (1990), p. 631.

Prostitutes were generally considered to be physically and psychologically different from 'virtuous' women. They were thus the foil to the idealized wife/mother, and also a caricature of female sensuality, greedy, plump and mindless. Much of the attraction for men must have been that this was a fake relationship in which they could play out their fears, frustrations and fantasies while still safely maintaining control through cash.

FAMILY

Marriage is in general a means of increasing one's credit and one's fortune and of ensuring one's success in the world.

Essai sur l'art d'être heureux, 1806[36]

Familles, je vous hais!

André Gide, Les Nourritures terrestres, 1897

Social identity was derived principally from families. As noted above, the Revolution had temporarily broken down the boundary between the public and the private, and this brought attempts, by counter-revolutionaries, liberals and republicans, to define where that boundary should be rebuilt. All agreed that the family marked the limit of the public, and that the family was the basic social cell: this was 'the newest political idea of the day'.[37] Counter-revolutionaries saw it as a microcosm of the divine monarchical order, with the father as king. Liberals saw it as the safeguard of individual liberties and interests. Republicans regarded it as a model for true democracy. Socialists saw it as the microcosm of a free community. So universal was approval for family values that even the least familial of institutions, such as the army and prisons, were obliged to pay lip-service to them and present themselves as 'one big happy family' showing 'paternal solicitude'.

The practical function of the family, however, at all levels from peasant to grandee, was economic: 'need and greed', in Weber's words.[38] This was true in every country, but it was given a unique dimension in France because of the millions of families who owned land or businesses. Hence the preservation, augmentation and transmission of the patrimony formed a solid core for an extended family, and the basis of stable social identity over generations. Parents and children, brothers and sisters were linked (or divided) by the handing on and division of family property. Landowning families large and small followed strategies to increase and protect their holdings. Business and professional families needed capital and contacts. Marriages were alliances, corporate mergers and demonstrations of status. Families and clans, especially among peasants, showed absolute solidarity towards the outside world, however much they might quarrel behind closed

36. Zeldin (1973), vol. 1, p. 288.
37. Perrot (1990), p. 100.
38. Weber (1977), p. 176.

doors. Their status and honour had to be displayed and defended, if necessary by violence. Jones, describing the society of the Massif Central, notes that in mid-century cases of murder, manslaughter or grievous bodily harm phrases such as 'he spoke of our house with a sort of smile that we could not tolerate' crop up constantly in court records.[39]

Marriage was a key move in the family's collective socio-economic strategy, to which the desires of individuals were necessarily subordinate: 'beauty can't be eaten with a spoon'; 'the pretty girl's the one who works and earns', said the proverbs.[40] This is not to say that arranged marriages were usually forced or reluctantly accepted: the idea of what constituted an honourable or at least acceptable marriage was so internalized that the choice of the family and the prospective couple no doubt generally converged. Whether for lord or peasant, shopkeeper or artisan, a *mésalliance* brought shame and ridicule: the freedom of choice of the twentieth century, after all, produces comparably symmetrical results. Caroline Brame's diary[41] shows how matter-of-factly a naive and dutiful middle-class daughter would accept her parents' choice, bearing out Maupassant's view that girls married 'from ignorance, fear, obedience, carelessness'. Besides, they would be allowed to meet few other eligible men. Romantic ideas of love seem not to have altered this behaviour, but perhaps placed a rose-coloured tinge on it and raised expectations of what sort of relationship could be expected. During the second half of the century, however, there are some signs that children became less willing to submit unquestioningly to family interests. Migration, greater urbanization, better education and wider job opportunities made it easier for individuals to imagine other social, economic and emotional possibilities, and to follow them through. A decline in dowries and marriage contracts late in the nineteenth century seems to show that couples were concerned more with each other, and less with economic calculation: marriage became less a career, more a relationship. Flandrin has argued that rising figures for pre-marital conception show marriages based more on love, or anyway on sexual attraction.[42]

Rules, strategies and rituals for negotiating marriage were often very sophisticated. Among the nobility, vast networks of kinship and delicate assessments of wealth and lineage continued to determine marriages irrespective of the legal and psychological impact of the Revolution; wealthy heiresses of non-noble stock could be married as an investment opportunity, but that was nothing new. Old bourgeois families behaved similarly. So did peasant landowners: over the century, nearly 70 per cent of children of *cultivateurs* married children of other *cultivateurs*.[43] Newer owners of industrial wealth formed dynasties of their own; best known are those of the

39. Jones (1985), p. 106.
40. Weber (1977), p. 170.
41. Perrot and Ribeill (1985).
42. Flandrin (1975), p. 243.
43. Dupâquier and Kessler (1992), p. 161.

textile families of the north, where family relationships amounted to business networks. Among artisans too, especially in towns, marriage was often within the trade. For the upwardly mobile, marriage was a crucial step, bringing money and enhanced career prospects. For example, the poor but promising politician Adolphe Thiers married the fifteen-year-old daughter of his *nouveau riche* patrons in 1833, and in return for financial backing for his career he gave them profitable State employment and vertiginous social ascent.

Marriage and family patterns among the landowning peasantry, unlike other social groups, differed greatly from region to region, being determined principally by variations in inheritance customs. The Code Civil gave all children right to a nearly equal share to the family inheritance. But where land was involved this was often circumvented in accordance with older practices, especially in the south. Children were persuaded to forego their legal rights, or to accept compensation in cash, often after deliberately underestimating the value of the patrimony. Traditions were often utterly different from the legal norm. In the Basque country, for example, the house was seen as embodying the family lineage, and one child, male or female, was chosen to inherit house, land, name and honour: the other children had to marry heirs of other families, or emigrate (doubtless the main reason why Basques were France's most numerous emigrants). If it was a girl who became *etcheko anderia*, mistress of the house, she had to marry a non-heir reputed a capable farmer. The relative status of husband and wife, and of parents – who might or might not be part of the household, and might or might not retain control of the property – varied according to regional custom.[44] In regions where the patrimony was customarily not divided equally, 'double marriages' took place between the siblings of one family and those of another, with careful matching of heirs/heiresses and non-heirs/ non-heiresses. In regions of equal inheritance, there were commonly marriages between relatives to keep property within the family. Dowries were an essential part of the marriage strategy: young girls went out to work to save their dowries when their families could not provide them.

Types of family varied geographically in accordance with these different inheritance patterns and ancient systems of land tenure. Nuclear families were most common in the northern third of the country; various patterns of extended family were the norm in the south-west and Massif Central, and in certain parts of Brittany, the north and the north-east. These were ancient and durable patterns which long survived the changes made by the Revolution. Le Bras and Todd have linked a range of social and political phenomena, from birth rate to voting patterns, to these family types, which they associate with authoritarian or egalitarian attitudes.[45] Historians are invariably suspicious of monocausal explanations, and look at a range of factors in explaining regional cultural variations, as will be seen in Chapter 14.

44. Segalen (1983), pp. 69–70.
45. Le Bras and Todd (1981).

Only in those urban working-class families where the transmission or protection of property was not at issue (many working-class families outside the cities did have small property) was marriage relatively simple: a household needed two adult wages, and in due course those of children, to survive. During the early decades of urban industrialization, in the 1830s and 1840s, workers' family structures in growing cities seem to have been rather unstable. This has sometimes been interpreted as increased liberty of choice of partner, but in reality meant insecurity, especially for women and children. In the second half of the century city workers showed the same eagerness to set up stable families as other social groups, partly, no doubt, in emulation of other classes, but also as an assertion of self-respect in often difficult conditions. But in older, more stable industrial communities family structures were often very solid, and, in a manner comparable with peasant families, formed the basis for economic and social existence. For example, in the ceramic industry of the small town of Nevers, husbands, wives and children worked together and families intermarried in the same quarter of the town for centuries. When such miniature societies as these came under strong pressure in the 1880s and 1890s from competition and 'rationalization' – which among other things usually meant the exclusion of family members from the workshop and sometimes greater geographical separation between home and work (preventing workers from going home for meals, for example) – the family and the local community could mount a formidable resistance.

When the function of families was primarily economic, and especially in conditions of great poverty, relations within the family were frequently harsh. Segalen[46] gives a rather optimistic picture of peasant families, in which each member had a complementary and necessary role. Weber, however, argues that complementary was very far from equal, and that utilitarian attitudes inhibited affection. Meals were brief and silent. Useless mouths were resented: children had to pay their way as early as possible, and the old were not expected to linger on uselessly; in-laws and non-family members were at the bottom of the pile. One little girl, boarded out with Sologne farmers, remembered that 'she was not unhappy: worse . . . You're cold? Work hard, you'll get warm. You're hungry? There's a potato left in the dresser . . . And then a slap here, a slap there, not out of cruelty – but children have to be trained.'[47] Fiction such as Jules Vallès's *L'Enfant* (1879), Jules Renard's play *Poil de Carotte* (1894) and Louis Pergaud's *La Guerre des Boutons* (1912) portray harsh parental discipline. Patriarchs reigned: within living memory, men in rural households were served at table by their womenfolk, who remained standing. Fathers and husbands were '*vous*', and often referred to as '*notre maître*'. No proverbs did women honour, remarks Weber; their births were less welcome and their deaths less mourned. As was seen in Chapter 8, the customary authority of fathers had powerful legal reinforcement, ultimately the reformatory, the lunatic asylum and the prison.

46. Segalen (1983).
47. Weber (1977), p. 171n.

Families were often ruthless in eliminating unwanted additions: the large number of foundlings and high infant mortality were two signs of this.

Marriage contracts could create tension between husband and wife; inheritances could cause jealousy between siblings and resentment between generations. Open violence was not uncommon. The best known historical example is Pierre Rivière, who in 1835 slaughtered his mother, sister and brother, but there were about ten to fifteen cases of parricide annually.[48] When family quarrels began to be taken to the law courts during the nineteenth century, it was a sign that traditional inhibitions were weakening. There were other causes and signs of change. Some economic possibilities narrowed, and others opened up. The surplus rural population – in practice, the children of poor peasants – began to seek jobs in the towns from the 1840s onwards. Lower-middle-class girls had more opportunity to become teachers after 1870 and civil servants after 1900. Landowners' sons looked more to business or the professions when the depression in agricultural rents after 1880 made their patrimony less adequate. Attendance at school, becoming general if sporadic after 1860, and even extended military conscription after 1875 opened up wider horizons: many boys did not return to their villages after the army, but found jobs in the rapidly growing railways and post office.

Nevertheless, if it lost some of its raw economic function, the family remained of enormous importance in determining the lives of its members. In spite of a few celebrated exceptions – self-made millionaires such as Aristide Boucicaut, sometime pedlar who founded the Bon Marché department store; or plebeian statesmen such as the grocer's son Gambetta – the status and economic position of a family largely determined that of its children, and often their beliefs and political loyalties too. The family had to provide funds, or at least give time, for education. For peasant children, the need to help on the farm especially at harvest time kept attendance relatively low throughout the century. Secondary and higher education was reserved for a small number whose families could afford the fees and forego adolescents' earnings: only about 2 per cent of secondary school pupils in the 1860s were sons of unskilled workers; and only 2.4 per cent of all boys passed the baccalauréat in the 1900s.[49] Career prospects largely depended on family contacts. A peasant boy or girl going to look for a job in town would probably follow the itinerary of relatives or neighbours who had already made the trip and also rely on them for help in finding work. Large industrial, mining or utilities firms commonly preferred to recruit relatives of existing workers. Among artisans, 45 per cent followed in their fathers' footsteps.[50] Young notables' career prospects depended very largely on family contacts and encouragement. At the turn of the century, for example, between 20 and 50 per cent of members of various civil service departments were sons of civil

48. Foucault (1978), p. viii.
49. Price (1987), pp. 342–3.
50. Dupâquier and Kessler (1992), p. 154.

servants.[51] Hence, dynasties, both humble and illustrious, were created, from the small peasant wine growers of Provence to the substantial tenant farmers of the Ile de France, who rented land from generation to generation, and tended to dominate (and even employ) the 'landlords' of the holdings they rented; or business dynasties such as the de Wendels, the Schneiders or the Foulds.

The political loyalties of the family were also passed down the generations, its status and prospects linked with the success of a particular party. Among those who appear elsewhere in these pages, there are ancient grandee families such as the Broglies, pulled towards liberal royalism by marriage ties with the Necker/Staël clan: Duc Victor de Broglie served Louis-Philippe, and Duc Albert was prime minister under MacMahon. There were newly prominent provincial *notables* such as the Periers, who grew enormously rich during the Revolution, who provided deputies or ministers for the Restoration, the July Monarchy, the Second Empire and the Third Republic, all of a conservative liberal tendency, and reached the presidency of the Republic in 1894. There were more purely political families, prominent because of the outstanding activity of one or two individuals during the Revolution, such as the Cavaignacs and the Carnots, both descended from members of the 1792 Convention: a Cavaignac descendant was a leading republican in the 1840s, another ruled France in 1848, a third was a minister in the 1890s; and a Carnot became president in 1887, largely because of his 'republican name'. Odilon Barrot, leader of the Dynastic Left under the July Monarchy, as a baby had been ceremonially presented to the National Guard at the Tree of Liberty of his home town; his grandfather was murdered by White Terrorists in 1800; and his father, a moderate member of the 1792 Convention, lost his job after Napoleon's Hundred Days. At a humbler level, the socialist Proudhon derived his first ideas from his republican parents and his cousin, an ex-priest turned Jacobin; the stonemason Martin Nadaud, deputy in 1848, learned his as a child from his Bonapartist uncle, wounded at Waterloo; the CGT leader Jouhaux's father had been a *Fédéré* drummer-boy in 1871, and his grandfather had been shot in 1848. In cases such as this, ideas learned at an early age, the expectations of family and friends, certain opportunities opened up by the prestige of a name, and, conversely, the hostility of governments of rival parties, made political loyalties practically hereditary. This could be seen at the very lowest grass-roots level: a list of republicans in a village in the Lozère department in 1889 reads 'mayor; mayor's father; mayor's brother; mayor's cousin; mayor's father-in-law; mayor's uncle'.[52] Segalen finds the same in Britanny to the present day, and there is no reason to think Britanny unusual: 'Not only are council members related to each other; they are related to their predecessors and their successors'.[53] The extent of social and economic change over the century

51. Charle (1987), p. 74.
52. Jones (1985), p. 252.
53. Segalen (1983), p. 273.

gave rise to a large literature and widespread discussion concerning supposed
crises of the family. Pessimists lamented the falling birth rate and the increase
in 'immorality'. But the cold eye of statistics suggests a different picture. In
the early twentieth century, the number of unmarried men was about the
same as half a century earlier; the number of illegitimate births was slightly
lower. Abortion and divorce were still rare to the point of marginality. In
short, 'the French family remained solid'.[54]

54. Fine, in Dupâquier *et al.* (1988), p. 458.

CHAPTER 13

COLLECTIVE IDENTITIES: COMMUNITY AND RELIGION

COMMUNITIES

Rural communities

There are no friends in the countryside, only relatives or neighbours.[1]

If the family marked the boundary between the 'public' and the 'private', for most people throughout our period the public was the small community in which they lived, moved and had their being. In 1846, 75.6 per cent of the population was defined as rural, which meant that they lived in a *commune* (the smallest administrative unit) whose main centre of population had fewer than 2,000 inhabitants. In 1911, 55.8 per cent still fell into this category. Many of the 38,000 *communes* had very small populations indeed, and they got smaller as agriculture shed some of its labour force in the late-nineteenth-century depression. Between 1876 and 1936 the number of *communes* with fewer than 200 inhabitants rose from 3,948 to 8,670. They also grew socially more homogenous as many *notables*, craftsmen and landless labourers left. Most people lived in *communes* with between 500 and 2,000 inhabitants; about as many lived in *communes* with under 500 as in large towns of over 100,000. Even these figures are misleading as to the actual size of communities, because a *commune* was an area, not a single village or parish: the *commune* of Mazières-en-Gatine, for example, had some 900 inhabitants in the 1840s, but the village itself had only 200, the other 700 living in outlying hamlets and isolated farmsteads. Nationally, some 14 million people in 1880 lived in similar isolation. In small settlements, family and community tended to be synonymous. Social life was given, not chosen, for most people spent their lives in one place: even in the last years of the century, over 60 per cent of the whole population lived in the *commune* where they were born, and over 80 per cent in the same department. Simply because of the immobility of peasants, most marriages were within the local

1. Mendras, in Weber (1977), p. 167.

community. Averaged over the century, over 60 per cent of married couples came from within the same *commune*, and in remote regions far more: in one district of Lozère in the 1810s, about a third of those marrying lived less than one kilometre apart; by 1900 it was still a quarter.[2]

There were two broad types of settlement: concentrated and dispersed. The former featured large 'urban villages' with 1,500–5,000 inhabitants (often termed *bourgs*) and was typical of parts of the Paris basin and the north and east, and of the Garonne basin, the Rhône valley and the Mediterranean littoral: not untypical was Florac (Lozère) which in 1855 was recorded as having 362 houses, 185 pigs and 112 manure heaps. The latter type, with much of the population isolated in farms and hamlets, was typical of the *bocage* country of the west and of the Massif Central. These patterns were very ancient. Concentrated settlement descended from Gallo-Roman communities in the south, medieval defence needs in the fortified *bastides* of Gascony and Languedoc, and open-field agriculture in the north, which survived the enclosure decrees of the Revolution. Dispersed settlement was linked with the trickle of population into less fertile regions. The difference between the two types of settlement was, and still remains, very evident. Communal social activities – festivals, religious confraternities, and during the nineteenth century drinking clubs, political groups and sports clubs – were much more developed in the urban villages. Sociability was sparser in the dispersed habitat. It has been argued, notably by Agulhon, that this accounts in part for political developments: peasant sociability became the basis for collective solidarity, resistance and political organization, whereas the weaker social structures of a dispersed population helped to maintain the authority of *notables* and clergy.

The local community, along with the family, defined and policed acceptable behaviour among its members. *Veillées* – when family and neighbours met to work together in the evenings, sharing lighting and heating – were the traditional place for stories, songs, gossip and flirtation. Books or newspapers would be read out. This practice remained common until the 1880s. Peer groups, especially of young men, punished transgressions against community custom (such as marriages of women with younger men and marriages with outsiders) with public mockery at carnival time and *charivaris*, noisy demonstrations outside the offenders' houses. This often caused friction with the clergy and local authorities. The young men also organized the festivals that helped to create community identity, and which were similarly often disapproved of by local authorities. Especially in the first half of the century, violence was frequent and often savage, not least at festival time. We should not think of village communities as too cosy: they united against the outside world; within, relations could be vicious.

Communities were often bitter rivals with their neighbours. The origins of

2. Statistics from Price (1987), p. 88; Weber (1977), p. 168; Dupâquier *et al.* (1988), p. 511; Thabault (1971), p. 32; Burns (1984), pp. 12–13; Dupâquier and Kessler (1992), p. 354; Jones (1985), p. 113.

some of these frequently ferocious quarrels were lost in the mists of time; others could be traced to the events of the Revolution. They were learned young: Pergaud described elaborate guerilla war between schoolboys waged with sticks, stones and catapults in the 1900s. But often they were material disputes involving local power and the use of common land: demands by villages to form separate *communes* and thus gain control of resources was one of the great local political issues. This inevitably took political form, with villages voting consistently for rival candidates and parties. 'When St Jean votes black, St Paul votes white', a prefect reported of two rival communities in 1865.[3]

The church was the main social centre and source of official authority until the 1880s and in some regions it retained this role throughout our period. Its festivals and pilgrimages, often with a specifically local significance (for example to a local shrine), were the big community gatherings. The priest possessed magical powers, necessary to guard against malign forces. He presided over great family ceremonies (baptisms, first communions, marriages and funerals). He exerted moral influence through confession, could apply the public stigma of refusal of the sacraments and even criticized individuals from the pulpit. All this gave him formidable authority, which was often exercised pretty roughly. From mid-century onwards, if he received decreasing support from the civil authorities (see p. 139) his influence was buttressed by modern institutions such as church schools and a network of charities and societies from sports clubs to trade unions. This very power caused resentment and sometimes open contestation, especially when priests attempted to interfere in communal amusements or private behaviour: trying to stop dancing or traditional 'pagan' festivals and rituals; replacing traditional religious-cum-social confraternities of laymen (such as the Penitents in the south) with newer organizations run by the clergy; giving unpalatable political instructions; or waging war on contraception. Much male anti-clericalism at a village level was certainly a response to clerical power; it was not necessarily anti-religious, indeed in some cases it insisted on perpetuating traditional religious activities which priests condemned as un-Christian.

The State was represented in every *commune* by the mayor and his entourage: the schoolteacher (who in the second half of the century developed much influence), village watchman (*garde champêtre*), postman and roadmender. The mayor, already chosen in part for his economic and social prominence, was a considerable figure within the *commune*, as was seen in Chapter 5, sometimes in rivalry with the priest. Finally, other organizations, such as the National Guard and their successors the volunteer Pompiers (fire brigades), *chambrées*, festival committees, brass bands and towards the end of the century sports clubs and agricultural cooperatives also helped to structure community life.

During at least the first half of the century, many rural communities were dominated socially, economically, culturally and politically by *notables*: the

3. Jones (1985), pp. 246–8.

larger landowners, both noble and 'bourgeois', who combined economic predominance with a near monopoly of political and administrative office. They alone had the ability to communicate with the wider society outside the village. In some parts of the country – such as the legitimist west and south, where *notables* and peasants shared a common ideology and where there remained a high proportion of noble mayors even after 1945, and in regions of large estates and sharecropping tenancies where their economic power was too strong to resist – their political lead was deferred to more or less willingly. Consequently, universal male suffrage in 1848 strengthened their position. Elsewhere, especially where there were long-running and often very bitter disputes over forest rights or land ownership, sometimes with sporadic legal action against *seigneurs* going back well before the Revolution, *notable* power was resisted by the community. It was further weakened by rivalry among *notables*, by the arrival of new kinds of *notables*, such as businessmen, and by the efforts of State officials to counteract the influence of politically hostile *notables*, as was done by the Second Empire and Third Republic. A vote for Louis-Napoleon Bonaparte from 1848 to 1870 was for many peasants a vote against the legitimist or Orleanist *notables*, and was sometimes backed up by violence. A vote for republicans after 1870 was similarly aimed against the old *notables*, accused of plotting to restore feudalism – an accusation that many seem to have believed. Resistance to the influence of *grands notables* was often led by new petty *notables*, whom Gambetta referred to in 1872 as 'new social strata' who would provide leadership for the republic: lawyers, doctors, smaller landowners. The republican victory has often been considered 'the end of the *notables*', and it did indeed mean a permanent loss in most of the country of local offices (especially those of mayor, prefect, judge and deputy) that had bolstered the authority of the old elites. Moreover, the long agricultural depression that began in the 1870s caused many to sell their estates to their former tenants and move to the towns. Even though an unquestioned hierarchy of property remained, it was a hierarchy of *agriculteurs*: those who worked the land. The decline of the *notables*, real though it was, should not be exaggerated. They maintained influence in new ways, for example by running some of the new farmers' *syndicats*.

The community was a powerful propagator of belief, custom and behaviour. To take one example: the control of adolescents. Girls were strictly watched in the country, not only by their own families. They were not allowed to wander about freely: older people would often ask them where they were going, and they had to be home by seven, when the Angelus rang (a custom that lasted until the Second World War). Suspect girls were closely watched for signs of pregnancy, including by the mayor and *garde champêtre* determined to forestall abortion or infanticide. Village women and young men constituted a sort of sexual police force, using customary humiliations. The *curé* too was involved, insisting that girls should attend vespers on Sunday afternoons (the usual time for walks and meetings with boys). The sanction could be severe: exclusion from the Children of Mary, which meant that no music was allowed at their wedding. Community customs dictated remarkable differences in people's most intimate lives, for example in courtship practices and sexual behaviour. In the Vendée considerable freedom was normal between courting boys and girls, including pre-marital sex. Elsewhere, this was unthinkable. In the patriarchal 'Latin' south, the strength of family and community pressures meant a low rate of rural illegitimacy, and a correspondingly high rate of abortion, infanticide and abandoning of infants, suggesting greater fear of social reprobation. There was more illegitimacy but less infanticide in the less oppressive north and east. Yet overall social control in rural communities was so effective that illegitimacy and infanticide were largely confined to the poor, illiterate, and isolated, for example female farm servants away from their home village and thus uncontrolled and unprotected from seduction or rape. To escape community disapproval, pregnant girls who were unable to marry continued the old custom of escaping to the relative freedom, anonymity, loneliness and insecurity of towns.[4]

Urban communities

On crie vive l'indépendence
On a l'coeur bête et content
Et on nage dans l'abondance
A Ménilmontant.

Aristide Bruand, 1910

France was a less urban society than its northern European neighbours: in 1910, some 78 per cent of Britons lived in towns, 60 per cent of Germans and only 44 per cent of French.[5] French towns were smaller, and there were fewer large cities: in 1851 only three (Paris, Lyons and Marseilles) had over 100,000 inhabitants. The speed of urbanization continued to be slower, and there were few mushrooming industrial cities comparable with Birmingham, Essen, Pittsburg or Kharkov. Indeed, small towns grew faster than large ones. The only big city was Paris, with over a million inhabitants by mid-century: a Great Wen, envied, feared, resented and isolated.

The urban geography of France was thus built on pre-industrial foundations: ancient centres – Paris, Lyons, Marseilles, Lille – remained dominant, and expansion was superimposed on old urban structures. Towns retained their traditional links with their regional hinterlands, and much of their established occupational structure and hierarchy, with silk weaving and luxury trades continuing to dominate in Lyons and Paris. Consequently, urban communities were not entirely alien worlds even for new arrivals. But the practical problems of urbanization – health, housing, utilities – were aggravated by the existence of this ancient urban fabric.

For the upper classes, men's social life revolved round *cercles* – from the

4. Fine, in Dupâquier *et al.* (1988), pp. 436–58; Segalen (1983), pp. 15, 21–7.
5. Fine and Sangoï (1991), p. 96.

café of a provincial *bourg* to the pinnacle of fashion, the Paris Jockey Club –
and that of women often round church and charities, and well regulated
mutual visiting. Parisian Society (what was called '*le monde*', or later '*le tout
Paris*') was itself a collection of often hostile coteries, marked by political and
religious, as well as social and economic, differences. The classic division
between the aristocratic and legitimist Faubourg Saint-Germain on the Left
Bank and the financial, and more liberal, elite on the other side of the Seine,
round the Chaussée d'Antin, persisted throughout the July Monarchy. The
upper crust of the 'noble Faubourg' largely boycotted the 'upstart' court of
Louis-Philippe, despised the vulgarity of the Second Empire and had nothing
to do with the Republic. This divorce between the social elite and the rulers
of the State created a 'society' separate from the 'court', based on wealth,
leisure and celebrity, and devoted to high culture, certain sports, amusement
and self-celebration. This was the world of Proust, and it lasted until the First
World War, after which it was to 'fragment and disperse'.[6]

Middle-class groups ran the towns. About one-twentieth of the population
fell into this category. In a middle-sized town such as Limoges, with 30,000
inhabitants, there were in the 1830s about 500 people who controlled the
municipal council and the National Guard, including doctors, lawyers,
businessmen, journalists and priests.

The urban population was overwhelmingly an immigrant population – 14
million out of the total urban population of 18.5 million in 1914.[7] People
generally moved no further than they had to, to the nearest town or city, and
maintained links with their families and community of origin. Relatives or
compatriots (*pays*) helped to find lodgings, loans, French lessons and jobs.
The Auvergnats in Paris were particularly well organized. They had clubs and
a newspaper, *L'Auvergnat de Paris*. Two *communes* in Cantal specialized in
sending tinkers and scrap-metal collectors, who settled round the Rue de
Lappe, near the Bastille. Masons from Creuse, who came to Paris seasonally
for building work, lived and ate together in dormitories and did not integrate.
Later immigrants often settled near the railway stations where they arrived:
traces remain even now, if only in the restaurants serving *choucroute* and
beer near the Gare de l'Est and *crêpes* and cider near the Gare Montparnasse.
Multiculturalism was characteristic of nineteenth-century cities.

The separation of social classes into distinct areas within towns, although
not new, increased with urban modernization: in old city centres, including
Paris, rich and poor had to some extent mixed, with the poor occupying
upper floors and garrets. Although this mixing did not entirely disappear, and
indeed was fairly common in parts of Paris until recently, new areas on the
city outskirts were much more socially homogenous. Even small towns had
their '*quartier nouveau*' or '*faubourg*'. The price of land and level of rents
created a gradation of socially distinct areas, until in the wealthiest the only
workers were domestics and providers of other services. In Paris, expensive

6. Martin-Fugier (1990) p. 394.
7. Bourillon (1992) p. 142.

residential districts were developed on the less smelly western side of the city from the 1830s onwards; and as industry expanded, vast areas of cheap tenements, railway yards, warehouses and workshops grew up on the eastern, northern and southern sides. In these districts, although there remained a *bourgeoisie populaire* such as shopkeepers and publicans, who often played a prominent leadership role, workers predominated. Class divisions were increasingly expressed in the fabric of the city, its architecture, facilities and smells, and even, after 1870, in street names. These differences found more serious political expression too, and in crises such as those of 1834 in Lyons, or 1848 and 1870–71 in Paris, these could lead to violent confrontations between inhabitants of the different *quartiers*.

There was constant movement in large cities, as people sought work and better or cheaper lodgings, or failed to pay their rent. In Paris, in the central 3rd *arrondissement*, largely white-collar workers and skilled craftsmen, about one-third of the inhabitants, changed lodgings every year; in 1892, for the whole city, the figure was nearly one in five; and in working-class Belleville, mobility seems to have speeded up after 1900. Yet people did not go far. Of the inhabitants of the Rue Nationale, in the working-class 13th *arrondissement*, 89 per cent moved between 1896 and 1906, but over half stayed in the same *arrondissement*. Jobs held them: the most stable groups were from two major local industries, sugar refining and railways.[8] The growth of family ties no doubt contributed too. But a move from one part of the city to the other, like that of the socialist activist Victorine Brocher from Montmartre to the 13th in 1869 (across the Seine – another world), was a complete break, even in her political activities. In the cities, there was therefore no urban 'community', but a mosaic of shifting 'communities' of street and *quartier*, and intersecting circles of sociability based on work and leisure. It was complex, mobile, divided and pretty anonymous.

What articulated it were either small cells of immediate neighbours, relatives, or workmates in the same trade, or else formal organizations, such as trade unions, the National Guard (essential as the organizational framework for insurrection in 1848 and 1871) or political groups. The importance of the craft as a basis for sociability can be seen in the occupations of marriage witnesses: in the 1860s among the furniture makers of the 12th *arrondissement* of Paris (including part of the Faubourg Saint-Antoine) half the friends and relatives who witnessed marriage acts worked in the same trade, although it employed only one-fifth of the workers of the district. Friendships, concludes Berlanstein, were 'less class-orientated and more craft-bound', though by the end of the century these links had weakened.[9] In smaller towns there could be more cohesive communities: communities in the conventional sense, in which family, work and neighbourhood overlapped. Such communities often put up determined resistance to attempts to alter their lives, whether through disruptive urbanization or relocation of work in factories.

8. Ibid., pp. 152–3.
9. Berlanstein (1984), pp. 19–20.

In large towns, neighbourhood communities began to coalesce after a period of severe strain caused by the early phase of rapid urban immigration and, especially during the 1840s, social disorganization and instability. This was marked by unstable or non-existent families, epidemics (the first cholera epidemic occurred in 1832), a high level of criminality and violence, high birth rates and high infantile death rates. Traditional social institutions, particularly the Church, were swamped by the change, and religious attachment declined. Outside the workplace, male sociability to the disapproval of social commentators centred on the cafés or cabarets, 'the worker's church'. They provided centres not only for drinking and talking, but for a range of social and political activities (socialist militants frequently ran cabarets), including friendly societies, trade unions and singing clubs. Women met at water fountains, markets and wash-houses; children spent much of their time in the street. During the second half of the century, although mobility and immigration were no less marked, urban working-class communities created more stability for themselves. The family became more stable. Both death rates and birth rates fell. Violence, both political and criminal, lessened. *Concubinage* (common-law marriage), which was very rare in rural society, was fairly common in cities among workers and even the lower-middle classes, possibly in part due to difficult and costly formalities and also to a degree of sexual 'liberation' for men in a mobile and anonymous society. But as the century progressed there developed a strong tendency for workers to set up stable, legally recognized marriages.

It was in the old cities such as Paris and Lyons, with traditional high-skill industries and a literate workforce, that social and political life seems to have been earliest and most strongly developed. The system of apprenticeship, initiation ceremonies and *compagnonnages* (the archaic journeymen's brotherhoods which until mid-century still included the traditional 'tour de France' by which young journeymen travelled round the country learning the craft) created a strong *esprit de corps*, which until mid-century commonly involved violent clashes with other trades. Men's and women's crafts became part of their identity, recorded in official documents. The political results were ambiguous. Such corporate solidarity stressed the value and status of manual skill, one source of class consciousness; on the other hand, its encouragement of rivalry between crafts may have been a barrier to class organization.

In all these ways, community identity developed. By around 1900, which Louis Chevalier has described as the golden age of the working-class community, a social life had developed that may surprise those used to the grim descriptions of the 1840s to the 1860s. In Paris's drab industrial suburbs, Saint-Denis had a 1,300-seat theatre presenting modern drama such as *Cyrano de Bergerac* and opera, two music-halls showing variety and films, and dozens of dance-halls; Ivry had at least seven subsidized athletics clubs. In the northern textile towns such as Lille and Roubaix, Flemish tradition encouraged a characteristic community sociability, with co-ops, brass bands, choral societies, pigeons, beer and football clubs. Sports groups were usually class-based, and workers attended the music hall on different nights from the middle classes. Socialist parties encouraged and ran social activities, which local authorities often subsidized, and which in turn created a sense of political and social identity. Community, class and politics were entwined in the city as they were in the village.

RELIGION

The character of the inhabitants . . . is in no way remarkable; they are religious without fanaticism in normal times . . . They try to avoid hell rather than deserve heaven.

Gendarme sergeant, Lourdes.[10]

The Revolution brought about an upheaval in religious life, its most profound social effect. As has been seen, the Revolution itself took on certain religious characteristics, and at its most radical phase attempted to 'dechristianize' France. Catholicism ceased to be the State religion; this had the long-term consequence, notes Gibson, of making Catholic practice no longer automatic.[11] Conversely, the small Lutheran, Calvinist and Jewish communities were given recognized status. The Catholic Church turned against the Revolution; many Protestants and Jews (though they also suffered during the Terror) became its sympathizers. This gave a permanent political coloration to religious affiliation that was deeper and more antagonistic than, for example, the differences between Nonconformity and Anglicanism in England.

Napoleon brought all the denominations within his newly designed bureacratic structure, but did not attempt to repair the ravages of the Revolution. As an institution, the Catholic Church began the nineteenth century poor, dilapidated and disorganized, with a decimated and ageing clergy: in 1814, 42 per cent of priests were over 60.[12] As a community of believers, it was in an ambivalent position: a generation was growing up which had received little or no religious instruction and had not taken part regularly in official worship; and yet partly as a reaction against persecution and as a response to the trials of civil and foreign war, religious fervour was strong, often led by women. Catholics and Protestants were affected by a revivalism that touched the whole of the western world.

The nineteenth century was not, consequently, a century of progressive decline of religious institutions. On the contrary, as was seen in Chapter 6, it saw remarkably successful and sustained efforts to restore organized religion, with the assistance of the State. The Catholic Church effectively regained the position recognized in the 1830 constitutional charter – that of the religion 'professed by the majority of French people'. Catholicism was an essential element of their individual and collective identity. But behind this impressive achievement lay huge variations: of region, of gender, of class, and of the significance and level of commitment, for religious practice was ceasing to be

10. Cholvy and Hilaire (1985), vol. 1, p. 181.
11. Gibson (1989), p. 54.
12. Cholvy and Hilaire (1985), vol. 1, p. 39.

an aspect of 'mentality', automatic and unquestioned, and becoming a matter of opinion, even of choice.

Regional variations

There were huge regional variations in religious practice. Historians now agree that they were not a simple consequence of socio-economic differences, but that religion was an autonomous cultural variable. This was so before the Revolution, and investigation of causes has to look back into the eighteenth century and earlier. Catholic strength and weakness had no correlation with obvious social and economic characteristics such as literacy, land tenure, urbanization or economic development. Some remote and backward regions were barely Catholic because the Church was barely present. Some advanced regions were anticlerical because it was present too much. Factors include the powerful influence of the Counter-Reformation in the formerly Spanish-ruled north; the stimulus of rivalry with Protestantism in the south and east; the neglect of their dioceses (especially in the Paris region) by generations of bishops who were absentee court nobles; the varying degree of implantation of Catholic schools; the eighteenth-century extent of Jansenism, with its austere and generally unpopular morality (again strong in the Paris region); the local economic importance of the Church, which could be a source of strength, as in the west and in some cathedral cities, or of weakness, as in Burgundy, where monastic ownership of vineyards caused envious resentment; and the social influence of the parish clergy, particularly great in the west where priests were numerous, locally recruited and important within the community.

The Revolution put these differences under strain and politicized them very dramatically, through communal violence, torture, massacre, reprisals and wholesale destruction. This alone was enough to cause enduring differences in religious practice. But in addition, during the nineteenth century, the evangelizing efforts of the Church tended in the same direction. Greater effort was made in areas seen as fruitful; more priests were sent, more churches and schools built. Consequently, by the 1850s, areas that had originally been 'more Chouan than pious' had become pious too.[13] People whose loyalty to the Church was at first political or social became, or their children became, more sincerely committed. On the other hand, regions that were seen as less obedient were progressively neglected. The extent of variations was very wide: at the end of the nineteenth century in Catholic strongholds such as Britanny and parts of Languedoc, over 80 per cent of men received communion at Easter; in the 'dechristianized' Paris region, for example Chartres or Meaux, only 2 per cent did so.[14] Huge differences existed between areas only a few miles apart.

Political and religious attitudes continued to be entwined. Religious belief did not necessarily mean clericalism, in the sense of obedience to the clergy

13. Lagrée (1977), p. 128.
14. Gibson (1989), pp. 39, 174–6.

in political matters. There were still 'Blue' (left-wing) Catholics in the west in the 1830s, and indeed the 1990s, and the clergy were well aware, as their self-assessments in the 1870s showed, that 'good' Catholics could be politically independent. The royalism of the Church eventually repelled many left-wingers, whether 'Blue' Catholics in rural Britanny or workers in towns, who tended to abandon church-going. Alternatively, in the Massif Central and the south-east, there were several cases in mid-century of entire villages deciding to become Protestant as a protest against clerical conservatism and interference. Later in the century, a different but equally clear reaction to the political stance of the Church can be seen: in Lorraine, the areas annexed by Germany in 1871 saw a striking increase in Easter communions, because Catholic church attendance was associated with patriotic fidelity and resistance to Prussia; but in the areas that stayed French, there was an equally striking fall, because the Church was associated with reactionary opposition to the Republic.[15]

Gender and religion

A mother's heart is the Creator's masterpiece.[16]

Religious conformity and even belief became increasingly female characteristics. There were portents during the Revolution, when mass resistance to dechristianization was led by women: arguably women's major political act in French history. Regional differences greatly affected the behaviour of both sexes, but did not alter the basic gender difference: far more men in the Vendée went to mass than women in for example the Paris region; yet more Vendéen women went than Vendéen men (roughly eight to five in the late part of the century), and vastly more women than men in the Paris region (roughly ten to one).[17] Indeed, by the end of the century in many regions practically no man except the priest set foot in church. By the 1870s nuns were outnumbering male clergy three to two. Of the thousands of pilgrims who flocked to confess to the *curé* of Ars, two-thirds in the 1850s were women.

Various explanations have been proposed, none conclusive. On one hand it has been suggested that men were repelled by the clergy's interference in politics, sexual matters, economic activity (for example by condemning Sunday work) and popular festivities. It has been further suggested that men resented the authority of other men, whereas women were brought up to accept it. On the other hand, it has been suggested that women were attracted by a companiable refuge from demanding and domineering men; by metaphysical explanations of life more appealing to female culture; and by careers the Church offered to women, whether in traditional contemplative

15. Jones (1985), p. 268; Gibson (1989), p. 237.
16. Doucet, in Mills, in Tallet and Atkin (1991), p. 39.
17. Gibson (1989), p. 174.

orders, or increasingly in new orders engaged in social work. Forms of piety underwent changes that have also been seen as responding to women's preoccupations, sociability and cultural habits. For example, the frightening, repressive and guilt-ridden style of eighteenth-century French Catholicism, influenced by Jansenism, was slowly replaced from the 1830s onwards by the 'Ultramontane' practices promoted in Italy by the theologian Liguori, stressing love and forgiveness. Brightly coloured, sentimental (indeed vapid) paintings and statues of female saints, the Sacred Heart and the Virgin and Child outshone in countless country churches both the usually turgid and obscure academic paintings provided by the State and ancient, rustic and miraculous statues.

There were spectacular manifestations of female mysticism. In 1830, Catherine Labouré had a vision of the Virgin Mary in her convent in Paris. In 1858 Bernadette Soubirous saw visions of the Virgin at Lourdes. There were several other comparable apparitions, the most famous at Redon-Espic, La Salette and Pontmain, involving children, mostly girls. They seem to show the spontaneous reaction of simple people to traumatic political events and fears, especially political conflict and war; they were fantasies of punishment and redemption. All caused mass religious fervour: less than a month after Bernadette's vision, 20,000 people had visited the site. Pilgrims, and those cured, were overwhelmingly women. In every case the clergy was at first hesitant, but in the cases of Catherine and Bernadette gave their approval; both were eventually canonized, as were two other (if strikingly different) models of French female piety: Joan of Arc and Thérèse Martin, a Carmelite nun who died of tuberculosis at Lisieux in 1897 aged 24. All became focuses of popular veneration and the subjects of mass-produced religious imagery and literature. Nearly a million copies of Thérèse's short biography and her spiritual notebooks – the quintessence of the new childlike, sentimental and guilt-free piety – and 30 million pictures of her were distributed during the 30 years after her death.

The feminization of Catholicism was clear to contemporaries. The Church was determined to maintain its dominance of girls' education, for this had become its principal means (boys being a lost cause) of influencing the future of society: 'Within the family, it is the wife who, by her gentle and tender piety, perpetually calls back to God those who forsake Him'.[18] Conversely, anticlericals aimed to break that dominance for precisely the same reason. Meanwhile, the Third Republic and its supporters refused to give women the vote on the grounds that women were Catholic and hence reactionary. Piety was seen as a normal part of female identity; and therefore to be shunned by men. Much of the language of anticlericalism is deeply misogynistic. This was one aspect of the derogatory image of male Catholics common on the Left. It portrayed them as 'effeminate', ignorant, schemingly hypocritical, morally and physically soft, often (especially priests and monks) addicted to shameful vices: any sex scandal concerning the clergy was gleefully publicized.

18. Bishop of Angers, in Mills, in Tallet and Atkin (1991), p. 42.

Muscular patriotic republicans of Gambetta's generation longed to snatch French boys from the feminizing grasp of Church schools.

Meanings of religion

They pray to God fervently when they are ill; when they believe themselves bewitched; when their cattle are sick; they ask God for temporal benefits, but never for spiritual benefits.

Priest, Orléans district, 1850[19]

Analyses of religious affiliation necessarily focus first on visible and measurable acts: attendance at church or school; reception of the sacraments, and religious celebration of the rites of passage – baptisms, marriages and funerals. It is less easy to say what these signified to those undergoing them: a commitment to Christian teaching, magical ritual, social conformity?

As was noted above, the Revolution harmed the Church more than it weakened religion. In the absence of priests, lay women and men celebrated rituals without worrying much about their sacramental validity; on the other hand, they often regarded (quite uncanonically) sacraments administered by clergy who took the 1791 oath as invalid. These are only two of many signs that popular belief and ritual had tenuous connections with the doctrines, ethics and disciplines of the Church. Ritual was the heart of popular religion, and it was seen in utilitarian terms as a necessary grappling with invisible everyday forces more than as a mystical symbol of relations with the eternal. Witchcraft coexisted with Christianity as a way of averting bad spells; as late as the 1830s there occurred cases of violence and even murder of suspected witches in several parts of the country, not only the most remote: in one case in 1835, an old woman was reportedly burnt in a village square in the Nord department in the presence of local authorities.[20]

The Church's sacraments were only a part of the required ritual; the priest, often seen as a particularly powerful caster of spells, and the church building were important but not exclusive elements. In addition there were pilgrimages to local holy places – wells, streams, shrines – many of which specialized in particular effects (marriage, conception, cure, avoidance of military service and so on). Similarly, those who approached the famous Abbé Vianney at Ars often had practical as well as spiritual concerns, for he was regarded as a saint, a miracle worker and an oracle: 'Father, should I take on more workers? Should I sack my servant? Should I sell my land? Should I get rid of my shop?'[21] There were many propitiatory acts, such as the erection of wayside crosses and statues (still omnipresent in the French countryside, and certainly still being built in the 1960s), the blessing of cattle and crops to ward off diseases and accident, and the ringing of church bells to keep off hailstorms, essential in wine-producing areas. If necessary, this

19. Cholvy and Hilaire (1985), vol. 1, p. 103.
20. Devlin (1987), p. 118.
21. Boutry and Cinquin (1980), p. 74.

could be done without, and even against the will of, the clergy; many priests before and after the Revolution attempted to stop what they regarded as pagan practices. This priestly scepticism could cause extremely hostile reactions, though few as spectacular as in Haute-Savoie in the 1850s. Dozens of women in 1857–58 suddenly showed symptoms of collective diabolical possession, including acrobatics, speaking in tongues and prophecy; but the clergy denied that these hysterical symptoms were supernatural. In response, dozens of women and girls assaulted the bishop and priest in church, and the sub-prefect reported that '. . . throughout the commune, in the cemetery, in the village square and on the roads, and inside the church, women were to be seen having dreadful attacks of convulsions'.[22]

At the grass-roots level, anticlericalism or indifference to church-going did not necessarily mean atheism; indeed, 'superstition' was arguably more prevalent in areas where the official Church was weak. The 'Voltairianism' and later 'positivism' of left-wing militants was largely confined to the middle classes (caricatured as Flaubert's Monsieur Homais) and skilled working class. In the Limousin and Orléanais regions, for example, people did not go to mass, but they did frequent miraculous springs and believe in magic spells. In 1874, the *curé* of a Limousin parish had to be rescued by *gendarmes* from an angry crowd after he had refused to lead a traditional procession to avert hailstorms – and it duly hailed.[23] Many regions and social groups were 'declericalized', says Lagrée, but not 'dechristianized'. In the north, coalminers' attitudes were complex. In the 1860s they held ceremonies to bless the pits; in the 1880s and 1890s strikes often had anticlerical overtones; but it was not until the end of the century that the dying commonly refused the last sacraments and had secular funerals.[24]

A rather different, if overlapping, motivation for religious activity was that of group solidarity. Until the 1880s, introduction of the 14 July holiday all festivals were nominally religious, and to take part in them was to participate in the collective life of the community. They were also fun – one reason why the clergy tried to change them. The festivals of the parish saint, reported one prefect:

> usually attract a large number of persons of both sexes . . . most of them drawn by the prospect of enjoying themselves . . . They habitually turn up on the evening before the solemnity concerned and . . . take care to arrange things in such a way as to find the time neither long nor disagreeable.[25]

Especially in the south, religious confraternities such as the Pénitents remained in mid-century one of the major forms of male sociability and mutual aid.

Another factor was that a minimum of religious conformity was at times a necessary sign of respectability, the lack of which could have damaging

22. Devlin (1987), p. 137.
23. Gibson (1989), p. 140.
24. Lagrée (1977), p. 90; Hilaire (1976), pp. 1024–5.
25. Gibson (1989), p. 143.

effects. The great majority were at least baptized (over 70 per cent even in Paris in 1900, and over 90 per cent in Marseilles); even in dechristianized Limousin in the 1920s, unbaptized girls could find marriage difficult – 'We've got enough animals like that in the cowshed, we don't need any in the house'.[26] Children were expected to make their first communion, a sort of graduation ceremony demonstrating a degree of education and good behaviour without which it might be more difficult to find a job, even if boys rarely attended thereafter. 'First Communion is at once an end of school, an end of catechism, an end of religion, in short, an end of childhood', lamented the bishop of Chartres in 1842.[27]

Under the Restoration, the July Monarchy and the Empire, state employees attended church on certain occasions, a sign of the mutual respect that State and Church jealously demanded of each other. The decline in church attendance after about 1880 is a sign that the wind had changed, and that prudence now counselled non-attendance, at least by men. The decline in numbers of priests ordained, sharp after the 1830 revolution (after a peak in the late 1820s), and sharp again during and after the Church–State conflict of the 1900s, shows among other things that political adversity made the Church a less viable career for ambitious sons of large Catholic peasant families.

Some indication of the proportion of people who were truly pious in a manner approved by the Church is the proportion who attended communion frequently. There were great differences of geography, age and sex (girls being the most pious), but the overall size of the 'fervent nucleus' towards the end of the century was between 1 and 10 per cent of the population, varying by region.[28] As to those who were truly dechristianized, the main centre was Paris: here, by around 1880, about a quarter of children were unbaptized, a similar proportion of couples married outside the church, and over a fifth were buried without a priest.[29]

The modernization of religious activity

> The church wants everything, soul and body . . . to attract the young it knows how to create an attractive, modern image. Its motto is, make them play to make them pray.
>
> Le Progrès, 1913[30]

As we have seen, the post-revolutionary Church waged a long and remarkably successful campaign to rebuild its institutional power. Part of this involved conscious modernization of its own practices. 'Ultramontane' piety has already been mentioned: there was a conscious desire to make the

26. Ibid., p. 165.
27. Cholvy and Hilaire (1985), vol. 1, p. 274.
28. Gibson (1989), p. 169.
29. Cholvy and Hilaire (1985), vol. 1, p. 238.
30. Arnaud, in Tombs (1991), p. 187.

Church more tolerant of popular needs and feelings, as opposed to the austere and forbidding practices of Jansenist tradition. Hellfire sermons, browbeating confessions; intransigent penances, humiliating refusals of the sacraments and dismissal of popular 'superstition' were progressively replaced from the 1830s and 1840s onwards by a stress on the love of Jesus, symbolized in the Sacred Heart, and especially on the merciful intercession of Mary. Sexual morality was somewhat less obsessively stressed from that time too, and many priests decided to draw a veil over the embarrassing question of birth control.

Popular religion was less readily dismissed as superstition, and instead accepted as showing a genuine if unsophisticated 'instinct for religion', as one *curé* put it in the 1860s.[31] The great success of the late-nineteenth-century Church was to direct this 'instinct' into orthodox liturgical forms and bring it under clerical control. This was epitomized by Lourdes. Healing springs and apparitions were the stuff of popular religion, and this one followed that conventional pattern. Now, however, after brief hesitation, Lourdes was officially approved, developed by the Church, and became a centre for organized mass pilgrimages by rail centred on the vast and hideous basilica (1876), with clergy-led processions, sacramental liturgy, organized immersions and medically certified cures (most were of tuberculosis).

The lay organizations of the Church were also modernized and brought increasingly under clerical control. The Pénitents, for example, had been independent, convivial and often rowdy, like those still existing in Spain. But the new organizations – charities, clubs, pious confraternities – were sober and disciplined bodies under the direct supervision of the bishops and parish clergy. From the 1870s onwards, this growing network of societies was intended, in the face of a hostile State, to form the basis of a 'Catholic counter-society' (see p. 142), by which Catholics from childhood onwards, through schools, youth groups, higher-education institutes, sports clubs, trade and agricultural syndicats, and newspapers, could be kept within a Catholic environment shielded from irreligious influences.

However utopian this vision, its degree of success should not be underestimated. By around the turn of the century, Catholic schools had over 1 million pupils, 20 per cent of the total. The newspaper *La Croix* had a circulation of 170,000. More than twice as many people went to Lourdes as went on strike; and up to 200,000 a year visited the shrine of the Sacred Heart at Paray-le-Monial. The Catholic sports federation included 1,500 clubs with 150,000 members by 1914. The Catholic agricultural federation of the south-west had 500 affiliated *syndicats* by 1913 with 125,000 members (out of 800,000 agricultural families).[32]

The existence of 'two Frances', Catholic and republican, was one of the unique features of the post-revolutionary period. Religion, which was simultaneously an expression of family, community, regional and political

31. Gibson (1989), p. 141.
32. Cholvy and Hilaire (1985), vol. 2, pp. 63, 84, 211; Arnaud, in Tombs (1991), p. 186.

identity, remained fundamental to the way people thought of themselves and each other. And this lasted: religion, not class, occupation or income, was the most reliable predictor of voting choices as late as the 1960s; probably the largest ever demonstrations in French history were those in favour of independent Catholic schools in 1984; and Catholic support for 'Europe' arguably swung the result in the 1992 Maastricht referendum.[33]

33. Derivry and Dogon (1986), pp. 157–81; and *L'Express*, 9 Oct. 1992, pp. 16–17.

CHAPTER 14

REGION AND 'MENTALITY'

What has principally determined the beliefs and political loyalties of French people since the Revolution has been the part of the country where they lived. The already discussed influences of family and immediate community usually (though not always, as will be seen later) reinforced an identity shared over a much wider area. The way that different regions experienced the Revolution marked them durably; and the political shocks and economic changes of the nineteenth and twentieth centuries modified but did not efface these differences. The political map of France therefore shows a continuity more striking and complex than that of Britain with its 'Celtic fringe', Italy with its Mezzogiorno or the United States with its Southern particularism. Fundamental contours fixed in the 1790s remained with slight modification at least until the mid-twentieth century, a graphic illustration of the long-term influence of the Revolution at the deepest level as both 'revealer' and 'creator' of political identities.[1]

THE REVOLUTION AND THE EMERGENCE OF POLITICAL 'MENTALITIES'

What the Revolution revealed were diverse and complex variations – social, economic, cultural, anthropological – that affected the way in which regions experienced and responded to its impact. The most important socio-economic factors included: patterns of land tenure and agricultural organization; the degree of economic development; rates of literacy; types of settlement; accessibility from the outside; the role of the Church; the level of integration into the State administration; and the degree of 'feudal' conflict. Yet these did not determine responses in any simple way. There is no 'centre'/'periphery' division, for example, nor one between French and non-French cultures (Bretons rejected the Revolution, but Catalans supported it). Some refractory regions where anti-feudal troubles had been common and where the

1. Vovelle (1993), p. 341.

demands by the Old Regime for taxes and conscripts had been stubbornly resisted (for example, the west and parts of the Massif Central) also resisted similar demands from the revolutionary authorities. Some regions which had been obedient and law-abiding under the Old Regime (such as the north and east) remained so under the Revolution. The diverse economic effects of the revolutionary wars were also important: sea-ports greatly suffered; some manufacturing cities benefited.

The clearest overall division corresponds to the varying regional strength of pre-revolutionary Catholicism, whose causes were discussed in the previous chapter, and which the Revolution made a political shibboleth. The choice, however, was not always simply a reflection of religious fervour: circumstance was crucial. In the early stages of the Revolution the most strongly Catholic areas showed no greater attachment to the Old Regime. Even the pattern of reactions to the 1791 Civil Constitution of the Clergy – undoubtedly a watershed in French history, for it began to set the Revolution against Catholicism – only partly prefigures the post-revolutionary political map. It was later events – civil war in the west, Catholic/Protestant conflict in the south, the federalist revolt, the Terror, foreign war and invasion – which modified the map in a way that could not be predicted from pre-revolutionary conditions and structures. In this way the Revolution 'created' as well as 'revealed' differences.

There were unpredictable variations. Some districts, unusually pious before the Revolution, accepted the 1791 Civil Constitution of the Clergy and supported the Revolution. Still in the 1830s and 1840s, especially in the west, these 'Blue Catholics' clung both to their left-wing and their Catholic loyalties. They addressed their *curés* as '*citoyen*'; religious processions, tricolour flag flying, were escorted by the mayor, with the National Guard firing ceremonial volleys at important moments. In rural areas of the Flemish north half a century later there were even church-going radicals and socialists. Conversely, parts of the remote rural west, notoriously irreligious and lawless in the eighteenth century, turned to 'White' Catholicism as a badge of resistance to the conscription and taxation of the Revolution; and although most people there in the early nineteenth century attended the major religious festivities, evidence of more intimate religious belief was lacking.

Several historians, most notably Michel Vovelle in a recent and ingenious statistical analysis,[2] have attempted to analyse and classify the range of variables, and draw up a satisfactory map of revolutionary politics and the emergence of durable political 'mentalities'. Although all such attempts are necessarily simplifications, Vovelle's findings are impressive for their comprehensiveness and valuable, especially from the point of view of the period with which we are concerned, in being able to illuminate the origins of a far wider range of responses than a simple dichotomy between 'Left' and 'Right', between support for or rejection of the Revolution. This makes the complexity and fluidity of post-revolutionary political identities more

2. Ibid.; see also Hunt (1984).

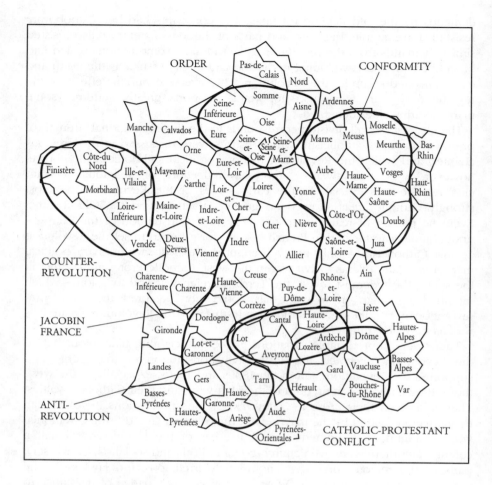

Figure 14.1 The Revolution and political mentalities
After Vovelle (1993), pp. 328, 280–92.

comprehensible. He classifies the fundamental divisions of the 1790s as
'Jacobin', 'counter-revolution', 'anti-revolution', 'order' and 'conformity', each
of which had its geography based on social, economic, cultural and historical
specifics. What follows is an attempt to draw out the implications of his
findings for the nineteenth century.

Jacobin France

Left-wing France, and especially its hard core, was, in Vovelle's words,
'sparsely populated, little urbanized, slowing down demographically, above
all poorer, and culturally under-developed'.[3] It extended from central France

3. Vovelle (1993), p. 310.

on the upper Loire, forming a crescent down the western side of the Massif Central, and into the central Pyrenees, regions that were fairly inaccessible from Paris, and were associated with small peasant landownership and often with oppressive share-cropping tenure (*métayage*) on large estates; with extended family systems; with a history of tax evasion and resistance to military service (what Vovelle calls 'le mauvais gré paysan', peasant ill-will); with weak Catholicism and readiness to accept the Civil Constitution of the Clergy.

'Counter-revolutionary' and 'anti-revolutionary' France

There were three principal and quite different areas of resistance to the Revolution. First, in the south, from the south-eastern part of the Massif Central to the Mediterranean, where reactions were coloured by the long and bitter antagonism between Catholics and Protestants. Protestants, given full citizenship in 1790–91, took over local power in several areas, and most importantly in the textile town of Nîmes. Protestant nobles and businessmen, supported by Protestant workers and peasants, came into bloody conflict with their Catholic neighbours as early as June 1790 in the notorious '*bagarre de Nîmes*'. Smouldering violence – riot, insurrection, terror and reprisal – continued throughout the 1790s, with Catholic death squads terrorizing Protestants and Jacobins.

Second, there was the west: Britanny and what became known as the '*Vendée militaire*', south of the lower Loire. Although a very distinct region in its culture, family structures, land tenure and strong Catholicism, conflict was less predictable than in the south, and arose largely from circumstance. A spontaneous revolt in 1793 against conscription (which caused unrest all over the country) here turned into the most serious of the counter-revolutionary outbursts, that of the Vendée. Eventually it spread into four departments, mobilized an armed horde some 80,000 strong and lasted sporadically until 1796. The rebels adopted Catholicism as their ideological justification: although not the original cause of the violence, defence of the old religion was both a genuine and an expedient rallying cry. Rebel fighters wore the Sacred Heart symbol sewn on their jackets. The movement always kept its popular character (one of the leaders, Cathelineau, was a pedlar, another was a gamekeeper) but the rebels also called on local nobles to lead them. Hence, the 'Royal and Catholic Army' was a true alliance of people, Church and nobility against a remote, alien, demanding and ultimately savagely repressive Republic. It produced the worst bloodshed in the two centuries of the 'Franco-French war', with grisly murders by the rebels and terrible reprisals by the 'Blues'. Finally 200,000 people died and vast areas were systematically devastated by republican punitive columns. Guerrilla resistance (*chouannerie*) continued in many parts of the west throughout the decade.

Less spectacularly, there were 'anti-revolutionary' areas, particularly the poor and remote highlands of the Massif Central, marked by apoliticism and a non-ideological though occasionally violent resistance to State demands, notably taxation and conscription. In their social structure and many of their attitudes they were not dissimilar to the Jacobin area to the west, or the strongly Catholic and counter-revolutionary southern highlands. But their greater degree of inaccessibility, and the absence of a Protestant 'enemy', meant that they never emerged from the 'deep silence' of passive resistance.

The France of 'order' and 'conformity'

The area of north-central France, centred on the Paris region and extending to the Normandy coast, is characterized by Vovelle as 'the France of order'. Economically it was the most developed and wealthy region, highly populated, urbanized, with relatively productive commercial agriculture based on large tenant farms, paid agricultural labour and large 'urban villages'. It was integrated into the State system: taxes were obediently paid and conscripts mustered. There was tension between employers and labourers, but the larger tenant farmers maintained political and economic control. Catholicism was generally weak. Several major aspects of the Revolution were welcomed and supported: the end of seigneurial dues and church tithes, the sale of church land, and 'dechristianization'. But the Terror and social and economic upheaval were rejected. The region therefore swung from 'Left' to 'Right' during the 1790s.

Not dissimilar was the north-east, which Vovelle characterizes as conformist. Like its western neighbour, it too was economically and culturally developed, with a very high rate of literacy, and law-abiding. There was no resistance to the Revolution, but it was accepted rather than supported: there was less political participation than in the Paris region. Nearness to the frontier and the resulting large military presence kept any opposition silent. It too moved toward the Right during the 1790s, but without any counter-revolutionary extremism or 'White Terror'.

PERSISTENCE AND DEVELOPMENT OF POLITICAL 'MENTALITIES', 1814–51

As we have seen, the power of kinship and of local communities were crucial in the creation of identity, and certainly served among other things to transmit political traditions. Forms of sociability – the evening *veillées*, the male *chambrées* – doubtless transmitted common political memories. Traditional festivities and rituals, such as carnivals and *charivaris*, could be used for political purposes, to make propaganda or enforce conformity. Local hierarchies and chains of dependence of landlord and tenant, or farmer and labourer, were not essentially changed by the Revolution, and they remained as sources of potential solidarity or of conflict. Sometimes tenants were forced more or less grudgingly to follow their masters' political orders, as in Britany in 1876, when

Vicomte de Kergariou informs the tenants . . . that he is charged by his relatives the landowners to make all without exception vote for Comte de Mun. He is to inform himself of how this order is carried out and report on it to the landowners, who will certainly remember it.[4]

But such pressure (beside the fact that it was not always exerted in favour of the same party) could equally cause resentment and revolt. As a means of propagating a certain political mentality, it only worked when most landlords and tenants shared the same basic sympathies, as in Britanny they did.

Far from weakening regional political mentalities, the processes of modernization entrenched and formalized them. The influence and rivalry of families and clans and the often long-established enmity of neighbouring communities took political form once elections and the power of the State became matters of common concern, as they did in various stages between the Revolution and the end of the nineteenth century: during the Revolution itself, after 1830 with the partial democratization of local government, and after 1848 with the introduction of manhood suffrage. Newspapers were local and regional (even today these are immensely more important than in a culturally and politically centralized society such as England). Literacy and mechanical printing meant access to more sophisticated propaganda. The 'cult of memory' was consciously and systematically developed, for example through the writing of history, the building of museums and memorials, the naming of streets and the erection of innumerable statues. Hence, in the Vendée, it was only in the 1880s that the inhabitants became collectively conscious of the full extent of the horrors experienced by their great-great-grandparents and only then in reaction to the republicans' 'mania for commemoration'.[5] Perhaps most important of all, the Catholic Church, as was seen above, successfully rebuilt and consolidated its influence after 1815. It became increasingly the unifying and identifying element of a counter-revolutionary political mentality.

Apart from these general factors, a succession of events contributed to the evolution of political mentalities. Although they are narrated in detail in Parts IV and V, their specifically regional dimensions are relevant here.

'Blues' and 'Whites', 1814–48

The period of the fall of Napoleon, the Bourbon Restoration, and the liberal monarchy of Louis-Philippe saw the revival, if in a lower register, of the quarrels of the 1790s, often involving the same men or their immediate descendants. The regional political mentalities created by the Revolution were thus reinvigorated, especially where local struggles had been most bitter.

In the south, Napoleon's return from Elba in February 1815 rekindled sectarian violence culminating in a 'White Terror' against defeated Bonapartists (often Protestant) that left memories and resentments which

4. Weber (1991), p. 370.
5. Martin, in Vovelle (1990), vol. 2, p. 1161.

persisted until well into the twentieth century. The strength of popular
Catholic counter-revolution carried over into determined opposition to the
July Monarchy, seen as a 'Protestant' regime. In the west, bitter antagonism
between the 'Blues' of towns such as Rennes, Nantes and Le Mans, little
republics that had been literally besieged by the hordes of rebel Vendéens,
and the mainly rural 'Whites' remained. Here too, Napoleon's 'Hundred Days'
rekindled violence that was carried over into the Restoration and the July
Monarchy. For decades, both under the Bourbons and Louis-Philippe, 'Blue'
towns such as Le Mans, Nantes and Angers were electoral strongholds of the
left-wing opposition, who opposed any return to power of 'Whites'. In 1832,
a small-scale though bloody revolt followed the arrival of the Bourbon
Duchesse de Berry, and the government sent large numbers of troops to
occupy the Vendée which was placed under martial law. In the 1840s 'Blue'
anger was aroused when the Guizot government appointed the son of a
Chouan rebel as tax collector – a post that gave ample opportunity for paying
off old scores. When 1848 brought universal male suffrage, the 'White'
majority of peasants swept the 'Blue' bourgeoisie from power and made the
west an electoral bastion of the Right for over a century. In the 1990s, a
Charette, descendant of the rebel leader of the 1790s, sat as conservative
deputy for Maine-et-Loire, as well as being mayor of the village where the
defeated rebels escaped across the Loire, and where 14 July is not celebrated.

But in the east, simultaneous events had quite opposite consequences. The
frontier provinces had long been patriotic and military, fruitful recruiting
grounds for the royal army. After 1789, support for the Republic and later for
Napoleon meant defence against foreign invasion. Napoleon, returning from
Elba in 1815, had to skirt Marseilles – one of the great ports ruined by the
war – but found a welcome further up the Rhône valley and in the east. The
defeats of 1814 and 1815, with their massive invasions and lengthy
occupation by Prussians and Austrians of this eastern region, who looted,
requisitioned and raped, and who were allies of the Whites, were a formative
experience. Nationalistic Bonapartist-republicanism reappeared in conspiracies
against the Bourbons in the 1820s and against Louis-Philippe in the 1830s,
involving soldiers and civilians, and centred on the garrison towns of
Strasbourg and Lunéville. The liberal parliamentary opposition to the
Bourbons and later to Louis-Philippe and Guizot also had strongholds in
Dijon and Auxerre. Nationalism, whether in liberal, Bonapartist or republican
guise, was to last here throughout the century.

The Second Republic, 1848–51

The revolution of February 1848 marked a new episode in the formation of
political mentalities. From 1849, a new phenomenon emerged on the Left: the
démocrates-socialistes, or 'démoc-socs'. Led by urban left-wing politicians
they were a mass party in the provinces, appealing to peasant needs at a time
of severe hardship in agriculture and forestry. Their success, as Figure 14.2
shows, went well beyond the area of 'Jacobin France' in the 1790s, though it

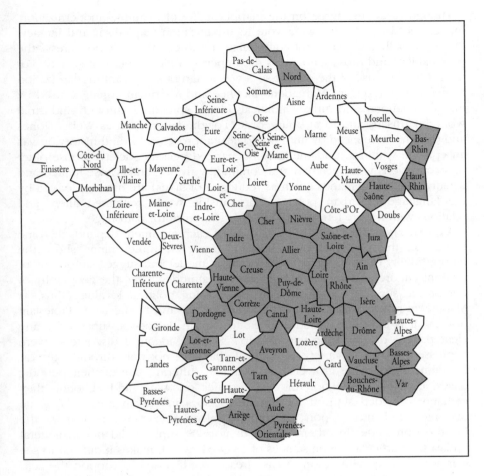

Figure 14.2 The démoc-socs, 1849 (over 40% of the vote, 13 May 1849)
After Lévêque (1992) p. 316

clearly built on that foundation. This was still the relatively undeveloped, sparsely populated and poor central and highland region, where démoc-soc promises to reduce taxes accorded with the tradition of 'le mauvais gré paysan', angry with government tax increases. They had also conquered support in the left-wing areas of the south whose existing revolutionary tendencies were spurred by the crisis in the wine trade, of increasing importance in the Mediterranean littoral. The rapid growth of the 'démoc-socs', and the geography of the insurrection they inspired against Louis-Napoleon Bonaparte's coup d'état in December 1851 – the most widespread popular uprising of the nineteenth century, involving some 100,000 people in some sort of protest and over 25,000 in actual violence[6] – has inspired much study and not a little unresolved controversy.

6. Margadent (1979), p. 8.

Though historians agree on the inapplicability of a simple 'modernization' model, ascribing the left-wing vote to urbanization, capitalism and literacy, there is still an important difference between those who stress the permeability and those who stress the impermeability of peasant society. For the former, the rise of the démoc-socs was a sign of significant modernization of peasant attitudes, as Margadent, McPhee and Merriman argue,[7] caused by market relations and urban political ideas, spreading through industrial workers, artisans and local bourgeoisie. For the latter, such as Weber, Jones and Corbin,[8] influenced by anthropological approaches to rural history, it was an episode within a fundamentally unchanged peasant society, whose older preoccupations with sectarian and community rivalry, and whose limited and usually negative demands (such as reduction of taxes) are merely cloaked by the language of urban politics. The outside world remained alien, and relations with it were left to local *notables*, in return for patronage.

As is so often the case, the plausibility of each argument depends to some extent on the particular area studied. However, three things show the inapplicability of any simple 'modernization' model and suggest autonomy of peasant culture and important continuity of attitudes. First, the geography of démoc-soc support was shaped by pre-existing political loyalties: thus, as Margadent notes, resistance to the coup d'état was most cohesive in Protestant districts. It is difficult, concludes Jones, to explain démoc-soc support 'by any clear pattern of economic relationship'.[9] Second, identical discontents were expressed through a variety of political channels, not only through support for démoc-socs: wine growers, for example, suffering one of their periodic crises, demanded abolition of excise duties on wine; and although they certainly provided support for the démoc-socs in certain areas, the same discontent fed into support for Louis-Napoleon Bonaparte or even for the Bourbon pretender in others. Third, démoc-soc support did not in general outlast the particular circumstances of 1849–51, which makes it difficult to see it in terms of modernization. Areas already predisposed to support the Left, which were embittered by repression both before and after the 1851 coup, remained a base for left-wing political growth for the rest of the century and beyond. But elsewhere, Jones suggests, support for the démoc-socs was a temporary reaction to severe economic crisis: a 'tide' that 'rose and fell leaving few traces'.[10] In several regions, such as the south-west and parts of the Massif Central, démoc-soc voters switched immediately to Bonapartism, which proved a more powerful and durable mobilizer of peasant support.

Bonapartism and the 'France of order'

Vovelle's 'France of order', as we have seen, covered those parts of the country that accepted the religious and political changes of the Revolution,

7. Ibid.; McPhee (1992:b); Merriman (1978).
8. Weber (1991), chs 7–8; Jones (1985); Corbin (1995).
9. Margadent (1979), p. 143; Jones (1985) p. 245.
10. Jones (1985), p. 237.

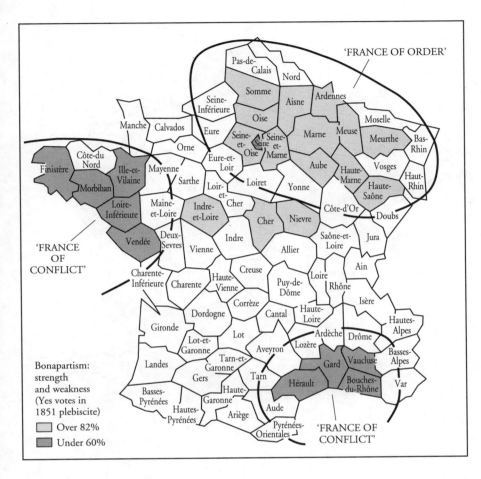

Figure 14.3 Bonapartism: strength and weakness
Based on statistics in Mènager (1988), pp. 433–4.

but resisted economic or social upheaval and prolonged political instability: in other words, a centrism that sometimes allied with the Left against counter-revolution, sometimes with the Right against revolutionary disorder. This found perfect expression in Bonapartism: not that of Napoleon I in 1813–15, which threatened war and upheaval, but that of Louis-Napoleon Bonaparte, which emerged suddenly as a mass phenomenon in the summer of 1848. This promised to maintain universal suffrage and oppose a royalist restoration while resisting further upheaval; and also to promote economic modernization.

Bonapartism was so successful electorally in 1848 that it almost obliterated pre-existing political maps, winning a majority in all regions. However, if we focus on the core areas of highest continuous electoral support – where Bonapartism won an astonishing 80 per cent of the vote or over in three

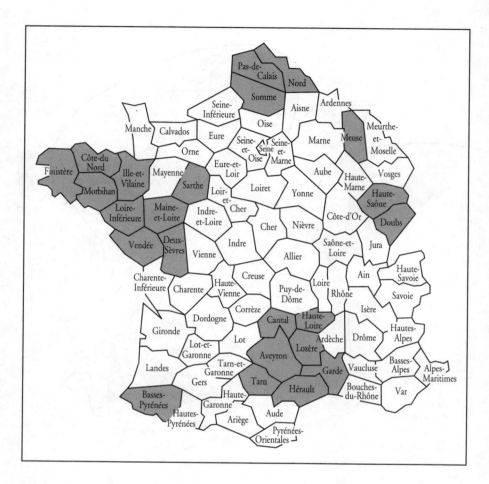

Figure 14.4 Extreme Right, 1870s (departments electing at least one Legitimist deputy) After Locke (1974), p. 258.

plebiscites over two decades – we see that they are those of Vovelle's 'France of order'. The small areas of Bonapartist weakness are the west and the south, the areas of most violent conflict during the Revolution, and hence of extreme polarization between counter-revolutionary and revolutionary traditions, where the centrist character of Bonapartism had relatively weak appeal: and each side suspected it of being too sympathetic to the other.

NEW WINE IN OLD BOTTLES, 1871–*c.*1940

The fall of the Second Empire and the eclipse of Bonapartism led to a political struggle between royalists and a broad republican coalition during the 1870s. However, the republicans soon fragmented into opportunists,

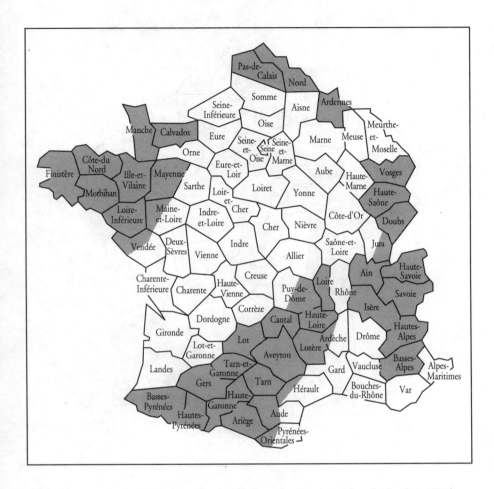

Figure 14.5 Catholicism (areas where religious practice considered 'good', *c.*1877)
After Gadille (1967), vol. 1, pp. 152–3.

radicals and later socialists. The 'Jacobin' regions of the centre and the south developed into strongholds of radicalism and socialism. Moderate opportunist republicans set out to capture the centre ground, in effect replacing Bonapartists as the spokesmen of the 'France of order' in the north and east. However, unlike Bonapartism, moderate republicanism remained ideologically part of the Left, with anticlericalism at the heart of its programme. Catholicism became the clearest political shibboleth, as the Right, especially the legitimists, made defence of the Church its rallying cry.

Catholicism and conservatism

However, there was not a complete and lasting correlation between Catholicism and the Right in the 1870s and 1880s. There were large areas

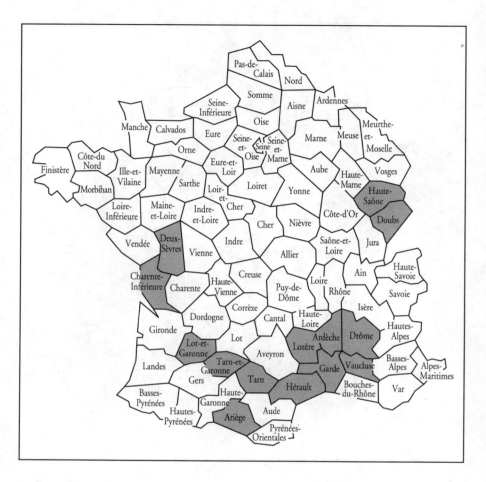

Figure 14.6 Protestantism, 1876 (highest number of Protestant ministers in proportion to population, 1876)
After Le Bras and Todd (1981), p. 374.

where people went to church but did not follow their priests' political instructions: these regions were willing to accept the moderate Republic from the 1870s onwards, and especially after the *ralliement*, when the Church officially accepted the Republic. The strongholds of the legitimist Right were not therefore all regions of piety, but those where Catholicism was a counter-revolutionary political banner. However, the political contours of Catholicism became firmer at the end of the century, when the results of the Dreyfus affair (see pp. 462–70) placed religion at the centre of political controversy. The map of Catholic France then became the map of resistance to the Left, as can be seen in Figure 14.9. This division persisted in the twentieth century, in opposition to a militantly anticlerical or atheist Left of radicals, socialists and later communists; and so it remained until the 1960s.

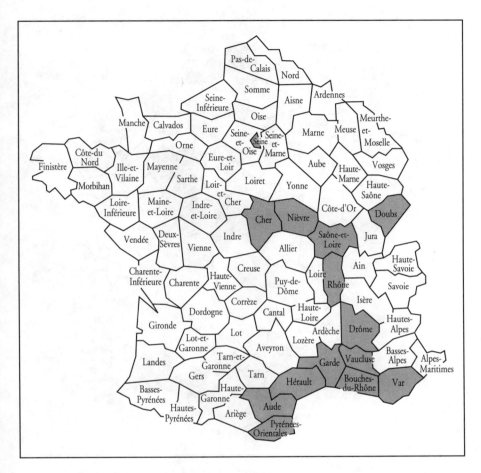

Figure 14.7 Radicalism, 1871–1901 (departments electing at least one radical deputy to every parliament)
After Bouju (1966), p. 118.

The Left: radicals and socialists

The strength of the re-emerging 'extreme Left', which from the 1860s onwards consisted of radicals (the most democratic and secularist republicans) and a variety of socialist groups, had like its predecessors in the 1790s and 1849–51 a strong geographical character, based on the large cities, the industrial north, and parts of the south and centre.

First, the cities. Paris and Lyons, since the 1820s, had developed a working-class militancy based on the major craft industries and probably on older republican links going back at least to 1815 and even to the 1790s. Second, the north. Here working-class radicalism and socialism were more recent developments, based on the textile towns such as Lille and Roubaix and coalmining villages such as Fourmies and Anzin, and favoured by the

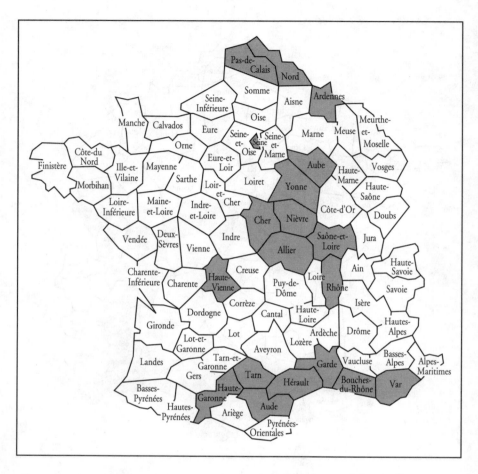

Figure 14.8 Socialism, 1914 (over 15% of registered electors voting for, in general election of April 1914)
After Bouju (1966), p. 119.

characteristic sociability of the Flemish north, more like Belgium, Germany or Britain than elsewhere in France. Third, the south. Often called '*le Midi Rouge*', it continued its unique sectarian in-fighting which caused some arcane political variations. Radicalism there, as Figure 14.7 shows (compare with Figure 14.5), was essentially anti-Catholic and often Protestant, and so Catholics, including workers and coalminers in some southern towns such as Carmaux, continued until the 1890s to vote royalist. When royalism finally became a lost cause, they preferred in some cases to vote socialist rather than see the detested radicals win. On the other hand, the 'red' tradition of the non-Catholic Midi encouraged radicals along the Mediterranean littoral and the Rhône valley to move on to the 'redder' version, socialism, which inherited a strong anti-Catholic colouring and Protestant connections. This was a persistent tradition: of the 21 departments that continuously supported the Left from 1871 to 1946, fourteen were in the *'Midi Rouge'*.[11] Fourth, radicalism and socialism also implanted themselves in the old Jacobin and dechristianized centre, where sometimes they found a first foothold in Protestant communities (for example in the northern part of the Cher department) among small peasant proprietors and woodcutters, a cohesive group hit by a collapse in timber prices in the 1880s and who became stalwart supporters of Blanquism.[12]

The main economic stimulus to change was the long-drawn-out crisis of the 1880s–1900s affecting the wine industry, agriculture and forestry which first moderate opportunists and then radicals were unable to solve. The failure of Clemenceau's radical government (1906–9) to remedy the crisis led to radicals being 'almost swept out of the Midi' by socialism,[13] though some radical party bosses survived by becoming socialists themselves, such as Dr Ferroul, long-serving mayor and deputy of Narbonne.

The importance of regional 'mentality' as opposed to class is quite clear in the case of the implantation of the Marxist Parti Ouvrier Français in the centre and south. Willard .concludes that support was motivated 'much less by conscious adhesion to collectivism than faithfulness to the republic'. Workers were under-represented and peasants over-represented: in the most Marxist rural department, Allier, 42.6 per cent of its election candidates were peasants. In general, the 'cradle' of Marxism in both the north and the south was an older radical, anticlerical tradition. Where the Church was strong (for example, industrialized Lorraine) Marxism made little progress. 'Inherited ideology' was 'a brake or a springboard', concludes Willard; 'whatever the social category of the region, the past leaves its mark on the present'.[14]

Nationalism

Nationalism made a significant change in the mentalities and regional maps of both Right and Left from the 1880s onwards. Boulangism (see pp. 447–53) was able to synthesize elements from Right and Left, in particular the counter-revolutionary tradition of the west and south and the anti-bourgeois radicalism of the cities, who found a common enemy in the 'bourgeois Republic'. In 1902, Paris was won by the nationalist Right for the first time. In the late 1890s, in traditionally republican regions of eastern France enough voters and politicians swung to the Right during the Dreyfus affair to alter the allegiance of the region: traditionally having associated nationalism, support for the army and defence of the Fatherland with the Left, they now associated it with the Right. The aftermath of the affair brought renewed conflict between Church and Republic. Consequently, in this period we see a clear and lasting polarization between the 'two Frances': the Right is now clearly

11. Loubère (1974); Sagnes (1982); Willard (1965).
12. Pigenet (1993); see also Pennetier (1982).
13. Loubère (1974), p. 187.
14. Willard (1965), pp. 267, 323.

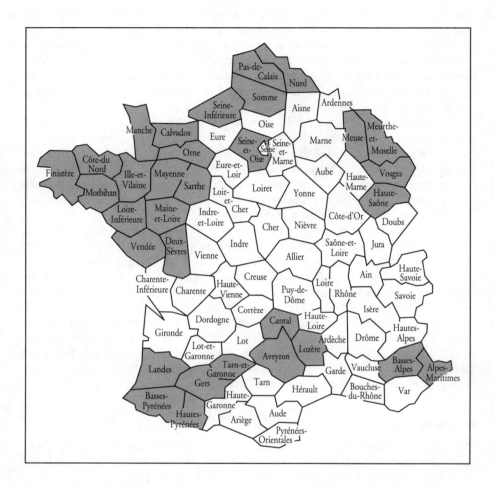

Figure 14.9 Polarization: the 'two Frances' (majority of seats won by Right, elections of May 1898)
After Goguel (1970), p. 37.

based on Catholic France, the Left on the old dechristianized 'Jacobin' regions and those of Protestantism.

Regional political 'mentalities' both preceded and outlasted socio-economic transformations, and shaped the political response to them, whether through a high level of consensus, as in the Catholic and Protestant regions of the Midi and the west, or by tipping the balance of electoral advantage by influencing a proportion of voters, or by creating new alliances, as in the Boulangist successes of the 1880s. Some parts of the country remained consistently on the 'Right' and others on the 'Left', however much the programmes, slogans and labelling of parties changed.

CHAPTER 15

IMAGINED COMMUNITIES: CLASS

The concept of 'class' has become a problematic one for historians. The idea of class as the fundamental socio-economic, cultural and political structure emerging inevitably from the upheavals and sufferings of the Industrial Revolution – a view that still colours many general accounts – has been discarded by most specialists. First, the traditional idea of the 'Industrial Revolution' as a rapid plunge into factories, towns and proletarianization is no longer tenable: the process was a far more complex and gradual one, with much continuity with 'pre-industrial' craft manufacture and small-scale production. One conclusion could be, as also has been suggested for Britain, that the period at which an industrial working class as conventionally understood emerged (permanently employed in large factories, living in segregated areas, unionized and politically represented by a militantly class party) was much later than previously supposed – around the time of the First World War.[1] Second, changing historical approaches, in particular the interest in culture and language as the creators of social identity, have demolished the determinism that regarded certain sets of attitudes and beliefs as a direct product – 'consciousness' – of economic conditions. Third, a recognition of the complexity of social, political and economic life, which included cooperation and solidarity between 'classes' and diversity and antagonism within them, has blurred the lines of division. Fourth, a recognition of the potency of other conceptions of belonging, such as people, community, religious denomination, political party or nation, shows class to be only one among several 'imagined communities' that make up our composite identity.

If we accept some or all of this revisionism, we must consider whether the political upheavals and violence of nineteenth-century France can be considered as manifestations of class struggle, and whether the traditional chronology of class warfare (1830–34, 1848–51, 1871) can still be accepted. Clearly this requires a different understanding of what 'class' is and what creates it: we can hardly regard it as a product of 'industrialization', 'proletarianization' etc., if these changes had not yet occurred. Another

---

1. Noiriel (1986), part 4.

question is whether France was a special case. In this context comparison is often made with Britain. Britain is commonly seen as epitomizing peaceful containment of class conflicts, while France experienced their violent and radical expression in both words and actions. Was France really unusually violent and if so why? Again, can an explanation be sought in special socio-economic conditions, or in political culture?

It is now widely accepted that the language of 'class' was created by ideological and political conflict. However, that leads to the danger of circular argument: political conflict creates class; class creates political conflict. It also begs the question as to whether 'class' remains a useful analytical concept: if 'class conflict' or 'class identity' are regarded as political and cultural constructs, and cannot 'in some sense be anchored in the socio-economic condition of workers',[2] then does the concept of class have any historical validity? Here one answer is suggested by Cottereau:[3] that nineteenth-century conflict in France between employers and workers stemmed from unremitting attempts by the former to increase productivity within an economic system that had not undergone technological transformation and maintained many of the methods of craft production. In short, the 'class consciousness' of French workers was a result of their resistance to economic changes, not a result of those changes once made.[4]

Another sense in which the idea of class retains undeniable historical importance is that contemporaries used class language and imagery. In Stedman Jones's phrase, it was a 'discursive' reality whether or not it was an 'ontological' reality.[5] In political theory, literature, painting and popular imagery, intense interest was shown in the portrayal of social types, as the French strove to identify, classify and ascribe certain characteristics to what seemed novel and often disturbing phenomena. This sustained cultural activity covers a vast range of style and medium: the voluminous series of prints *Les Français peints par eux-mêmes* published in the 1840s (from 'the worker' to 'the peer' via 'the grocer' and 'the poet'); over half a century of 'realistic' social novels or plays by Balzac, Sue, Scribe, Pyat, Dumas *fils*, the Goncourts, Flaubert, Maupassant and Zola; the satirical plays of Labiche and later Feydeau; the photography of Nadar; the naturalist paintings of Courbet and Millet in the 1840s and 1850s, continued over the next generation by the dedicated 'painting of modern life' of the Impressionists; and not least political speeches and propaganda (newspapers, pamphlets, cartoons, songs). All testify to an obsessive need to create a language through which a seemingly new and changing society could literally be 'classified' and made comprehensible.

To pursue these questions further, we shall first survey the 'labouring classes' as they were during most of the nineteenth century; second, the

2. Joyce (1991), p. 4.
3. Cottereau, in Katznelson and Zolberg (1986).
4. Mann (1993), vol. 2, p. 227.
5. Stedman Jones (1983).

political conflicts and languages of class during the 'era of revolutions' culminating in 1871; and third the crucial and turbulent period at the end of the nineteenth century when the economic and political meanings of class were transformed.

THE *CLASSES LABORIEUSES* IN POST-REVOLUTIONARY FRANCE

The Revolution profoundly and durably affected property and labour. It considerably increased the number of small landowners by a vast redistribution of land. Although much went to urban investors or large landowners, much was resold over the next decades, and probably about half of all agricultural land belonged to peasant farmers by the end of the process. This did not make them all prosperous yeoman: most landowners had small holdings, 85 per cent (in 1862) under 10 hectares. But it did create enduring social and economic characteristics: a large rural population owning land, aspiring to own land, or struggling to acquire more land; a low birth rate, and hence persistent labour shortages throughout the economy; the sturdy persistence of craft industry in town and country; a pattern of 'household economy' sustained by the labour of all its members in a diverse and overlapping range of activities; and perennial conflict between employers trying to increase productivity and workers determined to defend their identity, independence and control over work practices.

The largest element of the *classes laborieuses* was the agricultural labour force (7.3 million in the 1860s) which included a wide and complex range of wealth and status. Over half (3.8 million) were landowners, but less than a quarter of these had enough land to be independent. Substantial peasant-proprietors (*laboureurs*) and also larger tenant-farmers employed labourers and overlapped in status with the rural 'bourgeoisie'. Smaller landowners (about 2 million) had also to rent extra land or work part-time for other farmers or in industry; as did many small tenants (387,000) and sharecroppers (202,000). About 40 per cent of the agricultural labour force were wage earners: labourers (1.2 million in 1892) and farm servants (1.8 million).[6] These wage earners themselves formed a complex hierarchy of age, gender, skill and expectations, from foreman on a large farm to shepherd-boy or milk-maid; many owned some land themselves, or could expect in due course to inherit, buy, or marry into it.

The smallness of holdings meant that much farm work was only part-time: women and men had other occupations to keep the 'household economy' functioning. This variety of work was an essential characteristic of the *classes laborieuses*. Much textile manufacturing was done at home. In the Haute-Loire department alone, 40,000 women made lace, one of the major female skilled craft industries. The mighty Lyons silk industry, France's major

6. Clout (1980), p. 31.

exporter, employed over 300,000 people in the 1860s, but more than half were spread over a radius of 100 miles round the city in a highly complex system of 'putting out'. Technical innovation was absorbed into the system: mechanical spinning increased the demand for part-time rural handweavers, for example. Overall, handweaving actually increased over most of the century, in striking contrast to Britain. Around 1860, France had 200,000 handlooms, when Britain had only 3,000; and in many important textile regions, handweaving kept pace with mechanical looms until the last decades of the century.[7] Even in large-scale industrial enterprises 'proletarians' were also 'peasants'. In mid-century, workers at the Peugeot hardware works in Valentigny came from 364 families, of whom 151 owned land.[8] Similar forms of organization extended to many important industries including metallurgy, glass, ceramics and mining. Textile mills, sugar refineries, coalmines and factories were often seen as a way of filling in during bad weather and agricultural slack periods. In the Franche-Comté region, peasant families made clocks during the winter. But when agriculture needed hands, industrial employment, whether at home or in factories, was abandoned.[9] Periodic migration was another way of finding supplementary sources of income when agricultural earnings were insufficient. Highland areas supplied migrants for a range of specialized occupations: building workers, pedlars, street musicians, chimney sweeps, even schoolteachers. In mid-century over 800,000 migrated annually, including the celebrated stonemasons from Creuse – 40,000 out of a total population of 220,000.

Post-revolutionary society was in several ways geared to this pattern. The owners of small plots of land required extra earnings to live; and rural society was left with a hunger to buy land that industrial earnings helped to feed. Cash was needed to compensate siblings for foregoing their share of the family farm. Working full-time in industry was often associated with a particular phase in life: boys before military service, or girls saving their dowries, both aiming to set themselves up eventually on a family small-holding. It was not a permanent condition or one that separated industrial workers from the rest of the rural community as an industrial 'working class'.

This might seem to be a transitional stage between 'archaic' and 'modern' employment patterns (though similar diversity of work has been found in far more 'modern' Britain at the same time); but it was in any case a very long transition. Landownership among industrial workers actually increased over the century, and was encouraged by large industrial employers who provided loans to buy smallholdings as a means of stabilizing the workforce and keeping wages down. In the 1870s it was noted that 'as soon as these workers have a few savings, they buy a house or a bit of land'.[10] Workers were determined to

7. Perrot, in Reynolds (1986), p. 75; Cottereau, in Katznelson and Zolberg (1986), p. 116.
8. Statistics from Noiriel (1986) and Moulin (1988), passim.
9. See the following important works: Trempé (1971); Reddy (1984); Sewell (1980).
10. Perrot (1974), vol. 1, pp. 212–13.

preserve ways of working that allowed them to keep their ties with the land, spread the risk of economic disaster, support the household economy, and (for craft workers) maintain corporate status and control of production. Time and again, the offer of higher wages did not change their minds; nor did the threat of lay-off or dismissal. Consequently, much of the permanent industrial labour force were women, children and immigrants.

The principal division within the 'labouring classes', argues Noiriel, was not between 'proletariat' and 'peasantry', but between urban and rural workers, which was not at all the same thing. Rural workers were often involved both in agriculture and in large 'modern' activities such as mining and metallurgy. Urban workers were usually engaged in small-scale skilled craft industry such as furniture-making, printing, lock-making, building and clothing. Urban crafts *métiers* had strong corporate identities, developed by heredity of occupation (in Paris in the 1860s, in several trades over 70 per cent of sons followed in their fathers' footsteps[11]), geographical concentration, long apprenticeships, rituals, oral traditions, lavish collective festivities, a high degree of literacy and politicization, self-help organizations and distinctive costumes – a sign of corporate pride that Jules Vallès, in exile after the Commune, noted contemptuously that London workers, who dressed like the middle classes, had abandoned. There was no permanent division between employers and employees (the distinction was not regularly made in official statistics) who in small workshops laboured side by side. As in the case of rural workers, wage earning was (or was intended to be) a periodic condition, often a stage in a craftsman's career, or a necessity imposed by hard times. A high proportion of craftsmen were self-employed or worked for very small family firms: in 1860s Paris, of some 100,000 *patrons*, 31,000 employed from two to ten workers, and 62,000 employed one worker or worked alone.[12] Firms might consist of an older *patron*, himself a working craftsman; a wife who kept the books; and an apprentice or journeyman, who might well marry the *patron's* daughter and eventually take over the business. Even in 1906, 60 per cent of all manual workers worked at home or in firms with fewer than ten employees.[13]

It is tempting to idealize these patterns of rural and urban work, and when things went well they clearly gave immense satisfactions, social, cultural and even economic. This is shown by the determination with which they were defended, and the disorientation caused by their eventual erosion during the long economic depression of the 1880s–90s. But it was also a hard, insecure and unstable existence marked by fluctuations of overwork and lay-offs, bankruptcy and unemployment. Very few small firms were truly independent, perhaps only 3 per cent in mid century;[14] the rest depended for credit and orders on larger firms. Economic slumps in France (the late 1840s, the late

11. Berlanstein (1984), p. 75.
12. Rougerie (1971), p. 13.
13. Perrot, in Reynolds (1986), p. 72.
14. Poulot (1980), p. 70.

1860s, the 1880s) were perhaps particularly devastating, and politically so dangerous, because they were not merely cyclical downturns but marked the permanent demise of swathes of traditional industries. Moreover, this must not be thought of as a timeless, 'archaic' world. As Cottereau shows, it was under unrelenting pressure to raise output. Handweaving continued not as a picturesque survival, but because it was able to increase productivity: the ribbon and velvet makers of Saint-Etienne, for example, consumed 6.8 kilos of raw material per head in 1839, 26 kilos in 1855 and 59 kilos in 1895.[15] Such productivity gains were made under pressure of foreign and domestic competition, piece-rate wage cuts, division of labour, attempts to impose controls over work practices, and technical innovation. This, Cottereau argues, is the origin of a characteristically French (or at least Latin) pattern of conflict between employers and workers. Events that at first sight may seem trivial, such as bitter disputes over meal breaks, take on a new meaning: at stake was whether workers or employers should control the pace and method of production. Attempts to 'discipline' workers went on throughout our period, but the particular characteristics of the French economy and its labour force – above all the combination of agricultural and industrial work, and the relative shortage of labour – made workers' resistance much longer drawn out than for example in Britain, and they often won at least temporary successes in preventing innovation in products or methods. The demise of handweaving, which took only about ten years in Britain, took 70 in France; and Perrot notes that it took 'sixty years of daily struggle . . . to transform peasant-miners into miner-peasants and then into just plain miners'.[16]

Workers' resistance took many forms. Open conflict meant strikes, riots, or collective demands for employers to respect traditional working practices or agree a negotiated wage structure, a *tarif.* This would usually involve not only employees of a particular company but a whole community. Passive or covert resistance to new methods included go-slows and sabotage. But the most effective was labour mobility: rural workers would return to agriculture; urban workers would change bosses. 'You've only got one workshop; we've got more than 200 in the streets of Paris.'[17]

POLITICS AND LANGUAGES OF CLASS DURING THE 'ERA OF REVOLUTIONS'

Disputes over work may explain social tensions, and economic crises that devastated traditional industries may explain widespread unrest. But neither explains 'class conflict', which implies that participants have a sense of wider solidarities, and of taking part in systematic conflict of interests and values,

15. Cottereau, in Katznelson and Zolberg (1986), p. 118.
16. Perrot, in Reynolds (1986), p. 79.
17. Poulot (1980), p. 187.

often described in teleological, even millenarian terms. Indeed, the *classes laborieuses*, with their multiple activity, overlapping hierarchies and strong attachment to local community, were arguably unlikely to conceive of society as divided into 'classes'. And yet from the 1830s onwards, French workers seem to have been particularly radical in ideas and behaviour – a durable characteristic that has attracted the attention of many scholars. However, attempts to explain this in purely socio-economic terms have not proved successful.[18]

We must also look at political culture, marked by those obsessions discussed in the first part of this book. For 'class' in France derived meaning from the Revolution, and hence always had primarily political significance. From the very beginning, the Revolution, and subsequently its nineteenth-century aftershocks, were explained as class conflicts. One of the most familiar statements about the Revolution was that it replaced a society of orders (clergy, nobility, third estate) with a society of classes (bourgeoisie, proletariat, peasantry); and this seemed to be demonstrated from the first constitution of 1791 until 1848, when property was the qualification for full political rights. Critics saw this as creating a new privilege of wealth, a 'new feudalism' (a phrase used throughout the nineteenth century) by which the 'bourgeoisie' oppressed the unenfranchised 'helots' or 'proletarians'. Class thus became a widely accepted means of explaining the workings and failings of government and society, and indeed a key to the meaning of history as a succession of class struggles.

The Left: emancipating 'the producers'

Ouvriers, paysans nous sommes
Le grand parti des travailleurs;
La terre n'appartient qu'aux hommes,
L'oisif ira loger ailleurs.

J.-B. Clément, 'L'Internationale' (1871)

The Revolution and its interpreters cast 'the people', most commonly seen as those who worked and produced, in a leading political role as pillar of revolutionary radicalism, a role that from 1789 to 1871 Parisian craft workers above all fulfilled. Revolutionary ideology also explained to workers that they had been cheated of their rights, and gave them the hope that they could resist unwanted economic and social change by revolutionary victory which would usher in the reign of liberty, equality and fraternity promised in 1789. Added to this was lyrical celebration of the moral superiority of manual labour prominent in Enlightenment and Romantic ideas of virtue and creativity. The suffering of 'this Christ that they call the people' would redeem humanity and create a better world. A self-consciousness was being

18. For discussion, see Gallie (1983); Sewell (1980).

expressed among workers which asserted that they were the sole producers 'of all the wealth of the nation'.[19]

All this fostered a moral, political and cultural idea of class among republicans and socialists. It was a very broad idea, however. Saint-Simon's vision of society divided between 'producers' (from factory owners to farm labourers) and 'the idle' (les oisifs) was widely accepted, and taken up by later socialists such as Proudhon and his many followers. 'Property is theft', wrote Proudhon in 1840, meaning property from which people lived without working, as opposed to 'possessions' earned by work and used productively. 'Les prolétaires' were usually seen as all those working for wages, and hence including peasants, teachers, clerks, journalists, and certainly left-wing intellectuals such as Blanqui, who spoke of 'proletarians like me'. As the socialist Dezamy wrote in 1843, 'I name proletarians the workers of the towns and the peasants of the countryside'; while the future Communard Lissagaray could still write in 1870, 'peasant, worker, proletarian, once slave to the chateau, today serf of a social system'.[20] As has been seen, the actual pattern of work in France fitted such broad definitions.

The July 1830 revolution heightened the political significance of class. The victory had undeniably been won mainly by Parisian workers. Democrats believed that this gave them certain rights, including economic protection. However, both political and economic requests, for example to ban mechanical printing presses in Paris or sanction a wage tarif in Lyons, were refused. This led to violent confrontations in Paris and Lyons between the State and workers, culminating in major insurrections in 1831 and 1834 which arose from collective defence of conditions of employment in the silk industry and the attempt by the State to repress workers' organizations. This struggle added to a sense of popular solidarity in the face of a hostile and unjust 'bourgeois' regime. This was strongly articulated by workers themselves and their spokesmen, who were indignant at being exposed to 'the humiliations of a Helot or a Muscovy serf'.[21] There is a clear contrast here with the British experience, when Peel and Gladstone calmed Chartist radicalism by repealing the Corn Laws and cutting taxes on workers' consumption, thus convincing them that the State was not hostile to popular claims.[22]

These conflicts of the 1830s have usually been seen as the foundation of French working-class consciousness. In several important ways, however, it was more far-reaching than 'class consciousness' as traditionally understood. It was broad enough to include all 'producers' and also the republican concepts of 'people' and 'nation'. The French nation was seen as having an essential role in achieving freedom and equality for all humanity. The workers' paper L'Atelier stated in 1841, 'Those who sincerely want the reign

19. Fritz (1988), pp. 106, 112.
20. Dubois (1962), p. 387.
21. Bezucha (1974), p. 112.
22. Stedman Jones (1983).

of fraternity . . . must above all devote themselves to the nation that has the mission of realizing it'. This nationalism included xenophobic hostility to foreign workers and English and Jewish capitalists, and it stigmatized 'aristocrats' and 'bourgeois' who put their own material interests before those of the nation. The exclusion of 'the people' not only from the electorate, but also from the National Guard, the repression of labour organizations and strikes and the progressive silencing of political organizations and newspapers created a sense of injustice that combined class, republican and national consciousness. The severe economic crisis of the late 1840s was inevitably interpreted as a consequence of this injustice, and increased the desire to change the 'bourgeois' monarchy which neglected popular well-being.

The desire to be accepted and integrated as full citizens of a democratic Republic was briefly fulfilled after the February 1848 revolution. The worker militant 'Albert' joined the Provisional Government, the 'right to work' was proclaimed and an official commission was set up to study workers' demands for social reform. Workers hoped that the socialist ideas of Louis Blanc and Proudhon would be put into practice, and the 'National Workshops' (see pp. 379–83) seemed to be a first step towards the recognition by the 'social and democratic' Republic of the rights of workers. Sewell suggests that the privileged dockers of Marseilles, until then royalist and Catholic, turned to republicanism precisely because its democratic rhetoric offered workers 'a new dignity in the state'.[23] The principal workers' demand was for the 'organization of work', which meant control over production through cooperative 'associations', which in due course would supersede capitalism. The collapse of these hopes in April and May 1848 created a veritable atmosphere of class war culminating in the June 1848 insurrection in Paris. However, the 'June Days' rising was not a class conflict in simple terms: Gossez, Caspard and Traugott have all in different ways shown 'the diversity of social antagonisms'.[24] Many on both sides saw themselves as fighting not for a class, but in the interests of the Republic, democracy and progress for the benefit of all. Further repression of left-wing '*Montagnards*' and '*démocrates-socialistes*' in both town and country, culminating in the coup d'état of 1851 and mass arrests and transportations, led to resentment, fear and disillusion. It created, says Perrot, a workers' self-identity centred on victimhood, oppression and economic injustice.

For nearly a generation, however, there was quiescence, caused certainly by disillusion and repression, but also helped by a major economic upturn during the 1850s and 1860s, and accompanied by genuine sympathy for Bonapartism. Napoleon III tried to win the support of workers and peasants, and in 1864 stopped prosecutions of strike organizers – a perennial source of conflict between workers and State. However, this populist 'caesarism' had

23. Sewell (1980), p. 634.
24. Gossez (May 1956) and (1967); Caspard (July–Sept. 1974), pp. 891–106; Traugott (1985).

very partial success. City workers (especially in Paris) were already strongly republican, while the economic development fostered by the Empire inevitably caused the kind of disruption that many groups of workers opposed. In Paris, for example, the vast urbanization programme of the 1850s and 1860s forced workers out into new suburbs, a move that was disliked for several reasons (cost, inconvenience, a sense of being exiled); moreover, living in architecturally and socially homogenous districts was a tangible expression of 'class'. In Marseilles, major port modernization in the 1850s and 1860s destroyed the privileges of the dockers. The late 1860s saw a reappearance of worker militancy, with strikes, activity by the Internationale (the London-based federation of workers' societies, whose French leaders were prosecuted in 1870), and considerable political agitation in the cities. Coal strikes in 1869 saw severe measures by prefects and troops: workers were arrested, troops moved coal stocks. Resulting riots were met with bullets: thirteen were killed at La Ricamarie on 16 June, and fourteen at Aubin on 8 October, bloodshed that was never forgotten.[25] However, appeals for exclusively working-class political assertiveness met little response, even in Paris. Most workers, ignoring or indeed shouting down the urgings of some socialist leaders, voted for 'bourgeois' republicans. In provincial towns and rural areas many workers remained, as in 1848, open to the populist charisma of 'the people's Napoleon', and glad to accept the mediation of the authorities: miners at Carmaux still shouted 'Vive l'Empereur!'[26] The war of 1870 showed that the most revolutionary workers and their spokesmen were still enthusiastic exponents of revolutionary nationalism. 'In the presence of the enemy', proclaimed the Blanquists, 'no more parties or divisions.'[27]

The Paris Commune of 1871 (see pp. 426–31) was the last and biggest armed Parisian insurrection, and in the words of one of its participants, 'the third defeat of the French proletariat'. Was it 'proletarian' in composition or in ideology? Did it demonstrate 'class consciousness' among Parisian workers? These questions have long been debated, and the answers are now clear. Most of its participants were certainly workers, unskilled, skilled and white-collar; the rest of the population kept out of the fight or left the city. Leadership of the movement was 'popular', rather than proletarian. At all levels, from Commune Council (to which not a single unskilled worker was elected) to National Guard companies, it reflected a familiar hierarchy. Professionals (journalists, doctors, lawyers, teachers), 'popular bourgeoisie' (small businessmen, shopkeepers), white-collar workers and skilled craftsmen led; unskilled workers followed.

Organization was based on neighbourhood – a typical feature of 'pre-industrial' society – not on occupation or workplace. In one National Guard battalion, for example, most officers were shopkeepers from the main streets of their *arrondissement*; NCOs were shopkeepers from the backstreets;

25. L'Huillier (1957), p. 27.
26. Trempé (1971), vol. 2, p. 916.
27. Rougerie (1971), p. 37.

Table 15.1: Leadership in Commune National Guard (percentage of main participating occupational groups who were officers or NCOs)

White collar	36.8
Printing	31.9
Shopkeepers etc.	23.3
Wood	19.2
Metal	16.9
Building	7.3

After Rougerie (1964), p. 129

Table 15.2: Main occupational groups of those arrested for participation in Commune compared with those arrested in 1851 (percentage of total arrests)

	1871	1851
Building	15.7	6.1
Unskilled	14.9	5.0
Metal	11.9	6.7
White-collar	8.0	6.4
Wood	8.0	8.6
Luxury goods	6.9	6.7

After Rougerie (1964), p. 127

rank and file were manual workers. Nor was a 'new' proletariat prominent: workers in large modern enterprises (engineering, railways) were under-represented, probably because many were excused or could avoid National Guard service. Craft workers, idle because of the civil war, had a variety of motives for taking part: politicization, corporate loyalty, neighbourhood ties and economic distress – an echo of the National Workshops in 1848, as was seen above (Figure 1.1, p. 23). This socio-economic profile confirms that it was not a 'proletarian' movement: it reflected the whole Paris working population, with a substantial participation of white-collar workers and shopkeepers.

Was the Commune 'proletarian' in its ideology? It certainly spoke in the name of *les travailleurs*, but in the broad Proudhonist sense of producers from 'the workshop and the counter'. The principal Communard newspapers spoke of 'the labouring bourgeoisie (*la bourgeoisie travailleuse*) and the heroic proletariat fighting together to defend the Republic against 'royalists'; the revolution was the 'people's wedding' between the 'bourgeoisie and the proletariat'.[28] Deeds matched words. The Commune strove to persuade or force non-workers to participate in its struggle, seen as involving all good citizens. It protected shareholders' interests when permitting certain small

28. *La Révolution Politique et Sociale* (3 Floréal/23 April 1871), *Le Père Duchêne* (30 Ventôse Year 79).

items to be redeemed free of charge from the city pawnshop. It was reluctant to interfere in free collective bargaining between workers and employers. When it permitted workers' cooperatives to take over abandoned factories, the result was scarcely distinguishable from small 'capitalist' enterprises, and they paid compensation to the previous owners. The real enemy was elsewhere: the oppressive State and its overpaid lackeys, soldiers, policemen and priests (commonly nicknamed *les corbeaux* – the crows); the idle rich and the landlords (*les vautours* – vultures). What really demonstrates popular social ideology, notes Rougerie, was the identity of victims of popular violence: dozens of policemen and priests, a few army officers, one judge, a journalist, and a banker accused of fomenting the 1867 Mexican war. In the words of 'L'Internationale', written by a Commune member:

> How many gorge on our flesh!
> But if the crows and vultures
> One morning disappear,
> The sun will always shine.

In short, the Commune represented not a new proletarian consciousness but the demands of popular radical republicanism: 'the Republic and victory over the invader, bread and a roof for all, justice and social solidarity, recognition of their rights and dignity, and, crowning all, liberty'.[29] It marked the end of a characteristically Parisian insurrectionary tradition, 'dusk, not dawn'.[30]

The merciless crushing of the Commune is usually thought to mark a turning point in the class-consciousness of French workers, whose attitude thereafter was one of bitterness and alienation from the 'bourgeois republic'. This is a plausible view, though one frequently asserted rather than demonstrated. As the anti-Communard forces were usually described as royalists, *ruraux* (rustics) and even *chouans* (the peasant rebels of the 1790s) it is far from clear that the conflict was seen as one of 'bourgeois republic' versus 'proletariat'. Certainly, there remained a hard-core of revolutionary Parisian workers, but it is not clear that it was much altered in size or ideology by the Commune. Parisian workers and their leaders, including former Communards, gravitated to a whole range of rival political options: republican, radical, socialist, anarchist, nationalist. The Commune may have ended a tradition; but it began not one but several.

The Right: repressing the 'dangerous classes'

Ouvrier: Toujours honnête quand il ne fait pas d'émeutes
Flaubert, Dictionnaire des Idées reçues

In the face of both political threat and the perceived social and health problems of urbanization – a cholera epidemic in 1832 killed 18,000 in Paris,

29. Serman (1986), p. 571.
30. Rougerie (1964), p. 241.

and crime became an obsession – conservatives developed during the 1840s the idea of the 'dangerous classes' (see p. 13). These were not 'real workers', seen as 'always honest when not rioting' as Flaubert ironically observed, but a depraved and criminal underclass threatening 'society' and property. A quasi-racist feeling of fear and hatred existed. Workers themselves, Cottereau has suggested,[31] were influenced in their own self-image and behaviour by these views. Some stressed their respectability and moderation, some played up to the 'dangerous' imagery of conservative stereotype.

The period 1848 to 1851 intensified this fear, as the grave reality of political conflict, economic depression and mass unemployment was aggravated by the clash of ideologies. While the Left took an optimistic view of revolution as emancipation and fraternity, conservatives, influenced by memories of the Revolution and the Terror, and by the newer stereotype of the 'dangerous classes', interpreted events as a class war. This is why the avoidable tragedy of the June Days revolt inspired such fear and revulsion among even sensible and moderate conservatives:

> the whole of the working class was engaged, either in fact or in spirit, in the struggle . . . The spirit of insurrection circulated from one end to the other of this immense class . . . as the blood does in the body . . . and from the first [the insurrection] left us no alternative but to defeat it or to be destroyed ourselves.[32]

The 1871 conflict was interpreted in very similar terms. Rank-and-file supporters of the Commune were accused of being a criminal underclass that flocked to the urban jungle of Paris for an orgy of drinking and looting. Caricatures, for example by Doré, showed the Communards as hideous and bestial.[33] This was not just propaganda: it was acted on. Sûreté agents checked Communard prisoners for known criminals and 'thought they recognized many ex-convicts and dangerous people'. General de Cissey, one of the principal commanders, believed that the 'hard core of fanatics [was] recruited among the vagabonds and idle workers'; some had 'most ugly faces', which seemed to indicate 'a long habit of evil-doing'. Large numbers of men suspected of belonging to this imaginary hard core were summarily shot, often identified by their supposedly criminal appearance. A British journalist reported 'it was not a good thing on that day to be noticeably taller, dirtier, cleaner, older or uglier than one's neighbours. One individual in particular struck me as probably owing his speedy release from the ills of this world to his having a broken nose.'[34] But killing a largely imaginary enemy gave at best temporary reassurance. Fear of revolution and of criminality persisted, and in the 1890s was above all incarnated by anarchists, who inspired another round of fear and repression.

31. Perrot, in Reynolds (1986), pp. 95–6.
32. Tocqueville (1948), pp. 168, 170.
33. Doré (1979), pp. 93–103.
34. *Daily News*, 8 June 1871, p. 6.

Images of the bourgeoisie

One overthrows the nobility, which is a privilege; one does not overthrow the bourgeoisie, one joins it.

Jules Simon, 1878[35]

I call bourgeois all that thinks basely.

Flaubert

The bourgeoisie is one of the most potent cultural creations of the nineteenth century, and also one of the most ambivalent. Defined in Larousse as the 'intermediary middle class between the working class and the noble class', it was constantly subdivided. From *grande bourgeoisie*, via *bonne bourgeoisie* and *bourgeoisie professionelle* to *petite bourgeoisie* and *bourgeoisie populaire*, it covered a vast diversity of wealth, interests, beliefs and ways of life from millionaire landowner to village blacksmith, from merchant banker to grocer; and to it the nineteenth century gave a variety of contradictory definitions, from the 'aristocrats of money' to the 'vanguard of universal suffrage'.[36]

At the end of the nineteenth century, all these categories (including dependants) totalled about 10 million people, over a quarter of the population. About 1 million belonged to upper or middle bourgeois families: 50,000 families headed by large landowners, 50,000 by professionals, 40,000 by substantial businessmen, 45,000 by civil servants and officers, 20,000 by company executives. Far more numerous (over 2 million) were *petits commerçants*: shopkeepers, innkeepers, rural artisans and small manufacturers, who with their families totalled some 9 million people.[37] Many of these were on the fringes of the bourgeoisie, as were white-collar workers and minor civil servants, their status primarily defined not by income or property but by manner and dress. Clerks employed by the Paris Gas Company, for example, asked for higher pay than manual workers on the grounds that 'the demands of his condition require the clerk to have proper and costly attire. His wife and children spend more' than those of workers.[38] Economic modernization increased the size of these groups: in total, they formed about a third of the population of Paris in 1881, but half by 1900.

Contemporaries and historians have been unsure how to analyse this social conglomeration. A common approach has been to isolate the richest elements as a true bourgeoisie, supposedly culturally and economically dominant, living off its income, as distinct from the *classe(s) moyenne(s)* and the *petite* or *populaire* bourgeoisie, who worked for their living. However, Daumard shows that the truly 'idle', apart from the retired, were a tiny and uninfluential minority, a few thousand.[39] The label 'idle' was polemical rather than

35. Simon (1878), vol. 1, p. 380.
36. Dubois (1962), pp. 231–3.
37. Price (1987), pp. 123–4.
38. Berlanstein (1984), p. 161.
39. Daumard (1987), p. 72.

descriptive, stigmatizing occupations regarded as unproductive: senior civil servants, judges, bankers, big businessmen. The upper bourgeoisie was part of the *notable* class, in which at least until the 1850s, landowners were the wealthiest. In 1840, of 57 men nationwide who paid over 10,000 francs in tax, 45 were landowners, six merchants or bankers, and three industrialists. Landowners possessed the most visible, prestigious and potent form of economic power. At the end of the century, even in economically advanced Pas-de-Calais, 77 per cent of a sample of merchants and industrialists had inherited or bought land.[40]

Strata within the bourgeoisie were not strictly definable in terms of wealth, source of income or occupation, but depended on style, correct manner, and acceptance in different *milieux* (for example belonging to certain *cercles*); on being known and having influence; on dress, servants, housing (the possession of certain rooms and furnishings – 'a piano in the salon' – and a country house). Many of these things could be imitated or bluffed, hence the famous reluctance (far from extinct) of French families to invite casual acquaintances to their homes, where symbols of status can be appraised. Apart from such 'horizontal' divisions, there were 'vertical' divisions of profession, sector and perhaps above all geography: most of the bourgeoisie was local in its sphere of activity. Daumard, after exhaustive analysis, comes down finally to a cultural criterion: 'What made a French bourgeois [was] the will to succeed and the sense of his duties and rights'.[41]

Changes over the century stemmed from the same causes as those affecting other classes: political changes and structural crises in the economy. Land declined as a source of income, especially after 1880; landowners' wealth declined relatively, unless they added more productive investments. By the end of the century, rich landowners in Pas-de-Calais held over 50 per cent, and in Seine-et-Marne over 70 per cent of their capital in liquid form.[42] Small business remained remarkably stable throughout the period, especially outside the cities, where it accounted for about a quarter of the total workforce. Occupations connected with the State grew, especially in communications and teaching. Political office became practically a bourgeois monopoly.

It is hard to think of a single issue on which 'the bourgeoisie' and only 'the bourgeoisie' agreed, or a single interest they all shared. And yet this heterogeneous mass was conceived as a 'class', not only with distinct economic interests, but with common culture and mentality. Indeed, 'bourgeois' was only used as an economic rather than a socio-cultural category at the end of the nineteenth century, presumably under Marxist influence. Society was commonly described as 'bourgeois', yet the bourgeoisie was defined by what it was not: neither aristocracy nor people. It was a highly ambiguous concept, implying respectability, solvency, solid unostentatious worth (as in *cuisine*

40. Price (1987), pp. 98, 100.
41. Daumard (1987), p. 389.
42. Price (1987), p. 101.

bourgeoise, maison bourgeoise); and also materialism, cowardice, corruption, red faces and pot-bellies. The bitterest jibes against the bourgeoisie came from its own members, many of whom made intense efforts to escape from its stereotype. This wistful aspiration was perfectly and rather laughably expressed by the man called 'the most complete representative of the caste', Adolphe Thiers: 'By birth I belong to the people . . . By tastes and habits and associations I am an aristocrat. I have no sympathy with the bourgeoisie.'[43] Ironically, this was a typical bourgeois assertion.

The bourgeoisie was also defined by what was seen as its historic political role as victor and beneficiary of the 1789 Revolution, seen as its initial victory over the nobility, and that of 1830 which finally confirmed its power. Saint-Simon had predicted that future society would be governed by a class of entrepreneurs. The conservative liberal Doctrinaires argued that the *classe moyenne* (their preferred term) was the representative part of the nation, and could legitimately govern on behalf of all. All this placed the idea of class at the centre of political debate, and so the failings and disappointments of the July Monarchy were ascribed to its 'bourgeois' character. However, most of its electorate were inheritors of landed wealth, past middle age and far from the dynamic entrepreneurial class imagined by Saint-Simon. The very term *bourgeois* was frequently taken to mean only *rentiers* living off their property, not *négociants* engaged in business.[44] Opposition to the regime was supported by unenfranchised members of the middle class, including what were called *les capacités* (holders of professional and educational qualifications) who considered themselves at least as fitted to take part in politics as the enfranchised minority.

This disaffection from the 'bourgeois monarchy' of a large section of the *classe moyenne* partly explains the elaboration between 1830 and 1848 of an influential, durable and highly derogatory stereotype of 'the bourgeoisie' by writers, artists and politicians who were themselves 'bourgeois'. Examples abound: Balzac's ignoble schemers; Michelet's unpatriotic and cold-blooded materialists; Henri Monnier's pompous buffoon 'Monsieur Prudhomme' (1830) perorating in carpet slippers; the drawings of a brilliant generation of caricaturists, led by Daumier, Doré and Gavarni. Daumier portrayed villainous lawyers and grotesquely ugly politicians, and the actor Frederick Lemaître's farcical stage portrayal of the bandit Robert Macaire, also published in cartoon form by Daumier in *Le Charivari*, reached a vast public ('What a crew of Robert Macaires!' a worker was heard to exclaim when seeing the funeral procession of a minister in 1847).[45] No less popular was the rambling underworld fantasy of Eugène Sue's *Mystères de Paris*, a heart-rending tale of the honest poor preyed upon by wicked bourgeois. Petty acts of violence against individual bourgeois – stones thrown, mud splashed – were common. By 1848, 'the bourgeois' had a very recognizable image, and it was not flattering.

---

43. Senior (1878), vol. 1, p. 39.
44. Agulhon (1994), pp. 4–13, at p. 6.
45. Chevalier (1973), pp. 416–17.

The events of 1848, however, led to a more assertive bourgeois consciousness in the face of the perceived threat of violent social revolution. The idealistic historical view of the progressive role of the middle classes elaborated by the Doctrinaires – which collapsed with the February 1848 revolution – was replaced, Rosenvallon argues, with a class consciousness based on the defence of property.[46] This class consciousness was very sharp and simple: it saw 'a war of those who have nothing against those who have something'. The 'party of order' united those with something to lose. A series of conservative measures to restrict popular education, to control the press and to reduce the size of the electorate reflect this determination to defend 'society' and property. The 'party of order' superseded the old ideological divisions between legitimists and Orleanists, and supported the election of Louis-Napoleon Bonaparte as the best defence against revolution.

However, the 'bourgeoisie' did not preserve its political unity of 1849–50: the 'party of order' never became a French Tory party. The 'bourgeoisie' was too heterogeneous to constitute a united force. Like the working class, it was fragmented along ideological and religious lines. Though much of the bourgeoisie supported the parties of the Right, the republican party in the 1870s was by far the most bourgeois in its leadership, and it also attracted support from business circles displeased with Napoleon III's economic policies. Its leader Gambetta caused a sensation by proclaiming in 1872 that the new Republic would produce its own new ruling elite from among the 'new social strata'. He like many republicans would not use the term *classe* – classes no longer existed in a republic. His message was that the lower-middle class would take over power. His language and his argument show that the 'bourgeoisie' and 'middle class(es)' or 'strata' were not considered, and did not consider themselves, a single group. Small businessmen were indeed commonly radical republicans, and later many were socialists.

Sniping at the bourgeoisie continued without a pause. Economic expansion from about 1850 to 1880, the growth of consumer culture, the remodelling of whole cities in part to permit conspicuous display of wealth gave ammunition to critics of materialism. The newly invented department stores became a symbol of the new society: big, impersonal, opulent and available to all with money. Zola's novels about the Rougon-Macquart family aimed to paint the turpitudes of a bourgeois dynasty during the Empire, ending with the merited 'débâcle' of 1870–71. Maupassant gave an equally sinister impression of cynical corruption under the Third Republic. Genuine financial scandals, most notoriously the Panama scandal of 1889–93, added to the picture of a crooked 'bourgeois Republic'.

Painters as well as novelists wished to portray modern life. These works are far from being uncomplicated celebrations of 'bourgeois society' and its pleasures. The street scenes of Renoir, Caillebotte, Monet and Pissarro, even if sometimes on a monumental scale, seem distant and detached, more concerned with the fabric of new boulevards, buildings and bridges than with

46. Rosenvallon (1985), esp. ch. 10.

the doings of people. The paintings of Manet, Renoir, Degas and later Toulouse-Lautrec and Seurat, whether of crowds at cafés, dance-halls or the opera, of smaller groups or of individuals, were deliberately unsettling. The hallmarks are anonymity, ambiguity of status, uncertainty of relationships, promiscuity of contacts, and the interplay of money, power and pleasure. Although later generations have sentimentalized many of these images, if we look closely we see a rather menacing and friendless world, close to the imaginations of the Goncourts and Zola, Manet's friends, and sometimes not far from the anti-bourgeois caricatures of Gavarni's 'Masks and Faces' series or Daumier's grotesques. Theirs is a 'bourgeois' society above all in its fluidity: a place of passers-by, of customers and vendors who join it by paying their way, in cash or in kind. The more lyrical paintings are escapist and intimate: fields, lanes, gardens of country houses, women, children and flowers – the feminine sphere of bourgeois society perfectly expressed by Morisot.

Finally, the bourgeoisie was a symbol of disillusion, of depressing reality. It represented the post-revolutionary status quo – moderate, cautious, satisfied – in contrast to the exhilarating ideals and romantic gestures of the utopians of Right and Left. In that sense it was not primarily a social category: for Flaubert, a worker could be 'bourgeois', while he and his like (bourgeois though refusing the label) could see themselves as 'the People, or more precisely, the tradition of Humanity'. Taine could admire 'the fine and opulent bourgeoisie of the 18th century', aristocratic in taste and manner, while despising the 'Prudhomme-style petty bourgeois' of his own day.[47] Not surprisingly, sensitive and elegant members of the bourgeoisie modelled themselves on the nobility. This is doubtless part of the explanation for the post-1870 vogue for duelling. Those who were not quite gentlemen – shop assistants, journalists, politicians – were particularly eager to share in what Nye calls 'the culture of the sword'[48]: some Paris department stores gave their male staff fencing lessons. Bourgeois sons aimed at careers in the State service, not in business. The richest tried to marry their daughters into the nobility.

The nobility, a fairly diverse group superficially defined by possession of a title or the *particule nobiliaire* 'de', had survived the Revolution with much of its wealth and some of its prestige. A high proportion of the largest landowners were nobles (including 39 of the 58 highest taxpayers in the 1840s[49]) and this gave them undeniable social and political power as *grands notables*. The vicissitudes of the revolutionary and imperial periods had arguably increased their sense of cohesion, both social and political. They had their own milieux, which were exclusive to the point of tedium. They cultivated a much admired manner of 'exaggerated affability'[50] and particular styles of speech and pronunciation; they were careful about pedigree; they remained royalist and Catholic. They still inspired fear and envy. The fear of an impossible return to 'feudalism' was potent enough to inspire peasant

47. Agulhon (1994), p. 9.
48. Nye (1993), p. 148.
49. Zeldin (1973), vol. 1, p. 404.
50. Duchesse de Saulx-Tavannes, in Foster (1971), p. 179.

violence and left-wing peasant votes. The envy is shown in the widespread copying of a noble style, clearest in the frequent affectation of pseudo-noble titles and the *particule* (as a general rule, the longer the name, the more doubtful the claim). Since the eighteenth century, nobles had been prominent investors in industry, and their titles, as in other countries, won them company directorships during the nineteenth: railway company boards were 30 per cent noble in 1902.[51] The agricultural depression of the 1880s led to sales of estates and hence the absorption of many nobles into urban and capitalist society. What above all continued to mark them off as a group was snobbery and legitimism. M. Casimir-Perier and the Duc d'Audiffret-Pasquier were brothers-in-law who lived next door to each other in identical houses: that one chose the Republic in 1875 and the other supported a Restoration manifested a historical and ideological, not a socio-economic, boundary. 'Rank', not class.

What does it mean then to say that France was a 'bourgeois society'? If, as has been suggested, 'bourgeois' had become a synonym for society as it was, then it was a tautology. If 'bourgeois' meant the possessors of wealth and power, then it was a truism. If we compare France with Britain, the bourgeoisie was far less clearly the source of an 'ideal' (in Parkin's terms) which oriented political activity: there was no equivalent of the British Anti-Corn Law League, for example, crusading against the landed interest under the banner of free trade. Rather, class issues and class institutions tended to be disrupted by ideological divisions. If all (or nearly all) bourgeois were for the protection of property, the lowest common denominator of bourgeois 'consciousness' (though of course not confined to the bourgeoisie), more significant, and more interesting, is that they did not agree as to how property should or could be protected.

In what way was the French bourgeoisie different from that in other European countries? Socio-economically, in the stability of small businesses, due to the slow transformation of the 'French model' and to 'Malthusian' demography. Politically, in that its elite occupied the highest political and bureaucratic posts after 1830, and its expansion and influence was tied to the expansion of the State. Economic stability and political upheaval, in short, combined to make the bourgeoisie the *classe dirigeante*. Here, perhaps, is the French bourgeoisie's 'ideal': to serve and preserve the State, and hence the social order and their own status.

Peasants

> You don't need to go to America to see savages. Here are the redskins of
> Fenimore Cooper.
>
> *Balzac, 1844*[52]

'The peasant' as a type, whether stigmatized or idealized, was a creation of

51. Zeldin (1973), vol. 1, p. 405.
52. Weber (1977), p. 3.

non-peasants. Historical accounts of peasant revolt – the fourteenth-century *jacquerie*, the sixteenth-century revolt of the *croquants* – were underlined by more recent memories of the *château*-burning *grande peur* of 1789, and the Vendée and Chouan revolts of the 1790s. The savage nature of peasant revolt and the brutishness of peasant life were central themes of (urban) literary and administrative accounts. Peasants were regarded as primitive, as the derogatory connotation of *paysan* and its numerous synonyms (*rustique, plouc, péquenaud, cul-terreux, bouseux*) show. The difference between peasants and town-dwellers was described as if it were racial. Peasants were smaller, darker, dirtier; they dressed differently, and because of their stiff homespun clothes and clogs moved awkwardly and with a characteristic shuffle. They ate different food, frugal, poor and monotonous. Their living conditions were often worse than the worst urban slums. They spoke languages that were dismissed as *patois*, a sign of uncouth backwardness. Even now, the French cinema never uses rural accents, except the re-assuring brogue of the Midi.[53] The novelist Daudet (who wrote amusingly about rural life) warned of the dangers of employing them as servants, '. . . with their rough voices, their incomprehensible speech, their strong smell of the stable': however much they were washed and instructed the 'brute will reappear'.[54] In return, peasants, aware of and perhaps even accepting the derogatory urban description of themselves (so that by the late nineteenth century the word *paysan* was rejected in favour of *cultivateur* and later *agriculteur*), resented, envied and despised townspeople as soft, privileged and, when outside the urban environment, inept and gullible. Events of the nineteenth century kept urban fears alive: chronic unrest in forest regions in the 1820s and 1830s; serious lawlessness following the 1830 revolution, with numerous attacks on excise offices and enclosed woodland; anti-tax riots in 1848. The 1851 insurrection evoked the usual stories of peasant savagery. Much of the educational effort of the century was aimed at 'civilizing' the peasant masses.

In unresolved contradiction was the image of the peasant as pure and unspoilt: the same primitiveness, but this time idealized as the honest and healthy embodiment of the best of French and human values. Expressed in the rhetoric and ceremonies of the Revolution, this vision was eloquently taken up by Michelet, for whom the peasant instinctively loved nature, the land and France. A pictorial example was the very widespread patriotic imagery of 'the soldier-ploughman'. The 1840s novels of George Sand, herself a substantial landowner, portrayed romanticized peasants. After mid-century, paintings such as the officially approved works of Millet, so much more touching and reassuring than the rough *réalisme* of a Courbet, showed laborious peasant men and women ennobled by toil and piety. Sentimentalization of the peasantry became dominant in the twentieth century, just as their real social and economic importance was declining,

53. Coquet (1995), pp. 14–17.
54. Weber (1986), p. 62.

witness the maudlin rhetoric of Marshal Pétain and the cloud-cuckoo-land of the Common Agricultural Policy.

These contrasting visions were not easily reduced to politics. Moderate republicans remained throughout attached to the ideal of a democratic society based on small peasant proprietors, schooled, secularized, washed and Gallicized. Yet the support given to Napoleon III by most peasant voters during the 1850s and 1860s meant that the most virulent anti-peasant diatribes came from the urban Left. Some even wished to restrict their right to vote. Anticlericalism was partly a consequence of the fear of the peasants as a primitive horde manipulated by the clergy. The Right – although frequently disappointed by lack of peasant support for monarchy – made idealization of the peasantry an untouchable element of their vision of the eternal France of which they claimed to be the natural leaders. Some legitimists were early supporters of male suffrage for this very reason.

But the rural population did not fit any urban mould. The reality, as we have seen, was the vast economic, social, cultural and political diversity of the rural *classes laborieuses*. Arguably, the idea of a peasant 'class' is a contradiction in terms, as peasant society was composed of communities, not merely geographically distinct but culturally too. Language, religion, kinship, rivalry and honour were focused on the local community. What altered this to some extent was the impact of the State, and of politics: a 'colonization by the nation-state' to which peasants were obliged to react.[55]

The 'republic in the village' – the introduction of formal politics into rural life that came with the election of local councils in 1831 – inevitably focused on local matters and local men. About 1 million qualified to vote, which meant that a town such as Draguignan, in the Var, had 499 electors of whom 139 were farmers. In small *communes*, half the electors were farmers, including small peasants. Even during the Restoration, most mayors were involved in agriculture, and as farmers rather than mere landowners. Rather than 'national' politics erupting into rural life, it was local concerns, loyalties, hatreds and memories that determined reactions to the remote national scene.[56]

After February 1848, however, the importance to rural life of political events in Paris became clearer than at any time since the fall of Napoleon. Was this great political turmoil as important in creating elements of class solidarity for peasants as it was for 'proletarians' and 'bourgeois'? The imposition by the new Republic of a 45 per cent land-tax surcharge was universally resented as exploitation of the peasants by the towns, and led to widespread and frequently violent unrest, especially when the authorities attempted to seize and sell peasant property to meet tax arrears. Peasant turnout in the April 1848 elections was often round 90 per cent; the men marched to the polls in a body and voted *en bloc*. But far from being a 'class' vote, it created local alliances of peasants and rural *notables* against the urban republicans.

55. Jones (1985), p. 325.
56. Agulhon (1979), pp. 263–4; Moulin (1988), pp. 107–8.

This alliance was shaken when in 1849–51 the *démocrates-socialistes* branched out from their urban bases with a campaign consciously aimed at the peasantry. Although this had some startlingly rapid successes, they were limited to certain regions, as was seen in Chapter 14: it was not a peasant party with a general 'class' appeal. The most successful appeal to the peasantry came from Louis-Napoleon Bonaparte, who managed to create the image of the 'peasants' emperor', who would not only bring prosperity – the 1850s and 1860s were a golden age of peasant agriculture, with high prices and expanding markets – but also protect them against the 'feudalism' of the nobility, the interference of the Church and the turbulence of the *'partageux'* in the cities.

Peasant support for Bonaparte marked a significant step in the political formation of 'the peasantry': 'today they have been born into political life', commented Proudhon.[57] However partial was the view of Bonapartism as emancipation, and however dependent on favourable economic circumstances, it was politically unbeatable. For the first time in the 1860s, spontaneous peasant violence aimed to defend a government against its (and their) enemies. There was a wave of violent attacks on churches suspected of encouraging legitimist plots, and in 1870 a nobleman in the Dordogne was beaten and burnt to death by a crowd of loyal Bonapartist peasants who accused him of being a republican and a Prussian spy, an incident that aroused fears of a *jacquerie*. The fall of the Empire in 1870 did not end peasant Bonapartism, because neither the royalism of the *notables* nor the moderate republicanism of the urban middle class won peasant affections. Yet Bonapartism, however wide its support, can hardly be called a class movement.

A further stage in the politicization of the peasantry, argues Jones, was the 1870s and 1880s, the victory of the Republic. At a general level, the republicans won partly by default, and partly by offering peace and stability. Jones argues for more than that, however: that the republican regime 'shattered the cultural universe' of the peasant, especially in the more remote regions.[58] On one hand, through compulsory schooling and anticlericalism, a direct attack on what was in many regions the keystone of peasant society. On the other, through the offer of material inducements (see p. 106), which, carrying on from the practices of the Empire, taught peasants that their vote was literally worth something. Yet opportunism remained too much associated with the towns and the *notables* to win peasant loyalty, even though it sometimes extorted or bought their votes. Besides, politicization of the peasants did not create or express 'class consciousness'. Their political loyalties still covered the whole spectrum from legitimist to Marxist. A mosaic of regional political 'mentalities' re-emerged after 1870, above all among the 'peasantry': if most 'bourgeois' were on the Right, and most 'proletarians' on the Left, peasants differed by religion, region and community.

57. Tudesq (1965), p. 229.
58. Jones (1985), p. 296.

CRISIS AND CONFLICT, c.1880–1910: THE MAKING OF 'PROLETARIAT' AND 'PEASANTRY'?

The long economic depression of the last quarter of the century was, says Noiriel, the 'decisive period' in French working-class history.[59] Indeed, it was a crucial period in the formation of all class identities. Intense international competition in manufactures and primary products, falling prices, quicker and cheaper international and domestic transport of goods, new technology and competitive new methods of retailing demolished the big urban and rural craft industries, ruined small, technically unsophisticated producers of textiles and metals, impoverished landowners and bankrupted thousands of shopkeepers, who formed organizations to demand aid and protection from the State. The viability of household economies was destroyed as several of their diverse sources of income simultaneously dried up. The overall unemployment rate probably reached 10 per cent. Thus, the labour shortage in industry, which had been one of the most persistent features of the French economy and which had long strengthened workers' ability to resist unwanted changes, was now catastrophically reversed.

The making of the proletariat?

For the first time employers could recruit a relatively stable workforce increasingly dependent on industrial wages. Coalmining became a permanent occupation; the children of miners began to be recruited into the pits. Industrial workers ceased to be part-time farmers. Big employers extended the 'paternalist' systems that had previously had only limited success in disciplining their workers. Company housing and schools brought workers closer to the plant: of the 10,000 workers at Le Creusot in 1884, 6,000 lived within ten minutes' walk. Pensions and medical care were provided to attach workers to their employers. All provided potent means of pressure: children of strikers could be thrown out of school, families evicted, pensions lost. Most firms were too small to afford this kind of inducement. Their patriarchal attitude was no less marked, but was upheld more crudely. Strikers' delegates (and their families) were insulted, intimidated, sacked and even threatened with weapons. Bosses fought tooth and nail to resist unionization, and were reluctant to negotiate disputes face to face. Suspected troublemakers, especially if members of a union or involved in politics, were blacklisted.

This seems to demonstrate the chronic difficulty in France of finding a system of labour relations other than paternalism or authoritarianism. Face-to-face paternalism (which in the past had often worked) was breaking down. Owners of companies frequently no longer lived 'above the shop', and management was increasingly in the hands of salaried executives and foremen, who were often resented by workers: the notorious killing in 1886

59. Noiriel (1986), p. 83.

of the mining engineer Watrin (thrown out of a window by a violent crowd) was an example of this. 'The boss' was increasingly seen as a remote and parasitical monster, caricatured as a fat, greedy and idle man with cigar and top hat: this new level of hatred of the boss as oppressor and parasite was, says Perrot, a significant stage in the making of 'proletarian' identity.[60] The reality was less one-dimensional. Bosses were divided among themselves. To join an employers' organization was regarded as a humiliating sign of weakness, and the frequent rivalry between firms made lock-outs and blacklisting relatively ineffective. Employers even subsidized strikes against competitors paying lower wages. By the early twentieth century, a range of employers' organizations had come into existence, but most did little more than organize an annual dinner.

The impact of the depression was equally severe on urban craft workers. Mechanization destroyed some traditional skills, and although many were preserved within modern industrial processes, the old corporate identity and solidarity of the *métier* faded. Change was not all negative: living standards rose with modernization. Nevertheless, there was a 'profound identity crisis' among skilled urban workers, says Noiriel. Symptoms included the collapse of the apprenticeship system and a sharp decline in the number of boys following their fathers' trades. In 1869, for example, 78 per cent of cabinetmakers were the sons of cabinetmakers; by 1903 only 48 per cent. There was an alarming growth in drinking (especially of absinthe) and violent crime, a consequence of more money combined with social breakdown.[61]

The overall effect of these changes was to begin the creation of a more permanent, more homogenous industrial labour force. Few workers, in spite of increased schooling and republican meritocratic rhetoric, could expect social mobility for themselves or their children. In the 1890s, probably less than 2 per cent of *lycée* pupils were workers' sons. Of those in the Nord department who attended the more accessible senior primary schools (*écoles primaires supérieures*) about 60 per cent still went into manual jobs.[62]

This more stable workforce was also a more combative one: the 1890s–1900s saw one of the highest levels of strike activity in French history, violent conflict with the State and the creation of much larger socialist and trade union organizations. Was this a sign that a proletarian identity had been created? To attempt to answer this question, we shall look at three areas: first, that of ideas, symbols and culture; second, that of political organization and action; and third, that of labour organizations and their strategies.

The major new influence on ideas of class was Marxism, significant in France only from the 1880s. Marxism (preached by Guesde's Parti Ouvrier Français) fitted neatly into the experience of these years with a new variety of revolutionary utopianism. Its analysis of conflict, capitalist crisis and proletarian impoverishment must have struck chords among workers

60. Perrot, in Dufrancatel *et al.* (1979).
61. Noiriel (1986), p. 95; Berlanstein (1984), p. 75.
62. Robert Gildea (1983), pp. 291, 298.

experiencing the wrenching upheaval of the depression. Its vision of a future of Statist collectivization of large industry plausibly fitted the perspectives of the new 'proletarianized' working class, more than the decreasingly relevant Proudhonist aspiration towards independent skilled-workers' cooperatives. Its conception of the 'proletariat', the suffering, alienated vanguard of the future, does seem to have affected the image of the worker. And yet its appeal was limited and uneven. Its authoritarian methods and ideology were resisted by anarchists, who though never numerous were influential in the 1880s and 1890s, and by reformist 'republican socialists'. Where older traditions of French socialism were established, for example Paris, the Marxists made little headway. Moreover, a significant part of Guesde's support came in practice from peasants and the lower middle class.

Symbols of the separate identity of the proletariat, often called 'the Fourth Estate', were visible and recognized. The banned red flag and the song '*L'Internationale*' marked off the workers' cause from that of the 'bourgeois republic' symbolized by the tricolour and '*Marseillaise*'. Annual rallies from 1880 onwards at the Mur des Fédérés (the shrine to slaughtered Communards at the Père Lachaise cemetery in Paris) were a reminder of how 'the bourgeoisie' treated 'the proletariat', though the brawls between rival socialist groups that became part of the tradition were also a reminder of how proletarians treated each other. The 1 May demonstrations, originated by the Guesdists in 1890, formed a focus for ritual confrontation between frightened 'bourgeoisie' and vengeful 'proletariat'. This day also helped to crystallize the anarcho-syndicalist vision of *le grand soir*, the revolutionary general strike that would sweep away bourgeois society. This was different from the '*sans culotte*' tradition of the barricades, which involved all 'the people'. A proletarian iconography emerged, for example naturalistic drawings in the satirical *Assiette au Beurre* of grim-faced strikers and their families in cloth caps, shawls and clogs. A more symbolic style of bare-chested and brawny workers constituted an increasingly masculine imagery which, as Perrot points out, accompanied an increasingly masculine organization and ideology from which women workers were displaced.

Identity was also defined by sociability, but here the class dimension is less clear-cut. New forms of commercial entertainment and new sports (football, cycling, boxing) developed. Although originally upper class, sport soon proved particularly attractive to city workers. Football took root in the textile towns of the north thanks to their links with the mill towns of northern England. Although still in 1904 society ladies went to watch cycle races at Paris's Vélodrome d'Hiver, in which a son of the Comte de Vogüé was riding, one of them found it 'brutal, smelly and barbarous', and most competitors and all the champions were apprentices, delivery boys and shop assistants. Professional sport became a major part of male working-class culture, and for some a route to fame and fortune: a chimney sweep won the first Tour de France and its 6,125 franc prize.[63] Professional fixtures and separate workers'

63. Weber (1986), p. 200.

sports clubs (some of them sponsored by socialist parties and subsidized by left-wing local authorities) were becoming by 1914 a vibrant part of a new urban, masculine, 'proletarian' sociability. So on one hand sport was contributing to a working-class culture; but on the other, the message of sport was non-class, non-ideological, integrative and patriotic.

Political organization and action is our second vector of class identity. The republican victory over the Right in 1879 permitted the open and legal organization of unambiguously socialist parties: not coincidentally, it was in 1879 that a workers' congress at Marseilles openly adopted a hybrid Marxist and Proudhonist programme. Moreover, the defeat of royalism made a united republican front less necessary and brought social divisions among republicans to the fore. In the 1890s, as will be seen in Chapter 26, it seemed that politics were being recast along class lines. The Marxist POF became the largest of the socialist parties, strongest in the principal industrial region of the north.

However, the ostensibly class parties remained in fact socially heterogeneous, weak and spectacularly fragmented. The socialist movement was divided from 1881 until 1905 into several antagonistic parties. Besides anarchists (who rejected politics as fraudulent) there were Guesdists, 'possibilists' (reformists stressing local government action), Allemanists (proletarian and anti-authoritarian) and Blanquists (still waiting for insurrection). Each appealed to different regions, to different ideological traditions and to some extent to different occupational groups. Furthermore, some of the most popular socialist writers and politicians, such as the ex-Communard Benoît Malon, the first socialist deputy Clovis Hugues, and the prominent deputies Alexandre Millerand and Jean Jaurès, remained outside the parties as independents. There was enduring division over theory: was revolution the only road to socialism, or could gradual reform produce the same result? No less important were disputes over control: Guesde and his followers wanted a centralized socialist movement controlled by themselves, a claim rejected by all the others. These differences had important practical consequences: political (could local socialist parties make electoral pacts with radicals and so win more seats?); material (who would run local party organizations, and the jobs in local government that some of them controlled?); and personal (the various leaders had their political fiefs that they were unwilling to surrender).

These issues caused recurring recrimination. The Blanquists split in 1889 over whether to support Boulangism in the hope of bringing down the 'bourgeois' Republic. The Dreyfus affair again brought out disagreement about whether 'class' was the overriding political issue. Guesde at first dismissed the affair as a bourgeois quarrel. Even after the socialists had joined the Dreyfusard cause to defend the republic, many were angry when Millerand, a leading parliamentary socialist, became a minister in 1899 in the same government as a general who had been prominent in slaughtering Communards in 1871. Indeed, in 1904 Millerand was expelled from the party, which officially condemned participation in 'bourgeois' governments. Only in

1905, at the prompting of the International, did socialists form a single party, the Section Française de l'Internationale Ouvrière (SFIO).

Socialist parties and the socialist electorate remained very small until the 1890s, and only attracted a fraction of the 3 million workers' votes. In the 1890s, all the socialist parties combined had only 30,000 members, about half of them Guesdists. However, in the 1900s socialists steeply increased their votes and seats; and by 1914 the SFIO was the second-largest party in parliament, with 1.4 million votes and 103 seats. The timing of this take-off might appear to fit the chronology of 'proletarianization' surveyed earlier. Was it indeed a sign of a class-conscious and politically assertive proletariat? In one sense yes: radical governments in power after 1905 clashed with strikers, and many dissatisfied radical voters switched to the socialists. In other senses no. Most workers did not vote socialist: even in working-class districts of Paris and its suburbs in the 1890s–1900s it was rare for even half of the workers to vote socialist.[64] Conversely, a significant part of socialist support, and nearly all its leadership, came from outside the 'proletariat': of eighteen Marxist deputies elected 1893–99, only one was a worker. White-collar workers, public-sector employees (teachers, postmen), small businessmen (especially shopkeepers and publicans) and especially peasants featured among party members and voters in the 'Red' regions such as the Midi, where only 13–15 per cent of activists were workers.[65] Here socialism had become the party of radical republicanism, taking over the issues of anticlericalism and defence of small property, rather than remaining the party of 'the proletariat'. Moreover, the increased popularity of socialist parties seems to have been conditional on their following a moderate and reformist strategy, and playing down their revolutionary and proletarian rhetoric. The socialist rank-and-file, even in the Guesdist heartland of Lille-Roubaix, supported Millerand in 1899 in the hope that he as minister would carry out reforms, and he was invited to speak at the Guesdist strongholds of Lille and Limoges in defiance of the party leadership. It was the relative failure of Millerand in office, followed by major clashes between strikers and a radical government under Clemenceau, that set the socialists on a collision course with 'bourgeois' governments. Clearly, this was a consequence of political circumstances rather than intransigent 'proletarian consciousness', and is in that sense comparable with the reaction of the ideologically infinitely more moderate British labour movement to the legal penalties imposed on them by the Taff Vale and Osborne judgments of 1901 and 1909. Politics created class consciousness at least as much as the other way round.

The clearest expression of class identity is in the third area to be examined, that of workers' organizations. Their development was profoundly influenced by the attitude of the State. Workers' combinations were illegal and activity was either clandestine, often under the guise of workers' friendly societies, or, rarely, depended on the tolerance of employers and local authorities, as in

64. Berlanstein (1984), pp. 164–5; see also Brunet (1980), p. 84.
65. Willard (1965), pp. 365, 289.

the case of the Marseilles dockers. Strike activity frequently led to prosecutions and not infrequently to violence. Only in 1864 did Napoleon III order legal toleration of strike activity, and only in 1884 did the Republic formally legalize trade unions (*syndicats*), though under the surveillance of the authorities and without legal capacity to own property or funds. This history partly explains the fragile organization of the *syndicats* in later years.

Syndicats were local groups of workers in the same trade, and on average in the late nineteenth century had only 100–200 members. During the 1880s some began to federate regionally and then nationally, forming in 1895 the Confédération Générale du Travail (CGT), which had anarchist leaders. Simultaneously, *bourses du travail* were being established, in which Blanquist leaders were prominent, beginning in Paris in 1887. These labour exchanges, subsidized and given premises by left-wing local authorities, became headquarters for the labour activity of their districts, to which local *syndicats* affiliated. By 1900 there were about 50. There was rivalry between the two parallel labour movements, and only in 1902 did they join in a united CGT. Worse, however, was their tussling with the socialist parties, particularly the Guesdists, who tried from the late 1880s to take over the labour movement mainly as a propaganda vehicle. This tug-of-war had, of course, an ideological justification. The Guesdists believed that only political action could lead to revolution. The *syndicats*, especially under the influence of anarchist leaders Pouget (for the CGT), Pelloutier and Yvetot (for the *bourses*), declared that a general strike would bring down bourgeois society.

Conflicts with employers were often bitter and violent after 1880, with the use of firearms on both sides. Perrot points out an important explanatory factor linking this turn-of-the-century militancy with the demise of the old industrial system during the 1880s depression: it was former handweavers, now forced unwillingly into the mills of the industrial north, that made Roubaix the strike capital of France; and it was small beleaguered workshops of the Paris craft industries that became nests of anarcho-syndicalist militancy.[66] Rural wage-labourers, especially woodcutters and vine-dressers, also became very militant. The cause of conflict was not just wages, but organization: rules, wage structures, discipline. Employers attempted to increase productivity and specialization; workers rejected 'paternalism', the bossiness of foremen and managers, and work rationalization. They often attempted, when conditions permitted, to return to the job mobility of pre-depression practices, that unanswerable form of worker resistance. At the turn of the century at Decazeville, 65 per cent of workers left after less than a year; at the Cail engineering works, 75 per cent;[67] mining especially saw mass desertion by workers, despite 'paternalist' strategies long followed by big employers.

French workers clung to revolutionary rhetoric. Even moderates processed to the Mur des Fédérés; Allemane called for the demolition of Notre Dame to

66. Perrot, in Reynolds (1986).
67. Noiriel (1986), p. 109.

make way for a Palace of Labour; and syndicalists annoyed their British counterparts by criticizing them for not supporting Irish terrorism. Their view of labour relations stressed class conflict and rejection of bosses' authority. But they did not form strong organizations like British, German or American workers. By 1901–2, of some 11.4 million wage-earners, of whom 3.8 million were male industrial and transport workers, only 614,000 were *syndiqués*, and of these only 100,000 were in the CGT.[68] Still in the 1990s France has the least unionized workforce of any western country. This is an enduring puzzle to historians and social scientists, especially those attempting to formulate a general model of working-class movements. Various solutions have been suggested. Was revolutionary rhetoric a substitute for action, the fantasy of the *grand soir* a consolation for weakness? Was extremism a cause without rebels, confined to a minority of militant leaders and not shared by a rank-and-file interested by concrete reforms? There is some substance to these views. Strong trade unions (miners, printers) were the most reformist, as in Britain or America, and in fact made up the majority of CGT members. Most workers did ignore the urgings of anarcho-syndicalist leaders, who were only in office because of an unrepresentative election system. Most workers voted for moderate socialists, radicals, or even parties of the Right. The Leftist ideology of anarcho-syndicalists did put off many workers, who did not affiliate to the CGT, especially in conservative and Catholic regions such as Britanny and among immigrants in Paris suburbs; some were attracted to Catholic or nationalist trade unions.

But it would be misleading to see the French experience as merely a collective error, a failure to measure up to a German, British or American norm of big, rich, regimented unions. Cottereau points out that French workers habitually used a variety of tactics: informal 'invisible' resistance (as mentioned earlier, passive resistance and job mobility) and also political action within the community, demonstrations, petitions, even riots. This needed not permanent organizations, but broad temporary alliances to bring in the largest possible number of people in support: workers in several firms, their families, local shopkeepers, left-wing politicians. *Bourses du travail* were well suited for this sort of action, and so union-led strikes involved over three times the number of participants as non-union actions. Friedman brings out the key political difference between the United States and France: that French workers needed to, and could, involve the State in industrial disputes.[69] Between 1895 and 1914 the State intervened in 20 per cent of disputes, and when it did workers gained at least some of their demands in 70 per cent of cases. Nearly half of State interventions were at workers' request, and only 3 per cent at the request of employers, who were six times as likely as workers to refuse State mediation. The role of *syndicats* was, therefore, to maximize the number of people involved, which they did successfully, to make blacklegging difficult and to make favourable State

68. Ridley (1970), p. 77.
69. Friedman (March 1988), pp. 1–26.

intervention more likely. Revolutionary rhetoric and even violence served both these ends: prefects wished above all to maintain or restore order, and they were willing to put pressure on employees to make concessions, using the carrot of tax rebates or railway subsidies, for example, or the stick of threatening to remove troops and leave factories and blacklegs at the mercy of violent strikers. Friedman points out that in the United States local authorities and courts were more willing to use or permit sometimes savage repressive measures. Hence American strikers had to face long and bitter disputes, which required strong unions and large strike funds; French strikers usually needed neither. In short, revolutionary rhetoric about *le grand soir* was not merely a daydreaming compensation for weakness, it could be made to serve the practical aim of winning concessions. The syndicalist leaders' conception of revolution as a mobilizing 'myth' is thus more understandable, as is the willingness of workers to go along with it.

Also more understandable is the persistent ambivalence of an ostensibly revolutionary and class-conscious 'proletariat' towards the 'bourgeois' republic which often favoured their demands. Workers often had wider social and ideological links that diluted or even negated any exclusive sense of class. Membership of freemasonry and of freethinkers' societies remained popular, and linked workers with the radicals, for whom many voted. Although socialists and syndicalists criticized the 'bourgeois republic', when it was threatened – by Boulangism, by the Dreyfus affair, and by war in 1914 – most socialists and workers rallied to its defence. Each of these events posed again the fundamental question: for or against the Republic. The patriotic response in 1914 was not only an emotional reflex; it was a decision effectively made in advance. This is not to say that the French working class had wholeheartedly rejoined (if it ever really left) the bosom of the Republic and the nation. But what these examples do demonstrate is that the exponents of class politics were divided ideologically, and that the French 'proletariat' was diverse and liable to fragment under the strain of divided loyalties, contradictory political traditions, and overlapping identities: corporate, local, national, ethnic, sexual, religious.

As in Britain, some essential aspects of class only emerged during and after the First World War, namely, accelerated industrial concentration, the emergence of the factory as the basis of organization, the founding of an unambiguously class party (the Communist Party, 1920), and the mushrooming of new tracts of factories and cheap housing, especially Paris's *banlieue rouge* circling the city from Saint-Denis to Billancourt.

The making of a peasant 'class'?

The Republic will be a peasants' republic or it will cease to be.

Jules Ferry, 1884

The 'great depression' was earlier, deeper and longer in agriculture than in the rest of the economy, and had permanent social and economic effects. It was comprehensively devastating for the traditional rural economy that relied, as has been seen, on earnings from a variety of activities. Starting in the late 1860s, disease hit silkworm production (a major source of women's employment in the south), and was followed by competition from Asia; the whole industry had been wiped out by 1914. In the same region, cultivation of the profitable vegetable dye *garance* (madder) disappeared within five years in the 1870s when a chemical substitute was invented. Worst of all, the vine-killing insect phylloxera appeared in 1863, and from 1870 onwards began inexorably to destroy region by region the whole wine industry, which extended to 72 departments and provided France's largest agricultural export. Agricultural goods from the Americas, Russia, and British and French colonies now began to arrive in bulk by steamship. Imported wheat, equal to less than 1 per cent of national production in the 1850s, rose to 10 per cent in the 1870s and 19 per cent by 1890, just at a time when the stagnant population was eating less bread. For over two decades there was a general and catastrophic fall in agricultural prices and farm incomes: in Loir-et-Cher, for example, they fell by 20–30 per cent.

The area of cultivated land shrank as corn gave way to pasture or timber. Labour-saving technology was introduced, even if only, for small farms, a plough to replace hoes and scythes to replace sickles. The full-time male labour force actually increased; but there was less work for part-timers, women and children. At the same time, industrial depression reduced the part-time handicraft, factory and mining work that had helped maintain rural families. A 'rural exodus' of about 130,000 a year began: daughters and sons left home; temporary migrants became permanent. Falling rents (down 30–50 per cent between 1875 and 1900) caused 'bourgeois' landowners in several regions to sell out to their tenants or labourers. A third of all arable land changed hands during the 1880s, and so the number of farms reached a record level of 3.5 million in 1880. Thus rural society became more than ever typified by full-time landowning farmers, though still marked by great inequality of ownership and income. In 1892, over 70 per cent of landholdings were under 5 hectares, but they only accounted for 2.7 per cent of the area; only 15 per cent were over 11 hectares, but they accounted for 75 per cent of the area.[70]

The 'great depression' thus created a more specialized agricultural labour force just as it had made a more specialized industrial labour force. And as it had with workers and the middle classes, it made peasants more militant and more organized. Nevertheless, there were deep conflicts of interest, not only between rich and poor, landowner and tenant, and net seller and buyer of food, including those who had too little land to support their needs, but also between those who produced for export or the home market (and disagreed over tariff policy), and those who grew competing crops such as sugar-beet and grapes (putting sugar in wine provided a lucrative market for northern beet growers but lowered prices for southern grape growers). However, the

70. Cleary (1989), p. 8.

weight of opinion among farmers was such that the moderate republican governments of the 1880s and 1890s realized that they had no choice but to introduce tariffs.

The voting strength of peasants and the overwhelming ideological commitment of politicians to the defence of agriculture and small property (which even the hitherto largely urban-based Marxists joined in 1892) provided a powerful political base. The largest cross-party pressure groups in parliament included the Groupe Agricole, Groupe Oléicole (sic), Groupe Républicaine de Défense Paysanne, Groupe Sucrier, etc. The large Groupe Viticole in parliament counted conservatives and republicans among its organizers. There were, however, limits to the power of even the wine lobby. The problems of the southern wine industry – Europe's first wine lake – led to demands for State help backed by a mass civil disobedience campaign in 1907 (see p. 471), but extracted only limited action to prevent sugaring and other adulteration.

Trade union legalization in 1884 permitted the spread of agricultural *syndicats* including large and small farmers, though predominantly controlled by the former. They quickly built up a range of functions, including insurance, credit, cooperative buying and selling – in short, 'fertilizers, finance and moral exhortation'.[71] By 1914 they had over 1 million members, ten times the CGT. Recruitment was spurred on by ideological rivalry. Two federations, the conservative (Catholic crypto-royalist) Société des Agriculteurs de France and the republican Société Nationale de l'Encouragement de l'Agriculture, struggled for influence. They nevertheless agreed in promoting basically the same agrarian policy: a good example of how in France 'class' interests did not supersede ideological division, but also that ideological division did not prevent cooperation on class issues. Vitally important for the structure of peasant agriculture in the long run was the spread of cooperatives for buying, processing and selling, which the *syndicats* developed. This development (similar to other small-farming countries such as Denmark, Ireland and Russia) determined the survival and future of peasant agriculture, as well as constituting a new set of institutions within rural society and giving expression to peasant identity. Was this 'class consciousness'? Community still remained the focus, and new organizations often incorporated older communal structures. Moreover, the peasantry still remained complex and hierarchical. What it did have, however, was a solidarity, however grudging, between its different strata, parties, interests and localities in the face of common dangers and what was perceived as a hostile or indifferent urban world. This meant that 'the agricultural interest' was more comprehensively organized and more powerful than any other sectional group, and certainly more than industrial workers or bosses. This was to have permanent effects on the peasantry, the State and indeed the French (and eventually European) economic system.

71. Ibid., p. 40.

CONCLUSION: CLASS, STATE AND REVOLUTION

Many of the processes described above – in shorthand terms economic and social modernization and the creation of cultural stereotypes of class – were happening in every western country. One could easily find very similar language concerning 'bourgeoisie', 'proletariat' and 'peasantry' all over the Continent, and analogous concepts in Britain or America. What seems to be specifically French is the importance of the role of the State and of the ideological inheritance of the Revolution in the development of class identities.

As was seen in Chapters 3 and 5, the post-revolutionary State assumed the role of regulator of society. It intervened to conciliate, police and repress, not as the instrument of a class but 'following goals and banishing spectres of its own choosing'.[72] At a time when the other major democratic or liberal states, America and Britain, tended to withdraw from the operations of civil society, France held back the development of autonomous institutions by which civil society might have regulated itself. Social conflicts were therefore inevitably politicized because of the involvement of the State. The theorizing, organization and action of various groups was above all focused not on influencing each other but on influencing the State. Any sign of political change or government weakness could set off waves of combined political and strike action by workers who felt that at last they stood a chance of making their demands heard: for example 1830–34, 1840, 1869–70, 1885, 1900 and 1906–7.

This placed State authorities in a difficult position. As workers had no legal organizations for most of the century and mostly weak ones thereafter, they often resorted to violence, usually to protest against the arrest of leaders or to prevent strike-breaking. This was the way organizational weakness led to extremism. In an attempt to defuse violence, prefects quite often tried to persuade employers to make concessions. Employers responded by demanding deployment of police and troops against strikers, particularly to protect blackleg labour. This was a recurring pattern, from Lyons in the 1830s (the prefect was sacked for not being tough enough), during the Second Empire, when the government often encouraged prefectoral mediation, and even in the Third Republic, when prefects often had genuine sympathy with workers' complaints. However, it was a dangerous game: well-meaning official exhortation was a weak instrument, and the hope of bringing in the State on their side encouraged brinkmanship among employers and workers who did not negotiate face to face. When conflicts got out of hand, the consequences could be bloody: the insurrections in Lyons crushed by the July Monarchy have been mentioned; as we have seen, during the Second Empire troops fired on strikers at La Ricamarie and Aubin in 1869; and during the

72. Shorter and Tilly (1974), p. 39.

Third Republic there were shootings at Fourmies in 1891 and Draveil and Villeneuve-Saint-Georges in 1908. This explains the relatively bloody record of French labour disputes, much worse than Britain, though far less bad than Russia or the United States. When the State, in the name of public order, freedom of work, and the rights of property, sided with employers, workers were forced into perpetual and dangerous opposition, beginning with their turn towards republicanism in the 1830s.

Bringing social disputes into the political arena was an important part of making them into 'class', rather than merely local or sectional issues. This brings us to the question of ideology. Here comparison with Britain is instructive. In Britain, Perkin has argued, class 'war' was recognized to be a metaphor, because real class war was a disaster that all sides wished to avoid. Hence class conflict, seen as 'at bottom a struggle for income', was fairly easily institutionalized into mutually recognized political parties, pressure groups and trade unions which channelled conflicts 'out of the paths of violence into those of negotiation and compromise'.[73] The State took up a neutral attitude in order to depoliticize social conflict and demonstrate that it was not the protector of a single social group or interest: it was this that defused Chartism in the 1840s. The contrasts with France are stark. Some opponents of successive French regimes looked to class conflict as far more than just a struggle for income, but rather as fuel to re-ignite revolution. Those who feared renewed revolution tried to repress class institutions (most obviously trade unions) as too dangerous. Moreover, they often denied the very existence of class on the grounds that since the Revolution all were equal before the law: 'there is no more class here . . . there are only French citizens', said the republican Garnier-Pagès in 1847.[74]

Paradoxically, the centrality of the theme of revolution – still very vivid to the end of our period, when it formed an important aspect of 'proletarian' identity – had the effect of transcending class issues by focusing on politics. Would-be revolutionaries tried to maximize their political support by going beyond a 'class' constituency. This was clear in the case of the Paris Commune, and also for the Guesdists in the 1890s who, dogmatically certain that revolution must come, prepared for it by recruiting peasants, intellectuals and shopkeepers. Given the social composition of France this was inevitable as long as revolution was imagined as a political process: the exception here were anarcho-syndicalists, who relied on non-political action, the general strike. A clear indication of how 'class' was affected by politics was the tendency to overlook women, members of 'classes' but outside the polity. Women were pushed to the margins of socialist parties; they tended to be excluded from *syndicat*; the vast number of women shopkeepers were left out of middle-class organizations. The main political embodiment of the revolutionary tradition, republicanism, was all along explicit in its transcendence of class. It interpreted revolution in terms of 'people' and

73. Perkin (1969), p. 346.
74. Daumard (1987), p. 30.

'nation', not class; it made the struggle against the Church a central theme of politics; it propagated an attractive teleology of 'progress' through education and democracy. 'Proletarian' spokesmen frequently denounced this as a sham, but nevertheless were affected by it; ostensibly class parties were constantly pulled into the republican camp. At the very least, most working people regarded even the 'bourgeois republic' as better than its enemies and a step towards greater justice and equality.

CHAPTER 16

IMAGINED COMMUNITIES: THE NATION

France has made France, and the determinist element of race seems to me secondary. She is the daughter of her liberty.

Michelet, 1869[1]

If 'Italy', in Metternich's phrase, was merely a geographical term, then 'France' was a political one. In culture, family structure, belief and economic activity it was unusually diverse. The nineteenth century saw a prolonged effort by the State to create in reality the organic national unity which the Revolution had proclaimed in theory. It was aided in this by the various cultural and social processes – such as urbanization, widening literacy, economic integration, and the diffusion of the multiple symbols of nationality – that Gellner, Anderson and others have proposed as the creators of the 'imagined community' of the nation.[2] But the diversity of France persisted. The questions asked in this chapter, therefore, are when and to what extent did an idea of Frenchness become a significant aspect of the identity of the peoples of France? And what was Frenchness thought to involve?

PEASANTS INTO FRENCHMEN

The most basic divide was a line conventionally drawn between Geneva and Saint-Malo, and which marked off the north-eastern third of the country, which was economically more developed than the rest. This division accorded with many important criteria: wealth, literacy, physical size, agricultural productivity, manufacturing, premarital conception, steam-engines, suicide – in short, everything connected with 'modernity'. However, this division did not coincide with language, belief, politics (compare with figures in Chapter 14) or most of the criteria associated with culture. Here the picture is a mosaic, and it has been vividly recreated for the

1. Michelet (1869), p. viii.
2. Gellner (1983); Anderson (1991).

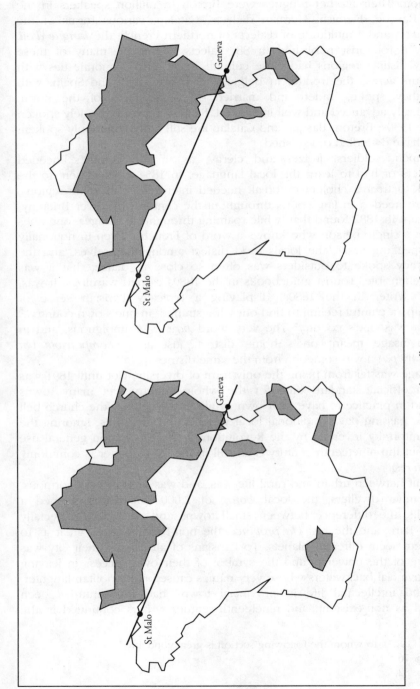

Figure 16.1: Physical size; over 40% of conscripts registered as tall,
(over 1.733m), 1819–26
After Aron (1972), p. 90

Figure 16.2: Literacy; over 70% of spouses signing marriage
contracts, (1854–55)
After Bouju (1966), p. 173

nineteenth century by Weber.[3] To take only language: official reports show that in the 1870s standard French was a foreign language for about half the population. Their mother tongues were Breton (a million speakers in the 1880s), Basque, Flemish, German dialects, Catalan, various forms of the *langue d'oc*, and a multitude of dialects of northern French, the *langue d'oïl*. In 1879, a folklorist published in 88 dialects. Moreover, many of these culturally distinct regions had close cultural, social and economic ties with neighbours across the frontier in Belgium, Germany, Italy and Spain, with whom they spoke, traded and married. In some parts of the north, economically advanced and well integrated, Flemish remained widely spoken until the 1930s; Breton, Basque and Catalan are still fairly commonly spoken; the rest have dwindled or vanished.

Policemen, soldiers, judges and clergy, as in the colonies, needed interpreters or had to learn the local language. In 1854, doctors sent to the Pyrenees to treat a cholera outbreak needed interpreters; in some regions, they were needed in law courts throughout the century. In lower Britanny, Maupassant in 1882 found that 'while roaming through the villages, one does not meet a single person who knows a word of French'.[4] Even in notionally French-speaking areas, the locals used dialect among themselves, and the French they spoke to outsiders was often so close to dialect that it was incomprehensible. Tourist guidebooks in the 1880s carried warnings. It was, noted a writer in the 1880s, displaying a typically Parisian sense of ownership, 'a painful feeling to find oneself a stranger in one's own country'.[5] But what was one's country? The very word *pays* was ambiguous, and in common usage meant one's home district, just as a *compatriote* (or colloquially *pays*) was someone from the same district.

Language was far from being the only form of diversity. Not until 1891 was there an official standard time for the whole country; yet many towns continued in practice to have their own, while in the country the church bell tolled the passing day. Traditional local weights and measures, ignoring the metric uniformity invented by the Revolution, were in common general use throughout the nineteenth century (and still in the 1990s butter is commonly sold in *livres*).

The gulf between urban and rural life was, and was seen to be, enormous. If, to hamlet dwellers, the local *bourg* of 2,000 inhabitants seemed a metropolis, the difference between small towns and cities, and especially between Paris and the rest (*la province*, the non-Paris) was so great as to make them seem different planets. To Parisians of all classes, their city was the centre of the universe, and the symbol of their own success in leaving those provincial backwaters whose very names caused metropolitan laughter. Social and intellectual life in provincial towns had for centuries been described as non-existent, and nineteenth-century writers continued in the

3. Weber (1977), to whom the following section is greatly indebted.
4. Ibid., p. 76.
5. Ibid., p. 82.

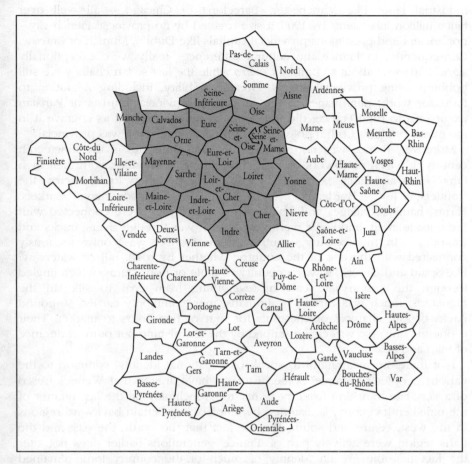

Figure 16.3: French-speaking France, 1835 (wholly French-speaking departments)
After Weber (1977), p. 68

same vein: 'grass growing between the cobblestones, now and again a
streetlamp lost in the night, a dismal solitude from 8 p.m. and often all day'
etc.[6] Most provincials never made the great pilgrimage to Mecca by the Seine:
those who did were often nicknamed 'le Parisien' for the rest of their lives.
While the great Parisian exhibitions attracted vast numbers – that of 1900 had
51 million entries[7] – many even close to the capital had never seen it. Similar
differences and prejudices existed in other countries. In France, however,
there was a unique degree of contrast between a large, traditional rural and
small-town society and a small, highly sophisticated, cosmopolitan and
concentrated urban world. For there were neither new commercial or

6. Taine, in Corbin (1992:b), p. 803.
7. Kaspi and Marès (1989), p. 39.

industrial cities like Manchester, Barcelona or Chicago – all well over half-a-million inhabitants by 1900, a size reached by no provincial French city – nor ancient and prestigious provincial capitals like Dublin, Munich or Cracow. Consequently, in France the cultural differences really were exceptionally stark: Paris was about to build its *métro* while the last sedan chairs were still bobbing along provincial streets. Greater mobility, including migration to Paris for work, pilgrimages to the capital by provincial tourists or Parisian excursions to rural France, did not so much reduce the gulf as engrave it in the minds of all: as Corbin notes, the countryside realized it was provincial.[8]

Moreover, France was not an economic unit until late in the nineteenth century: it was a patchwork of local and regional economies, with their own fairs, banks and stock exchanges. Those on the periphery looked across the frontiers; a few – Bordeaux, Lyons – catered for inter-continental markets. Farms, hamlets, villages and small towns, where they were connected with the outside at all, and some were very little, it was through rivers, tracks and footpaths. In mid-century, south-western France was only tenuously connected with the rest of the country, whether by road, rail or waterway; like Spain and Greece, it was a country of mule or pony trains, which jingled through the countryside carrying everything from coal to silk. In the highlands, much was carried by humans: men commonly carried 50-pound packs of salt, charcoal or chestnuts for four or five hours to market. Their economic universe was circumscribed by the astonishing but puny endurance of man and beast.

Is it therefore meaningful to speak of a 'national identity' common to the various peoples of France? Some historians have argued that Weber's fresco of a very late transition from 'peasants' to 'Frenchmen', in the last quarter of the nineteenth century, is distorted by emphasizing certain backward regions in the west, centre and south. But the fact that the north, the east and the Paris region were actively part of 'France' generations earlier does not alter the fact that the French identity of much of the country long remained theoretical. The well-meaning confusion of schoolchildren is eloquent: in 1864, an inspector in Lozère was horrified that children could not say which nation they belonged to: 'thought doesn't go beyond the radius of the poor parish in which they live'. No less significant is the confusion in the mind of an older boy, nearly a generation later, between the real local and the dimly imagined and abstract national: 'The fatherland is the *pays* where we are born . . . and our dearest thoughts lie; it is not only the *pays* we live in, but the region [*contrée*] we inhabit; our fatherland is France'.[9] This child might at least have seen a map of France: they were practically non-existent until the 1880s, when wall maps were issued to schools. Significantly, most maps were of regions, and only on the eve of the First World War did people become familiar with the shape of France and their own position inside it.

To create a nation was a central political aim of the Revolution. The

8. Corbin (1992:b), p. 807.
9. Weber (1977), pp. 111, 333.

abolition of the old provinces, the creation of uniform departments, national weights, measures, money and taxation, and the aspiration to a single language were all part of the new order. 'Federalism and superstition speak Breton; emigration and hatred of the republic speak German; counter-revolution speaks Italian and fanaticism speaks Basque.'[10] Those who shared the 'values of 1789' shared these ambitions, and so, from 1830 onwards, all regimes set in motion an institutional effort to create a unified nation, while often proclaiming that such a nation already existed, and had existed at least in essence since the days of Vercingetorix, Clovis and Charlemagne. But to make the nation a reality required more than rhetoric or even State schools. The efforts of politicians, intellectuals, schoolteachers and administrators merely bounced off impermeable localism until everyday life acquired 'national' dimensions through work, communication and movement.

The State promoted integration by building a communications network far beyond the means or needs of local interests or collectivities. This network did not merely follow or anticipate economic need, but consciously shaped a national system of power and economic relations: 'Profit was subordinated to the national interest'.[11] The first trunk road system, begun under the Old Regime, extended under Napoleon and largely completed under Louis-Philippe by the late 1840s, and the trunk railway system, begun under the Railway Law of 1842, both radiated out from Paris. They were intended to permit the projection of power, both through normal administrative communication and, if necessary, through the movement of troops to areas of possible rebellion, such as the west, where a road programme was undertaken following the troubles of 1832, and to key strategic points in case of war: the Channel, the borders and the Mediterranean ports.

But strategic communications were not enough to create the nation. In May 1836 the first law to regulate and subsidize local roads (*chemins vicinaux*) was passed, though only after 1881 was a dense network really begun, making local journeys possible in all weathers. In many regions, road stone had to be imported, and so railways had to precede metalled roads. A network of branch lines and narrow-gauge tracks was added late, again principally after 1881, in the Freycinet plan. Until then, the existence of only a main line could actually increase the isolation of villages along its route: for trains made coaches and barges obsolete, but trains, unlike coaches or barges, did not stop. Hence, villages near a railway but not connected with it found their population draining away. It was only in the quarter-century before the First World War, therefore, that vast remote areas of France could take part in a national economic network, buying and selling goods over long distances, and acquiring the contacts and language needed for such dealings. A national railway network made frontiers a reality: in the Pyrenees, for example, traditional exchanges across the mountains gave way to trade along the railways to the interior.

10. Barère, in Fritz (1988), p. 70.
11. Pinkney (1986), p. 36.

Economic life everywhere became more 'national': the Banque de France greatly increased its provincial branches towards the end of the century; local stock exchanges dwindled as that of Paris grew. More goods were moved, more cheaply and over longer distances: in 1845 the railways carried 102 million ton-kilometres, in 1860 3.14 billion. The volume of long-distance communication vastly increased: the small southern city of Albi, capital of the Tarn department, had a telegraph office which in 1859 handled on average fewer than two telegrams a day, mainly official dispatches; by 1897 it handled nearly 400 a day.[12] People moved too, although less in France than Britain. By the late 1860s, 100 million passengers were carried per year, and by the end of the century, 400 million. Until well into the second half of the century, long journeys were confined to certain groups: the wealthy migrated seasonally from city to country and to spas and later seaside resorts; men and women from the poor highland regions moved to find work; soldiers and officials went to new postings. Such movement, far from promoting a 'melting pot', could reinforce a sense of difference: the Limousin masons who migrated to Paris in the 1830s exchanged insults and sometimes blows with the locals on their journey, and lived together in dormitories while in Paris.

Towns and factories, when they attracted permanent migrants from a distance, did act as cultural melting pots: French necessarily became the common language for non-French speakers from inside and outside France. The influx of foreign workers too, which because of the low French birth rate was on a scale unique in Europe (some 1.1 million by 1900) may thus have helped to promote the adoption of French. It certainly increased a sense of Frenchness as a by-product of xenophobia, and 'helped nationalist mobilization' among workers.[13] Hostility and sometimes violence towards foreign workers persisted throughout the period. In 1848 the targets were British, Belgians and Savoyards. In the 1880s and 1890s, when the economic depression again made relations tense, Belgians and Italians were the main targets. In 1892, Belgian workers and their families had to flee by the trainload. There was repeated violence against Italians in the south. The worst single incident was the notorious riot in Aigues-Mortes (Bouches du Rhône) in 1893 when Italians were stoned, clubbed and shot at by crowds waving the red flag and shouting left-wing slogans; at least eight were killed.[14]

The word *immigration* was coined only in the late 1870s; a nationality law followed in 1889, and registration (the first step towards universal identity cards) in 1893. Before then, the law had been vague concerning the status of 'foreigners', and State bodies took little or no interest in the matter. The general tendency, however, especially during the Second Empire, was towards liberalization, and free trade treaties also provided for free movement of people. It was the question of military service that brought the matter before parliament in 1889, and the desire to conscript the sons and grandsons

12. Ibid., p. 47; Weber (1977), p. 220.
13. Noiriel (1988), p. 354.
14. Lequin (1992), pp. 380–5.

of immigrants altered the basis of French nationality from *jus sanguinis* (nationality by inheritance) to *jus soli* (nationality by residence). Acceptance of immigrants through intermarriage and modest social mobility seems to have been quite widespread, especially in the second generation. The Third Republic's 'melting pot' of school and army doubtless affected foreign immigrants as it did peasant immigrants – two groups not easy for town-dwellers to tell apart. On the whole, immigrant workers took the work that natives refused: this is doubtless a general rule. The specifically French variant is that, due to the resistance to economic change that shaped the 'French model', the unwanted work included a large area of modern industrial and mining work; on the other hand, immigrants and even their children tended to be excluded from the usual French route to social advancement – from agriculture to the public sector and thence to the professions.

The army acted as a giant mixer, the 'school of the nation'. Until the 1880s, men from different regions were deliberately mixed and posted away from home; regiments were kept on the move from garrison to garrison. In 1870 peasant soldiers on their way to the front were amazed to see regions and customs they had never known. In 1889 near universal military service was adopted, not only for military reasons but also in the hope of creating a sense of patriotism and certainly providing a practical course in spoken French. By 1914, most of the male population had done their two or three-year service, lived away from home and mixed with men from other communities and classes. This was often the route away from the farm and the village and into jobs on the railways or in the post office.

Over the course of the century, more people began travelling for pleasure. In mid-century trips off the beaten track were somewhat risky. Two adventurous Cambridge undergraduates who stopped for a meal in an Alpine valley in 1858 found that there was no meat, no cutlery and the inn 'was very like a cow-house – dark, wooden and smelling strongly of manure'.[15] Much changed over the next 30 years. Cheaper railway fares, the expensive but affordable bicycle after 1890, and the very expensive motor car created tourism, with all its paraphernalia of maps, guide-books, picture postcards and touring clubs and its spin-offs of decent roads, restaurants and hotels. It also fostered a self-conscious 'regionalism' of recognized tourist attractions and supposedly traditional folk-costumes and cuisine, mostly nineteenth-century inventions. People could only become conscious of their regional peculiarities when outsiders came to experience, and even better pay for them: highlanders in the Cévennes only began to see their landscape as beautiful rather than 'bad country, all rocks' when tourists told them so. Far from conflicting with a wider sense of nationhood, picturesque variety was celebrated as one of the special glories of France, variations on a rich national theme. Most of the country, however, was untouched by tourism, which was largely confined until the last decades of the century to the Norman and

15. *The Eagle* (St John's College), vol. 1 (1859), p. 249.

Breton coasts, the Riviera (especially for the English), mountain spas and the Loire valley.

The effects of economic and cultural integration were facilitated by a range of State and other institutions. Most important were the schools. Whether State, Church or private, they propagated the French language and patriotic values. An example of this is that most popular of schoolbooks, already mentioned in Chapter 6, *Le Tour de la France par Deux Enfants* (1877), one of the most widely read books of the century which had sold 6 million copies by 1901. Written to inculcate republican patriotism, it told of two orphaned brothers from Lorraine, whose father's dying wish was that they should escape from German occupation to the Fatherland. The story told of their journey round France, and it included elementary geography, history, science and copious doses of republican propaganda, all bound together by the basic patriotic lesson: *'J'aime la France'*. Although for practical reasons some classes had to be given in languages other than French, it was always a prime aim of the schools to replace what was contemptuously termed *patois* with French, the language of civilization and progress. Children were commonly ridiculed and punished for using the forbidden languages. Yet all these efforts had limited results until the use of French became necessary and desired in adult life: otherwise, children never used it outside school, at best became semi-bilingual, and often simply forgot their French once they left the classroom behind.

This changed as society changed. French became the language of a new, desirable and now accessible life, urban, commercial and literate. Eventually, people spoke French because they wanted it and needed it: to understand regulations and laws, even if only those of the bowls club; to read newspapers and novels; to follow national politics; to take new kinds of jobs; to travel; to follow sport – an entirely new popular phenomenon with its own mass press, a national football championship in the 1890s, the Tour de France cycle race (1903), and boxing, which produced a French world heavyweight champion, Georges Carpentier, in 1913. French had become the language of good manners and of being up-to-date: at village dances, boys would ask girls to dance in French. *Patois* became restricted to familiarity, to farmwork, to the elderly, the unfashionable and the parochial: 'once patois came to be widely scorned its fate was sealed', notes Weber.[16] After 1890 it was increasingly rejected, like regional costume, by the young, by women, and by the socially ambitious.

The victory of French was not, therefore, simply a victory of the State colonizing its own provinces. But nor was it an inevitable consequence of economic and social change: Flemish more than survived in Belgium, as did Basque and Catalan in Spain. In France, however, the vernaculars had long been abandoned among the educated, and so once-great literary languages fragmented into purely oral local dialects. When regionalists, most prominent among them the Provençal 'Felibrige', founded in 1854, attempted to revive

16. Weber (1977), p. 89.

regional languages by creating a new literature, the *patois*-speaking masses could not read it, and most of the upper classes no longer wished to: 'What a pity that this masterpiece should be written in the language of our servants', was one reaction to Frédéric Mistral's epic poem *Miréio* (1859).[17] The Flemish Society seems to have regarded its language as of purely antiquarian interest: the society's own journal was in French. The policy and prestige of the State and of official culture was obviously crucial here, as was its active discouragement of linguistic particularism, completely excluded from secondary and higher education. Interestingly, the revival of cultural interest in Provence seems less to have promoted a sense of separateness than to have created the idea, visible in political writings (for example of the nationalist Maurras) and in the painting of Cezanne, Van Goch, Matisse and others, that the Latin Midi was the essential France, rather than the damp northern plains where most people lived and worked.

Long lacking was any clear sense of why the vernaculars should be preserved. Since 1789, they had been tarred with the brush of reaction and obscurantism. The clergy was keen to continue teaching and preaching in languages people actually understood, but this was politically damaging in further associating *patois* with 'reaction', and it called down official retribution under the Third Republic. This doubtless goes far in explaining the weakness of ethnic militancy until well into the twentieth century. Every political party stood for France 'one and indivisible', and the Left was the most vocal of all in pressing for linguistic unity as a means of emancipation. It meant not only modernity, progress, fashion and science, but also democracy, republicanism and socialism.

The loss of so many vernacular languages by millions of people was certainly traumatic, especially as it formed part of the economic and political turmoil of the final decades of the nineteenth century. 'The peasant cannot say what he sees, what he feels', wrote one contemporary in 1896. For a good half of the population, the natural means of expression, 'simple, concise . . . full of images', was replaced by a partly or wholly foreign, school-taught language. Only the generation born in the 1890s, to parents who themselves had been exposed to universal schooling in French, was wholly French-speaking, suggests Weber; and indeed, the complete triumph of French may have been even later, with the spread of mass secondary education.[18] The overall cultural effect has been largely overlooked by historians, and is perhaps incalculable. It may still be palpable in the characteristic French concern with linguistic correctness: using French is not a game involving choice, ambiguity, allusion and invention, but a set of rules and definitions to be learned and applied.

17. Ibid., p. 80.
18. Ibid., p. 94. I am grateful to Tim Baycroft for information on Flanders.

NATIONHOOD AND NATIONALISM

The French nation, to which we have the good fortune to belong, is the most
civilised, the most generous, the greatest of nations; it is also the most polite . . .
The French . . . have natural kindness, decency, honesty . . . a marvellous aptitude
for science and literature and an exquisite taste for art, a burning courage, a
natural wit.

Théodore Barrau, La Patrie, 1864[19]

If processes of economic and cultural homogenization made the fact of being
French more relevant to the mass of the population, and if it made a French
'identity' possible, it did not determine how people understood that identity,
what it consisted of, and what its political implications were. What events,
symbols and places composed a usable national 'memory'? What did the
French see as their own characteristics? What was being French supposed to
involve?

The starting point was the conviction that French civilization was in
important ways universal. The French were not merely a nation; in a sense
they were *the* nation, *la grande nation*. Michelet expressed this plainly: a
nation was not merely a biological race, and not merely a geographically
defined population, but a personality that created itself through its history;
and French history had been the greatest such act. 'All other history is
mutilated; only ours is complete.'[20] This idea of universality originated from
French cultural and political hegemony during the seventeenth and
eighteenth centuries. This, for patriots, defined the modern age: 'Once there
was a Greek world and a Roman world', declared Carrel in 1831, 'for a
century now there has been a French world.' At the end of the century
another nationalist, Charles Maurras, developed the similar idea that France
was the core of the 'Helleno-Latin West', guardian of the glorious heritage of
the ancient world. The French language was commonly declared to be the
most perfect of languages, uniquely 'harmonious', 'sweet', 'precise' and 'clear'.
France was uniquely complete and beautiful, a microcosm of nature,
bounded by 'natural frontiers', 'symmetrical, well proportioned and regular'.
These were not the ideas of nationalist extremists, but the commonplaces of
speeches and school textbooks.[21] Much flowed from this conviction of
universalism: a sense of mission to less favoured nations; a belief that French
(in practice Parisian) civilization was the most polite and sophisticated, its
women the most charming and elegant; that French products,
characteristically those of craft industries such as clothing, cooking and
furniture, showed the greatest quality and taste. The desire to protect French
culture from inferior foreign influences (whether Lancashire cotton, the
operas of Wagner or more recently the products of Hollywood) was not

19. Citron (1987), p. 4.
20. Ibid., p. 19.
21. Maingueneau (1979), p. 255; Weber (1991), pp. 58–9.

always crude chauvinism: it was often urbane chauvinism. Debussy and d'Indy, and not only nationalist yahoos, deplored the influence of Wagner.

There was a painful awareness that things were changing, and that the world was no longer recognizing French cultural tutelage, just as in 1813–15 it had thrown off French power. Within France itself there were periodic vogues for foreign styles, and these were taken to be, and indeed often were, deliberate rejections of French tradition, hence the passions they aroused. Romanticism had been just such a revolt against French classicism. Consequently, the nineteenth-century national self-view was shaped by nagging fears about decline, even decadence. Patriots wanted to diagnose the malaise, rediscover the sources of greatness and foster the true national identity. There were two overarching themes, which were described in an earlier section as collective obsessions: revolution and war.

The Revolution had created a new definition of what a nation, and first and foremost the French nation, was: the association of free citizens who had asserted their right to constitute the sole source of sovereignty. The Fête de la Fédération of 14 July 1790 had proclaimed and symbolically enacted the unity of the nation. For democrats inside and outside France, the French nation was above all the revolutionary nation, the prophet and standard-bearer of political progress and hence in a new way the universal civilization: 'The Fatherland, my fatherland, alone can save the world'.[22] The nation's enemies were not only external opponents of France and the Revolution, but also all those inside France who betrayed the nation by putting their own interests first. Such selfishness, if unchecked, would destroy the nation itself: it faced 'decay' as a society and 'death' as a race, thought Quinet in the 1830s. Only national pride, it was widely argued, could keep the nation united, and prevent a collapse into materialism, factionalism and moral decadence. Accusations of treason were made by republicans against the aristocracy ('who have no fatherland', said Cabet), Catholics ('Can a Catholic be a patriot?' asked Gambetta), the 'bourgeoisie' ('their fatherland begins at their counter and ends at their cash-box', said L'Atelier) and Jews ('their fatherland is the London stock exchange', wrote Michelet). Catholic nationalists at the end of the century would make similar accusations against socialists, freemasons, Protestants and Jews. As Michelet summed it up, 'devotion of the citizen to the fatherland is my measure for judging men and classes'; but nationalists, of course, themselves decided what devotion to the nation involved, and who qualified as its members.[23]

Revolution and war, both as cultural obsessions and as periodic events, meant that a large part of the population was constantly made aware of belonging to the nation. From 1789 to 1815, in 1830, 1848 and 1870–71, involvement in national life was broad and deep to an extent probably unique to France, which also, after 1848, was the only large country to involve most adult males in elections, a high proportion of whom regularly

22. Michelet (1946), p. 271.
23. Cabet (1840), p. 22; L'Atelier (Nov. 1842); Michelet (1946), pp. 123, 121.

voted. Although one could find conscripts in the 1890s who had never heard of the Franco-Prussian War, highland peasants who thought that Napoleon III was still emperor, and even candidates for the *baccalauréat* who did not know that the Germans had annexed Metz,[24] huge numbers of people had been actively involved in what they realized were national events. In June 1848, 100,000 part-time National Guards mobilized themselves to march on Paris to put down the June Days revolt, and in December 1851 another 100,000 people took up arms to defend the Republic. People who cared little about politics could not but realize that great events far away in Paris affected their own lives. As noted above (p. 244), a series of mystical visions by peasant children showed that even they had a hazy awareness of national political events. In short, even political disunity reminded people that they were French, and showed them one aspect of what Frenchness meant.

Not all national events were violent: following the example of the 1790s, governments organized grandiose festivities to instil a sense of unity and also to shape the national 'memory'. These included great Parisian fêtes, such as the tenth anniversary of the 1830 revolution (for which Berlioz wrote his Grande Symphonie Funèbre et Triomphale); the 14 July celebrations begun by the Republic in 1880; the ceremonial 'pantheonization' of Republican heroes (that of Victor Hugo in 1885 became a huge popular ceremonial); the centenary of the Revolution in 1889 (which included the doubtless highly memorable parade and banquet of 15,200 mayors); and the Parisian exhibitions of 1867, 1889 (for which the Eiffel Tower was built) and 1900. Such festivities, complete with military bands, fireworks and dancing in the streets, were reproduced on a smaller scale in towns and villages throughout France, which paraded, harangued, planted trees of liberty, rang bells, unveiled statues and inaugurated innumerable Places de la République and Rues Nationales the length and breadth of the land.

Conservatives tended to share the view that the French had become a revolutionary nation, though of course they deplored it as a betrayal of the nation's true identity. Their vision of France was based essentially on its Catholicism: the 'eldest daughter of the Church', chosen as the protector of the papacy after the miraculous conversion of Clovis and his baptism by St Rémi at Rheims on Christmas Day 496, with an ampoule of oil brought from heaven by a dove. Thereafter France was governed by a divinely protected line of kings, the creators of her greatness: 'while other nations fell by the wayside, she would prepare herself to lead the other European peoples, as queen of the civilized world', in the words of a bishop of Orleans.[25] 'Toujours en France les Bourbons et la foi', went the royalist hymn. Joan of Arc, a heroine claimed by both sides, eventually became the foremost symbol of Catholic patriotism, evidence that God paid special attention to French prayers. A similar message is proclaimed in the mosaic inside the dome of the Sacré-Coeur at Montmartre (begun 1876), which shows the Messiah on

24. Weber (1977), p. 110.
25. Krumeich, in Tombs (1991), p. 68.

amicable terms with royalist politicians and army officers. As the legitimist Bishop Pie summed it up in 1859, 'there will never be anything national in France except that which is Christian'.[26]

In the face of these conflicting ideas of what the nation meant, the rhetorical insistence that it was 'one and indivisible' was, suggests Girardet, a kind of exorcism to ward off open division.[27] However, the fact that both sides shared the conviction that France was unique, the nation that led mankind, or ought to, could form a basis for reconciliation, or at least coexistence. Taught one school textbook,

> It is generally in France that the great ideas that interest humanity are born, or at least first applied. Thus the country is sometimes much disturbed! But its sufferings benefit the whole world, which often does not appreciate this, and by ingratitude or jealousy mocks our country exhausted by its efforts.[28]

Thus, the 'disturbances' and conflicts could be combined into a hybrid saga of greatness featuring Vercingétorix, Charlemagne, Joan of Arc, Louis XIV, Danton and Napoleon: this was the view adopted by nationalists such as Déroulède and Barrès in the 1890s.

War, as we have seen, was another obsessive theme, and it too greatly shaped French national identity. Though every contemporary western state glorified military virtues and used military ceremony and symbolism, the experience of France – the long Revolutionary Wars, mass conscription, Napoleon's victories, and finally defeat and occupation in 1814 and 1815 – made war a stark reality to large numbers of people. The cult of Napoleon was a major consequence, and it provided one of the century's great moments of national communion: the 'retour des cendres' in December 1840, when Napoleon's remains were brought back from St Helena and taken slowly up the Seine to the crypt of the Invalides. Before the days of mass politics, mass literacy and mass media, hundreds of thousands of people waited fervently in the freezing cold to welcome 'l'empereur': 'the people, the genuine people ... cried "Vive l'empereur", wanted to unharness the horses and pull the funeral car. A suburban [National Guard] company went down on its knees; men and women kissed the drapes of the catafalque.'[29] It was perhaps the century's biggest and largely spontaneous expression of national identity, and it showed how much a sense of being French owed to the Napoleonic epic.

Real wars under Napoleon's nephew in 1854, 1859 and 1870 were also focuses of national feeling, with emotional patriotic demonstrations, especially in the cities. Napoleon III's departure for the Italian front in 1859, and the victorious army's triumphal return, brought out cheering crowds in Paris, especially among the working-class districts, not usually supporters of

26. Gadille (1967), vol. 1, p. 57.
27. Girardet (1986), p. 161.
28. Maingueneau (1979), p. 70.
29. Hugo (1972), p. 189.

the government: the Italian cause combined the warlike and the revolutionary themes in French patriotism, and so won support even among political opponents on the Left. The war of 1870 also inspired large patriotic demonstrations. Audoin-Rouzeau argues that the response of the French people to the war of 1870 demonstrated the existence of a developed national identity, for they accepted from the beginning that the war was the concern of all, not just of the government and the army.[30] The implication is that a widespread sense of nationhood existed even before the completion of the integration processes that turned 'peasants into Frenchmen', and before the sustained patriotic indoctrination of the Third Republic. Be that as it may, marked differences soon emerged between bellicose town and war-weary country, between chauvinist Left and defeatist Right, and to some extent between patriotic north and indifferent south.

At least from the Revolutionary Wars until 1914, military virtues were central to French views of themselves. For Michelet France had the only 'serious' army in Europe because it drew on the unique fraternal solidarity of the nation. The French considered themselves a naturally martial race, who made the best soldiers in the world because they were excitable, quick to anger, violent, chivalrous and intellectually adventurous, traits inherited from 'our ancestors the Gauls', and which similarly inclined them to discouragement, quarrels and revolution. As both Left and Right agreed, the French, unlike the phlegmatic English or stolid Germans, were a brilliant but dangerous people, bristling like their moustaches – typically French appendages, wrote Maupassant, redolent of wine, women, horses and battles. The warrior self-image carried over into civilian life: juries were indulgent to men or women whose crimes of violence were explained as consequences of passion or honour. Susceptibility and hot temper, if sometimes regrettable in their consequences, were considered national attributes to be excused, even cherished.

The defeat of 1870 affected the language of national identity. Many believed, as we saw in Chapter 2, that it proved at least a degree of cultural inferiority, of national decadence. The falling birth rate too was seen as a symptom of profound national malaise. Nationalist language became more pessimistic: 'I feel French nationhood diminishing, disappearing', wrote Barrès.[31] Diagnoses followed the familiar political battle lines. For the Right, the culprits were revolution, democracy, godlessness and materialism; for the Left, lack of civic spirit, insufficient education and Catholicism. This was the context in which a new political phenomenon emerged in the 1880s and 1890s, an alliance of Right and Left explicitly using the new term 'nationalist', seeking a remedy for French decline and stigmatizing political opponents as betrayers of the nation. These themes were not wholly new, but the tone had altered: it was a nationalism of 'dissatisfaction, of tension and of protest'.[32]

30. Audoin-Rouzeau (1989), p. 56.
31. Girardet (1983), p. 17.
32. Ibid., p. 276.

politically and culturally pessimistic (for example in its rejection of modernity, democracy and the individual, and its acceptance of racial determinism). By giving the nation 'absolute priority' as a political value, it tried to transcend existing political divisions and create a movement attracting a diverse range of adherents: impatient socialists, desperate royalists, intellectuals, bankrupt shopkeepers and populist priests. It was embodied above all in extra-parliamentary leagues such as Paul Déroulède's Ligue des Patriotes (1882), and later the Ligue de la Patrie Française (1899) and Action Française (1908).

Nationalists attempted to redefine national identity. As noted above, the 1889 nationality law redefined legal nationality, though for practical rather than ideological reasons. The Republic offered foreigners an implicit contract: they would be accepted as equal citizens on condition that they abandoned ethnic identity and accepted French culture and French (republican) principles. But for new nationalist thinkers, this was far from sufficient. In a famous phrase of the most influential nationalist writer of the 1890s, Maurice Barrès, the essence of a nation was 'la terre et les morts': it was the organic creation of generations of ancestors inhabiting the same soil. While this again was not entirely new – there are echoes of Michelet and Renan, for example – it was interpreted in a far more racial and deterministic sense: 'There are no personal ideas . . . the individual disappears to find himself again in the family, in the race, in the nation . . . I can only live according to my dead. They and my land demand a certain activity of me.'[33] This concept was used to exclude as inherently and irremediably non-French, 'foreigners', freemasons, Protestants and above all Jews such as Alfred Dreyfus. The stress on race also transcended the two rival interpretations of the nation that we have seen above, the Catholic royalist and the revolutionary.

These, however, were too deeply rooted to be easily replaced. One reason why the new nationalism had limited appeal, suggests Sorlin, was that older concepts of nationalism were too well established in the language.[34] It was also difficult to find a recognizable symbol of the nation distinct from the symbol of the Republic: symbols of France tended to take on the attributes of 'Marianne', including her revolutionary phrygian bonnet.[35] The new 'integral' nationalism was as likely to be absorbed into the older traditions of republicanism or Catholicism as it was to replace them. Nevertheless, it injected into the language of national identity a virulently xenophobic element that was to remain at least until the Second World War as a way of explaining national decline, reaching an infamous climax in the persecutions of the Vichy years. At a symbolic level, suggests Agulhon, 'integral' nationalists and fascists sought a masculine symbol (they would eventually find Pétain) to replace the feminine symbol of the Republic, seen by them as corrupt and weak.

33. Ibid., p. 185.
34. Sorlin, in Tombs (1991), pp. 86–7.
35. Agulhon (1989), pp. 320, 340–5.

THE LIMITS OF NATIONAL IDENTITY

The geography of patriotism

In spite of the tide of national exhortation from 1789 onwards, many remained indifferent to the idea of the nation and regarded the obligations of nationhood as an alien imposition to be avoided. As with so many French phenomena, this can be mapped. Broadly speaking, in the first half of the century dutiful France was the north and north-east, which paid its taxes and performed its military service. Recalcitrant France was the centre and south-west, which evaded taxes and went to great lengths to keep out of the army; running away, chopping off the trigger-finger or knocking out front teeth (needed until the 1860s to bite open paper cartridges) were common stratagems. Clearly, this was a reflection of differing degrees of integration into the nation: both subjective (feelings of duty), and objective (the ability of the administration to enforce obedience).

Feelings are more difficult to judge than acts. Military reports on popular attitudes towards the army show patriotic France to be the north and especially north-east, close to threatened frontiers, frequently a battleground, studded with fortresses and barracks, and a provider of warriors from Joan of Arc to Charles de Gaulle. Indifferent, and even unpatriotic, France is that of much of the west and south, perhaps where the Paris-centred French-speaking nation and its international struggles were seen as serious liabilities.[36] These were deep-rooted differences. During the 1780s, ten times as many soldiers were said to come from Alsace as from Gascony; during the war of 1870 and the First World War, there were still persistent allegations that southerners were less patriotic.

Attitudes to war, then, were taken by contemporaries and by many subsequent historians to be the true touchstone of patriotism. Yet there is no straightforward link between national integration in the social and economic sense and bellicosity. Reactions to war were influenced by belief and judgement. Hence, in 1814–15 and 1870–71, people judged the war according to their own private circumstances (of course), but also in terms of their commitment to emperor, king or republic and their assessment of the political, social and economic consequences of winning, losing or just continuing the struggle. The remarkable unity in the face of war in 1914 (which will be discussed in the final chapter) may partly be a result of the transformation of 'peasants into Frenchmen'; but we must remember that 1940 saw no such unity. What had changed was that in 1940 there was a very different set of political, moral and military circumstances. In short, 'national sentiment' is a political variable, not a socio-economic product.

36. Weber (1977), pp. 104–8.

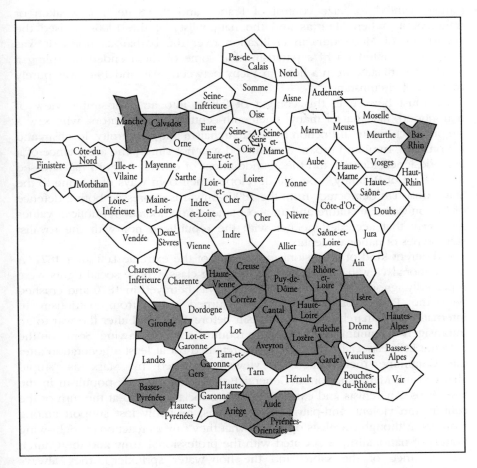

Figure 16.4: Limits of patriotism (areas of most frequent evasion of military service, 1819–26)
After Aron (1972), p. 80

Rival identities: region and class

We have seen above that local and regional identities were deep. Yet a dog that did not bark during the nineteenth century, or only rarely growled, was regional separatism. If at times of crisis – 1815, 1870, 1940 – there were murmurs of Breton, Savoyard or Provençal particularism, and although the uncomfortable position of Alsace as a bone of contention between France and Germany led to a fairly widespread current of autonomism, there was no major and sustained campaign to break away or even to demand formal autonomy from the 'one and indivisible'. The reason seems to be the absence of any ideological vision to justify political regionalism. All the major political

parties wanted to seize control of France and the State, not weaken or
fragment it. When Maurras and the nationalists of the 1900s praised the
superiority of Mediterranean civilization over the barbarous north, it was
without any intention of separatism: that some of them ended up ruling a
southern mini-state from a hotel in Vichy between 1940 and 1944 was purely
by force of circumstance.

We must beware in this context of falling into an over-simple view of
nationhood, like that of many nineteenth-century commentators, who saw a
simple black/white distinction between archaism and modernity, localism and
nationalism, rural and urban. Nationhood was not simply the acceptance of a
Paris-designed identity and the abandonment of others. As Ford has stressed
in the case of Britanny,[37] people developed their own ways of relating to the
State: Christian democracy from the 1890s onwards expressed both a defence
of Breton Catholic culture and an acceptance of democratic republican values
in a way that accorded neither with the republican nor with the royalist
stereotypes of national identity.

A different kind of secessionism was that of the extreme Left after 1871. A
conventional view has been that the working class, whose social rights were
repeatedly ignored, and whose patriotism was betrayed in 1870 and crushed
with the Paris Commune in 1871, turned away from patriotism to
internationalist anarchism and socialism before 1914, and after the war to an
intransigent communism. This picture requires some redrawing. Some on the
extreme Left, especially the Blanquists, retained for at least a generation after
the Commune their nationalist views, dismissed by Marx as 'stupid
chauvinism'. Many supported General Boulanger's patriotic populism in the
late 1880s. Anarchists and extreme left-wing socialists, who at the turn of the
century ran violent 'anti-patriotic' campaigns, probably lost support among
workers. Although socialists opposed what they saw as reactionary right-wing
brands of nationalism, associated with the professional army and the Church
('the alliance of the sabre and the holy-water sprinkler'), they always
defended the right of national defence. 'France attacked will have no more
ardent defenders than socialists', proclaimed the Guesdists.[38] Even an
anarcho-syndicalist such as Griffuelhes was proud of the record of French
workers and disliked Germans. The republican tradition of nationalism,
linked with the defence of democracy at home and the emancipating mission
of France abroad, was always a potent magnet at least until 1914. Howorth
concludes that French workers were nationalist in their 'hearts and guts'.[39]

37. Ford (1993).
38. Derfler (1977), p. 94.
39. Howorth (1985), pp. 71–95, at p. 73.

The depth of a common culture: demography as an indicator

> O French mothers, make children, so that France may keep her rank, her strength
> and her prosperity for it is necessary for the world's salvation that France should
> live, for from her came human liberty, from her will come all truth and all
> justice! . . . I would like every household to have twelve children, to cry out
> human joy in the face of the sun.
>
> *Emile Zola, 1899*[40]

French society was unique in its early adoption of birth control (*le Malthusianisme*), which brought about an unparalleled slow-down in population growth. Fertility fell by 42 per cent between 1800 and 1910, giving France the lowest birth rate in Europe. From being the second most populous country after Russia in 1800, by the 1900s she had become the fifth, her 39 million being overtaken by Germany (65 million), Austria-Hungary (51 million) and Britain (41 million).[41] This was an immensely important collective decision involving the most fundamental levels of behaviour. It had consequences for many aspects of French society and culture, from the survival of traditional economic activity to the widespread fear of decadence. It can tell us much about the changing patterns of identity that have been discussed in this section: individual self-awareness, the relationship between women and men, the influences of family, community, religion and geography, the growth of class differences, and the degree of national integration.

The first signs of systematic birth control within marriage occurred during the eighteenth century. However, the period of the Revolution accelerated and propagated it. The important change – the 'real break in behaviour' – came in the 1790s–1800s when the fertility rate among married women turned sharply down, falling by 26 per cent between the 1780s and the 1810s.[42] During the 1830s the birth rate fell below 30 per thousand, 'generally considered as marking the beginning of a regime of controlled fertility'.[43] The fall continued: in 1831, every 1,000 married women gave birth to 195 children; in 1901, to 138.[44]

There were major regional variations, but taken overall, the social groups which most limited their fertility were the peasantry and the non-industrial middle classes. Of men reaching maturity at about 1860, every 100 living on private incomes would have 292 children, every 100 white-collar workers would have 302, while bosses of firms would have 395 and workers, 402; coalminers had nearly twice as many children as teachers in the 1900s.[45]

40. *La Fécondité*, 1899, in Dupâquier *et al.* (1988), p. 492.
41. Mitchell (1978), pp. 4–8.
42. Dupâquier *et al.* (1988), p. 364.
43. Fine and Sangoï (1991), p. 40.
44. Gégot (1989), p. 65.
45. Bardet, in Dupâquier *et al.* (1988), p. 370.

There are many hypotheses. Was it a sign of the greater importance and equality of women, less willing to endure multiple pregnancies? The usual method of birth control, *coitus interruptus*, has often been interpreted as a proof of male dominance, but could as easily be a sign of mutual agreement and trust. But this view seems weakened by the fact that working-class women, usually said to have been the most equal to their men, had more children than other groups. Was it a sign of greater importance given to children and their upbringing, causing a decision to have fewer children so as to look after them better? But this does not square with the widespread abandonment of babies, their boarding out with wet-nurses, or the high rate of infant mortality. Was it a sign of liberation for women? The prevalence of backstreet abortions and even infanticide suggest constraint rather than liberation. Was it a sign that couples regarded their sexual relationship as more aimed at pleasure than at mere reproduction? Family planning in France (children being conceived early in marriage, followed by the use of birth control) might suggest a less repressive form of self-denial than other forms of birth control (late marriage or, as in Britain, spacing of conceptions over a longer period within marriage by sexual abstinence). On the other hand, there were marked regional and social variations, and it is hard to imagine that peasants and clerks were more hedonistic than businessmen and workers, or that Bretons were more erotically charged than Provençaux. Moreover the timing of the phenomenon (as we have seen, the 1790s) predates the 'eroticization of marriage' placed by Corbin after 1860 (see p. 225).

Was it due to secularization of values and the decline of Church influence? Here there are undeniably strong links: the least Catholic regions (compare Figure 14.5, p. 261) were also the least fertile; it seems clear that Catholicism inhibited contraception. However, this correlation emerged rather late. In mid-century there is no apparent geographical pattern, but by the 1900s the map of high birth rates is practically identical with that of religious practice. The late emergence of this pattern may be because birth control did not come to the attention of the Church, the State or political and moral commentators until the 1860s when population growth visibly slackened, and especially after 1880 when the population itself stagnated and even fell. Priests assumed that husbands were mainly responsible for the grave sin of onanism, and priestly criticism probably contributed to the growth of male anticlericalism, including Michelet's obsession with the confessor. On the other hand, priests realized that their influence was limited. It was perhaps the norms of Catholic communities, rather than the direct influence of the clergy, that counted. One might note in passing that Catholicism was more successful than the republican State (which tried to exhort, induce or even force – by making contraception difficult – its citizens to have more children) in affecting private behaviour.

Therefore, while the influence of Catholicism did much to form the regional pattern of fertility between the 1880s and 1940s – and incidentally confirms all that we have seen on the importance of Catholicism in forming regional mentalities (the 'two Frances') – it did not alone explain the origins of the decline nearly a century earlier.

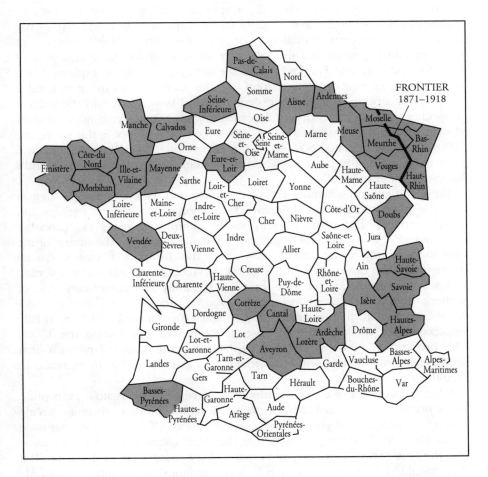

Figure 16.5: High fertility, 1911 (more than 2.75 children per woman)
After Le Bras and Todd (1981), p. 323

   The earliest and most influential general hypothesis concerns the Code Civil
and its requirement to divide inheritance between all children. This is
assumed to have induced landowners to limit the number of their children so
as not to fragment the family holding. However, there are basic problems
with this hypothesis. The demographic downturn predated the Code Civil
(1800). Besides, in areas where other inheritance customs were entrenched,
the code continued to be circumvented, a demonstration of the resistance of
local cultures to the homogenizing ambitions of the nation-state. Moreover,
other groups who had no concern with fragmented landholdings, such as
minor civil servants and white-collar workers, were even more 'Malthusian'
than peasant proprietors. Wrigley has suggested that a fall in mortality during
the eighteenth century put pressure on agricultural resources, to which birth

control was the least difficult response.[46] This accounts for its eighteenth-century beginnings, and for its rural spread. But alone it does not account for regional variations, or for the strict Malthusianism of non-agricultural groups and the relatively affluent, or for the uniqueness of the French experience. Nor can the falling birth rate simply be explained as a consequence of economic stagnation, for the French economy generated a demand for labour: from the Napoleonic period onwards it had the highest proportion of immigrants of any European society. There were huge influxes at times of economic expansion: the 1840s, the Second Empire, the 1870s, the 1900s. The total reached 800,000 in the 1870s and 1.13 million in 1911 and grew even more after the First World War, when France became the world's largest importer of people.[47]

There is, then, no generally accepted explanation. Fine and Sangoï suggest that the phenomenon has different explanations for different regions and social groups, but that overall some cultural change is 'probably determinant'.[48] Some general points can be made, however. The timing of the downturn in the birth rate suggests that the Revolution was a crucial accelerator. The destructive effects of the Revolution include the weakening of traditional norms and controls by Church, family and community, and of systems of charitable support, and the sudden uprooting of men through mass conscription: this traumatic effect might be compared with the equally unprecedented demographic collapse in Eastern Europe during the 1990s. The breakdown of social controls explains too the seeming paradox that increasing birth control within marriage was paralleled by an increase in illegitimacy.

A long-term effect of the Revolution may have been to create a perception of opportunity for social advancement, however modest, through saving money, acquiring land and investing in education, all of which necessitated fewer children. It seems plausible that the 'Malthusian' lower-middle classes and the landowning peasantry were particularly susceptible to this view. But they imagined advancement within a closed economic system: there was only so much land and so many professional and civil-service jobs. Much of the work in new industries was left to immigrants. Moreover, we have seen how the growth of 'class consciousness' among rural and urban workers took place in the context of defence of a 'household economy' against pressure to increase productivity: this resistance often entailed a defensive Malthusianism. In contrast, those groups that were more prolific, such as miners, industrial workers and businessmen, were involved in expanding sectors, demanding ever more participants and offering work prospects to children. Few French people emigrated to find better opportunities in the New World: this too distinguished them from every other people in Europe. Millions of French families wanted both to better themselves and to stay put.

46. Wrigley (1985), pp. 31–60, 131–9.
47. Lequin (1992), pp. 322, 325.
48. Fine and Sangoï (1991), p. 60.

These demographic variations demonstrate how important were the cultural differences among the peoples of France, and how the Catholic/*laïc* divide came to shape personal behaviour. Yet while the divide between the 'two Frances' persisted, the degree of difference lessened: a sign of increasing national convergence. Both the persistent difference and the growing similarity are proof that at the deepest social and cultural level, being French, from the 1790s to the 1960s, was a distinctive experience.

PART FOUR

THE ERA OF REVOLUTIONS, 1814–1871

After me, the Revolution – or, rather, the ideas which formed it – will resume their course. It will be like a book from which the marker is removed, and one starts to read again at the page where one left off.

Napoleon I, 1813

CHAPTER 17

THE IMPOSSIBLE RESTORATION, 1814–30

The brief period of the Bourbon Restoration was the moment when France tried, and failed, to return to normality after a quarter of a century of revolution and war. It may seem in retrospect, after so many subsequent revolutions and wars, that there was in fact no normality to return to: that hatreds were too bitter and expectations too high, and that France had become ungovernable. Or was it rather that blunders were made and opportunities for reconciliation missed: that France was not ungovernable, but badly governed?

FRANCE AND THE BOURBONS, 1814

In seeking thus to relink the chain of time . . . we have wiped from our memory, as we would that we could wipe them from history, all the evils that have afflicted the fatherland during our absence.

Louis XVIII, preamble to Charter, 1814

The political direction on which France set out in 1814 was determined not by the French, but by the British, Russians, Austrians and Prussians. Their decision was remarkably pragmatic. As candidates for the throne the British preferred the Bourbons, but the Austrians considered a regency for Napoleon's son, and the Russians thought both of the Duc d'Orléans (the Bourbon's progressive-minded cousin) and the King of Sweden (Napoleon's former Marshal Bernadotte, son of a cooper from Pau). The Allies still negotiated with Napoleon himself, in February 1814 offering to allow him to keep the throne, with France retaining her 1792 frontiers (that is, losing what remained of the conquests Napoleon had made, but keeping the small gains made in Belgium and western Germany during the early Revolutionary Wars). Napoleon refused: a fatal decision for himself and France: 'My reign will not outlast the day when I have ceased to be strong and therefore to be feared'.[1] He did not want to make peace, and perhaps, as Schroeder suggests, did not know how to.[2]

1. Johnson (1991), p. 74.
2. Schroeder (1994), p. 469.

Napoleon, dictator since his coup d'état of 18 Brumaire Year VIII (9 November 1799) and emperor since 1804, was still the master of France, though a France increasingly sullen, mutinous and exhausted. His strength was due to military success, but also to his imposing an effective compromise regime after the turmoil of the 1790s, suppressing both revolutionary extremism and royalist reaction. He had placated rebellious Catholics by permitting the open practice of Catholicism and signing the 1802 Concordat with the pope. He had won the support, however conditional, of many of the old ruling class: most émigré nobles had returned, and some of the younger men and women made enviable careers in his service as administrators, courtiers, diplomats or soldiers. Yet Napoleon was the enemy of the old monarchy, and under him the gains of the Revolution – civil equality, office, land, wealth – were safe in the hands of those who had won them.

None of this counted, however, unless he could fight off the Allies. Although unable to oppose him openly, many of the emperor's officials and ministers realized that the war was lost and that he was an obstacle to negotiations. Talleyrand, aristocrat, ex-bishop, veteran of the Revolution, arch-intriguer and most seductive of diplomats, an improbable caricature of those who had done well out of the Revolution – 'shit in silk stockings' said Napoleon – made contact with the Allies as spokesman of the French political class. He urged the restoration of the Bourbons in the person of the Comte de Provence, brother of Louis XVI. The Allies doubted that the Bourbons had enough support in the country. They were largely forgotten after more than twenty years' exile: one might as well have been talking about the children of the emperor of China, recalled Chateaubriand. However, there were pro-Bourbon demonstrations because the Bourbons meant peace. This convinced the Allies that they might be viable; there was not much alternative. On 12 March, as British and Portuguese troops arrived in Bordeaux, Lynch, the mayor, hoisted the Bourbon white flag amid shouts of *'Vive le Roi!'* from a large crowd. Such scenes were repeated in Marseilles, Toulouse and most importantly in Paris, which made no resistance to the Allies when they arrived on 30 March. Napoleon abdicated.

Behind the chicanery and stage-managed demonstrations, what most French people wanted was peace, and if that meant the Bourbons, so be it. The costs of a generation of revolution and war had been huge: perhaps 1.5 million deaths.[3] More than one in three of all boys born between 1790 and 1795 were killed or wounded. Thousands of deserters were on the run, living often as brigands, and conscripts had to be dragged to barracks roped together. Inflation, heavy taxation, requisitions and the British naval blockade caused economic devastation. The last three years of the war had been particularly hard, with serious food shortages and unemployment, with long-term damage to the health of children. The arrival of the Allies and the fall of Napoleon were therefore greeted with relief. Toulouse greeted Wellington as a liberator; Louis XVIII's brother the Comte d'Artois rode in

3. Charle (1991), p. 16.

triumph into Paris; Caen feted the Duc de Berry, his nephew; the Agen district reported 'joy everywhere'. The Bourbons encouraged this enthusiasm with imprudent promises to abolish conscription and cut taxes. The popular songwriter Béranger had expressed the country's war weariness in cheeky praise for the 'King of Yvetot' (1813), who cared nothing for glory, got on with his neighbours, and left his subjects in peace: 'What a good little king was he!'

In the vital matter of the liquidation of the war, there was some cause for satisfaction. Louis XVIII's government was being treated gently by the Allies, who had no wish to undermine it. Moreover, Britain and Austria wished to keep France relatively strong as a barrier to Russian hegemony. The First Treaty of Paris was rapidly signed on 30 May 1814. France was to keep her 1792 frontiers; there was to be no occupation and no indemnity; even art treasures looted by Napoleon's armies were to stay in Paris. At least on the surface, France was once again an equal diplomatic partner.

However, some were happier than others to see the return of the Bourbons and their entourage. First, these differences reflected contrasting attitudes towards the Revolution itself. Those who still held to the 'principles of 1789' might accept Napoleon as emperor – he was, after all, a creation of the Revolution, and could be seen as its inheritor and continuer – but they were chary of a possible return to the Old Regime. Second, attitudes were shaped by the uneven economic effects of the war, which in some regions had disrupted the economy, and in others had provided a stimulus. The third element shaping public feeling was the Allied armies. They were not seen as liberators for long. The Germans especially had suffered for years from the presence of French troops on their soil and they had no hesitation in paying French civilians back in their own coin: seizure of food, money and other property, wanton destruction, insults, violence, rape. Most of the sufferers, especially those who tried sporadically to stand up to the invaders, seem to have reflected that Napoleon had tried to fight them off, while the Bourbons regarded them as Allies. One who was affected was the nine-year-old Auguste Blanqui, whose father, prefect of Alpes-Maritimes, lost his job and his department (annexed to Sardinia) and had Prussian soldiers billetted in his house by the royalist authorities. When he reached his teens, Blanqui joined the opposition to the Bourbons – the beginning of a life of unyielding revolutionary activism.

Certain groups were more likely to be loyal to Napoleon and fear the Bourbons. Soldiers, civil servants, those involved in certain industries, all faced an uncertain post-war future. Those who had bought *biens nationaux* (former Church land, nationalized and sold from 1791 onwards, or land confiscated from émigrés) feared for their new property when the Bourbons returned. They were many, perhaps a million families. About 7–10 per cent by value of all the land of France had been sold, 2.8 billion francs' worth. About one-quarter had gone to the peasantry, the rest mainly to middling landowners and professional men, often the very same who had risen politically during the revolutionary years and ended up under Napoleon as a mayor, prefect or magistrate. Finally, the mass of small and middling landowners who, before 1789, would have had to pay seigneurial dues and tithes to the Church feared anything that suggested a return to 'feudalism'.

Most eager for a Bourbon Restoration were those who had lost most. Nobles who had lost privilege, land and wealth, who had risked death or imprisonment, or had vegetated in exile in Germany or England. The clergy, whose institutional wealth had gone, whose numbers had dwindled, who had risked persecution if they refused to accept the revolutionary Civil Constitution of the Clergy, and had been subject to the dechristianization campaign of 1793. Small peasants who had mostly been unable to afford to buy *biens nationaux*, whose rents had risen, whose churches had been closed, whose sons had been conscripted, maimed or killed. Merchants and artisans ruined by the wartime disruption of trade. People such as these welcomed the Bourbons, sometimes with enthusiasm. But they expected miracles: jobs, pensions, the return of lost estates, the end of high taxes and conscription, in short, some compensation for their sufferings and losses.

It is hard to see how the Bourbons could have avoided disappointing their supporters and antagonizing their opponents. They could not, given the immense cost of the war and occupation, reduce taxes at a stroke. There were excise riots not only in lukewarm Dijon, but also in royalist Bordeaux: the interests of the wine trade outweighed ideology. Nor could the government restrain the Allied troops, however hard local authorities tried. Where it could, the new regime behaved with circumspection. A constitutional Charter was published in June 1814, guaranteeing legal equality, civil liberties, a parliament, the security of the *biens nationaux* and official 'oubli' of all acts committed during the Revolution. There were no mass sackings of civil servants; some former enemies were even given medals. But symbolic acts spoiled the effects of the concessions. The tricolour was replaced by the Bourbon white flag. The king insisted that he was Louis XVIII, in the nineteenth year of his reign, successor of 'Louis XVII', the little son of Louis XVI who had died wretchedly in a Paris prison. He was 'King of France' by divine right, not 'King of the French' by the nation's will. Worst of all, the preamble to the Charter declared that it was a 'concession and grant' (*octroi*) to 'our subjects', 'voluntarily and by the free exercise of our royal authority'. These were just words, for the Charter had in fact been a condition of the restoration, but by implying that what had happened since 1791 was null and void, and by denying the contractually binding nature of the Charter, Louis aroused the fears of those inclined to suspect the Bourbon's intentions: 'they resented the nineteenth century', wrote Hugo, 'they were grudging. The people saw it.'[4]

Moreover, Louis could not wholly ignore or control his followers. Emigré nobles understandably felt that they had returned as victors, and this was resented: 'See this old marquis bloke, Treats us like conquered folk', sang Béranger. While Napoleonic regiments were disbanded and officers put on

4. Hugo (1967), vol. 2, pp. 351–2.

half pay, former Chouans and émigrés were given commands. Priests felt that the cause of the Church had triumphed, and set out to restore religion to France. 'Expiatory festivals' and open-air processions offended the sceptical 'Voltairian' middle classes, not least because many priests and nobles, often with the support of the mass of the population, put pressure on the possessors of *biens nationaux* to return their ill-gotten gains to the former owners. However strongly the king might insist that there was no threat to the *biens nationaux*, neither side was convinced. 'I must not be the king of two peoples', said Louis. But he was. 'To say "the regicides" or to say "those who voted"; to say "the enemies" or to say "the allies"; to say "Napoleon" or to say "Buonaparte" – that placed a huge gulf between men.'[5] Much that was done by the king or in his name – the ceremonies of expiation, the anniversaries of the deaths of Louis XVI and Marie Antoinette – symbolically widened that gulf and made it impossible for the Bourbons to become a symbol of unity, making Louis's ambition to 'relink the chain of time' a vain hope.

NAPOLEON'S HUNDRED DAYS, FEBRUARY–JUNE 1815

I may lose my throne. But I shall bury the whole world in its ruins.

Napoleon, 1813[6]

The Tiger has broken out of his den
The Ogre has been three days at sea
The Wretch has landed at Fréjus . . .
The Invader has reached Grenoble
The General has entered Lyons
Napoleon slept at Fontainebleau last night
The Emperor will proceed to the Tuileries today
His Imperial Majesty will address his loyal subjects tomorrow

Paris broadsheet[7]

Napoleon was in genteel exile as ruler of Elba, with a pension, a retinue and a little army, playing at enlightened despotism in miniature, and worrying about his future. Emissaries informed him of the Bourbons' growing unpopularity with the army, among possessors of *biens nationaux*, among non-Catholics, and among workers hit by a post-war slump and British imports. On 26 February he left Elba with 700 men, and landed at Golfe-Juan, near Cannes. Avoiding royalist areas, he made his way to the pro-Bonapartist city of Grenoble, greeted by joyful demonstrations in a region that had recently suffered the Allied occupation. At Lyons he was welcomed by demonstrations of silk workers. Troops sent to stop him refused to fire. Marshal Ney, who

5. Ibid., vol. 1, p. 145.
6. Johnson (1991), p. 75.
7. Chandler (1980), p. 19.

had promised to bring him to Paris in an iron cage, could not control his men when they met Napoleon on 17 March at Auxerre, a hotbed of Napoleonic fervour, and Ney went over to the side of his former master. During the night of 19 March, Louis XVIII left the Tuileries and made for the northern frontier. At 9 p.m. on the 20th, Napoleon arrived. The following day, a large crowd assembled outside the palace to cheer the emperor and wave the tricolour. The Powers declared Napoleon an outlaw, and on 25 March renewed the Treaty of Chaumont to prosecute the war against him. Within France, the conflicts which Louis XVIII had tried tentatively to calm burst out again. 'Nothing surprised me more on returning to France', said Napoleon, 'than this hatred of the priests and the nobility which I find as universal and as violent as at the beginning of the Revolution.' Napoleon's own proclamations used unmistakably revolutionary language.

Although many soldiers, workers and even peasants had cheered him, the middle classes and the politicians were chary. As the slippery revolutionary veteran Fouché, Napoleon's former police chief, predicted, 'That man has learnt nothing and has returned just as despotic, just as thirsty for conquest, in fact just as mad as ever . . . The whole of Europe will come down on him . . . and he will be finished inside four months'. Napoleon knew, like Louis XVIII, that he had to make political concessions. He too had a constitutional document, the Acte Additionnel, drawn up, largely by the liberal Benjamin Constant, which promised civil equality and individual liberties, and again guaranteed the 'inviolability' of the *biens nationaux*. Public reaction was unfavourable. Many were sceptical of Napoleon's sudden conversion to liberalism. His supporters on the Left disliked the Act's provision of a hereditary Chamber of Peers and its refusal of universal male suffrage. When put to a plebiscite, it received 1.5 million Yes votes to only under 6,000 Noes; but at least 5 million voters abstained.[8] The Yes vote was concentrated in the east and north, in Paris and in the Protestant areas; it was principally rural (with buyers of *biens nationaux*) rather than urban; and the urban voters were mainly civil servants and former soldiers. When a Chamber of Representatives was elected, many abstained, and those who voted elected only 80 thoroughgoing Bonapartists out of 629 deputies.

Napoleon's partisans, being a minority, were active. In the regions of former civil war in the west and south they organized armed federations. Their leaders were lawyers and officials who had previously held local power under the Republic and Empire. They were often beleaguered minorities (a few hundred in towns the size of Nantes or Toulouse) armed and organized for self-defence against royalist violence and foreign invasion, often with support from workers and some peasants. In Paris, the Federation of the Faubourgs, by far the largest spontaneous movement of support for Napoleon, reached some 20,000 men, overwhelmingly workers. The *fédérés* proclaimed that Napoleon had come to save France from 'the inquisition of the monks and the tyranny of the nobles'. In Dijon they declared their

8. Bluche (1980), p. 107.

opposition to 'the feudal nobility . . . seigneurial rights . . . tithes [and] a privileged religion which could threaten *biens nationaux*'.[9]

The deciding factor, as in 1814, was not political but military. Napoleon wanted rapid victories to induce the Allies to negotiate – a vain hope. He thrust into Belgium, surprised Wellington's mainly Anglo-Dutch army at Quatre Bras on 16 June, inflicted a serious semi-defeat on Blucher's Prussians at Ligny the same day, and having separated the two returned to finish Wellington. They met on 18 June near a village just south of Brussels: Waterloo. Napoleon, with 72,000 men, had to smash the 67,000 British, Dutch, Belgians and Hanoverians. He nearly did in a bloody slugging match described by Wellington as a damned near-run thing. Napoleon gambled everything on the final throw. Massive cavalry and infantry attacks, in which 25,000 men (one-third of the army) were killed or wounded, failed to break through Wellington's lines. Twenty years of struggle were consummated in a few acres of damp farmland; for a few minutes, the fate of Europe seemed to turn on whether the giant Lieutenant Legros, '*L'Enfonceur*', could smash open the gate of Hougoumont farm. He failed. As evening approached, the Prussians arrived to attack the French flank and rear, and Wellington ordered a general advance that turned the French failure into a rout. Waterloo was more than just a battle lost: in Hugo's words, the universe changed direction. France lost her primacy in Europe, a verdict that generations of nationalists would dream of reversing. Yet even if Napoleon had won, it might only have galvanized his enemies to redoubled efforts:[10] his time, and that of French hegemony, had passed.

Napoleon escaped and hurried back to Paris. Ministers, generals and the Chamber were unwilling to continue the war. The working-class Parisian *fédérés*, however, were full of fight, and ready to intimidate the emperor's domestic opponents. But he, unwilling to be only 'the emperor of the rabble', was once again persuaded to abdicate in favour of his son. The city surrendered on 3 July, and the stock market rose. With the Allied armies came the Bourbons. The second restoration was again lubricated by the intrigues of the two ex-priests Talleyrand and Fouché, 'vice leaning on the arm of crime', who met Louis XVIII on 6 July at Saint-Denis: 'the trusty regicide [Fouché] placed the hands that had caused the head of Louis XVI to fall between the hands of the martyr-king's brother; the apostate bishop [Talleyrand] guaranteed the oath'.[11] Louis XVIII was sufficiently cool-headed – and cold-hearted – to resign himself to such grotesque reconciliations. As in March 1814, he had no choice but to ally himself with the post-revolutionary ruling class of France, whom Fouché and Talleyrand represented.

9. Alexander (1991), passim.
10. Schroeder (1994), p. 537.
11. Chateaubriand (1947), vol. 4, book 5, p. 41.

'PARDON AND OBLIVION', 1815–20

> Legitimate monarchy would re-enter Paris behind those red uniforms which had
> just renewed their colour in Frenchmen's blood!
>
> *Chateaubriand*[12]

The Hundred Days reopened the wounds left by the Revolution. Royalists
were deeply divided over whether to treat them by ointment or cauterization.
Moderates believed Napoleon's return had been possible because many
people had felt threatened by counter-revolutionary extremism. Quite
opposite was the view of hard-liners, for whom it had happened because
unreliable men had been left in key positions. They should now be swept
away, opposition crushed, and seditious ideas uprooted. The dispute was no
easier to resolve because both sides were partly right.

The moderates, led by Louis XVIII and backed by the Allies, believed that
the restored monarchy could only survive if it could win the general loyalty,
or at least acquiescence, of the uncommitted, who would accept the
Bourbons if they guaranteed peace, order and secure enjoyment of the fruits
of the Revolution. The king, doubtless sharing Talleyrand's view that in
present circumstances treason was 'a question of dates', showered honours
and favours on useful former enemies who had guessed correctly during the
Hundred Days on which side their bread was buttered. Marshal Ney, who got
his dates wrong, was shot; General Bourmont, who defected to Napoleon but
defected back again just before Waterloo, was promoted. Robespierre's
former secretary was put in charge of political intelligence.

The hard-liners, or 'ultraroyalists' as they came to be called, included
members of the royal family itself, most importantly the heir to the throne,
the king's brother the Comte d'Artois. Ultras in the south launched a new
'White Terror' on those involved in the Hundred Days, especially where the
fédérés had themselves used violence. It recalled the earlier 'White Terror'
against the Jacobins in the 1790s. Indeed, the people involved were often the
same: Catholic death squads of peasants and workers, with noble and
bourgeois encouragement, such as that led by the notorious '*Trestaillons*'. In
Toulouse, Marseilles, Nîmes, Lyons, Perpignon, Albi, Toulon, Avignon and in
rural districts, these royalist bands – the '*Verdets*', from their green cockades,
colour of the Comte d'Artois – made hundreds of arrests, pillaged houses and
massacred prisoners, most notoriously Marshal Brune in Avignon and General
Ramel in Toulouse. Two or three hundred were killed and thousands fled.
The local authorities were unable or unwilling to restrain their partisans, until
the king and his ministers, alarmed at the violence and its effects on public
and foreign opinion, sent moderate officials to take control: some, such as
Rémusat, sent as Prefect to Toulouse, former servants of Napoleon. This
outraged hard-line royalists; some of them dreamed briefly of an autonomous

12. Ibid., vol. 4, book 5, p. 15.

'White' Midi governed by the Duc d'Angoulême. In the general elections of August 1815, they turned out in large numbers to elect thoroughgoing royalists to the Chamber of Deputies: they emerged with a huge majority, which prompted the king to call it 'une chambre introuvable'. The Chamber threw out the Talleyrand-Fouché government and insisted on a legal White Terror to follow up the mob violence of the previous weeks. Some 50–80,000 officials (a quarter or a third of the whole civil service) were sacked or otherwise punished, as were some 15,000 army officers.[13] Special summary courts (*cours prévôtales*) passed 6,000 sentences. Sedition laws gave the prefects arbitrary powers. This repression was substantial though not enormous by earlier or later standards, but it created martyrs, and created a horde of resentful men whose careers had been blighted. It was these men who had backed Napoleon during the Hundred Days and suffered for it during the 'White Terror' who formed the core of the opposition to the Bourbons during the next fifteen years, and finally defeated them in 1830.

The Hundred Days had greatly worsened France's, and the Bourbons', position. After Waterloo, 1.2 million foreign soldiers descended on two-thirds of the country and the sufferings of the 1814 invasion were redoubled. Many Allied commanders and soldiers were more than ever convinced that the French, by their renewed support for Napoleon, had forfeited all sympathy. Royal officials, and the Bourbons themselves, were treated with contempt. The occupation did not end until 1818, a crushing burden. A new treaty, the Second Treaty of Paris, shrank France to her 1790 frontiers by removing Savoy and several strategic border areas and fortresses, and imposed an indemnity of 700 million francs. French patriots thought this outrageously harsh, and it left a permanent grievance. The treaty was a blow for the king, who had been brought to Paris not by even a semblance of popular acclaim, as in 1814, but 'in the Allies' baggage-train'. He was held responsible for the terms he had no choice but to accept. One article of the treaty returned the art treasures seized by the French during the previous wars, and which had caused a sensation when exhibited to Parisians (though a German visitor deplored the negligence with which they were treated in the 'lumber room' of the Louvre). This extra humiliation the king resisted, so British troops simply removed them, including the Byzantine bronze horses that Napoleon had taken from Venice and placed on the Arc de Triomphe du Carousel, plus 2,000 paintings (among them 75 by Rubens, dozens of Rembrandts and Van Dycks and fifteen Raphaels) and 300 statues. The association with defeat and humiliation, and dependence on the hated foreign enemy was an affliction that the Bourbons were never able to shake off.

The indemnity, added to the 500 million francs that the Allied occupation cost, meant that not only could the government not cut taxes, as it had promised in 1814, but it had also to reduce expenditure. Jobs and salaries in the civil service were cut. The army shrank, adding to the discontents already created by the 1815 purge; insult was added to injury by the creation of a

13. Bertier de Sauvigny (1970), pp. 135–6.

new highly paid Royal Guard. Financial policy, directed by a former minister of Napoleon, Baron Louis, was regarded by experts as a model of prudence; but it was not popular. On top of this came a harvest failure in 1816–17 which caused widespread hunger, market riots and attacks on grain convoys, and the ominous rumour of a 'pact of famine', the old story, last heard in 1789, that people in high places were deliberately causing the dearth.

Louis XVIII chose caution. He was not interested in the details of politics, which he regarded as beneath him, but he did not want trouble and he strongly resented the ultras' disobedience. Moreover, the Allies encouraged a moderate political course. In September 1816, after a series of clashes between the king's ministers and the ultras in parliament, the 'chambre introuvable' was dissolved. There was relief in the country and (a good indicator of feeling in Paris) the stock market rose. The electorate had calmed down since the Hundred Days, and obeyed the promptings of the government, which had been using all its powers of patronage and influence against the ultras: 146 'constitutional royalists' were returned, and only 92 ultras. The turnout among the tiny electorate, however, had been low. In four departments, so few voted that no deputies could be elected. In February 1817, the government pressed its advantage by passing a new electoral law, aimed at weakening the ultras. This sort of gerrymandering, which had started during the Revolution, was regularly resorted to by the governments of the Restoration; the electoral system remained a political football under all subsequent regimes.

The youthful Elie Decazes, minor official under Napoleon, protégé of Fouché, minister of police and then the dominant minister from 1818 to 1820 as Louis XVIII's favourite (probably the last minister in French history, at least until the Fifth Republic, to occupy such a position), carried out one of the biggest administrative purges of the century. Fourteen prefects and 30 sub-prefects, all ultra sympathizers, were sacked. His new appointments, and a new batch of peers, were liberals, many of whom had supported Napoleon in 1815. Moreover, 39 per cent of deputies elected to parliament between 1817 and 1819 had supported Napoleon during the Hundred Days. Prominent among them were critics and even enemies of the Bourbons: Lafayette, veteran of the American War of Independence and hero of the 1789 Revolution; Manuel, former republican and who had rallied to Napoleon; Constant, who had drafted Napoleon's Acte Additionnel; and even Grégoire, former member of the Convention that had condemned Louis XVI to death. Such elections, in old revolutionary and Bonapartist strongholds such as Grenoble, the Sarthe and Dijon, were rightly seen to be acts of defiance. They were doubly so, in that ultras who detested Decazes voted for left-wing candidates to spite the government. In short, in favouring the election of liberals in the hope that they would support them against the ultras, the government found itself facing a new left-wing opposition whose loyalty to the Bourbons was slight. By 1819, half the Chamber – ultras and liberals combined – was in opposition.

Decazes decided that they were getting the worst of both worlds, especially at a time when student agitation in Germany and military revolts in Italy and Spain revived memories of revolution. He proposed to modify the electoral law again, this time to hamper the liberals. But in February 1820, before this switch had taken effect, came a stunning blow: the Duc de Berry, third in line to the throne and the last of the Bourbons, was murdered by a Bonapartist who aimed to destroy the Bourbon dynasty. The pro-liberal policy followed since 1814 was now utterly discredited: it seemed only to have helped the enemies of the monarchy. Decazes's 'feet slipped on the blood', commented Chateaubriand.

A new government, under the Duc de Richelieu, introduced emergency laws on press censorship and detention without trial. The electoral law was again altered to give a double vote to the wealthiest electors. The University was reorganized, with some courses and teachers suspended, including the liberal royalist Guizot, and the Ecole Normale Supérieure was closed. Of more importance than the government's measures was the electorate's reaction. A sizeable section was convinced that the liberals were ·after all dangerous, and, as after the Hundred Days, there was a swing towards the ultras. In the November 1820 general election the liberals won only 80 of the 450 seats.

THE RULE OF THE ULTRAS, 1821–27

> I have heard of men banging their heads against a wall, but it is rare to see men build a wall specially to bang their heads against.
>
> *Chateaubriand*

The ultras, led by the Comte de Villèle, now came to power, replacing Richelieu in December 1821. The ultras were typically provincial landed nobles, often former émigrés. If not attempting to turn the clock back to 1788, the ultras would have been glad to stop it at about 1790. Their strength was greatest among the wealthier electors, mainly nobles, and, of course, in the White west and south. In times of crisis as after the Hundred Days, or the murder of the Duc de Berry, they could attract wider support from a frightened electorate; in calmer times, the electorate was frightened of them. They were linked together by local Catholic societies and committees (*sociétés royales*). The most important ultra organization, the Chevaliers de la Foi, was a secret society originally founded to resist Napoleon. At its peak, it counted 120 members of parliament. Its leaders, the Duc de Montmorency and Bertier de Sauvigny, had the ear of the Comte d'Artois, later Charles X. Artois was always the ultras' patron and chief hope. As heir to the throne, he was proof that the cautious preferences of Louis XVIII would not last for ever.

Villèle's period of office (six years) is one of the longest in modern French history. He was of typical ultra background: southern squire, mayor of the royalist stronghold of Toulouse. But he was no fanatic, had a good grasp of the business of government, and a huge capacity for work. His character and ability made him one of the major politicians of the century; but they did not save him from being one of the most unsuccessful. The ultras were by no means devoid of talent; but they were a diverse collection, whose disunity was aggravated by conflicts of ambition. Some portents were good. Seven months after Berry's murder, a posthumous son, *l'enfant du miracle'*, was born to carry on the Bourbon line. In case the miracle was doubted, his mother sent out for witnesses when she was about to give birth, including a bewildered National Guard sergeant on sentry duty at the Palace and fetched in to provide street credibility. The following year, Napoleon died in exile on St Helena; Bonapartism thus lost its focus, for the emperor's only son was safely in Austrian hands and showed no inclination for madcap political adventures.

Conspiracies were a running sore during the early 1820s. Bonapartists plotted in the army: attempts to stage a coup failed lamentably, but added to tensions. The Charbonnerie (a secret society based on the Italian Carbonari) organized ineffectually for revolution, attracting some 60,000 adherents, including leading liberal politicians such as Lafayette. Ultras were convinced that some liberals were incorrigibly seditious, and liberals accused the government of fabricating plots with agents provocateurs. Both were right.

The arena in which the political contest took place was small. The electorate (men over 30 paying over 300 francs in direct tax) totalled some 110,000, which government gerrymandering reduced to some 80,000 by 1827; 60 per cent were landowners. Most constituencies were centred on small or medium-sized towns, and had some 200–400 electors; Corsica had only 40. Only men over 40, and paying 1,000 francs in tax, were eligible – only 15,000 in all, three-quarters of them landowners; some departments had only a dozen possible candidates. In these circumstances, politics turned not only on ideology or interest, but also on personal and family rivalries, and direct personal advancement.

With the administration so greatly centralized by Napoleon, posts and benefits over a vast field lay within the gift of the government and its agents (see p. 98–99). 'The State owes justice to all but favours only to its friends' was a saying coined under the Restoration, though it was equally applicable under succeeding regimes. Decorations – the *'ruban rouge'* of the Legion of Honour or the *'cordon bleu'* of the Order of St Louis – were also marks of political favour, visible proof of belonging to the in-group, a sign of victory over local rivals or enemies, and an augery of benefits to come. At a time of budget cuts, professional overcrowding, a growing younger generation eager for employment, and a ruling class riven by recent conflicts, the partisan use of State patronage helped to prolong the rifts by dividing the upper class into insiders and outsiders, and perpetuating divisions from one generation to the next.

The strength of the government and the regime was greatly enhanced in 1823 by a successful military intervention in Spain. A revolt against the Spanish Bourbons led the conservative European powers to support intervention. For the ultras, this was an opportunity not only to strike a blow against revolution and support the Bourbons' Spanish kin, but also to rally patriotic support by winning back the influence in Spain lost to the British by Napoleon. In spite of Villèle's misgivings, 100,000 French troops marched into Spain in 1823. Attempts by the Left to provoke mutiny failed. The French met little opposition, and successfully restored royal authority. There was even a satisfactory little battle when they stormed the Trocadero fortress at Cadiz. The army was pleased, and there were no more military conspiracies. Patriotic opinion was delighted with a show of strength that had been 'an affront to the pride of England'. This had been principally the idea of the foreign minister, the saturnine romantic novelist Chateaubriand, who dreamt of winning the monarchy popularity by a bold foreign policy: 'I wanted . . . to win the French by great things, to lead them to reality through dreams; that is what they love'.[14] Villèle, however, preferred diplomacy that was 'not very brilliant . . . but safe'. This dilemma, glory or safety, would perplex every French regime. Louis XVIII's answer was to sack Chateaubriand, creating a dangerous opponent. The Spanish success brought signs of a new acceptance of the regime: there were fewer reports of seditious shouts among the masses. The electorate, worried by the antics of the Charbonnerie, thoroughly gerrymandered by the prefects, and pleased by the success in Spain, was equally docile. In the general elections in March 1824, the royalists won 410 seats, the liberals only 19: this was 'la chambre retrouvée'. Ironically, the ultras' triumph contributed to their downfall and eventually that of the monarchy, for they now had the power to carry out a counter-revolutionary programme. When Louis XVIII died in September 1824, the last feeble restraint was removed. The ultras had a king, Charles X, to crown their parliamentary majority.

The ultras' aim was to strengthen the influence of the Church and the landed nobility, the two social forces most antithetical to the Revolution. The events of the 1790s had shown how powerfully the Church had served as a rallying point for enemies of the Revolution. Since the 1790s, while the revolutionary government had tried to de-Catholicize or even de-Christianize France, a religious revival had spontaneously begun, in which women were particularly active, and continued through the early 1800s. It was natural for a royalist government to swim with the tide and encourage religious revival as a pillar of the Throne. However, this again emphasized that the French had become 'two peoples', and that Crown and government represented only one party: the Church's stress on the sinfulness of the Revolution required a recantation and penitence that much of the nation was not prepared to make. Even the apolitical were annoyed at vehement priestly attacks on dancing, usury and bad books (such as Voltaire).

In 1825, against Villèle's better judgement but on the insistence of the Chevaliers de la Foi, a Sacrilege Law was passed. It punished the deliberate desecration of the consecrated eucharist as parricide: cutting off the right hand followed by decapitation. It was an inapplicable, purely symbolic

14. Yvert (1990), p. 116.

measure, but it caused predictable outrage. The coronation of Charles X in May 1825 strengthened anticlerical paranoia. Although Villèle had modernized the ceremony (with four of Napoleon's marshals playing a prominent role – a remarkable gesture, especially as one of them was Soult, Napoleon's chief-of-staff during the Hundred Days), it was of course religious and archaic. Though Romantic poets like Hugo and Lamartine found it moving, and Rossini wrote a fashionable comic opera to celebrate it, critics found it alarming and burlesque. Charles was anointed with the sacred oil brought down from heaven by a dove in the year 496, a smear of which had providentially been 'rediscovered' after revolutionary vandalism. He prostrated himself before the altar. He also 'touched', rather reluctantly, a number of people suffering from scrofula (the 'king's evil') who had spontaneously turned up; five were reported cured. All this was taken as proof of the new king's clericalism and superstition: 'The Coronation of Charles the Simple', Béranger called it. Anticlericals related that he had become a clandestine Jesuit, and secretly celebrated Mass. No oil was holy enough nowadays to make kings sacred, mused Chateaubriand.

A flood of anticlerical, and particularly anti-Jesuit, propaganda appeared in the 1820s, from the learned historical treatise of the eccentric Comte de Montlosier to the scurrilous popular songs of Béranger and the mocking pamphlets of Paul-Louis Courier, hawked the length and breadth of the land. By attacking clerical influence, the liberals could avoid risky direct criticism of the monarchy and even pose as its true defenders; but the king and the government were deliberately tarred with the clerical brush. There were anticlerical demonstrations and attacks on churches. Juries refused to convict anticlerical authors, and when magistrates' courts did so they simply turned the accused into heroes: Béranger, sentenced to nine months' imprisonment in 1828, had tens of thousands of the prosecuted songs snapped up.

The second element in the ultra programme was to strengthen the landed nobility, pillar of a stable society. The Revolution, by its confiscation of émigrés' lands, and its legal requirement that all children must inherit an equal share, deliberately undermined great noble estates. Villèle wanted to compensate former émigrés, and help them to build up new estates. Moreover, compensation would tardily pay a debt of honour owed by the Bourbons to those who had suffered in their cause. Finally, it would settle the vexed question of the *biens nationaux*. The émigrés, once compensated, would no longer press the new owners for the return of their confiscated land; the new owners would be reassured, and the market price of such property, up to 30 per cent below its real value because of the uncertainty and stigma attached to it, would rise. Everyone would be happy. Then, a law to restore a measure of primogeniture would enable the restored estates to pass on from generation to generation.

The main proposal was to indemnify former émigrés for their confiscated lands. To raise the money without increasing taxation, Villèle planned to convert government debt (the *rente*) from 5 per cent to 3 per cent bonds, saving the State 30 million francs per year in interest payments. This was reasonable if looked at dispassionately, for investors who a few years earlier had bought their *rentes* cheaply were getting an over-generous return. But nothing in France in these years was looked at dispassionately. Villèle was accused of robbing the *rentiers* to reward the émigrés: loyal Frenchmen were being penalized to profit those who had deserted to the enemy. Villèle's opponents stressed the suffering that would be inflicted on small investors – the little old ladies living on their life savings. The political damage was enormous, especially in Paris, where most *rentiers* lived. The bill was defeated in the Chamber of Peers, where there were many liberals created by Decazes before 1820.

In spite of the defeat of *rente* conversion, the bill to indemnify the émigrés went ahead in April 1825. The value of confiscated land was estimated at nearly 1,000 million francs ('*le milliard des émigrés*') and an amount approaching this (600 million) was to be reimbursed in bonds bearing interest at 3 per cent. So in cash terms, some 18 million francs per year would be paid by the State to those compensated. This caused another storm. The debate was carried on outside parliament, in the newspapers and in pamphlets. Finally the government carried the bill, in a vote that closely reflected the personal interests of members of parliament: not a good augery for a measure which had been justified as one of justice and reconciliation. In practice, the law proved a damp squib: it did not transform the situation of the government's friends, and certainly did not permit the old nobility to reconstitute its estates. Apart from a handful of enormous beneficiaries (notably the Duc d'Orléans, the Bourbons' liberal cousin) most received paltry sums: one-quarter got less than 250 francs per year. The State paid up slowly, and the market value of the bonds fell sharply. Many staunch supporters of the Bourbons (for example the Vendéen peasants whose houses and farms had been devastated) received nothing, for the law covered only confiscation; all other forms of loss remained unindemnified. Critics could rightly argue that only a small privileged group was being aided at the expense of the country as a whole. The main beneficiaries were in fact the million or so purchasers of *biens nationaux*, many of them vocal critics of the bill, for the security and value of their property rose.

Villèle's last controversial measure was the inheritance bill of 1826, aimed to protect landed estates from being split up over the generations through the shared-inheritance provisions of the Code Civil. It too was a relatively cautious proposal, to make it automatic for owners of large estates, unless they expressly chose otherwise, to bequeath a larger share to their eldest son. This too caused a mighty storm of protest. It was, in the liberal Duc de Broglie's words, a 'revolution against the Revolution',[15] aiming to restore feudalism. The bill was defeated by liberal nobles in the Chamber of Peers, which led to triumphant demonstrations in Paris. 'The Charter is saved', proclaimed the liberal paper *Le Constitutionnel*. So much damage was the regime suffering from the polemic its legislation had aroused in the press, that

15. Bertier de Sauvigny (1970), p. 387.

it introduced in December 1826 a law to curb it, unhappily described in the official *Moniteur* as 'a law of justice and love', a label that the opposition ironically adopted. Once again, a storm of criticism broke. Dissident ultras, led by Chateaubriand, joined forces with the liberals to attack Villèle. The bill had to be withdrawn, and again the opposition demonstrated triumphantly in the streets.

These proposals aroused such vehement opposition because they were believed to signify an attempt to return to the Old Regime. As one humble buyer of *biens nationaux* put it, 'I don't know what all this will lead to, but as the nobles and priests are laughing, it's sure that we have to weep'.[16] When, in 1825, a financial crisis hit France, Villèle's financial measures, especially the '*milliard des emigrés*', were inevitably blamed. The government's political situation was then truly in ruins: it had 'as many supporters as the plague would have if it gave pensions'.

THE LIBERAL REVIVAL, 1825–27

> I have my flag in my cottage
> When shall I shake off the dust
> That dulls its noble colours?
>
> *Béranger, Le Vieux Drapeau (1820)*

The liberal opposition, decimated in 1820 and 1824, was revived by the campaign against Villèle's legislation. The term 'liberal' covered a diverse coalition united by hostility to the ultras, and thus, as Alexander says, 'willing to support several alternatives to the current regime'.[17] There were intellectuals such as Benjamin Constant, the historian François Guizot and the Doctrinaire group. There were veterans of the diverse factions of the 1790s and even earlier, such as the Duc de Choiseul, Marquis Voyer d'Argenson, Marquis de Lafayette and Prince de Talleyrand. There were Bonapartists such as General Lamarque and General Foy, with a large popular following in the country. There were *nouveau riche* notables such as the Perier brothers and the Duc d'Orleans' banker, Jacques Laffitte. There were discreet republicans, mostly students or elderly survivors of the Convention of 1792 and their descendants; it was not only the nobility whose politics were hereditary. Among them were the Garnier-Pagès and Cavaignac brothers, and the future socialists Cabet, Raspail, and Blanqui. Many of these families, and thousands more obscure, had governed France at various levels during the Republic and the Empire, often acquired wealth (through office or *biens nationaux*) and still retained influence and prestige in regions such as Burgundy, the east and the Alps, where memories of the Republic were associated not with Terror and civil war, but with democracy and patriotism.

It was all these men that the ultras were trying to displace, in order to

16. Gain (1929), vol. 1, p. 184.
17. Alexander (Dec. 1994), pp. 442–69, at p. 447.

recreate the power of nobles and clergy, often former émigrés who had their own pressing reasons (not least financial) to take over public employment. The ultras used State patronage to weaken the liberals' influence and deny them a future: their sons risked finding themselves excluded, or at least greatly disadvantaged, in finding a career. This was the world brilliantly caricatured by Stendhal and Balzac, in which the belief that 'the Congregation' or the Jesuits controlled appointments to jobs was a central theme of anticlericalism. Moreover, the ultras tried to humiliate the liberals by denying the legitimacy of their beliefs and past services to a Republic and an Empire officially denounced as criminal by both State and Church.

The liberal alliance came together in self-defence. They used the legal methods of parliament and the press when these were effective, but were capable of illegal methods when press censorship or government gerrymandering seemed to turn the political balance permanently against them, as in the period after Waterloo, or the four years after the murder of the Duc de Berry. Then, underground groups such as the Charbonnerie and the Chevaliers de la Liberté planned revolution. Such methods, which invariably failed, caused dissension and recrimination and frightened off middle-of-the-road electors, helping to ensure the success of the ultras in 1820 and 1824. In response to the rule of the ultras, the opponents of the government reorganized. The conspiracies of the early 1820s had failed, but the networks remained. In the Rennes district, for example, former *fédérés* from the Hundred Days sat on the municipal council; in the Sarthe, Goyet, a Jacobin in the 1790s, still led the local liberal movement which had secured the election of Lafayette and Constant. Committees and newspapers were re-established. Candidates again presented themselves with some prospect of success.

Coordination throughout the country was provided in part by an electoral association set up in 1827 by François Guizot, a vigorous young Protestant historian from Nîmes, son of a Girondin guillotined in 1794, who had remained loyal to Louis XVIII in 1815 but who deplored ultra extremism. If its name, *Aide-toi le ciel t'aidera* ('Heaven Helps Those Who Help Themselves'), recalled cloak-and-dagger conspiracy, its function was legal and peaceful: to provide information and expertise to liberal groups and candidates struggling to stop local officials from pruning the electoral registers and harassing liberal sympathizers. Even more important was the press. Pamphlets could evade the legal controls on newspapers, and provided an immense amount of propaganda. Newspapers provided not merely news and comment but also offices, personnel and leadership, for example by designating lists of approved election candidates. The number of subscribers was small, but the number of readers was increased through cafés, clubs and reading rooms. Provincial papers tended to echo the message of their Parisian counterparts. 'Opinion', wrote Balzac, 'is made in Paris; it is manufactured with ink and paper.' This put the government at a disadvantage, for Paris and its newspapers were predominantly liberal. Of 65,000 press subscriptions in 1825, only 20,000 were to pro-government papers. Villèle tried to counteract this by secretly buying the shares of Parisian newspapers with money from the secret service funds, but with little effect. He and his successors were excessively alarmed at the hostile tide of press propaganda. The consequences of this for their morale, and their tendency to extreme pessimism and hence to over-reaction, was not the least effect of press polemic in the second half of the 1820s.

Liberal discontent found expression in the arts. The relative freedom of the Restoration, and the post-war impact of British and German Romanticism encouraged an explosion of artistic and literary creativity. Yet it was the opposition which benefited. The Romantic movement, inherently rebellious, had during the later years of the Empire tended to be attracted to traditionalism, in particular to aesthetic Catholicism and a royalism coloured by the novels of Scott. The fashionable young poets Hugo, Lamartine and the guards officer Vigny were at first fulsomely loyal to the restored king. Yet even those who remained loyal tended, like Chateaubriand or the young priest Lamennais, to criticize the reality embodied by the inglorious, workaday or philistine figures of the dropsical, gourmandizing, whist-playing Louis XVIII, the book-keeping gradgrind Villèle and the vacuous bird-slaughtering Charles X – a Restoration that was 'cold, petty and without poetry', in Balzac's words.[18] Young artists such as Hugo, Delacroix and Berlioz found themselves in conflict with a conservative artistic officialdom. Hugo proclaimed that Romanticism was liberalism in art, and he changed his life accordingly. Vigny noted in his diary

> He has told me that on thinking things over he has decided to leave the Right . . . The Victor whom I loved is no more. That Victor was a bit of a fanatic for religion and royalism, as chaste as a young girl . . . Now he has taken a fancy to bawdy talk and has become a liberal.[19]

His play *Hernani,* with its deliberately shocking language and flouting of the hallowed conventions of French classical drama, rallied the long-haired shocktroops of Romanticism, led by young Gérard de Nerval and Théophile Gautier resplendent in scarlet waistcoat, against the bald-headed defenders of convention. The 'battle of Hernani' was fought nightly in February 1830 with boos and cheers at the Théatre Français, temple of classical tradition.

How much more attractive than Restoration decorum was in retrospect the epic of Napoleon – '*quel roman que ma vie*', he had exclaimed – when young men of genius had achieved prodigies. The Hundred Days, Waterloo and St Helena were transmuted into a Romantic defiance of malevolent fate, and Napoleon into a Prometheus, punished for his daring by 'the vulture England gnawing at his heart'. A cult of Napoleon had already begun in the first years of the Restoration, propagated by demobilized soldiers. It was to reach millions, both through high and mass culture, songs, pictures, memoirs, poems. Hugo published the *Ode à la Colonne* in 1827, marking his personal and political conversion. Koechlin, the liberal mayor of Mulhouse, built

18. Hollier (1989), p. 650.
19. Johnson (1991), p. 962.

himself a house modelled on Napoleon's residence at St Helena and commissioned the sculptor Rude's masterpiece 'Napoleon waking to glory'. The published and oral stories of old soldiers, and the hugely popular songs of Béranger spread the message that the emperor had been the people's friend and the nation's protector.

The study of history too, itself partly a product of the Romantic fascination with the past, inculcated liberal themes of progress and condemnation of reaction as futile and destructive. The Revolution was rehabilitated as the epoch-making event of modern times. Augustin Thierry in 1825 explained French history as a national conflict of the Gauls (the people) against the Franks (the nobles), culminating in 1789. Assuming that history followed logical patterns, its significance for the present and the future was clear. English history seemed to point out the path for France to follow: Hugo's play *Cromwell* (1827) was followed by increasingly blunt press and pamphlet references to James II and the Glorious Revolution of 1688. The first widely read histories of the French Revolution, stressing its historic necessity, were published by two rising young liberal journalists, François Mignet and Adolphe Thiers in 1823. Far from condemning the Revolution as a crime, as Restoration propriety required, Thiers daringly praised it as a moment of lost greatness: 'Frenchmen, we who have seen since then our liberty stifled, our country invaded, our heroes shot or betraying their own glory, let us never forget those immortal days of liberty, greatness and hope!'

The strength of liberal feeling in Paris was strikingly shown in April 1827 when Charles X reviewed the National Guard. The liberal press and liberal politicians (a number of whom were officers in the force) had urged the men to shout 'Vive le Roi! A bas les ministres!', in the hope of convincing him that he was personally popular, but that the government was detested and ought to be dismissed. However, some National Guardsmen shouted 'A bas les Jesuitesses!' as the king's devoutly Catholic niece drove past, and part of the force, led by well known liberal officers, demonstrated outside Villèle's office. Villèle may have feared that the National Guard was planning a coup d'état; he certainly believed that only strong action could save the government's face. He persuaded the king to disband the Guard: a public admission that the Parisian middle class had turned against the government.

In November 1827, Villèle tried to shore up his position by a general election. No one was optimistic about the result, but waiting seemed worse still. The election campaign, during which the law required that press censorship should be suspended, was marked by violent attacks not just on the government – 'the most corrupting and the most corrupt that the world has ever seen', said *Le Journal des Débats* – but on the monarchy itself, for Charles X had become personally associated with the government's unpopularity. Opposition papers made allusions to the English revolution of 1688. 'Are we enlightened', asked *Le Constitutionnel*, 'like the English . . . under James II?'[20] The electoral organizations of both the liberals (Aide-toi le

20. Ledré (1960), pp. 76, 77.

ciel t'aidera) and of Chateaubriand's dissident royalists (Les Amis de la Presse) had worked hard on the electoral registers, and got some 25,000 new voters (25 per cent of the total) inscribed. In 20 departments the press of both oppositions designated the same candidates. The turnout was high: 85 per cent. The outcome was more disastrous for the government than expected. A likely estimate is: Villèle supporters, 195; liberals, 199; dissident Right, 31. Villèle had lost his majority, but it was not clear who had won. The news of Villèle's defeat caused joyful demonstrations in Paris. These turned into riots in the working-class districts, the first popular mobilization since the Hundred Days. Barricades were built in the districts that were to revolt in 1830: it was a dress rehearsal for revolution.

The king tried to maintain Villèle in power, but this prolonged the confusion. Finally, in January 1828 the king accepted a weak compromise government led by a relatively liberal former minister of Villèle, Martignac. It tried to win some liberal support by grudging concessions: loosening press controls, modifying the system for preparing electoral registers, taking steps to restrict Catholic schools and expelling Jesuits. This delighted the Left, who were encouraged to demand more, while angering the Right.

CHARLES X REIGNS AND RULES, 1827–30

These fools are in serious trouble and they think everything is going wonderfully.
British ambassador (attrib.)[21]

Charles X now made his political debut. His sympathy for ultra-royalism was strong, but he had neither the intelligence nor the strength of character to dominate politics. He had been glad to cling to the advice of Villèle and play the role of constitutional monarch, for which his gracious affability fitted him. With the eclipse of Villèle and the lack of a clear parliamentary majority he was obliged to play a more prominent role. For this he was worse than ill prepared. From being a frivolous and dissolute young man, he had become a frivolous and pious old man, remarks Brogan.[22] His reckless counter-revolutionary intrigues in 1789–91 had contributed to the first overthrow of the Bourbons. His disastrous choice of advisers and ministers – 'blind tactlessness or deliberate provocation', concludes Bury[23] – precipitated their second and irretrievable downfall. Admittedly, the political situation was so insoluble that a crisis was inevitable.

He rightly saw the Martignac government as a temporary expedient. His closest advisers – men of the far Right such as Bertier de Sauvigny, of the Chevaliers de la Foi, the Prince de Polignac, and the intemperate reactionary La Bourdonnaye – persuaded him that a government backed by all royalists, followers of Villèle, Chateaubriand and even Decazes, was possible, and

21. Beach (Jan. 1964), pp. 87–146, at p. 133.
22. Brogan (1957), p. 11.
23. Bury (1967), p. 38.

would enjoy a majority of 40. From January 1829, Polignac began secret negotiations to form it. In April, the king was happy to see the Martignac government humiliatingly defeated in the Chamber over a bill to make local government elective, thanks to the combined hostility of the liberals (for whom the measure was not enough) and the extreme Right (for whom it was too much). This confirmed the king in his view that compromise had failed.

In November 1829 he appointed his old friend Polignac to head a new government. Although he was not quite the lunatic religious visionary of legend, he personified for the opposition the worst of ultra vices: he had been an émigré, belonged to one of the most aristocratic Old Regime courtier families, had plotted to kill Napoleon, was 'Jesuitical' (that is, a devout Catholic) and a tool of the English (having been ambassador in London and having a Scottish wife). He chose as colleagues the loud-mouthed but ineffective White Terrorist La Bourdonnaye and the competent but detested 'traitor of Waterloo' General de Bourmont. Chateaubriand would not serve under him and so he could obtain no majority in the Chamber, and Chateaubriand's influential *Journal des Débats* added to the chorus of invective:

> Here once again is the Court with its old rancour, the émigrés with their prejudices, the priesthood with its hatred of liberty . . . Turn [the government] round whichever way you like: from every side it frightens, from every side it angers . . . Squeeze it, wring it: all that drips out are humiliations, misfortunes and dangers.

On both sides of the political arena, men began thinking of a coup d'état: ministers and officials began discreetly to discuss it; royalists in the provinces wrote to the king to urge it; prominent liberals began to plan a tax strike in response to it. The government was less threatening than bumbling. At cabinet meetings 'the king would cut up paper into bizarre shapes . . . MM. de Polignac and de Montel covered the notebooks in front of them with pen sketches . . . If someone fell asleep the king, laughing, would order them not to be woken.'[24]

In March 1830, parliament reassembled. The king's speech stigmatized the opposition's 'blameworthy manoeuvres'. The deputies replied with an address condemning the government, which was voted by 221 deputies, and delivered to the king by a delegation including known enemies of the Bourbons. Charles considered this a challenge to his prerogative, and he dissolved the Chamber in irritatingly paternalistic terms: 'As father of my people, my soul was wounded, as king I was offended'.[25] New general elections were called for June–July 1830. In retrospect, these appear the first steps towards revolution.

Charles and many of his advisers were convinced that France had reached a crisis. The combined opposition of the liberals and Chateaubriand's group on the Right made government impossible. The opposition press was preaching what they considered sedition throughout the country and

24. Bertier de Sauvigny (1970), p. 272.
25. Pilbeam (1991), p. 33.

undoubted enemies of the Bourbons were being elected to parliament. If nothing was done, they believed, France would drift into revolution. 'Better to mount our horses than mount the scaffold', said the mild-mannered Duc d'Angoulême; 'I do not want to ride in a tumbril like my brother', echoed Charles.[26] No extreme measures were immediately decided, however. The king was convinced of his own popularity among ordinary people out in the country. Even if this was correct, it was irrelevant: only the 100,000 electors and the people of Paris counted. But the king recklessly became involved personally in the political crisis, which led him to be attacked and ridiculed by the opposition press.

The government's strategy was to rally patriots. The success of Spanish intervention in 1823 showed the advantages. Charles X had heady and preposterous plans for doing a deal with the Russians to redraw the map of Europe and gain Belgium and the Rhine for France. Expeditions were sent to Greece and Madagascar. The latest scheme was an expedition against the Dey of Algiers, who had long been an irritant and who had imprudently slapped the French consul with his fan. Over 50,000 men were dispatched to take the city, and news of victory arrived in Paris in early June. However, it had little impact on the electorate. To the surprise and horror of the king and his ministers, the election results of June–July 1830 were appalling. Of the 221 deputies who had voted the hostile address, 202 had been re-elected in spite of all the government's efforts; total opposition seats were 270 to the government's 145. It had been reiterated officially that the elections were a contest between Revolution and the monarchy: between those who had been responsible for 'the profanation of churches, imprisonment, deportations, executions, drownings, shootings' and those who would 're-establish the throne and the cross, peace and liberty'. And the result was clear: 'No doubt about it, the Revolution has triumphed. Charles X is on the road that his unhappy brother took, and at the end is the scaffold . . . Safety for . . . France lies only in the unchangeable will of the king', concluded the ultraroyalist *Drapeau Blanc*. Charles agreed: 'If I gave in this time', he told ministers, 'they would finish by treating us as they treated my brother'.[27]

THE 'THREE GLORIOUS DAYS', 27–29 JULY 1830

Peuple français, peuple de braves,
La liberté rouvre ses bras,
On nous disait: soyez esclaves!
Nous avons dit: soyons soldats!

Casimir Delavigne, 'La Parisienne' (1830)

On 25 July, the ministers presented Charles with four draft ordinances (emergency decrees) ordering yet another dissolution of parliament and

26. Furet (1992), p. 321.
27. Tulard (1985), p. 321.

general elections, strict press controls and slashing the electorate by three-quarters to 25,000. Ministers argued that article 14 of the Charter applied, which gave the king power to 'make ordinances necessary for . . . the safety of the State'. It nonetheless amounted to a coup d'état. Polignac was serenely confident: 'I do not anticipate disorder, but in any case, the forces on hand in Paris are of sufficient strength to guarantee the public peace'.[28] The king took a leaf out of Louis XVI's book and went shooting at Saint Cloud.

The ordinances were published on 26 July. Minor disturbances broke out in Paris, in which printing workers, their jobs threatened by the new press restrictions, took a lead. The next day, the first of *les trois glorieuses*, there were more demonstrations and the first shots were fired, but the situation calmed down in the evening. Opposition politicians vacillated, fearing both government repression and popular revolution, and suggested a tax strike. Liberal journalists, prompted by Thiers, co-editor of *Le National*, drafted a protest. Decisive action was taken from daybreak on the 28th by workers who, waving the tricolour and shouting '*Vive l'Empereur*', began seizing arms, building barricades, and attacking the troops. 'It's no longer a riot', said the army commander Marmont, 'it's a revolution.'

The crowds had no leadership from the political class: deputies, journalists and disbanded National Guards mainly remained as onlookers, or tried vainly to arrange a compromise. A few republican or Bonapartist students were involved (though Berlioz was swotting for his exams), but casualty figures show that it was workers who did the fighting. The combattants doubtless included members of workers' societies such as the *compagnonnages*, former soldiers, probably many of the *fédérés* of 1815. As the Hundred Days had shown, many Paris workers had never accepted the Bourbons, and since then falling wages (by 30 per cent), food shortages, economic depression and unemployment over the last three years gave further reasons for anger.

The garrison was outnumbered and unprepared. Much of the army was in Algeria. No reinforcements had been brought up so as not to give warning of the coup. There proved to be only 13,000 men available, just over half consisting of the Royal Guard. As the history of the nineteenth century would repeatedly show, outnumbered troops could not be relied on in a civil conflict. Moreover, the line infantry were discontented over pay and promotion and resented the privileged Guard, which included foreign mercenaries. They began to fraternize with the crowd, and even join the revolt. The Guard, isolated, ran from the crowds assaulting the Tuileries Palace on the 29th and in a faint but disturbing echo of 10 August 1792 a few Swiss were butchered. Talleyrand, watching the scene, looked at his watch and remarked 'At 5 past 12, the elder branch of the Bourbons ceased to reign'. By the early afternoon of the 29th the fighting was over. About 150 soldiers had been killed and 600 wounded; another 1,750 had deserted. Among the Parisians, over 500 were killed, and over 1,500 wounded; the great majority were skilled workers – carpenters, joiners, locksmiths,

28. Beach (Jan. 1964), p. 141.

stonemasons, printers – aged 25–35.[29] There were very few middle-class combattants.

On 1 August, Charles X abdicated in favour of his infant grandson, the 'miracle child', and appointed the Duc d'Orléans Lieutenant-General of the Kingdom. In the provinces, even in the royalist heartlands of the Vendée and Provence, there was no significant action in support of the Bourbons; in Toulouse, Villèle stayed at home. Disappointment with the government, surprise, despair and fear had taken their toll. All over the country, liberals took control unopposed. Charles's troops were deserting; he retreated to Rambouillet, further from Paris, pursued by a motley crowd of National Guards and revolutionaries. From there he and his dwindling entourage trudged slowly to Cherbourg, and thence to exile at Holyrood. Etiquette survived revolution: round tables in houses en route had to be hastily cut square for the king to sit at them.

CONCLUSIONS

The idolatry of a name is abolished; monarchy is no longer a religion.

Chateaubriand, 1830[30]

Death is a sure symptom of illness.

Guizot

The question of whether the Restoration had a chance of survival is impossible to answer with certainty. Recent historians take various views. Few share Bertier de Sauvigny's regrets at the Bourbons' passing, but Mansel agrees that at first (until Louis XVIII's death) the prospects were good. Menager notes the decline of open dissidence after the successful intervention in Spain. Few if any now regard 1830 as the preordained 'bourgeois revolution', which leads us to focus on circumstances (such as the economic depression of the late 1820s) and, as always, on the indisputable political errors of the Bourbons and their ministers, from Villèle's detested legislation of the mid-1820s to the last fatal contortions of Charles X and Polignac.

The Bourbons had the advantage of being in place, enjoying the baleful support of the Allies, with no widely accepted alternative, and with no significant force working for revolution. However, they had few other positive advantages. At best, they were accepted without enthusiasm by most of the country, and hence were at the mercy of the sort of political errors and accidents we have seen. Always there *faute de mieux*, tepidly welcomed because they seemed to offer peace and quiet, they could never provide a focus of loyalty for the post-revolutionary nation, never offer a positive

29. Pinkney (1972), pp. 253–9.
30. Furet (1992), p. 325.

vision, never make themselves part of the country's history since 1789, except as leaders of a counter-revolutionary party that, except in a few regions, proved to be a minority even of the tiny political nation. The rhetoric, the ideology, the ceremony of the Restoration constantly referred to the sins of the revolutionary period. The very presence of the Bourbons recalled, for those who had lived under, participated in and often gloried in the Revolution and Empire, defeat, civil war and invasion. They even seemed to menace the collective and private gains the Revolution had bought at such terrible cost.

Yet these sixteen years are not merely a dead end: in many ways they were the beginning. In 1814, royalty had been forgotten, the Empire was collapsing, Catholicism was withering, the Revolution was barely a memory, representative government an exotic and unpredictable experiment. By 1830, during this time of relative freedom, the practice of parliamentary politics began, fundamental political lines were drawn and ideologies and myths elaborated: Catholic, anticlerical, liberal, Bonapartist, revolutionary, counter-revolutionary. They were to remain the foundations of French political culture throughout the century.

CHAPTER 18

THE JULY MONARCHY, 1830–48

An absolute monarchy is as impossible as an absolute republic . . . Moderation in
all things is the true source of the happiness and prosperity of nations.

Louis-Philippe[1]

The July Monarchy has few friends among historians, and ever since its own
day has been caricatured contemptuously as a 'bourgeois monarchy'. Yet its
leaders had high-minded intentions: to safeguard liberty and peace, and set
France on the high road of progress, a road marked out by the working
models of Britain and America. Few regimes have been run by such
remarkably intelligent men: its politicians' writings still repay reading, for this
was the Indian summer of French political thought. No other nineteenth-
century French regime had perspectives that seem, from the end of the
twentieth century, so 'modern': to protect the individual, to maintain
international peace and to foster economic growth. But a system similar to
that which prevailed in most of north-western Europe failed in France,
politically, intellectually and morally.

THE BEST OF REPUBLICS: THE INVENTION OF
ORLEANISM, JULY–AUGUST 1830

The July Monarchy . . . British liberty in French society, realized all our ideas.

Charles de Rémusat[2]

As the Bourbon regime disintegrated in the turmoil of the Paris streets few
were confident about what to do next. The parliamentary opposition had
been liberal monarchists whose aim had been to defeat Charles X and
Polignac, not to start a revolution. Most of those who had fought were
instinctively Bonapartist: 'Vive l'Empereur' and 'Vive Napoleon II' were the
frequently heard rallying cries; and when the fleet off Algiers received news

1. Paignon (1848), pp. 125–7.
2. Pilbeam (1991), pp. 6–7.

of the revolution, they too cheered 'Napoleon II'. However, the emperor's nineteen-year-old son was in the hands of the Austrians, and any attempt to restore the Bonaparte dynasty might lead to a repetition of 1815. A Republic too had adherents, including young journalists and students who had been with the fighters in the streets, but they had limited popular support even there, for the word 'Republic' evoked memories of violence and terror.

There was a possible solution long familiar to politicians: the Duc d'Orléans. As early as 1814 he had been thought of as an alternative king. Descendants of Louis XIV's brother, the House of Orléans had long cultivated popularity and eyed the throne. Their Paris residence, the Palais Royal, had been a centre of popular agitation in 1789. The then duke had sat in the revolutionary Convention as Philippe Egalité and acquiesced in the death of Louis XVI, whom he subsequently followed to the guillotine. His son, the present duke, had served with the revolutionary armies at the victories of Valmy and Jemappes (something his supporters harped on) and though forced to flee the Terror he had never fought in the émigré armies against France. Instead, he had travelled in Europe and America, even earning his living as a teacher. During the Restoration, he had been on lukewarm terms with the Bourbons, and had cautiously made his progressive sympathies known, the Palais Royal again becoming a meeting place for liberal politicians, fashionable artists and journalists. During the 1820s, pamphleteers had alluded to him as the William III of a French 1688, should Charles X be foolish enough to imitate James II. But there was no 'Orleanist' movement, and during the July fighting, the duke went into hiding.

A few of his acquaintances, including his banker, Jacques Laffitte, and a few politicians and journalists (the Duc de Broglie, Guizot, Thiers) acted. Thiers drafted a poster that on 30 July was all over Paris, and which defined the popular pretensions of what would become Orleanism:

> The Republic would expose us to frightful divisions: it would embroil us with Europe. The Duc d'Orléans is a prince devoted to the cause of the Revolution . . . The Duc d'Orléans is a Citizen King. [He] has carried the tricolour under enemy fire . . . he accepts the Charter as we have always wanted it. It is from the French people that he will hold his crown.

First, he had to win over the street. Many Parisians regarded him as just another Bourbon. He had to overcome the suspicion of the Bonapartists and republicans (not easily distinguishable) among the combatants. Their chief was the Marquis de Lafayette, aged hero of the American War of Independence, prominent in the 1789 Revolution and in the liberal opposition of the 1820s. He was the only popular leader to emerge from the Paris revolution. He admired the American Republic, rural and patriarchal. His experiences during the French Revolution, when he narrowly escaped the guillotine, testified to his lack of sympathy with extremism. That he should be the idolized leader of the Left in 1830 shows how little support anything smacking of Jacobinism enjoyed. Orléans rode through the turbulent streets on 31 July to meet him at the Hôtel de Ville. They agreed in admiring the

American system, for which, alas, they thought France was not yet ripe. Orléans promised 'a popular throne surrounded by republican institutions' which Lafayette agreed was 'the best of republics'. Both appeared, draped in a large tricolour, on a balcony above a cheering crowd, and the marquis embraced the duke: 'Lafayette's republican kiss made a king'.[3]

Chateaubriand's ironical epigram sums up the Janus face of Orleanism. Like all post-revolutionary regimes in France, it had to try to find some compromise between Right and Left. Orleanists saw themselves as seeking the middle way (le juste milieu) to avoid both 'anarchy' and 'despotism'. But this was regarded as a betrayal by those who soon formed a left-wing Orleanist opposition or turned to outright republicanism: the Revolution, they said, had been escamotée, conjured away. On the other hand, ignoring Charles X's instruction to proclaim his grandson king was to loyalists an unforgivable act of treachery never forgiven or forgotten, and it meant that for half a century France would have two rival royalist parties.

On 9 August the final step was taken: after a vote by the Chamber of Deputies (219 for, 33 against; but with more than 150 absent), Orléans was proclaimed Louis-Philippe I, King not of France but 'of the French', hinting at a popular mandate but deliberately ambivalent as to whether he was the heir of the Bourbons or king of the barricades. The ceremony of enthronement was appropriately secular: the 'Citizen King', in National Guard uniform, pledged before parliament to uphold the Charter and signed in triplicate. There was one significant link with the pomp of Charles X's coronation: four of Napoleon's marshals were prominent in the ceremony, proof that all regimes believed that they needed to gild themselves with national glory, even at second hand. Here too the juste milieu was to be elusive. The new monarchy had to present its installation as a patriotic victory, the overthrow of the system imposed after Waterloo: 'Remember', the young republican Godefroy Cavaignac told Orléans forcefully on 31 July, 'this is a national revolution'.[4] And yet it also proposed itself as a government that could keep the European peace.

Those who mattered in the country accepted Louis-Philippe without difficulty as the man to maintain peace, order and the post-revolutionary status quo. Only in Nantes was there significant bloodshed. There was a frantic rush for jobs at all levels as Bourbon supporters were purged. The first government were nearly all former officials or soldiers of Napoleon, and several had served the First Republic too. The army and local administration were similarly taken over by men who had opposed the ultras in the 1820s, had usually supported Napoleon in the federations during the Hundred Days, and had not infrequently been active during the Revolution.

The Charter was revised. The emergency powers that had permitted Charles X to launch his coup were deleted, as was the divine right language of the preamble. The tax qualification for the franchise was lowered from 300 to 200

---

3. Chateaubriand (1947), vol. 5, book 15, p. 237.
4. Girardet (1983), p. 12.

francs, and the minimum age for election to parliament from 40 to 30. This was intended to bring in liberals, including active supporters of the new regime such as Thiers, who was now just old enough (though only rich enough thanks to a large soft loan from his future father-in-law) to enter the Chamber. But it was not intended to transform the system: democracy was a pejorative term, and no one thought of universal suffrage. So the electorate rose from 90,000 extremely rich elderly men to 170,000 very rich middle-aged men: 5 electors per 1,000 inhabitants, less than one-sixth the proportion enfranchised by the 1832 Reform Bill in England.

Did the new regime merit its ambivalent label 'bourgeois monarchy'? This question inspired much contemporary polemic, and has not ceased to concern historians.[5] The new rulers carried out a wholesale purge of officials – 83 per cent of prefects and sub-prefects were sacked, for example – and in many cases this meant that nobles were replaced by commoners. Similarly, many nobles left or were ejected from parliament: in 1821, 58 per cent of deputies were noble, but in 1840, only 40 per cent. However, this was largely a reaction against the ultraroyalists' preference for nobles in the 1820s, and represented a return to the position of the early Restoration and Empire. Moreover, the post-1830 'bourgeois' officials and politicians were over-whelmingly men who had served before: under Louis XVIII, very often Napoleon, not infrequently the Republic, and sometimes even Louis XVI; not a few looked back with pride to many generations of hereditary state service.[6] Laffitte and Perier, both bankers (though the Periers were also an Old Regime legal family), were prime ministers in 1830–31; but far from being harbingers of a new business elite they were the last bankers to hold that office for half a century. As the years passed, increasing numbers of nobles returned to parliament and the bureaucracy. In short, those who ran the July Monarchy were the *notables* of birth, wealth or ability who had emerged from the Revolution and Empire. Except for professional men and businessmen in the cities, principally Paris, most voters, officials and deputies were and remained landowners and members of the traditional professions. They were certainly not a new class of capitalists or industrialists, and it has proved difficult to identify any precise policies they adopted that served the exclusive interests of such a group, itself divided by interest and belief.

It has been argued, nevertheless, that the July Monarchy saw a new bourgeois 'style' or 'ethos', and this was certainly reflected in literature, the arts, political discourse, and in the calculated symbolism of Louis-Philippe's bourgeois play-acting with frock-coat and umbrella. Both friends and enemies of the regime declared it to be the reign of the bourgeoisie or the *classe moyenne*. This was so in a primarily ideological sense. The Revolution had waged war on privilege, especially the 'feudal' status of the nobility.

5. Among recent writings, see Magraw (1983), ch. 2 for a single-minded attempt to resuscitate Marxist orthodoxy, and Pilbeam (1991) and Furet (1988) for discussion of the problematic concept of 'bourgeois revolution'.
6. Pilbeam (1991), pp. 133–49.

'Aristocrats' (an ideological term as elastic as kulak for a Bolshevik) had become the enemy, and many nobles (though not the nobility as a whole) joined the Bourbons' counter-revolution in exile. Their ultraroyalism led to advancement during the Restoration and to dismissal after 1830. But many leading nobles had never been active counter-revolutionaries, and some, such as Lafayette and Broglie, were prominent liberals who supprted the new regime. The *classe moyenne* who became the official pillar of the new order was also an ideological invention. Liberals tended to explain history in class terms: both 1789 and 1830 were seen as victories of the bourgeoisie over the aristocracy. Guizot conceptualized a *classe moyenne* lying between the nobility and the people, educated and hence best fitted to rational and moderate politics. But in reality, it comprised only a small section of the actual property-owning class, and included many nobles. The July Monarchy was to have the disadvantages of being ideologically a 'bourgeois' regime without the political advantages of really representing property owners as a whole.

The 1830 revolution was not the triumph of one socio-economic class over another, but of one socio-political faction over another, that of the majority of *notables* who had accepted and gained from the changes of 1789, over the ultraroyalist minority that had rejected them and lost. The victors were, as Thiers put it later, the 'party of the Revolution'; but for them the Revolution was now over. They explained their triumph in historical terms: 1830 corresponded to the English 'Glorious Revolution' of 1688, setting France once again on the road to the future.

POST-REVOLUTIONARY CONFLICTS, 1830–34: 'MOVEMENT' AND 'RESISTANCE'

The belfry of Notre Dame chimed out, on 29 July, the hour of our liberation! The cannon of Paris has silenced the cannon of Waterloo!

General Lamarque[7]

There has been no revolution; there has merely been a change in the person of the head of state.

Casimir Perier

The divisions that were to persist throughout the July Monarchy emerged at the beginning. The starting point was the meaning of 1830: was it the beginning of a new era of revolution, or a return to normality? Two questions emerged: the 'social question' and the 'national question'. The social question – the combination of the hopes for social progress aroused by revolution with awareness of the problems posed by economic modernization – led to demands that the new regime should protect urban workers against

7. In parliament, 15 Jan. 1831.

undesired economic change. The national question – hopes that France could recover her position as the mistress of a liberated Europe – led to excited calls to arms. The decision facing the new rulers was to what extent, and how, they should go along with or resist these post-revolutionary aspirations.

The 20,000 Parisian workers who had fought to save a Charter that gave them no political rights had done so because they wanted the defeat of the Bourbons, the priests, and the victors of Waterloo. This was not all, however. Popular hatred of the Bourbons had been partly caused by falling wages and unemployment. The victory of July, admitted to have been the people's victory ('C'est le peuple qui a tout fait', wrote *Le National* on 30 July), was expected to bring a government that would look with benevolence on the plight of those to whom it owed its existence. Consequently, in July, August and September 1830, the new authorities were faced with a succession of demands to ban machinery, expel immigrants, guarantee wages, limit competition, or fix hours. The printing workers, for example, recalling 'the active part we played in the events of 27, 28 and 29 July, when several of our brothers shed their blood for the cause of liberty', drew up a petition against mechanical printing, which they intended to 'place at the foot of the throne, on which the nation has set a prince whose civic actions are a certain guarantee that our demands will be listened to'.[8] Such approaches were met by the authorities at first with smug paternal advice: 'I said appropriate things which they received well', noted the Prefect of Police, '. . . they want things that are against their own real interests. I am neglecting nothing to convince them.'[9] To liberals convinced of the indisputable benefits of economic freedom, the only explanations of such demands were the ignorance of the workers, and the sinister activities of political *provocateurs*, whether republican or Carlist.[10] They were especially alarmed as in September serious riots broke out when ministers of Charles X were put on trial. In the provinces peasants occupied common land, wrecked tax offices and ransacked forests, and town-dwellers attacked church buildings. The government provided money for job-creation schemes and food subsidies, and hoped that the economy would pick up.

On 25 August 1830, revolt broke out in Brussels and led to a declaration of independence from the Netherlands. On 17 November, revolt against the Russians broke out in Warsaw. The example of the successful revolution in Paris, the expectation of French aid, and the belief that Europe was entering another period of upheaval reminiscent of the 1790s, encouraged revolt. Belgium and Poland mattered to French nationalists. Both had been satellites of France during the Napoleonic Wars. The Belgians were regarded by many Frenchmen as being in reality French; their reunion with France would be a triumph, securing part of her 'natural frontier', the Rhine. The Poles had fought loyally under Napoleon all over Europe. Consequently, French patriots

8. Festy (1908), pp. 39–40.
9. Newman, in Merriman (1975), pp. 26–7.
10. Supporters of Charles X, later called legitimists.

felt a special debt to Poland, 'the France of the North'. Moreover, they were convinced that only the Polish revolt was preventing the Russians from marching west. Polish and Belgian liberation would protect France from the machinations of the 'Holy Alliance', which, they asserted, was only waiting for a favourable moment to invade.

The government reacted prudently. To attempt to gain Belgium would bring British and Prussian intervention, with Russian and Austrian support. France, disrupted by revolution, was in no condition to fight. The army was ill trained, disorganized by the revolution, and too small. A British general reported to Wellington that 'a month's campaigning would send a third of the army into hospital . . . it would require two years to fit them for war'.[11] Moreover, every politically aware person knew that war in the 1790s had led to dictatorship, civil war and terror; Louis-Philippe and his ministers had no desire to follow that road. On the other hand, they were pressed by the Left to assert French interests and defend European freedom. The dangers of angering nationalists, especially in Paris, were clear at a time when the trial of Charles X's ministers was causing threatening demonstrations. Besides, it was conceivable that France might be forced into war. In that case, support among liberals within enemy countries, who might turn on their own reactionary governments as the Poles and Belgians had done (this scenario was particularly dear to the French Left), might give France a victory that would solve all the new regime's mounting problems. Rémusat, a supporter of the government, was 'convinced that a war would be useful, if one could limit it, naturally; I would be ready to risk it'. Louis-Philippe was not so ready to gamble and sent Talleyrand as ambassador to London – the fifth regime he had represented there – to negotiate a settlement based on 'non-intervention'.

Revolts in Italy early in 1831 added more fuel to the flames, and encouraged the French Left in their belief that Europe was on the verge of revolution. 'It is to deny the mission of France', wrote the young Edgar Quinet, 'to confine the consequences of her revolution within her own frontiers.'[12] In Le National Armand Carrel, one of the most vocal nationalists, demanded destruction of the 1815 settlement, seizure of 'natural frontiers' and aid to revolts abroad. War, the Left argued, was inevitable anyway, because the reactionary monarchies of Europe would not dare to let a revolutionary regime survive. France must therefore seize the most favourable moment to fight, which was while the Poles, the Belgians and the Italians were still up in arms: 'Make this war, make it as soon as possible [and] settle the quarrel between the old and the new Europe'.[13] In Paris and some 60 departments, sociétés nationales enrolled tens of thousands of members, including deputies, soldiers and civil servants, to organize for war: many members, disillusioned with the government's pacifism, soon turned to republicanism. Tens of thousands more flocked to the colours of the National Guard.

11. Cox (1994), p. 99.
12. Thureau-Dangin (1884–90), vol. 1, p. 52.
13. Ibid., vol. 1, p. 174.

Faced with the turbulence of the social and national questions, with strikes and demonstrations in Paris and the provinces showing that the revolution was not over, the Laffitte government appeared to be losing control. In February 1831, riots broke out in Paris when Carlists held a memorial service for the Duc de Berry. Several churches were attacked and the archbishop's library thrown into the Seine. Government officials stood by and prevented troops from intervening. Laffitte considered a cabinet reshuffle to strengthen left-wing sympathizers, and then a general election: this shift to the Left, in a bid to keep up with the radicalism sparked off by the revolution, was to be called the policy of 'Movement', and it raised the spectre of a snowballing of demands at home and intervention and war abroad. Here the king, for the first but not the last time, drew the line and in March 1831 replaced Laffitte with Perier, who was to turn the regime decisively in a conservative direction with what was called the policy of 'resistance': toughness against opponents at home combined with firm if careful action abroad.

Perier, far from being a revolutionary, had tried to arrange a compromise with Charles X, and then accepted the Duc d'Orléans as a way of maintaining order. He was a man of stern determination who for ten months dominated the king, his colleagues and the Chamber of Deputies – the only prime minister to do so throughout the regime – and halted the apparent drift into chaos and war. He stopped the king's political and diplomatic initiatives, to the latter's intense annoyance, and forced the Chamber into obedience by votes of confidence, dissolution and once by briefly resigning. His aim was to create a disciplined majority. 'He was ignorant and brutal', pronounced a colleague; 'these qualities saved France.'[14]

Perier did not want war. There was, he asserted, no obligation to aid foreign revolutionaries: 'the blood of Frenchmen belongs only to France'. He welcomed the neutralization of Belgium. There was no help for Poland. In September 1831, Warsaw fell to the Russians, and four days of rioting ensued in Paris. But Perier took calculated steps to defend French interests and save the regime's prestige at home in the face of intense nationalist criticism. He dispatched a force to Portugal; sent 70,000 troops into Belgium in August 1831 to force the Dutch out of Antwerp, awarded to Belgium by the London Conference; and in January 1832 occupied the port of Ancona, in the Papal States, to counteract the influence of Austria. But nationalists were angry that Belgium had not been annexed, and outraged that the French troops had not even blown up the Allies' monument, the Lion of Waterloo.

In November 1831, insurrection broke out in Lyons, caused by the government's refusal to sanction a wage-fixing agreement demanded by the silk-workers. Prominent in the rising were nationalist volunteers whom the government had prevented from going to fight on the side of Italian rebels. Many of the silk-workers were Italian. Repression of disorder was an essential part of the policy of 'resistance', and the rising was suppressed by military force.

14. Ibid., vol. 1, p. 367.

The link between domestic and foreign crises was dramatically demonstrated in May and June 1832. The Duchesse de Berry, mother of the child pretender 'Henry V', landed in legitimist Provence and made her way in disguise to the equally 'White' Vendée to raise revolt, hoping that if war broke out over Belgium the legitimists could bring down the regime. The local Carlists, however, were not prepared; the peasants were not suffering from religious oppression and mass conscription as in the 1790s, and only a few hundred took up arms and were quickly crushed by the army. The widowed duchess was caught hiding up a chimney in Nantes, and was shortly found to be pregnant. The scandal tarnished her romantic image, and she was deported. Carlist opposition remained, but threat of peasant revolt had proved hollow.

More serious were events in Paris. The first ever cholera epidemic in 1832, which killed nearly 20,000, had added to tensions, as rumours were rife that conspirators had caused it by poisoning drinking water. Several suspects were lynched. The disease killed Perier himself, arguably the most effective minister the July Monarchy ever had, and also the nationalist leader General Lamarque, whose funeral on 5 June became a mass demonstration, which republican secret societies turned into an insurrection, building barricades in working-class districts where some of the heaviest fighting in July 1830 had taken place. Although the rising was defeated, it showed that the regime now had bitter enemies on the Left as well as the Right. It was an unfortunate epitaph for Perier. There had been no slide into revolution and war; the maniac bellicosity of the Left had been rejected; France's interests abroad had been firmly if prudently asserted; and popular revolt had been crushed. But the brief fraternity of July 1830 had gone. Perier's insistence that the only answer to workers' demands was denial had meant that in Paris, Lyons and other cities, they turned against the regime for good. Some of them, and the republicans and nationalists who hoped to lead them, turned to violence and conspiracy more sustained and dangerous than any the Bourbons had faced.

Republican societies existed in Paris, Lyons and the patriotic east, the biggest and best known being the Société des Droits de l'Homme. After the death of Napoleon's only son in 1831, many crossed the thin dividing line from Bonapartism to republicanism. Led by youthful intellectuals and professional men they recruited several thousand members, mainly among skilled workers of the cities and small towns, who were literate, highly politicized and disillusioned with the government's refusal to listen to their economic and political demands. The years 1833 and 1834 saw exceptional strike activity, which republicans (and where they could Carlists/legitimists) were eager to encourage. The government responded by prosecuting left-wing newspapers and tightening the law forbidding associations. The authorities, as usual, were interpreting primarily economic unrest – such as attempts of the Lyons silk-workers to protect wages and working conditions in the face of foreign competition – as political sedition. The consequence was to turn many workers towards republicanism.

On 9 April 1834, several Lyons workers were put on trial for belonging to a trade union, and demonstrations in their support turned into another insurrection. At the same time, there were disturbances in Strasbourg and reports of political unrest in the army. In Paris, 150 leaders of the Société des Droits de l'Homme were arrested, but this precipitated an uprising on 13 April in the central working-class districts of the capital, the scene of fighting in 1830 and 1832. During the night of 13 April, troops moved in, and by next morning, the fighting was over. Soldiers pursuing a sniper attacked a house and killed several innocent people. This 'Rue Transnonian Massacre', immortalized in a lithograph by Daumier, remained a standing reproach against the regime, and a slogan for its enemies. For the moment, however, the government had won. The uprisings in Lyons and Paris had been crushed, and mass arrests of secret society members were carried out in Paris, Lyons and Strasbourg. The electorate, alarmed by the prospect of civil war, rallied to the government in the June 1834 general elections.

Enemies of the regime struck back. On 28 July 1835, as the king rode to a National Guard review to mark the anniversary of the 1830 revolution, a 24-barrelled 'infernal machine' blasted the procession with lumps of metal, killing fourteen but leaving Louis-Philippe with only a bruise. It was the worst of the eight assassination attempts against him. Joseph Fieschi, a Corsican ex-convict, former Bonapartist and police spy, now linked with the Société des Droits de l'Homme, had carried it out. The government passed sweeping repressive measures, the September Laws. They defined new offences (such as insulting the king, inciting insurrection, publicly adhering to another form of government), increased penalties, and changed legal procedures to facilitate prosecutions. The revolutionary Left and the legitimist Right, their societies outlawed and their press curbed, were hamstrung. With the propertied classes fearful of upheaval, the rural population largely indifferent, the artisans of Paris and Lyons beaten, and unemployment alleviated by an economic upturn, they were anyway swimming against the current. 'Resistance' had won its pyrrhic victory, but the 'popular throne surrounded by republican institutions' seemed a bad joke.

1840: THE TURNING POINT

As early as the 1834 elections, part of the electorate had shown that it wanted a thaw in the policy of 'resistance' by electing a growing number of deputies to form a Third Party, later called the *Centre-Gauche*, aiming to occupy the middle ground between resistance and movement (the constitutional elements of which now formed a 'loyal opposition' called the *Gauche dynastique*). This tendency strengthened once the threat of war and revolution had receded. The resistance 'party' splintered and its former leaders, most notably Guizot, Broglie, and Thiers, jockeyed for power. The confusion meant a succession of short governments and permitted Louis-Philippe to play an increasingly active and controversial political role. He was supported by the mass of non-party conservative deputies who saw him as a guarantee of peace and stability; they included a sizeable contingent of civil servants and businessmen. However, an opposition 'coalition' of most of the prominent parliamentary leaders, including Guizot, Thiers and Broglie, culminated in a crescendo of political clashes in 1839–40, in which Louis-Philippe himself was openly criticized for his political role. He was finally forced to call on Thiers, young, clever, hardworking, pushy and somewhat unpredictable, to form a government.

Thiers's brief period of office, from March to October 1840, was a turning point for the July Monarchy. His appointment marked a victory of parliament over the Crown, and also for the Left-Centre policy of 'transaction': winning over the dynastic Left by favours at home and a 'national' policy abroad. As Rémusat, minister of the interior, told the prefects, the government intended 'transaction . . . conciliation and the bringing together of the parties'. Yet they had no intention of taking risks: Rémusat wrote to his friend Guizot, ambassador in London, that the government 'will seem . . . especially for the first month, to be moving towards the Left. These will be the appearances . . . but I answer for the reality on the essential points' – no electoral reform and no dissolution of parliament. This balancing act included jobs for members of the dynastic Left: unfriendly prefects were removed and jobs given to left-wing *notables* and their clients. Economic legislation pleasing to the Left was introduced, concerning canals, harbours, steamship services, and the first State guarantee of interest on railway bonds.

The rhetorical keystone of the new policy was nationalism. In Thiers's words, 'have a great patriotic interest, a great motive of national honour, and you will see . . . that fine enthusiasm of the first days of our revolution reappear'. His idea was to bring back Napoleon's remains from St Helena: this was to be one of the great patriotic ceremonies of the century, the grandiose culmination of the Napoleonic gestures that the July Monarchy, at Thiers's prompting, had been making for years: completing the Arc de Triomphe, replacing Napoleon's statue on the Vendôme Column etc. But nationalism was a dangerous tool: by the time Napoleon's remains returned in pomp to Paris in December, Thiers was out of office amid foreign and domestic crisis that was fuelled by nationalist excitement. France had long supported the Albanian pasha of Egypt, Mohammed Ali, who ruled most of the Levant. He was seen as a francophile, a modernizer, and a bulwark against British and Russian expansion. In 1839, he had fought a successful campaign against his overlord, the Sultan of Turkey, and the Great Powers intervened to save the Ottoman Empire from collapse. France, while ostensibly joining with the other Powers, held up action in the hope of winning concessions for Mohammed Ali. The other governments finally lost patience and on 15 July 1840, without informing France, signed a convention that threatened force against Mohammed Ali unless he withdrew from Syria. The convention caused an immense outcry in France, where it was interpreted as a deliberate insult and a return to the hostile four-power 'Coalition' of 1815. Even the conservative *Journal des Débats* (29 July) called it 'a piece of insolence that France will not endure . . . It is necessary for her to prepare for war.' The police reported 'lively indignation, even among usually calm and peaceful people'. The poet Heine felt around him in Paris 'a joyful warlike enthusiasm . . . Frenchmen have rallied round the tricolour, and their unanimous cry is: War on perfidious Albion!' The enthusiasm of 1830 that Thiers had promised had returned with frightening force. Tocqueville warned him that 'there is no government, indeed no dynasty, that would not be exposing itself to destruction if it wished to persuade this country to stand idly by'.[15]

It was not Thiers's intention to stand idly by. He set out to intimidate foreign governments by sabre-rattling. He threatened to invade Germany, which responded with an unprecedented outburst of nationalist fervour, and Italy; Louis-Philippe talked of 'unleashing the tiger' of revolution so that oppressed peoples would revolt and call for French liberation. The bluster had effect: the Prussians, the Austrians, Queen Victoria and several British ministers wanted compromise. But Palmerston, the foreign secretary, refused to take Thiers or Mohammed Ali seriously (promising that the latter would be 'chucked into the Nile') partly because Louis-Philippe and Guizot were quietly hinting that France would not fight. In September, British steamships landed troops near Beirut and, with the help of Lebanese rebels, forced the Egyptians to retreat.

When this news reached Paris in October it further inflamed public bellicosity: 'The government has our fleets and our armies at its disposal . . . [France] will respond on the Continent, if need be, as in the Mediterranean', wrote the left-wing *Siècle* (3 October). There were nationalist demonstrations in the streets and theatres. The stock market and export trade were hit. An unprecedented strike wave broke out in response to economic difficulties but also clearly encouraged by the sudden climate of revolution. Louis-Napoleon Bonaparte, the late emperor's nephew, landed at Boulogne to try to raise military revolt. Mass demonstrations demanded electoral reform. There was another attempt to assassinate the king: the attacker, when arrested, muttered something about Beirut. In short, France had returned to the turmoil of the early 1830s that it had taken years of resistance to subdue. Thiers's answer was to continue to ride the tiger. Threats and military preparations continued, in the belief that the Powers would offer concessions to avert a European war. Louis-Philippe, however, saw things differently. Conservatives, appalled at the looming spectre of war and revolution, were looking to him to save the situation. He shared their alarm, and was eager to regain his active role in policy. Moreover, he and Guizot had convinced themselves that if Thiers went, the Powers would offer concessions in relief and gratitude. As a Russian diplomat put it, a policy of begging replaced that of threatening. On 21 October, the king refused to make a bellicose speech written for him by the government (it ended 'No sacrifice would be too great to keep [France] her position in the world . . . and your king . . . wishes to leave intact to his son that sacred heritage of independence and national

15. Ibid., vol. 4, pp. 232–4; Bury and Tombs (1986), p. 68.

honour which the French Revolution has placed in his hands'[16]) and it resigned. Guizot replaced Thiers.

The 1840 crisis was a fateful turning point for the July Monarchy. 'Transaction' – the attempt to regain popularity by conciliating the moderate Left – had failed. Louis-Philippe and the majority of the electorate had been badly frightened. The king was determined that there should be no repetition, and set his face against any political reform that might bring Thiers and the Left to power. 'I hope that people will understand that war, revolution and [Thiers] are synonymous', wrote a conservative critic.[17] On the other hand, the Left were embittered by what they saw as cowardly betrayal of the national interest by the king, Guizot and 'the bourgeoisie': as he had feared, Louis-Philippe was stigmatized as 'the foreigners' king'. But the foreigners' king, and the king of the conservative party, he was now determined to be, seeing the alternative as war and anarchy.

LOUIS-PHILIPPE AND GUIZOT, 1840–48: THE DANGERS OF PRUDENCE

> Louis-Philippe . . . would be counted among the most illustrious rulers of history if he had loved glory a little, and had a feeling for what is great to the same degree as a feeling for what is useful.
>
> *Victor Hugo[18]*

> I understand passions, shady interests, even vices. I do not understand stupidity, and do not resign myself to it.
>
> *François Guizot[19]*

For the next seven years, the alliance of Louis-Philippe and Guizot dominated politics with ultimately fatal and far-reaching consequences. Both were outstanding men by ability and character who inspired both admiration and hatred. Hugo gives a remarkable portrait of the king, whom he knew well:[20]

> simple, calm and strong; adored by his family and household; . . . singing the Marseillaise with conviction; impervious to depression, to weariness, to the beautiful and the ideal, to daring generosity, to utopias, to chimaeras, to anger, to vanity, to fear; . . . brushed eight times by regicide, and always smiling; . . . worried only by the prospect of a European upheaval; . . . governing too much and not reigning enough; . . . having something of Charlemagne and something of a pen-pusher.

Guizot, the weightiest historian and a leading political thinker of his time, a

16. Rémusat (1958), vol. 3, pp. 482–4.
17. Tudesq (1964), vol. 1, p. 510.
18. Hugo (1967), vol. 2, p. 361.
19. Johnson (1963), p. 433.
20. Hugo (1967), vol. 2, pp. 358–65.

man of austere personal integrity but unscrupulous political methods, the dominant intellectual and political leader of mid-century liberalism, was effective head of government from October 1840 onwards.

Their predominance, however, was never secure, even within the restricted political nation. In the 1842 Chamber, the pro-government conservatives had 185 seats and their Doctrinaire allies 25; Thiers's Left-Centre and Barrot's dynastic Left, the main opposition, had 100 each, while the 'non-dynastic' opposition, legitimists and crypto-republicans, had 20 each. The government, therefore, with only 210 firm supporters against 240 of the various opposition parties, needed the floating votes of independent deputies. Their supporters included a large number of civil servants (primarily judges and state prosecuters) who sat as deputies for small, poor, rural constituencies, where State patronage could easily sway votes. In contrast, the opposition represented for the most part Paris, the more urbanized and industrial north and east, and the 'Blue' towns of the west. It was not new for civil servants, especially magistrates, to sit in the Chamber. Nor was it new for governments to use threats or inducements to deputies. But with the political class bitterly divided by the 1840 crisis, anger and impatience grew towards what was attacked as an abuse of the royal prerogative and a perversion of the parliamentary system. Enemies portrayed the king as a greedy cynic, and the Calvinist Guizot as an arrogant hypocrite, like 'an honest woman who keeps a brothel'.[21] In 1842 came a blow to the dynasty more serious than any struck by would-be assassins of the secret societies: the heir to the throne, the dashing and popular Duc d'Orléans, was killed in a road accident. His death made the long-term survival of the regime more doubtful: Louis-Philippe was ageing and unpopular; the new heir was a child.

On the credit side, the 1840s saw some of the most rapid economic growth in French history. The later 1830s had seen the beginning of an extensive road-building programme, and uncertain steps towards the construction of railways. The decisive step was the Railway Law of June 1842. For ten years, railways had been inconclusively debated: vested interests (boat and stage-coach owners), regional jealousies and disagreement concerning the proper role of the State had delayed them. The government was now strong enough to force a decision: under the new law the State would carry out most of the building, and then concede the lines for a limited period for private firms to run. This enabled the State to decide the layout of the network (with military and political considerations in mind) as well as supplementing insufficient private enterprise. By the spring of 1843 contracts for rails and equipment were being awarded and by 1844 the railway companies were being set up. By April 1846, the Compagnie du Nord, the largest, had placed orders worth 25.8 million francs, and it employed 40,000 people. The orders for materials were placed largely in France, protected against English imports by tariffs, and encouraged the growth of large, modern engineering and metallurgical firms: Schneider, Anzin, de Wendel, Gouin and Cail were, or

21. Rosenvallon (1985), p. 335.

soon became, famous names. By 1847, 900 miles of railway had been built, a modest total compared with British or German programmes but a sizeable economic stimulus. Other industries shared in the boom: between 1839 and 1846, production in the mining, metal, chemical, cotton and silk industries grew by 61 per cent.[22]

Economic and social change, however, was endured at least as much as it was enjoyed. Although the birth rate was falling, total population was still growing, as all over Europe. From 1801 to 1846, it increased by 30 per cent to 35.4 million. Growth was strongest in the countryside, and the rural population reached its highest ever level in the 1840s. The numbers living on the margins of destitution increased: workers regularly migrated from the highland regions for seasonal work; children of small peasant farmers or landless labourers scraped a living from odd jobs or traditional rights such as common pasture or gleaning. So delicate was the balance that successive governments restrained enclosure of commons; but as in all developing rural societies, the management of woodland proved a constant source of conflict between local people for whom it was an essential resource, landowners who wanted commercial management, and governments wanting to prevent deforestation and avoid disorder. Although food production increased, this was due less to improvements in method and productivity than to the increased use of labour in reclaiming previously uncultivated, and often poor, land. The symptoms, especially in the more backward southern half of the country, were underemployment, hunger or the fear of hunger, frequent unrest (above all over taxation and forest laws) and migration. In 1847, for example, 20,000 left for the United States; far more moved to the towns. The last insurrection against grain shortages, a centuries-old phenomenon, took place at Buzençais, on the Loire, in 1846; the ringleaders were guillotined. Population and economic growth caused problems in the cities too. There were acute problems of overcrowding and health, as in all other developing countries, and their visibility and novelty caused widespread concern. What was specific to France was not the nature of the problems but the manner in which they were understood and the political conclusions that were drawn. Since the upheavals of the Revolution, politically aware Frenchmen of all opinions had been conscious of, indeed tended to exaggerate, the changes France had undergone, the fragility and fragmentation of French society, and the dangers of social violence. As was seen in Chapter 3, all political tendencies had in common a utopian desire to create a stable and coherent 'new order'. Economic changes seemed, especially to those not obviously benefiting, to aggravate the dangers by destabilizing society, and promoting greed, selfishness and conflict. Both Catholic paternalists and republican democrats championed those who felt themselves harmed or threatened by economic development.

Friends and enemies, as we have seen, agreed that 1830 had made France a 'bourgeois' society. Many accused the king and Guizot of exploiting, indeed

22. Pinkney (1986), ch. 2.

epitomizing, 'bourgeois' vices. The regime's cautious encouragement of economic growth, its stress on property as the qualification for political functions, its encouragement of self-help and workers' savings, were attacked as bourgeois materialism. Its political methods were stigmatized as corrupt. Its refusal to take risks in foreign affairs was attacked as the egotism of those who thought more of their property than of their country. These attacks were reiterated in parliament and the press, and backed up by a powerful range of literary and artistic propaganda (see pp. 280–85). Lemaître's celebrated stage performances as Robert Macaire, the comic bandit who caricatured bourgeois vices, were stopped when he began to mimic Louis-Philippe's appearance and mannerisms. A famous series of caricatures showed Louis-Philippe's head as a pear, and when the artist Philipon was prosecuted he naturally turned the trial into a farce, and the pear henceforth became a universally known symbol. It was this climate that made many Orleanists so eager for the regime to win prestige by a display of boldness abroad.

Nothing better illustrates the obsessions of the time than the emotions aroused by the trivial Pritchard affair of 1842. Pritchard, a former British vice-consul in Tahiti, where he was an influential nonconformist missionary, was unceremoniously expelled by French naval officers who had declared the island a protectorate. When London complained, Guizot expressed regret and agreed to pay compensation. Collective apoplexy at this supine capitulation to perfidious Albion ensued in parliament, the press and the armed services; even the king's sailor son, Joinville, published a pamphlet. In an angry debate in January 1845, the government was reduced to its hard-core supporters (nicknamed the *pritchardistes*) and had a majority in the Chamber of only eight votes. Nearly three-quarters of the *pritchardistes* were civil servants, which inspired further demands for parliamentary reform to disqualify them from sitting. The Pritchard affair sealed an anti-Guizot alliance of all the opposition groups: legitimists, republicans, dissidents among Guizot's own party, and the dynastic opposition of Barrot and Thiers.

The other emotive subject concerned religion, more precisely church schools, though it came to focus on the Jesuits. This brought together several of the issues of ideology spiced with paranoia that were discussed in earlier chapters, and provided a handy stick with which to beat Guizot. In brief, 'liberal' Catholics led by Montalembert claimed that political liberty should include liberty of education, meaning an end to the monopoly of the *Université* in secondary education, and freedom for the Church to run secondary schools on an equal footing. This led to a counter-attack on clericalism, focusing on the educational activities of 'unauthorized congregations' (religious orders which had not been officially recognized by the State), above all the Jesuits, the spine-chilling *'hommes noirs'* of left-wing mythology. Michelet and Quinet gave sensational lecture courses denouncing Jesuit machinations, opposition politicians led by Thiers and Barrot joined in, the minister of education had a breakdown and believed he was being followed by Jesuit agents, and Guizot, trying as usual to steer a middle course, pleased no one. His estrangement from the Orleanist Left meant that he was relying increasingly on Catholic legitimist voters, which further angered Blues at grass roots level.

However, in spite of the Left's rather histrionic wrath, 1846 and the general elections of July passed fairly quietly, with two now almost routine assassination attempts on Louis-Philippe. A well-wisher asked one of the royal family whether he might congratulate the king on his escape: 'Certainly', came the answer, 'we always do'. Thiers complained that the government was interested only in 'sugar cane, beetroot and budget', but so, apparently, was the electorate. France, once a great nation, sighed the historian Mignet, 'now only wishes to be a prosperous nation'. The government side gained 25–30 seats, bringing their strength to about 290, more than half of them salaried officials. Against this, the opposition mustered 123 of the dynastic opposition (which won all the seats in Paris), 37 quasi-republicans and 18 legitimists.[23] In spite of opposition diatribes, the government and the regime seemed solidly installed within the boundaries of the political nation. What, after all, did mass popularity really matter? No government in Europe depended on the love of its subjects.

The government's electoral success was due, at least in the eyes of its opponents, to its mastery of corruption: it had won only 10,000 more votes nationally than the opposition, but had carried many small constituencies where 'you can nominate a horse if we get a railway'.[24] The result led to fresh demands for parliamentary reform (the restriction of eligibility for State officials) and an extension of the franchise. The government had no desire to change the rules of a game it was so obviously winning. Yet the refusal of Guizot, the king and their supporters to contemplate reform rested on deeper causes. Had they been merely opportunists, their attitude would have been less dangerously inflexible. Guizot, as was noted above, believed that the aim of a political system was to produce rational politics; and he honestly believed that it was doing so in his hands. Change was not only unnecessary, it might unleash irrational forces at present kept in check, and France would be on the slippery slope to war and revolution. Guizot was willing to exploit the 'passions' and 'interests' of his electorate, but not compromise with the 'stupidity' of his opponents.

The 'loyal opposition', including Thiers, Barrot and Tocqueville, liberals and elitists though they were, had a different conception of politics, which necessarily involved the emotional as well as the rational. To reject all change and ignore popular 'passions' was to create the danger of revolution.

> Do you think that one can govern free peoples by nullifying and enervating all their passions? For me . . . there is only one way of taming evil passions, that is to oppose them with good passions . . . But to try to struggle simultaneously against the patriotic spirit and the revolutionary spirit is beyond the strength of any man.[25]

23. Estimates vary; I have followed Tudesq (1964).
24. Ibid., vol. 2, pp. 858, 886.
25. Tocqueville in Chamber of Deputies, 30 Nov. 1840.

They wished to give the country the impression, perhaps only the impression, of openness to political change by modest parliamentary reform and extension of the franchise to more of the middle classes. They also wanted to win popularity through patriotic policies. Guizot and the king, they believed, by their resolutely prudent foreign policy, increasingly aligned with conservative Austria, exposed themselves to the greater danger of revolution. As the young Duc d'Orléans had put it pithily: 'Better to die on the banks of the Rhine than in a Paris gutter'.

Everything went wrong for the government after 1846, abroad and at home. Spain had long been a problem, but by the summer of 1846, Guizot believed he had won a success against Britain. After labyrinthine intrigues in which politics, diplomacy and dynastic ambition were mixed, it was arranged that the young Queen Isabella should marry an ageing cousin (a match that seemed unlikely to produce an heir) while her even younger sister should marry Louis-Philippe's son the Duc de Montpensier, whose children could be expected to succeed to the throne. The British were outraged at what they considered French duplicity. However, far from pleasing Anglophobes at home, Guizot met further criticism: when he had been in the right, over Pritchard, he had given way, but now he had angered Britain by a shabby intrigue, which put the interests of Louis-Philippe's family before national honour. Moreover, the cooling of the '*entente cordiale*' pushed the French closer to Austria, which led Guizot to favour the Catholic conservative side in the Swiss civil war (who lost anyway), to make only a mild protest at Austria's annexation of independent Cracow, and to seek to discourage radicals in Italy. All this seemed to bear out Chateaubriand's scathing words: 'Philippe is a policeman; Europe can spit in his face; he would wipe himself and say thank you'.[26] But international tension made the king and Guizot determined to hang on to power at all costs, while it added to the severe crisis of confidence in financial circles caused by speculative investment in railway shares in both England and France, which was greatly aggravated by the appalling harvest of autumn 1846, the worst for 25 years.

The whole of the industrializing world was heading for a unique economic disaster that combined one of the last traditional subsistence crises (caused by crop failure) with one of the first great financial and industrial slumps, due to business and investment cycles. The first symptoms, from October 1846 onwards, were falls in share prices and lay-offs among railway construction workers and in the iron and coal industries. Crop failure caused basic food shortages and steep price rises (potato prices rose up to 400 per cent), and a consequent fall in mass consumer spending. This hit textile, wine and meat producers. In the textile town of Roubaix, for example, in May 1847 8,000 out of 13,000 workers were idle. Balance-of-payments problems caused by imports of dear food brought a rise in bank rate for the first time since 1815, which further hit small businesses and the building trade, causing more insolvency, bank failures and unemployment. Most food prices returned to

26. Furet (1992), p. 352.

normal in 1847, but the crisis left a trail of bankruptcy, debt, mass unemployment and lack of confidence which prevented industrial recovery, and led in turn to a collapse of agricultural prices in the autumn of 1847 when production recovered but consumption did not.

All over Europe, governments faced crisis, but the July Monarchy was peculiarly vulnerable. It had encouraged capital investment, and now was blamed by investors who had lost their money. Furthermore, Guizot and his supporters had justified their conservatism as a guarantee of prosperity: 'Remember what state France was in on 29 October 1840', they had argued during the 1846 elections, 'look at its state now, and choose!' He had advocated prosperity as the antidote to French 'passions': 'Let us not speak to our country of territories to conquer, of great wars, of taking vengeance. Let France prosper, live in freedom, rich, intelligent, tranquil, and we shall have no need to complain that she lacks influence in the world.'[27] He had made the call 'Enrichissez-vous'. Even when the prosperity was undeniable, his opponents had attacked him for encouraging crass materialism. But now that the bubble had burst he seemed to be condemned out of his own mouth. In business circles, usually supporters of the government, the severity of the crisis was widely blamed on government policies. It was accused of encouraging over-speculation, of reckless public spending, and of mishandling the Spanish, Swiss and Polish crises, which had caused a war scare and stock market panic. If there had been a larger electorate, wrote Le Siècle, 'industry and commerce would regain their proper rank in the State' and the government would pay more attention to their interests.[28] 'It's the government's fault if bread is dear', said the workers' paper L'Atelier, and there were food riots in eighteen departments.

The parliamentary opposition began in 1847 a reform campaign to disqualify officeholders from the Chamber of Deputies and double the electorate, inspired by the success of anti-Corn Law agitation in Britain in 1846. They held banquets (a way of circumventing legal restrictions on public assembly) to demonstrate public support. Over the next few months, 180 banquets involving more than 20,000 people were held in 28 departments, especially in the opposition heartlands of the north, Burgundy and the Paris region.[29] As the campaign proceeded, republicans became more prominent in it, especially the barrister Ledru-Rollin and the poet and historian Lamartine, a former legitimist turned romantic democrat. They refused to make any gesture of loyalty to the king and began to use the rhetoric of revolution. At a banquet at Mâcon in July 1847, Lamartine attacked 'the spirit of materialism and wheeler-dealing' of this 'regency of the bourgeoisie' and he threatened 'a revolution of contempt'.[30] Lamartine also published a wonderfully timed book, L'Histoire des Girondins (1847), a rose-tinted history of the Revolution,

27. Julien-Laferrière (1970), pp. 98, 140.
28. Tudesq, in Labrousse (1956), p. 28.
29. Tudesq (1964), vol. 2, p. 967.
30. Collingham (1988), p. 398.

which became a sensational bestseller, greatly outdoing the almost simultaneous history by the socialist Louis Blanc. Alexandre Dumas's revolutionary melodrama *Le Chevalier de la Maison Rouge* played to packed houses in Paris. Clearly, the idea of revolution, far less negatively portrayed than ever before, was in the forefront of many people's minds.

At the worst possible moment, a series of scandals broke. In July 1847 two former ministers, Teste and General Despans-Cubières, were convicted of grubby financial corruption. Both were typical dignitaries of the July Monarchy: Teste, the scion of a family that had done well out of the Revolution, had made speeches as a twelve-year-old patriot at Jacobin clubs in the 1790s, and he had governed Lyons for Napoleon during the Hundred Days; Cubières was a soldier of Napoleon. In August a leading Orleanist peer, the Duc de Choiseul-Praslin, gruesomely murdered his wife and then took poison. Even the newly ennobled Baron Victor Hugo was caught with his trousers down, and had to escape through a window. Not only did the scandals cause public disgust, they also shook the self-confidence of the regime's supporters. Commented a former minister, 'Our civilization is sick indeed, and nothing would surprise me less than a good cataclysm to put an end to it all'.[31] Guizot himself had bouts of pessimism. The king's son, the Prince de Joinville, wrote to his brother the Duc de Nemours, 'We have to face parliament with an appalling domestic situation, and a foreign one that is no better. All that is the work of the king alone, the result of the old age of a king who wants to govern, but who lacks the strength to take a virile decision.'[32]

But the regime's supporters were divided over the remedy. Some pressed Guizot to make concessions on reform, or even resign, but he insisted on postponing any move while the situation in Switzerland and Italy remained dangerous. Louis-Philippe refused all urging, even from his own family, to make concessions to 'blind and hostile passions': he told Guizot that he would refuse the royal consent to a reform act even if one were passed. He, like Guizot, was convinced that reform, followed by a general election, would bring Thiers and the Left to power, which risked leading France into a war. The reform campaign, he insisted, was 'a storm in a teacup': the opposition was divided, the government had a safe majority and it could easily repress any disorder. He was right on every point except the last.

THE UNSCHEDULED REVOLUTION, 22–24 FEBRUARY 1848

You will be the Polignac of the July Monarchy.

Member of parliament[33]

The opposition leaders' private view of the situation differed little from that of

31. Ibid., p. 395.
32. Julien-Laferrière (1970), p. 121.
33. *L'Atelier*, Feb. 1845.

the king. Though the extreme Left was eager as ever to get out and build barricades, parliamentary republicans and the dynastic Left feared that disorder would be crushed and that this would strengthen the government. Consequently, when a reform banquet planned in Paris by left-wing National Guard officers for 22 February 1848 was banned, most of the opposition decided to obey with verbal protests but secret relief. To put a brave face on their retreat, some of the parliamentary opposition proposed to impeach the government, but only 53 deputies signed. In spite of the apocalyptic talk of the previous months, revolution was not on the agenda: liberals knew that 1688 had no sequel.

Marrast, republican editor of *Le National*, however, urged civilians and National Guardsmen to turn up at the banquet to demonstrate their opposition to the government; but other republican leaders urged calm so as not to give the government 'a bloody success'. The government, sure that their firmness had cowed the opposition, kept the troops in barracks to avoid provocation, and when on the morning of 22 February groups of workers and students appeared in the streets, no strong measures were taken to disperse them. During the night and next morning, the 23rd, everything changed. Extreme left-wing groups, espousing mixtures of utopian socialism, Jacobinism and nationalism, had several thousand followers concentrated in Paris and Lyons. Several hundred belonged to conspiratorial cells eager to overthrow the regime by force. Though few in number, they were able to catalyse violence by going into the streets with weapons and building barricades, as they had in 1832, 1834 and 1839. Following usual practice, the government called out the National Guard, to provide not only military strength but, more important, the political legitimacy conferred by using the citizen militia to defend the regime. This time, however, the citizens mostly stayed at home; those who mustered shouted 'A bas Guizot! Vive la réforme!', drafted manifestos and even obstructed the regular troops. Only two of the twelve legions proved reliable. No one had expected this disaster, which suddenly showed the regime's vulnerability. It proved that the Paris middle classes, most of whom the government had stubbornly refused to enfranchise (there were only 18,000 Paris electors, though 180,000 newspaper subscribers), who had suffered in the economic crisis for which the government was blamed, and who were certainly affected by criticism of the government's supposed corruption, egotism and lack of national spirit, refused to defend it against 'the people'. Louis-Philippe was stunned by this defection. Pressed by his family and advisers to make concessions before it was too late, and determined not to attempt mass repression with regular troops (who were anyway unprepared), he agreed in mid-afternoon on the 23rd to dismiss Guizot.

At 10 o'clock that night, shots were fired on celebrating demonstrators in the Boulevard des Capucines, and some 20 civilians were killed.[34] This made the streets uncontrollable. Consequently, the king's replacement of Guizot

34. Stern (1985), p. 123.

with Molé, the conservative opposition leader, then of Molé with Thiers and Barrot, then with Barrot alone, and finally his decision to abdicate, proved always too little and too late: 'the feeling of absolute powerlessness weighed on everyone', recalled Rémusat.[35] The regular troops, hemmed in by large crowds and barricades, obstructed by the National Guard, and without clear orders, were helpless; many joined the demonstrators. A bemused Louis-Philippe slipped away from Paris, legend has it in a cab. The demoralization of the Orleanists and the gap left by the death of the Duc d'Orléans six years before were fatally obvious: had he still been alive, he might have been able to establish a popular nationalist monarchy, thus anticipating the Second Empire by four years. The last hope for the Orleans dynasty was his German-born widow and her ten-year-old son the Comte de Paris. She risked going to the Chamber with the boy in the hope that the deputies would proclaim him king. But republican and legitimist deputies (taking long-awaited revenge for 1830), led by Lamartine and the republican Ledru-Rollin, and backed up by a crowd who invaded the Chamber, prevented this. Instead, a Provisional Government of republican politicians and journalists was proclaimed. As in 1830, there was no resistance to the Parisian revolution in the rest of the country or even in Algeria, where the army was commanded by Louis-Philippe's son the Duc d'Aumale. When a regime lost Paris, it lost France.

CONCLUSION

The system that has served England so well only appeared in France to demonstrate its impossibility.

Thiers

The philosopher-historian finally turned out to be stupider than Polignac.

Sainte-Beuve[36]

Saint-Beuve's bitter and patently untrue verdict raises an interesting point. Why did such different men as Polignac and Guizot, and indeed Charles X and Louis-Philippe, representing such different beliefs and systems, meet such a similar fate? Why did a political system that worked not only in Britain, as Thiers observed, but in all the politically advanced countries in Europe, fail in France?

An obvious part of the answer is the actions of governments, which under both regimes refused to try to buy off opposition with calculated concession and so made a divided and rather timid parliamentary opposition into a reluctant catalyst of revolution. Both began as essentially compromise regimes, but both came to regard themselves as immutable and refused further

35. Tudesq (1964), vol. 2, p. 982.
36. Rosenvallon (1985), p. 335.

compromise. This was because both judged and misjudged the forces
opposing them in similar ways: they exaggerated the long-term political
consequences of concessions, believing that they would set France on a
slippery slope towards revolution and/or war (dangers that we should not
discount); but they equally underestimated the short-term danger of
intransigence, dismissing the threat of popular disorder and assuming that the
'silent majority' must rally to their support.

Apart from the obvious fact of unpopular and unrepresentative
governments becoming isolated from the true state of public opinion, there
was a comparable ideological foundation to their failures. However different
their beliefs, all regarded politics as a struggle of right against wrong in which
they represented right and legitimacy, and their opponents unreason, chaos
and disaster; they were believers, not schemers. If Charles was God's
anointed, Louis-Philippe felt no less consecrated by his unique political
experience. If Polignac was confident of divine assistance, Guizot was no less
certain that reason, history and Providence were behind him: 'He always
thought that the facts must sooner or later obey the theory'.[37] He was never
able to understand why they had not.

Yet the failure of constitutional monarchy had causes deeper than the
errors of its governments. It was, Rosenvallon has suggested, nothing less
than the failure of 'moderation' as a tendency in French political culture,
which could only envisage power in the forms of absolute monarchy or
radical republic.[38] Hence, the July Monarchy could never be more than what
it had begun as: a political stopgap. But as a stopgap it was rather successful.
Unlike its successors, it staved off major civil war and steadfastly refused to
embark on foreign war. These were the negative successes of an
eighteen-year rearguard action. More positively, it practised genuine
parliamentary government, which confirmed certain political rules (such as the
need for a parliamentary majority, approval of the budget, scrutiny of
government actions) that every future regime had eventually to accommodate.

37. Ibid., p. 350.
38. Rosenvallon (1994), pp. 179–80.

CHAPTER 19

THE SECOND REPUBLIC, 1848–51

LOST ILLUSIONS, FEBRUARY–JUNE 1848

I prefer '93 to '48. I prefer to see Titans wading through chaos than nincompoops dithering.

Hugo, March 1848[1]

With the fall of Louis-Philippe, power moved away from the *notables* and towards Parisians, particularly the crowds in the streets. Significantly, the Chamber of Deputies was deserted by 4 o'clock on 24 February, as the provisional government nominated by the deputies went to the Hôtel de Ville to be consecrated by crowd acclamation. To republican deputies, several of them sons of members of the 1792 Convention or veterans of the struggles of the 1820s – Ledru-Rollin, Lamartine, Arago, Garnier-Pagès, Crémieux, Carnot, Dupont de l'Eure (whose parliamentary career had started in 1797) and Marie – were added four non-parliamentary members: the editors of the republican paper *Le National*, Marrast, and the socialist-leaning *La Réforme*, Flocon; the prominent socialist intellectual Louis Blanc; and a token worker, Alexandre Martin, known under his *nom de guerre* in the left-wing underground Société des Saisons, 'Albert'. The leader of the government was Alphonse de Lamartine. A former legitimist, sometime diplomat, distinguished Romantic poet, scathing critic of the July Monarchy and author of the bestselling *Histoire des Girondins* (1847), which convinced republicans that he was a sincere ally, he enjoyed enormous popularity. He had the experience and standing to represent the new republic internationally as minister of foreign affairs. Moderates and conservatives throughout the country considered him a bulwark against extremism and war.

The new government, though republican to a man, hesitated to proclaim a republic, fearing adverse reaction in the provinces and abroad. But on 25 February, a massive demonstration forced their hands. On 5 March they decreed 'universal' (male) suffrage. They accepted socialist demands to promise 'work to all citizens' and the right of workers to 'associate together to

1. Hugo (1972), vol. 2, p. 314.

enjoy the legitimate profit of their labour'. A commission of enquiry, the Luxembourg Commission, composed of workers' delegates was set up under Blanc's chairmanship to propose social reforms. National Workshops – in practice militarized work gangs – were announced on 26 February to create jobs, keep unemployed workers under control and provide strong-arm support for the government if required. However, calls for the tricolour to be replaced by the red flag were resisted. The death penalty was abolished for political offences, in part to show that this republic was not that of the Terror.

In the provinces, news of revolution led to spontaneous attacks on tax offices, machinery, railways, foreign firms and workers, and in Alsace on Jews. What was considered common pasture and woodland was forcefully returned to popular use, sometimes with whole villages ceremoniously destroying hated walls and fences. Local authorities, clearly fearing the consequences of resisting the apparently invincible revolution, hastened to affirm their active loyalty. Such new-born supporters were scornfully nicknamed '*les républicains du lendemain*' (republicans the day after the revolution) as opposed to '*les républicains de la veille*' (those who had already been republicans the day before). Many kept their jobs, though of course the prefects, as the key political officers, were replaced by renamed *commissaires de la république*. Ledru-Rollin, the minister of the interior, appointed 110, recruited across the whole range of left-of-centre politics: typically, the new officials were professional men (lawyers or doctors), members of republican secret societies in the 1820s or 1830s, National Guard officers and supporters of the banquet campaign.[2]

In Paris, the general acceptance of the new regime caused immense relief among republicans – the socialist Cabet described it as 'miraculous' – and no less among royalists and property owners who had feared violence and pillage:

> We no longer even have a guard on the door . . . The Princesse de Bauffremont is as republican as Carnot or Ledru-Rollin. She told me yesterday that there could be no more question of Bourbons or royalty in France . . . The jealousy that was once shown for the upper classes has completely disappeared.[3]

Priests blessed trees of liberty, noble ladies took street collections for those wounded in the February fighting, and a spirit of optimism and fraternity – the 'spirit of '48', later recalled ironically as naive – prevailed. Dozens of new newspapers and hundreds of political clubs were founded; the novelist George Sand, locked out of her flat, could not find a locksmith to open the door as they were all at club meetings. Post-revolutionary optimism, always somewhat forced, was short-lived, for the new regime faced dangers at home and abroad reminiscent of those that had followed 1830, but worse. Its most urgent task was to face a potentially hostile Europe; its most intractable, to

2. Pilbeam (1995), p. 190.
3. Apponyi (1948), p. 27.

survive an economic crisis that the revolution had both inherited and aggravated.

The proclamation of a republic in France raised the spectre of a European war. Many at home and abroad expected it to emulate its terrible ancestor, especially as the men now in power had bitterly criticized the timidity of the July Monarchy and called for repudiation of the 1815 settlement, seizure of 'natural frontiers' and the forcible liberation of oppressed peoples. The Austrian ambassador reported that 50,000 French troops were about to march into Italy. Belgium appealed to the Great Powers for protection. Throughout Germany, troops were mobilized. In Russia, the tsar's son noted in his diary, 'for us only blood is visible on the horizon . . . A repetition of the terrible events of the end of the last century'.[4]

Lamartine and his colleagues, nationalistic though most were, had no intention of embarking on war. The army and the treasury were in appalling disarray. Yet the government could not ignore the strength of nationalist feeling on the Left. They fell back on Lamartine's skill with words: he published a 'Manifesto to Europe' on 7 March asserting the rights of France and of oppressed peoples, renouncing the treaties of 1815 in theory but accepting them in practice, and promising that France would not breach the peace. Foreign diplomats were discreetly told, reported the British ambassador, that 'public impatience [had to] be fed by high-sounding phrases'. The March uprisings in Germany, Austria (partly a consequence of fears that Metternich was preparing for war with France), Hungary and Italy, and the subsequent dispute between Prussia and Russia over the future of Poland, reduced the danger of war.

Domestic problems were more intractable. The government found itself torn between the aspirations of the republican minority, especially in Paris, and the conservatism of the majority, and the parallel conflict of urban and rural interests at a time of extreme economic dislocation: 54 per cent of Paris workers were jobless, in some trades 70 per cent. The revolution aggravated the crisis of confidence, marked by a collapse of government stock and railway shares, cessation of credit, a run on the banks, hoarding of coin, and a near standstill of business. The government faced a daunting situation: its reserves of money were almost exhausted, the collapse of the bond market meant that it could raise no loans, and tax receipts dried up as taxpayers defaulted and excise offices were burnt down. Yet the State was called upon to furnish credit to save firms and jobs, to provide unemployment benefit, to fund job-creation schemes including the National Workshops, and to strengthen the armed forces. Its immediate need was reckoned at 100 million francs. As it could not borrow and as indirect taxes were not coming in, it had to levy a direct tax. A new income tax was considered, but would take months to prepare. There seemed no practical alternative to a surcharge on existing taxes, including the land tax. A 45 per cent levy (known as the '45 centimes') was decided on 18 March to raise 160 million.

4. Lincoln (1978), p. 279.

These comprehensible decisions had disastrous political consequences. The government, mainly city republicans, were painfully aware of the sufferings of the towns, but underestimed those of the rural areas, which had suffered first from bad harvests and dearth, and then from bumper harvests, glut and price collapses, as a still depressed economy could not absorb the increased production of food, wine, brandy, silk, dyestuffs and timber. Rural industry and seasonal employment had been ruined by the same crisis that affected the cities. The government was trying in effect to transfer the burden of supporting urban unemployment and industrial credit to the countryside. There was no easy alternative, given the economic and political pressures the government faced in Paris.

Militant republicans mistrusted the provisional government's moderation. They knew that some of its members had hesitated over proclaiming the republic and recognizing the 'Right to Work'. They realized that the only effective force wholeheartedly in favour of the republic, especially the 'democratic and social republic' that would abolish poverty and inequality, was the Parisian Left. To create this ideal republic, they had to maintain political dominance within Paris by mobilizing mass popular action, democratizing the National Guard, keeping the regular army out of Paris, and postponing general elections to a Constituent Assembly at least until left-wing groups had time to organize a national campaign to inform the benighted peasantry of the benefits of the Republic.

On 17 March, 150–200,000 people – the largest rally of the entire period of the revolution – demonstrated their support for the Republic and presented the demands of the clubs. The government made minor concessions, notably postponing the general elections, but only for two weeks until 23 April. On 16 April, some trade union and club leaders tried again, staging a march on the Hôtel de Ville. The marchers were unarmed, but nevertheless aroused fears that they were planning a coup. This split the forces of the Left, some of whose leaders helped to call out the National Guard to stop the marchers, who were surrounded and jeered at by a large force of National Guards, including working-class units. For the first time since the revolution, the Left had failed to dominate the street. 'Today we are the defeated', Blanqui admitted. Lamartine recalled later, 'From that day . . . everything became easy'.

Elections to a constituent assembly were called for 23–24 April, and this brought divisions within the country into the open. Throughout the country the economic situation undermined support for pro-government republicans, and the 45 per cent tax levy – seen as a left-wing measure to favour idle Parisian workers at the peasants' expense – was fatal. While the government had always intended to provide rebates for small rural taxpayers, these were administered by mayors and local tax collectors. Their decisions were seen as arbitrary and unjust, sometimes rightly, and there was widespread refusal to pay. Attempts to seize defaulters' property caused serious, often violent, resistance, not infrequently with the connivance of local authorities and the National Guard. Conflict was worst in poor highland areas and the major wine-producing regions, hit by glut. By the end of May, only 44 million had been collected. The political damage was irreparable. 'Nothing is more frightening than the speed with which republican enthusiasm is collapsing around us', reported one official.[5] Moreover, peasant rejection of what they saw as narrowly urban and anti-rural republicanism lasted for decades, with far-reaching consequences.

The consequences were visible in the election results. The first free vote since 1792 by a mass electorate (9 million) produced a high turnout: 84 per cent. In many villages, the voters assembled after Mass and marched in a body to the nearest town where balloting took place, often led by the mayor or parish priest. Sometimes they were met by pickets of republican workers giving rather muscular hints to vote for 'good republicans'. Though all 900 members of the new Constituent Assembly called themselves republicans, fewer than 300 seats were won by moderate *republicains de la veille*', and the extreme Left won only 70–80. There were fourteen veterans of the Convention of 1792, and over 30 workers. Lamartine won a personal triumph by being elected in ten departments, though invariably with conservative support; he was clearly the royalists' favourite republican. Most Parisian workers were still loyal to the provisional government: there proved to be only about 50,000 extreme left-wing voters in the capital.

Nearly 300 crypto-royalists, mostly Orleanists, were elected. Socially, the new Assembly was similar to July Monarchy parliaments: most deputies were rich enough to have been eligible under Louis-Philippe, and about half had actually held elected office, or were close relatives of men who had. The predominantly peasant voters chose more landowners, nobles and priests than had the limited electorate of the July Monarchy. Indeed in some regions, particularly the counter-revolutionary west and south, they threw out the 'Blue' liberal politicians who had dominated politics since 1830. But also in the economically more developed north, support for the Republic was limited. Those who wished to 'bring back 1793 and its monstrous cortège' had been ousted, commented a conservative paper. The results provoked riots by disappointed workers in Limoges, Elboeuf, Amiens, Nîmes and Rouen, where there occurred the first serious violence since the revolution, with artillery used against the rioters.

THE ROAD TO CIVIL WAR: MAY–JUNE 1848

You who don't know what poverty is, you reproach us for the 23 sous per day that we are given by the state. We don't earn them, you say. Well, by God, we know that as well as you, and that is what leads us to despair . . . But we have to eat, and we have to feed our families

National Workshops members, 27 May[6]

The Provisional Government handed over to the new Assembly, which

5. Tudesq (1964), vol. 2, p. 1053.
6. Traugott (1985), p. 153.

returned it to office as the Executive Commission, shorn of its socialist members Blanc and Albert; Ledru-Rollin was kept on the insistence of Lamartine, who hoped his presence might avert a clash with the extreme Left. In this he was disappointed: the Paris clubs reacted angrily to the election results and sought an opportunity to confront the new Assembly and prevent it from turning away from the 'democratic and social republic'.

The first clash came over Poland, which had remained a danger point on the European scene and the cause of passionate debate in France. Early in May, Polish rebels were being bombarded in Cracow by the Austrians and harried in Posen by the Prussians. The extreme Left organized a mass demonstration in favour of Poland, which some hoped would also give them the chance of imposing their will on the Assembly. On 15 May, over 20,000 marched, unarmed, to the Place de la Révolution, just across the Seine from the Constituent Assembly. Apparently spontaneously, about 3,000 made a rush across the bridge and burst into the Assembly. There followed several hours of noisy and sweaty tumult, with the deputies keeping their seats and the intruders attempting to make speeches. The leaders Raspail, Barbès and Blanqui demanded the immediate dispatch of an army to Poland (thus starting a European war), a billion-franc tax on the rich and the removal of regular troops from Paris. Finally, the noise of drums was heard outside as the Garde Mobile and Garde Nationale came to the Assembly's rescue, the crowd dispersed, and many of the leaders were arrested. This failed parody of the *journées* of the 1790s was serious because it frightened and angered moderate republicans and conservatives. They believed that extremist agitation had to be defeated, and more troops were quietly brought into Paris. Cooler heads might have realized that the political danger was now receding. But the Assembly took measures that created opposition even among Paris workers who had so far supported the government against the extremists. On 16 May, it ordered the dissolution of the Luxembourg Commission, the centre of Paris radicalism. A few days later, it was the turn of the National Workshops.

The numbers enrolled in the Workshops had ballooned from 28,000 to 120,000. Unpopular with taxpayers and liberal economists as expensive, unproductive (for there was no real work for them) and a distortion of the labour market, they had been tolerated only as a temporary crisis measure. For some on the Left, however, the Workshops, although unsatisfactory in operation, were the first step towards a socialist 'organization of labour', and the concrete result of the February pledge of the 'right to work'; they also put bread on the tables of tens of thousands of families. The Executive Commission, alarmed at their spiralling cost, and harassed by anti-tax revolts in the provinces which reached a peak in June, was eager to move some of their members on to railway construction and land reclamation away from Paris, while encouraging private employers and the army to take on as many as possible. The events of 15 May led conservatives to press the government to act quickly to remove what they saw as an 'army of revolution'. In fact, the Workshops had kept most of their members out of militant politics, and the failures of the extreme Left were partly due to the Workshops' continuing loyalty to the government. Yet after long and violent debate on 19, 20 and 21 June, the Assembly decided to abolish them. Their men were given the choice between the army and land reclamation in central France.

The next day, 22 June, Workshop men with their company banners held protest meetings. On the 23rd, barricades were built in the working-class eastern quarters. The National Guard of those districts, largely working-class and with elected officers, sided with the insurgents. The minister of war, General Cavaignac, refused to commit his forces at once, fearing a repetition of February when small dispersed units had been cut off by crowds and barricades. The rebels were thus given time to prepare. Consequently, when serious fighting began on the 24th, it was a real urban battle: large bodies of troops with artillery assaulting the barricaded rebel-held districts in the south and east of the city: the Pantheon, the Barrière d'Italie, above all the Faubourg Saint-Antoine. It has often been suggested that this was a deliberate trap to eliminate the Paris Left; but professional military caution seems a more likely explanation. On the rebel side, some 40–50,000 people were involved, with perhaps 15,000 actually fighting.[7] About half were men of the Workshops, many of them also National Guards. The resistance was spontaneous, with improvised leaders – Workshop officers, National Guards, club officials – known only in their own districts. Even the highest estimates of numbers show that the insurgents were a minority among over 200,000 workers in Paris and even among the National Workshop members. Most of these stayed out of the fighting on the urging of their officers and with the encouragement of the government, which continued their pay. Most parts of the city were untouched by the fighting. Republicans and workers faced a painful dilemma: while some joined the rebels, others saw the revolt as an attack on the republic and on universal suffrage, fomented by monarchists or foreign agents. But some rebels too believed that they were fighting to defend the republic against a monarchist coup: it was rumoured that the Bourbon white flag was flying over the parliament building. Fighting did not end until the morning of the 26th, when the Faubourg Saint-Antoine surrendered. The total of casualties (killed and wounded) is not known precisely, but one estimate is 4,000 for the government troops and 6,000 for the insurgents.[8] This was the bloodiest fighting Paris had yet seen.

Leading the fight against the rebels was the Garde Mobile. This 14,000-strong force, set up after the February revolution, was regarded as a left-wing body, like the Workshops themselves, and in social composition it was nearly identical with the rebels. Two 'armies of the poor' fought each other across the barricades.[9] Does this show that the conflict was not a 'class war'? In the eyes of the elite it was precisely that. They saw it as the eruption of a profound social malady, a 'servile revolt' of the *classes dangereuses*, a

7. Ibid., pp. 201–2; Tilly and Lees, in Price (1975), p. 186.
8. Chesnais (1976), p. 167.
9. Traugott (1985); see also Gossez (May 1956).

warning of horrors to come. 'It suddenly showed terrified society monstrous and unknown forms', wrote Hugo. It was 'civilization attacked by cynicism and defending itself by barbarity. On one side, the despair of the people, on the other, the despair of society.' But he had no doubt which side had to win: 'Saving society, as Paris did in June, is one might almost say saving the life of the human race'.[10] This was, as Flaubert realized, 'an outburst of fear. They took vengeance on newspapers, clubs, meetings, on all that had exasperated them in the past three months.'[11]

In the provinces too, the revolt caused panic. *Notables* and peasants mounted guard in case the 'Reds' were coming. National Guards from 53 departments, fearing a Parisian socialist dictatorship, turned out to fight the rebels; eventually over 100,000 made it to the capital. On their return home they were feted as saviours: 'The scoundrels who yearned for the deaths of good citizens, for pillage, arson, theft, the abolition of the family, have been beaten', wrote a Bordeaux paper.[12]

Myths of the Terror were easily revived. An army general and the archbishop of Paris were both shot in confused circumstances while trying to parley with the rebels, and the events were luridly reported as proof of mob savagery. Army prisoners were said to have been burned alive or sawn in two. So the stage was set for repression. Many rebel prisoners were shot; others were held in appalling conditions without trial, and 5,000 transported en masse to Algeria. The gulfs between Paris and the provinces, and between urban workers and the rest of the country, were further widened. 'Paris must finally realize', wrote one provincial paper, 'that it is only one-thirty-sixth of France, and that the provinces, while they look to it for a lead, will not leave in its hands a tyrant's sceptre or a slave-driver's rod.' For the first time since 1789, notes Furet, France was governing Paris.[13]

The Assembly voted full powers to General Cavaignac. France had found a sterner saviour than Lamartine. In the provinces, the *notables* increasingly resumed the leadership of a frightened population. The men and the measures associated with revolution – the 'Right to Work', tax reform, railway nationalization – were all tarred with the brush of the July revolt. In the Constituent Assembly, conservatives organized as the 'Party of Order': 300–400 deputies, under the party leaders of the July Monarchy (Thiers, Molé, Berryer) and controlling a network of conservative committees and newspapers. During the summer and autumn of 1848, they set out to roll back the tide of political and social radicalism that had emerged since February. In July, Proudhon, the now very isolated socialist deputy and theorist, proposed to the Assembly a programme to solve the economic crisis and to begin to transform France into a socialist society. He advocated universal cheap credit and the reduction of all rents by two-thirds: the

10. Hugo (1972), vol. 2, pp. 346–7.
11. Brogan (1957), p. 97.
12. Tudesq (1964), vol. 2, p. 1110.
13. Vidalenc (1948), pp. 83–144, at p. 84; Furet (1992), p. 409.

Assembly, by 691 votes to 2, condemned Proudhon's plan as 'an odious attack on the principles of public morality'. However, two new populist movements were rapidly to transform the political scene.

THE SURPRISES OF DEMOCRACY: BONAPARTE AND THE DÉMOCRATES-SOCIALISTES

The triumph of Louis-Napoleon Bonaparte

> The other day I asked a little child of five what Napoleon was. He answered 'Well, he's our emperor; he's the best'.
>
> Victor Hugo, 1834[14]

> The name of Napoleon is a programme in itself.
>
> Louis-Napoleon Bonaparte, 1849[15]

A new political force, unexpected and irresistible, emerged suddenly in the summer of 1848, just as Hugo's five-year-old was about to become a voter: Bonapartism. Napoleon-worship had immense emotional force, but no political focus. When Louis-Napoleon Bonaparte, the emperor's nephew, had tried in 1836 and 1840 to seize power, he had failed humiliatingly. Sentenced to life imprisonment after the second attempt, he had escaped in 1846. Little was heard of him until 1848, although he was known to have progressive ideas for relieving social problems, as is the wont of pretenders. The political class did not take him seriously: there was no logical reason why a mediocre nephew should inherit the prestige of a man universally acknowledged as a genius. The first shock came in June 1848, when Bonaparte was elected to the Constituent Assembly. In response to criticism, he quietly resigned, protesting that he had no intention of causing disquiet. In by-elections in September, however, he was re-elected by five departments, coming top of the poll in Paris.

The press and the political class were dumbfounded. Their almost unanimous contempt for Bonaparte had been ignored by a broad cross-section of voters: one of his posters was signed by a 'notary', a 'merchant', a 'manufacturer', two 'ex-Luxembourg delegates' and a 'worker'. The Assembly could still have scotched his chances. It had decided, with some misgivings, to have a president of the Republic in its new constitution, and to make him eligible by universal suffrage, rather than nominated by parliament. It could have barred members of former ruling families from standing, but after a debate decided against it. The time-honoured explanation is that when Bonaparte himself spoke he appeared such a tongue-tied nonentity, short, unimpressive and with a German accent, that it seemed unnecessary to bar him. There were other, more plausible, reasons

14. Hugo (1972), vol. 1, p. 139.
15. Rémond (1968), vol. 1, p. 105.

not to exclude fallen dynasties, however: some conservatives liked the idea of a tame Bonaparte as puppet president, former Orleanists hoped that one of Louis-Philippe's sons would be elected, and idealistic republicans were reluctant to place limitations on the people's choice.

Once the presidential election campaign got under way, it became clear that Bonaparte would win; one of his aides even ordered furnishings for the Elysée. The other candidates were unpopular, or simply unknown to the mass electorate. Some voters were said to think that Lamartine was a woman named Martine, and Ledru-Rollin *le duc Rollin*. It is not just that the Bonaparte name was universally recognizable, important though this doubtless was. A Bonaparte also embodied shared memories, ideas and aspirations. It says much about the importance of political tradition that both the main candidates were principally qualified by descent: Cavaignac was the son of a regicide member of the 1792 Convention. The Party of Order decided to climb on the bandwagon, prompted by Thiers, who thought Bonaparte 'a cretin' who would make a docile figurehead. Whatever the politicians did or did not do made little difference: Rémusat thought that all their efforts added perhaps 50,000 votes to the 5,000,000 he would have won unaided.

The vote, on 10–11 December 1848, was truly astonishing – 'not an election, but an acclamation':[16]

Bonaparte	5,534,520
Cavaignac (moderate republican)	1,448,302
Ledru-Rollin (radical republican)	371,431
Raspail (socialist)	36,964
Lamartine (moderate republican)	17,914
Changarnier (conservative)	4,687 [17]

Bonaparte won a majority in every department except four: two in the west and two in the south, where memories of past conflicts left voters too polarized to be attracted to the Bonapartist synthesis (see pp. 258–60). Everywhere else, he triumphed. This was not merely sentimental voting for a famous name, but a peasant revolt against the whole political class and the *notables*. Significantly, there were shouts of 'Vive Napoléon! A bas les riches!', for just as they believed that Napoleon I had been a people's emperor, so they believed his nephew would be a people's president: 'Napoleon will be their saviour. Napoleon will get rid of all their burdens . . . So away with the priest, the lawyer, the landlord, the gentleman, the moneylender, the rich!'[18]

The Party of Order (alias Union Libérale) were happy with the rout of the republicans. They regarded Bonaparte as their creature. He was new to the country, unfamiliar with its political personnel and the workings of its

16. Girardin, in Bury (1969), p. 82.
17. Bluche (1980), p. 265.
18. Proudhon's *Le Peuple* (9 Dec.), in Tudesq (1965), p. 229.

government. In recognition of this, he dined at Thiers's house on the night of his victory. More importantly, he took Thiers's advice and appointed Barrot, Louis-Philippe's last ephemeral prime minister, to head his first government. It must have seemed that the revolution of 1848 had been consigned to the scrapheap of history. So the Party of Order, reassured that Bonaparte could please the masses while they exercised real power, set about rooting out the remnants of revolution, and erecting the bulwarks of a more conservative future society.

It was in Italy in April 1849 that their first dramatic action took place. During 1848, revolts across Italy, including the Papal States, had set up independent city republics, while Sardinia had tried to increase its own power at Austrian expense by invading Lombardy. Against the odds, Austria managed to restore its power in northern Italy and defeat Sardinia in August 1848. Though French republicans supported Italian liberation, and French patriots generally opposed Austrian influence, they had avoided involvement for fear of a major war. Bonaparte now wanted an international Congress to discuss the whole Italian question, in the hope that he could alter the 1815 settlement without war. Britain and Austria were unsympathetic. With Austrian power largely restored, the likelihood arose that the Roman Republic (which had forced the pope into exile) would be attacked by Austria. No French government would willingly permit such a humiliating extension of Austrian power, and in April 1849 a French expeditionary force was sent to Rome. They were supposed to mediate a settlement between the pope and the revolutionaries that would satisfy both republican and Catholic opinion in France: an attempt to square a circle that would prove typical of Bonaparte. However, the Roman republicans fought off the French advance. Bonaparte had no intention of letting his first venture into foreign policy end with a humiliating defeat. Moreover, the general elections to the Legislative Assembly in May 1849 had increased the majority of the Party of Order, which detested the Roman republic. So the French troops were ordered to fight their way into Rome. They did, the Republic fell, and the pope returned.

On 13 June there were demonstrations in Paris and Lyons against this betrayal of republican values. They were suppressed. Conservatives accused the demonstrators of attempting a coup d'état, and the leaders, including Ledru-Rollin (to whom was attributed the immortal comment 'I am their leader, I must follow them'), fled abroad. Bonaparte, however, was not willing to act simply as the instrument for restoring oppressive papal rule. He could not change his government's policy, given the strength of the Party of Order, but he wrote a letter, leaked to the press, in which he attacked the evils of papal government and called for fundamental reforms. This caused a furore among Catholics at home, and the whole government resigned. Far from begging for mercy, Bonaparte appointed a new government, this time not chosen by the Party of Order. He also declared that policy would follow 'a unique and firm direction' – a Bonapartist one. This was his first rift with the Party of Order, and a sign of things to come.

Nevertheless, the Party of Order in the National Assembly pursued its policy of eradicating revolution at home, what one called 'a Rome expedition in the interior'. There were three major areas to which conservatives turned their attention. In July 1849 a new press law was voted, aimed at restricting socialist propaganda. In January 1850, the Assembly debated proposals for social reform produced by its Public Assistance Commission whose spokesman was Thiers, pursuing his crusade against socialism. As an antidote to socialism, the Commission, influenced by Catholic philanthropy, were eager to improve charitable provision and show that they were sensitive to the sufferings of the poor, though the concrete results were small (see p. 179).

The third area was education. The conservatives wished to prevent the school system from being used for propaganda by the Left, and ensure that it would be used to inculcate conservative values. Here again, Thiers took the leading role as chairman of the parliamentary commission, which struck a bargain between non-Catholic Voltairians such as himself and Catholics eager to extend the Church's educational activity. Thiers's indiscreet remarks are a revealing guide to the thinking of frightened conservatives in the aftermath of 1848.[19] Education was socially dangerous if too widely extended: 'education is a beginning of affluence, and affluence is not reserved to all'; 'I consider things as they are: I cannot consent to light a fire under an empty pot'. Schoolteachers, the only rival to the influence of the clergy in the villages – 'veritable anti-priests' – were dangerous sources of left-wing propaganda, and must be severely controlled. In fact, 1,200 were suspended or sacked.[20] Conversely, the role of the clergy in elementary education, though not in secondary or higher, was extended. The Falloux Law was voted on 15 March 1850 after bitter debate. It cut back the elementary school curriculum to religious instruction and the three Rs, Catholic influence in the State system increased, and independent Church schools expanded over the next generation. This was a landmark. It made control of schools a major political battleground for a century. It allied the Catholic Church once more with conservatism, and helped make anticlericalism an essential characteristic of the Left.

An immediate response to this legislation came in by-elections in March and April 1850, marked by the victory of four 'Reds' in Paris. The winning candidates horrified conservatives: de Flotte, an insurgent in the June Days; Carnot, former left-wing minister of education whose election was clearly a protest against the Falloux Law; Vidal, an associate of the socialist Louis Blanc and a supporter of the utopianism that the Assembly had recently ostentatiously rejected; and Eugène Sue, bestselling novelist who romantically vindicated the goodness of ordinary people, and denounced the dastardly machinations of the Jesuits to whom the Falloux Law had just given a foothold in French education. Conservatives suddenly realized that the Reds were still not defeated, and that the 250 seats they had already won in the May 1849 elections were only a beginning.

19. Chenesseau (1937), pp. 31–2, 39–40, 153–4, 192.
20. Price (1972), p. 257.

Their response was the law of 31 May 1850. This reflected the social fears of mid-nineteenth-century conservatives: it disfranchised all men with judicial records, all those with less than three years' residence, and all those who could not prove their residence from the tax registers: a way of reintroducing a property qualification by the back door. As some realized, not all those disfranchised would be Red voters: many would be deferential peasants and loyal old retainers. But to most conservatives, the enemy to be feared were the rootless, the propertyless, and the criminal, what deputies called 'the army of evil', 'the dangerous people', and what Thiers, once again summing up conservatives' feelings in a notorious phrase, called *'la vile multitude'*.[21] While not ostensibly contravening the constitutional guarantee of universal (male) suffrage, the law reduced the electorate from 9,680,000 to 6,800,000. Hugo bitterly mocked the Right:

> Take away three million electors, take away four, take away nine . . . What you will not take away are your own mistakes, all the contradictions of your policy of repression, your fatal incapacity, your ignorance of the country today, the antipathy that you feel for it and it feels for you.[22]

Indeed, the 1850 law, the culmination of a policy of negation, was the mark of a Party of Order that was not only frightened but which, for the most part, could not think how to manage a mass electorate except by repression. They succeeded only in alienating moderate republicans, driving the Reds underground and galvanizing them to determined efforts to defend their votes, and handing an effective weapon to Bonaparte, who was soon to present himself as the defender of universal suffrage, and who would eventually emerge as the real victor in the conflict.

The rise of the démoc-socs

> Good villagers vote for the Mountain,
> . . . The taxes on drink will disappear,
> . . . Without charge you will have schools
> And money at most at 3 per cent.
>
> *Song of the Vine-growers, 1850*[23]

The growth of a new republican-socialist movement, aiming to mobilize mass support in the country, not just in one or two cities, had been galvanized by Bonaparte's landslide victory in December 1848. The left-wing *Réforme* admitted 'No one had given a thought to the countryside since the First republic. From now on we shall have to.' For the first time, the extreme Left, led by *Montagnard* (Mountain) deputies (a term copied from the 1790s) set out to win over and organize the mainly rural mass of the nation behind a

21. Raphael (Nov.–Dec. 1909), pp. 277–304; (May–Oct. 1910), pp. 44–79, 297–331.
22. Dautry (1977), p. 245.
23. Price (1972), p. 251.

programme to meet their grievances. They created a movement, the *démocrates-socialistes* or 'démoc-socs', that combined traditional elements of peasant belief and modern politics in the language of utopian Christian socialism.

The economic crisis of agriculture, now three years old, created a very favourable opportunity for a populist movement. In many parts of the country, especially (so Margadent and others have argued) those producing for the market, such as the main wine-growing areas, peasants were desperate for some remedy, and as the election of Bonaparte had shown, they were ready to look to something new. The collapse of their markets had revived familiar complaints concerning excise duties on alcohol, lack of cheap credit, and communal and forest rights, to which was added outrage at the '45 centime' tax surcharge. Barrot's government attempted to repress this activity, restricting political clubs and the press, and harassing suspected subversives: wearing a red tie became a risky activity. The movement organized clandestinely. Some of the areas in which it put down roots stayed loyal to the Left for the next hundred years (see p. 256).

Démoc-soc strategy aimed at organizing overwhelming support for the dual elections, for president and Assembly, due in 1852. They intended to assert the right of universal male suffrage: the 3 million men disfranchised by the law of May 1850 would vote, by force if necessary. This, they hoped, would lead to a revolution through the ballot box, with the Left winning both the presidency and the chamber; 1852 was portrayed in millenarian manner as the start of a golden age.

Conservatives began to get frightened again, especially when, for example, at a carnival in the south floats carried figures with ropes round their necks carrying the placard '1852'. When a friend of Hugo's told him that she had had a nightmare in which a burning coach was dragged over a cliff by bolting horses, he replied, 'You have dreamt of 1852'.

Bonaparte crosses the Rubicon, December 1851

> I appeal to the whole nation . . . If you still have confidence in me, give me the means to accomplish the great mission you gave me.
>
> *Proclamation, 2 December 1851*[24]

At the same time as the conflict between the démoc-socs and the Party of Order was developing, an insoluble political dilemma came to a head. The 'prince-president's' term of office was to end in 1852, and the constitution forbade re-election. But he was clearly the only candidate with mass support in the country; there was no very credible successor. For him to leave office would be the end of the ambition of his whole life; it would also mean personal ruin because he had run up huge debts before and since his assumption of office. He and his supporters campaigned for a revision of the

24. Girard (1986), p. 147.

constitution to permit a second term. Many conservatives were willing to comply, fearing a constitutional crisis, a coup d'état, or even worse a Red revolution in the political vacuum that would be created if Bonaparte were excluded in 1852.

From the summer and autumn of 1850 onwards the president toured the provinces, was fêted by supporters, and criticized the ungenerous policies of the Party of Order. He also held military reviews at which the troops were encouraged to shout 'Vive l'Empereur!' and plied with cigars and cold chicken. He progressively replaced army commanders and ministers with his own men. He was gaining the whip hand, and by the early months of 1851 it was becoming evident that he might use it. The majority of the Assembly were willing to amend the constitution to permit his re-election, but the republican minority and an Orleanist group led by Thiers mustered enough votes to prevent the amendment from getting the necessary three-quarters majority. But these opponents of Bonaparte mistrusted each other, and so attempts by the Assembly to guard against a coup d'état – to limit the president's control of the army, to lay down a procedure for impeaching him if he broke the constitution – came to nothing. As Thiers had said in a vehement but useless speech in January 1851, there would soon be only one power in the State, the president, and then 'the Empire is made'.

Bonaparte and his advisers decided on 'Operation Rubicon'. To demonstrate that he was the real representative of the nation, he ostentatiously asked the Assembly to repeal the law of May 1850 and restore universal male suffrage. They refused, but in doing so weakened their own democratic legitimacy and made Bonaparte the champion of democracy: as he put it himself, he had waited until the Assembly was over the precipice, and then cut the cord. A coup aimed at a coterie of unpopular politicians in the name of the national will was an obvious step, and widely expected. Into key offices were brought fellow conspirators. Bonaparte's half-brother Morny (illegitimately descended from Bonaparte's mother and, separately, from Talleyrand) became minister of the interior, one of the coolest and most cynical scoundrels ever to hold that great office, which is saying a lot. A penniless and unscrupulous general, Saint-Arnaud, became minister of war. His civilian equivalent, Maupas, became Prefect of Police: a successful coup had to go through the proper channels. On 2 December 1851, the anniversary of Napoleon's great victory at Austerlitz, Operation Rubicon began. The timing took everyone by surprise. George Sand, passing the Elysée that evening, saw no lights and only a single sentry, and concluded that 'it's not for tomorrow'. Thiers assured a dinner party that the president would not dare disturb the Christmas and New Year festivities.

But that very night, Thiers and other key deputies (army officers, Montagnards, Orleanists) were efficiently arrested in their beds. The Imprimerie Nationale printed proclamations under military guard, and police squads posted them up. The National Assembly was occupied and astonished deputies were turned away next morning; those who resisted were marched off to a nearby barracks. A few barricades were built in working-class districts, and a few hundred militants rallied. A Montagnard deputy, Baudin, was shot dead in the Faubourg Saint-Antoine. But observers were struck by the indifference of the population, many of whom had voted for Bonaparte, and whose experiences since February 1848 seem to have left them little enthusiasm for politicians. Legend – probably apocryphal but still revealing – has it that workers said 'Why should we die for your 25 francs?', the daily parliamentary salary, fabulous wealth for workers and peasants, and which had done much to foster political cynicism. The most serious bloodshed in Paris occurred on the elegant Boulevard des Italiens when nervous troops fired indiscriminately at onlookers, many seated on café terraces, killing several dozen.

The revolt of the démoc-socs

> The male population of the commune, with the exception of a few old men, the sick and the children, all departed [to fight]; the commune was left in the hands of God.
>
> Mayor of village in Drôme, 1851[25]

In central and southern France, however, there was a popular reaction that few had anticipated, and which changed the whole character of the coup. In dozens of villages and small towns, little groups of men turned out with shotguns and pitchforks to defend the Republic: the ideal future Republic of 1852, 'la belle'. In the confusion, however, it seems that some thought that they were turning out to defend 'the people's Napoleon' from his enemies. Led by local démoc-socs – labourers, farmers, craftsmen, shopkeepers, a few professional men and politicians – little columns marched on the local prefecture or sub-prefecture. In all, some 70,000 men took up arms and nearly 30,000 were involved in fighting: the largest provincial uprising of the century.[26] Nevertheless, it was too uncoordinated, too limited in area and too remote from Paris to constitute a threat to the government. Troops were sent and the rebels scattered. After a few days the rising was over.

If 'the fighting in December did not amount to much . . . the purge that followed would be impressive indeed'.[27] For the rising was widely interpreted not as a defence of the republican constitution, but as an abortive *jacquerie*, a peasant revolt against property and order which it was assumed the Reds had been planning. Morny encouraged this belief, telling the prefects that they had 'just withstood in 1851 the social war that was to have broken out in 1852. You must have recognized it by its arson, banditry and murder. If you have defeated these enemies of society, it is because they were taken by surprise.'[28] Even many of Bonaparte's enemies concluded that he had saved

25. Margadent (1979), p. 263.
26. Ibid., p. 8.
27. Ibid., p. 301.
28. Weill (1928), p. 272.

society from a terrible revolutionary uprising. Newspapers printed horrific stories of fictitious atrocities – pillage, rape, torture: once again, the Right proved more class conscious than the Left, for the rebels in reality had been respectful of property and lives, except for those of a few gendarmes unfortunately in the wrong place at the wrong time. There were mass round-ups: 27,000 were arrested; 15,000 summarily sentenced by special Mixed Commissions of officials and soldiers; nearly 10,000 were transported to Algeria or Cayenne, the rest interned or placed under police surveillance.

The coup, conceived as a surgical operation against an unpopular Assembly in the name of popular sovereignty, had thus gone seriously wrong, resulting in gratuitous bloodshed in Paris, a mass rising in the provinces, and harsh repression. Bonaparte rapidly moderated the zeal of his officials, having sentences revised and giving pardons. It was too late: 'Deux Décembre' went into history as an act of violence and terror. In the short term, this made the coup more effective. Opposition disappeared: the Left was terrorized and the Right convinced that the president had forestalled a revolution. Most people welcomed or acquiesced in the replacement of the Republic by an authoritarian regime promising order and normality.

Bonaparte, his conscience clearly pricking, announced that universal suffrage had 'absolved' him from his act, and pleaded that he had 'acted illegally to ensure justice'.[29] And yet the stain of the coup was never effaced. However popular he remained with most of the French people, he could never overcome the hatred of a minority: the Reds, of course, but also the elite of the 'old parties', Orleanist, legitimist and republican. Hugo expressed this with inimitable venom in a whole volume of verse, Les Châtiments:

> Great nation, at this time you can enjoy,
> While in the dark men suffer, weep and die,
> . . . Illuminations, games, and fun galore:
> Your wages as this wretched fellow's whore!

CONCLUSION: THE POLITICS OF THE IMPOSSIBLE

> If the people make a mistake . . . frightened by the grandeur of . . . the republic and the difficulties of its institutions . . . well, too bad for the people! It will not be we but they who lack perseverance and courage.
>
> Lamartine, October 1848[30]

The failure of the Second Republic was even worse than that of the Bourbon and Orleanist monarchies, and seemed to demonstrate the truth of liberal fears that 'anarchy' led inevitably to 'despotism', and that in French conditions a republic was impossible. It had faced formidable social and economic

29. Girard (1986), pp. 165, 156–7.
30. Nicolet (1982), p. 141.

problems, though no worse than most of Europe at the time. Much of Europe went through a similar period of turbulence. France's special extra problems were the fears and also the expectations that it inherited from the Revolution. The 'politics of the impossible' that Tocqueville regarded as the revolutionary legacy collided with the pessimism of the Right, so that, as Furet puts it, France was caught in the trap of its own spectres.[31]

Republicans, in February 1848 a small minority of intellectuals, hereditary Leftists, professional revolutionaries, organized workers and city dwellers, never won the confidence of the electorate, as was shown as early as April 1848; and their economic policies, above all taxation, confirmed peasant suspicions of them as an alien townsmen's party. Though Lamartine was able to dismiss this superciliously as the people's fault, many republicans were shocked into a change of attitude. They realized that the republican idea had to win wider popular support: but should it be by greater radicalism, as in the millenarian propaganda of the démoc-socs, or by greater moderation, making the Republic, in Thiers's celebrated phrase of 1850, the government that 'divides us least'? This was to prove a long-drawn-out dilemma for the republican party. But they had a whole generation to resolve it: for the people had turned their backs on the Republic to follow 'the Great Man's nephew'.

31. Furet (1992), p. 405.

CHAPTER 20

THE TRIUMPH AND DISASTER OF BONAPARTISM, 1851–71: CLOSING THE ERA OF REVOLUTIONS

> My mission is to close the era of revolutions by satisfying the legitimate needs of the people and protecting them from subversive passions.
>
> *Louis-Napoleon Bonaparte[1]*

> 'Era of revolutions'. Still open, for each new government promises to close it.
>
> *Flaubert[2]*

Bonapartism is the great synthesis of post-revolutionary French political culture. All French politics since 1814 had turned on a series of restorations, of imitations of past models by self-conscious heirs. All were intended to be the final restoration, the end of the cycle. Bonapartism came closest to achieving this by its seductive eclecticism: the combination of Right and Left, of glamour and safety, of revolution and order, of democracy and authority. It attracted unequalled popular support through a charismatic leader appealing to 'the people'. By showing that a mass electorate was not a recipe for anarchy it made universal male suffrage a permanent feature of French politics. It restored 'order' after violent conflict: the usual and logical end to revolutions. It constituted a strong authority that was accepted and indeed desired, because it purported to be neutral between the conflicting factions of the 'old parties' that had been struggling since 1814. For it was neither Red nor White, neither revolutionary nor counter-revolutionary. Rémond considers Bonapartism as part of the Right; Girard considers it basically on the Left;[3] the answer is surely that it was neither – and both. It was therefore acceptable to the mass of voters as that arbitrating power that post-revolutionary French society needed, as Hoffmann has pointed out, in order to function. Finally, it promised to establish France on an advantageous footing with the outside world – the other major problem bequeathed by the Revolution. It thus became, says Nicolet, 'the matrix of modern France',[4]

1. Girard (1986), p. 147.
2. Flaubert (1991), p. 513.
3. Rémond (1968); Girard (1986).
4. Nicolet (1982), p. 146.

though in my opinion in more ways than he concedes. For a generation it ended the Revolution.

And yet it contained the seeds of its own downfall. How could charismatic leadership be sustained in the humdrum circumstances of normal politics, subject to age, sickness and criticism? How could the myth of national unanimity and of an authority 'above' politics be reconciled with the inevitable conflicts of interests within any society? Above all, how could the Bonapartist aura of national glory be sustained in a changing Europe where the economic and demographic power of France was being overtaken?

LOUIS-NAPOLEON BONAPARTE: THE POWER OF FANTASY

> March at the head of the ideas of your century, and those ideas will strengthen and sustain you; march behind them and they will drag you after them; march against them and they will overthrow you.
>
> *Napoleon III*

> France's first mistake was to take him for an idiot; her second was to take him for a genius.
>
> *Victor Hugo*

Louis-Napoleon Bonaparte, who became Napoleon III in 1852 at the age of 44, had a personal impact on France and Europe equalled by no Frenchman between Napoleon I and Charles de Gaulle. This in itself is extraordinary. He was shy, slow-speaking, stolid and not obviously outstanding. As the discerning Rémusat saw it,

> He lacks so many of the qualities of an ordinarily able man [yet] he has a rare and powerful faculty . . . He who can bring his imagination to bear on the affairs of the world and produce or modify events by virtue of his fantasy possesses [a] gift of daring and power that singles him out and places him in the ranks of historic figures.[5]

This 'fantasy' and 'daring' seem explicable only as a consequence of his genuine belief in the legend of Napoleon I and his own mission as his uncle's self-appointed political heir. That the mass of the nation also believed that the Bonaparte name implied a solution to crisis made success possible. The genuinely populist nature of Bonaparte's conception of legitimacy, derived from the Revolution and fundamentally different from that of legitimist traditionalists or Orleanist liberals, was shown by his calling two plebiscites and a parliamentary election within a year of his seizure of power. The first plebiscite, under restored universal (male) suffrage, was an integral part of the coup d'état itself, held on 21 December to 'make the entire people judges'

5. Caron (1985), p. 16.

of his act. Shortly afterwards, in February 1852, there were elections to the new Corps Législatif. Finally, on 21 November 1852, a second plebiscite was called to approve his restoration of the Empire as Napoleon III.

The will of the people was recognized as sovereign; but, unlike in a republic, it needed to be guided by, and expressed through, a charismatic leader. Charisma was backed up by intimidation and bribery. Much of the country was under martial law; opposition was gagged; thousands were awaiting trial after the coup. Undisguised hints of the dangerous consequences of a No vote were given, and the secrecy of the ballot was a fiction. Community pressures too discouraged dissidence. Opposition was usually demonstrated by not voting. Yet it has never been seriously suggested that Bonaparte's support was not genuine. 'There was terror and calumny to excess', noted George Sand, 'but the people would have voted as they did without that.' In the plebiscite called to approve the coup d'état in December 1851, some 7.4 million (78 per cent) voted Yes, more than had elected him president; 1.4 million (15 per cent) abstained; 600,000 (7 per cent) voted No, nearly a third of these in Paris. The power of the State was again used to influence the parliamentary elections. 'Official candidates' were designated, and they obtained 83 per cent of votes cast, though only 53 per cent of the total electorate. Paris and other large cities still showed opposition by electing several republicans, who refused to take their seats. Three legitimists were also elected. In the November 1852 plebiscite called to approve the restoration of the Empire, 7.8 million voted Yes, 250,000 voted No.

These three votes showed that Bonaparte enjoyed the support of an unprecedented, increasing and never again equalled majority. In 1848 people hoped that he could restore peace and prosperity; in 1851 he seemed to be doing it; by 1852 he seemed to have done it. The coup and the success of the first plebiscite had encouraged a burst of pent-up economic activity, and peasants, landowners, workers and employers showed their relief at the ballot box.

Many former opponents rallied to the new regime, hence the increasing majorities. Fear of revolution and civil war was the first motive. 'Hatred of the Red', one prefect reported, had united 'the other two colours',[6] the republican Blues and the legitimist Whites. To many conservatives and liberals, it seemed that France had faced the classic dilemma, teetering between anarchy and despotism; forced to choose, they preferred the latter. As Morny put it, 'This country is so tired of revolutions that all it wants today is a good despotism. That's just what it's got.'[7] Some areas that had voted démoc-soc in 1850 and even fought against the coup in December 1851 now voted Yes. For many peasants, a vote for the Reds and for Bonaparte had the same aim: to reject the domination of the *notables* and the towns, and to get a government that would be on their side. Peasant Bonapartism was an expression of peasant identity catalysed by the conflicts of the Second Republic. The complexities

6. Ibid., p. 90.
7. Girard (1986), p. 182.

are shown well in the case of the Gers department, in the rural south-west. It had the sixth highest 'No' vote; but it was legitimist districts that voted No, while formerly left-wing districts gave an overwhelming 'Yes'; and the region remained strongly Bonapartist for generations.[8]

The Constitution of 1852, based on that of the Year VIII (1799), gave far greater power to Napoleon III than those enjoyed by the restored Bourbons or Louis-Philippe. He was 'responsible before the People, to whom he has always the right to appeal', thus bypassing parliament through plebiscites. Ministers were responsible only to the emperor: he would often listen to their views in silence, then make his own decision later. The Senate (unlike the old Chamber of Peers) was merely the guardian of the constitution and largely inactive. The lower house, renamed Corps Législatif, had its numbers reduced and its debates were given minimum publicity. The Council of State, originally founded by Napoleon I, was given an extended role as the emperor's advisory body of technical experts, who would help to put his general ideas into legislative form. But he alone could introduce legislation.

He believed like many of his contemporaries that he had understood where history – 'the ideas of your century' – was going. As an outsider he was less respectful of the vested interests of the *notables* than his predecessors. Nevertheless, his powers were limited in practice. First, by his own shortcomings. Even before illness reduced his personal activity in the 1860s he always lacked the technical knowledge to ensure the execution of his projects, partly due to his upbringing, partly due to a certain indolence and preference for grand ideas over details. Bismarck noted that

> he has a succession of *idées fixes* and never knows where they will lead him. One would say that he has thought about them for a long time and is carrying them through to his goal. But in their execution, he shows how weak his preparation is, as if he suddenly woke up in charge of a locomotive that he did not know how to drive.[9]

Thiers put it more succinctly: 'He confuses the verb to dream with the verb to think'.

This would become disastrously clear in his foreign policy of the 1860s, but can be seen to some extent throughout his reign. Contemporaries put it down to his imaginative personality and his long career as a conspirator; but it was also due to political, as well as personal, isolation. He knew that many of his entourage, his ministers, and most of the political class of the country disagreed with, and came increasingly to fear, his ideas and intentions. 'How do you expect the Empire to run smoothly?' he is supposed to have said, 'The Empress is a Legitimist, Morny is an Orleanist, my cousin Napoleon is a Republican, I am a socialist; only Persigny [a faithful minister] is a Bonapartist and he is mad.' While there were political advantages in thus appearing to be different things to different people, it raised problems in actually governing.

8. Soubadère, in Feral (1990), p. 620.
9. Caron (1985), p. 16.

Conservatives had rallied to him for fear of Red revolution, not to experience Bonapartist radicalism. The politicians and bureaucrats with whom he had to govern were nearly all inherited from the July Monarchy. They frequently watered down or blocked his wishes. Even many faithful supporters were unwilling to back his wars.

Napoleon III knew that his support was among the masses, and an important aspect of his rule was a dialogue with them. Tours of the provinces and public political speeches were a new and important aspect of the style of the regime. Cheering crowds were often orchestrated, just as elections were managed, but much of the support was real. The emperor studied public opinion through reports of local officials, and decisions and announcements were tailored accordingly. Although the centralized administration was a powerful instrument for influencing public opinion (or at least its outward expression), the Empire and its servants were often in practice compromisers, finding out what people intended to do and then ordering them to do it.

'THE EMPIRE MEANS PEACE': PROMOTING ECONOMIC GROWTH

The empire means peace . . . We have immense tracts of uncultivated lands to clear, roads to open, ports to create, rivers to make navigable, canals to finish, our railway network to complete . . . These are the conquests I am contemplating, and all of you . . . you are my soldiers.

Louis-Napoleon Bonaparte, 1852[10]

'Satisfying the legitimate needs of the people' included economic improvement. Bonaparte, partly through enforced study in prison, had formed an eclectic economic outlook, influenced by his interpretation of Napoleon I's policy as one of economic modernization, by his experience of both wealth and poverty in Britain and by the influence of the leading socialists of the 1840s. As emperor he agreed with his economic adviser, the former Saint-Simonian Michel Chevalier, that 'it is one of the most absolute conditions for the stability of the State and society that . . . the mass of goods and services . . . should always grow in comparison with the population, so that each can obtain a better return for his labour, and consequently be better fed, clothed, heated, lit'.[11] Also, economic growth would benefit and win the support of the upper classes. The ideas were not new, but the desire to act and achieve quick results was. The Restoration had feared the social and political consequences of rapid economic change. During the July Monarchy, Guizot never spoke on economic matters and rarely attended economic debates: they were beneath the chief minister. But Napoleon III would say 'We must do . . .', 'The government will do . . .': the Bonapartist State wanted

10. Bordeaux speech, 15 Oct., in Furet (1992), p. 448.
11. Caron (1985), p. 37.

to take the lead.[12] As early as 1852, steps were taken to expand the credit system, accelerate railway building, and remodel the cities.

It was widely accepted that a stronger credit system was required for the French economy to match the rapid industrialization of Britain, Belgium and Prussia. France had no national banking system, but only sparse regional networks of small banks and discount houses. It was hard to raise working capital or even pay bills over long distances: many transactions required payment in coin, which was hoarded or exported at times of crisis, when money (as in 1848) ran physically short. The Empire's reforms were fundamental for the banking system over the next century. The first, and most famous, step was to encourage the establishment in 1852 of the Crédit Mobilier bank, by the visionary Saint-Simonian Pereire brothers. During the 1850s and 1860s a series of joint-stock clearing banks were set up, including the Crédit Industriel et Commercial, the Crédit Foncier, the Crédit Lyonnais, and the Société Générale. Equally important was the change in the status of the Banque de France, which was required to increase the number of its regional branches, which then became the centres of a greatly enlarged, though still rather conservative, banking system.

The government acted with similar speed over railways, still convalescent after the shock of 1846–48. In 1852, the concessions of the companies were extended to 99 years to give them longer to pay off their debts and so have a far better prospect of returns. Freight charges fell and traffic increased. The State also promoted company mergers and guaranteed a minimum profit on new lines. As early as 1852, railway building resumed. In return the companies undertook to build branchlines for which there was no immediate prospect of profit, but which the government wanted in order to develop rural areas and to win political gratitude.

The most spectacular and characteristic project was the transformation of Paris. It was the emperor's personal concern, and, typically, combined a philanthropic but not fully worked out desire to improve the condition of the population and create jobs, with a political wish to dazzle, concern for public order and a dynastic-nationalist ambition to make Paris the greatest city of Europe, as under Napoleon I. Changes were in any case necessary. Traffic problems were appalling in a commercial and manufacturing centre crammed into a partly medieval infrastructure. Streets and houses, however picturesque, were cramped and filthy. The water supply was inadequate and polluted: drinking water came from, and sewage returned to, the Seine, hence cholera epidemics. Death rates were significantly higher than in London. Slum districts were difficult to police, were hotbeds of revolt (in 1827, 1830, 1832, 1834, 1848 and 1851), and were dangerously close to the centres of government. A buccaneering official, Haussmann, was appointed prefect of the Seine to implement the emperor's plans. Over the next two decades, wide, straight streets such as the Boulevard de Sébastopol, squares, government buildings and fortified barracks cut swathes through the ancient

12. Plessis (1976), p. 86.

rookeries of the centre and remodelled it with bureaucratic tastefulness. Ranks of apartment buildings stood to attention along the Grands Boulevards; opulent mansions lorded it round the Etoile; uniform workers' flats sprang up on the eastern, southern and northern outskirts for people displaced from the centre or attracted from the provinces; monumental railway stations, huge gloomy churches, wedding-cake theatres like the Palais Garnier, pretentious department stores, landscaped parks with lakes and rocks, and cavernous sewers proudly open to tourists completed the flashy 'Americanized' Paris, the showplace of a dynamic new France ruled by a modern and forceful government. Behind the new facades, however, much of the ancient city remained. That prestige and profits were not the only concern of the author of *L'Extinction du Pauperisme* was shown by projects for workers' housing, hospitals and welfare institutions for the aged; their effect was more symbolic than utilitarian. Other cities and towns of the Empire followed in the wake of the capital. Even the humblest would soon boast a new *mairie*, market, barracks, church or school – the ubiquitous symbols of the French State, and of the emperor's power and solicitude.

He was rewarded by a halcyon period of rapid growth. Industrial production nearly doubled in the 1850s. In 1851, 4.4 million tons of coal were mined; in 1860, 8.4 million. During the same period, pig-iron production rose from 446,000 tons to 898,000. The length of railway lines open rose from 2,915 kilometres to 9,063; the freight they carried leapt from 462 million ton/kilometres to 3,120 million, and the number of passengers from 20 million to 50 million.[13] Agricultural production and consumption rose by about a quarter during the 1850s and 1860s. Naturally, the government received much of the credit, some of it deserved. But the idea that Napoleon III had created an economic transformation – which many contemporaries, friends and enemies believed – is fallacious. The growth of the 1850s was not unique either in French experience or in the context of other countries at the same time; while the Empire's economic policies were less spectacular than they seemed. The economy had restarted growth and modernization during the later years of the Restoration, after the appalling damage done by the domestic and foreign turmoil of the revolutionary and Napoleonic years. Under the July Monarchy, that growth had accelerated, particularly in the 1840s, reaching record levels, then faltering in 1847 and 1848. The performance of the early 1850s was so impressive because it followed a disastrous slump; compared with the whole of the previous decade it was less prodigious. So too if compared with the rest of the world, which was experiencing a boom caused by railway building and monetary growth created by Californian and Australian gold discoveries. Consequently, French growth was helped by a great increase in exports of luxury goods to the expanding markets of Britain and North America. Yet the growth in per capita income during the 1850s was far below that in Britain, Belgium, Switzerland or Germany. Far from being the 'beneficent motor' of economic growth

13. Mitchell (1978), passim.

through its direct macro-economic activity, the State actually reduced its non-military spending as a proportion of gross domestic product to a level below that of the Guizot years.[14] Moreover, while the famous banking reforms may have signalled to investors that the time had come to take out the gold coins from under the bed, the direct results were limited: the new banks became great national institutions only in the 1880s and after. In short, some spectacular policies obtained for the Empire the image of a dynamic regime promoting wealth. But its most important contribution was to create a climate of relative stability and optimism after the slump of the late 1840s, which had been prolonged in France by fears of political and social turmoil. The country was thus able to share in the worldwide boom of the 1850s.

The political consequences were great, but mixed. The sudden resumption of growth consolidated that element of support for the regime that had originally been based on dislike of the alternatives. Many who had been cool towards Bonaparte rallied. In the Nord department, workers and employers in the large textile industry voted strongly for the Empire in the two plebiscites and the elections of 1853. Above all, agricultural France became the solid electoral basis of the Empire, for railway-building, urbanization and industrial modernization provided expanding markets, the transport to bring produce to the consumer, and rising prices. But not all reactions were favourable. Napoleon III was an outsider and a visionary: he paid far less attention to vested interests and stability than his predecessors. Economic change created losers; and many feared that the regime's ambitions would damage them and the country. These included taxpayers and liberal economists who deplored State spending. During the 1860s, the liberal and republican opposition would become vocal spokesmen of this view. Industries supplying the home market, and used to the featherbedding provided by tariffs against British imports opposed any breach, such as the exemptions given for iron rails to speed railway building, and rightly feared that Napoleon III would move decisively towards free trade. Many Parisians – romantic antiquarians, tight-fisted ratepayers, hard-pressed tenants – regretted 'Haussmannization', which swept away picturesque streets and insanitary but cheap accommodation and put up rents, prices and taxes. Employers, especially in agriculture, protested that their workforce was being lured away by high wages and shorter hours on the Paris building sites. Conservatives feared that a concentration of workers in the capital could lead to social and political dangers. Critics characterized the '*fête impérial*' as a squalid orgy of meretricious courtiers and brassy speculators even worse than the 'joint stock company' of the July Monarchy. Many Bonapartists merited the invective. Morny was greedy and unscrupulous in his business affairs: he had boasted to his mistress at the time of the coup, 'We are going to know, you and I, a degree of prosperity that you cannot imagine'.[15] There were many like him who revelled in the new opportunities to get and spend – such a reaction

14. Plessis (1976), p. 89.
15. Girard (1986), p. 175.

after a period of economic depression is perhaps not unusual. Naturally, the regime was blamed for the unacceptable face of capitalism just as it was praised for growth. Throughout the 1850s, however, the balance was heavily on the credit side.

SOWING THE WIND: THE PRINCIPLE OF NATIONALITIES, 1854–60

Prince, the roots of your power cling to a revolutionary stem. Be strong enough to assure independence and liberty, they will make you invulnerable.

Plea at Orsini trial, 1858[16]

'The Empire means peace', the emperor had promised in 1852. He was convinced, like all faithful Bonapartists, that Napoleon I had been forced into war by the intransigent opposition of the forces of reaction, led by Britain, and that the emperor's ultimate dream had been peace, prosperity and freedom. Napoleon had said so himself from St Helena! But Waterloo and the treaties of 1815 had left patriots with a bitter grievance, and French governments, even Polignac's, dreamed of redrawing the map of Europe. The Left especially had burned to reassert France's mission as leader and liberator (see pp. 35–42). Napoleon III shared that goal, but as with so much else, had no precise idea of how to achieve it. He had three general principles, however. The first, taken as usual from his uncle's pronouncements, was that the 'principle of nationalities' was one of those invincible ideas of the century that must be espoused as the basis of a new European order. Nations would struggle for self-determination, and France, by aiding them, would overturn the old order, gain allies, even satellites, among newly freed nationalities (for 'a great nation is like a star – it cannot live without satellites', he said in 1859), and perhaps recover her 'natural frontiers', the Rhine and the Alps. The second principle was that a repetition of Napoleon's fatal European wars must be avoided, and that the European reconstruction should be pursued where possible through international congresses. The third principle was the need to have Britain as an ally. Her enmity had been the root cause of Napoleon's defeat ('all my wars came from England'), whereas no European coalition against France could succeed without British participation.

These beliefs, despite the alarm of the public and the vacillation of the emperor himself, took France into war with Russia in 1854. The roots of the conflict went deep. Russian expansion towards the south, with Constantinople as the great future prize, had long caused foreboding in France, as well as in Britain and Austria. Napoleon I had stated that if Russia took Constantinople she would become 'mistress of the world'. Since the mid-eighteenth century, France and Russia had used religion to win influence, respectively claiming protectorates over Latin and Orthodox Christians in the

16. Caron (1985), p. 139.

Ottoman domains. Hence, the trivial quarrel over the rights of Latin and Orthodox in the Holy Places had diplomatic implications which the Russians inflamed by invading the Ottoman Danubian provinces. Napoleon III was eager to find a diplomatic solution. French public opinion, as he well knew, provided no support for starting a major war. He was pushed into it largely by Britain, whose alliance he wanted to keep, but was careful to present France as fighting only due to Russian provocation. This seems to have had an effect: in the populous industrial Nord department, for example, war was 'well accepted by all', especially the left-leaning, nationalistic lower-middle and working-class population of the towns, for whom Russia was the enemy of liberty.

The Allies decided to attack Sebastopol to destroy Russian naval power in the Black Sea. An expeditionary force was landed on the Crimean peninsula, and under abysmally incompetent Anglo-French command found itself involved in a long siege. Reports of feats of courage by the troops were tarnished by heavy casualties, disease and chaotic administration. The government was aware of growing war weariness, and fear of tax rises and conscription, aggravated by food shortages, which could not now be alleviated by imports of Russian corn. The emperor decided to go to the Crimea and take command, which caused near panic among all those who saw in him France's only hope of political stability. The danger was averted by the fall of Sebastopol in September 1855. There was rejoicing at the victorious peace, but clear evidence of a desire among the public, the press, and ministers not to risk further hostilities with Russia: Russian diplomats were cheered in Paris and shown marked courtesy by the emperor, to the chagrin of the British. The peace conference held in Paris in February 1856 seemed to demonstrate that imperial France was for the first time since 1812 the leading Power of Europe, and Napoleon the arbiter of the future. The solidarity of the Allies of 1815 against France had been broken. Both Britain and Austria were estranged from Russia. The Russians seemed ready for a rapprochement with France. To crown Napoleon's triumph, a son and heir was born on 16 March from his 1853 marriage with a slightly raffish Spanish lady, Eugenia de Montijo, now Empress Eugénie. Paris crowds cheered at the baptism: sentiment apart, it seemed to show that the Empire might last beyond the life of Napoleon III (there were at least five assassination plots) and that for the first time for over 200 years a son might succeed his father on the French throne.

In 1857 came the first general elections since the proclamation of the Empire. The government intended to make them a demonstration of popular loyalty amid the atmosphere of victory. No opposition campaign was permitted; the press was strictly controlled. 'On no account must people in France and Europe be able to say that the Imperial government has lost ground among the masses', declared the minister of the interior. But the vote on 21 June showed no improvement on 1852: although official candidates won 5.5 million votes (some 90 per cent of those voting) still about one-third abstained. The emperor and the government were far from pleased, and were horrified that known republicans won a handful of seats. Five republicans, soon known as '*les Cinq*', took their seats in parliament, three from Paris, one from Lyons, one from Bordeaux. A minister reported that 'the Paris elections have greatly alarmed the emperor. He seems inclined to act more severely in future.' Haussmann, angry that Paris still contained enemies, was eager to hasten the rebuilding, 'an eminently strategic work', and remove industry and the working-class population from the capital.[17]

In this rather overwrought atmosphere occurred a nearly successful attempt on the emperor's life. On 14 January 1858, three bombs were thrown at his carriage on the way to the opera. Eight people were killed and nearly 150 injured. When regimes were short-term expedients, dependent for their durability on a single individual, assassination offered tempting rewards for discontented groups as well as deranged individuals, as the Bourbons and Louis-Philippe had discovered. The opera (featuring plots and assassination) was performed as normal; but the emperor's habitual impassivity concealed fear and anger. In February a Law of General Security was introduced. On the pretext that opponents of the regime advocated the emperor's assassination, anyone arrested previously for political acts could now be re-arrested, exiled or transported. A violent row with Britain began when it was discovered that the plot had been hatched in London, and the bombs made there; a London jury added insult to injury by acquitting one of the accomplices. For a time, even war seemed possible. The alliance of the Crimea was no more, and a naval arms race began. The British government raised volunteers and fortified the southern ports. This estrangement was to cost France dear in future years. The bomb-throwers were caught: four Italians led by a romantic professional revolutionary, Felice Orsini. His aim had been to bring back a republic which would, he hoped, aid Italian unity. He was visited in prison by the prefect of police, the left-wing Bonapartist Piétri, a former secret society member and Montagnard deputy, who persuaded him that Napoleon was not the enemy of Italy, but potentially its liberator. Orsini wrote to the emperor begging him to free Italy; his lawyer repeated the appeal at his trial. In an extraordinary turn of events, Napoleon resolved to act on the appeal of his would-be assassin.

The condition of Italy had been a concern of all French governments since 1815; to 'do something for Italy' was above all an ambition of Napoleon III, in his youth a member of the Carbonari, the nationalist secret society. Opposition to his rule still persisted in France, and neither repression nor economic growth had eliminated it. Napoleon, visionary, fatalistic, now decided, encouraged by Piétri and his cousin Jerome Napoleon, to follow his first instincts and win support and prestige at home by further demolishing the 1815 settlement through the 'principle of nationalities', and so disarm his enemies on the Left. He announced that the Law of General Security would be left in abeyance, and sacked the hard-line minister of the interior.

Italy showed how decisive Napoleon's 'imagination' and 'fantasy' could be

17. Plessis (1976), p. 190.

in major affairs of State. It also showed the limits on his power and his ways of circumventing them. He wanted a war with Austria to free Italy, and to increase the territory of Sardinia-Piedmont with Lombardy and Venetia, taken from the Habsburgs. France would become the protector of Italy, organized as a confederation of weak states under the nominal presidence of the pope. France, showing at last that 1815 had been superseded, would gain Savoy and Nice, and thus her 'natural frontier' on the Alps. All this was agreed with the Piedmontese prime minister Cavour at a secret meeting at Plombières in July 1858. The Foreign Ministry was only informed afterwards. However, it was not clear that the emperor could get what he wanted. His first hints of war caused a stock market fall, worried press comment, and alarming reports from officials about public opinion. The marriage of the King of Sardinia's daughter to the emperor's cousin caused further alarm, for it was correctly interpreted as the sign of a (still secret) alliance: there was a cold reception when the couple drove through Paris – 'Not a cheer, not a wave of the handkerchief', reported the British ambassador.[18] The appearance of a pamphlet, *L'Empereur Napoléon III et l'Italie*, known to have been inspired by Napoleon, outlining his plans for Italy and referring to the possibility of war with Austria, caused renewed uproar in political and financial circles. When the emperor opened parliament three days later the deputies' reception was 'icy'. The ministers, the emperor's personal entourage and even the army opposed him. Catholics feared that the papacy might lose its independent sovereignty. Financiers feared for their shares. Foreign governments were suspicious. Queen Victoria wrote a warning letter. The emperor retreated and decided on a European congress – his invariable expedient in times of trouble. 'To divide my enemies and win the neutrality of part of Europe, I have to show clearly my moderation and desire for conciliation.' At the same time he inspired a press campaign to try to convince public opinion that war might be necessary if Austria were the aggressor, in spite of his efforts for peace. On 20 April, Austria obligingly fell into the trap, delivering an ultimatum to Sardinia demanding that she begin disarming in three days. This had a marked effect on public opinion and gave Napoleon the pretext without which he was unable to act. French troops began leaving for Piedmont, and on 10 May the emperor left to take command. He was seen off by cheering crowds of Parisians, especially in the working-class districts. ·

Napoleon's promise that 'the Empire means peace' had been shown to be hollow. As nationalist demonstrators shouted 'To the Rhine!'[19] more foreign adventures were on the cards. The campaign was victorious, the French winning two big battles at Magenta and Solferino (see pp. 42–43). But rather than risk being drawn into a long and difficult war with the possibility of Prussian intervention, Napoleon signed a rapid truce with the Austrian Emperor Franz Josef at Villafranca: fortunately for him, the Austrians were unwilling to be rescued by Prussia, who would expect in return to be

18. Case (1954), p. 58.
19. Ibid., p. 178.

recognized as Austria's equal in Germany. They preferred to accept the loss of Lombardy which was ceded to France, and thence to Sardinia. Not having obtained Venetia too, as originally promised, France did not receive her 'tip', Nice and Savoy.

This hasty compromise settled nothing: Napoleon and the Sardinians were dissatisfied, and central Italy was in turmoil. A congress (as usual) was to be held to discuss Italy's future. However, in December 1859, Napoleon had another pamphlet published, *Le Pape et le Congrès*, urging the end of the papal government in central Italy. This provoked rude comments from Pius IX and the Austrians refused to attend the planned congress. The fate of central and southern Italy remained open, and it proceeded to solve itself. Nationalists organized plebiscites, and obtained large votes, including in the papal states, for annexation by Sardinia. In March 1860, an agreement with Sardinia recognized her annexation of central Italy. In return, France would receive Nice and Savoy if the population agreed. This was still not the end. In September 1860, the Italian nationalist freebooter Garibaldi invaded Sicily, then the mainland. Cavour, determined to prevent a revolutionary nationalist state in the south, sent troops to occupy all of central and southern Italy except the city of Rome, where papal sovereignty was protected by a French garrison. Italy became a kingdom, ruled by Victor Emmanuel II of Sardinia. Savoy and Nice now became French: their largely French-speaking inhabitants, at first far from convinced of the benefits of joining Napoleon's authoritarian empire, were persuaded by the two governments and the clergy that all other possibilities were worse. Thus France made her last major territorial acquisition, the only part of her 'natural frontiers' ever to be regained. The 1815 treaties were no more.

1860: THE WATERSHED

It is the fix in which H.M. finds himself with regard to the Italian question which has brought the matter to a crisis.

British ambassador[20]

Napoleon had played the sorcerer's apprentice in Italy. The Italian war and its unplanned and uncontrollable aftermath began a new era in external and internal politics not only for the Second Empire, but in the longer term for France and Europe. In three fundamental ways, it is the most significant watershed of the century for France. First, it marked the high tide of French expansionism and power: having defeated Russia in the Crimea she had now also defeated the second most powerful continental State, and seemed clearly to be the dominant European power. The defeat of 1815 had thus been wiped out, and a new Europe principally shaped by France seemed to be coming into being. Second, it was significant because this very success

20. Ibid., p. 295.

created new and intractable problems. Napoleon III had alarmed other
countries, especially the German states and Britain, with his annexation of
Savoy and Nice: they took it to be the first step towards other claims along
the Rhine. The weakening of Austria strengthened Prussia, whose rise would
dominate not only French diplomacy but even the domestic life of the French
people for generations. Finally, it was also significant as the internal political
repercussions of these events would bring about permanent changes in the
political system.

The widespread belief in Europe that Napoleon would aim for further
aggrandizement did not – as would have happened at any time between
Waterloo and the Crimea – cause the other Great Powers to unite to oppose
her. The combination of the revolutionary explosions of 1848 and the
Crimean War had brought in a period of cynical and anarchic power politics
which left each country occupied with its own advantage and willing to
bargain and betray without compunction. Russia saw French expansionism
now not as a threat to the general order to be combatted, but as a force to be
exploited so as to obtain the abrogation of the 1856 Treaty of Paris
demilitarizing the Black Sea. Prussia was indifferent to the Near East or Italy,
unless Austria would buy her help with acceptance of her dominance of
northern Germany; alternatively, she was willing if necessary to bargain with
France over parcelling out Germany and the Low Countries. Austria, in spite
of her defeat, would soon be willing to discuss common action with the
French over Poland, the Near East and even Germany, and to go along
half-heartedly with Napoleon's hare-brained plan – 'the great idea of the
reign' – to set up a satellite empire in Mexico with the Habsburg Archduke
Maximilian on the throne. Britain, though suspicious of French designs on
Belgium and Franco-Russian collusion in the Near East, was ready to
cooperate with Napoleon over the Lebanon, China or Mexico. But the naval
arms race, begun at the time of the Orsini affair, continued, with the British
government and public opinion seriously convinced that the French might
attempt a surprise invasion with their new steamship fleet. Napoleon, without
wishing to, had lost the alliance with Britain which, drawing lessons from his
uncle's experience, he had believed vital to France's security.

Almost as important, the direct and indirect consequences of the Italian war
were to place Napoleon III on the defensive at home. In domestic politics,
while the war had been popular with left-enclined city-dwellers, it aroused
anger and alarm within the political class, as we have seen. Catholics
deplored the spoliation of Church territories, which they blamed on
Napoleon, and feared the final extinction of papal sovereignty. Liberals and
republicans feared that the Empire would consolidate its power by appealing
to popular jingoism. Property owners feared higher taxation and economic
disruption. Peasants feared conscription. Open opposition appeared in
parliament, not only from the minority of die-hard opponents of the regime,
but from supporters who, along with some of Napoleon's close advisers and
officials, set out to restrain the emperor's activities. Thus began the unsteady
but irreversible consolidation of the liberal and democratic political system,

with an increasingly free press, openly operating parties, and a democratically elected parliament, that France would retain (with the exception of 1940–44) thereafter.

An immediate offshoot of tension with Britain had major consequences for domestic politics and the economy: namely, free trade. With occasional hesitations, Napoleon believed in trade liberalization; it was part of the Centre-Left package from which many of his opinions were taken. Progressive economists believed it would increase prosperity, and lower the cost of living for the masses. However, the reason for acting at once appears to have been his concern to repair relations with Britain after the events of 1859 and the annexation of Savoy and Nice. Every Frenchman knew how to butter up the nation of shopkeepers. The 1852 constitution gave the emperor the power to make treaties, and so, after secret negotiations in which the English liberal Richard Cobden and the former Saint-Simonian Michel Chevalier acted as go-betweens, a free trade treaty was signed on 23 January 1860, an 'economic coup d'état', which was extended over the next seven years, without parliamentary sanction, through trade treaties with most of Europe. The great exporting industries of Lyons silks and Bordeaux wines were traditionally in favour of liberalization, especially of trade with England. The port and railway companies were also favourable, wishing to increase international traffic, and to obtain cheaper rails and coal. But other major industries, particularly coal, metallurgy, wool and cotton, had fought liberalization for decades. They now mounted a protectionist campaign, which became throughout the 1860s a pillar of the opposition to the authoritarian power of the emperor. They had money, emotional arguments in favour of 'national jobs', and powerful spokesmen. Investors, employers, workers and those who depended on them in the coal and textile regions of the north and east constituted a new and powerful reinforcement to the opposition, especially when economic slowdown in the 1860s, partly due to foreign competition, created discontents that were easy to blame on the emperor's tariff policy.

The growth of effective parliamentary opposition was facilitated by the emperor himself, beginning with decrees of November 1860 permitting the Corps Législatif to reply to the Speech from the Throne, and allowing its debates to be published in the press, and of December 1861 permitting a parliamentary vote on each section of the budget. It has been argued[21] that these changes were the emperor's free decision – certainly his ministers opposed them. But generally they have been seen as conciliatory moves after the embarrassing developments in Italy. This was to be the pattern of the 1860s: concessions to parliament were made to reconcile opponents, but even if they succeeded partially, they provided opportunities for open criticism which in the 1850s had been muzzled. Public debate through parliament, pulpits, the press and electoral manifestos brought politics back to life.

21. For example, recently in Caron (1985), pp. 166–7.

THE REVIVAL OF OPPOSITION AND THE
LIBERALIZATION OF THE REGIME, 1860–70

Sire, when one is acclaimed by 35 million people . . . there still remains one
inexpressible joy . . . to be the courageous and willing initiator of a great people to
liberty.

Emile Ollivier, 1861[22]

Opposition had several elements. First, the Catholic clergy and leading
laymen, often legitimist, were angry at the undermining of papal
independence caused by the unification of Italy: the so-called 'Roman
question'. Young men, 'the flower of French nobility and chivalry',
volunteered for the papal army, especially the famous Pontifical Zouaves.
Some were killed by the bullets of Napoleon's Italian protégés at
Castelfidardo in 1860, and their funeral ceremonies in France became
legitimist demonstrations. Catholics had previously supported Napoleon as a
barrier against revolution; to them, his Italian war showed that he had gone
over to the enemy. Furious episcopal letters, critical articles in Catholic
newspapers and occasional demonstrations in Brittany or Provence had little
effect on the country as a whole. Yet this 'clerical' opposition was
nevertheless significant, for it included influential landowning *notables* with
significant representation in parliament, and it caused the emperor perhaps
excessive worries about the effect on peasant voters. Also, some of the
Empire's leaders, including the empress and the foreign ministers Walewski
and Drouyn de Lhuys, sympathized with the Catholic viewpoint. A
smouldering dispute between State and Church which alternated between
periods of relative amity and periods of tension continued throughout the
1860s. The government began counter measures against clerical influence,
limiting their educational activity, restricting religious orders, banning
newspapers (including the widely read *Univers*), forbidding publication of
papal encyclicals, and even prosecuting members of the clergy. This tussle
reached its peak when the education minister, Victor Duruy, introduced
measures to bring church schools under State supervision and deliberately
broke the Church's quasi-monopoly of girls' education. Catholic opposition
was, however, kept within bounds by the fact that the only effective defender
of papal Rome was the French garrison, and also because most ordinary
Catholics proved to be little concerned by pontifical sovereignty.

The second element of opposition was republican. Although the Italian
policy had won approval from republican voters, and even persuaded some
prominent politicians, notably the deputy Emile Ollivier, that the Empire need
not be an enemy, a core of republicanism remained in the cities and in
certain rural areas. The coup d'état caused a bitterness that amnesties and
pardons failed to soothe, while relaxation of repression simply permitted

22. Girard (1986), p. 356.

more open expression of republican loyalty. From 1857 onwards, former abstainers ventured to the polls as republican as ever. The mainstay of republican electoral strength was the city working class, above all in Paris, where the emperor and some of his policies were not necessarily unpopular, but where the republican party was still seen as the people's voice.

The third element was liberal. It was led by a small elite of Orleanists who refused to rally to the Empire for reasons of pride or principle. They dominated the intellectual establishment – the French Academy, the quality press, learned societies – and conducted a powerful literary war against the Empire through works such as Thiers's massive bestseller, *L'Histoire du Consultat et de l'Empire* (1845–62), intended to show the dangers of despotic rule, Tocqueville's *L'Ancien Régime et la Révolution* (1856), Broglie's *Vues sur le gouvernement de la France* and Prévost-Paradol's widely read *La France nouvelle* (1868). During the 1860s they provided much of the leadership of the revived parliamentary opposition, winning electoral support by their criticism of military adventures in the Lebanon, China and Mexico and their opposition to tax increases and military spending. The force of their criticism caused the emperor to make one leading critic, the banker Fould, minister of finance in 1861. Liberal strength lay not in numbers, but in the standing of their leaders, and the fact that their ideas and fears were widely shared not only among the avowed opponents of the Empire, but also among its supporters and officials and even in Napoleon's own entourage, particularly by Morny. Such men believed that for the sake of the regime itself, the emperor's more dangerous initiatives had to be curbed by increasing powers of parliament.

The 1863 elections made the parliamentary opposition a significant force. That these elections mattered is clear from the number of opposition candidates (300) and the increased turnout of voters – half a million more than in 1857. The minister of the interior, Persigny, used familiar strong-arm methods, harassing the opposition press, confiscating opposition literature, redrawing boundaries, ordering the prefects to use every trick of pressure and influence, and refusing to designate as official candidates sitting deputies who had opposed government measures. These procedures, effective against a beleaguered republican minority at a time when the Empire was popular anyway and overwhelmingly supported by clergy and *notables*, now proved relatively ineffective. It was impossible to intimidate or buy off powerful and influential men who felt their fundamental interests and beliefs threatened. Indeed Persigny's tactics backfired by turning friendly critics into opponents and giving the opposition a unifying theme.

This they sorely needed. Catholics and republicans were as ever campaigning against each other as much as against the government. There were efforts to form opposition alliances against official candidates, which occasionally brought Catholics and moderate republicans together under the banner of the Union Libérale. However, this sometimes aroused dark suspicions among Bonapartist peasants, who thought that an alliance of nobles, priests and republicans boded no good for them. The great majority

of voters, especially in rural areas, voted obediently for 'our emperor'. Most
opposition successes, as in 1857, came in the cities where they won
seventeen seats. In Paris Thiers and eight republicans swept the board.
However, divisions, especially over Italy, made a truly united opposition a
distant prospect.

As in 1857, a modest success for the opposition was taken by the regime as
a major setback. A regime that had carried out a coup against what were
officially referred to as 'the former parties', and whose legitimacy was based
on its claim to represent the national will, tended to exaggerate the dangers
of opposition. Sometimes officials tried to defeat their critics with the familiar
electoral tricks. Sometimes, unsure that this would work, they tried to win
over opponents by promising changes of policy and even adopting moderate
critics as official candidates. Sometimes, when neither tactic seemed
promising, they were reduced to a humiliatingly neutral stance, unable to put
up an official candidate with any chance of winning, and letting the
opposition candidate stand unopposed: anything rather than publicly backing
a loser.

Over the next six years a series of reforms dismantled many obviously
authoritarian aspects of imperial rule: one set concerned political activity, the
other, social, and particularly working-class, activity. The motives were not
identical, and reflected disagreement among supporters of the regime. One
current of opinion, fearing a resurgence of republicanism after the results of
the 1863 elections, wished to win over liberal critics of the regime in a
common front against the 'Reds'. This was Morny's view. To give greater
power to parliament would satisfy the liberal aspirations strongly held among
the educated and provide a means by which major interest groups could
restrain the emperor from controversial, dangerous and costly initiatives.
However, another current of opinion, most vocally represented by the
emperor's radically chic cousin Prince Jerome Napoleon ('Plon-Plon'),
believed that the Empire was fundamentally populist, and should cultivate the
support of the mass electorate against liberal and conservative critics. Support
for nationalities abroad had been one way, social reform was another. This
was dubbed 'caesarism' by opponents. There was, however, a third tendency,
stubbornly defended by the minister of state Rouher: to maintain authoritarian
government, and make no concessions to the opposition. The emperor was
temperamentally inclined to populism, but also to vacillation; moreover, his
health deteriorated after 1864, and his attention was also much occupied with
growing difficulties abroad. Above all, he wanted to assure the future of the
Bonaparte dynasty. Consequently, he listened successively, even
simultaneously, to divergent opinions and followed the path of expediency,
which led to liberalization.

Prévost-Paradol quipped that the emperor could not be both Thiers and
Proudhon, meaning that he could not favour both conservative liberalism and
social transformation. In the early 1860s, he leant towards Proudhon.
Important concessions were made to the working-class Left, who were still
voting against government candidates in elections, but who had

enthusiastically supported the Italian war and in many cases kept their affection for the emperor himself, first shown in 1848. In the early 1860s, the predominant influence among the feebly organized working class was Proudhonist. Proudhon (who died in 1865) had once hoped that Bonaparte would act as patron of socialist reforms, and urged a largely apolitical, peaceful path towards a socialism based on decentralized cooperatives. Nothing in the emperor's background was inimical to a dose of socialist experiment, especially if divorced from republican politics. It might win the loyalty of workers, or at least wean them away from middle-class liberal and republican politicians. In this he was encouraged by Jerome Napoleon, whose residence, the Palais Royal, was the centre of the left-wing Bonapartist 'Palais Royal Group'. This group prompted the government to sponsor a delegation of workers to the London Exhibition in 1862 and prepare a report on labour questions. More than 200,000 Paris workers voted to select the delegation, which was led by the Proudhonist bronze sculptor Tolain. These contacts led to their being co-founders of the International Working Men's Association, L'Internationale. Their report urged the government to recognize the right to strike. In February 1864, Tolain and other delegates drafted a Manifesto of the Sixty repudiating violence, calling for social reforms and declaring that workers' political interests should be represented by workers themselves. This was published in Jerome Napoleon's newpaper *L'Opinion Nationale*, and promptly attacked in the liberal and republican press as 'caesarist'. In April, the government introduced a bill to legalize workers' coalitions. It was presented by a young former republican, Emile Ollivier, now becoming reconciled to what he considered a progressive-minded Empire. The immediate consequence was a sharp increase in strikes, mainly for higher wages: 80 per cent were successful, affecting one-tenth of all workers.[23] The authorities generally urged employers to compromise. In February and March 1866 the government instructed local authorities to permit strike meetings and trade union associations. The same year the Code Civil was modified to give workers' and employers' evidence equal standing in case of disputes. The emperor also moved towards the abolition of the *livret*, the much-criticized workers' pass-book.

These acts were a deliberate challenge to the liberal opposition. For them this was the classic bread-and-circuses tactic of 'caesarist' despotism: war in Italy, big public spending, and now concessions to socialism. The 'absoluto-democratic party', as Thiers called it, was using democracy, or being used by it: 'if the emperor gives himself completely to the revolution, he can raise the vile mob against us'. They were all the more determined to use parliament to stop him. On 11 January 1864, in a resounding speech in the Corps Législatif, Thiers, newly returned to politics, set the liberal programme, which he defined as 'the necessary liberties': of the individual, of the press, of elections, and of parliament to initiate legislation and to call ministers to account. If the Empire granted these, he said, it would be accepted by all citizens; but if it

23. Caron (1985), p. 173.

refused them, one day the nation would 'require' them. Both Rouher and the emperor rejected Thiers's demands as the 'exaggerated tendencies' of a destructive and outworn parliamentarism.

However, the government and most of its critics dreaded another revolutionary conflict, and in spite of harsh words the climate was for compromise rather than intransigence. Over the next six years, the government had much success in disarming opponents by political and social reforms, although not every reform pleased all critics: conservatives, for example, deplored concessions made to the workers' movement and disliked press freedom. But most could be reconciled, however grudgingly, to a regime that seemed capable of change. The insoluble problems came not from domestic but from foreign developments in Poland, Italy, Mexico and Germany, whose stunning impact at home weakened the regime, leading it into further domestic concessions and diplomatic intrigues without ever being able to reassert control or win back its original prestige.

REAPING THE WHIRLWIND, 1863–67

> One of my greatest reproaches against Italian unity is that it is destined to be the mother of German unity.
>
> *Thiers, 1865.*[24]

Napoleon III powerfully contributed to the instability of Europe by committing France to supporting the 'principle of nationalities', admirable in theory and a Pandora's box in practice. It opened opportunities to those such as Bismarck and Cavour who were prepared to exploit nationalism for purposes of power politics, and set up a chain-reaction of events that led Napoleon into increasingly dangerous expedients in a vain attempt to master the situation and win compensating gains for France.

The first casualty was France's post-Crimean rapprochement with Russia, damaged by Napoleon's response to the re-emergence of the Polish problem. In January 1863, another revolt broke out in Poland. The Poles enjoyed the passionate sympathy of French nationalists and Bonapartists; unlike the Italians, they also had the support of Catholics (the Church had played a part in the outbreak of the revolt). Thousands of petitions flooded in pressing the government to act. However much it clung to the *entente* with Russia, it was forced to protest in April against Russian repression, as did Austria and Britain. The Russians understood this and accepted it philosophically, but Napoleon, unable to resist the temptation of fishing in troubled waters, suggested armed intervention to Austria and Britain, to bring about Polish independence and a redrawing of the map of Italy, the Balkans and the Rhineland – the sort of breathtakingly unrealizable project he loved – and in August, the French government declared its *entente* with Russia over. With

24. In Corps Législatif, 13 April.

Britain and Austria of course unwilling for war, Napoleon, as was his wont, called in November for a congress to discuss Poland and other European problems: 'The treaties of 1815 have ceased to exist', he declared, and a new order must be created to replace them. This was well received at home, but Britain, suspicious of French expansionism, refused to attend. Consequently, without benefit to France or the Poles, Napoleon further soured relations with Russia and Britain. This meant that none of them were in a position to prevent or influence the 1864 war of Prussia and Austria against Denmark, which annexed Schleswig and Holstein to the German Confederation.

In September 1864, wanting to extricate himself from the Roman Question, Napoleon signed a convention with Italy to withdraw the French garrison on condition that Florence became the capital of Italy, the implication being that Rome would be left to the pope. The reward for Italy would be to obtain Venetia, still in Austrian hands. Thus would Napoleon fulfil his pledge made in 1859 to free Italy 'to the Adriatic'. To bring this about without fighting another war, he found an accomplice in the newly appointed minister-president of Prussia, Bismarck, intent on preparing the ground for the looming conflict with Austria over primacy in Germany. In October 1865, Bismarck met Napoleon at Biarritz. They wished to make sure that neither would support Austria: that Prussia would not support her in retaining Venetia, and that France would not support her in resisting Prussian ambitions in northern Germany. They talked of the possibility of France annexing Luxembourg or Belgium. This was the usual Napoleonic three-horse accumulator, wonderful if everything went according to plan. He urged his Italian protégés to sign a secret alliance with Prussia on 8 April 1866 for a war against Austria. Napoleon thus made a major war possible and imminent: Bismarck would not have risked a conflict with Austria in less favourable circumstances, and Italy would not have signed the alliance without French encouragement. Public opinion proved overwhelmingly hostile to any direct French involvement. On 3 May Thiers made a widely reported speech arguing that now there were dangers for France in a European upheaval overturning the remnants of the 1815 settlement, and that the new danger to France was Prussia. The emperor replied in a speech three days later at Auxerre (an old Bonapartist stronghold), in which he said that he 'hated the treaties of 1815, which some wished to make the sole basis of our foreign policy'. This caused a sensation, with press outcry, alarmed reports from prefects and anger among ministers. The stock market fell, and Rothschild coined a much-quoted witticism parodying Napoleon's famous Bordeaux speech of 1852, 'l'Empire, c'est la baisse'.[25]

The emperor fell back on his usual ploy of demanding a European congress, hoping that there might be some redistribution of European territories in which Italy would receive Venetia; Austria, compensation in the Balkans; Prussia, Schleswig-Holstein; and France, as honest broker, would at

---

25. A pun on the phrase 'L'Empire, c'est la paix'; 'la baisse' was the fall in the stock exchange.

least see a neutral buffer-state established in the Rhineland, and possibly gain actual territory. Austria refused. In fact, the Austrians and Napoleon believed that in the event of a German war, Austria would almost certainly win. Napoleon expected such a war to be long and exhausting, leaving him the arbiter. After encouraging Prussia the previous year, he now, with child-like duplicity, made a secret bargain with Vienna on 12 June that he would remain neutral and agree to a victorious Austria annexing Silesia. In return, Italy would receive Venetia and France her Rhenish buffer.

In June 1866 Prussia declared war on Austria and most of the other German states. The French government took very careful soundings of public opinion. A Belgian diplomat reported that 'everywhere the answer was an ardent desire for peace. His majesty did not conceal the impression produced on him by this result.'[26] Italy had declared war on Austria as Prussia's ally, but on 24 June was decisively defeated at Custozza. Prussian troops marched rapidly into Bohemia, and defeated the main Austrian army on 3 July at Sadowa/Königgrätz. When this news reached Paris it caused consternation: 'we felt that something in the soil of old Europe had just crumbled'.[27] Austria asked for French mediation, and agreed to cede Venetia to Napoleon, who would transmit it to Italy. For a moment, French opinion regarded this as a brilliant bloodless victory: Napoleon was hailed as a diplomatic genius, the liberator of Italy, the arbiter of Europe. He and his ministers had no such illusions: the Prussian victory had stunned them and completely altered the prospects for the future of Europe. Though the ministers of war and foreign affairs urged sending all available troops – a mere 80,000 – to the eastern frontier to enforce a settlement favourable to France, all the other ministers were opposed. The army was hamstrung by commitments in Algeria and by the endless campaign in Mexico; moreover, urged the minister of the interior, public opinion was overwhelmingly opposed to French involvement. In any case, it was unthinkable for France to risk war with Prussia and Italy, exponents of the principle of nationalities that was central to Bonapartist foreign policy. As Jerome Napoleon secretly reminded his cousin, it would be 'the negation of the empire's whole policy, and would undo what the emperor had so gloriously done in 1859'; Napoleon must not become the 'representative of reaction and clericalism' but remain true to his historic mission as 'enlightened leader of the Revolution, never deserting its great principles of liberty and nationality'.[28]

The official French line, therefore, was that the Prussian victory, far from damaging France's interests, was a desirable step towards a reconstruction of Germany that would give France a friendly and satisfied north German neighbour and (it was hinted) soon bring France an increase in territory along the Rhine. In the words of a pro-government paper, 'a Protestant power, Prussia will not seek to extend her action beyond the river Main. In all this it

26. Case (1954), p. 205.
27. La Gorce (1894–1905), vol. 5, p. 12.
28. Rothan (1879), pp. 454–6.

is impossible to see even a shadow of danger for France.'[29] However, over the next few months, as Prussia ignored French 'mediation', set up the North German Confederation under her domination, and signed military treaties with the independent south German states, an uncomfortable realization grew that 1866 had been a great setback. Worrying reports came in concerning the effect on public opinion: in Montpellier people 'had hoped for territorial concessions to France'; in Toulouse 'people say we played the game badly'; Dijon reported that 'faith in the star and good luck of the Emperor have weakened . . . we are far from the days of self-satisfied pride following the Italian campaigns and the annexation of the Savoy provinces and Nice.'[30]

Napoleon was forced to make further political concessions to retain support. A decree of 19 January 1867 permitted the formal questioning (*interpellation*) of ministers by deputies, and allowed all ministers to address parliament. This was quite inadequate to repair the damage. The Speech from the Throne was given a cold reception. On 15 March 1867 Thiers made a devastating attack on the government's whole foreign policy, which he said had undermined French security: they had permitted a new power of 40 million people to be established on France's frontier, 'young, active, bold and devoured by ambition'. Now France must become the defender of the threatened European status quo, and so gain allies. 'There is not', he told the Chamber in a much-repeated phrase, 'a single mistake left to make.'

The government needed a success abroad, and they hoped that the acquisition of Luxembourg would do the trick, giving France a major German fortress on her ever-vulnerable eastern frontier, and proving that the emperor had not been left empty-handed after all. Bismarck encouraged them to proceed with negotiations with the King of Holland to purchase the territory, but then sabotaged the deal by announcing that he could not accept the transfer without the agreement of the German states (as Luxembourg had been part of the old German Confederation) and the other Great Powers. A conference held in London would only agree to Luxembourg being neutralized and demilitarized. In France there were expressions of relief that war had been avoided, but informed observers realized that over the whole German question Napoleon had been outmanoeuvred: 'For France the game is lost', admitted a diplomat, 'and lost for a long time'.[31]

The political damage caused by foreign entanglements was far from exhausted. The emperor felt obliged to propose expansion of the army to match Prussia (see p. 43), which proved the most unpopular thing he ever did. Its passage through parliament was not helped by the humiliating news that the Emperor Maximilian of Mexico, Napoleon's protégé, had been captured and shot in June 1867 by republican forces after French forces had withdrawn – further evidence of Napoleon's blundering. Italian problems still caused trouble: in November 1867 an expedition led by Garibaldi into the

29. *Revue Contemporaine*, May 1866.
30. Case (1954), pp. 216, 226.
31. Ibid., p. 233.

remaining papal territory was defeated by a hastily dispatched French force at Mentana, where Garibaldi himself was wounded. The French general's tactless report that 'the chassepot rifles worked wonders' confirmed the republicans' anti-military sentiments. Many concluded that Napoleon could not be trusted with a larger army; besides, most people complacently took it for granted that France was still the world's leading military power, and Prussia, even enlarged, was still seen as in the second rank with 'an army of lawyers and oculists',[32] mere amateurs. The most vocal opposition to army expansion came from the republicans, whose objections included cost, humanitarianism and anti-authoritarianism. The Empire was based, as they never for a moment forgot, on a military coup. The reforms as finally passed were 'drawn within the narrow limits of what was politically possible for a people which grudged every penny spent on the army, distrusted its own rulers and was deeply divided in itself'.[33] It showed how much resistance could be mounted to the emperor's will even among his officials and political supporters, and demonstrated the waning of his prestige and authority since 1860. The road to further political concessions was clearly marked out.

TOWARDS A 'LIBERAL EMPIRE', 1867–70

You will avert the threat of revolution, you will set liberty and order on a solid footing, and you will make it easier for the crown to be passed on to my son.

Napoleon III[34]

You are nothing but a bridge between the Republic of 1848 and the Republic that is to come, and we shall cross that bridge!

Léon Gambetta[35]

Other problems were piling up. The general economic situation, which had begun to deteriorate in 1860, now took an unmistakable turn for the worse. Underlining the point, the Crédit Mobilier, the pioneering bank set up with the emperor's support in the halcyon days of 1852, collapsed. Protectionist critics blamed Napoleon's free-trade policy since 1860. Strikes against lay-offs and wage cuts multiplied, facilitated by the emperor's policy of conceding trade union rights. In many strikes, especially in the provinces, there was no political overtone, and local authorities still acted as conciliators. Shouts of 'Vive l'Empereur!' were sometimes heard from strikers. This, of course, had always been Napoleon's intention. But in Paris and the largest cities, radical republicanism and socialism maintained a strong influence among organized workers, and the strikes of the late 1860s permitted them to consolidate it. The International, though still a weak organization, provided a rallying point

32. General Bourbaki, in Howard (1967), p. 29.
33. Ibid., p. 31.
34. Proclamation, 1870, Furet (1992), p. 490.
35. In Corps Législatif, 10 Jan. 1870, Furet (1992), p. 489.

that grew increasingly revolutionary in its aims as the older Proudhonist generation of leaders were replaced by men such as Varlin, Duval and Assi, who combined trade-union militancy with revolutionary ambitions.

Republicans attacked the Empire's economic policies. In 1868 Jules Ferry published an attack on Haussmann's financial methods – he had used many short cuts in a pioneering example of creative accountancy – called *Les Comptes fantastiques de Haussmann*. By implication this stigmatized all the financial methods which the Empire was thought, rightly or wrongly, to use, with all the corruption, profiteering, favouritism and instability that ensued. In the provinces, republicans mounted familiar opposition warhorses: conscription, alcohol duties, 'mad expenditure', centralized bureaucracy.

Attacks on the government were facilitated by further loosening in 1868 of restrictions on the press and assembly. In Paris above all, a new style of polemic and a new set of political celebrities emerged in a ferocious, and sometimes amusing, anti-government press and also through public meetings, organized in theory to discuss non-political matters, but which took on a radical tone, discussing the iniquities of the Church, class struggle and the coming revolution. The star of the new journalism was Henri Rochefort, whose paper *La Lanterne* provided satire and scurrility eagerly sought by a public long deprived of the pleasure of seeing their rulers mocked. A subscription for a memorial to Baudin, the deputy killed in the 1851 coup, led to a prosecution, and the defence barrister, another rising young star Léon Gambetta, made his speeches in court an indictment of the Empire and the 1851 coup, details of which were now for the first time being published. This political commotion in Paris was, as always, given great, and perhaps excessive, attention. The effect was two-edged. While it alarmed many supporters of the Empire, and led to gloomy speculation about its long-term prospects, it also worried many moderate opponents, particularly in the provinces, and hindered the development of a united opposition. Left-wing candidates lost support among voters terrified of another revolution. Among peasant Bonapartists, anti-republican and anti-Parisian feeling increased. This was to have grim consequences in 1871.

The government could hardly have been in a worse condition to face the general elections of May 1869. So bad were the prospects that in a quarter of the constituencies no viable official candidate could be found, many possibles refusing to be designated as official because it was now an electoral handicap. An increasing proportion of the electorate voted for candidates demanding further liberalization of the political system to give greater authority to parliament and reduce the personal power of the emperor. The results were by far the worst ever for the regime. Forty per cent of votes went to the opposition, and many others to men who, though supporters of the regime, were critical of many of its principal policies. Of the 292 deputies, only about 90 were Bonapartist loyalists; there were about 40 republicans, mainly from Paris, the other cities, and the traditional left-wing rural areas. The mass of deputies, however, were centrists, liberal Bonapartists (about 130), Orleanists or legitimists. When the new Corps Législatif met, 116 members signed a motion calling for further liberalization and 'responsible government'. Napoleon had no choice but to concede. With a clear-sighted willingness to grasp the nettle such as Charles X or Louis-Philippe had never shown, he conceded further powers to parliament and on 27 December 1869 he called on the former republican, Ollivier, to form a government 'faithfully representing the majority of the Corps Législatif'. That strange hybrid, the 'liberal empire', had arrived.

The new ministry represented what had been the regime's 'loyal opposition'; it was also supported by men considered Orleanists. They had little choice but to welcome a liberalization they had long demanded. Their leader Thiers had predicted back in 1860 that if the Empire liberalized 'we are quite simply prisoners of the regime, and we must honestly surrender'. The essence of liberalism was parliamentary government, which was now seen as an effective antidote to Napoleon's adventures. What was new and historically significant about the liberalism of the 1860s, however, was that it was no longer the overtly anti-democratic ideology of the July Monarchy. However grudgingly, Orleanists and republicans (themselves not unconditional supporters of the sovereignty of the ballot box if it meant peasants voting for royalists or Bonapartists) had accepted that parliament elected by manhood suffrage was the only viable expression of national sovereignty, and the best counter-weight to 'caesarism'. Ironically, this was a lesson they had learned partly from the emperor, who had grasped the fact that political extremism would be 'extinguished by the immensity of universal suffrage'.[36] The opposition's gratifying electoral successes in the 1860s – the first time that Orleanists or moderate republicans had really started to win elections – confirmed that they had made the right choice. In short, liberal parliamentary democracy was becoming the basis of a new political consensus extending from moderate legitimists to moderate republicans.

Compared with these fundamentals, the figurehead of the State seemed less important. Orleanists such as the Duc de Broglie, who had acquiesced in Bourbon rule and been a senior minister of the July Monarchy, now accepted a liberalized Empire while regarding with equanimity the possibility of a republic when the ailing Napoleon died. As Broglie pointed out, no French monarch had succeeded his father since Louis XIV, hence the very basis of monarchy had faded and France was already in practice a republic. Tocqueville's view that the inevitable trend of modern society was towards democracy had been widely accepted. As liberals from Constant onwards had taught, the important thing was not the form of the regime, but its substance, and its ability to avoid the extremes of anarchy and despotism. That this parliamentary liberalism was a reaction against 'caesarism' was clear from the policies adopted by Ollivier's government: moving back towards protectionism; prosecuting the leaders of the International; sacking Haussmann; dropping the planned abolition of the workers' *livret*; and cutting the army budget – all disavowals of Bonapartist initiatives.

36. Speech from throne, Feb. 1867.

The 'liberal empire', however, was a precarious fudge: whether it would prove viable, and in what form, was unpredictable. Ollivier, who had formed its government, was merely minister of justice, not prime minister. It was Napoleon who still presided over ministerial meetings. The amended constitution stated that ministers were 'responsible', but omitted to say whether to parliament or the emperor; but they 'depended' only on him. Napoleon continued his own policies and his own diplomacy without the whole government being informed. He quietly opposed certain government policies: for example, privately urging deputies to oppose cuts in the army budget and getting his old enemy Thiers to speak against them. Most of all, he retained the plebiscite: the amended constitution stated that he was 'responsible to the people, to whom he has always the right to appeal'. He showed that he had not lost his political shrewdness: like de Gaulle in 1969 he intended to prove that he retained the arbitrating role in the State; unlike de Gaulle, he pulled it off. In January 1870 he asked the electorate whether they approved the liberal reforms, but everyone took this as a vote of confidence in the regime. Many of his ministers and most liberals strongly disapproved, regarding a plebiscite as a Caesarist trick to undermine the authority of parliamentary government, which of course it was. Liberals and the extreme Left urged their supporters to vote No or abstain. In the provinces, Bonapartists urged a Yes vote, arguing that the alternative to the emperor was revolution: 'the return of the Terror, the ruin of the countryside for the benefit of the towns . . . the National Workshops'.[37] The result was an overwhelming majority of Yesses: 7.3 million, against only 1.5 million Noes. The country as a whole, it was clear, was happy with a liberalized Empire. Napoleon was delighted; and in Gambetta's disabused opinion, the Empire was stronger than ever.

Its government, however, was weak. The centrists backed Ollivier, but the Orleanist tendency was angry about the plebiscite, and their two ministers resigned. Many republicans regarded Ollivier as a turncoat, while the extreme Left in Paris was increasingly turbulent. The Victor Noir affair, in which a journalist was shot in strange circumstances by a dissolute cousin of the emperor, Pierre Bonaparte, brought out the full forces of the Parisian Left to demonstrate at his funeral. Ollivier moved in troops, and the crowds dispersed; but it was obvious that the liberal Empire had not won over the Parisian Left. On the other hand, the Bonapartist Right (nicknamed 'arcadiens' or 'mamelukes'), hoped for an opportunity to wreck the liberal experiment and return to authoritarian government. It is fruitless to speculate about whether this hybrid of liberalism and Bonapartism might have survived. For, as with the First Empire, it was not the domestic but the foreign problems inherent in the nationalist aspect of Bonapartism that destroyed it.

37. Soubadère, in Feral (1990), p. 635.

THE ROAD TO SEDAN, JULY–SEPTEMBER 1870

For four years I have heard people constantly regretting Sadowa. Well, now France
has not only a pretext . . . not only a favourable opportunity, but an imperative
motive for making war.

Deputy in Corps Législatif, 15 July 1870

On 4 July 1870, Paris learnt that Prince Leopold of Hohenzollern-Sigmaringen,
a distant relative of the King of Prussia and an officer in the Prussian army,
was a strong candidate for the vacant Spanish throne. Spain was regarded by
the French as their sphere. In the tense atmosphere following 1866, when
many expected war with Prussia, a Prussian King of Spain would at the least
force the French to split their army to guard the Pyrenees. Ollivier told the
British ambassador that no French government could consent. This was
probably true, but the Ollivier government was under more pressure than
most: they 'must show firmness and spirit or we shall not be able to cope
with revolution and socialism at home', he confided.[38] The foreign minister,
Gramont, told the Corps Législatif on 5 July that unless the candidature were
withdrawn, the government would fulfil its duty 'without hesitation or
weakness'. Bismarck, who was secretly implicated in the candidature, thought
that 'this certainly looks like war'.[39] Both sides began to prepare their armies,
the French on 9 July recalling troops from Algeria. King William of Prussia
was unwilling to force the issue, and the candidature was withdrawn, greatly
to the relief of the unenthusiastic Leopold: being King of Spain was no bed of
roses. Equally relieved were Napoleon and his ministers. Yet when Ollivier
gave the news to the Corps Législatif, instead of cheers he met scornful
criticism from his enemies the Bonapartist Right, who said the government
had been duped: there was nothing to stop the Prussians from renewing the
candidature later unless the French government forced them to give a public
undertaking. Moreover, French patriots felt that the Prussians had provoked
them, and deserved a lesson. The Austrian ambassador reported that 'public
opinion appears to push the government so hard that peace appears
henceforth impossible'.[40]

On 12 July, the emperor and Gramont, without the consent of the
government, instructed their ambassador Benedetti to obtain a promise from
the King of Prussia that he would forbid any future candidature. Benedetti
met the king informally at Ems on 13 July and asked him for his assurance.
The king, rather annoyed at what he considered an unreasonable and
somewhat insulting request, refused, though he later let Benedetti know that
he gave his 'entire and unreserved approval' to Leopold's withdrawal.
Bismarck published an edited account of the meeting that same day, the

38. Zeldin (1963), p. 174.
39. Howard (1967), p. 51.
40. Case (1954), p. 256.

notorious Ems telegram, which suggested to the Prussians that their king, and to the French that their ambassador, had been affronted, and that diplomatic relations had been practically severed. When this reached Paris, the French government assumed that the Prussians were bent on war. Each side realized that the other had already begun some military preparations, and the French minister of war, Marshal Leboeuf, threatened to resign unless he was allowed to mobilize the army; this was finally agreed on 14 July, the day before the Prussians mobilized.

The publication of the Ems telegram unleashed noisy demands for war in the press and parliament. Few dared to dissent, and they, notably Thiers, Gambetta and the republican Jules Favre, were howled down in parliament. Parisians, believing victory certain, marched through the streets shouting 'A Berlin!' War was declared on 19 July. Ollivier, justifying his actions on the grounds that he, who had never in the past supported an anti-German policy, now believed that war was necessary, used a phrase that he immediately corrected, but which, in the coming disaster, stood as a never-forgotten condemnation of him and the regime: he entered the war, he said, 'with a light heart'.

A handful of critics at home and many more abroad said that with the withdrawal of Leopold's candidature France had no justification for war: in Thiers's words (shouted down in the Chamber) the government was going to war in 'a fit of pique'. Indeed, domestic politics and light-headed chauvinism did play a major part, but the French reaction can only be understood in the context of tension with Prussia following the latter's victory in 1866. The belief that France now had an opportunity to redress the balance was based on the widespread conviction that the French army was superior, and ready to march into southern Germany before Prussia could mobilize its reserves. Then, optimists declared (and they included the emperor and Gramont), the south German states and Austria would openly ally with France to cut Prussia down to size. The North German Confederation would be broken up, and France would at last have the opportunity to expand to her 'natural frontier' on the Rhine.

This baseless confidence collapsed with the first battles in August. The emperor, very ill with gallstones, went nominally to command the army. The Ollivier government fell, and was replaced by a Bonapartist general, Cousin-Montauban, the Comte de Palikao, with the empress as regent. They refused to permit a retreat on the fortress of Paris, for fear that it would lead to revolution – a decision that turned a crisis into a catastrophe. It led on 2 September to the defeat and capture of an entire army, including the emperor himself, at Sedan. The news immediately caused uprisings in the left-wing strongholds of Marseilles, Nîmes and Mâcon. It reached Paris on 4 September. While deputies deliberated, the Paris crowd for the third time since 1815 took the initiative. Bourgeois, workers and National Guards invaded the Corps Législatif. The empress-regent and her government slipped away unheeded. France had its one bloodless revolution; the only casualty was a man who fell off some scaffolding. The republican leaders, following the ritual, proclaimed a republic at the Hôtel de Ville, and installed a Government of National Defence composed of the republican deputies for Paris. The provinces received another government by telegraph through the agency of Gambetta, self-appointed minister of the interior. Sedan destroyed the most widely supported post-revolutionary regime, now rightly blamed for having begun and lost a war. Napoleon's 'mission' to end the era of revolutions through national unity had ended ignominiously. The political future was again in the melting pot.

THE POLITICS OF WAR, 1870–71

Let us win in Paris, the rest is a detail.

Prefect, Lille, 1870[41]

Sedan and the proclamation of the Republic, to the surprise of many on both sides, did not end the war, the military aspects of which have been described in Chapter 2. Many republicans, who had opposed what they considered the emperor's war, assumed that they could make peace easily with the Germans, whose national aspirations they accepted. But German nationalism and Prussian patriotism had fed on images of the war of 1813 and threats of invasion from French nationalists claiming 'natural frontiers'. The prospect of conflict with France, especially in 1840 and 1866, had stimulated German nationalism to a 'Watch on the Rhine'. Bismarck was not alone in considering the French aggressive, arrogant and untrustworthy; he intended to guarantee future security by thoroughly defeating and weakening France. When the new government asked Bismarck's peace terms, they were appalled to discover that he intended to annexe Alsace and part of Lorraine, including the fortresses of Strasbourg and Metz, as a barrier against future French attack. They pledged to surrender 'neither an inch of our territory nor a stone of our fortresses', and continued the struggle as a great republican national crusade.

Behind the patriotic fervour, however, lurked mistrust. Republicans believed that to pursue victory, as in the 1790s, would enable them to complete the revolution of September. Gambetta, who left beleaguered Paris by balloon in October to galvanize resistance in the provinces, was compared with Danton. He appointed ardent republicans as prefects, who purged local government of men who had served the Empire. They stressed decisive action, not consultation. Gambetta's reluctance to hold elections and readiness to dissolve uncooperative local councils led to accusations of dictatorship. The cities, strongholds of radicalism, supported Gambetta, and further alarmed conservatives by arming workers and closing Catholic schools; and the Paris police were ordered to shave off their 'imperial' whiskers. Many conservatives feared that the Left aimed to bring about real revolution, and concluded that the only way to stop them was to stop the

41. Audoin-Rouzeau (1989), p. 178.

war. This view was widespread in rural areas and small towns, especially in the traditionally less patriotic rural south, but also in the areas occupied by the Germans. These divisions emerged as the prospect of victory dwindled. The general fall in morale is shown by the numbers volunteering for the army: 36,000 in August, 17,000 in October, 6,000 in January.

The stark alternative facing the government was personified by Thiers and Gambetta. Thiers had gone round the European capitals in October in a vain attempt to enlist diplomatic support: the other governments felt that France had brought her troubles on herself, and would go no further than to urge negotiations. He was convinced that fighting on was hopeless: 'every day of resistance will be paid for . . . A prompt peace, if we are not counting on a miracle, could be paid for with one province and two billion; a delayed peace will be two provinces and four or five billion, plus a month or two of dreadful devastation'. It was an accurate forecast, but too bleak for the government to accept in the face of left-wing pressure to fight. They preferred Gambetta's view that with ruthless determination the war could be continued in the provinces until the Germans were so worn out that they would offer easy terms. The Germans were indeed growing impatient, but were more inclined to greater harshness than to conciliation. So the war continued, sustained above all by the stoical determination of Parisians, who pressed the government to fight on, in spite of cold, hunger and bombardment. Only when Paris was practically out of food on 28 January 1871 did the government sign an armistice, not just for Paris but for the whole country: a course of action which the indomitable Gambetta accepted with great reluctance.

Defeat left a political vacuum, deep divisions, economic disruption, psychological trauma, a vast quantity of uncontrolled weaponry (more than 300,000 rifles and 600 cannon in Paris alone) – in short, all the ingredients of crisis. This was reflected in the results of elections held on 8 February to a National Assembly to meet at Bordeaux. The elections were to decide war or peace. The peace party was a reincarnation of the 1849 Party of Order of monarchists and moderate republicans. The war party was Gambetta and his supporters, strong in the provincial cities, and a large part of the population of Paris, especially the Left. The peace party, which had been preparing for months, won decisively. But party divisions were not simply about the war: the eclipse of Bonapartism inevitably revived the 'old parties', eager to fill the political vacuum:

Orleanists	214 seats
Legitimists	186
Republicans	150
Independents	80
Bonapartists	15[42]

42. Rudelle (1982), p. 18.

The royalists were *notables*, many returning to public life for the first time since 1851 or even 1830, many quite new to parliament. They were 'the old France . . . squires, gentlemen . . . their picturesque appearance made the Bordelais laugh'.[43] They owed their election to their local prominence, to their wartime leadership, for example, commanding local Gardes Mobiles, and to their opposition to Gambetta's war. Thiers, always an opponent of the war and advocate of a quick peace, had been elected by 26 departments: a never equalled feat. The Assembly duly elected him chief of the executive power of the French Republic when it met in Bordeaux on 13 February 1871. The Republic seemed doomed: already unpopular after the failures of 1848, it was now associated with war and defeat. Thiers, however, had long thought it possible that France would become a republic, if only because of the quarrels of royalists. In 1850 he had coined the famous definition of the Republic as 'the government that divides us least'. Even in the dark days of 1871 he believed that the Republic had a chance: 'if we succeed in this reorganization [of France] it will be done under the form of the republic and to its profit'. The tasks in which they had to succeed were formidable: to make peace, end the German occupation, repair the devastation of war, restore State finances and the administration and rebuild the army. Until this were done, urged Thiers, no decision could be taken concerning the country's future form of government. This political truce, the 'Bordeaux Pact', was agreed by the Assembly on 19 February.

THE FINAL ERUPTION: THE PARIS COMMUNE, MARCH–MAY 1871

Debout les damnés de la terre
Debout les forçats de la faim,
La raison tonne en son cratère,
C'est l'eruption de la fin!

Eugène Pottier, 'L'Internationale', 1871

The improbable success of the Commune will bring back the Prussians. The hardly doubtful success of the government will be the signal for an intense reaction.

Republican politician, 1871

Paris, however, was not a party to the Bordeaux Pact. As we have seen in earlier chapters, the capital, and to a lesser extent other large cities, had long been politically far more radical than the rest of the country. The experience of the war, when Parisians, cut off from the rest of the country, had felt they were fighting almost alone, had deepened this separation. The provinces voted overwhelmingly for peace; but Paris elected to the Assembly a pro-war left-wing contingent: veterans such as Blanc, Hugo (back again as

43. Halévy (1937), vol. 1, pp. 10–11.

self-appointed national conscience), Garibaldi and Delescluze; young radicals such as Gambetta and Clemenceau; socialists such as Tolain. They voted against the preliminary peace terms that Thiers and Favre had negotiated with Bismarck: the loss of Alsace and much of Lorraine, and an indemnity of 5 billion francs. Thiers kept the fortress of Belfort in exchange for a German parade down the Champs Elysées. The Assembly, by 546 to 107, consented amid intensely emotional scenes. Some of the hard-line patriots walked out; a deputy from Strasbourg, about to be ceded to Germany, died of a heart attack.

Many Parisians considered the treaty a betrayal. The National Guard organized itself independently of government authority into a Republican Federation. Angry at the prospect of German troops entering Paris, and believing that hostilities might recommence, National Guards seized rifles, ammunition and cannon which were hauled off to working-class districts, principally Montmartre and Belleville. As well as being anti-German, the National Guard Federation was also determinedly republican. The two things went together: they saw the peace as both unpatriotic and reactionary. The royalists, they believed (not entirely without reason), were eager for peace because, with Prussian connivance, they planned to restore a monarchy. Demonstrations, arms seizures and attacks on the police became daily occurrences; the government, with few armed troops in the city following the armistice, was helpless. The court martial of some left-wing leaders, the banning of radical newspapers and an Assembly measure to end the wartime moratorium on commercial debts, which threatened small businessmen, aggravated the situation. In the circumstances, the royalist majority in the Assembly refused to meet in Paris, menaced by 'the paving-stones of the mob', as one deputy put it, and voted to sit at Versailles.

Thiers sent troops to take back the several hundred cannon seized by the National Guard Federation. Was this deliberate provocation, as has often been suggested? The strongest evidence against such a view is that the government was militarily so unprepared. Rather, it was a fatally reckless attempt to defuse the crisis at a stroke. Instead, it precipitated the last great Parisian uprising. Early on 18 March, crowds of women, men and children turned out to block the path of the outnumbered and half-hearted troops who were trying to haul dozens of cannon down the steep cobbled streets of Montmartre. Many soldiers fraternized with the crowd. A regular army general, Lecomte, and a former commander of the National Guard, a veteran republican of 1830 and 1848, Thomas, were shot by the insurgents. These scenes, reminiscent of February 1848, caused the generals and the government to panic, and they fled to Versailles. Evacuation of the city in case of serious disturbance was a familiar idea, and one that Thiers had spoken of in the past. But on this occasion it had certainly not been planned, and it had the immense disadvantage for the government of abandoning the fortifications of Paris and its huge arsenal of artillery, gunboats, armoured trains, machine-guns, rifles and millions of rounds of ammunition into the hands of the insurgents. Never had a revolution won so great a prize and at such little cost.

The National Guard Federation (the *fédérés*) were as unprepared as the government. Only a few, particularly the Blanquists, wanted to force a crisis; others feared a repetition of the 'terrible June days' of 1848. After strained attempts to negotiate a compromise, elections were called for a Paris Commune. Some 230,000 people voted, just under half the electorate. The election, far from leading to a peaceful solution, precipitated conflict. Many middle-class voters had left the city; conservatives and many moderates boycotted the vote. The Commune Council was dominated by the extreme Left: veterans from 1848 such as Delescluze and Pyat, youthful Blanquists such as Eudes, Ferré and Rigault, working-class activists such as Varlin, Malon and Assi, revolutionary intellectuals such as Vallès, Vaillant and Vermorel. All had been prominent in campaigns against the Empire in the late 1860s, but the siege had given them a much wider constituency within Paris as uncompromising partisans of national defence and the Republic. The insurgent population of skilled workers and the *bourgeoisie populaire* (see p. 276) was typical of Paris radicalism since the Revolution.

The improvised revolution needed a programme. The name Commune evoked the heritage of 1792; it also echoed Proudhonist ideas of local autonomy. The main statement of its aims was the Déclaration au Peuple Français (19 April), a synthesis of radical republicanism and Proudhonian socialism, much more precise in its political than its socio-economic agenda. The stated intention was to break down the oppressive State and its expensive unproductive pillars: police, army, bureaucracy, Church. 'The Free City of Paris' was to become a model republic, governed directly by its male citizens as electors and National Guards. It was also to be autonomous, a fundamental right of all communes, and hence would remain republican whatever the rest of France did. Social intentions were less ambitious. The declaration referred vaguely to 'measures to be taken to improve the social welfare of the citizens'. Since 1848, there had been a reaction against utopianism, and a stress on gaining power first: this was true over the whole spectrum of the extreme Left, from Gambetta to Blanqui. Moreover, there were disagreements over what social measures were desirable. Finally, the need to maximize support among the republican middle classes in Paris and the provincial cities may have encouraged prudence. Social measures taken were therefore limited and pragmatic. The pressure of debt built up during the war was somewhat alleviated by extending the moratorium on payments and handing back small articles pledged at the municipal pawnshop. Night work in bakeries was banned. Some socialist members believed that a government should not interfere in free collective bargaining; but intervention was considered proper in this case because bakers were forbidden by law to strike. Abandoned workshops were to be handed over to workers' associations to be reopened, but the original owners would be paid compensation; there was no suggestion of expropriating going concerns. There was no class war: 'the hard-working bourgeoisie, honest and robust' was 'the sister of the proletariat', proclaimed the largest Communard newspaper *Le Cri du Peuple*. The Commune authorities maintained good relations with many private firms producing arms and equipment, and courteous ones with the Bank of France, from which it obtained funds. One member of the Commune, the Hungarian Frankel (one of only two or three Marxists), exclaimed impatiently, 'unless the Commune does something for working people I cannot see its justification'.

But its primary justification lay elsewhere: defence of the Republic against 'reaction'. That the Republic should be made permanent and the 'rights of Paris' guaranteed were always the fundamental demands. From early April onwards, Paris was at war, in the minds of many Communards, with the descendants of the Chouans and aristocrats of the 1790s. The main activity became military. It has been traditional to stress the Communards' inefficiency and indiscipline, though it is hard to see by what criteria they should be judged. If compared with the Red Army in 1917 or the republican militia in Spain in 1936, their performance would probably look rather good. Moreover, the National Guard was a real citizen army: one of the few in history not to maintain discipline by killing its own men. In any case, a defence was improvised capably enough to keep the regular army (eventually over 130,000 strong) out of Paris for several weeks: no mean achievement. In the long run, the fight was hopeless, but this the Communard leadership could never bring itself to accept, hoping to the last for a miraculous *levée en masse* or rising in the provinces to save it. But its allies in the provinces were few: sympathetic uprisings in several towns – Marseilles, Lyons, Narbonne, Limoges – lasted only days or hours, and most republicans, far from entering the fray, urged both sides to negotiate. The Commune's fight against 'reaction' within their gates was principally directed against the Church, sinister conspirators of reaction, corrupters of youth, whose influence had to be eradicated if the Republic was to progress towards the golden future. Most fervent here were the Blanquists, who as self-proclaimed experts in revolutionary power had taken over the Prefecture of Police (abolished by the Commune, and so officially the 'Ex-Prefecture'). Evidence of priestly crime was sometimes manufactured to arouse public indignation. Church schools were closed, nuns ejected from their jobs in hospitals and prisons, convents and monasteries searched for arms, and parish churches ransacked. The archbishop of Paris and other priests were taken as hostages and 24 eventually shot.

There were opportunities for more beneficent initiatives amid the usually well-meaning and amiable semi-anarchy of Paris under the Commune. For example, model schools were established, in which women had a rare opportunity to take a leading role. The painter Courbet helped set up an artists' federation. The distinction between State and citizen was intended to disappear, with all officials being elected. Citizens as National Guards were to defend and police Paris, a democratic 'dictatorship of the proletariat' applauded by Marx and Engels, which in practice meant wearisome nights of guard duty, arresting prostitutes, gamblers and drunks or confiscating illegally baked bread, as well as fighting in the trenches. Because the Commune was such a big and kaleidoscopic happening, largely run by workers, suggestive of possibilities but not long enough to be disappointing, so luridly dramatic in its end and above all because it was the last, it has come to occupy a prominent position in historical writing in which myth and reality were and are frequently difficult to distinguish.

The Commune's existence was one of constant emergency and improvization. The only clear political division that emerged was on 1 May between the 'majority' (mainly 'neo-Jacobin' radicals and Blanquists) which favoured a dictatorship by a Committee of Public Safety, and a 'minority' that insisted on democracy and rejected the language of the 1790s. In this debate, personality, ideology and tactics were inextricably mixed, and in any case it was cut short (like so many of the Commune's debates) by the irruption of events outside. Broadly speaking, the Communard view of revolution stressed the spontaneous fervour of the people, the *levée en masse* based on the legend of 'our forefathers' of 1789 and 1792. This vision, both rhetorical device and genuine conviction, seems to have helped to keep the insurrection going in manifestly hopeless circumstances.

On 21 May, after a five-week siege, government troops slipped through the city ramparts. What followed – *la Semaine Sanglante* (Bloody Week) – was the worst civil bloodshed in Europe between the 1790s and the 1940s: a week of street-fighting that saw the burning of buildings by the retreating rebels (including the Tuileries, the Hôtel de Ville and part of the Louvre), mass executions of captured *fédérés* and reprisal killing of hostages. The army, applauded by politicians, intellectuals and the press, slaughtered thousands, determined to wipe out the 'dangerous class' whom they believed responsible for a criminal revolt against a defeated France (see pp. 18–19).

Thiers told the Assembly that he hoped these horrors would serve as a lesson: they did, though not quite as he intended. The French Left, radicals and most socialists, did indeed give up the idea of an old-style revolution on the barricades. In Furet's words, 'the last great uprising . . . the one which created the most fear and shed the most blood . . . formed the ultimate exorcism of a violence which had been an inseparable part of French public life since the end of the eighteenth century'.[44] But the Left now had new legends and renewed hatreds: of royalists, the army, and moderate republicans, once again, as in 1848, slaughterers of the people. Some of its leaders were more ready to look to international working-class solidarity in place of the old revolutionary nationalism. The effects would be felt well into the next century.

Most of the country, however, seems to have remained more detached from the Parisian conflict than in 1848 or 1851. Voters were less willing to be frightened than 20 years earlier, and failed to respond to the alarmist warnings of royalists that a republic necessarily meant disorder. 'All is saved', exclaimed Clemenceau, 'the provinces have not been frightened!'[45] On the contrary, most provincial voters gravitated towards the Republic that had defeated the Commune, as by-elections in July proved.

44. Furet (1992), p. 506.
45. Nicolet (1982), p. 157.

With the defeat of the Commune the Revolution had, as Furet puts it, been 'tamed'.[46] The 'era of revolutions' was over, at appalling cost. Crushing military defeat had demolished one revolutionary myth: that of France's destiny to lead Europe. The two sieges of Paris, by the Prussians and the Versaillais, had buried another revolutionary myth: that of the people's invincibility. Napoleon III's aspiration to end the era of revolutions thus came true with terrible irony: it was not his successes that had brought it about, but his military and political failures.

46. Furet (1988), p. 494.

THE GOVERNMENT THAT DIVIDES US LEAST, 1871–1914

CHAPTER 21

THE SURVIVAL OF THE REPUBLIC, 1871–90

The Republic exists, it is the legal government of the country: to want anything else would be a new revolution, and the most fearsome of all.

Thiers, November 1872

The era of revolutions had ended; but that is clear only with hindsight. For those living in 1871, political collapse, defeat and revolution began a period of uncertainty. The Left feared a monarchical reaction; the Right, a return of the Commune. All feared another war. Above all, the electorate wanted a safe option. That proved to be the Republic, the lowest common denominator, the status quo. This 'conservative republic' for the first time conquered the support of the majority. Many historians, especially in France, present the 'triumph' of the Republic as the natural, logical and even inevitable conclusion of the Revolution and the embodiment of the 'values of 1789': 'the French Revolution was coming into port', concludes Furet.[1] This rather whiggish approach seems to have been reinvigorated by the abandonment of Marxist teleology over the last generation, and by a desire, admirable in its way, to reaffirm liberal 'republican' values. We should take such political piety with a pinch of salt. The 'values of 1789' were widely accepted, and had been practised in some form since the fall of the Jacobin dictatorship (which had practised a more totalitarian form of democracy). Legal and religious equality had been consecrated in the 1814 Charter. National sovereignty had been successfully asserted in 1830. Parliamentary government had laid down its rules between 1815 and 1848. Universal male suffrage dated from 1848. In that sense, the Revolution had been coming into port ever since its journey began. The 'values of 1789' prevailed piecemeal as a result of practical political need, like the 'necessary liberties' won in the struggles of the 1860s. The Third Republic certainly claimed to be the legitimate heir of the revolutionary tradition (though as was seen in Part I dispute continued about precisely what this

1. Furet (1992), p. 537.

involved). And it did single-mindedly pursue certain aspects of the revolutionary heritage – freedom of expression, secularism, education, cultural homogenization. However, republicanism was deliberately diluted with a large dose of consensus liberalism influenced by British and American models, the 'values of 1688' and the 'values of 1775', so to speak. Finally, the Third Republic succeeded politically by stepping into the empty shoes of popular Bonapartism, offering order, democracy and patriotism deliberately shorn of the utopianism of 1848 and 1871. Its survival was less a victory of ideology than a product of circumstance, a victory by default.

MONSIEUR THIERS'S REPUBLIC, 1871–73

The Republic will be conservative or it will not be.

Thiers, November 1872

The two years that followed the end of the German war and the civil war were a period of surface calm, which is what most people desperately wanted. The political nation, restrained by the 'Bordeaux Pact', turned its collective mind to repairing the terrible damage caused by the war. Thiers was irreplaceable, less because of his considerable skill in the business of government than because of the confidence his reputation as an elder statesman and as the man who had defeated the Commune inspired at home and abroad, not least in Germany. A clever, diminutive, self-made Marseillais, amusing, vain, exasperating and irrepressibly loquacious, rather resembling Mr Punch in appearance and even manner, now 73, but still frenetically energetic and dominating, he exerted for two years a personal grip on the direction of the State unequalled since Napoleon I.[2] 'Monsieur Thiers', as he was universally called (whether respectfully or sarcastically), had played an important role in every regime since the Restoration – and on the whole a destructive one. He was detested personally and politically by many royalists and republicans, who regarded him as the archetype of the vulgar and soulless bourgeois on the make, without principles, imagination or ideas. His determination to follow a *juste milieu* that would reject both revolution and counter-revolution, and could accommodate universal suffrage while avoiding the populist risks of Bonapartism, did much to remould popular perceptions of what a republic could be. Above all, he provided reassurance to an electorate terrified of war and upheaval: he was the first in a line of old men to whom the French turned in times of crisis. In Furet's barbed conclusion, he was 'the greatest French statesman of the nineteenth century' because he had 'finished by wearing out the Revolution'.[3]

The first priority was to sign a peace treaty. The Treaty of Frankfurt was

---

2. Napoleon III, whose impact was greater, never tried to control the minutiae of government.
3. Furet (1992), pp. 513–14 – a stimulating pen portrait.

signed on 10 May, confirming the cession of Alsace-Lorraine and an indemnity of 5 billion francs. Many experts believed that the sum was too huge to be paid quickly or even at all (it was the equivalent of two-and-a-half times the annual state budget) and that it would permanently weaken French finances and prevent large military spending. However, the defeat of the Commune began a remarkably quick return of confidence. Two international loans, the largest ever raised, were floated in June 1871 and July 1872, and greatly over-subscribed. This success, taken as evidence of French recovery, and portending the end of the German occupation, caused public rejoicing. It was a personal triumph for Thiers, and also a success for the Republic. As Reuters put it, 'eagerness country entrust savings state proves that, under Thiers Republic, order, law, property will be respected and that France has confidence in its destiny'.

Thiers's intention was to encourage calm. This meant keeping the Republic and not undertaking reforms. As we have noted, he considered a republic the government 'that divides us least'. Liberal writers such as Tocqueville, Laboulaye and Prévost-Paradol had all looked to America as a model: to the Republic of Washington and Jefferson, not that of Danton and Robespierre. Thiers announced a conservative republic, at first sight a contradiction in terms. But thinking that a trend towards democracy was inevitable, he believed that only a republic would be popular enough to control the masses: 'the only government . . . that can speak to democracy with sufficient authority'. He wanted the Assembly to draw up a republican constitution with institutional checks and balances: a strong presidency and a senate. If the July Monarchy had been designed as 'the best of republics', Thiers's Republic was to be the best of monarchies. He was perfectly satisfied with 'material order' – calm in the streets and economic recovery – and had no sympathy with the wishes of many on Right and Left for fundamental reform. He blocked indefinitely a whole list of measures: local government decentralization ('a syringe in my prefects' backsides'), income tax ('civil war by finance') and universal short-service conscription. While he was involved in negotiations over the evacuation of German troops with Bismarck (who made it clear that he trusted Thiers and no one else), his position was impregnable, and the Assembly had to bow the knee.

This moderate conservatism reassured much of the 'silent majority', but reassurance was less easy to promote among the political class. The issues raised by the war and the Commune had further polarized it. Both poles, royalist and republican, were horrified by France's downfall, and aimed to regenerate what they considered a decadent society and state, though in quite different ways. For royalists, regeneration meant a restoration of monarchy, religion, tradition and a paternalistic social hierarchy – in short, a 'moral order' of society. For republicans, it meant on the contrary creating free citizens by breaking the influence of the Church and the *notables* – a different kind of moral order (see p. 50). Moreover, the political upheavals of the past months, and in particular the vacuum left by the eclipse of popular Bonapartism, convinced both sides that victory was within their grasp. The

1871 elections had given a large royalist majority. But by-elections since showed a string of republican successes: of 38 held between January 1872 and May 1873, republicans won 31.[4]

The two royalist parties, legitimist and Orleanist, had managed to arrive at a common strategy after four decades of rivalry or worse. Together they had a majority in the Assembly; but their political ideas were really no more alike than when they divided in 1830. True legitimists, followers of 'Henri V', the Bourbon Comte de Chambord, grandson of Charles X, the 'miracle child' of 1820, detested republicanism as a godless abomination. Many had become fervently ultramontane since mid-century, with a mystical devotion to the Church and the papacy as well as to a divine-right notion of monarchy. The Orleanists were liberals who saw constitutional monarchy as a desirable source of stability and dignity; their king was a functionary, not a priest, and certainly not an absolute authority. Many Orleanists had been prepared to contemplate a republic if it could guarantee liberty, order and property, but the war and the Commune had frightened them: they did not think that Thiers's 'conservative republic' would last. Their unexpected electoral victory in 1871 provided a tempting opportunity to restore a monarchy as a bulwark against radicalism and socialism. They were prepared to put Chambord on the throne in the knowledge that he had no children, and that Louis-Philippe's grandson, the Comte de Paris, would succeed him. The royalists expected, probably rightly, that the country, exhausted by war and civil strife, would acquiesce. France, they liked to repeat, was by nature a monarchy: its republics had always been short-lived and unhappy, for the French wanted and needed strong and stable government. Besides, no Great Power could function as a republic.

On 5 July 1871, however, the Comte de Chambord published a manifesto saying that he would not ascend the throne unless the tricolour was replaced by the white flag of the Bourbons, 'the standard of Henri IV, of François I and of Joan of Arc . . . I received it as a sacred trust from the old king my grandfather, dying in exile. It floated over my cradle, I wish it to shade my grave. Frenchmen, Henri V cannot abandon the white flag of Henri IV.' He had said the same thing in the past. But in the present circumstances, the majority even of legitimists thought that for the good of France he would be prepared to sacrifice a matter of personal sentiment, for 'when the white flag is waved, the people think that privilege and feudalism are returning, and equality being suppressed'. But Chambord was deaf to political expediency: he would be king on his own terms or not at all. The legitimists were disheartened, the Orleanists furious. Restoration stopped in its tracks. Thiers was elated: Chambord, he joked, would go down in history as the French Washington – the founder of the Republic.

The following month, August 1871, Thiers signalled that he was out to establish the Republic permanently. One of his supporters, Rivet, proposed to the Assembly that Thiers should be formally entitled president of the

4. Mayeur (1984), p. 31.

Republic, a motion passed by 491 to 94 (the latter being legitimists). This was the first sign of a strategy that Thiers was to follow over the next 21 months: to push the Assembly into voting a conservative republican constitution by agreement of the centre groups, Orleanist and republican, against the resistance of the extremes, both legitimist and radical republican.

In March 1873, Thiers concluded a convention with Bismarck agreeing on the departure of German occupation troops. His popularity in the country was confirmed as 'the liberator of the territory'. The Pact of Bordeaux was therefore ending, and the Assembly would have to vote a constitution. However, the conclusion of negotiations with Germany also meant that he was no longer essential: a colleague told him that he could now say his *Nunc Dimittis*. In April, Gambetta and the radicals put up a well-known anticlerical, Barodet, in a by-election in Paris against Thiers's old friend and foreign minister, the aristocratic liberal Rémusat. Barodet won. Not for the first time, a Paris by-election was taken as a portent. Alarmed conservatives, including those who had been willing to go along with Thiers's conservative republic, now decided that any sort of republic was dangerous: Thiers could not control the radicals, who, they thought, were preparing another Paris Commune. Only uncompromising conservatism, they thought, could save them from the 'Reds'. So they voted Thiers out of office on 23 May.

His fall marked another defeat for liberalism, and of another attempt to create a centrist consensus superseding the great ideological division bequeathed by the Revolution – something that Louis XVIII, Decazes and Benjamin Constant would have understood. Paradoxically, the Third Republic would be in many ways conservative, but it would never be centrist: it would always be ideologically a regime of the Left. Thiers wrote to a royalist opponent 'I am more conservative than any of you ... It was necessary to pacify, and you have angered. That is what has been done for fifty years, and no government can become established ... You have all served the radicals more than the conservatives.' The Third Republic would indeed prove in time to be essentially the regime of the radicals: democratic, secularist, anti-socialist.

THE DUKES' REPUBLIC, 1873–77

We were monarchists and the nation was not.

Vicomte de Meaux

The Duc de Broglie, scion of a great liberal dynasty which included Necker and Staël, had led the attack on Thiers. He then played a leading part in that episode ironically called '*la république des ducs*', when royalist nobles, in power for the last time, tried to restore a monarchy and ended by creating a republic. Until Chambord saw reason or died, the pass had to be held. A soldier would be head of State: another duke, Marshal de MacMahon, Duc de Magenta, hero of the Crimea and Italy, gallant loser at Sedan and, perhaps more important, conqueror of the Paris Commune. The political brains were provided by Broglie. His aim was to resist the rise of the radicals and if possible bring Henry V to the throne, and thus (in the words of the statement he wrote for MacMahon) put France back on the path of 'moral order', that elusive utopia of harmony and authority.

The problem was the legitimists: counter-revolutionary fervour proved fatal to conservative common sense. Attempts were made to persuade Chambord to make concessions – for example, to have a flag that would be white on one side and tricolour on the other – but in vain. Chambord, a man of no experience or visible talents, reputed unable to tie his own shoe-laces, and who knew nothing of France, apparently intended to rule as an absolute monarch. That ended all prospects of his restoration; but the legitimists would not countenance any other king while he lived. 'So we've been dreaming', sighed one royalist. They had no option but to keep MacMahon in power, and voted him a long seven-year term of office. This was to make him a barrier against the Left, and keep the route open, if Chambord died in time, for the restoration of the Comte de Paris. Part of the electorate, however, had quite another restoration in mind: in another portentous by-election on 24 May 1874 Bourgoing, a former equerry of Napoleon III, won a seat from the republicans. This brought home to royalists and republicans that voters who mistrusted a republic and feared a monarchy might go back to their old love: 'the people's Napoleons', able to offer authority without dukes and democracy without reds. The Orleanists and Gambetta's Union Républicaine decided that they must fix a constitution. The Orleanists would agree to a republican constitution; in return Gambetta would agree to conservative checks and balances, most importantly a Senate, heavily over-representing rural France, and with a proportion of life senators as a quasi-peerage. On 30 January 1875, the momentous symbolic line was crossed: the liberal Wallon proposed an amendment that defined the regime as a republic and became the second article of the constitution: 'The President of the Republic . . . is elected by the Senate and the Chamber'. It passed by a single vote. Broglie led the bulk of the Orleanists to join nearly all the republicans to pass a series of constitutional laws over the next five months. Against were 200 die-hard royalists, 30 Bonapartists and a few extreme radicals under Clemenceau. However, there was more duplicity than genuine compromise: most Orleanists and republicans looked forward to revising the constitution in favourable circumstances, the former to replace the president with a king, the latter to create a truly democratic republic.

General elections to the two new chambers in February and March 1876 saw a collapse of the royalists: to the 360 seats won by the various republican groups they had only 76, while the Bonapartists more than doubled to 75. Governments were formed first by Dufaure then by Jules Simon, both former ministers of Thiers. Dufaure had been a minister under Louis-Philippe; two of his colleagues, Casimir-Perier and Bardoux, were relatives of leading July Monarchy politicians. Simon came from the most moderate wing of the old republican party. This was a 'conservative republic' with a vengeance, which neither Gambetta and his keen young followers nor the extreme-Left ginger-group led by Clemenceau could stomach. The clerical issue, that raw nerve of French politics, brought down first Dufaure, defeated in the Chamber by the Left for being too soft on clericalism, and then Simon, sacked by MacMahon for being too soft on anticlericalism – an act that became known as the coup d'état of *seize mai* (16 May) 1877.

The only hope of Broglie, back in power, was to win a general election, for neither he nor MacMahon were prepared to contemplate a real coup d'état. Conservatives liked to believe that a determined government, using its powers of coercion and inducement, could influence ordinary voters, whom they presumably regarded as having no firm opinions. Here they had clearly learnt nothing and forgotten rather a lot: they intended to use the methods they had condemned under the Empire, but overlooked both the genuine popularity of Bonapartism, and the failure of those methods during the 1860s, not to mention their own failures during the Second Republic. Unreliable prefects and mayors were removed. Newspapers were prosecuted, civil servants enlisted as auxiliaries or threatened with dismissal, conservative propaganda circulated by government agencies, and that of the opposition forbidden. Owners of republican meeting-places were threatened. This was a repetition, in short, of the struggle against the démoc-socs in 1849–51. The great difference in 1876 was that the Right had no Bonaparte to provide a positive appeal to the electorate. The only nationally popular politicians were both on the Left: Gambetta and Thiers, now allies. Thiers's death at the height of the campaign set republicanism on a more radical track, but his funeral in Paris, the city he had crushed in 1871, became a grand ceremony of republican unity. The result of the general elections on 14 October 1877 showed how gravely the monarchists had miscalculated: republicans retained a majority of 317 seats to 199.

Gambetta publicly warned MacMahon that he would have to 'se soumettre ou se démettre' (submit or resign), and the marshal gave in and recalled Dufaure. In January 1879, elections to the Senate gave the republicans a majority there too. The party was now impatient to have its own men in national and local power. MacMahon resigned. There was a great purge of officials and a new generation of politicians and civil servants took power. The 'dukes' republic' had come to an end not with a bang but a whimper; it was the end of the old *notables* as a ruling class, for they never again held so many seats, and certainly never again dominated a government. This, ironically, was precipitated by the romantic royalism of Chambord and his followers, who had wrecked the last chance of a restoration. As Halévy remarked, this was very different from the pragmatic tradition of the French monarchy, not least that of Henri IV for whom Paris was well worth a mass; but with 'Henri V' royalism left the realm of politics for that of myth. Thiers's prediction in 1871 that the future would belong to 'les plus sages' (the most sensible) had proved correct.

The republican victory was not overwhelming: a large minority of the electorate – over 3 million, to the republicans' 4 million – voted for the Right.

The Bonapartists made an extraordinary recovery, becoming the strongest of the monarchist parties from 1876. The Republic had some remarkable luck: after gallstones and the British medical establishment had killed Napoleon III in 1873, the Zulus, inadvertently abetted by the British army, killed his son the Prince Imperial on 1 June 1879, leaving the Bonapartists divided and adrift. The Right, having briefly had three candidates for one throne, had to wait 60 years for another effective figurehead.

THE REPUBLICANS' REPUBLIC, 1879–85

For the first time in the history of the world, the French Republic is governing and leading a great people without God or King.

Revue Occidentale[5]

By 1879 the republicans had for the first time won a consistent series of victories by popular vote: they had to some extent lived down the suspicions of the rural electorate and replaced the Bonapartists as the people's friends. They celebrated by showing the country and the world that the Republic had arrived: the 'Marseillaise', hitherto banned, became the national anthem; 14 July was proclaimed the national holiday; parliament returned from Versailles to Paris; full amnesty for the remaining Communard transportees was proclaimed; as if to balance the picture, the army, guarantee of internal order as well as national security, was paraded at Longchamps on 14 July. The Longchamps review became the great annual ritual of a Republic that made patriotism its core value and the war of 1870 its new epic. In thousands of villages, especially in the traditional republican regions, 14 July in miniature became a truly popular festival.

A large part of the victory was due to the leadership of Léon Gambetta, son of an Italian grocer at Cahors, a bearded, scruffy, beer-drinking barrister from the Latin Quarter, the unlikely hero (or to some the 'raving madman') of the doomed war effort of 1870–71, and also a shrewd politician who had realized that republicanism needed to be sold to a timid electorate. He had appointed himself its 'travelling salesman' in tireless provincial speaking tours, when his exuberant personality, it was said, made the temperature rise when he entered a room. He had also worked to make the republican party – especially his faction, the Union Républicaine – fit to govern.

The 'republican party' was a heterogeneous coalition, socially and regionally, from landed notables to factory workers, from Lille to Provence. Its leaders were determined to disprove the taunt that a republic meant chaos. All could agree on a general programme: republicanizing the State; realizing the 'principles of 1789'; and regenerating the nation after the catastrophe of 1870. Not all could agree on exactly how to do all this, and how quickly. Should they concentrate on reassuring a barely convinced

5. Nicolet (1982), p. 242.

electorate that the Republic was safe? Or should they use their power to weaken the sources of opposition and remake France as a truly republican nation? Almost at once they fragmented.

The moderate wing were called 'opportunists' by their critics and 'government republicans' by one of their leaders, Ferry. Both names are revealing: reforms must come when they were 'opportune', said Gambetta. The eagerness to shoulder government and abandon the republican tradition of perpetual opposition was their defining characteristic. But they themselves were divided. The largest republican group was Gambetta's Union Républicaine, 204 members in 1881. Next came the Gauche Républicaine, led by Jules Ferry and Jules Grèvy, 179 deputies in 1881, most obviously defined by its suspicion of Gambetta and his followers. This dated from Gambetta's radicalism of the late 1860s, his wartime 'dictatorship', and his radicalism in the early 1870s which helped cause the fall of Thiers and the temporary rule of 'the dukes'. In spite of his recent circumspection in domestic or foreign affairs, they did not regard him as safe or respectable. He and his closest followers were career politicians, closer to the Rue du Croissant, Paris's Grub Street, than to the French Academy, and one would hesitate to invite them to spend the weekend at one's *château* (though Gambetta did come to be on good terms with the Prince of Wales, who was clearly less fastidious).

The radical wing of the party, called *radicaux* or *intransigents* were themselves subdivided into *Gauche radicale* and *extrème Gauche*. They included veterans of the 1840s such as Louis Blanc (d. 1882), and a younger generation from the democratic opposition of the 1860s. Prominent were the journalist Rochefort, who made a lifelong career out of extremist provocation, and the young doctor Clemenceau, equally ruthless with tongue, pen and pistol, who had close links with the socialist fringe from the Marx family to the ageing revolutionary Blanqui (d. 1881), who regarded him as his successor. Radicals regarded themselves as the pure republicans, fighting both the intrigues of reaction and the corruptions of office. Many of them had sympathized, usually at a distance, with the Paris Commune, and they campaigned throughout the 1870s for an amnesty for convicted Communards; they detested those (including Jules Ferry) who had sided with Versailles. They were strongest among the small businessmen and skilled workers of Paris and the other cities, with support in the strongholds of the south-east and 'Blue' west.

Jules Grèvy, first republican president of the Third Republic, was a *notable* of starchily respectable appearance who symbolized rejection of the personal rule of a Bonaparte or a MacMahon. He promised parliament that he would never oppose its will by dismissing a government or dissolving the Chamber: a significant step in the creation of the Third Republic's constitutional conventions, by which the president became a non-executive symbol 'paid to wear evening dress during the day'. But Grèvy still took part in the political game, discreetly playing off the various factions when governments were formed. This too set a precedent for his successors. Grèvy and his circle were determined to keep Gambetta out of power, in spite of his electoral popularity and his power within the party. Instead, Grèvy chose the obscure centrist Waddington, notable chiefly as the only Cambridge rowing blue so far to head a French government. This set another important constitutional precedent: the president was not required to invite the main party leader to form a government. After republican success in the 1881 elections, however, which strengthened Gambetta's Union Républicaine, Grèvy was forced to give in. Gambetta, who had waited so long and worked so hard to win power, and to prepare himself and his supporters for it, planned to form a 'grand ministère': a cabinet including all the major republican leaders. However, personal rivalry and fears of Gambetta's intentions in foreign policy and over railway nationalization made them refuse to serve. Gambetta had only his own youthful and inexperienced supporters, which opponents sarcastically called his 'grand ministère'. The combined opposition of moderates and radicals to Gambetta's proposals to reform the constitution forced him to resign in January 1882 after only 73 days in office. It was effectively the end of his career, for he died suddenly after an accident in December, aged only 45. This was more than just a personal tragedy of unfulfilled promise. He was the only man who still had a chance, however slim it had become by 1882, to reunite the mass of the republican party in parliament and the country, and provide both effective and popular government. Jules Ferry, who succeeded him as the principal republican leader, provoked violent opposition that was to prove fatal to him, and almost fatal to the regime.

Despite these growing divisions, a series of measures were taken which established some of the principal features of the Third Republic. Life senators were abolished and a few other constitutional changes made, though too few for the radicals. Controls on the press and public houses (often the venue of republican meetings) were relaxed: popular consumption of scandal and alcohol increased. Monarchist pretenders were banished. A policy of colonial expansion began, something dear to Gambetta and Ferry. The mayors of all communes except Paris were made elective. There were symbolic and concrete attacks on Catholicism: Sunday work was legalized; divorce was introduced; cemeteries and hospitals were secularized; the crucifix was removed from law courts. Religious orders (congrégations) – theoretically illegal under the 1810 law on associations – had the law applied to them after a long period of tolerance. The Jesuits were expelled. Other orders were instructed to apply for State authorization or suffer the same fate: on their refusal, police and troops invaded the cloisters and ejected their occupants. An exception was made in the case of the Trappists, whose strict vow of silence made them an improbable source of sedition, and womens' orders, who were socially useful and politically insignificant. The greatest measure – Ferry's principal achievement, for which he is now remembered – was to 'republicanize' (that is, secularize) the school system, a saga discussed in Chapter 6. However, Ferry resisted radical demands for a total break with the Church. The Concordat remained; diplomatic relations were kept with the Vatican; and Catholic schools, with Catholic teachers, remained. Even in the State system, Ferry urged moderation. To the radicals, these were half-measures; and half-measures when the Republic at last had the power to enforce its will, were treason. Just as bad was the constitutional revision introduced by Ferry in 1884. Republicans, as we saw, compromised with the royalists in 1875, accepting the Orleanist checks and balances of presidency and Senate, with the intention of changing them as soon as possible. However, opportunists now saw dangers in changes that might give too great a scope to the extreme Left, while realizing that now that most electors voted republican, the checks and balances buttressed the new status quo which they controlled. Radical demands to abolish the Senate and the presidency were ignored. The enormous over-representation of rural and small-town France and its local political oligarchies remained, a barrier against the radicals whose strength lay in the cities.

Radical impatience was fuelled by the economic crisis that had appeared in the mid-1870s, and which all over Europe caused a turning away from liberalism towards more radical politics of Right and Left. After a post-war boom, financial crashes in America, Austria, Britain and Germany, partly due to financial instability caused by the French war indemnity, marked the onset of a long period of worldwide economic slowdown. Causes included the slackening of railway-building and the arrival in European markets of agricultural products from the Americas, Australasia and eastern Europe. The French economy was hit particularly hard. Population growth was negligible, and so urbanization and the home market provided little buoyancy. Its traditional high-quality exports suffered. Obsolescent rural industries were almost wiped out. Most seriously of all, agriculture was devastated not only by foreign imports (the price of wool, corn and oils fell continuously from 1873 to 1895), but by natural disasters: silk-worm disease and phylloxera, which attacked vines. For several years the wine industry was ravaged – 63 per cent of the Côtes du Rhône were affected for example – and parts disappeared for good. In consequence, agricultural incomes fell by over 20 per cent between 1873 and 1894; foreclosures, land sales, falling land prices, and falling rents meant an exodus from the land to the towns. Depressed demand also affected manufacturing and building: industrial production fell by 15 per cent in 1874–77. Unemployment in metallurgy reached about 20 per cent in the mid-1880s. There were strikes against wage cuts, and demonstrations against immigrants.

The opportunists were not inactive. They produced a bold industrial policy, the Freycinet Plan, begun in 1879. It was a public works programme for railways, roads and canals, a familiar idea but on a gigantic scale. It aimed to build 8,700 kilometres of railway, later raised to 17,000, in a continuation of the Empire's policy of building a dense network of branchlines to bring remote rural areas into the national economy. It was popular but expensive and unlikely ever to be profitable. However, the stimulus was short-lived: the completion of the main part of the programme, the financial difficulties it caused, and the consequent reductions in public spending elsewhere meant that stagnation continued in the 1880s after a serious financial crash in 1882. The other principal government policy was the reintroduction and augmentation of tariffs in 1881, 1885 and 1887. Otherwise, the opportunists hoped for recovery: there was, Gambetta had said, 'no social question'; nor, said Ferry, was there any economic panacea.

Many workers and peasants turned against the opportunists in the mid-1880s, looking to radicals or socialists for more potent economic remedies. Radicals and socialists attacked the opportunists for timidity and for putting up food prices by tariffs, the 'bread tax', to 'starve the people' to benefit 'a few rich agriculturalists'. Instead, they proposed nationalization of the 'Jesuit-controlled' railway companies, tax reform and increased trade-union rights.[6] But the first step, to make these measures possible, was to democratize the 'monarchical' constitution by abolishing the conservative Senate.

The radicals' battle with the opportunists came to a head over a quite different issue, however: colonial policy. Gambetta and his followers were determined that the defeat of 1870 had to be repaired, but direct 'revenge' on Germany was for the time being impossible. Colonial expansion would give the French nation a new goal and vitality (see pp. 200–06). In May 1881, pressed by Gambetta, Ferry had forced the Bey of Tunis to accept a French protectorate. Parliament showed no enthusiasm. When in June a revolt required the dispatch of more French troops, radical and conservative deputies accused Ferry of misleading the Chamber, and implied that the profits of a few were being allowed to compromise the national interest. Only Gambetta's support had won a majority for the policy. However, the anger over Tunis was a sign of things to come. The Right played on the indifference of the rural electorate for colonies and their fear of military adventures. Radicals and socialists, eager to damage the opportunists, combined idealistic criticism of colonial aggression with a stress on the German threat, from which overseas adventurism drained men and money. Clemenceau's paper *La Justice* alleged that it 'left Bismarck master in Europe'.[7] The same view was taken by the new nationalist lobby, whose most important organization was the Ligue des Patriotes. This body, founded with Gambetta's blessing in 1882 by the quixotic soldier-poetaster Paul Déroulède to promote gymnastics and military training in schools, now began to flex its political muscles, insisting that France must fix her attention on 'the blue line of the Vosges' and concentrate her forces at home for the coming war of revenge.

Ferry, after Gambetta's death the acknowledged leader of the opportunists, began to extend French influence into Tonkin, claimed as a protectorate since 1873. War with China ensued in 1883, and a major naval and military expedition was sent. As with north Africa, this caused angry criticism on Left and Right, but as long as the policy seemed successful Ferry's majority was safe: only 60 deputies voted against war credits. In March, confused reports reached Paris of a minor French military defeat at Lang-Son. This gave Ferry's radical, royalist and nationalist enemies their chance. Clemenceau took the lead. He and Ferry detested each other. This stemmed from 1870–71, when

6. Kayser (1962), p. 129.
7. Derfler (1977), p. 23.

'Ferry-famine', mayor of Paris, was blamed for food shortages during the Prussian siege, and also when Ferry had favoured repression of the extreme Left. This had culminated in March 1871, when he supported Thiers's decision to seize the cannon at Montmartre while Clemenceau, who was mayor of Montmartre, was trying to negotiate a peaceful settlement. Ferry had regarded Clemenceau as a tool of the revolutionaries; Clemenceau regarded him as an ally of the detested 'Versaillais', the butchers of Paris. Since then, nothing had happened to bring them together. Ferry considered Clemenceau 'as rabble-rousing, as scheming, as reckless as before the Commune', and the radicals as 'the flower of stupidity . . . sinister and grotesque'.[8] Clemenceau regarded him as a crypto-conservative who was stifling the potential of the Revolution.

On 30 March 1885, Clemenceau interpellated the government. A violent and bitter debate ensued. Clemenceau warned that sending troops to Asia left France exposed to a surprise attack by Germany, and he demanded Ferry's impeachment: 'We cannot, we will not, discuss the interests of our country with you . . . [You] are accused of high treason'.[9] Underlining his threats, the shouts of an angry crowd could be heard from outside the Chamber. Clemenceau had made it clear to opportunist deputies that if they supported Ferry they would suffer the electoral consequences: the radicals would oppose them in the general elections due in October. Opportunists who had been elected in marginal constituencies led a rush to abandon Ferry, who was defeated in a vote of confidence by 306 to 149. The anti-Ferry majority was made up of 220 republicans and 86 conservatives.[10] Ferry left the Chamber, characteristically insisting on walking out through the hostile mob that was threatening to lynch him. This defeat was the beginning of the end of his career; he never held ministerial office again and lost his seat in 1889. Shortly afterwards, a nationalist's pistol bullet condemned him to semi-invalidity and to a premature death. After Gambetta, Ferry too had been defeated by the combined forces of conservatism and radicalism. This *de facto* alliance was about to bring forth alarming progeny.

GENERAL BOULANGER AND THE EMERGENCE OF RADICAL NATIONALISM, 1886–89

With a flash of thy sabre awake the pale dawn,
And to our young banners come show the way forth,
To march for the Rhine, to march for the Rhine:
Appear, we await thee, O General Revenge.

Popular song[11]

In October 1885, general elections took place. Radicals and the Right stressed their opposition to Ferry's war, which won them both many votes. Recent

8. Kayser (1962), p. 124; Chevallier (1982), p. 274.
9. Watson (1974), p. 94.
10. Rudelle (1982), p. 113.
11. Dansette (1938), p. 72.

quarrels had disorganized the republicans: in Paris, for example, there were at least four rival 'radical' lists of candidates, and four rival socialist lists.[12] But the Right, for the first time since 1879, were organized and united, thanks in part to the deaths of Chambord (in 1883) and the Prince Imperial, which caused most to rally to the Comte de Paris, though royalist aspirations were discreetly played down. Consequently, on the first ballot, 176 right-wing deputies were elected (compared with their total of less than 100 in the previous Chamber), while all republican factions totalled only 127. The shock caused a closing of republican ranks for the second ballot, so that only one republican list should be presented for each constituency. This allowed their national superiority to emerge, for despite the dissensions of the last few years, republicans of all shades loyally voted for the common lists with what was termed 'republican discipline'. The radicals, strengthened by their anti-war and anti-Ferry campaign, tripled their seats to 144, with only a small increase in votes. Although the republicans finally totalled more seats than the Right (367 to 201) the Right had made a remarkable recovery in overall votes, and was only 400,000 short of the republican total.

The 1885 elections created a Chamber loosely divided into three groupings: conservatives, opportunists and radicals. The opportunists had lost their majority. An attempt to govern with the tacit support of conservatives lasted only a few weeks. The alternative of a coalition with the radicals, what was to be called 'concentration', was tried for the first time – a landmark in Third Republic history – under Freycinet, an opportunist acceptable to the radicals and to President Grèvy. As the price for radical support, the government included three of Clemenceau's protégés, including as minister of war an almost unheard-off phenomenon, a radical general. This was Georges Boulanger, youngish, unscrupulously ambitious, and a brilliant self-publicist. His task, as the radicals saw it, was to democratize the army and take a bolder stance towards Germany, in contrast to Ferry's dastardly rapprochement. This Boulanger did with gusto, and soon proved an effective parliamentary performer and minister. Solid achievements included revising mobilization plans and hastening the introduction of the Lebel rifle (which gave some 30 years' service). Flashier initiatives included painting sentry-boxes blue, white and red (a durable innovation), throwing the Orléans princes out of the army, and allowing soldiers to grow beards, both modish and republican. Growing one himself was, suggests Brogan, one of the most important decisions he ever made. He was soon a popular figure, and after leading the 14 July parade in 1886 achieved stardom through a hugely popular song, 'En rev'nant de la revue', which contained the couplet: 'Moi, j'faisais qu'admirer / Not' brav' général Boulanger!' More than 370 other songs were written about him over the next three years. Soon, his popularity was being used to sell toys, soap, cheese and an apéritif 'containing no German product, putting fire in the belly'.[13] It was soon to be used to sell a new brand of politics.

12. Kayser (1962), pp. 139–40.
13. Dansette (1938), p. 88.

Above all, this popularity came from his resolute attitude to Germany. Ever since 1871, there had been a nagging fear that Germany might provoke another war before France could regain her military strength. Early in 1887, two crises blew up in which this suddenly seemed in prospect. First, Bismarck declared that Boulanger was a threat to Germany, and backed up the statement with an alarmist press campaign. Then, in April 1887, a French police officer, Schnaebélé, on frontier duty which included espionage, was lured across the border and arrested. Again, Boulanger urged a vigorous response, suggesting movement of troops and calling up reserves, and again he was restrained by his colleagues. However, when the Germans released Schnaebélé, the patriotic press lauded Boulanger as the hero who had frightened off Bismarck.

Politicians were far less impressed. Opportunists, royalists and some radicals began to worry. The two dreadful memories they all shared were the coup d'état of 1851 and the war of 1870: a nationalistic demagogic general gave pause for thought. Ferry and 70 opportunists voted against the government, forcing its resignation in May 1887. Boulanger lost his ministry and was posted off to a command in Clermont-Ferrand. A crowd, organized by the extreme-Left Blanquists and the Ligue des Patriotes, blockaded the Gare de Lyon, lying on the tracks in an attempt to keep him in Paris. 'Boulangism' was born, a new and heady combination of Left and Right: a tawdry mixture of the intrigue of ambitious radicals, the revolutionary nostalgia of ageing Blanquists, the desperate cynicism of failed royalists, and the weekend jingoism of Parisian office-boys. There was a new element too, which would increase in importance over the next ten years: antisemitism, whose potential appeal was shown by the huge sales of *La France Juive* (1886), an interminable antisemitic diatribe by Edouard Drumont.

Boulangism was helped on its way by a scandal in October 1887. Daniel Wilson, son-in-law of President Grèvy and a brazen republican fixer, had been selling honours. The Right asserted that this showed the squalid reality behind the holier-than-thou facade of republicanism. Grèvy was forced to resign. Ferry was the obvious successor; but he was feared and detested by Catholics, nationalists and radicals. The Blanquists, proclaiming that 'revolution had begun', rioted in Paris alongside the Ligue des Patriotes. The royalists were eager to believe that the Republic was in terminal decline. Boulanger, willing to do anything to keep Ferry out so that he could return to office, offered his services promiscuously to radicals and royalists. When parliament met in December 1887 to elect a president, some of Ferry's supporters were scared enough of insurrection in Paris if he were elected that they voted for a compromise candidate acceptable to the radicals, Sadi Carnot, grandson of the Jacobin organizer of the revolutionary armies. Clemenceau was reputed to have said 'Let's vote for the stupidest'. His actual words were more significant: 'He's not very bright but he has a republican name'.

A republican figurehead did not mollify General Boulanger and his new backers from the inner circles of the extreme Left: Naquet, architect of the divorce law; Laguerre, Clemenceau's astute former lieutenant and husband of a leading feminist; Rochefort, star journalist of the Left since the 1860s and director of *L'Intransigeant*; and Eudes and Granger, the leaders of the Blanquists, the old comrades' association of the Paris Commune. Militant patriotism was part of their heritage, and they abominated Ferry and lukewarm opportunism. They saw Boulanger's popularity as a weapon to institute a truly radical, even revolutionary, regime. Marxists and other small socialist groups either supported Boulangists or refused to oppose them; Paul Lafargue, Marx's son-in-law, refused to stand against Naquet. The Société des Droits de l'Homme split, with rank-and-file socialists leaving it because its leaders opposed Boulanger. His most effective allies were the organized heavies of Déroulède's Ligue des Patriotes, who wanted him to throw out the parliamentary moderates and become the charismatic head of an authoritarian nationalist Republic.

While the Left provided Boulanger with brains and brawn, he also needed the Right: they could offer the votes they commanded in the Catholic west and south and, even more important, lots of money. Most came from the Duchesse d'Uzès, a formidable amazon from a stratospherically noble family, a descendant of Charles X's last prime minister, a muscular feminist and France's first woman motorist. In return for her 3 million francs (her mother inherited the Veuve-Cliquot champagne fortune) and another 2.5 million from the Comte de Paris, Boulanger was to sponsor the latter's restoration as Philippe VII. Not all the Right approved of this flirtation with populism: traditional Orleanists were too attached to peace, order and parliamentary institutions. But many did: the Bonapartist tendency, always eager to ride on popular emotions; those legitimists who could not bring themselves to accept a democratic Republic on any terms; and the Comte de Paris, who was sceptical of Boulanger but felt that this was a heaven-sent opportunity to give the moribund Republic its coup de grâce.

Radicals and royalists were ignorant of each other's precise links with Boulanger and uncertain of his real intentions. Had he truly allied himself with conservatism, as Irvine argues; or were his promises to support an Orleanist restoration merely a 'linguistic convention', in Levillain's words?[14] He himself may never have really worked out his plans, but ridden the tide and trusted to luck. In any case, while the Boulangists had diverging aims, they agreed totally on the means: to destroy the opportunist Republic. Their slogan, invented by the left-wing paper *La Cocarde*, was 'Dissolution, Révision, Constituante'. Boulanger would demand the dissolution of the Chamber, propose revision of the constitution, and insist on elections to a new Constituent Assembly. The plan was that Boulanger would stand for parliament, repeatedly and in a large number of constituencies, using his popularity and the support of his right and left-wing allies to win a string of victories that would force a dissolution. Then would come the election of a Constituent Assembly, which each accomplice hoped to win and thus grab the political spoils.

14. Irvine (1988); Levillain (1982), p. 174.

The scheme began in the spring of 1888. The government dismissed Boulanger from the army for his political activities. Though amply deserved, this enabled him to pose as a martyr and made him legally eligible for parliament. He immediately stood in by-elections in the Aisne and Bouches-du-Rhône departments: he won in the former but made no impact on the strong traditional republicanism of the latter. In April he stood in the Nord, Dordogne and Aude departments, winning in the first two. There was a pattern here. Boulanger could win under his own steam in regions where there were no strong political traditions or organizations, Right or Left, as in Aisne, where he attracted a protest vote which had no other effective channel. Where strong political traditions and organizations did exist, he could only win with their support, as from Bonapartists in Dordogne and the combined forces of Catholics and the urban Left in the Nord. If they did not support him, as in Vendée, where he was said to be too 'clerical' for the Blues and not clerical enough for the Whites (reminiscent of Louis-Napoleon Bonaparte's relative failure in the west), he lost. Radicals and socialists were split. They were being forced to make a historic choice: either for the Republic, but a bourgeois Republic; or against the bourgeois Republic, but in alliance with the Right.

The new deputy made his first speech on 4 June 1888, calling for dissolution of the Assembly and a revision of the constitution, to be ratified by the people. Only 181 deputies voted for his motion, 159 of them royalists. During the angry debate he traded insults with the prime minister, the radical Floquet, who accused him of aiming to be another Bonaparte, but 'at your age . . . Bonaparte was already dead'. After further clashes, they fought a duel, which ended with the civilian's rapier through the general's neck, almost bringing his career to a premature end. Throughout July 1888 strikes and Blanquist agitation in Paris kept the country in a state of excitement. In August, Boulanger won three more by-elections. His greatest triumph came in Paris on 27 January 1889. The republican candidate, Jacques, was backed by opportunists and anti-Boulangist radicals. The anti-Boulangist socialists put up a Blanquist, Boulé, who later went over to Boulanger. An expensive American-style campaign was launched by the Boulangists, who plastered the city with 5 million posters. The result was a stunning victory, Boulanger winning 245,236 votes, Jacques 162,875, and Boulé 17,039.[15] The highest vote for Boulanger came in the newer working-class suburbs where factory workers, won over by the Blanquists, joined forces with white-collar republicans. He did least well in the older central districts, where the official radical party was deeply rooted in the artisan republican tradition.

That evening, when the result became known, an excited crowd of supporters cheered Boulanger and his lieutenants who were dining at a smart restaurant in the Place de la Madeleine, only a short walk from the Elysée Palace. Looking back on events, some Boulangists thought that they had missed their chance to stage an easy coup; there may have been shouts of 'A

---

15. Rudelle (1982), p. 232.

l'Elysée!', but few at the time thought seriously of illegal action, least of all Boulanger. Contemporary reports noted the light-heartedness of the occasion, and neither press nor police reports mentioned a coup d'état.[16] Arguably, Boulanger's republican upbringing had left him with a repugnance for the 1851 coup, while recent memories of the Paris Commune made his left-wing allies chary of barricade building. But above all, there was no need to take such risks: Boulangism was on the crest of a wave, with a general election victory expected in the autumn.

Here the Boulangists proved naive: their opponents had no intention of letting them win. Less than a fortnight after Boulanger's great Parisian victory, the Chamber voted a return to single-member constituencies (*scrutin uninominal*) so as to increase the weight of local issues and personalities, and in July it banned candidates from standing for more than one constituency, as national political figures had so often done in the past. With Boulanger limited to a single small constituency, his heterogeneous supporters could never find and agree on candidates who could match his charismatic appeal. The interior minister, Constans, a clever and unscrupulous political operator, decided to finish Boulanger off by forcing him outside the pale of legality, preventing him from re-entering parliament, humiliating him and frightening off his supporters. Boulanger proved to be a moral and political lightweight, easy meat for Constans. In February 1889, legal proceedings were begun against his chief lieutenants. The Boulangists were portrayed as conspirators against the State and warmongers: 'if you want war, vote for Boulanger'. Constans leaked the news that Boulanger was about to be arrested and tried for high treason. This was bluff, but the general had no stomach for a cell and feared assassination. Appropriately on April Fools' Day 1889, Constans leaked a false order for his arrest. Although some of his advisers (not all) urged him to escape, as did his mistress, the plump adoring Mme de Bonnemains, the inglorious decision was his: he fled to Brussels, and thence to Jersey. Admirers were dismayed. In August, after a farcical show-trial in his absence, he was sentenced to transportation for life.

The general elections of September–October 1889 were a more serious trial, but given the new rules of the game, there could only be one verdict. Boulanger won in Paris, an important symbol, but he was simply disqualified and his defeated opponent, the socialist Joffrin, was declared elected. Although nationally the Boulangists and the Right totalled only 11,673 votes fewer than the republicans, the Boulangists won only 43 seats, half of them in Paris, to the Right's 162, and the republicans' 350.[17] In terms of votes, the largest party were the royalists (3.1 million), who had gained considerably from their purchase of Boulanger. The parliamentary majority belonged to the combined opportunists (3 million votes) and radicals (1 million).

These results show that Boulangism combined two distinct elements. First,

16. On this much-discussed point see Levillain (1982), pp. 142–3.
17. Rudelle (1982), pp. 257–8. The loyalties of many deputies were not entirely clear, and other books give different estimates.

in the provinces, it was a broad movement of dissatisfaction among conservatives and centrists who were dissatisfied with sectarian and unstable republican governments. Boulanger's criticism of the parliamentary system, along with promises of an 'open' (i.e. not anticlerical) republic of the whole nation, was attractive in regions outside the traditional heartlands of royalism or republicanism. Second, in the cities, Boulangism was a pregnant amalgam of familiar elements of the Left (nationalism, socialism, popular militancy) and the Right (authority, order), with roots going back through the Paris Commune and Bonapartism respectively, but also foreshadowing the extreme Right of the twentieth century. The leading Boulangists – Déroulède, the novelist Barrès, Rochefort – belonged to this tendency. They made a dominant impact in Paris, and enjoyed an intellectual influence throughout Europe far greater than their parliamentary strength. After Boulanger's fall, they remained prominent, having attracted 700,000 votes, forming the core of what Barrès termed 'national socialism', violent, anti-establishment, populist, anti-individualist, anti-capitalist, anti-Semitic.

Boulanger's personal eclipse was as rapid as his rise. In the 1890 Paris municipal elections, his supporters won only two seats. His furtive relations with the royalists were disclosed by a disillusioned former supporter. His entourage was split by quarrels and desertions. Boulanger himself, ambitions dashed, financially ruined, and distraught by the death of his mistress from consumption, shot himself on her grave in a Brussels cemetery in September 1891.[18] Clemenceau, sometime friend and patron, commented with lucid malice: 'Here lies General Boulanger, who died as he lived: like a second-lieutenant'.

CONCLUSION

How beautiful the republic was – under the empire.

Georges Clemenceau (attrib.)[19]

The Third Republic thus survived its most serious peacetime challenge, and without shedding blood. In 1889 it celebrated the centenary of the Revolution with a brilliant international exhibition (which registered over 30 million visits) and the building of the Eiffel Tower. But despite the display of triumph, it still appeared vulnerable and unstable. All over western Europe, the 1880s had begun a new and unexpected era of political and intellectual turbulence in which the fundamental beliefs of republicans – democracy, equality, science – were to be questioned. Economic stagnation, in contrast with the worldwide boom of the 1850s and 1860s, widened the audience both of conservatives who had lost power and of radicals and socialists who were still excluded from it. Workers' organizations revived. Nationalism,

18. A few years ago it was still decorated with flowers – plastic ones, which seems an apt symbol.
19. Derfler (1977), p. 272, n. 11 suggests the origin of this famous quip.

socialism, antisemitism, none of them new ideas, were rejuvenated by political and economic dissatisfaction and spread by a new cheap mass press. In France, the target was the 'conservative Republic' launched by Thiers and adopted tacitly by Gambetta and Ferry. Although economic and social issues were always present, they did not structure the political debate: the fundamental question remained the system of government, because the 'conservative republican' was not seen as the last word. It was a compromise – not a flattering term in French political vocabulary – and, like the Bourbon Restoration and the July Monarchy, only accepted by the country *faute de mieux*. Many on the extreme Left thought that a revolutionary situation was taking shape. The Right agreed that support for the Republic was crumbling. Consequently, ideology, not policy, took centre stage: religion, the constitution and the legitimacy of the regime pushed debates over tax reform, tariffs or social welfare into the background.

These issues came to focus on the uncomprehending and ephemeral figure of General Boulanger. Because Boulangism was about more than 'the brave general', it survived his inglorious end, and had repercussions he could never have imagined. It permanently altered the political scene. Monarchists realized that they had a political future: they could function effectively without a monarch. In this sense, suggests Levillain, Boulanger was 'the grave-digger of the monarchy'. Ex-Boulangists remained as the core of a new 'revolutionary Right', originally a radical form of republicanism which was now on the verge of breaking away from the republican fold and allying permanently with the extreme Right. Most radicals had turned against Boulanger, and to defeat him they allied with the opportunists, choosing to support the 'conservative Republic'. This historic decision made them permanently a more centrist and rural party, for they lost much of their working-class following, which went first to the Boulangists, and then towards socialism. This helped the socialists make a small comeback nationally with some 80,000 votes, their first significant advance since 1851. Yet they too had fragmented over Boulanger: their largest group, the possibilists, had split when the leadership decided to cooperate with radicals and opportunists to keep Boulanger out; the Blanquists too split, most of them siding with Boulanger. Indeed, most of the few socialist deputies remained on close terms with the Boulangists, and they tended to vote together.

The opportunists had survived, and were confirmed as the natural party of government, the safe option, though many of their old leaders (including Ferry, who lost his seat in 1889) had faded away. The 1875 constitution, designed by Orleanists, now became sacrosanct for republicans: proposals to change it were taken as threats to the Republic itself. Just as the Comte de Chambord had despite himself helped to found the conservative Republic, so Boulanger, notes Dansette, 'without wishing to, did more to perpetuate it than a Gambetta or a Ferry'.[20]

20. Dansette (1938), p. 384.

CHAPTER 22

NEW POLITICS AND OLD,
1890–1911

The revolutionary spirit, which one flattered oneself had been destroyed in 1871, has recovered its ardour, activity and power.

Le Siècle, 11 February 1892[1]

The 1890s seemed the dawn of a new political era. What was seen nostalgically in post-war years as *la Belle Epoque*, and which we often imagine through the pink and blue haze of Renoir's late paintings, was for those experiencing it a tense and worrying time. The May Day demonstrations of 1890 caused ludicrous panic. Anarchist bomb outrages in March 1892 in Paris began a sensational and frightening phase. The fear of socialism, Sorlin notes, was 'one of the dominant characteristics of French political life' in this period.[2] Politics nationally, for the first time since 1848, were apparently becoming structured along class lines.

The persistent economic stagnation, and then its lifting at the end of the 1890s, formed the context. The erection of trade barriers by Germany and Italy brought forward the divisive question of tariffs: while their imposition helped vulnerable industries and agriculture, higher prices for consumers fuelled left-wing protests. Labour militancy scared business and property owners. A younger generation of politicians began to arrive on the scene proclaiming that a new approach to politics was necessary, going beyond the obsolete struggles of republican and monarchist, Catholic and anticlerical. The Boulangist turmoil had cleared the way for new alignments. The Panama scandal seemed once again to show the fragility of the regime and its corruption. To what extent did this new approach to politics prove viable? Did not the turn of the century see a decisive turn back to the old politics of ideology?

1. Sorlin (1966), p. 358.
2. Ibid., p. 359.

NEW ALIGNMENTS, *c.*1890–98

The Pope wants appeasement and so does our government.

Eugène Spuller, 1893[3]

Practical royalists and circumspect Catholics drew swift conclusions from the failure of Boulangism. Fantasies of restoration were dangerous and led nowhere. It was necessary to work within the republican system. Those Catholics more concerned with the Church's religious mission both inside and outside France than with its function as a pillar of romantic royalism were eager for accommodation. They included many of the clergy, such as Cardinal Lavigerie, missionary bishop of Carthage, and Pope Leo XIII, eager to restore good relations with the French government. The aim was an understanding with moderate republicans, who would abandon anticlericalism in return for Catholic support against radicalism and socialism. Jacques Piou, a disenchanted royalist deputy, set up in 1890 a small Droite Constitutionelle parliamentary group, mainly landowners and businessmen from the north and north-west, with a programme of spending cuts, administrative decentralization, religious teaching in schools and tariff protection, intending 'to show the country that there is a constitutional opposition composed of sober conservatives'.[4] On 12 November 1890, at a reception for naval officers in Algiers, Lavigerie shocked his mainly royalist guests by proposing a toast to the Republic, backed up by the band of the White Fathers' mission school playing the 'Marseillaise'. Reaction among French Catholics to his gesture was chilly. The pope, however, soon made clear that he supported this rallying to the Republic – the *ralliement*. In February 1892 he published an encyclical letter, *Au Milieu des Sollicitudes*, urging French Catholics to cooperate with 'wise and sensible' republicans.

The *ralliement* weakened royalism permanently. Some royalist politicians retired in despair from public life 'betrayed by king and pope', or else, like Comte Albert de Mun, obeyed the pope's call and joined Piou in the renamed Droite Républicaine. However, obstacles remained in the path of an alliance with moderate republicans to form a 'French Tory party', the dream of generations of conservatives, or even a Catholic party on the lines of the German Centre. Die-hard royalists defied the pope's urgings – royalist nuns prayed for his conversion. Middle-of-the-road Catholic voters tended to bypass the *rallié* politicians and, accepting the logic of the *ralliement*, simply voted tactically for opportunists or even socialists as the best way of defeating anticlerical radicalism. Catholics who were not social conservatives were eager to go much further towards the Left in the hope of rechristianizing the masses: prominent among these were the '*abbés démocrates*', Lemire and Gayraud, who had no desire for an alliance with the opportunists. On the

3. Sedgwick (1965), p. 124.
4. Ibid., p. 34.

other side of the political fence, the opportunists were less eager to respond to the *ralliement* than its protagonists had hoped. They were suspicious of anything clerical and Roman, and feared that any concession to the Church would cause their voters to defect to the radicals.

The Panama scandal, which burst in September 1892, added to the political shake-up. The Panama Canal Company, directed by France's greatest engineers, Ferdinand de Lesseps and Gustave Eiffel, had met enormous construction problems. It needed ever more capital, which it obtained by raising a special loan with the support of politicians and the press. This support was paid for in cash. Two prime ministers and the radical leader Clemenceau had accepted contributions to their anti-Boulanger campaign; many other deputies had taken money for less high-minded purposes. The company went bankrupt in 1889, leaving stupendous losses and many angry shareholders. In September 1892, Boulangists, lusting for revenge, alleged that 104 deputies had taken bribes. A financier, Reinach, killed himself; others fled; Lesseps, Eiffel and a former minister were convicted of corruption. The reputations of the Republic and of parliament were permanently damaged. Leading figures were forced out of politics. Clemenceau, savaged in parliament by Déroulède, with whom he fought a serious duel, was defeated at the polls. Monarchists and nationalists were heartened: why rally to a Republic that was tottering?

The elections of August–September 1893 showed the effects of these tremors: 190 new deputies entered the Chamber, replacing the founding fathers of the Republic. The *ralliement* was put to its first test, with disappointing results for its promoters. Many Catholics stayed away from the polls and the Right lost nearly half its votes and half its seats. At the grass roots, republican prefects, mayors and local activists had no intention of treating the *ralliés* as long-lost brothers, and indeed regarded the whole business as a Jesuitical trick: three-quarters of *rallié* candidates were opposed by opportunists. Both Piou and Mun were defeated. The opportunists, in short, were the major beneficiaries of the *ralliement* at no cost to themselves, except a few conciliatory statements. Moderate republicans won over 300 seats, usually benefiting from Catholic votes in the second round, and again had a majority without the radicals.

Many of the new generation of republicans saw themselves as forward-looking and non-sectarian, and were soon to take the name *progressistes*. They were more ready than the older opportunists to ally with Catholics, more ready to accept tariffs if necessary, and critical of the power of the Chamber and the weakness of the executive. Among them was Raymond Poincaré, elected in 1887 as a republican, but who had made much in his campaign of the fact that his grandfather had been an Orleanist deputy under Louis-Philippe – an open appeal for conservative votes. The new men were more aware of, or afraid of, social problems and class conflict, and espoused a moderate reformism intended to dish the radicals and the socialists. But in the short run they were unable to take the place of the opportunists of the great age of Gambetta and Ferry: they were poorly organized, had no national programme and few leaders of stature.

The elections had seen what Siegfried termed '*sinistrism*' (see p. 111): a series of switches of votes to the Left. Many Catholics had voted opportunist; so suspicious republicans voted for the radicals as the party of republican purity and the revolutionary tradition. Some radicals, feeling that the party was becoming too moderate, shifted to socialism, often in traditional republican strongholds such as the rural Midi. The radicals won 122 seats, and the socialists, marking their first major parliamentary success for generations, 49.

The socialist movement, a quarrelsome collection of parties and sects – Broussists, Guesdists, Allemanists, Blanquists, independents – began to move hesitantly towards its own form of opportunism in these years, hanging on to revolutionary ideology but combining it with spadework in local government and parliament. The first independent socialist deputy, the poet Clovis Hugues, had been elected on a radical list in 1881. During the 1880s, a small Groupe Ouvrier was formed in the Chamber, mainly of left-wing radicals but with six socialists; it split over Boulangism. Relations with the radicals were crucial for the socialists. The success of one was likely to be at the expense of the other; but outright conflict between the two at election time would mean a split vote and common defeat. Although their long-term aims differed, with the radicals espousing a small-property-owners' democracy and the socialists various forms of State or worker-controlled collectivism, their immediate programmes were similar – democracy, secularization, income tax, some nationalization – and their constituencies overlapped. Their personal relations were often close. They frequently wrote for the same newspapers, such as *La Justice* and *La Cocarde*, and cooperated in parliament. At the grass roots, activists were linked by membership of freemasonry and anticlerical Sociétés de Libre Pensée. Left-wing voters – workers, artisans, white-collar workers, small farmers, the lower-middle classes – divided their allegiance between radicals and socialists, and shifted from one to the other for tactical or personal reasons. The Marxist leader Jules Guesde was elected to parliament with radical support. Sitting radical politicians in constituencies with a growing socialist vote often renamed themselves 'socialist radicals'. Socialists too had a variety of labels, including 'Boulangist socialist', 'anti-semitic socialist' and 'republican socialist'.

In the early 1890s, the socialists began to make small advances into national politics. As has been seen, dissatisfied radicals attracted by Boulangism often gravitated thereafter to socialism. The Panama scandal, implicating leading radicals, encouraged the drift. Labour militancy in the 1890s, encouraged by the end of the slump, and aggravated by industrial restructuring and fiercely anti-union employers, helped the socialists to emerge as the chief political representatives of striking workers. Events such as the army's shooting at a crowd of stone-throwing May Day strikers at Fourmies in 1891, when nine people were killed, encouraged polarization. Two future leaders, Alexandre Millerand, a left-wing radical deputy involved in the legal defence of strikers, and Jean Jaurès, originally an opportunist, both moved to socialism after Fourmies. However, the trade-union leadership, much influenced by anarchism, rejected socialist interference and many condemned parliamentary politics as a bourgeois trick: this division between political action and workplace militancy persisted until the eve of the First World War. Socialist gains in the 1893 general election confirmed the revolutionary optimism of the Marxists, especially as their leader Guesde had been elected. He proclaimed that the road to power lay through elections, though he believed that in the case of a successful revolution in the streets, a seat in parliament would ensure a call to lead it, as in 1848 and 1870. However, more than the Guesdists or the other socialist parties, it was independent socialists such as the Communard Benoît Malon and Jaurès who gained, winning 21 seats to the 16 won by all the parties combined.[5] Leadership of the socialist movement therefore went to them.

At the other end of the political spectrum, attempts were made to form a working entente of moderate republicans and *ralliés*. Governments headed by Dupuy and Casimir-Perier (grandson of the July Monarchy minister) cut public spending and closed down the Paris Bourse du Travail, the anarchist-led trade union headquarters in July 1893. In December 1893, an anarchist, Vaillant, threw a bomb into the Chamber (the Boulangist Duchesse d'Uzès promised to look after his daughter after he was sentenced to death), and there were more bombs in Paris in February and April 1894. In June, President Carnot was murdered in Lyons by an Italian anarchist. The impact on public opinion was immense, and fear of revolution was rekindled among the timid. Carnot became a republican martyr, with statues throughout the country. His successor was Casimir-Perier. Stronger repressive legislation was introduced, and these '*lois scélérates*' were strongly opposed by radicals and socialists. Some socialists shared the conservative belief that revolution was around the corner, and refused to give their enemies further powers of repression. To ensure Catholic support in the Chamber, Spuller, the veteran Gambettist minister of public instruction, declared on 3 March 1894 that a 'new spirit' of tolerance reigned, and relaxed enforcement of anticlerical legislation. Remarkably, even in the exaggerated atmosphere of social crisis, ideological antagonism still outweighed class solidarity. Catholics were impatient that the 'new spirit' was not spreading far or fast enough; republicans were unwilling to abandon projects such as the taxation of religious orders. Many moderate republican deputies came under pressure from their electors to reject an alliance with Catholics. Attacks led by radicals and socialists on Casimir-Perier led him and the prime minister Dupuy to resign.

These parliamentary manoeuvres were not disturbed by the arrest in September 1894 of an obscure staff officer, Captain Alfred Dreyfus. A court-martial found him guilty of giving secrets to the Germans and sentenced him to solitary confinement for life on Devil's Island, in conditions that an American newspaper described, not inaccurately, as 'mental and physical vivisection'.[6] There was some antisemitic comment, but the political class was

5. Derfler (1977), p. 83.
6. Feldman (1981), p. 85.

united for once in execration of the criminal. The avuncular Jaurès seemed regretful that the bourgeois traitor had not been shot.

The first ever all-radical ministry to take office, that of Léon Bourgeois in November 1895, announced a programme of economic and social reform bearing the label 'solidarism', and intended as the radical response to the challenge of socialism. The major element was income tax. The government introduced a bill providing for a progressive rate of 1 to 5 per cent for incomes over 2,500 francs. This raised a storm of opposition against the principle of progressivity and against 'inquisition' by local tax committees who would know everyone's business and who would be politically biased. This was a familiar and not unfounded suspicion. Opposition was led by the Senate, the stronghold of socially conservative provincial republicanism, and for a time the dispute became one between the two chambers. However, support among deputies and in the country was lukewarm (70 department *conseils généraux* voted disapproval of the tax bill) and when the Senate refused to vote credits for the military expedition then occupying Madagascar, Bourgeois resigned. He was the first prime minister to be overthrown by the Senate – an important precedent. The radicals could bring down centrist governments, but not govern themselves.

After the radical defeat, the conservative forces in parliament – moderate republicans, *ralliés* and even unconverted monarchists – united by a fear of income tax, radicalism, socialism and anarchism, provided a solid majority for Jules Méline, opponent of income tax and successful advocate of tariffs, who became prime minister on 29 April 1896 and remained in office for 26 months, three times the average. His advocacy of tariffs had won him strong rural support ('veneration', says Caron) which firmly attached peasant voters to the Republic, after defections to the Right in 1885 and 1889.[7] His ministers were all republicans (no *ralliés*), and would not alter Ferry's lay laws; but they were willing to allow dissolved religious congregations to reassemble *de facto*, and put no pressure on local authorities in Catholic areas to secularize schools. They enacted a set of cautious reforms: laws on industrial accident compensation, aid to friendly societies (*mutuels*) and to agriculture, and judicial reform to aid the defence. Méline's majority gained reinforcements from both Right and Left. Attacks from an increasingly angry Left had no effect, and indeed were counter-productive, in that the government majority tended to close ranks. It looked as though Méline might manage to do what so many politicians since Villèle had vainly attempted: to create a sensible conservative party, as opposed to an extremist reactionary party.

Socialists continued their electoral gains. In the local elections of May 1896, they won control of Marseilles, Lille, Roubaix, Dijon and another dozen towns. In celebration, Millerand's supporters gave a banquet for him in his Paris constituency. His after-dinner speech, known as the Saint-Mandé Programme, was a manifesto to unite all the socialist groups in a manner acceptable to a wide electorate, while defining what made them different

7. Caron (1985), p. 481.

from the radicals. Based on a quasi-Marxist analysis of the inevitability of socialism, it made no mention of revolution but rather stressed that universal suffrage was the sole means of obtaining power, after which a socialist society would be created by nationalization. He also stressed that socialists were patriots as well as internationalists. The programme was welcomed by the two major spokesmen of the revolutionary tendency, the Marxist Guesde and the Blanquist ex-Communard Vaillant, and adopted by the socialist group in the Chamber by 27 votes to 4. 'Parliamentary action', declared Guesde, 'is the socialist principle *par excellence.*' The Left, like the Right, seemed to be abandoning the gratifications of extremism for the benefits of pragmatism.

Méline's government was strengthened by an event that overshadowed all others in 1896, and indeed was one of the great public events of the century: the state visit in October of Tsar Nicholas II. The *rapprochement* with Russia and the secret but widely rumoured alliance had been the major diplomatic change since 1870. The tsar's visit was its public consecration, proof that France was no longer alone and vulnerable to German aggression, and that the Republic was respected by the Great Powers. The tsar was given a triumphal reception (even though President Faure's desire to have a royal blue uniform for the occasion was turned down by the government). Nearly a million visitors flocked to Paris to see the tsar's ceremonial entry, marked by banquets, fireworks, parades, visits to the tombs of Napoleon and the martyr Carnot, and genuine popular rejoicing.

Political life seemed to be taking a new track, in which the old ideological struggles were being replaced by largely peaceful, if tense, contests of economic interests. The government's majority had increased to a comfortable 50–80. But out at the grass roots, those 36,000 Clochemerles where politics turned round unforgiving clannish struggles for influence, status and patronage, where *instituteur* was pitted against *curé* and *maire* against *notable*, progressist commitment to the 'new spirit' was wobbling. Radicals and socialists accused Méline and his supporters of betraying the Republic to clerical wolves in *rallié* clothing. *Rallié* Catholics suffered similar attacks from die-hard royalists, intransigent Catholics (led by those modern missionaries, the Assumptionists, controllers of a large newspaper network) and anti-parliamentary nationalists. All these groups were looking for a way to break up Méline's unholy cohabitation with the *ralliés*. It was anyway a rule of the political game for centrist alliances made in the middle of parliamentary terms to crumble when elections approached (the next were for 1898) and ideological rhetoric re-emerged. On this occasion, Alfred Dreyfus, dead to the world in his solitary hut on Devil's Island, unwittingly became a weapon for intransigents of Right and Left, and the means by which the great ideological conflicts of the past were given a new relevance and vigour.

THE DREYFUS AFFAIR AND ITS AFTERMATH, 1894–99:
THE LAST TRIUMPH OF THE REVOLUTION

> I was only an artillery officer whom a tragic error prevented from pursuing his normal
> career. Dreyfus the symbol . . . is not me. It is you who created that Dreyfus.
>
> *Alfred Dreyfus*[8]

Since Dreyfus's sentence in 1894, his family and a few sympathizers had been working quietly and unsuccessfully to prove his innocence. In 1896, a new head of army intelligence, Colonel Picquart, discovered that the real traitor was another officer, Esterhazy. Late in 1897, independently and by chance, Dreyfus's brother Mathieu made the same discovery. As a miscarriage of justice, the Dreyfus case could have been corrected quite simply. But the Dreyfus 'affair' was never primarily about Dreyfus as an individual, and it soon ceased to be much concerned with him at all.

The army staff, first through prejudice and carelessness, then through self-preservation, had undertaken from the beginning a barely conceivable series of subterfuges to convict Dreyfus and then to keep him on Devil's Island. Picquart was silenced, evidence fabricated and Esterhazy exonerated. The army's obduracy was applauded by antisemitic and nationalist newspapers for whom Dreyfus's guilt was unquestionable and Esterhazy, a former Pontifical Zouave, the victim of a Jewish plot. Most newspapers accepted Dreyfus's guilt. Most politicians washed their hands of the case: 'There is no Dreyfus affair', stated Méline, taking the convenient view that it was for the courts to decide. Republicans of all shades were loyal to the patriotic cult of the army. Socialists were indifferent to the fate of a rich Jewish officer, triply antipathetic. Most people took little notice.

The 'affair' really began on 13 January 1898 when the novelist Emile Zola published an open letter to the president of the Republic in Clemenceau's paper *L'Aurore* under the headline *J'Accuse*. He accused the high command of abetting a miscarriage of justice, and blamed it on their reactionary prejudices: 'clerical passion' was the culprit. Although the generals responsible were in fact republicans, not Catholic royalists, it was by attacking 'religious passion, military spirit, hierarchy, that Zola made the affair into the latest round of the century-old political and ideological struggle of Right and Left.[9] His prosecution, conviction and flight to England caused an international sensation, arousing violence both verbal and physical in the Paris streets and the antisemitic press ('It must smell really nasty, grilled yid' – *La Libre Parole*). His trial exposed irregularities in the Dreyfus case that army and government had tried to cover up. It also caused a growing number of *intellectuels* (a new word) and politicians on both sides to take up a public position.

8. Wilson (1982), p. 1.
9. Bredin (1983), p. 235.

The Dreyfus family found their cause being turned into a left-wing crusade, led by Clemenceau and Jaurès. The socialist Léon Blum hoped to form 'a permanent army in the service of human right and justice'; with that intention the Ligue des Droits de l'Homme was re-founded in 1898. The 'Dreyfusards' saw the affair as a struggle against reaction, the Church and the aristocratic-military caste – 'the forces of the middle ages', in Clemenceau's words – and an opportunity to break up the Méline coalition and create a new left-wing alliance. The 'anti-Dreyfusards' replied with the Ligue de la Patrie Française, which claimed 100,000 members, including 10,000 workers in Paris. For them, it was a struggle against forces undermining national unity and the great national institutions, the army and the Church. They convinced themselves that a vast 'Jewish syndicate' was determined to whitewash Dreyfus by bribing journalists, officers, politicians and judges, with the connivance of the Germans. Evidence and argument had no effect: when Esterhazy admitted his guilt, they said he too had been bribed; if officers had lied and forged evidence, it was to protect a truth too dangerous to be told.

During January and February 1898 there were 69 antisemitic riots or demonstrations in most big towns, including Paris, Nantes, Rennes, Saint Malo, Nancy, Epinal, Dijon, Châlons, Marseilles, Toulouse and Algiers: a significantly new combination of the conservative and Catholic west; the republican, patriotic, militaristic and antisemitic east, where the highest incidence of violence occurred; and the radical, newly antisemitic south; worst of all Algiers, where there was a serious pogrom. The Antisemitic Group in the Chamber of Deputies included members coming from Right and Left.[10] The Catholic press, especially that run by the Assumptionists, joined in. La Croix described itself as 'the most anti-Jewish newspaper of France' and peddled a reeking brew of Jew-hatred, anti-liberalism and anti-capitalism, supported by abbés démocrates, the left-wing political priests: 'Judas Dreyfus has sold France . . . the Jews have taken over everything, soiled everything, destroyed everything'.

There has been much debate about when and to what extent the affair made an impact on ordinary people in the provinces. The 1898 general election, it has usually been argued, was scarcely affected by the affair. If 85 per cent of the press was hostile to Dreyfus, only 30 per cent gave the case prominence at all, and the campaign was dominated, argues Caron, by agricultural policy, taxation, pensions and religion in schools.[11] Certainly, most politicians were cautious and opposed reopening the case: 'We are with the crowd and not at all with the intellectuals', said a radical manifesto. The election results did not change the balance in the Chamber, at least on the surface. Méline promised 'neither reaction nor revolution' and his supporters won 250 seats, making them by far the largest party. The socialists failed to make the breakthrough they had expected, having under 50 seats in spite of frantic scrabbling for electoral pacts with radicals and antisemites; Guesde

10. Wilson (1982), pp. 107–8, 114, 217.
11. Caron (1985), p. 462.

was devastated. But there is evidence that the Dreyfus affair was already having repercussions out in the country,[12] as well as in Paris and among politicians. The electoral map of 1898 (see p. 266) shows that the country had now polarized along ideological – that is, religious – lines. Beneath the surface, Méline's centrist position was fragile, and the Dreyfus affair turned out to be the last straw.

For months at grass-roots level, die-hard Catholics, ralliés and republicans had been at each other's throats; one-third of progressist candidates wanted to return to a 'republican concentration' coalition with the radicals, the principal opposition to Méline. Conservative politicians in town and country seized on antisemitism as a way to modernize their political appeal: that Jews were infiltrating the Republic and controlling the economy became the explanation and scapegoat for anything unpopular, from conscription to farm prices. Some radicals and socialists replied with anti-Semitism of their own. Prominent Dreyfusards, including Jaurès and Guesde, lost their seats. The progressists split. Fifty, now fearing the revival of the Right more than socialism or radicalism, abandoned Méline and demanded a government based on 'an exclusively republican majority': that is, depending on radical, not rallié, support. Méline resigned. Ideology had once more replaced interest as the substance of politics. The Dreyfus affair, of growing impact in the provinces, increasingly dominated the political world of the capital: the Chamber, the press, the parties and ligues, the churches, the cafés, the salons and the streets. It was now simply 'l'Affaire', a worldwide sensation.

In August 1898 a new minister of war, Cavaignac, scion of a great republican dynasty and a patriotic anti-Dreyfusard, discovered to his horror that crucial evidence against Dreyfus had been forged. The forger, Colonel Henry, was arrested and cut his throat. Nationalists proclaimed him a martyr and launched a subscription in his honour, which produced, along with money, a nauseating flow of antisemitic ravings. In 1899, tragicomedy struck. In February, President Félix Faure, a bon viveur who revelled in the female admiration inspired by fame, died suddenly in what one newspaper called, with unconscious precision, the performance of his functions.[13] His successor, Emile Loubet, favoured a new trial for Dreyfus. The extreme Right, notably Déroulède's Ligue des Patriotes and Guérin's thuggish Ligue Antisémitique, decided to use Faure's state funeral on 23 February to stage a coup. They were encouraged by the pretender, the fatuous (the British ambassador's term) Duc d'Orléans. All was hastily improvized: Déroulède alerted his cohorts by sending out 4,000 postcards. He believed he had secured the cooperation of at least part of the army, which, with a few thousand of his men, would be enough to occupy government buildings and raise the nationalist banner. The generals, however, proved less angry with the government, or at least less daring, than Déroulède hoped. General Roget,

12. Fitch (Feb. 1992), pp. 55–95.
13. This occasioned much humour, e.g. Doctor (called in haste): 'Le Président a-t-il encore sa connaissance?' Footman: 'Non, docteur, elle est sortie par la porte de côté.'

commander of the funeral escort, whose bridle he seized with a cry of 'A l'Elysée!', retreated into the nearest barracks with an excited Déroulède still trotting alongside. The embarrassed soldiers tried to persuade him to go away, but he insisted on being arrested for high treason. After declaring in court that if released he would try again, he was triumphantly acquitted by a Paris jury. On 4 June, the nationalists staged a demonstration against Loubet at the Auteuil races which culminated in his being struck on the head with a walking stick, severely denting the presidential top hat. Republicans were not amused by these antics. On 11 June, the radicals and socialists replied with a mass counter-demonstration of some 100,000. The hat-basher was given four years' gaol, and Déroulède, whatever the jury said, was arrested again, along with other nationalist leaders.

Earnest republicans were now angry and alarmed at the turbulent agitation in the capital. Waldeck-Rousseau formed a government of republican defence on 17 June. To bring the army to heel he chose as minister of war General the Marquis de Galliffet, a hero of 1870 who had rallied to Gambetta and the Republic, and had since remained a solid, if eccentric, pillar of legality. He was equally famous, however, as one of the butchers of the Paris Commune, whose exhibitionistic sadism had been widely reported in the press and pilloried in Lissagaray's *Histoire de la Commune*. To placate the Left, Waldeck also brought in Millerand as minister of commerce, the first socialist to hold office since 1848. This pleased many socialists, who saw it as a breakthrough. However, some leaders and militants were unhappy at this abandonment of the revolutionary tradition, and when they realized that 'the murderer' Galliffet was also to be in the government there were angry scenes in the Chamber, and the beginning of a socialist rift. Nevertheless, so grave did the threat to the Republic seem that even the anti-Millerand socialists led by Vaillant (a veteran of the Commune) and Guesde did not vote against the government. The new parliamentary Bloc Républicain included all deputies for whom the defence of the Republic against 'reaction' was the overriding political cause. A parliamentary caucus, the Délégation des Gauches, representing all the pro-Waldeck parties and in which Jaurès played a prominent part, was set up to coordinate support. It included the radicals, now the party of republican tradition *par excellence*, stressing democracy and secularism; most socialists, who, as at the time of Boulanger, had rallied to the 'bourgeois' republic for fear of something worse; and those elements of the old opportunist centre who had decided that the danger from the Right for the moment exceeded that from the Left. This position was typified by Waldeck-Rousseau himself, a former minister of Gambetta, a wealthy lawyer from the 'Blue' city of Nantes, who had inherited a suspicion of both Whites and Reds, but considered Jesuits more dangerous than socialists.

On the other side was a newly assembled Right. It included the remnants of the old royalists and ex-*ralliés* led by Albert de Mun, who combined Catholic paternalism with militaristic patriotism; those progressists unwilling to follow Waldeck-Rousseau, who were concentrated in the traditionally Catholic, patriotic and anti-Semitic east and in Normandy; the Ligue de la Patrie

Française, including successful literary men and the academic establishment; and the knuckle-dustered nationalist riff-raff. The affair confirmed radical nationalism as a distinct form of anti-liberalism. Essentially urban, indeed mainly Parisian, it took its street politics and xenophobic patriotism from the old Parisian Left, and fed on the economic discontent of the self-employed, especially shopkeepers and certain groups of workers such as butchers. It was egged on by a ruthlessly amoral popular press, often left-wing in origin, and typified by Rochefort's *L'Intransigeant*. Its most active leaders were a strange collection: old-style republican patriots such as the quixotic Déroulède, who glorified the revolutionary heroes of 1792; intellectual nationalists such as Barrès and the neo-royalist Charles Maurras, who believed they were defending civilization against the corruption of cosmopolitan modernity; crooks such as Jules Guérin, who organized the Ligue Antisémitique for money; and aristocratic royalists who held their noses and paid up in the desperate hope that they could buy popularity by patronizing antisemitism.

Waldeck-Rousseau, an unemotional man ('a pike in aspic'), was well suited to lead the republican bloc and settle the affair because, though a moderate he did not believe in a socialist threat, though a republican did not exaggerate the power of the Church, and though a patriot regarded the nationalists with contempt. At first delayed by the burlesque 'siege of Fort Chabrol', when Guérin barricaded himself in his Paris headquarters, supplied with food by nationalists from the top decks of passing buses, Waldeck hauled a collection of nationalist leaders, including Déroulède and Guérin, before the Senate sitting as High Court. He ensured their conviction and banishment, ironically for a Dreyfusard lawyer, by having evidence forged. He banned the ligues and prosecuted the Assumptionists under the long-defunct article 291 of the penal code forbidding unauthorized associations (they were fined 16 francs). Dreyfus, brought back a physical wreck from Devil's Island totally unaware that he had become the most famous Frenchman since Napoleon, was retried by court martial at Rennes in August–September 1899.

The Rennes trial was the climax of the affair, which now dominated the press across the globe. The army high command presented a quasi-ultimatum: if the country had no confidence in the honour of its soldiers, they declared, they could no longer ensure its defence of the nation. Faced with such a choice, the court martial again found Dreyfus guilty but salved their consciences by finding 'extenuating circumstances' and giving him a short sentence that he had already nearly completed. One officer remarked 'I am convinced of Dreyfus's innocence but . . . I would convict him again for the honour of the army'.[14] This preposterous verdict caused an explosion of international protest. Demonstrations were held in Hyde Park; international boycotts were threatened. The government offered Dreyfus a pardon, which he and his family, though still protesting his innocence, accepted: he was too

14. Bredin (1987), p. 536.

ill to return to Devil's Island. Those Dreyfusards for whom the cause was infinitely more important than the man were shocked: 'We were willing to die for Dreyfus', said the left-wing writer Charles Péguy loftily, 'but Dreyfus was not willing to die for Dreyfus'. The pardon deflated the agitation surrounding the affair, and Galliffet declared that 'the incident is closed'. Its long-term effects, however, had only just begun.

For generations, the Left had seen Catholicism as the taproot of reaction, the 'redoubtable enemy that picks up, reassembles and revitalizes the wreckage of the defeated parties and keeps them ready to launch an assault on liberty'.[15] This time they were determined that the Church would be rendered harmless. The first round was the July 1901 Law on Associations. This was aimed at the religious orders, about which many on the Left had long been paranoid, seeing them as fabulously wealthy conspiratorial organizations and the worst culprits of the affair, both through the disgraceful propaganda of the Assumptionists, and through the more insidious influence of former pupils of Jesuit schools who were believed to have infiltrated the army and the civil service. Under existing laws, all associations of more than 20 members were illegal, unless expressly authorized by the State, but the law had largely fallen into abeyance. Thousands of unauthorized associations existed, including religious orders, and were tolerated or even recognized *de facto* by the State. The new law expressly gave recognition to all associations *except* religious orders, which were required to seek authorization under strict controls. Waldeck-Rousseau, whose aim was to reduce the clergy to obedience, not engage in a religious war, indicated that for most orders authorization would not be refused.

The new law removed the legal obstacle to a wide range of organizations of citizens, including political parties, which could now own property and receive gifts, for example. The change coincided with the need to redefine and reorganize political forces. The affair had dissolved old alliances, such as opportunism, and shifted the electoral balance. The radicals, the great electoral gainers of the affair, and the socialists, had received a flood of new recruits, which party leaders wished to organize and discipline in view of the crucial elections of 1902. The radicals held a founding congress in June 1901, the *ralliés* formed Action Libérale in July, and the socialists formed two rival parties in 1901–2. The rapid increase in left-wing votes was a mixed blessing. Any candidate considering himself an 'advanced republican' could adopt the radical or socialist labels to win votes, and many did; but they accepted no obligation to obey any discipline or support any legislative programme. Party structures aimed to bring some order and discipline.

In the case of the socialists, their long-standing disagreement over strategy – whether socialism could be built through parliament – was brought to a head by Millerand's membership of the government. He was bitterly attacked by Guesdist and Blanquist leaders. He was, however, warmly supported by much of the rank and file, including Guesdists, and by ordinary workers, as

15. Paul Bert, in Sorlin (1966), p. 221.

well as by reformist socialists such as Jaurès. Millerand's aim was to show that socialist participation in government could win major gains, and in this he was fairly well supported by Waldeck, who wished to bring the workers firmly inside the republican fold. His hope was to set up a system of compulsory arbitration, under the aegis of the State, to limit and control industrial conflict. Many workers' leaders, however, had no wish to consign their dreams of revolution to the scrapheap of history, and employers resisted giving recognition and concessions to organized labour. The project foundered in the 1900 strike wave brought on by a sharp economic revival. Millerand's other aim, to establish a pension system, was blocked by the Senate.

While not negligible, the results of his ministry were insufficient to fulfil the expectations of his supporters, and far from sufficient to disarm his critics. 'Millerandism' was rejected by the socialist movement, and he himself expelled in 1904. Two socialist parties were formed, corresponding broadly to those who had attacked and those who had defended Millerand, the Parti Socialiste de France ('the party of revolution') led by Guesde and Vaillant, and the Parti Socialiste Français (for 'social transformation and republican defence') led by Jaurès. The latter was far more successful electorally. Only in 1905 did socialists form a single party, the SFIO (Section Française de l'Internationale Ouvrière). But this did not really resolve the ideological, emotional and political problem: were they stepping into the radicals' shoes as the left-wing parliamentary opposition, or were they a revolutionary movement? The solution adopted was to be the former in deeds and the latter in words: an interesting challenge to Jaurès's practical mind and tirelessly lyrical tongue. In the case of the radicals, a single party was formed, but one very broad in its programme and loose in its structure, as was shown by its composite title, Parti Républicain Radical et Radical-Socialiste. Divergent tendencies within the same structure were never able, or willing, to adopt a tight organization or programme. Hence it relied on the unifying power of republican tradition, and especially anticlericalism: 'our programme . . . was fixed by our forefathers'.[16] Many radicals remained outside the party, including their leading figure, Clemenceau.

THE RADICALS' REPUBLIC, 1902–9

Radical comes from radish, red outside, white inside.

Manuel du parfait radical, 1896[17]

The 1902 elections, like those of 1877 and 1889, brought 'the two Frances' face to face: Left against Right, the Republic against its enemies. The fate of the Church had become the defining and only significant issue. Income tax,

16. Nordmann (1977), p. 42.
17. Kayser (1962), p. 179.

pensions, and tariffs faded into the background. There were few centrist candidates to blur the divide: 415 out of 589 constituencies elected a deputy on the first round, and only 9 had more than two candidates for the second round. Although the Right polled well (only 200,000 short of the Left in the first round), the Bloc des Gauches won a majority of 80–90.

Waldeck-Rousseau, in weak health, hoping perhaps to be elected president, and realizing that the new Chamber would be further to the Left than he was, resigned. Emile Combes formed a new government with a single priority: the Church question. 'Le petit père Combes' was an elderly country doctor, a radical, a freemason (like all his cabinet). There was more to him than a reincarnation of Flaubert's atheistic chemist M. Homais, however. Ironically, he had trained for the priesthood and taught in an Assumptionist school, and was a *spiritualiste*, believing in a numinous universal spirit. He also wrote verse and enjoyed a sentimental correspondence with an aristocratic nun, Princess Bibesco (a revelation that left the pope literally speechless). But his anticlericalism was bitter and aggressive. If Waldeck-Rousseau's government was one of republican defence, his was to be one of republican offence. His anticlerical passion was shared by rank-and-file republicans of all parties.

The question was how to proceed. The Church under Napoleon's Concordat obtained certain benefits, especially financial, but in return came under State supervision. A disestablished Church would lose its benefits, but would also be dangerously free. Combes's original intention was to destroy the hated religious orders, dismantle their school system, and bully the Vatican into accepting a rigorous interpretation of the Concordat. The Law on Associations provided the means to tackle the orders. Requests for authorization were refused en bloc, and unauthorized orders dissolved, where necessary by force: 1,500 colonial troops were sent to mop up three Breton convents, and 3,000 soldiers successfully besieged a monastery near Tarascon. In 1904 a further law forbade all teaching activity by any member of a religious order. The courts fell in behind the government, interpreting the laws with great severity, and thousands of schools and religious houses were closed. The Vatican, worried that weakness would encourage attacks from other states, fired back two thundering encyclicals, *Gravissimo officii* and *Vehementer nos*, and refused compromise. Consequently, Combes, pressed by his majority, was pushed towards abrogation of the Concordat and legal separation of Church and State. A separation bill was passed in September 1905. Its repercussions were felt for years, especially over property. Attempts by officials to draw up inventories of church treasures caused sometimes violent resistance by Catholics, and the government eventually abandoned the attempt: candlesticks, said Clemenceau, were not worth human lives. Much real property was confiscated, but the Vatican made things worse for French Catholics by forbidding them until 1924 to form *associations cultuelles* (worship associations) to which the government was willing to hand back churches rent free. The material loss to the Church ran into many hundreds of millions, and recruitment to a more poverty-stricken clergy slowed. But it was far from being, as anticlericals had hoped, a death blow.

The rest of Combes's programme concerned further 'republicanization'. There was another purge of the administration, in addition to officials who resigned rather than execute the new laws. The army, the other villain of the Dreyfus affair, was also to be republicanized. However, this involved a purge of personnel, not a reform of the institution: courts martial, directly responsible for the injustice to Dreyfus, remained unchanged. Rather, 'reactionary' officers were to be rooted out. The new minister of war, General André, made use of newly acquired powers over promotions to favour 'republican' officers. He used a card-index (*fiches*) containing information acquired from other officers, freemasons and civil servants, concentrating on the religious affiliations of officers and their families. Practising Catholics were suspect. There was nothing new about this procedure, but when it became public in October 1904 it precipitated Combes's defeat a few weeks later.

The Bloc des Gauches scarcely outlasted him. During the second half of his long tenure of power his parliamentary support had already begun to fray. The defeat of the (much exaggerated) right-wing threat and the conclusion of Church disestablishment left the Bloc without a common purpose. At the same time, problems arose that put its fraying cohesion under strain. As has been seen, economic growth from the late 1890s onwards increased workers' bargaining power; new methods and new foreign competition caused employers to attempt, often high-handedly, to increase productivity by attacking restrictive practices. With labour organizations weakly organized, covering only a minority of workers, and led by revolutionaries, this was a recipe not merely for industrial conflict, but for wildcat action, blacklegging and violence. A major strike wave in 1904 placed severe strains on the Bloc, whose most moderate elements were highly suspicious of socialism and revolutionary extremism. A new phase in the international situation, dramatically signalled by the Moroccan crisis of the summer of 1905, placed a terminal strain on the Bloc, torn between the republican patriotism of the radicals and Alliance Républicaine Démocratique, and the internationalism of the socialists, tinged with anti-militarism, anti-colonialism and 'anti-patriotism' on their extreme wing. The formal break with the socialists came when Jaurès left the parliamentary caucus, the Délégation des Gauches, in February 1905, after the Amsterdam congress of the International condemned socialist participation in 'bourgeois' governments. By this time he had little to stay for, and his departure was the price of unification with the Guesdists to form the SFIO.

The Bloc des Gauches still operated as an electoral alliance, however, and the 1906 elections demonstrated its efficacy. 'Republican discipline' meant that the candidates who received the most votes in the first ballot, whether radical, socialist or centrist – the ex-progressists were now discreetly called the Alliance Républicaine Démocratique (ARD) – would not be opposed by the others in the second round. In consequence, they made further gains, and the radicals became the largest party. However, they did not have a working majority. The SFIO would neither join a coalition nor dependably vote for the government. The ARD was eager to do both, but on its terms, which many radicals were happy to accept: opposition to strikes, restraint on public spending especially for pensions, and extreme prudence in fiscal reform.

Clemenceau, the master of parliamentary mayhem, veteran radical, nicknamed 'the tartar' both for his mandarin-like impassivity and his calculated ferocity, in October 1906 formed his first government at the age of 65. It was to be taken up largely with combatting strikes, so that he ironically described himself as 'le premier flic de France'. It was a classic dilemma for a radical who combined a genuine concern about working-class conditions with opposition to socialism and a neo-Jacobin devotion to the sovereignty of the State. From 1905 to 1907, Clemenceau faced a series of confrontations with public sector workers, some demanding the right to form unions affiliated with the anarchist-led CGT. Previous governments had evaded the tricky question of public sector unions, sometimes tolerating them, sometimes banning them, often fudging. Clemenceau would not permit affiliation with the CGT, on the grounds that civil servants were the instruments of the State, and could not be allowed to join a movement ostensibly aiming at its overthrow. This conflict led to a bitter succession of strikes, violence, repression, and mass sackings. Yet he resisted demands from his own side to ban the CGT.

In the spring and summer of 1907 came conflict of a quite different nature: the revolt of the southern wine growers. After the devastation of phylloxera, a very different industry had emerged, with a near monoculture of vines mass-producing cheap wine along the Mediterranean coast. This, combined with Algerian, Spanish and Italian production, had glutted the market and caused catastrophic price falls, in spite of a disquieting increase in consumption of alcohol, in which France led the world. In the past, wine growers had demanded tax cuts or restraints on production, but now they demanded a far greater degree of government intervention. In 1907, the wine-growing south was in a state of largely peaceful quasi-insurrection with huge demonstrations (up to 500,000 people) and the mass resignation of local councils and mayors. A locally recruited infantry regiment mutinied. Clemenceau handled the crisis with considerable adroitness ('brutality and trickery', in Rebérioux's opinion[18]) and the largely peaceful 'revolt' died down without serious bloodshed: proof of how times had changed since 1848 or 1851.

These events, though interesting as portents of durable future problems concerning wine-lakes and public-sector corporatism, are of little consequence in the light of the high drama of the past decade, let alone the hopes, fears and struggles of the previous century. For the next few years, until the approach of war, politics became complicated, trivial, sterile, and frankly dull. It is a postscript to our period. Let us pass over the details and look for a meaning.

18. Mayeur and Rebérioux (1987), p. 252.

CONCLUSION: FROM MYSTIQUE TO POLITIQUE

Tout commence en mystique et finit en politique.

Péguy

As the aftermath of the Dreyfus affair petered out, Clemenceau inherited an authority based on the crumbling ideological solidarity of the Left and found himself using it to break strikes. Even though he was good at it, it was a clear sign that politics had lost coherence. Why was the Left carrying out the policies of the Right? There were many other symptoms of incoherence during the period between 1911 and 1914. There were eleven governments between July 1909 and August 1914, and four in 1913 alone. The radical party made the introduction of income tax its core objective, but in spite of repeated attempts could not get its own members to vote a bill. Briand became the new parliamentary star and headed four governments. An ex-socialist who had moved to the centre-left ARD, his qualities were astuteness, affability and apparent lack of principle.

The fundamental reason for this incoherence is fairly plain. During the 1890s, as was seen, there were attempts to restructure politics along lines of interest. But the drama of the Dreyfus affair restored the primacy of ideology: again, revolution struggled with reaction, and the Republic was successfully defended against its enemies. But this last great victory of the Revolution was something of a sham: although for a time, as the British ambassador reported, the nation appeared to have gone mad, 'returning to the frame of mind of one hundred years ago', it all ended in Clemenceau's counting of candlesticks and General André's petty snooping.

The 'republican discipline' that remained was enough to rule out the formation of a moderate conservative government in the footsteps of Méline. A large part of the political spectrum was thus permanently excluded from participating in government, even though its various organizations relabelled themselves 'democratic', 'republican' and 'left' – a sure sign in these years of being on the Right. Only a 'left-wing' government could conceivably command a majority, but the ideological Left now extended so far into the socio-economic centre (including such pillars of anti-socialist moderation as Waldeck-Rousseau, Poincaré and the orthodox economist Caillaux) that there was no conceivable left-wing consensus on how to govern, especially once the cathartic disestablishment of the Church had removed its great uniting cause. As the journalist Séverine pointed out, 'You have shut up heaven but not opened the bakers' shops'.[19] It was in these confused circumstances that France was faced with a revived threat from Germany.

19. Brogan (1967), p. 266.

CHAPTER 23

TO THE SACRED UNION, 1914

The Republic summons us;
We shall conquer or perish;
A Frenchman must live for her,
A Frenchman must die for her.
Le Chant du Départ, 1794

PROLOGUE: FROM SEDAN TO MOROCCO, 1870–1905

We never saw the return of spring without the sinister croak: 'War is coming'.
Romain Rolland[1]

In her disastrous war with Germany in 1870, France had been given no help and not much sympathy by the other Great Powers, and in her weakened state had no prospect of finding future allies. She remained vulnerable to any future German aggression. For the republicans who came to power in the 1880s, though direct war of revenge was unthinkable in the foreseeable future, to abandon the hope of 'revanche', or at least of some redress against the Treaty of Frankfurt, was just as unthinkable. For the myth of republican resistance in 1870–71 was both the glory and the burden of the Third Republic. Much of its legitimacy came from its patriotism; patriotic celebration was at the core of its political culture. The assertion of French greatness – including, even above all, military power – was felt as an imperative.

Germany has been the central problem of French foreign relations from the 1860s to the present day. The questions posed were unchanging and terribly simple. How could French security best be ensured in the face of German power? Should France accept German hegemony and seek coexistence, and even eventually junior partnership? Or could she compete with German power, and seek allies to do so? Though these questions were widely discussed, the key decisions were taken by a small number of men, usually with little public scrutiny, occasionally in defiance of public opposition, often in secret. The answers they gave, naturally, were complex. French security, it

1. Digeon (1952), p. 519.

was almost universally accepted, required her to fortify the frontier and strengthen the army to try to keep pace with that of Germany. Yet the superiority of German military power was tacitly accepted. There was moreover a recurring desire to reduce tension with Germany; and the economic ties between the two were close. However important a theme of French nationalism the notion of conflict with Germany remained, all practical idea of a war of revenge was dropped. A wit suggested that Gambetta's famous dictum should be reversed: 'speak of it always, think of it never'.[2] Alsace-Lorraine remained as an obstacle to rapprochement, but most French people would probably have been satisfied if the 'lost provinces' had been given some autonomy within the German empire, with recognition of French language rights.

Politicians and soldiers realized that France could not guarantee her own security unaided: an alliance with Russia was essential to force Germany to divide her forces. The idea of such an alliance had been nursed by French politicians and soldiers since 1870. But as Thiers had realized then when vainly soliciting Russian aid, France had nothing to offer a Russia that had no grievances against Germany and suspected the French Republic of being at best unreliable and at worst a hotbed of revolution. Bismarck had played on this fear by signing the Dreikaiserbund with both Austria and Russia. His fall in 1890 led to change of policy in Berlin: the decision that the vital alliance with Austria was incompatible with an alliance with Russia. The possibility of a future war with Austria supported by Germany caused Tsar Alexander III and his generals, with the support of Russian nationalists, to swallow their monarchist scruples and seek an informal military understanding with the French Republic, which was formalized by treaty in 1892. The clinching attraction for the Russians, however, was access to the French money market for loans, a facility denied by Germany in 1890. Although details of the treaty were kept secret, signs of friendship were greeted with public rejoicing, traditional left-wing anti-tsarism notwithstanding. When in 1893 a Russian naval squadron visited Toulon, its officers and men were hauled off for a lavish round of entertainments, culminating in a magnificent fête in Paris hosted by the left-wing Municipal Council and attended, among others, by the former Communard Marxist leader Paul Lafargue and his wife, Karl Marx's daughter. It was widely, though wrongly, believed that Russia had dissuaded Germany from pre-emptive attacks on France in 1875 and 1887; now, it seemed, the alliance had made the German threat recede. The defensive intentions of the treaty are demonstrated by the fact that during the 1890s relations with Germany improved.

Briefly, Russian autocrat and republican president seemed to wallow in the same requited emotion: 'It is for always'.[3] By the late 1890s, however, the relationship had gone stale. France and Russia had too few interests in common: Russia was not interested in supporting French colonial ambitions;

2. Doise and Vaïsse (1987), p. 24.
3. Andrew (1968), p. 119.

indeed, the two were potential rivals in the Near East. Among prominent French politicians, only Théophile Delcassé (foreign minister 1898–1905) was determined to revive the alliance. Only the Russians' need for French money kept them faithful, so Delcassé forced his colleagues to facilitate the river of cash, allowed Russians to bribe French newspapers into printing glowing accounts of investment prospects, and put pressure on the banks to cooperate. In return, he got the Russians to build a railway to Tashkent to frighten the British with a threat to India, and to sign an extension to the treaty, which he brought back from St Petersburg in 1899 inside his underwear for safe-keeping.

Colonial expansion seemed to provide a way of increasing French power and self-confidence without risking a clash with Germany. As has been seen, that was why nationalists originally objected. As they anticipated, perfidious Albion for some years equalled or replaced Germany as France's *bête noire*. Resentment began after 1882 when Britain imposed hegemony over Egypt. Round the turn of the century the colonialist tail was wagging the diplomatic dog, as a series of incidents dangerously poisoned relations with Britain. Most serious among them was the Fashoda incident of 1898, which seven-year-old Charles de Gaulle experienced as the most traumatic event of his childhood. A small French military expedition under Captain Marchand had been sent overland from west Africa to try to forestall the British on the upper Nile. There ensued in November an absurdly unequal armed confrontation between the handful of French and a sizeable army under Kitchener. Contacts remained polite: Marchand gave Kitchener some of the warm champagne he had carefully carried across Africa; Kitchener maliciously gave Marchand some French newpapers containing the latest details of the Dreyfus affair, which reduced the French officers to tears. Had shooting started the consequences would have been incalculable; fortunately everyone was too sensible to start a major war. But there followed French attempts to organize international pressure on Britain during the Boer War. This, like the Marchand expedition, was optimistically aimed at levering the British out of Egypt, but was no more successful. The realization of the futility of such ploys by the colonial lobby themselves, and the knowledge that Germany and Russia would not aid their colonial ambitions against Britain, caused a change in policy of the utmost importance: a compromise with London. In return for recognizing British predominance in Egypt, they wanted Britain to recognize theirs in Morocco. This bargain led to a convention in 1904, soon referred to as the Entente Cordiale (a name resurrected from the 1840s). It soon took on global significance as an informal alliance against Germany.

Morocco became the cause, or pretext, for serious Great Power conflict which fundamentally altered Franco-British and Franco-German relations. Morocco was the latest territory to be cast as the French India, 'the last chance that remains for us to extend the space occupied by our race on the world's surface'.[4] The German government challenged France's ambitions

4. Ibid., p. 105.

there largely as a diplomatic gambit, to prove to the French that neither their Russian ally nor their new British partner would help them, and that a rapprochement with Germany was their only way of obtaining Morocco. The kaiser went on a visit to Tangier in March 1905, where he expressed support for Moroccan independence. As the Grand Vizier put it, 'Whilst in the act of ravishing Morocco, France has received a tremendous kick in the behind from the Emperor William'.[5] The German government unofficially conveyed threats of war. Russia was unwilling to risk war on this issue, and was anyway crippled by her defeat by Japan and internal upheaval. Delcassé was forced to resign by frightened colleagues in June 1905 as a sop to Germany. Germany's triumph was short-lived, however, for both Russia and Britain, concerned at what seemed German provocation, stood by France, and at an international conference at Algeciras France's claim to supervise Moroccan affairs was upheld. Germany's ploy recoiled on her, for Russia and Britain, convinced that Germany was set on mischief, sought to strengthen their links with France and improve relations with each other.

MILITARY PRECAUTIONS

Inside France, the Moroccan crisis had mixed effects. The French government and army panicked: 'There is nothing, no ammunition, no equipment, no stocks of provisions, and morale in the army and the country is in an even worse state'.[6] Delcassé was widely attacked by Left and Right in parliament and the press for risking war. But the determination of the colonial lobby to secure full control of Morocco was unabated. In May 1911 French troops occupied Fez, and in response the German government sent a gunboat to Agadir, ostensibly to protect German residents (a 'resident' was sent specially). Although settled peacefully through a deal with Germany which recognized a French protectorate over the whole country, this incident confirmed a growing perception among writers, soldiers, students, diplomats and politicians that Germany was plotting a war, and that France must take precautions (see pp. 56–58).

Many politicians, alarmed by the dangerous conduct of foreign and colonial policy and by ministerial instability at home, wanted a firm hand on the tiller, 'to make France's position felt in any international crisis',[7] but also to prevent any lurch into war. This led to the appointment of the moderate republican Raymond Poincaré as prime minister and foreign minister in January 1912, and then to his election as president of the Republic by a majority including Left and Right in February 1913. Poincaré, determined to strengthen the Russian alliance, assured Russia of support in the Balkans, where the First Balkan War began in October 1912.

5. Ibid., p. 274.
6. Ibid., p. 289.
7. Keiger (1983), p. 139.

The army staff pressed Russia to improve its mobilization plans and coordinate them with the French. The alliance from the beginning had required France and Russia in case of war to begin operations against Germany as soon as possible, to prevent her from defeating them in turn. French politicians and soldiers regularly urged the Russians to prepare for a rapid attack, and provided large loans for railway building to help them do so. But during both the Moroccan crises, the French generals firmly told their government that their own army was in no state to fight Germany.

The great political battle of the immediate pre-war period came over the government's proposal in 1913, on which the generals were very keen, to increase the period of military service from two years to three. The debate inside and outside parliament was intense. Most socialists and some radicals suspected the government of ulterior motives: plotting aggression, preparing domestic repression, or at least using defence as an issue to try to split the Left. They therefore opposed the law, but did not wish to appear indifferent to national security. Very few of the Left advocated *l'antipatriotisme* and rejection of any participation in national defence. Most held to the republican patriotic tradition which saw France as the home of liberty, equality and fraternity that democrats should defend. Those who had tried to negotiate a joint plan with German socialists to prevent war had been disappointed to find the Germans as patriotic as themselves. Therefore, although official socialist policy was to prevent war from breaking out, if necessary by an international general strike, there was no intention to sabotage the national defence if war actually began, and certainly not to take unilateral action in France. Otherwise, as Guesde privately admitted, the countries where socialism was strong would be defeated by those where it was weak. Finally, the government won a majority for the three-years law in part by offering the radicals a deal, especially a commitment to income tax.

In the 1913 general election the socialists, the most vigorous opponents of the law, gained 300,000 votes and 30 seats; but overall a small majority of votes went to parties that supported the law.[8] After the elections there still remained a small majority in parliament for three-year service, especially as it was now being presented as a short-term emergency measure to deter German aggression and keep the peace. Opposition to the three-year term was largely confined to the ballot box: the expectation that there would be serious disturbances and even mutinies of conscripts largely failed to materialize. In short, conscription was unpopular, but most were ready to do their bit if they had to, however much they grumbled. There was no expectation that war was imminent.

8. Becker (1977), p. 78.

THE 1914 CRISES: TWO ASSASSINATIONS

France, once soldier of God, today soldier of humanity, will always be the soldier
of the ideal.

                                                                    Clemenceau[9]

In 1914 occurred two notorious assassinations. On 16 March the editor of *Le
Figaro*, Gaston Calmette, was shot dead in his office by Henriette Caillaux,
the wife of the finance minister. On 28 June the heir to the Austro-Hungarian
thrones, Archduke Franz Ferdinand, was shot dead in Sarajevo by Serb
nationalists. The latter killing caused a few raised eyebrows in France. The
former caused a sensation that monopolized the headlines and most of the
government's attention when her trial began in July. 'If the wives of statesmen
start shooting journalists', commented another journalist, 'a healthy impulse
may turn into an unpleasant habit.' Her motive was to prevent publication of
embarrassing letters written to her by Caillaux when they were both still
married to other people; the letters also showed him to be a cynical and
unscrupulous politician. Many believed that her real reason had been to
prevent publication of evidence of her husband's treasonable contacts with
Germany during the Agadir crisis. Caillaux, the most powerful political
advocate of détente with Germany, was forced to resign. He insisted that the
government arrange his wife's acquittal, and threatened to publish decoded
diplomatic dispatches proving underhand negotiations by ministers with
foreign governments if they did not. A chivalrous Paris jury acquitted her on
28 July: a decision that let the government off the hook. Foreign embassies,
realizing that their dispatches were being deciphered, changed codes and so
the French government was left in the dark at a crucial time. Furthermore,
this domestic distraction left politicians, including Poincaré and the new
independent socialist prime minister Viviani, a novice in foreign affairs, with
little time to think about the growing Balkan crisis, and left public opinion
oblivious of the danger.

Striking proof of unpreparedness was that Poincaré and Viviani set sail on
16 July on a previously arranged visit to Russia and Scandinavia: when the
crisis broke the French government was 'literally and metaphorically at sea'.[10]
Austria and Germany had decided on a war with Serbia over the Sarajevo
assassination, but delayed their ultimatum to Belgrade until the French
leaders had re-embarked from St Petersburg for Stockholm on 23 July. While
with the Russians, Poincaré appears not to have agreed a joint Balkan policy,
though he stressed France's commitment to the alliance which he believed
safeguarded peace and security by restraining German ambitions. He and
Viviani were only in very unreliable wireless contact with the shore, which
the Germans were also trying to jam, when the Russians decided to begin

9. Citron (1989), p. 24.
10. Keiger (1983), p. 147.

partial mobilization on 25 July and the Germans followed suit. French diplomats and ministers were very incompletely aware of what was happening. The French war minister, Messimy, and chief of staff, Joffre, urged the Russians on 27 July that in case of war they should 'take the offensive in East Prussia as soon as possible'.[11] Poincaré and Viviani only arrived back in Paris on 29 July.

Could the French have helped to calm the accelerating crisis? Should they, in particular, have sternly warned the Russians against beginning mobilization? They had reined in Russia during the Balkan crisis of 1908: could and should they have done so again? Did they even inflame the dispute? During and immediately after the First World War, left-wing and German propaganda pushed the line of French complicity: 'Poincaré la Guerre', the Lorrainer bent on revenge, so ran the argument, had sought the conflict to regain the 'lost provinces'. But there is no evidence that the French government was aiming for war. The circumstances just described show how little they were in a position to influence events. Decisions made in St Petersburg, and even more in Vienna and Berlin, were not materially influenced by anything the French did, or could have done.

But in the longer term had French policy helped to create fatal tensions in Europe? As we have seen, the defeat of 1870 had not been forgiven or forgotten. For years French generals had been urging their Russian colleagues to increase their military strength and the speed of their mobilization. French governments for a generation had placed the Russian alliance at the heart of their security policy, and would not risk destroying it. Poincaré believed that European stability required the maintenance of a balance of power founded on the alliance systems.[12] The growth of French and Russian military strength, instead of being a deterrent, was the reason why the German general staff decided that they wanted to fight a preventive war before they lost their military hegemony. The seriousness of this latest Balkan crisis was that it seemed in Vienna and Berlin that unless Austria reacted decisively, she could not survive as a Great Power. In that case, Germany would stand alone, 'encircled', as they saw it, by a hostile coalition of France, Russia and perhaps Britain.

But it must be remembered that it was Germany's own unpredictable and provocative policies over two decades that had created this 'encirclement', which was, in fact, very loose and uncoordinated. The only way of allaying German fears would have been openly to accept their supremacy and hope for German goodwill. It is not self-evident that such appeasement would have been a more reliable way of keeping the peace. As it was, German generals refused to contemplate the loss of their military superiority. They decided, whatever the cost, to force a decision in 1914. What began as a diplomatic and political crisis turned into a reckless scramble for military advantage without any clear conception of the aims or outcome of the conflict. Few

11. Kennedy (1979), p. 263.
12. Keiger (1983), pp. 153–4.

statesmen and not all soldiers realized that, so balanced on a knife edge were the military advantages, so finely calculated the days and hours of military planning, that any move towards mobilization by one would lead to mobilization by all, and that would inevitably lead to war. No diplomatic initiative could halt the juggernaut once it had started. The attitude in Berlin was, in the kaiser's words, 'now or never'.

Poincaré and Viviani, back in Paris, did warn the Russians on 30 July that they 'should not immediately proceed to any measure which might offer Germany a pretext for a total or partial mobilization of her forces'.[13] Such a warning was no longer relevant, but it does show what the French attitude was. In fact, a war in eastern Europe was by now inevitable. In the circumstances, the French were prepared to stand by their alliance with the Russians. The government could conceive of no alternative, and indeed, by this time there was none, other than surrender without a fight, permitting German troops to occupy French soil and frontier defences. On 30 July troops were ordered to cover the eastern borders, but were kept 10 kilometres back from the frontier. They were also ordered to make no move into Belgium. General Joffre was unhappy with such restrictions, and calculated that every 24-hour delay in mobilizing cost 15–20 kilometres of territory. But in France, unlike Germany, civilians were in charge, and the government was determined, for the sake of domestic and British public opinion, that France should not be an aggressor: 'let the Germans put themselves in the wrong' the cabinet decided.[14]

FRANCE GOES TO WAR: THE 'SACRED UNION'

Amour sacré de la Patrie
Conduis, soutiens nos bras vengeurs!
Liberté! Liberté cherie,
Combats avec tes défenseurs.

'Marseillaise'

France . . . represents today, once again, before the universe, liberty, justice and reason . . . . She will be defended by all her sons, whose sacred union in the presence of the enemy nothing will break.

Poincaré, 4 August 1914[15]

In every country, governments stated, and peoples believed, that they were responding to enemy aggression. The socialists, vocal critics of militarism, accepted this too. Their leaders knew that nowhere had socialist parties or trade unions managed to put a brake on the preparations, though the SFIO leader Jaurès still hoped that a conference of the International, called for 9

13. Ibid., p. 127.
14. Ibid., p. 127.
15. Message to parliament, Poincaré (1926), vol. 4, p. 546.

August in Paris, might help; he could not know that time had run out. He also accepted, as did his German and Austrian comrades, that their own government had not sought war: 'if we were in their place, I don't know what more we could do to assure peace'.[16] His murder by a deranged nationalist on 31 July was therefore as senseless as it was tragic.

At 3.55 p.m. on 1 August mobilization telegrams were sent from the Rue de Grenelle post office. An hour or two later, all over France, the notices carefully kept in every *mairie* were posted up, and, as a few old people still remember, church bells rang the tocsin to call workers from fields and workshops: 'That's the funeral bell for our lads'.[17] Most people were surprised that a diplomatic crisis in a far-away country had suddenly come to this. There was little patriotic elation; for most people, war, as always, was a disaster. Men aged between 20 and 48, 3,700,000 of them, left for their regimental depots; only 0.5 per cent, far fewer than the 10 per cent expected, hid away. There were few demonstrations, whether bellicose or pacifist: *carnet B*, the register of suspected subversives to be arrested, was not needed. This generation had been brought up to believe that duty to France was sacred, and that every male citizen must be ready to defend the Fatherland. Soldiers' letters home would speak of duty to country and community. War had not been expected by most people in 1914, any more than it had been expected in any particular year; but that an attack by Germany might come one day was an ingrained belief.

Germany declared war on France on 3 August. The tradition of republican patriotism now commanded practically universal assent: 'Because it's necessary, we'll go', said one worker, 'and we'll show how socialists can shoot Germans'.[18] Péguy, the socialist nationalist, put it more poetically: 'I go to fight, as a soldier of the Republic, in the last of wars and for general disarmament'.[19] Poincaré proclaimed a 'sacred union': there would be a truce in the 'Franco-French war' in order to fight the Franco-German war. The nationalist Barrès and members of the Ligue des Patriotes attended the funeral of their old enemy Jaurès, where the CGT leader Jouhaux made a speech declaring that the war was the responsibility of Germany and Austria. The Marxist leader Guesde accepted a seat in the cabinet. The former revolutionary anti-militarist Hervé changed his paper's title from *La Guerre Sociale* to *La Victoire*. Two old enemies, a *laïc* schoolteacher and a priest, met in a village in the Alps: 'So, this is it, then, Monsieur le Curé. Well, we're friends, we only hate the invader now.'[20]

As 600,000 Germans swept down through central Belgium and north-western France, where they were not supposed to be, their way barred only by the Belgians, the British Expeditionary Force and a few middle-aged

16. Becker (1977), p. 226.
17. An old Breton peasant woman, quoted in ibid., p. 295.
18. Becker (1977), p. 344.
19. Nicolet (1982), p. 505.
20. Becker (1977), pp. 373–4, 402.

territorials, the French were forced back in a desperate withdrawal from their
bloody and futile attacks on the eastern frontier (see pp. 59–60). Joffre now
showed skill and fortitude, sacking failed generals and improvising a vast
redeployment of forces to defend Paris. It was made possible by the energetic
determination of soldiers and civilians alike, such as had not been seen in
1870 and was not seen again in 1940. A British liaison officer[21] recalled that

> General Joffre and Field-Marshal Sir John French met in the palace of Compiègne;
> signallers were laying lines from picture to picture in the galleries. The noise of
> hammering was such they had to be told to stop. It was purposeful, intent and
> businesslike. They were the soldiers of an army which, though beaten, meant to
> fight on. Nothing else occurred to them, though they were less than 80 kilometres
> from Paris.

It was an army of civilians in uniform, mostly peasant soldiers, often led by
schoolteachers: the Republic in arms.

The Germans did not reach Paris. Its garrison sallied forth (some in
commandeered taxis) to join an allied counter-attack north-east of the capital
from 5–10 September: this 'Miracle of the Marne' turned the invaders back. As
in most miracles, it is difficult to separate myth from reality. The Germans
were anyway at the end of their tether after marching 300 miles, and were
short of food and ammunition; even had they not been exhausted, the
Schlieffen Plan was not seriously expected by its exponents to win the war.
But it did place northern France in German hands, and France's ability to
fight on depended on her allies.

Yet France and the Republic had survived, and war had reconciled the
followers of Joan of Arc and those of Marianne. This was the apotheosis of
the Third Republic, which, from being 'the government that divides us least'
had become the government of union, of national defence and eventually of
victory. The 'sacred union', however, did not last throughout the war: the
re-emergence of old political conflicts ended it by 1917. Moreover, the strains
of war created formidable new problems and resentments that emerged soon
after it ended. Nevertheless, 1914 marked another step in the long and
painful process of ending the Revolution.

21. Spears (1956), p. 483.

CONCLUSIONS

It cannot be repeated too often: the French Revolution has founded a society, but is still seeking a government.

Prévost-Paradol[1]

We began in an age of powdered hair and knee breeches; when English visitors found the French noticeably smaller and skinnier; when the population of central France lived principally on chestnuts; when it took four days to travel from Paris to the second city, Lyons; when agricultural methods and agricultural society were still medieval; and when people with scrofula still hoped to be healed by a king's sacred touch. As Pinkney puts it, the Revolution 'had left largely unchanged the fundamental aspects of French life'.[2] By the end of our period, there had been an immense transformation. People were bigger, healthier and lived longer; they were far more literate; more lived in towns; they travelled by train and motor bus; they took holidays at the seaside, listened to the gramophone and washed relatively frequently; Louis Pasteur had become in his own lifetime France's greatest scientific hero, the embodiment of the benefits of progress, and Marie Curie, first woman professor at the Sorbonne, had discovered radium. In 1830, the prime minister Jacques Laffitte crossed Paris by sedan chair; in 1912, parliamentary candidate Jules Védrine toured his constituency at the controls of an aeroplane, probably the world's first airborne campaigner (he lost). All the commonplaces about 'modernization' can thus be applied to France, as to her neighbours. But however important these changes, and even though France followed a somewhat distinctive pattern of economic and social change, this is not the essence of French history in the nineteenth century. In social and economic terms, France, appropriately enough, was somewhere between Britain and Italy – a pretty standard performance. It can be described and quantified, but there is not much to conclude from it. It is France's political experience that is unique, and here the story is as much one of continuity as of transformation: Laffitte and Védrine, however different

1. Prévost-Paradol (1869), p. 296.
2. Pinkney (1986), p. 3.

their technology, would have understood each other's politics. Indeed, it became a political cliché to assert that the same struggle was continuing from generation to generation.

This struggle was fundamentally about one thing: the consequences of the Revolution of 1789. It was long, bitter and often bloody, not because of class conflict or the strains of socio-economic change (from that point of view there was no reason for France to be more agitated than Belgium), but because of the tensions inherent in the traditions, beliefs, hatreds, solidarities, ideologies, rivalries, hopes and fears embodied in French political culture. The Revolution had begun a new era, but the substance of that era – the ideologies, institutions and parties that were to dominate the nineteenth and twentieth centuries – was created during the debates and struggles of the nineteenth century. All this greatly complicated and envenomed the problems of exercising power, ruling the State and policing society. On the one hand were what we might call negative problems: lack of legitimacy, lack of consensus. No regime could count on a general acceptance of its right to govern. On the other hand, constructive problems: how to meet a range of post-revolutionary aspirations that were frequently utopian (a society without poverty; a society of deferential paternalism) and also explicitly conflicting (a society 'without God or king'; a Christian monarchy). These connected problems of legitimacy, consensus and utopianism focused on the State, which the Revolution had made the master and creator of society, and hence simultaneously a threat and a prize.

The immense difficulty of creating a post-revolutionary polity is one that the late twentieth century shows to be one of the most urgent problems of the modern world. Post-colonial as well as post-Communist states have to face it. France may therefore be of more interest as a post-revolutionary than as a revolutionary model: the first modern State to have faced the problem, and to have both invented and exhausted a spectrum of possible solutions from religious traditionalism to revolutionary democracy. But however interesting, the French experience is – if I can be forgiven a truism – quin-tessentially of the nineteenth century: 'pre-modern' not 'post-modern', with hope and naivety outweighing cynicism and disillusion. Religious belief was of central importance. 'Progress' was dazzling and reassuring. It was an age of new and intoxicating ideologies, hence the prominence of political thinkers and prophets. Its economic, cultural and social 'modernization' was only beginning, which meant, as in some post-colonial systems, that political modernization (particularly universal male suffrage) came early and suddenly to a mainly rural and largely illiterate society in which local *notables* were important intermediaries. Economic life was relatively simple, economic needs seemed finite, and the economic function of the State was limited. Assumptions, expectations and the focus of politics were therefore quite different from those of the twentieth century. We shall see in the case of eastern Europe whether cynical twentieth-century materialism can provide a safer foundation for politics than naive nineteenth-century idealism.

Was the French quest for a post-revolutionary order successful? Yes, from the point of view of democratic liberals, for whom France had left behind the dangerous extremes of anarchy and despotism. No, from the point of view of revolutionary and counter-revolutionary idealists, who after the First World War had to seek their utopias elsewhere: in Italy, Spain, Germany or the USSR. The nineteenth century in France is a time of continually reduced and postponed expectations. By the end, the French had stumbled upon the Austro-Hungarian recipe for political stability: a state of universal mild dissatisfaction. They had finally constructed a political system not much different from the rest of western Europe; but at far greater human cost.

The Second Empire did not remodel a Europe of free nations, but it did remodel Paris; the Third Republic did not build a perfect democracy, but it did build the Eiffel Tower. Such achievements greatly impressed contemporaries, and helped to maintain France, particularly Paris, as one of the world's models of modernity: to call some aspiring backwater 'the Paris of the Orient' or 'the Paris of South America' was a universally acknowledged accolade. But it is difficult to go along with the effusive conclusions of some historians on the wider global significance of the Revolution. The Revolution certainly invented the very concept of 'revolution' as a sudden leap into a utopian future, and this has indeed had immense reverberations. But was the Revolution really 'the creation of a universal framework of political action in result of which the French Revolution has remained the master narrative of modernity'?[3] Liberals and conservatives everywhere saw France during and after the Revolution as an anti-model, stewing in violence, decadence and weakness; Britain, America and even Germany were far more influential models of modernity from Argentina to Japan. Although revolutionaries for much of the nineteenth century still looked to France as the torchbearer, ironically this was something that most French people were doggedly and successfully trying not to be. By the end of the century, the Revolution had neither triumphed, nor had it been expunged; it had, in Furet's word, been tamed.

How can we explain this modest culmination? French political culture was marked by a persistant utopianism restrained by a no-less-perpetual caution: in the famous joke, every Frenchman had his heart on the Left and his wallet on the Right. We can see this at every level of political thought and practice. There is a constant awareness of danger, particularly the dangers, real or imaginary, of a return to the 1790s, to terror, civil war and foreign invasion. Very few people (Blanqui is the most famous and persistent) ever positively sought to renew these ordeals; governments accidentally blundered into them, but politicians and voters quickly sought an exit. Events taught them caution. Every major political tendency saw its hopes dashed: legitimists in 1830, Orleanists in 1848, republicans in 1851, Bonapartists in 1870, revolutionaries in 1871. Political options were regularly eliminated by this political Darwinism, resulting in the survival of the blandest.

The intellectual form this took was liberalism. Liberalism was a powerful

3. A fairly widespread idea; this particular formulation is from Feher (1990), p. 5.

intellectual and political influence in its own right. It inherited many of the values of the Enlightenment and of 1789, and was buttressed by the examples of Britain and America. Indeed, Rosenvallon sees two parallel political histories of France, the 'Jacobin' and the 'English'.[4] Liberalism was invaluable as a defence against ideological adventure, especially when the adventurers were armed with the formidable power of the State. Hence, liberalism was the weapon of the opposition to ultraroyalism in the 1820s and to Bonapartism in the 1860s: it was the way to restrain rulers.

Why then did it take so long for a useful and inoffensive consensual liberal system to become established, certainly not before 1879 and arguably not before 1945? Rosenvallon suggests that post-revolutionary political culture was 'deeply illiberal', and that this explains the failure of constitutional monarchy, the standard European liberal form.[5] He argues that it was very difficult for French politicians even to conceptualize the idea of political moderation, whether based on the idea that the State should be neutral between parties, or on the idea that the State should incorporate the balanced representation of diverse interests. As we have seen, the State was hardly ever politically neutral, and political diversity was rarely regarded as ideal or even legitimate, for the State was supposed to define and represent the general interest (good) against the private interests of individuals and groups (bad). The only political models truly comprehensible in France, argues Rosen-vallon, were the absolutist monarchy and the democratic republic. If we apply this insight to events, we see that the Restoration fell when it tried to be the former, the Second Republic when it tried to be the latter, and the July Monarchy when it tried to be neither. Only Bonapartism solved the political conundrum by being both: absolutist and democratic.

Bonapartism has repeatedly shown itself to be the most convincing, though temporary, solution to the political and ideological problems bequeathed by the Revolution. This view contests or modifies two influential analyses of post-revolutionary politics, which we might call the 'Whig-Republican' and the 'Tory-Tocquevillian'. The 'Whig-Republican', which has recently enjoyed a revival in France, sees the Revolution as the inventor of modern democratic politics, whose legacy of liberty and equality reached its logical, desirable and seemingly predestined outcome in the Third Republic, when, in around 1880, the Revolution 'was coming into port'.[6] The 'Tory-Tocquevillian' sees the essential results of the Revolution to be the strengthening of the power and rights of the State, the weakening of the autonomous institutions of civil society (churches, corporations, communities, associations), and the creation of economic and social rigidity in what Hoffman terms a stalemate society permanently dominated by those who had come out on top in the revolutionary struggle.[7] The weakening of civil society meant that it could not

4. Rosenvallon (1994), p. 7.
5. Ibid., p. 179.
6. Furet (1992), p. 537.
7. Tocqueville (1967), p. 79; Hoffmann (1963), p. 9.

function without the exercise of State authority, and the price of political consent was that the State would use its authority to protect vested interests. 'For more than a century the political problem of France was to devise a political system adapted to the stalemate society.'[8]

These two interpretations are not incompatible with each other; but they are difficult to reconcile with the awkward phenomenon of Bonapartism, which perhaps in consequence is often downplayed.[9] There seem to me several connected reasons for regarding Bonapartism as the culmination of post-revolutionary political culture. First, it created a powerful post-revolutionary State. In an important discussion of the phenomenon of revolution, Skocpol has argued that its outcome is a regime 'more centralized and rationalized ... more potent within society and more powerful and ambitious ... within the international states system'.[10] Bonapartism fulfilled this role in France. Second, its plebiscitary authoritarianism proved the most workable political formula for the revolutionary myth of the 'general will', incarnated in the charismatic populist leader. Third, Bonapartism was the only ideology that managed to synthesize conflicting ideas and aspirations brought out by the Revolution: just as it could be both absolutist and democratic, it could also be both Catholic and anticlerical, populist and elitist, conservative and progressive. Fourth, a popular 'cult of Napoleon' was a particularly potent and seductive element of popular political culture, that 'symbolic over-investment in politics' (in Furet's phrase) which revisionist historians tell us was the essence of the Revolution. Bonapartism was thus too powerful to be overcome by any of its rivals within France: only external forces, including Wellington, Bismarck and the Zulus, could bring it down, and so begin again the search for a way to end the Revolution.

The crucial importance of Bonapartism seems to disprove both the 'Whiggish' interpretation that the Revolution logically engendered a republic, and the view that a 'stalemate society' was the inevitable solution to political instability. For the most popular regime of the nineteenth century was not a republic but the Second Empire, which was also the most deliberately dynamic, espousing economic modernization, introducing free trade (which seriously undermined the stalemate society) and owing much of its mass support to its willingness to use the power of the State to promote economic growth and to some extent to emancipate the masses from the influence of the post-Revolution elites. Bonapartism provided the strong authority that Hoffmann tells us society required, and it was accepted, even desired, because it purported to be and in a sense was neutral: neither 'Red' nor 'White', it guaranteed both the Revolution and order.

Yet Bonapartism's ending of the Revolution was of course temporary.

8. Hoffmann (1963), p. 12.
9. It is strikingly neglected in the massive collections that appeared to commemorate the Revolution in 1989, and also from Nora's seven-volume compendium (1984–93) of the great themes of national history.
10. Skocpol (1979), pp. 161–2.

Paradoxically, the process took place at least two, and arguably three, times: under the First Empire, the Second Empire and the Fifth Republic. Of the great problems left by the Revolution – internal conflict, relations between State and subject, and relations with the outside world – Bonapartism could solve the first two but not the third, because national glory was an essential part of its claim to legitimacy, and brought it into fatal conflict with its neighbours. Gaullism, of course, made great use of nationalist rhetoric, though mostly directed safely against France's allies.[11]

International relations are of fundamental importance in modern French history, even though historians often treat them as merely an occasional distraction from essential domestic issues. Recent reassessments of the Revolution have stressed the centrality of international power struggles in destroying the Old Regime and dominating the political process after 1791.[12] These problems did not disappear after Waterloo, even though they were held in check until the 1850s by a shared desire among European governments to ward off another catastrophic war. But in France, all governments came under pressure, at a time when nationalism was in the ascendant, to assert French power inside and outside Europe. Moreover, it was generally believed that success abroad would win them support and enhance stability at home. International power struggles have therefore been at least as important as any other factor in French political upheavals.

We should note in passing that France, despite its relative decline since the mid-eighteenth century, has been rather successful – though at vast human and financial cost – in exercising power outside its borders, and is the only European Great Power in the twentieth century to have maintained its territory. If weak neighbours and powerful allies have made this success possible, far from negligible has been the potency of the national, especially republican, myth of unity, determinedly promoted by successive regimes. Religious homogeneity inherited from the Old Regime has given substance to the idea of unity: ironically, 'the Republic One and Indivisible' is built on Catholic foundations. Nevertheless, international relations have proved a dangerous element because while political prestige required the maintenance of France's 'rank', its demographic and economic underpinnings were waning. This contradiction led to Sedan, the second failure of Bonapartism.

How do events after 1870 fit into this interpretation? The Third Republic stepped into the gap left by the defeat of Napoleon III: it was the only option left, 'the government that divides us least'. The circumstances that made its accession possible – desire for peace, fear of internal conflict, and not least the support of France's conquerors – invite comparison with the Bourbon

11. It will be interesting to see how the Fifth Republic deals with the only real – though peaceful – external threat to its power and legitimacy: European integration. The assumption so far, comparable with that of Napoleon III before 1866, is that European integration will enhance French power, not limit it.
12. See Blanning (1986) and (1996); Schama (1989); Mann (1993); Schroeder (1994); Skocpol (1979).

Restoration. Its political system was not a revival of the experiments of the Revolution: its parliamentary practice was derived from the Restoration and July Monarchy, and the important addition of manhood suffrage was as much Bonapartist as republican. Its attitude towards the Revolution was always uneasy, and the ideological links mainly symbolic. The Third Republic's political principles were above all the conscious and deliberate antithesis of the Second Empire: weak executive, dominance of parliament and mediation by parties.

Consequently, all who wanted 'strong' government could not but look, however shamefacedly, to Bonapartism as the alternative model: charismatic leadership incarnating 'the nation', a powerful executive 'above party', plebiscitary democracy, and contempt for parliamentary tactics and party politics. The crises of 1940 and 1958 brought a resort to 'strong' charismatic authority and a rejection of liberal parliamentary republicanism. De Gaulle's Fifth Republic, the first political system since the Revolution to have attained practically universal acceptance, is a new version, shorn of dynastic complications, of the Bonapartist formula of the 'republican monarch', 'the only chance for French democracy'.[13] In short, it is not the Republic in its 'weak', liberal, parliamentary form – 'the principles of 1789' – that has concluded the long post-revolutionary ordeal, but that characteristic French combination of 'active authority and passive democracy'[14] first exploited by Bonaparte: 'the principles of 1799' able to restrain the excesses of both Right and Left. As the consuls declared duplicitously after the coup d'état of Brumaire 1799, 'The Revolution is fixed to the principles that began it: it is over'.

13. Michel Debré (principal drafter of the Fifth Republic constitution), in Gildea (1994), p. 82.
14. Bluche (1980), p. 332.

FURTHER READING

This guide aims to be relatively concise, to reflect my own preferences and yet to provide a degree of comprehensiveness. One way of doing this is by marking with an asterisk works with important and up-to-date bibliographies. I have cited author and date so that full references can be followed up in the bibliography (pp. 500–26).

Contemporary authors I find particularly stimulating (all have several works cited below) are Weber, who combines ideas, scholarship and entertainment; Girardet, formidably intelligent, elegant – and concise; Rosenvallon, constantly shedding fresh light on political analysis; and the inexhaustibly original Corbin.

There has been a succession of important general works in English on France in the nineteenth century. Bury (1969) is lucid and elegant; Brogan (1967) robust and shrewd; Cobban (1965) sweeping and judicious; *Magraw (1983) opinionated and packed with information; Wright (1981) concise and comprehensive; *Furet (1992) pithy and erudite; Zeldin (1973) idiosyncratic and anecdotal.

On social history, *Price (1987) is encyclopedic and *McPhee (1992:a) lively and argumentative; on economic history, Asselain (1984) is a fine introduction.

PART I: OBSESSIONS

An introduction to the aftermath of the Revolution is Best (1988), especially the contribution by Weber. On tradition and memory, *Gildea (1994) is a lively survey, and *Nora (1984) a national monument. Recent research on post-revolutionary political culture is assembled in Vovelle *et al.* (1990), and Agulhon *et al.* (1992); individual contributions are Pessin (1992), Luzatto (1991), Gosselin (1992), Paulson (1983), Amalvi (1992) and Aubry (1988). On ideas of 'the people', Chevalier (1973) is seminal and Fritz (1988) invaluable; Barrows (1981) and Nye (1975) examine late-nineteenth-century perceptions. On political symbols, Agulhon (1981) and (1989) are essential. On revolutionary ideas, see Talmon (1960), unfashionable in approach but with a wealth of material and written with passion; Dalotel *et al.* (1980), Stuart (1992) and Steenhuysen (1971). On counter-revolutionary alarms, Roberts (1973) is important and concise.

On revolutionary events, works are listed under Parts IV and V. General consideration of revolutionary situations and their outcomes are Cobb (1969), Labrousse (1948), Pilbeam (1993) and Winock (1986). On violence, see Corbin (1992) and Chauvaud (1991). On repression of revolution, see Vidalenc (1948), Merriman (1978), Wright (1975) and Tombs (1981). Biographies of leading revolutionaries include works on Blanqui by Paz (1984) and Bernstein (1971), and on Malon, a revolutionary turned reformist, by Vincent (1992). Among the most vivid memoirs are Tocqueville (1948), Vallès (1972), Vuillaume (1971) and Brochet (1977).

On the politics and culture surrounding war, there is relatively little on the pre-1870 period – see *Puymège (1993) on the soldier image, and a collection edited by Viallaneix and Ehrard (1985) – and a profusion thereafter, particularly Girardet (1983), Digeon (1952), Weber (1959) and *Roth (1990). On economic and political consequences of war, see *Mann (1993). Case (1954) is indispensable for domestic reactions to Napoleon III's adventures. Military preparations have recently attracted serious attention. Griffith (1989) discusses ideas. Cox (1994) investigates planning after 1815, and *Doise and Vaïsse (1987) after 1870; in English see also Mitchell (1984). Williamson (1969), May (1984) and Kennedy (1979) are important for the military context to 1914.

The most studied war of the period is that of 1870. Howard (1967) is a classic of military history; *Roth (1990) and Audoin-Rouzeau (1989) are important on domestic repercussions, and Levillain and Riemenschneider (1990) analyse various aspects, including the economic. Ascoli (1987) is a vivid study from the soldiers' level. Holmes (1984) and Adriance (1987) investigate causes of defeat.

On ideas of a new order a stimulating introduction is Girardet (1986). There is no adequate introductory work in English on French political ideas. An important selection of thinkers is however discussed by *Hayward (1991); Coplestone (1977) is very useful for reference; Zeldin (1973) summarizes central themes. Charlton (1984) and (1963) are valuable on Romanticism and religion, and Crossley (1993) on Romantic historiography. On counter-revolutionary ideas, Rémond (1969) is an indispensable introduction; see also Locke (1974), Sutton (1982), Weber (1962) and *Sirinelli (1992). On the nagging fear of decline, see Swart (1964). On liberalism, there has been a recent boom: see Holmes (1984), Welch (1984), Siedentop (1994), *Kelley (1992), Johnson (1963) and Pitt (1995), and in French, *Rosenvallon (1985), Girard (1985) and Jardin (1984) and *(1985). On republicanism, see the welcome recent survey by *Pilbeam (1995); Lefranc (1973) is still useful. The major work on republican ideas is *Nicolet (1982); see also Auspitz (1982). Socialist ideas have a vast literature: good ways into it are through *Lovell (1992), Manuel (1962), Stedman Jones and Patterson (1996), *Vincent (1984) and (1992), Judt (1986) and Stuart (1992). On Comte, see Pickering (1994). On

Bonapartist ideas there is very little: see *Bluche (1980) and Bonaparte (1839), and on the 'cult' of Napoleon, Lucas-Dubreton (1960). On ideas of the nation, Fritz (1988), Girardet (1983) and (1986), and Nora (1984–93) are invaluable; in English, see Tombs (1991).

On paranoia, Girardet (1986) is again full of ideas. *Cubitt (1993) explores the Jesuit myth, and Parry (1993) examines the whole area of the Third Republic; both consider the roots of conspiracy theories. Roberts (1973) contains startling material. See also Rémond (1985) on anticlericalism, *Wilson (1982) on anti-Semitism and Mitchell (1980) on spies.

PART II: POWER

Introductory works in English on the State and its workings include Anderson (1977), Zeldin (1973), and the old but useful and amusing Bodley (1898); and in French, *Levêque (1992), *Lagoueyte (1989) and *Mayeur (1984). *Rosenvallon (1990) is important, and *Gueslin (1992) useful and concise; on thinking about the State, see Jones (1993). Electoral systems and elections are usefully surveyed by Campbell (1958) and electioneering by Zeldin (1973); major recent works are *Rosenvallon (1992) and *Huard (1991). The bureaucracy is best approached through the concise yet exhaustive *Burdeau (1994); in English, see Church (1981). Elites are analysed massively by *Tudesq (1964) for the period before 1848, and after 1880 by *Charle (1991), (1980) and (1987) and Estèbe (1982). 'High politics' and the details of tactics and policy attract few French historians; some angles have been studied by Julien-Laferrière (1970), Hudemann (1979), Smith (1980) and *Rudelle (1982). The social composition of various assemblies is analysed by Beck (1974), Higonnet and Higonnet (1967) and Higonnet (1968); for parliamentary life, see Guiral and Thuillier (1980); reference works are Robert, Bourloton and Cougny (1889–91) and Yvert (1990). The activities of pressure groups are little known. Smith again (1980) and Lebovics (1988) give fundamentally differing accounts. For agriculture, see Barral (1968), and for the important wine industry, Loubère (1978). The conjunction of politics, the bureaucracy and pressure groups can be seen in different areas in Andrew and Kanya-Forstner (1971), Auspitz (1982), Barral (1974) and Keiger (1983).

French historians have long been interested in the formation of political 'mentalities' and organizations. Pioneering works are Siegfried (1913), Thibaudet (1932) and Goguel (1946). For the Right, Rémond (1969) is seminal, and *Sirinelli (1992) exhaustive; valuable studies in English include a survey by Anderson (1974), Locke (1974), Kale (1994) and Rothney (1969). Indispensable on the 'new Right' after 1880 are *Sternhell (1978), Girardet (1983) and Weber (1962). The parties and organizations of the Left have received mountainous attention. As introductions, see *Pilbeam (1995) and the still valuable Lefranc (1977), Kayser (1962) and Weill (1928). Important detailed studies include for the radicals *Stone (1985), Berstein (1980) and Nordmann (1974); for socialism and syndicalism, Stuart (1992), Willard

(1965), *Magraw (1992), Judt (1979), Braque (1963), Baker (1967), Pennetier (1982) and Pigenet (1993). Liberal and centrist movements have inspired less interest, but recently Girard (1985), Jardin (1985) and Hamon (1986) have partly filled the gap. Local studies of politics rural and urban are far too numerous to list, but the genre is usefully surveyed by *Prost (1992); good examples in English include Loubère (1974), Scott (1974), Fitzpatrick (1983), Jones (1985), Merriman (1985), Hanagan (1989) and Aminzade (1993).

On the government of minds, Prost (1968) remains the best introduction to the schools question. On the struggle with the Church, Dansette (1961:b) remains the most accessible political narrative; on the Third Republic period, see also McManners (1972), Auspitz (1982) and Larkin (1974) and (1995). Schools and literacy have properly received much attention. Major syntheses are *Mayeur (1981) and *Prost (1982); on literacy, Furet and Ozouf (1982); on organization and teaching methods, *Giolitto (1983), and on what was taught, Maingueneau (1979). Good studies in English are Gildea (1983) and Anderson (1975). There has recently been much important work (much of it in English) on higher cultural realms: for example Fulcher (1987) on opera; Marrinan (1988) and *Mainardi (1993) on the State and art, while Wilson-Bareau (1992) is a fascinating case study; Nora (1984–93) on the creation of tradition; Agulhon (1981) and (1989) on symbols; Weisz (1983) on universities; Fox (1992) on science; Charle (1990) and Sirinelli and Ory (1992) on intellectuals; Osborne (1983) on elite training.

Economic history has long been controversial. In the 1950s, the problem seemed to be French 'retardation'; 'coal men', who stressed lack of natural resources, debated with 'culture men', who stressed resistance to industrialization. The debate has moved on, largely because of statistical research questioning the retardation thesis, and showing that per capita the French economy grew at a normal rate. Useful brief introductions in English are Fohlen (1973) and Crouzet (1974); and in more detail, Price (1981) and Caron (1979). O'Brien and Keyder (1978) is a still valuable revisionist essay, arguing that the French economy was more successful than the British. Some recent studies take a comparably optimistic view, notably *Asselain (1984). But *Lévy-Leboyer and Bourguignon (1990) redress the balance by diagnosing fundamental long-term weaknesses. The debate, therefore, continues. On the role of the State, see again *Rosenvallon (1990) and *Gueslin (1992). On the major question of tariff policy, see Smith (1980) and Verdier (1994). Valuable works in English on aspects of the subject are *Price (1983), Clout (1980), *Moulin (1991) and *Noiriel (1990).

Women's and gender history has seen an explosion of work in recent years. A good comparative introduction is Rendall (1985), while *McMillan (1981) provides a lively account focusing on the Third Republic. All Perrot's work is important: (1986:b) is an incisive summary. Rebérioux (1980:a) is a useful overview. Thomas (1967) and Schulkind (1985) discuss women during the 1871 Commune. *Hause and Kenney (1984) are indispensable for the suffrage struggle, as are *Hilden (1986) and Sowerwine (1981) for women workers' mixed experience of socialism. Important insights on women and religion are given by Mills and McMillan in contributions to Tallet and Atkin (1991). Other important aspects are covered by Mayeur (1979), Bidelman (1982), Smith (1981) and Segalen (1983). Harris (1989) and Berenson (1992) discuss perceptions of female deviance. *Nye (1993) embarks on the study of masculinity. Children's work experience is thoroughly analysed by *Heywood (1988), informative on social and economic conditions generally. Fuchs (1984) is harrowing on abandoned children.

Prisons, asylums and delinquency attract major attention. Foucault (1977) provoked controversy, reflected in the indispensable Perrot (1980). Wright (1983) covers the treatment of criminals; see also Nye (1984) and Machelon (1976). Pick (1989) analyses the scientific underpinnings of repression. Corbin (1990:b) analyses prostitution; see also Harsin (1985). Foucault (1978) and Chauvaud (1991) examine violence. Madness, the asylum and the psychiatric profession are studied by Goldstein (1987), Ripa (1990) and Castel (1988), and the power of doctors by Ellis (1990) and Crosland (1992).

The major modern work on Paris is the huge official *Nouvelle Histoire de Paris, especially the volumes edited by Bertier de Sauvigny (1977), Girard (1981) and Rials (1985); a useful short history is *Marchand (1993). Girard (1964) is indispensable on public order; see also Stead (1983) and Pinkney (1975). Urban development is covered very accessibly by Pinkney (1958), exhaustively by Gaillard (1977), by Sutton (1982), and (with photographs) by Evenson (1979). Architectural meaning is studied by Van Zanten (1994); changing literary and artistic images are masterfully analysed by *Chevalier (1973), *Herbert (1988) and Clarke (1985). For Paris in a comparative perspective, see Girouard (1985) and Olsen (1986). Collections of early photographs include Mellot (1991) and Beaumont-Maillet (1992). Late-nineteenth-century socio-economic change is explored by *Berlanstein (1984). Electoral politics are discussed by Girard (1960), Nord (1986) and Shapiro (1962).

There is no single up-to-date English work covering the army over the whole period. Porch (1974) summarizes the years before 1848, and also *(1981) provides an important reassessment of the Third Republic to 1914. There is also a brief survey by Horne (1984). In French, works by Girardet (1953) and Chalmin (1957) remain important. Military history has recently seen a surge of interest, synthesized in *Delmas (1992), *Pedroncini (1992) and Croubois (1987). Exhaustive analysis of the officer corps is provided by *Serman (1979), (1982) and (1994). On the domestic role of the army, for the 1830s see Pinkney (1975); for 1848, Girardet et al. (1955), Traugott (1985) and De Luna (1969); for 1871, Tombs (1981); for intervention in industrial conflict, Perrot (1987) and Loubère (1963). On the police, see Stead (1983), Payne (1966), Forstenzer (1981) and, for a comparative perspective, Emsley (1983) and Liang (1992).

On colonialism much of the best work is in English. An authoritative overview is *Andrew and Kanya-Forstner (1988). A useful comparative introduction is Baumgart (1982). Indispensable for imperialist ideas are Girardet (1972) and (1983), and Todorov (1993). On the crucial role of the military, see Kanya-Forstner (1969) and Porch (1986) and (1991). Bouche (1991) is a comprehensive narrative history of the century; Ageron (1991) is a concise history of Algeria. For important analysis of how the empire was governed and its impact on subject peoples, see Prochaska (1990), Marr (1981) and Asiwaju (1976). For its changing economic significance, Marseille (1984).

PART III: IDENTITIES

On private identities the starting point is *Perrot (1990), an important and fascinating collection. Zeldin (1973) is informative. On the rural family, Segalen (1983) and Weber (1977) give important and divergent views. On urban families, Perrot (1986:a). Rural communities are brilliantly discussed by *Weber (1977) and *Jones (1985). A celebrated case study is Thabault (1971), and a no less celebrated memoir is Hélias (1978). Urban communities are discussed concisely by *Bourillon (1992) and at length by *Agulhon et al. (1983).

The history of religion has produced much impressive work in recent years. *Gibson (1989) is an excellent synthesis, and major themes are discussed in Tallet and Atkin (1991). In French, *Cholvy and Hilaire (1985) provide substantial coverage of recent research, as do *Boutry et al. (1991) over a longer timescale. The fascinating arcana of popular religion are analysed by Devlin (1987) and Kselman (1983). On the feminization of Catholicism, see Arnold (1984), Langlois (1984) and Mills (1991). Of many massive regional studies in French, the most interesting include Marcilhacy (1964), Lagrée (1977), Boutry (1986) and Hilaire (1976).

Regional studies and political geography are characteristics of French historiography. Siegfried (1913) and Bois (1971) were influential on different generations in trying to analyse 'mentalities'; the recent analysis of attitudes to the Revolution by Vovelle (1993) is important. Enlightening regional studies in English are Agulhon (1982), *Jones (1985), Loubère (1974), Fitzpatrick (1983) and Ford (1993); among the vast number in French, particularly helpful are Corbin (1975), Ménager (1983), Sagnes (1982) and Pennetier (1982). Indispensable political maps are in Bouju et al. (1966) and Goguel (1970). A provocative anthropological hypothesis is Le Bras and Todd (1981), which contains a wealth of maps and statistics.

Class has inspired an immense literature. Surveys of social history are *Price (1987), *Charle (1994) and *McPhee (1992:a). On workers, begin with the brilliant essays by *Perrot (1986:a) and *Cottereau (1986), and the remarkable synthesis by *Noiriel (1990). *Magraw (1992) is a full chronological account in resolutely Marxist vein. For important comparisons with English experience, and new approaches to the history of class, see Stedman Jones (1983), Reid (1992) and Joyce (1991). On myths about workers, see Chevalier (1973) and Poulot (1980). On characteristics of French working-class history, see *Sewell (1980), Judt (1986), Reddy (1984), Gallie (1983) and Friedman (1988). A good survey of socialist political history is Lefranc (1977). Workers' memoirs include Nadaud (1977), Dumay (1976) and a useful collection edited by Faure and Rancière (1976). On workers' militancy, *Perrot (1987) is the major work; and for the formative earlier periods see Aguet (1954) and L'Huillier (1957). See also Magraw (1992), Jennings (1990), the informative Ridley (1970) and the statistical analysis by Shorter and Tilly (1974).

On peasants see the concise survey by *Moulin (1991), the massive collection by *Duby and Wallon (1976), and for the economic, social and geographical background, *Planhol (1994), *Price (1983) and Clout (1980). On politics and the peasantry, Agulhon (1982) is seminal; see also the brilliant analysis by *Jones (1995), essays by Weber (1991), and Corbin's gripping case study (1992). Margadent (1979) and McPhee (1992:b) disagree with Weber, Corbin and others who stress the enduring separateness of peasant culture and values. On rural economic organizations, see Barral (1968) and Cleary (1989).

On the bourgeoisie, *Pilbeam (1990) and *Crossick and Haupt (1984) provide valuable comparative studies. See also *Daumard (1987), a pioneer in the field, and *Charle (1987). On employers, see Stearns (1978). The nobility are surveyed by Higgs (1987). An interesting essay on images of the bourgeoisie is Agulhon (1994).

On national identity, the necessary starting point is the seminal and controversial Weber (1977), who portrays a belated process of national integration; some critics have argued that he gives excessive prominence to the least developed regions. Ford (1993) and *Lehning (1995) attempt to rethink the meaning of national and regional identity; a characteristically insightful overview is Agulhon (1980). The monumental *Nora (1984) maps the national 'memory' in somewhat elegiac vein; for a powerful critique, see Englund (1992), and for an astringent examination of the national myth, Citron (1987). Tombs (1991) covers several aspects of the question. Zeldin (1973) vol. 2 has useful material on French views of themselves and others. On how Savoy became 'French', see Guichonnet (1983). Weber (1991) is interesting on maps. On food, that potent national symbol and passion, see *Mennell (1985) and Pitte (1991). On image-making, see *Herbert (1988) and (1992), Clarke (1985), Higgonet (1992), and Antliff (1993). Generally on cultural history, see Hemmings (1971) and (1987), Allen (1981), and *Hollier (1989).

On nationalist ideas and politics, excellent concise analyses are Fritz (1988), Girardet (1983), and on the idea of unity, Girardet (1986). An analysis of thought on nationality and race is *Todorov (1993). On the late nineteenth century, see pioneering and controversial analyses by *Sternhell (1978) and (1994), who stresses the radical and subversive aspects of nationalism, and a contrasting account by *Irvine (1988), who regards it as essentially conservative. Pinto (1986) summarizes Sternhell's debate with his critics. See Nord (1986) for the grass roots of nationalism. See too the encyclopedic *Sirinelli (1992).

The question of the alienation or integration of workers is discussed by

Charle (1994) and Magraw (1983). *Noiriel's pioneering work on immigrants (1988) raises fundamental questions concerning national identity and its historiography. On workers and patriotism, see Howorth (1985), Winock (1973) and Kriegel and Becker (1964).

On demography, an excellent introduction is Fine and Sangöi (1991); a major collection of research is *Dupâquier et al. (1988). See also Wrigley (1985).

PART IV: THE ERA OF REVOLUTIONS

A full and sympathetic survey of the Restoration is Bertier de Sauvigny (1974); see also Jardin and Tudesq (1983). On the opposition, see important works by *Alexander (1991), *Pilbeam (1995), Ménager (1988), Sahlins (1994), Spitzer (1971) and Ledré (1960). Valuable regional studies are Higgs (1973), Neely (1986) and Fitzpatrick (1983). On the key 1827 election, see Kent (1975). Biographies or memoirs include Chateaubriand (1947), Fourcassié (1954), Cabanis (1972), Neely (1991), Mansel (1981) and Wolff (1993).

On the events of 1830 and their aftermath, see Pinkney (1972), *Pilbeam (1991), Merriman (1975) and Bertier de Sauvigny (1970).

The July Monarchy has recently had considerable attention, due mainly to a new interest in liberalism. The best general history is *Collingham (1988); see also Jardin and Tudesq (1983). Thureau-Dangin's voluminous work (1894) is still valuable. On liberal ideas, see works discussed under Part I. Tudesq's great study (1964) of the *notables* is indispensable, as is Agulhon's (1982) on popular politicization. On social and economic change see *Pinkney (1986) and Charle (1994); and on the fears change aroused, the seminal Chevalier (1973), and the great novels of Hugo (1967) and Sue (1989). There is a vast literature on the rebirth of republicanism, socialism and the labour movement. On republicanism, see *Pilbeam (1995) and also the durably valuable Weill (1928) and Kayser (1962). The best introduction to the workers' movement is *Magraw (1992); see also monographs by *Sewell (1980), Bezucha (1974), Aguet (1954) and Festy (1908). On early socialism, see *Lovell (1992), and works listed under Parts I and II. On the economic crisis of the late 1840s, see Labrousse (1956) and Tudesq (1964). This was a great period for political memoirs and diaries: those of Rémusat (1958) are among the most important of the century, and those of Tocqueville (1948) and Hugo (1972) among the most vivid. On leading individuals, see Johnson (1963) on Guizot; *Antonetti (1994) and Howarth (1961) on Louis-Philippe; Siedentop (1994) and Jardin (1984) on Tocqueville; Fortescue (1983) on Lamartine; *Bury and Tombs (1986) on Thiers. A thorough reference work is *Newman (1987).

The best survey of the Second Republic is Agulhon (1983). Many historians have focused on the dramas in Paris: Amman (1975), *Traugott (1985), the best recent study of the June Days, Gossez (1956), Caspard (1974) and Tilly and Lees (1975), and from the government side, De Luna (1969). Accounts by eye-witnesses include Stern (1985), Hugo (1972), Tocqueville (1948), again indispensable, as, in another way, is Flaubert's novel of disillusion,

L'Education sentimentale. On foreign policy, Jennings (1973) and Chastain (1988). Events outside Paris, especially linked with the rise of the démoc-socs, are discussed by *Berenson (1984), Weber (1991), and *McPhee (1992:b). The repression of démoc-soc activity is described by Merriman (1978) and Forstenzer (1981). The best account of the 1851 coup d'état is still Ténot (1868), and of resistance in the provinces, Margadent (1979).

Bonapartism has attracted much analysis in English since Simpson (1909), still worth reading; see also the concise biography by *McMillan (1991:b), the survey by Bury (1964), quirky comments by Zeldin (1973) vol. 1, and a sprightly biography by Ridley (1979). There is no more penetrating concise analysis than Rémond (1968). The best general survey of the Empire is *Plessis (1985). Major research in French is *Ménager (1988), indispensable for popular Bonapartism, and see also Lucas-Dubreton (1960); *Bluche (1980), on ideas and politics; Dansette (1961:a), a good narrative; Tudesq (1964) and (1965), indispensable analyses of electoral strength; and *Girard (1986), the best scholarly biography. On methods of government, see also Zeldin (1958) and Payne (1966). Foreign policy and its domestic repercussions have naturally received much attention. Case (1954) is indispensable, and also important are Isser (1974), Pottinger (1966), Barker (1967), Echard (1983), and *Goldfrank (1994). On the 1870 crisis and war, Sorel (1875) is still fundamental; see also Howard (1967), Zeldin (1963), *Audoin-Rouzeau (1989), Steefel (1962) and also works listed under Part I. For reference, see *Echard (1985) and the major work by La Gorce (1894).

On the Commune, the most important works are in French: Rougerie (1964), *(1971) and *(1988), Gaillard (1971) and *Serman (1986). In English the best narrative is Lissagaray (1886); see also Edwards (1971). Other works are listed under Part I.

PART V: THE GOVERNMENT THAT DIVIDES US LEAST

On the founding of the Third Republic, Halévy (1937) is superb; his main lines are taken up by *Mayeur and Rebérioux (1987). Voluminous and authoritative general histories are Agulhon (1993) and Caron (1985); for reference, Hutton (1986). On the principal actors, see *Bury's great work (1973) and (1982) on Gambetta; Bury and Tombs (1986) on Thiers; Chevallier (1982) on Ferry; Watson (1974) on Clemenceau; Goldberg (1962) on Jaurès. Recrimination and regret produced some fine memoirs, including Broglie (1938), Rémusat (1958), Lacombe (1907) and Barrès (1900). On the long-term political consequences of the war, see Mitchell (1979) and (1984).

On politics, a good general survey is *Mayeur (1984), and in English, Anderson (1977). On the party system, *Rudelle (1982) and Hudemann (1979); and for key electoral data, Gouault (1954). On republican political culture, see Agulhon (1989). On political parties see also works listed under Parts I and II; and for class and nationalist movements, see under Part III.

On developments of the 1890s, the *ralliement* is covered by Sedgwick (1965) and the Panama scandal exhaustively by Mollier (1991). There is no overall study of the new conservatism of the 1890s, though aspects are discussed by Smith (1980), Nord (1991) and Barral (1968); an important study of the renewal of liberal thought is Pitt (1995). On radical party reformism, see Stone (1985). A welcome biography of Poincaré is *Keiger (1996); there is no biography of Méline, though there is a fine biography of Waldeck-Rousseau by Sorlin (1966). A vivid panorama of the period is Weber (1986).

The Dreyfus affair has an immense bibliography. A full and gripping narrative which combines political analysis is *Bredin (1987). A good concise analysis is *Cahm (1996); see also Johnson (1966). An important collection of recent research is *Birnbaum (1994). Contrasting studies of popular reactions are Burns (1984) and Fitch (1992). The major study of anti-Semitism is *Wilson (1982). A sensitive history of the Dreyfus family is Burns (1992). On the anti-Dreyfusard Right, see Weber (1962), Larkin (1985) and contributions in Tombs (1991).

The period of the radical Republic is concisely surveyed in *Mayeur and Rebérioux (1987). Works on radicalism and socialism have been listed earlier. An original study of the role of the centrist ARD is *Wileman (1994). The conflict with the Church is summarized by McManners (1972), and analysed in detail by Larkin (1974) and (1995).

The origins of the First World War are one of the great modern historical problems. The best guide is *Keiger (1983); see also studies of Delcassé by Andrew (1968), of the Russian alliance by Kennan (1984) and of relations with Germany by Poidevin and Bariety (1977). For military considerations, see works listed under Part I. On the pre-war political context, see Weber (1959) and *Krumeich (1984), who analyses the debates surrounding the three-year law. The socialist attitude is discussed by Howorth (1985) and Kriegel and Becker (1964). Keiger (1995) lucidly analyses the decision to go to war. The national response is assessed by *Becker (1977).

On the themes evoked in the conclusion, Tocqueville (1988) is the best starting point. Few short essays have had more lasting impact than that of Hoffmann (1963) discussing characteristics of post-revolutionary society. On meanings of French politics, Girardet (1986) and Rosenvallon (1990) and (1994) are illuminating. Furet (1992) and Agulhon (1993) are admirable spokesmen for what I venture to call the 'Whig-Republican' interpretation. Skocpol (1979) is helpful in thinking about the context of the Revolution. On reincarnation of Bonapartism and its consequences, Gildea (1994) is shrewd, Englund (1991) takes a rather different view from mine, and Revel (1992) is a splendid philippic.

BIBLIOGRAPHY

Unless otherwise stated, French books are published in Paris and English books in London. Where possible, accessible modern editions of older works are cited, with the date of the first edition in square brackets after the title.

Adriance, Thomas J. (1987) *The Last Gaiter Button: A Study of the Mobilization and Concentration of the French Army in the War of 1870*

Ageron, Charles-Robert (1991) *Modern Algeria: A History from 1830 to the Present*

Aguet, Jean-Pierre (1954) *Les Grèves sous la Monarchie de Juillet (1830–1847)*, Geneva

Agulhon, Maurice (1979) *La République au village: Les populations du Var de la révolution à la IIe République*

Agulhon, Maurice (1980) 'Conscience nationale et conscience régionale en France de 1815 à nos jours' in J.C. Boogman and G.N. van der Plaat, eds, *Federalism: History and Current Significance of a Form of Government*, The Hague

Agulhon, Maurice (1981) *Marianne into Battle: Republican Imagery and Symbolism in France, 1789–1880*, Cambridge

Agulhon, Maurice (1982) *The Republic in the Village: The People of the Var from the French Revolution to the Second Republic*, Cambridge

Agulhon, Maurice, ed. (1983) *Histoire de la France urbaine: Vol 4 La ville à l'age industriel*

Agulhon, Maurice (1983) *The Republican Experiment, 1845–1852*, Cambridge

Agulhon, Maurice (1989) *Marianne au pouvoir: l'imagerie et la symbolique républicaines de 1880 à 1914*

Agulhon, Maurice *et al.* (1992) *Le XIXe siècle et la Révolution française*

Agulhon, Maurice (1993) *The French Republic, 1879–1992*, Oxford

Agulhon, Maurice (1994) 'Réflexions sur l'image du bourgeois français à la veille de 1848' *Quarante-huit Quatorze: Conférences du Musée d'Orsay 6* (1994), pp. 4–13

Alexander, Robert S. (1991) *Bonapartism and the Revolutionary Tradition in France: the Fédérés of 1815*, Cambridge

Alexander, Robert S. (1994) 'Restoration republicanism reconsidered' *French History* 8:4 (Dec. 1994), pp. 442–69

Allain, Jean-Claude (1976) *Agadir 1911*

Allen, James Smith (1981) *Popular French Romanticism: Authors, Readers and Books in the 19th Century*, Syracuse NY

Amalvi, Christian (1987) 'La Révolution et la France' *Revue de la Bibliothèque Nationale* 23 (Spring 1987), pp. 17–39

Amalvi, Christian (1992) 'Combats pour la mémoire à l'ombre du clocher et de la mairie: la révolution au village de 1870 à 1914' *Annuaire-Bulletin de la Société de l'Histoire de France* 505 (1992), pp. 23–40

Aminzade, Ronald (1993) *Ballots and Barricades: Class Formation and Republican Politics in France, 1830–1871*, Princeton

Amman, Peter H. (1975) *Revolution and Mass Democracy: The Paris Club Movement in 1848*, Princeton

Anderson, Benedict (1991) *Imagined Communities: Reflections on the Origin and Spread of Nationalism*, 2nd edn

Anderson, Malcolm (1974) *Conservative Politics in France*

Anderson, R.D. (1975) *Education in France, 1848–70*, Oxford

Anderson, R.D. (1977) *France 1870–1914: Politics and Society*

André, Roger (1924) *L'Occupation de la France par les Alliés en 1815*

Andrew, Christopher M. (1968) *Théophile Delcassé and the Making of the Entente Cordiale*

Andrew, Christopher M. (1984) 'France: adjustment to change', in Hedley Bull and Adam Watson, eds, *The Expansion of International Society*, Oxford

Andrew, C.M. and Kanya-Forstner, A.S. (1971) 'The French "Colonial Party": its composition, aims and influence' *Historical Journal* 14 (1971)

Andrew, C.M. and Kanya-Forstner, A.S. (1974) 'The groupe coloniale in the French Chamber of Deputies, 1892–1932' *Historical Journal* 17 (1974)

Andrew, C.M. and Kanya-Forstner, S. (1981) *France Overseas: The Great War and the Climax of French Imperial Expansion*

Andrew, C.M. and Kanya-Forstner, A.S. (1988) 'Centre and periphery in the making of the second French colonial empire, 1815–1920' *Journal of Imperial and Commonwealth History* 16:3 (May 1988)

Angenot, Marc (1993) *L'Utopie collectiviste: Le grand récit socialiste sous la Deuxième Internationale*

Antonetti, Guy (1994) *Louis-Philippe*

Antony, Alfred (1910) *La Politique financière du Gouvernement Provisoire, février–mai 1848*

Antliff, Mark (1993) *Inventing Bergson: Cultural Politics and the Parisian Avant-Garde*, Princeton

Apponyi, Rudolf (1948) *De la Révolution au coup d'état*, Geneva

Ariès, Philippe (1971) *Histoire des populations françaises et de leurs attitudes devant la vie depuis le XVIIIe siècle*

Armengaud, André (1962) *L'Opinion publique en France et la crise allemande de 1866*

Arnaud, Pierre (1991) 'Dividing and uniting: sports societies and nationalism, 1870–1914', in Robert Tombs, ed., *Nationhood and Nationalism in France from Boulangism to the Great War, 1889–1918*

Arnold, Odile (1984) *Le Corps et l'âme: la vie des religieuses au 19e siècle*

Aron, Jean-Paul *et al.* (1972) *Anthropologie du conscrit français*

Ascoli, David (1987) *A Day of Battle: Mars-la-Tour, 16 August 1870*

Asiwaju, A.I. (1976) *Western Yorubaland under European Rule 1889–1945: a Comparative Analysis of French and British colonialism*

Asselain, Jean-Charles (1984) *Histoire économique de la France du XVIIIe siècle à nos jours*, 2 vols

Aubry, Dominique (1988) *Quatre-Vingt-Treize et les Jacobins: regards littéraires du 19e siècle*, Lyon

Audoin-Rouzeau, Stéphane (1989) *1870: La France dans la guerre*

Auspitz, Katherine (1982) *The Radical Bourgeoisie: The Ligue de l'Enseignement and the Origins of the Third Republic, 1866–1885*, Cambridge

Baker, Robert F. (1967) 'Socialism in the Nord, 1880–1914: a regional view of the French socialist movement' *International Review of Social History* 12 (1967), pp. 357–89

Baker, Donald B. and Harrigan, Patrick J., eds (1980) *The Making of Frenchmen: Current Directions in the History of Education*, Waterloo, Ontario

Barbier, Frédéric (1991) *Finance et Politique: la dynastie des Fould, XVIIIe–XXe siècle*

Barker, Nancy N. (1967) *Distaff Diplomacy*

Barral, Pierre (1964) *Les Perier dans l'Isère au XIXe siècle*

Barral, Pierre (1968) *Les Agrariens français de Méline Pisani*

Barral, (1974) 'Les groupes de pression et le tarif douanier français de 1892' *Revue d'Histoire Economique et Sociale* 52:3 (1974), pp. 421–6

Barrès, Maurice (1900) *L'Appel au Soldat*

Barrows, Susanna (1981) *Distorting Mirrors: Visions of the Crowd in Late Nineteenth-Century France*

Baumgart, Winfried (1982) *Imperialism: The Idea and Reality of British and French Colonial Expansion, 1860–1914*, Oxford

Beach, Vincent W. (1964) 'The Polignac ministry: a revaluation' *University of Colorado Studies: Series in History* 3 (Jan. 1964), pp. 87–146

Beaumont-Maillet, Laure (1992) *Atget Paris*

Beck, Thomas D. (1974) *French Legislators, 1800–1834: A Study in Quantative History*

Becker Jean-Jacques (1977) *1914: Comment les Français sont entrés dans la guerre: contribution à l'étude d'opinion publique, printemps–été 1914*

Becker, Jean-Jacques (1986) *The Great War and the French People*, Oxford

Bédarida, François (1964) 'L'armée et la république: les opinions politiques des officiers français en 1876–1877' *Revue Historique* 232 (1964), pp. 119–64

Beecher, J. (1986) *Charles Fourier: The Visionary and his World*, Berkeley CA

Beltran, Alain and Griset, Pascal (1988) *La Croissance économique de la France 1815–1914*

Bénichou, Paul (1973) *Le Sacre de l'écrivain*

Bénichou, Paul (1977) *Le Temps des prophètes*

Bénichou, Paul (1988) *Les Mages romantiques*

Béranger, P.J. de (1857) *Oeuvres complètes*, 2 vols

Berenson, Edward (1984) *Populist Religion and Left-Wing Politics in France, 1830–1852*

Berenson, Edward (1992) *The Trial of Madame Caillaux*, Berkeley CA

Berlanstein, Lenard R. (1984) *The Working People of Paris 1871–1914*

Berlioz, Hector (1969) *Mémoires*, vol 1

Bernstein, Samuel (1971) *Auguste Blanqui and the Art of Insurrection*

Berstein, Serge (1980) *Histoire du parti radical*, 2 vols

Bertier de Sauvigny, Guillaume de (1970) *La Révolution de 1830 en France*

Bertier de Sauvigny, Guillaume de (1974) *Au Soir de la monarchie: La Restoration*, 3rd edn

Bertier de Sauvigny, Guillaume de (1977) *Nouvelle Histoire de Paris: La Restauration, 1815–1830*

Best, Geoffrey, ed. (1988) *The Permanent Revolution: The French Revolution and its Legacy, 1789–1989*

Bezucha, Robert J. (1974) *The Lyon Uprising of 1834*, Cambridge MA

Bidelman, Patrick K. (1982) *Pariahs stand up! The Founding of the Liberal Feminist Movement in France, 1858–1889*, Westport CT

Birnbaum, Pierre (1993) *'La France aux Français': histoire des haines nationalistes*

Birnbaum, Pierre, ed. (1994) *La France de l'affaire Dreyfus*

Blanning, T.C.W. (1986) *The Origins of the French Revolutionary Wars*

Blanning, T.C.W. (1987) *The French Revolution: Aristocrats versus Bourgeois?*

Blanning, T.C.W. (1996) *The French Revolutionary Wars*

Bluche, Frédéric (1980) *Le Bonapartisme: Aux origines de la droite autoritaire (1800–1850)*

Bodley, J.E.C. (1898) *France*, 2 vols

Bois, Paul (1971) *Paysans de l'ouest*

Bonaparte, Louis Napoleon (1839) *Des Idées Napoléoniennes*, London

Bouche, Denis (1991) *Histoire de la colonisation française*, 2 vols

Bouju, Paul M. *et al.* (1966) *Atlas historique de la France contemporaine, 1800–1965*

Bourillon, Florence (1992) *Les Villes en France au XIXe siècle*

Bourset, Madeleine (1994) *Casimir Perier: un prince financier au temps du romantisme*

Boutry, Philippe (1986) *Prêtres et paroisses au pays du curé d'Ars*

Boutry, Philippe *et al.* (1991) *Histoire de la France religieuse: Vol. 3, Du roi Très Chrétien à la laïcité républicaine (XVIIIe–XIXe siècle)*

Boutry, Philippe and Cinquin, Michel (1980) *Deux pèlerinages au XIXe siècle: Ars et Paray-le-Monial*

Braque, René (1963) 'Aux origines du syndicalisme dans les milieux ruraux de centre de la France' *Mouvement Social* 42 (Jan.–March 1963), pp. 79–116

Bredin, Denis (1983) *L'Affaire*

Bredin, Denis (1987) *The Affair: The Case of Alfred Dreyfus*

Brochet, Victorine (1977) *Victorine B . . . Souvenirs d'une morte vivante*

Broder, Albert (1993) *L'économie française au XIXe siècle*

Brogan, Sir Denis (1957) *The French Nation from Napoleon to Pétain*

Brogan, Sir Denis (1967) *The Development of Modern France, 1870–1939*

Broglie, Jacques Victor Albert, duc de (1938) *Mémoires*, 2 vols

Brunet, Jean-Paul (1980) *Saint-Denis, la ville rouge: socialisme et communisme en banlieue ouvrière, 1890–1939*

Bullen, Roger (1974) *Palmerston, Guizot and the Collapse of the Entente Cordiale*

Burdeau, François (1984) *Liberté, liberté chérie: l'idée de décentralisation administrative des Jacobins au maréchal Pétain*

Burdeau, François (1994) *Histoire de l'administration française du 18e au 20e siècle*

Burns, Michael (1984) *Rural Society and French Politics: Boulangism and the Dreyfus Affair*, Princeton

Burns, Michael (1992) *Dreyfus: A Family Affair, 1789–1945*

Bury, J.P.T. (1936) *Gambetta and the National Defence: A Republican Dictatorship*

Bury, J.P.T. (1964) *Napoleon III and the Second Empire*

Bury, J.P.T. (1969) *France, 1814–1940*

Bury, J.P.T. (1973) *Gambetta and the Making of the Third Republic*

Bury, J.P.T. (1982) *Gambetta's Final Years: 'The Era of Difficulties', 1877–1882*

Bury, J.P.T. and Tombs, R.P. (1986) *Thiers 1797–1877: A Political Life*

Cabanis, José (1972) *Charles X, roi ultra*

Cabet, Etienne (1831) *Péril de la situation présente, 14 octobre 1831: compte à mes commetans*

Cabet, Etienne (1840) *Lettres sur la Crise actuelle*

Cahm, Eric (1996) *The Dreyfus Affair in French Society and Politics*

Campbell, Peter (1958) *French Electoral Systems and Elections since 1789*

Canler (1882) *Mémoires de Canler, Ancien chef du service de sûreté*

Caron, François (1979) *An Economic History of Modern France*

Caron, François (1985) *Histoire de France: Vol. 5 La France des patriotes: de 1851 à 1918*

Carroll, E. Malcolm (1931) *French Public Opinion and Foreign Affairs 1870–1914*

Case, Lynn M. (1954) *French Opinion on War and Diplomacy during the Second Empire*, Philadelphia

Caspard, Pierre (1974) 'Aspects de la lutte des classes en 1848: le recrutement de la garde nationale mobile' *Revue Historique* 511 (July–Sept. 1974), pp. 81–106

Castel, Robert (1988) *The Regulation of Madness: The Origins of Incarceration in France*, Cambridge

Chaline, J.-P. (1981) *Les Bourgeois de Rouen*

Chalmin, Pierre (1957) *L'Officier français de 1815 à 1870*

Chandler, David (1980) *Waterloo: The Hundred Days*

Charle, Christophe (1980) *Les Hauts fonctionnaires en France au XIXe siècle*

Charle, Christophe (1987) *Les Elites de la République 1880–1900*

Charle, Christophe (1990) *Naissance des 'intellectuels', 1880–1900*

Charle, Christophe (1991) *Histoire sociale de la France au XIXe siècle*

Charle, Christophe (1994) *A Social History of France in the 19th Century*, Oxford

Charlton, D.G. (1963) *Secular Religions in France, 1815–1870*

Charlton, D.G. (1984) *The French Romantics*, 2 vols, Cambridge

Chastain, J. (1988) *The Liberation of Sovereign Peoples: The French Foreign Policy of 1848*

Chateaubriand, René, vicomte de (1947) *Mémoires d'outre-tombe*, ed. E. Biré and P. Moreau, 6 vols

Chauvaud, Frédéric (1991) *De Pierre Rivière à Landru: La violence apprivoisée au XIXe siècle*

Chenesseau, G. (1937) *A l'origine de la liberté de l'enseignement: la Commission extraparlementaire de 1849: texte inédit des procès-verbaux*

Chesnais, Jean-Claude (1976) *Les Morts violentes en France depuis 1826: comparaisons internationales*

Chevalier, Louis (1958) *Classes laborieuses et classes dangereuses à Paris pendant la première moitié du XIXe siècle*

Chevalier, Louis (1973) *Labouring Classes and Dangerous Classes in Paris During the First Half of the Nineteeenth Century*

Chevallier, Pierre (1982) *La Séparation de l'église et l'école: Jules Ferry et Léon XIII*

Cholvy, Gérard and Hilaire, Yves-Marie (1985) *Histoire religieuse de la France contemporaine*, 2 vols, Toulouse

Church, Clive (1981) *Revolution and Red Tape: The French Ministerial Bureaucracy, 1770–1850*, Oxford

Citron, Suzanne (1989) *Le Mythe national: L'histoire de France en question*

Clarke, T.J. (1973) *The Absolute Bourgeois: Artists and Politics in France 1848–1851*

Clarke, T.J. (1985) *The Painting of Modern Life: Paris in the Art of Manet and his Followers*

Cleary, M.C. (1989) *Peasants, Politicians and Producers: The Organisation of Agriculture in France since 1918*, Cambridge

Clément, Jean-Paul (1987) *Chateaubriand politique*

Clout, Hugh (1980) *Agriculture in France on the Eve of the Railway Age*

Cobb, Richard (1969) 'The coming of the French Revolution', *A Second Identity: Essays on France and French History*

Cobb, Richard (1970) *The Police and the People: French Popular Protest, 1789–1820*, Oxford

Cobb, Richard (1976) *Tour de France*

Cobban, Alfred (1964) *The Social Interpretation of the French Revolution*, Cambridge

Cobban, Alfred (1965) *A History of Modern France*, 3 vols

Collingham, H.A.C. (1988) *The July Monarchy: A Political History of France 1830–1848*

Collins, Irene (1959) *The Government and the Newspaper Press in France 1814–1881*, Oxford

Considérant, Victor (1840) *De la politique générale et du rôle de la France en Europe*

Considérant, Victor (1849) *L'Apocalypse, ou la prochaine rénovation démocratique et sociale de l'Europe*

Coplestone, Frederick (1977) *A History of Philosophy: Vol. 9 From Maine de Biran to Sartre*, New York

Copley, Anthony (1989) *Sexual Moralities in France, 1780–1980*

Coquet, Françoise (1995) 'Du muet à "la voix inouïe": les accents dans les films français' *French Studies Bulletin* 54 (Spring 1995), pp. 14–17

Corbin, Alain (1975) *Archaïsme et modernité en Limousin 1845–1880*, 2 vols

Corbin, Alain (1978) *Les Filles de noce: misère sexuelle et prostitution au 19e et 20e siècles*

Corbin, Alain (1990:a) 'Backstage', in Michelle Perrot, ed., *A History of Private Life: Vol. 4 From the Fires of Revolution to the Great War*, Cambridge MA

Corbin, Alain (1990:b) *Women for Hire: Prostitution and Sexuality in France after 1850*, Cambridge MA

Corbin, Alain (1992:a) *The Village of Cannibals: Rage and Murder in France, 1870*, Cambridge

Corbin, Alain (1992:b) 'Paris-Province', in Perre Nora, ed., *Les Lieux de Mémoire*, Vol. 3, pp. 777–823

Corbin, Alain (1994) *The Foul and the Fragrant: Odour and the French Social Imagination*

Corbin, Alain (1995) *Time, Desire and Horror: Towards a History of the Senses*, Cambridge

Cottereau, Alain (1986) 'The distinctiveness of working-class cultures in France, 1848–1900', in Ira Katznelson and A.R. Zolberg, eds, *Working-Class Formation: Nineteenth Century Patterns in Western Europe and the United States*, Princeton

Cox, Gary P. (1994) *The Halt in the Mud: French Strategic Planning from Waterloo to Sedan*, Boulder

Crafts, N.F.R. (1984) 'Economic growth in France and Britain, 1830–1910: a review of the evidence' *Journal of Economic History* 44 (1984), pp. 49–67

Crafts, N.F.R. (1985) *British Economic Growth during the Industrial Revolution*, Oxford

Crosland, M.P. (1992) *Science under Control: The French Academy of Sciences 1795–1914*, Cambridge

Crossick, Geoffrey and Haupt, Heinz-Gerhard (1984) *Shopkeepers and Master Artisans in Nineteenth-Century Europe*

Crossley, Ceri (1993) *French Historians and Romanticism: Thierry, Guizot, the Saint-Simonians, Quinet, Michelet*

Croubois, Claude, ed. (1987) *Histoire de l'officier français des origines à nos jours*, Saint-Jean-d'Angély

Crouzet, François (1974) 'French economic growth in the nineteenth century reconsidered' *History* 59:196 (June 1974), pp. 167–79

Crouzet, François (1990) *Britain Ascendant: Comparative Studies in Franco-British Economic History*, Cambridge

Crubellier, Maurice (1991) *La Mémoire des Français: recherches d'histoire culturelle*

Cubitt, Geoffrey (1993) *The Jesuit Myth: Conspiracy Theory and Politics in Nineteenth-Century France*, Oxford

Dalotel, Alain *et al.* (1980) *Aux origines de la Commune*

Dansette, Adrien (1938) *Le Boulangisme, 1886–1890*

Dansette, Adrien (1961:a) *Histoire du Second Empire*, 3 vols

Dansette, Adrien (1961:b) *Religious History of Modern France*, 2 vols, Freiburg

Daumard, Adeline (1970) *Les Bourgeois de Paris au XIXe siècle*

Daumard, Adeline (1987) *Les Bourgeois et la bourgeoisie en France depuis 1815*

Dautry, Jean (1977) *1848 et la deuxième république*

De Luna Frederick A. (1969) *The French Republic under Cavaignac 1848*, Princeton

Delabre, G. and Gautier, J.M. (1983) *Godin et le Familistère de Guise*

Delmas, Jean, ed. (1992) *Histoire militaire de la France: Vol. 2, De 1715 à 1871*

Derfler, Leslie (1977) *Alexandre Millerand: The Socialist Years*, The Hague

Derivry, D. and Dogon, M. (1986) 'Religion, classe et politique en France: six types de relations causales' *Revue Française de Science Politique* 36:2 (April 1986), pp. 157–81

Déroulède, Paul (1885) *Chants du Soldat*, 117th edn

Déroulède, Paul (1907) *1870: Feuilles de route*, 22nd edn

Devlin, Judith (1987) *The Superstitious Mind: French Peasants and the Supernatural in the Nineteenth Century*

Digeon, Claude (1952) *La Crise allemande de la pensée française (1871–1914)*

Doise, Jean and Vaïsse, Maurice (1987) *Diplomatie et outil militaire, 1871–1969*

Doré, Gustave (1979) *Gustave Doré: Versailles et Paris en 1871*

Doyle, William (1980) *Origins of the French Revolution*

Doyle, William (1990) *The Oxford History of the French Revolution*, Oxford

Doyle, William (1992) 'A culture shock for Louis', *Times Higher Education Supplement*, 6 March 1992, p. 24

Droz, Jacques (1966) *Le Socialisme démocratique, 1864–1960*

Droz, Jacques, ed. (1972) *Histoire générale du socialisme*, 2 vols

Dubois, Jean (1962) *Le Vocabulaire politique et social en France de 1869 à 1872*

Duby, Georges and Wallon, Armand, eds (1976) *Histoire de la France rurale*, 4 vols

Dufrancatel, Christiane *et al.* (1979) *L'Histoire sans qualités*

Dufresne, Claude (1993) *Morny: le roi du Second Empire*

Dumay, Jean-Baptiste (1976) *Mémoires d'un militant ouvrier du Creusot (1841–1905)*

Dupâquier, Jacques *et al.* (1988) *Histoire de la population française: Vol. 3 De 1789 à 1914*

Dupâquier, Jacques et Kessler, Denis, eds (1992) *La Société française au XIXe siècle: tradition, transition, transformations*

Duprat, C. (1980) in Michel Perrot, ed., *L'impossible prison: recherches sur le système pénitentiaire du XIXe siècle*

Echard, William E. (1983) *Napoleon III and the Concert of Europe*

Echard, William E. (1985) *Historical Dictionary of the French Second Empire 1852–1870*, New York

Ecotais, Yann de l' (1992) 'France prepares for battle', *The Economist: The World in 1993*

Edwards, Stewart (1971) *The Paris Commune of 1871*

Ellis, Jack D. (1990) *The Physician-Legislators of France: Medicine and Politics in the Early Third Republic, 1870–1914*, Cambridge

Emsley, Clive (1983) *Policing in its Context, 1750–1870*

Englund, Steven (1991) 'Le théâtre de la démocratie française', in Antoine De Baecque, ed., *Une Histoire de la démocratie en Europe*

Englund, Steven (1992) 'The ghost of nation past' *Journal of Modern History* 64 (June 1992), pp. 299–320

Eros, John (1955) 'The Positivistic generation of French republicans' *Sociological Review* 3 (1955), pp. 255–77

Estèbe, Jean (1982) *Les Ministres de la République 1871–1914*

Evenson, Norma (1979) *Paris: A Century of Change, 1878–1978*

Faure, Alain and Rancière, Jacques, eds (1976) *La Parole ouvrière, 1830–1851*

Faury, Jean (1980) *Cléricalisme et anticléricalisme dans le Tarn (1849–1900)*, Toulouse

Feher, Ferenc, ed. (1990) *The French Revolution and the Birth of Modernity*, Berkeley CA

Feldman, Egal (1981) *The Dreyfus Affair and the American Conscience, 1895–1906*, Detroit

Ferguson, Niall (1992) 'Germany and the origins of the First World War: new perspectives' *Historical Journal* 35:3 (Sept. 1992), pp. 725–52

Festy, Octave (1908) *Le Mouvement ouvrier au début de la monarchie de juillet (1830–1834)*

Field, Frank (1986) 'Jaurès, Péguy and the Crisis of 1914' *Journal of European Studies* 16 (1986), pp. 45–57

Fine, Agnès (1988) in Jacques Dupâquier *et al.*, *Histoire de la population française: Vol 3 De 1789 à 1914*

Fine, Agnès et Sangoï, Jean-Claude (1991) *La Population française au XIXe siècle*

Fitch, Nancy (1992) 'Mass culture, mass parliamentary politics, and modern anti-Semitism: the Dreyfus affair in rural France' *American Historical Review* 97:1 (Feb. 1992), pp. 55–95

Fitzpatrick, Brian (1983) *Catholic Royalism in the Department of the Gard, 1814–1852*, Cambridge

Flandrin, Jean-Louis (1975) *Les Amours paysannes: amour et sexualité dans les campagnes de l'ancienne France (XVIe–XIXe siècles)*

Flandrin, Jean-Louis (1976) *Familles, parenté, maison, sexualité dans l'ancienne société*

Flandrin, Jean-Louis (1981) *Le Sexe et l'occident*

Flaubert, Gustave (1991) 'Dictionnaire des idées reçues', in *Bouvard et Pécuchet*

Flora, Peter *et al.* (1983) *State, Economy and Society in Western Europe*, 2 vols

Flourens, Gustave (1863) *Histoire de l'homme: cours d'histoire naturelle des corps organisés, au Collège de France*

Fohlen, Claude (1973) 'France', in Carlo M. Cipolla, ed., *The Fontana Economic History of Europe*, vol. 4(1)

Ford, Caroline (1993) *Creating the Nation in Provincial France: Religion and Political Identity in Britanny*, Princeton

Forest, Philippe, ed. (1991) *Qu'est-ce qu'une nation? Text intégrale de E. Renan*

Forrest, Alan (1989) *Conscripts and Deserters: The Army and French Society during the Revolution and Empire*, Oxford

Forstenzer, Thomas R. (1981) *French Provincial Police and the Fall of the Second Republic*, Princeton

Fortescue, William (1983) *Alphonse de Lamartine: A Political Biography*

Foster, Robert (1971) *The House of Saulx-Tavanes: Versailles and Burgundy, 1700–1830*

Foucault, Michel (1977) *Discipline and Punish: The Birth of the Prison*

Foucault, Michel (1978) *I, Pierre Rivière, having slaughtered my mother, my sister and my brother . . .: a case of parricide in the 19th century*

Fourcassié, Jean (1954) *Villèle*

Fox, Robert (1992) *The Culture of Science in France, 1700–1900*

Friedman, Gerald (1988) 'Strike success and union ideology: the United States and France, 1880–1914' *Journal of Economic History* 48:1 (March 1988), pp. 1–26

Fritz, Gérard (1988) *L'Idée du peuple en France du XVIIe au XIXe siècle*, Strasbourg

Fuchs, Rachel Ginnis (1984) *Abandoned Children: Foundlings and Child Welfare in Nineteenth-Century France*, Albany NY

Fulcher, Jane F. (1987) *The Nation's Image: French Grand Opera as Politics and Politicized Art*, Cambridge

Fumaroli, Marc (1992) *L'Etat culturel: essai sur une religion moderne*

Furet, François (1986) *La Gauche et la révolution au milieu du XIXe siècle: Edgar Quinet et la question du jacobinisme, 1865–1870*

Furet, François (1988) *La Révolution: de Turgot à Jules Ferry, 1770–1880*

Furet, François (1992) *Revolutionary France, 1770–1880*, Oxford

Furet, François and Ozouf, Jacques (1982) *Reading and Writing: Literacy in France from Calvin to Jules Ferry*, Cambridge

Gadille, Jacques (1967) *La Pensée et l'action politiques des évêques français au début de la IIIe République*, 2 vols

Gaillard, Jeanne (1966) 'La Ligue d'Union Républicaine des Droits de Paris' *Bulletin de la Société d'Histoire Moderne* 5 (1966), pp. 8–13

Gaillard, Jeanne (1971) *Communes de province, commune de Paris 1870–1871*

Gaillard, Jeanne (1977) *Paris la ville, 1852–1870*

Gain, André (1929) *La Restauration des biens des émigrés (1814–1832)*, 2 vols, Nancy

Gallaher, John G. (1980) *The Students of Paris in the Revolution of 1848*

Gallie, Duncan (1983) *Social Inequality and Class Radicalism in France and Britain*, Cambridge

Gégot, Jean-Claude (1989) *La Population française aux XIXe et XXe siècles*

Gellner, Ernest (1983) *Nations and Nationalism*

Gibson, Ralph (1989) *A Social History of French Catholicism, 1789–1914*

Gildea, Robert (1983) *Education in Provincial France 1800–1914: A Study of Three Departments*, Oxford

Gildea, Robert (1994) *The Past in French History*

Gillis, John R., ed. (1989) *The Militarization of the Western World*

Giolitto, Pierre (1983) *Histoire de l'enseignement primaire au XIXe siècle*, 2 vols

Girard, Louis, ed. (1960) *Les Elections de 1869*

Girard, Louis (1964) *La Garde nationale, 1814–1871*

Girard, Louis (1981) *Nouvelle Histoire de Paris: La Deuxième République et le Second Empire, 1848–1870*

Girard, Louis (1985) *Les libéraux français, 1814–1875*

Girard, Louis (1986) *Napoléon III*

Girardet, Raoul (1953) *La Société militaire dans la France contemporaine*

Girardet, Raoul (1955) 'L'Armée et la Second République' *Bibliothèque de la Révolution de 1848* 18

Girardet, Raoul (1972) *L'Idée coloniale en France de 1871 à 1962*

Girardet, Raoul (1983) *Le Nationalisme français: anthologie, 1871–1914*, 2nd edn

Girardet, Raoul (1986) *Mythes et mythologies politiques*

Girault, René (1973) *Emprunts russes et investissements français en Russie, 1887–1914*

Girouard, Mark (1985) *Cities and People: A Social and Architectural History*

Goguel, François (1946) *La Politique des partis sous la IIIe République*

Goguel, François (1970) *Géographie des élections françaises sous la Troisième et la Quatrième République*

Goldberg, Harvey (1962) *The Life of Jean Jaurès*

Goldfrank, David M. (1994) *The Origins of the Crimean War*

Goldstein, Jan (1987) *Console and Classify: the French Psychological Profession in the Nineteenth Century*, Cambridge

Goncourt, Edmond de (1969) *Paris under Siege, 1870–1871: From the Goncourt Journal*, ed. George J. Becker

Goncourt, Edmond de (1978) *Pages from the Goncourt Journal*, ed. Robert Baldick, Oxford

Gosselin, Ronald (1992) *Les Almanachs républicains: traditions révolutionnaires et culture politique des masses populaires de Paris (1840–1851)*

Gossez, Rémi (1956) 'Diversité des antagonismes sociaux vers le milieu du dix-neuvième siècle' *Revue Economique* 5 (May 1956), pp. 439–58

Gossez, Rémi (1967) *Les Ouvriers de Paris: L'organisation 1848–51*, La Roche-sur-Yon

Gouault, Jacques (1954) *Comment la France est devenue républicaine: les élections générales et partielles à l'Assemblée nationale, 1870–1875*

Griffith, Paddy (1989) *Military Thought in the French Army, 1815–51*, Manchester

Gueslin, André (1987) *L'Invention de l'économie sociale*

Gueslin, André (1992) *L'Etat, l'économie et la société française XIXe–XXe siècle*

Guichonnet, Paul (1983) *Histoire de l'annexation de la Savoie à la France*, Roanne

Guillet, Claude (1994) *La Rumeur de Dieu: apparitions, prophètes et miracles sous la Restoration*

Guiral, Pierre and Thuillier, Guy (1980) *La Vie quotidienne des Députés en France de 1871 à 1914*

Halévy, Daniel (1937) *La Fin des notables*, 2 vols

Hamerow, Theodore S. (1983) *The Birth of a New Europe: State and Society in the Nineteenth Century*, Chapel Hill

Hamilton, C.I. (1993) *Anglo-French Naval Rivalry 1840–1870*, Oxford

Hamon, Léo, ed. (1986) *Les Opportunistes: Les débuts de la République aux républicains*, Auxerre

Hanagan, Michael P. (1980) *The Logic of Solidarity: Artisans and Industrial Workers in Three French Towns, 1871–1914*

Hanagan, Michael P. (1989) *Nascent Proletarians: Class Formation in Post-Revolutionary France*, Oxford

Harris, Ruth (1989) *Murders and Madness: Medicine, Law and Society in the Fin de Siècle*, Oxford

Harsin, Jill (1985) *Policing Prostitution in Nineteenth-Century Paris*, Princeton

Hause, Steven C. and Kenney, Ann R. (1984) *Women's Suffrage and Social Politics in the French Third Republic*, Princeton

Hayward, Jack (1991) *After the French Revolution: Six Critics of Democracy and Nationalism*

Hélias, Pierre Jakez (1978) *The Horse of Pride: Life in a Breton Village*

Hemmings, F.W.J. (1971) *Culture and Society in France, 1848–1898*

Hemmings, F.W.J. (1987) *Culture and Society in France, 1789–1848*, Leicester

Hemmings, F.W.J. (1994) *The Theatre Industry in Nineteenth-Century France*, Cambridge

Herbert, Robert L. (1988) *Impressionism: Art, Leisure and Parisian Society*

Herbert, Robert L. (1992) *Fauve Painting: The Making of Cultural Politics*

Herold, J. Christopher, ed. (1961) *The Mind of Napoleon: A Selection from His Written and Spoken Words*, New York

Heywood, Colin (1988) *Childhood in Nineteenth-Century France: Work, Health and Education among the 'Classes Populaires'*, Cambridge

Higgs, David C. (1973) *Ultraroyalism in Toulouse from its Origins to the Revolution of 1830*

Higgs, David C. (1987) *Nobles in Nineteenth-Century France: The Practice of Inegalitarianism*

Higonnet, Anne (1992) *Berthe Morisot's Images of Women*, Cambridge MA

Higonnet, Patrick L.R. and Higonnet, T. (1967) 'Class, corruption and politics in the French Chamber of Deputies, 1846–1848' *French Historical Studies* (Autumn 1967), pp. 204–24

Higonnet, Patrick-Bernard (1968) 'La composition de la Chambre des Députés de 1827 à 1831' *Revue Historique* 239 (1968), pp. 351–78

Hilaire, Yves-Marie (1976) *La Vie religieuse des populations du diocèse d'Arras, 1840–1914*, 3 vols, Lille

Hilden, Patricia (1986) *Working Women and Socialist Politics in France 1880–1914: A Regional Study*, Oxford

Hoffmann, Stanley (1963) *In Search of France*

Hoffmann, Stanley (1974) *Decline and Renewal*, New York

Hollier, Denis, ed. (1989) *A New History of French Literature*

Holmes, Richard (1984) *The Road to Sedan: The French Army 1866–70*

Holmes, Stephen (1984) *Benjamin Constant and the Making of Modern Liberalism*

Horne, Alistair (1965) *The Fall of Paris*

Horne, Alistair (1984) *The French Army and Politics, 1870–1970*, New York

Howard, Michael (1967) *The Franco-Prussian War: The German Invasion of France, 1870–1871*

Howarth, T.E.B. (1961) *Citizen-King: The Life of Louis-Philippe, King of the French*

Howorth, Jolyon (1982) *Edouard Vaillant : La création de l'unité socialiste en France*

Howorth, Jolyon (1985) 'French workers and German workers: the impossibility of internationalism, 1900–1914' *European History Quarterly* 15 (1985), pp. 71–95

Huard, Raymond (1991) *Le Suffrage universel en France, 1848–1946*

Hudemann, R. (1979) *Fraktionsbildung im französischen Parlament (1871–1873)*, Munich

Hugo, Victor (1870) *Les Châtiments*

Hugo, Victor (1938) *Oeuvres de Victor Hugo: Actes et paroles, vol. II (1852–1870)*

Hugo, Victor (1967) *Les Misérables*, 3 vols [1862]

Hugo, Victor (1972) *Choses vues*, 3 vols

Hunt, Lynn (1984) *Politics, Culture and Class in the French Revolution*

Hutton, Patrick H. (1981) *The Cult of the Revolutionary Tradition: The Blanquists in French Politics, 1864–1893*

Hutton, Patrick H. (1986) *Historical Dictionary of the Third French Republic 1870–1940*, 2 vols, New York

Irvine, William D. (1988) *The Boulanger Affair Reconsidered: Royalism, Boulangism and the Origins of the Radical Right in France*, New York

Isser, N. (1974) *The Second Empire and the Press: A Study of Government-Inspired Brochures in French Foreign Policy*

Jardin, André (1984) *Alexis de Tocqueville, 1805–1859*

Jardin, André (1985) *Histoire du libéralisme politique: de la crise de l'absolutisme à la constitution de 1875*

Jardin, André and Tudesq, André-Jean (1983) *Restoration and Reaction 1815–1848*, Cambridge

Jauffret, Jean-Charles (1991) 'The army and the appel au soldat, 1874–89', in Robert Tombs, ed., *Nationhood and Nationalism in France from Boulangism to the Great War, 1889–1918*

Jaurès, Jean (1947) *Anthologie de Jean Jaurès*, ed. Louis Lévy, London

Jennings, Jeremy (1990) *Syndicalism in France: A Study of Ideas*

Jennings, Lawrence C. (1973) *France and Europe in 1848: A Study of French Foreign Affairs in Time of Crisis*

Johnson, Christopher H. (1975) 'Economic change and artisan discontent: the tailors' history, 1800–1848', in Roger Price, ed., *Revolution and Reaction: 1848 and the Second French Empire*

Johnson, Douglas (1963) *Guizot: Aspects of French History 1787–1874*

Johnson, Douglas (1966) *France and the Dreyfus Affair*

Johnson, Paul (1991) *The Birth of the Modern: World Society 1815–1830*

Jones, H.S. (1993) *The French State in Question: Public Law and Political Argument in the Third Republic*, Cambridge

Jones, P.M. (1985) *Politics and Rural Society: The Southern Massif Central c.1750–1880*, Cambridge

Jones, P.M. (1988) *The Peasantry in the French Revolution*, Cambridge

Joyce (1990) 'Work', in F.M.L. Thompson, ed., *The Cambridge Social History of Britain 1750–1950*, vol. 2, Cambridge

Joyce, Patrick (1991) *Visions of the People: Industrial England and the Question of Class, 1848–1914*, Cambridge

Judt, Tony (1979) *Socialism in Provence 1871–1914: A Study in the Origins of the Modern French Left*, Cambridge

Judt, Tony (1986) *Marxism and the French Left: Studies in Labour and Politics in France, 1830–1981*, Oxford

Julien-Laferrière, F. (1970) *Les Députés fonctionnaires sous la Monarchie de Juillet*

Julliard, Jacques (1971) *Fernand Pelloutier et les origines du syndicalisme d'action directe*

Kale, Stephen (1994) *Legitimacy and Reconstruction*

Kanter, Sanford (1986) 'Exposing the myth of the Franco-Prussian War' *War and Society* 4:1 (May 1986), pp. 13–30

Kanya-Forstner, A.S. (1969) *The Conquest of the Western Sudan: A Study in French Military Imperialism*, Cambridge

Kaspi, André and Marès, Antoine (1989) *Le Paris des étrangers depuis un siècle*

Katznelson, Ira and Zolberg, A.R., eds (1986) *Working-Class Formation: Nineteenth-Century Patterns in Western Europe and the United States*, Princeton

Kayser, Jacques (1962) *Les Grandes batailles du radicalisme: des origines aux portes du pouvoir, 1820–1901*

Keiger, John F.V. (1983) *France and the Origins of the First World War*

Keiger, John F.V. (1995) 'France', in Keith Wilson, ed., *Decisions for War, 1914*

Keiger, John F.V. (1997) *Raymond Poincaré*, Cambridge

Kelley, George Armstrong (1992) *The Humane Comedy: Constant, Tocqueville and French Liberalism*

Kennan, George F. (1984) *The Fateful Alliance: France, Russia and the Coming of the First World War*, Manchester

Kennedy, Paul M., ed. (1979) *The War Plans of the Great Powers, 1880–1914*

Kent, Sherman (1975) *The Election of 1827 in France*

Kriegel, Annie and Becker, Jean-Jacques (1964) *1914: la guerre et le mouvement ouvrier français*

Krumeich, Gerd (1984) *Armaments and Politics in France on the Eve of the First World War*, Leamington

Kselman, Thomas A. (1983) *Miracles and Prophecies in Nineteenth-Century France*, New Brunswick NJ

Kuisel, Richard (1981) *Capitalism and the State in Modern France*, Cambridge

Labrousse, Ernest (1948) 'Comment naissent les révolutions?' *Actes du Congrès historique du centenaire de la Révolution de 1848*

Labrousse, Ernest, ed. (1956) *Aspects de la crise et de la dépression de l'économie française au milieu du 19e siècle, 1846–1851: Etudes de la Société de la Révolution de 1848*, vol. 19

Lacombe, Charles de (1907) *Journal politique*

La Gorce, Pierre de (1894–1905) *Histoire du Second Empire*, 7 vols

Lagoueyte, Patrick (1989) *La Vie politique en France au XIXe siècle*

Lagrée, Michel (1977) *Mentalités, religion et histoire en Haute Bretagne au XIXe siècle: le diocèse de Rennes, 1815–1848*

Landes, David S. (1969) *The Unbound Prometheus: Technological Change and Industrial Development in Western Europe from 1750 to the Present*, Cambridge

Langlois, Claude (1984) *Le Catholicisme au féminin: les congrégations françaises à supérieure générale au XIXe siècle*

Larkin, Maurice (1974) *Church and State after the Dreyfus Affair: The Separation Issue in France*

Larkin, Maurice (1985) 'La République en danger? The pretenders, the army and Déroulède, 1898–1899' *English Historical Review* 100 (1985), pp. 85–105

Larkin, Maurice (1995) *Religion, Politics and Preferment in France since 1890: La Belle Epoque and its Legacy*, Cambridge

Laux, James L. (1976) *In First Gear: The French Automobile Industry to 1914*, Liverpool

Lebovics, Herman (1988) *The Alliance of Iron and Wheat in the French Third Republic, 1860–1914*

Le Bras, Hervé and Todd, Emmanuel (1981) *L'Invention de la France: atlas anthropologique et politique*

Le Chartier, E. (1911) *La France et son parlement: annuaire des électeurs et des parlementaires*

Leclerc, Yvan (1991) *Crimes écrits: La littérature en procès au XIXe siècle*

Ledré, C. (1960) *La Presse à l'assaut de la monarchie 1815–1848*

Lee, C.H. (1986) *The British Economy since 1700: A Macroeconomic Perspective*, Cambridge

Lefranc, Georges (1967) *Le Mouvement syndical sous la Troisième République*

Lefranc, Georges (1973) *Les Gauches en France (1789–1972)*

Lefranc, Georges (1977) *Le Mouvement socialiste sous la troisième république*, 2 vols

Le Goff, Jacques and Rémond, René, eds (1991) *Histoire de la France religieuse: Vol. 3 Du roi Très Chrétien à la laïcité républicaine (XVIIIe–XIXe siècle)*

Lehning, James R. (1995) *Peasant and French: Cultural Contact in Rural France during the Nineteenth Century*, Cambridge

Le Men, Ségolène, ed. (1993) *Les Français peints par eux-mêmes: Panorama social du XIXe siècle (Les Dossiers du Musée d'Orsay)*

Lequin, Yves, ed. (1992) *Histoire des étrangers et de l'immigration en France*

Levêque, Pierre (1992) *Histoire des Forces Politiques en France, 1789–1880*

Levillain, Philippe (1982) *Boulanger, Fossoyeur de la monarchie*

Levillain, Philippe and Riemenschneider, Rainer, eds (1990) *La Guerre de 1870–71 et ses conséquences*, Bonn

Lévy-Leboyer, Maurice and Bourguigon, François (1990) *The French Economy in the Nineteenth Century*, Cambridge

L'Huillier, Fernand (1957) *La Lutte ouvrière à la fin du second empire*

Liang, Hsi-Huey (1992) *The Rise of Modern Police and the European State System from Metternich to the Second World War*, Cambridge

Lichtheim, George (1966) *Marxism in Modern France*, New York

Liebowitz, Jonathan J. (1993) 'Rural support for protection: evidence from the parliamentary enquiry of 1884' *French History* 7:2 (June 1993)

Lincoln, W. Bruce (1978) *Nicholas I: Emperor and Autocrat of All the Russias*

Lissagaray, Prosper-Olivier (1886) *History of the Commune of 1871*

Lloyd, Rosemary (1992) *The Land of Lost Content: Children and Childhood in Nineteenth-Century French Literature*, Oxford

Locke, Robert R. (1974) *French Legitimists and the Politics of Moral Order in the Early Third Republic*, Princeton

Loubère, Léo A. (1963) 'Left-wing Radicals, strikes and the military, 1880–1907' *French Historical Studies* 3:1 (Spring 1963), pp. 93–105

Loubère, Léo A. (1974) *Radicalism in Mediterranean France: Its Rise and Decline 1848–1914*, Albany NY

Loubère, Léo A. (1978) *The Red and the White: A History of Wine in France and Italy in the Nineteenth Century*, Albany NY

Louis, Marie-Victoire (1994) *Le Droit de cuissage: France, 1860–1930*

Lovell, David W. (1992) 'The French Revolution and the origins of socialism: the case of early French socialism' *French History* 6:2 (June 1992), pp. 185–205

Lucas-Dubreton, J. (1960) *Le Culte de Napoléon 1815–1848*

Lyons, Martyn (1994) *Napoleon Bonaparte and the Legacy of the French Revolution*

Luzzato, Sergio (1991) *Mémoire de la Terreur: vieux montagnards et jeunes républicains au XIXe siècle*, Lyon

Machelon, Jean-Pierre (1976) *La République contre les libertés? Les restrictions aux libertés publiques de 1879 à 1914*

Magraw, Roger (1983) *France 1815–1914: The Bourgeois Century*

Magraw, Roger (1992) *A History of the French Working Class: Vol. 1 The Age of Artisan Revolution, 1815–1871; Vol. 2 Workers and the Bourgeois Revolution*

Mainardi, Patricia (1993) *The End of the Salon: Art and the State in the Early Third Republic*, Cambridge

Maingueneau, Dominique (1979) *Les Livres d'école de la République: discours et idéologie*

Malo, Henri (1932) *Thiers 1797–1877*

Mann, Michael (1993) *The Sources of Social Power: Vol. 2 The Rise of Classes and Nation-States, 1760–1914*, Cambridge

Mansel, Philip (1981) *Louis XVIII*

Mansel, Philip (1988) *The Court of France, 1789–1830*, Cambridge

Manuel, Frank (1962) *The Prophets of Paris*, Cambridge MA

Marchand, Bernard (1993) *Paris, histoire d'une ville, XIXe–XXe siècle*

Marcilhacy, Christianne (1964) *Le Diocèse d'Orléans sous l'épiscopat de Mgs Dupanloup*

Margadent, Ted W. (1979) *French Peasants in Revolt: The Insurrection of 1851*, Princeton

Margadent, Ted. W. (1984) 'Tradition and modernity in rural France during the Nineteenth Century' *Journal of Modern History* 56, Number 4 (December 1984) pp. 667–97

Marr, David G. (1981) *Vietnamese Tradition on Trial 1920–1945*, Berkeley

Marrinan, M. (1988) *Painting Politics for Louis-Philippe*

Marseille, Jacques (1984) *Empire colonial et capitalisme français: histoire d'une divorce*

Martin, Andrew (1990) *The Mask of the Prophet: The Extraordinary Fictions of Jules Verne*, Oxford

Martin-Fugier, Anne (1990) *La Vie élégante ou la formation du Tout-Paris, 1815–1848*

Maupassant, Guy de (1975) *Bel-Ami* [1885]

May, Ernest R., ed. (1984) *Knowing One's Enemies: Intelligence Assessment before the Two World Wars*, Princeton

Mayeur, Françoise (1981) *Histoire générale de l'enseignement et de l'éducation en France: Vol. 3: De la Révolution à l'école républicaine*

Mayeur, Françoise (1979) *L'Education des filles en France au XIXe siècle*

Mayeur, Jean-Marie (1973) *Les Débuts de la IIIe République, 1871–1898*

Mayeur, Jean-Marie (1984) *La Vie politique sous la Troisième République*

Mayeur, Jean-Marie and Rebérioux, Madeleine (1987) *The Third Republic from its Origins to the Great War, 1871–1914*, Cambridge

McManners, John (1972) *Church and State in France, 1870–1914*

McMillan, James F. (1981) *Housewife or Harlot: The Place of Women in French Society, 1870–1940*, Brighton

McMillan, James F. (1991:a) 'Religion and gender in modern France: some reflections', in Frank Tallet and Nicholas Atkin, eds, *Religion, Society and Politics in France since 1789*

McMillan, James F. (1991:b) *Napoleon III*

McPhee, Peter (1990) 'La mainmise du passé: les images de la Révolution française dans les mobilisations politiques rurales sous la Seconde République', in Michel Vovelle, ed., *L'Image de la Révolution Française*, Oxford

McPhee, Peter (1992:a) *A Social History of France, 1780–1880*

McPhee, Peter (1992:b) *The Politics of Rural Life: Political Mobilization in the French Countryside, 1846–1852*, Oxford

Mellon, Stanley (1958) *The Political Uses of History: A Study of Historians in the French Restoration*, Stanford CA

Mellot, Philippe (1991) *Paris sens dessus-dessous: Marville et Nadar 1852–1870*

Ménager, Bernard (1983) *La Vie politique dans le département du Nord de 1851 à 1877*, 3 vols

Ménager, Bernard (1988) *Les Napoléon du peuple*

Mennell, Stephen (1985) *All Manners of Food: Eating and Taste in England and France from the Middle Ages to the Present*

Mérimée, Prosper (1973) *Carmen* [1845]

Merriman, John M., ed. (1975) *1830 in France*

Merriman, John M. (1978) *The Agony of the Republic: The Repression of the Left in Revolutionary France 1848–1851*

Merriman, John M., ed. (1982) *French Cities in the Nineteenth Century*

Merriman, John M. (1985) *The Red City: Limoges and the French Nineteenth Century*, Oxford

Michelet, Jules (1869) *Histoire de France*

Michelet, Jules (1946) *Le Peuple* [1846]

Mills, Hazel, 'Negotiating the divide: women, philanthropy and the "public sphere" in nineteenth-century France', in Frank Tallet and Nicholas Atkin, eds, *Religion, Society and Politics in France since 1789*

Mitchell, Allan (1979) *The German Influence in France after 1870: The Formation of the French Republic*, Chapel Hill NC

Mitchell, Allan (1980) 'The xenophobic style; French counter-espionage and the emergence of the Dreyfus affair' *Journal of Modern History* 52:3 (Sept. 1980), pp. 414–25

Mitchell, Allan (1984) *Victors and Vanquished: The German Influence on Army and Church in France after 1870*, Chapel Hill NC

Mitchell, B.R. (1978) *European Historical Statistics 1750–1970*

Mollier, Jean-Yves (1991) *Le Scandal de Panama*

Montaudon, Gen. Alexandre (1898–1900) *Souvenirs militaires*, 2 vols

Moulin, Annie (1988) *Les Paysans dans la société française: De la Révolution à nos jours*

Moulin, Annie (1991) *Peasantry and Society in France since 1789*, Cambridge

Nadaud, Martin (1977) *Léonard, maçon de la Creuse* [1895]

Neely, Sylvia (1986) 'Rural politics in the early Restoration: Charles Goyet and the liberals of the Sarthe' *European History Quarterly* 16 (1986), pp. 313–42

Neely, Sylvia (1991) *Lafayette and the Liberal Ideal, 1814–1824: Politics and Conspiracy in an Age of Reaction*, Carbondale IL

Newman, Edgar L. (1975) 'What the crowd wanted in 1830', in John M. Merriman, ed., *1830 in France*

Newman, Edgar L. (1987) *Historical Dictionary of France from the 1815 Restoration to the Second Empire*, 2 vols, New York

Nicolet, Claude (1982) *L'Idée républicaine en France (1789–1924)*

Noiriel, Gérard (1986) *Les Ouvriers dans la société française XIXe–XXe siècle*

Noiriel, Gérard (1988) *Le Creuset français: histoire de l'immigration XIXe–XXe siècle*

Noiriel, Gérard (1990) *Workers in French Society in the 19th and 20th Centuries*, Oxford

Nora, Pierre, ed. (1984–93) *Les Lieux de mémoire*, 7 vols

Nord, Philip G. (1986) *Paris Shopkeepers and the Politics of Resentment*, Princeton

Nord, Philip (1991) 'Social defence and conservative regeneration: the national revival, 1900–14', in Robert Tombs, ed., *Nationalism and Nationhood in France from Boulangism to the Great War, 1889–1911*

Nordmann, Jean-Thomas (1974) *Histoire des radicaux, 1820–1973*

Nordmann, Jean-Thomas (1977) *La France radicale*

Nye, Robert A. (1975) *The Origins of Crowd Psychology: Gustave Le Bon and the Crisis of Mass Democracy in the Third Republic*

Nye, Robert A. (1984) *Crime, Madness and Politics in Modern France: The Medical Concept of National Decline*, Princeton

Nye, Robert A. (1993) *Masculinity and Male Codes of Honor in Modern France*, Oxford

O'Brien, Patricia (1975) 'L'embastillement de Paris: the fortification of Paris during the July Monarchy' *French Historical Studies* 9:1 (1975), pp. 63–82

O'Brien, Patrick and Keyder, Caglar (1978) *Economic Growth in Britain and France: Two Paths to the Twentieth Century*

Ollé-Laprune, Jacques (1962) *La Stabilité des ministres sous la 3e République, 1879–1940*

Olsen, Donald J. (1986) *The City as a Work of Art: London, Paris, Vienna*

Osborne, Thomas R. (1983) *A Grande Ecole for the Grands Corps: The Recruitment and Training of the French Administrative Elite in the Nineteenth Century*, New York

Paignon, Eugène, ed. (1848) *Code des rois: Pensées et opinions d'un prince souverain sur les affaires de l'Etat*

Parry, David L. (1993) 'Conspiracy theory and the French Third Republic', University of Cambridge PhD

Paulson, Ronald (1983) *Representations of Revolution, 1789–1820*

Payne, Howard C. (1966) *The Police State of Louis Napoleon Bonaparte*, Seattle WA

Paz, Maurice (1984) *Un révolutionnaire professionel, Blanqui*

Pedroncini, Guy, ed. (1992) *Histoire militaire de la France: Vol. 3 De 1871 à 1940*

Péguy, Charles (1957) 'Eve', in *Oeuvres poétiques complètes*

Pennetier, Claude (1982) *Le Socialisme dans le Cher 1851–1921*

Perkin, Harold (1969) *Origins of Modern English Society*

Perkin, Harold (1989) *The Rise of Professional Society: England since 1880*

Perrot, Michelle (1974) *Les Ouvriers en grève: France 1871–1890*, 2 vols

Perrot, Michelle (1979) 'La femme populaire rebelle', in Christiane Dufrancatel et al., *L'Histoire sans qualités*

Perrot, Michelle, ed. (1980) *L'Impossible prison: recherches sur le système pénitentiaire du XIXe siècle*

Perrot, Michelle and Ribeill, G., eds (1985) *Le Journal intime de Caroline B.*

Perrot, Michelle (1986:a) 'On the formation of the French working class' in Ira Katznelson and A.R. Zolberg, eds, *Working-Class Formation: Nineteenth Century Patterns in Western Europe and the United States*, Princeton

Perrot, Michelle (1986:b) 'Women, power and history: the case of nineteenth-century France', in Sian Reynolds, ed., *Women, State and Revolution: Essays in Power and Gender in Europe since 1789*, Brighton

Perrot, Michelle (1987) *Workers on Strike: France 1871–1890*

Perrot, Michelle, ed. (1990) *A History of Private Life: vol. 4, From the Fires of Revolution to the Great War*, Cambridge MA

Pessin, Alain (1992) *Le Mythe du peuple et la société du XIXe siècle*

Pick, Daniel (1989) *Faces of Degeneration: A European Disorder, c.1848–c.1918*, Cambridge

Pick, Daniel (1993) *War Machine: The Rationalisation of Slaughter in the Modern Age*

Pickering, Mary (1994) *Auguste Comte: An Intellectual Biography*, Cambridge

Pigenet, Michel (1993) '*Ouvriers, paysans nous sommes . . .*': les bûcherons du centre de la France au tournant du siècle

Pilbeam, Pamela M. (1990) *The Middle Classes in Europe 1789–1914: France, Germany, Italy and Russia*

Pilbeam, Pamela (1991) *The 1830 Revolution in France*

Pilbeam, Pamela (1993) 'The insurrectionary tradition in France 1835–48' *Modern and Contemporary France* 1:3 (1993), pp. 253–64

Pilbeam, Pamela (1995) *Republicanism in Nineteenth-Century France, 1814–1871*

Pinkney, David H. (1958) *Napoleon III and the Rebuilding of Paris*, Princeton

Pinkney, David H. (1972) *The French Revolution of 1830*, Princeton

Pinkney, David H. (1975) 'Pacification of Paris: the military lessons of 1830', in John M. Merriman, ed., *1830 in France*

Pinkney, David H. (1986) *Decisive Years in France 1840–1847*, Princeton

Pinto, Antonio Costa (1986) 'Fascist ideology revisited: Zeev Sternhell and his critics' *European History Quarterly* 16 (1986), pp. 465–83

Pitt, Alan (1995) 'The evolution of liberal thought under the Third French Republic, c.1860–c.1940', University of Cambridge PhD

Pitte, Jean-Robert (1991) *Gastronomie française: histoire et géographie d'une passion*

Planhol, Xavier de (1994) *An Historical Geography of France*, Cambridge

Plessis, Alain (1976) *De la fête impériale au mur des fédérés, 1852–1871*

Plessis, Alain (1985) *The Rise and Fall of the Second Empire, 1852–1871*, Cambridge

Poidevin, Raymond and Bariéty, Jacques (1977) *Les Relations franco-allemandes 1815–1975*

Poincaré, Raymond (1926) *Au Service de la France*, 10 vols

Ponteil, Félix (1966) *Les Institutions de la France de 1814 à 1870*

Porch, Douglas (1974) *Army and Revolution: France 1815–1848*

Porch, Douglas (1981) *The March to the Marne: The French Army 1871–1914*, Cambridge

Porch, Douglas (1986) *The Conquest of the Sahara*, Oxford

Porch, Douglas (1991) *The French Foreign Legion: A Complete History*

Pottinger, E. Ann (1966) *Napoleon III and the German Crisis, 1865–1866*, Cambridge MA

Poulot, Denis (1980) *Le Sublime, ou le travailleur comme il est en 1870 et ce qu'il peut être* [1870], ed. A. Cottereau

Prévost, Marcel (1906) *Monsieur et Madame Moloch*

Prévost-Paradol, Lucien-Anatole (1869) *La France Nouvelle*

Price, Roger (1972) *The French Second Republic: A Social History*

Price, Roger, ed. (1975) *Revolution and Reaction: 1848 and the Second French Republic*

Price, Roger (1981) *An Economic History of Modern France, 1730–1914*, 2nd edn

Price, Roger (1983) *The Modernization of Rural France: Communications Networks and Agricultural Market Structures in Nineteenth-Century France*

Price, Roger (1987) *A Social History of Nineteenth-Century France*

Prochaska, David (1990) *Making Algeria French: Colonialism in Bône 1870–1920*, Cambridge

Prost, Antoine (1968) *Histoire de l'Enseignement en France, 1800–1967*

Prost, Antoine (1982) *Histoire générale de l'enseignement et de l'éducation en France: Vol. 4: L'Ecole et la famille dans une société en mutation*

Prost, Antoine (1992) 'What has happened to French social history?' *Historical Journal* 35:3 (1992), pp. 671–79

Psichari, Ernest (n.d.), *L'Appel aux armes*, in *Oeuvres complètes*, vol 2

Puymège, Gérard de (1993) *Chauvin, le soldat-laboureur: contribution à l'étude des nationalismes*

Quinet, Edgar (1840) *1815 et 1840*

Raphael, P. (1909) 'La loi de 31 mai 1850' *Revue d'Histoire Moderne et Contemporaine* 13 (Nov.–Dec. 1909), pp. 277–304; 14 (May–Oct. 1910), pp. 44–79, 297–331

Rebérioux, Madeleine (1980:a) 'L'ouvrière', in Jean-Paul Aron, ed., *Misérable et glorieuse: la femme du XIXe siècle*

Rebérioux, Madeleine (1980:b) 'Zola, Jaurès et France: trois intellectuels devant l'Affaire' *Les Cahiers Naturalistes* 54 (1980), pp. 266–81

Rebérioux, Madeleine (1984) 'Le mur des Fédérés', in Pierre Nora, ed., *Les Lieux de mémoire*, vol 1

Reddy, William M. (1984) *The Rise of Market Culture: The Textile Trade and French Society, 1750–1900*, Cambridge

Reid, Alistair (1992) *Social Classes and Social Relations in Britain, 1850–1914*

Rémond, René (1968) *La Droite en France: de la Première Restauration à la Ve République*, 2 vols

Rémond, René (1969) *The Right Wing in France from 1815 to de Gaulle*, Philadelphia

Rémond, René (1985) *L'Anticléricalisme*

Rémusat, Charles de (1958) *Mémoires de ma vie*, ed. C. Pouthas, 5 vols

Rendall, Jane (1985) *The Origins of Modern Feminism: Women in Britain, France and the United States, 1780–1860*

Resnick, Daniel P. (1966) *The White Terror and the Political Reaction after Waterloo*, Cambridge MA

Revel, Jean-François (1992) *L'Absolutisme inefficace: ou contre le présidentialisme à la française*

Reynolds, Sian, ed. (1986) *Women, State and Revolution: Essays in Power and Gender in Europe since 1789*, Brighton

Rials, Stéphane (1985) *Nouvelle Histoire de Paris: De Trochu à Thiers, 1870–1873*

Ridley, J.J. (1970) *Revolutionary Syndicalism in France: the Direct Action of its Time*, Cambridge

Ridley, Jasper (1979) *Napoleon III and Eugenie*

Ripa, Yannick (1990) *Women and Madness: The Incarceration of Women in Nineteenth-Century France*, Cambridge

Robert, A., Bourloton, E. and Cougny, G. (1889–91) *Dictionnaire des parlementaires français*, 5 vols

Roberts, James (1990) *Counter-Revolution in France 1787–1830*

Roberts, J.M. (1973) *The Paris Commune from the Right*, English Historical *Review* supplement 6

Ronsin, François (1980) *La Grève des ventres: propagande néo-malthusienne et baisse de la natalité en France, 19e–20e siècles*

Rosenvallon, Pierre (1985) *Le moment Guizot*

Rosenvallon, Pierre (1990) *L'Etat en France de 1789 à nos jours*

Rosenvallon, Pierre (1992) *Le Sacre du citoyen: histoire du suffrage universel en France*

Rosenvallon, Pierre (1994) *La Monarchie impossible: les chartes de 1814 et de 1830*

Roth, François (1990) *La Guerre de 1870*

Rothan, G. (1879) *La Politique française en 1866*

Rothney, John (1969) *Bonapartism after Sedan*

Rougerie, Jacques (1964) *Procès des Communards*

Rougerie, Jacques (1971) *Paris libre 1871*

Rougerie, Jacques (1988) *La Commune 1871*

Rudelle, Odile (1982) *La République absolue: aux origines de l'instabilité constitutionnelle de la France républicaine*

Sagnes, Jean (1982) *Le Midi Rouge: mythe et réalité: études d'histoire occitane*

Sahlins, Peter (1994) *Forest Rites: The War of the Demoiselles in Nineteenth-Century France*

Schama, Simon (1989) *Citizens: A Chronicle of the French Revolution*

Schroeder, Paul W. (1994) *The Transformation of European Politics, 1763–1848*, Oxford

Schulkind, Eugene (1985) 'Socialist women during the 1871 Paris Commune' *Past and Present* 106 (Feb. 1985), pp. 124–63

Scott, Joan W. (1974) *The Glassworkers of Carmaux: French Craftsmen and Political Action in a Nineteenth-Century City*, Cambridge MA

Sedgwick, Alexander (1965) *The Ralliement in French Politics, 1890–1898*, Cambridge MA

Segalen, Martine (1983) *Love and Power in the Peasant Family*, Oxford

Segalen, Martine (1991) *Fifteen Generations of Bretons: Kinship and Society in Lower Britanny 1720–1980*, Cambridge

Senior, Nassau William (1878) *Conversations with M. Thiers, M. Guizot, and Other Distinguished Persons during the Second Empire*, 2 vols

Serman, William (1979) *Les Origines des officiers français, 1848–1870*

Serman, William (1982) *Les Officiers français dans la nation, 1848–1914*

Serman, William (1986) *La Commune de Paris (1871)*

Serman, William (1994) *La Vie professionnelle des officiers français au milieu du XIXe siècle*

Sewell, William H. (1980) *Work and Revolution in France: The Language of Labor from the Old Regime to 1848*, Cambridge

Sewell, William H. (1988) 'Uneven development: the autonomy of politics, and the dockworkers of nineteenth-century Marseille' *American Historical Review* 93:3 (June 1988), pp. 604–37

Shapiro, David M., ed. (1962) *The Right in France: Three Studies*

Sherman, D. (1977) 'Governmental responses to economic modernization in mid-nineteeth century France' *Journal of European Economic History* 6:3 (Winter 1977), pp. 717–36

Shorter, Edward and Tilly, Charles (1974) *Strikes in France 1830–1968*, Cambridge

Siedentop, Larry (1979) 'Two liberal traditions', in Alan Ryan, *The Idea of Freedom: Essays in Honour of Isaiah Berlin*

Siedentop, Larry (1994) *Tocqueville*

Siegfried, André (1913) *Tableau politique de la France de l'Ouest sous la Troisième République*

Siegfried, André (1930) *Tableau des Partis en France*

Simon, Jules (1878) *Le Gouvernement de M. Thiers*, 2 vols

Simpson, F.A. (1909) *The Rise of Louis Napoleon*

Singer, Barnett (1983) *Village Notables in Nineteenth-Century France: Priests, Mayors, Schoolmasters*, Albany NY

Sirinelli, Jean-François (1992) *Histoire des Droites en France*, 3 vols

Sirinelli, Jean-François and Ory, Pascal (1992) *Les Intellectuels en France: de l'affaire Dreyfus à nos jours*, 2nd edn

Skocpol, Theda (1979) *States and Social Revolutions: A Comparative Analysis of France, Russia, and China*, Cambridge

Smith, Bonnie G. (1981) *Ladies of the Leisured Class: The Bourgeoisie of Northern France in the Nineteenth Century*, Princeton

Smith, Michael S. (1980) *Tariff Reform in France, 1860–1900: The Politics of Economic Interest*

Snyder, Jack (1984) *The Ideology of the Offensive: Military Decision Making and the Disasters of 1914*

Sorel, Albert (1875) *Histoire Diplomatique de la Guerre Franco-Allemande*, 2 vols

Sorlin, Pierre (1966) *Waldeck-Rousseau*

Sorlin, Pierre (1991) 'Words and images of nationhood', in Robert Tombs, ed., *Nationhood and Nationalism in France from Boulangism to the Great War, 1889–1918*

Soubadère, G. (1990) 'La république césarienne et le second empire', in Pierre Feral, ed., *Pays de Gers, coeur de Gascogne*, vol. 2, Pau

Sowerwine, Charles (1981) *Sisters or Citizens? Women and Society in France since 1876*, Cambridge

Spears, Sir Edward (1956) *Assignment to Catastrophe*

Spitzer, Alan B. (1971) *Old Hatreds and Young Hopes: The French Carbonari against the Bourbon Restoration*, Cambridge MA

Stafford, David (1971) *From Anarchism to Reformism*

Stead, Philip J. (1983) *The Police of France*

Stearns, Peter (1978) *Paths to Authority: The Middle Classes and the Industrial Labor Force in France, 1820–48*

Stearns, Peter (1975) *Lives of Labour: Work in a Maturing Industrial Society*

Stedman Jones, Gareth (1983) *Languages of Class: Studies in English Working-Class History, 1832–1982*, Cambridge

Stedman Jones, Gareth and Patterson, Ian (1996), *Fourier: Theory of Four Movements,* Cambridge

Steefel, L.D. (1962) *Bismarck, the Hohenzollern Candidacy and the Origins of the Franco-German War of 1870*, Cambridge MA

Steenhuysen, D. (1971) 'Quelques jalons dans l'étude du thème du "Grand Soir" jusqu'en 1900' *Mouvement Social* (April–June 1971), pp. 63–76

Stern, Daniel (1985) *Histoire de la Révolution de 1848* [1850]

Sternhell, Zeev (1978) *La Droite révolutionnaire 1885–1914: les origines françaises du fascisme*

Sternhell, Zeev *et al.* (1994) *The Birth of Fascist Ideology: From Cultural Rebellion to Political Revolution*, Princeton

Stevenson, David (1988) *The First World War and International Politics*, Oxford

Stone, Bailey (1994) *The Genesis of the French Revolution: A Global-Historical Interpretation*, Cambridge

Stone, Judith F. (1985) *The Search for Social Peace: Reform Legislation in France 1890–1914*

Stuart, Robert (1992) *Marxism at Work: Ideology, Class and French Socialism during the Third Republic*, Cambridge

Sue, Eugène (1989) *Les Mystères de Paris* [1842]

Sutcliffe, Anthony (1970) *The Autumn of Central Paris: The Defeat of Town Planning, 1850–1970*

Sutton, Michael (1982) *Nationalism, Positivism and Catholicism: The Politics of Charles Maurras and French Catholics 1890–1914*, Cambridge

Swart, Konrad W. (1964) *The Sense of Decadence in Nineteenth-Century France*

Szramkiewicz, Romuald and Bouineau, Jacques (1989) *Histoire des Institutions, 1750–1914*

Taine, Hippolite (1878) *Les Origines de la France contemporaine*, 5th edn, 6 vols

Tallet, Frank and Atkin, Nicholas, eds (1991) *Religion, Society and Politics in France since 1789*

Talmon, Jacob L. (1960) *Political Messianism: The Romantic Phase*

Tapia, Claude (1989) 'Paris, ville de congrès, de 1850 à nos jours' in André Kaspi and Antoine Marès, eds, *Le Paris des étrangers depuis un siècle*

Ténot, Eugène (1868) *Etude historique sur le coup d'état*, 2 vols

Thabault, Roger (1971) *Education and Change in a Village Community: Mazières-en-Gâtine 1848–1914*

Thibaudet, Albert (1927) *La République des professeurs*

Thibaudet, Albert (1932) *Les Idées politiques*

Thiers, Louis Adolphe (1831) *La Monarchie de 1830*

Thomas, Edith (1967) *The Women Incendiaries*

Thuillier, Guy and Tulard, Jean (1984) *Histoire de l'administration française*

Thureau-Dangin, Paul (1884–90) *Histoire de la Monarchie de Juillet*, 5 vols

Tilly, Charles and Lees, Lynn H. (1975) 'The people of June 1848', in Roger Price, ed., *Revolution and Reaction: 1848 and the Second French Republic*

Tocqueville, Alexis de (1948) *Recollections of Alexis de Tocqueville* ed. J.P. Mayer

Tocqueville, Alexis de (1967) *L'Ancien régime et la Révolution* [1856]

Tocqueville, Alexis de (1985) *Selected Letters on Politics and society*, ed. Roger Boesche

Tocqueville, Alexis de (1988) *The Ancien Regime* [1856]

Todorov, Tzvetan (1993) *On Human Diversity: Nationalism, Racism and Exoticism in French Thought*

Tombs, Robert (1981) *The War against Paris 1871*, Cambridge

Tombs, Robert, ed. (1991) *Nationhood and Nationalism in France from Boulangism to the Great War, 1889–1918*

Traugott, Mark (1985) *Armies of the Poor: Determinants of Working-Class Participation in the Parisian Insurrection of June 1848*, Princeton

Trebilcock, Clive (1981) *The Industrialization of the Continental Powers 1780–1914*

Trempé, Rolande (1971) *Les Mineurs de Carmaux 1848–1914*, 2 vols

Tudesq, André-Jean (1956) 'La crise de 1847 vue par les milieux d'affaires parisiens', in Ernest Labrousse, ed., *Aspects de la crise et de la dépression de l'économie française au milieu du 19e siècle*

Tudesq, André-Jean (1964) *Les Grands notables en France (1840–1849): étude historique d'une psychologie sociale*, 2 vols

Tudesq, André-Jean (1965) *L'Election présidentielle de Louis-Napoléon Bonaparte*

Tulard, Jean (1985) *Histoire de France: Vol. 4 Les Révolutions de 1789 à 1851*

Vallès, Jules (1972) *L'Insurgé* [1882]

Van Creveld, Martin (1977) *Supplying War: Logistics from Wallenstein to Patton*, Cambridge

Van Zanten, David (1994) *Building Paris: Architectural Institutions and the Transformation of the French Capital, 1830–1870*, Cambridge

Verdier, Daniel (1994) *Democracy and International Trade: Britain, France and the United States, 1860–1990*, Princeton

Verley, P. (1988) 'Exportation et croissance economique dans la France des années 1860' *Annales ESC* 1 (1988), pp. 73–110

Viallaneix, Paul and Ehrard, Jean, eds (1980) *Aimer en France (1760–1860)*, 2 vols, Clermond-Ferrand

Viallaneix, Paul and Ehrard, Jean, eds (1985) *La Bataille, l'armée, la gloire, 1745–1871*, 2 vols, Clermont-Ferrand

Vidalenc, Jean (1948) 'La province et les journées de juin' *Etudes d'Histoire Moderne et Contemporaine* 2 (1948), pp. 83–144

Vidalenc, Jean (1953) 'Lettres de J.A.M. Thomas, préfet des Bouches-du-Rhône, à Adolphe Thiers, 1831–1836' *Publication des Annales de la Faculté des Lettres, Aix en Provence* 5 (1953)

Vincent, K. Steven (1984) *Pierre-Joseph Proudhon and the Rise of French Republican Socialism*, Oxford

Vincent, K. Steven (1992) *Between Marxism and Anarchism: Benoît Malon and French Reformist Socialism*, Berkeley CA

Vovelle, Michel, ed. (1990) *L'Image de la Révolution Française*, 3 vols, Oxford

Vovelle, Michel (1991) *The Revolution against the Church*, Cambridge

Vovelle, Michel (1993) *La Découverte de la politique: géopolitique de la révolution française*

Vuillaume, Maxime (1971) *Mes Cahiers rouges au temps de la Commune* [1909]

Watson, David R. (1974) *Georges Clemenceau: A Political Biography*

Weber, Eugen (1959) *The Nationalist Revival in France 1905–14*, Berkeley CA

Weber, Eugen (1962) *Action Française: Royalism and Reaction in Twentieth-Century France*, Stanford CA

Weber, Eugen (1977) *Peasants into Frenchmen: The Modernization of Rural France, 1870–1914*

Weber, Eugen (1986) *France Fin de Siècle*, Cambridge MA

Weber, Eugen (1991) *My France: Politics, Culture, Myth*, Cambridge MA

Weill, Georges (1928) *Histoire du parti républicain en France 1814–1870*

Weisz, George (1983) *The Emergence of Modern Universities in France, 1863–1914*, Princeton

Welch, Cheryl B. (1984) *Liberty and Utility: The French Ideologues and the Transformation of Liberalism*, New York

Wileman, Donald G. (1994) 'Not the Radical republic: liberal ideology and central blandishment in France, 1901–1914' *Historical Journal* 37:3 (Sept. 1994), pp. 593–614

Willard, Claude (1965) *Le Mouvement socialiste en France (1893–1905): les guesdistes*

Williamson, Samuel R. (1969) *The Politics of Grand Strategy: Britain and France Prepare for War 1904–1914*, Cambridge MA

Wilson, Stephen (1982) *Ideology and Experience: Antisemitism in France at the Time of the Dreyfus Affair*

Wilson-Bareau, Juliet (1992) *Manet: The Execution of Maximilian: Painting, Politics and Censorship*

Winock, Michel (1973) 'Socialisme et patriotisme en France, 1891-1894' *Revue d'Histoire Moderne et Contemporaine* 20 (July–Sept. 1973), pp. 376–423

Winock, Michel (1986) *La Fièvre héxagonale: les grandes crises politiques 1871–1968*

Wolff, Jacques (1993) *Les Perier: la Fortune et les Pouvoirs*

Wright, Gordon (1981) *France in Modern Times*, 3rd edn

Wright, Gordon (1983) *Between the Guillotine and Liberty: Two Centuries of the Crime Problem in France*, Oxford

Wright, Vincent (1975) 'The coup d'état of December 1851', in Roger Price, ed., *Revolution and Reaction: 1848 and The Second French Republic*

Wright, Vincent and Le Clère, B. (1973) *Les Préfets du Second Empire*

Wrigley, E.A. (1985) 'The fall of marital fertility in nineteenth-century France: exemplar or exception?' *European Journal of Population* 1 (1985), pp. 31–60, 131–9

Yvert, Benoît, ed. (1990) *Dictionnaire des ministres de 1789 à 1989*

Zamagni, V. (1989) 'An international comparison of real industrial wages 1890–1913', in Peter Scholliers, ed., *Real Wages in 19th and 20th century Europe: Historical and Comparative Perspectives*, New York

Zeldin, Theodore (1958) *The Political System of Louis-Napoleon Bonaparte*

Zeldin, Theodore (1963) *Emile Ollivier and the Liberal Empire of Napoleon III*, Oxford

Zeldin, Theodore (1973) *France 1848–1945*, 2 vols, Oxford

Zysberg, A. (1980) in Michel Perrot, ed., *L'Impossible prison: recherches sur le système pénitentiaire du XIXe siècle*

MAPS

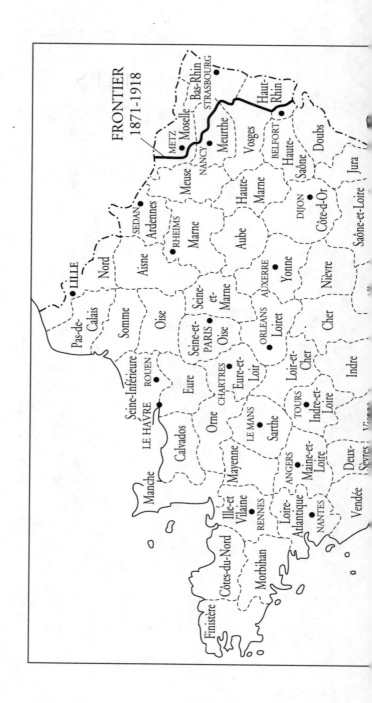

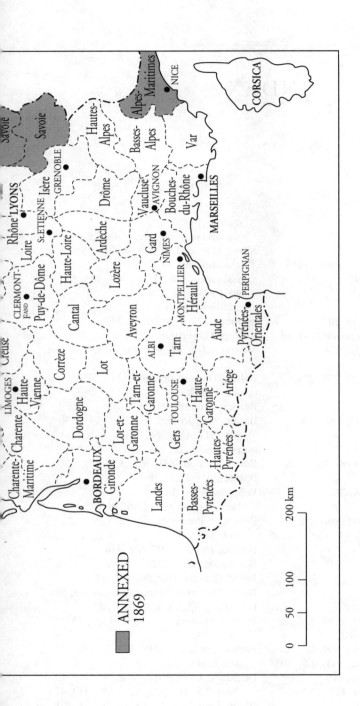

INDEX